THE NATIONAL INSTITUTE OF
ECONOMIC AND SOCIAL RESEARCH

Economic and Social Studies

V

THE DEVELOPMENT OF THE SOVIET ECONOMIC SYSTEM

THE DEVELOPMENT OF THE
SOVIET ECONOMIC SYSTEM

*An Essay on the Experience of Planning
in the U.S.S.R.*

BY

ALEXANDER BAYKOV

*Lecturer in charge of the Department of Economics
and Institutions of the U.S.S.R.,
Birmingham University*

CAMBRIDGE
AT THE UNIVERSITY PRESS
1946
REPRINTED
1970

Published by the Syndics of the Cambridge University Press
Bentley House, 200 Euston Road, London, N.W. 1
American Branch: 32 East 57th Street, New York, N.Y. 10022

PUBLISHER'S NOTE

Cambridge University Press Library Editions are re-issues of out-of-print standard works from the Cambridge catalogue. The texts are unrevised and, apart from minor corrections, reproduce the latest published edition.

Standard Book Number: 521 07769 9

First published 1946
Reprinted 1970

First printed in Great Britain at the University Press, Cambridge
Reprinted in Great Britain by John Dickens & Co. Ltd, Northampton

ANALYTICAL TABLE OF CONTENTS

1. *Industry*   *p.* 3

The position in industry as inherited by the Soviet Government. The Soviet Government's measures for the nationalization of industry and its actual course. The urgent need for a hasty total nationalization of industry. Sharp decline in industrial production.

2. *Agriculture*   *p.* 9

Essential characteristics of the agrarian problem inherited by the Soviet Government. Food shortages on the eve of the October Revolution. Measures taken by the Soviet Government for the nationalization of land. The actual process of land nationalization. In search of a solution of the food crisis. General results of the land nationalization and sharp decline in agricultural production.

3. *Internal and External Trade*   *p.* 24

Early measures taken by the Soviet Government were designed to control, but not to nationalize home trade. Hasty 'nationalization' of trade to avert food crisis. Rationing made unavoidable. The degradation of home trade. The foreign trade monopoly. Sharp decline in the foreign trade turn-over.

4. *Public Finance, Credit and Money*   *p.* 29

The Party's views on the nationalization of banks. The position in the field of State finance and credit as inherited by the Soviet Government. Hasty nationalization of banks caused by the opposition to attempts at controlling their activities. Emergency measures in the field of State finance. General deterioration in credit, monetary circulation and State finance.

5. *Labour*   *p.* 39

Attempts to put into effect the most advanced labour legislation. Actual developments in the field of labour.

6. *General Planning*   *p.* 44

First attempts at setting up planning institutions and planning the country's economic development.

SECTION III. *PERIOD OF EXTENSIVE IN-DUSTRIALIZATION, COLLECTIVIZATION OF AGRICULTURE AND RATIONING*

PREFACE

In the course of the last quarter of a century, hundreds of volumes have been written about the economic system of the U.S.S.R. and various aspects of it. These books—or rather, some of them—are worthy of the effort and the time spent on their perusal; I leave it to the reader to decide whether the publication of another study is justified or not, but I would like to explain how it came to be written.

Having left the U.S.S.R. in the summer of 1920, my personal impressions cover only the first three years of the new regime. Later I had the opportunity of meeting many people who had either just left the U.S.S.R. or had visited it in order to study its economic and social system. In 1922, having resumed my academic studies in Prague and having access to the abundant material received directly from the U.S.S.R. by the Russian Historical Archive, the Institute of Russian Studies, and the Russian Economic Study Centre of Prof. S. N. Prokopovich in Prague, I began to follow the development of the economic processes which were taking place in my native country. Many well-known Russian economists, sociologists and former statesmen worked in these institutions, whose object was to study developments in the U.S.S.R. From 1927 to 1939, as a member of the Russian Economic Study Centre of Prof. Prokopovich, and using the plentiful data regularly received there from the U.S.S.R., I contributed monthly articles on the development of industry, home and foreign trade, State finance and some other aspects of the national economy of the U.S.S.R. to the *Bulletin of the Russian Economic Study Centre of Prof. S. N. Prokopovich*, published in Prague, and later also memoranda for the Czech State Statistical Institute. From 1935 to April 1939 I lectured on the development of the national economy and economic system of the U.S.S.R. in the Faculty of Commerce of the Czech Technical University of Prague.

Years of study of the economic development of Russia and of the Soviet Government's economic policy have time and again forced upon me the conclusion that the appreciation of current economic events and measures, by myself as well as by other authors, was liable to be wrong, when these events and measures were considered in isolation and not in association with the *general course of development* of the entire national economy of the U.S.S.R. Many economic facts and many of the measures of the Soviet Government were considered at the time as inherent in the Soviet economic system, whereas they were only passing phases or temporary measures adopted to solve merely temporary difficulties or to achieve temporary aims. It is now recognized that the economic development of the U.S.S.R. and the Soviet system have already passed through four definite stages of development—the transition period, the period of the New Economic Policy, the period of rationing, and the period which began with the abolition of rationing and was brought to an end by the outbreak of war. In the course of these periods, the processes which took place in the national economy and the measures taken by the Government differ so widely that it is possible to speak of four systems. Each of these periods had its special aims, and the measures taken were designed to achieve these aims and to overcome the obstacles and complications peculiar to that stage. But at the same time, every stage left its permanent mark and influenced the economic system of the next period. Thus systematic study over many years of the development of the national economy and economic system of the U.S.S.R. has convinced me that only by adopting the historical approach in the study of the present-day economic system of the U.S.S.R. can one hope to avoid errors and pitfalls, and to find explanations conforming to reality, and moreover that this approach is equally necessary to enable economists and sociologists who are confronted with similar problems in other countries to understand the lesson of Russian experience.

The present study is an attempt at such an historical introduction to the contemporary economic system of the U.S.S.R., i.e. the system in force in the later pre-war years. It does not profess to be a history of the development of the national economy or of the economic system of the U.S.S.R., because such a history would run into thousands of pages; it is only an historical introduction to the description of the present-day system in its principal aspects and problems. Hence, only those facts in the development of the economy and the system will be mentioned which, in my opinion, must be known in order to understand and rightly appreciate the present-day system and its problems. This approach demands a certain simplification in the outline of events, a choice of facts and measures, which may be coloured by the author's sense of values. Processes are never as simple and straightforward as generalizations make them appear. Even the division into periods is only a rough approximation, and no attempt has been made here to differentiate the years 1917–18 from the 1917–21 period, and

similarly the transition years 1926–9 are included in the 1921–9
period. Therefore my references to sources and the additional
bibliography are not merely an indication of the material used in
this study, but should help the reader to find considerably more
detailed explanations of matters referred to only briefly in the
course of this book.

The development of the U.S.S.R. economic system can be
studied from various angles and for various purposes. The theoretical approach to the study of the Soviet system would be an
academic analysis parallel to that used in describing the functioning
of the competitive system and would tend to establish the similarities
and differences between the two systems. The political approach
would consider how far the Soviet economic system conforms to
'socialist ideals' and to 'communism', and would attempt to assess
its advantages on political and moral grounds when compared
with the capitalistic system, followed by discussions on 'freedom'
and 'compulsion', 'democracy' and 'dictatorship', as inherent
or not in a planned system 'on the basis of the experience of the
U.S.S.R.' The technical approach would involve an account of
planning technique, of the structure of the economic institutions,
of the administrative organization in various branches of the
national economy, of technical and economic methods applied to
different branches, and so on; generally speaking, it would be an
outline of the technical and economic machinery of administration
in the Soviet economic system. This study, however, pursues none
of these aims. Its object is to give an analysis of the Soviet economic
system as such, i.e. to give an account of the aims pursued, of
the measures taken to attain these aims, of the results achieved as
regards both the aims and the elaboration of basic principles on
which the functioning of the Soviet system is founded. Naturally,
such an approach leads me to touch upon technical problems, but
only in so far as this is necessary to explain the basic principles
on which the Soviet economic system is built. Generalized views
are given only in the concluding pages of each chapter in section IV,
and even so only on some problems debated in 'theoretical treaties'
and social and economic literature, problems which in any case will
have to be solved in any attempt to go over from the competitive
to the planned system. I hope the material presented will enable
the reader to draw his own conclusions and generalizations.

Though the commonly adopted method is to outline the development of each branch of the national economy separately for the
entire past period, I found it preferable to review in turn the processes which took place in the main branches of the national

economy of the U.S.S.R. and all the corresponding aspects of the U.S.S.R. economic system *during each period*. The reason is that in the course of each period definite aims were pursued and definite planned measures taken to attain those particular aims, and therefore events in various branches of the national economy of the U.S.S.R. were so interlinked that to describe them separately for the entire 25 years would artificially split an organic whole. Moreover, in every one of the four periods which have elapsed, distinct aims were pursued and the processes which took place in distinct branches of the national economy determined the development and legislation affecting the others; therefore, each of the four sections of the book devotes most attention to the analysis of those branches which in the given period were the fundamental, determining branches of the national economy. In the first section the stress is laid on the analysis of industry and agriculture; in the second on internal trade, State finance, credit and money; in the third on industry and agriculture; in the fourth on trade and industry. In connexion with such a method of exposition I was sometimes obliged to repeat statements made previously in another context. This method of exposition may give the impression of a certain lack of continuity. In that case I would suggest that the reader pick out from every section the chapters referring to a particular branch of national economy and then peruse the whole book section by section.

For this book I have used only original sources, i.e. studies, statistical material, various handbooks, journals on economics and law, technical periodicals, collected laws and departmental regulations, etc., published in the U.S.S.R. Works published abroad were consulted only to compare and check my observations and conclusions with those of other authors, but they were not used as sources of information. I do not share the view that Soviet statistical and other sources are less reliable than those published in other countries. On the contrary, systematic study over a number of years has convinced me that they can be used to analyse the economic processes and the economic system of the U.S.S.R. with the same degree of confidence as similar sources published in other countries. Only occasionally and temporarily some statistical data were not published, as, for instance, some information regarding agriculture in the period of collectivization. However, one of the greatest defects of the data published in the U.S.S.R. is the frequent changes in the forms of publication, which make it difficult and at times impossible to draw up statistical tables showing trends of evolution. This fact and the absence of much of the material

published in the U.S.S.R. from British libraries explain the somewhat disconnected and often incomplete data given in the tables
which refer to the later years, and for this I apologize.

I am quite aware of the shortcomings of this work, but in my
approach and method of treatment 'I was thinking alone'. If it
arouses further interest in the study of the problems touched upon
and leads to an exchange of views on these problems, its publication will have been justified.

In conclusion, I must apologize for the faulty English of this
book. Part of it, namely, chapters I–VI, was written by me in
English and revised by British friends; the other chapters were
translated from my Russian MS. by Miss E. Koutaissoff, B.Litt.
(Oxon), to whom I express my thanks for her endeavour to follow
my Russian text as closely as it was possible. Hence two styles.
Only the war conditions under which this study was written can
excuse its publication despite such an obvious technical defect.

I am very much indebted to the National Institute of Economic
and Social Research, without whose financial support and
technical help it would have been impossible for me to complete
this study and to prepare it for publication.

I am especially grateful and indebted to the Chairman of the
Institute, Professor Henry Clay, not only for his personal interest in
my research work but also for sacrificing his time in correcting the
main defects in the English of the whole MS., and for very many
valuable suggestions which greatly improved the text of this study.

With great pleasure I also express my thanks to the University
of Birmingham. The Honorary Research Fellowship which was
granted me by the University facilitated the continuation of my
research work after I left Prague. My personal thanks go to the
Vice-Principal of the University, Professor J. G. Smith, and to
Professor P. Sargant Florence for their interest in and friendly
support of my research work.

Some of the material which has been included in this study
has been published in the *Economic Journal, Economica* and the
London and Cambridge Economic Service Bulletin. I am indebted to
the editors of these Journals for their kind permission to use this
material.

The Index was prepared by Miss Beatrice Lawrence, M.A.,
to whom I express my gratitude for undertaking this formidable
task.

A. M. B.

March 1944
LONDON

SECTION I. *TRANSITIONAL PERIOD AND PERIOD OF 'WAR COMMUNISM'*

CHAPTER I. IDEOLOGICAL PREMISES AND AIMS UNDERLYING THE CHANGES IN THE EXISTING ECONOMIC SYSTEM

We shall not here attempt to describe the ideological aspect of the Russian Revolution of October 1917; to do so it would be necessary to go far back into the history of revolutionary movements, both Russian and international, and this would lead us very far from the main theme of this book. We must, however, establish some of the general premises with which the process of changing the existing economic system began.

The Bolshevik party aimed not merely at altering the economic system which then existed in Russia, but at completely superseding it by a Socialist system based on the main ideas expressed by Marx and Engels in the *Communist Manifesto*. It aimed at establishing a completely new organization of society, an organization in which industrial production would be directed, not by entrepreneurs competing among themselves, but by society itself, according to a plan designed to satisfy the needs of all citizens; society would expropriate from private ownership all means of production, transport, distribution, etc., and would dispose of them according to a definite plan and with a definite aim in view.*

It aimed at achieving this supersession of the existing economic system by seizing control of the 'commanding heights' of that system, and by using the existing economic organizations and retaining their managing and administrative personnel during the transitional period. There was no concrete plan for reconstructing the economic system on a new basis; the main ideas for guiding the economic system through a transitional period were clear, but not the forms which a permanent reorganization would take, or the methods by which such a reorganization was to be brought about. A period of experimentation, of trial and error, was accepted as inevitable until a suitable form of planned economy could be found.†

* K. Marx and F. Engels, *Communist Manifesto*, pp. 299, 304. Lenin, *Collected Works*, vol. XIV, pt. II, p. 336.

† Lenin, op. cit. vol. XV, pp. 280–1; vol. XVI, pp. 72, 103, 253–4; vol. XVIII, pt. II, p. 48; vol. XXIII, p. 484. *Stages in the Economic Policy of the U.S.S.R.* pp. 45–6.

The leading figures of the Soviet Government, in this period, proceeded on the following assumptions: (*a*) that in the near future social revolutions must be expected to take place in other countries, and that consequently the experiment of rebuilding the Russian economic system would not be an isolated one;* (*b*) that during the transitional period the State must base itself, not on the principles of parliamentary democracy, but on the 'Dictatorship of the proletariat', i.e. on the combined power of the Party and the Soviets, with the Communist Party as the 'leading vanguard of the proletariat'.†

From October 1917 up to the middle of 1918 the policy of the Soviet Government was not directed towards immediate wholesale nationalization, but towards the nationalization of certain branches only of the national economy, and that only to a certain extent.‡ From the middle of 1918 up to March 1921 was the period of so-called 'War Communism'. During this period the conditions brought about by civil war and foreign intervention, together with the rapid disintegration of the country's economy, caused the Soviet Government to resort to a hasty nationalization of the whole national economy, to an extreme centralization of the economic administration, and to the adoption of the principles of war economics. During this period of 'War Communism' the economic measures of the Soviet Government, under pressure of emergency (as well as, in many cases, under the influence of Marxist economic theories), took the form of an attempt to pass directly to a centrally directed system of production and distribution, to a system based on State-organized barter.

CHAPTER II. MAIN FEATURES OF ECONOMIC POLICY AND ECONOMIC DEVELOPMENT

Soviet economic policy and economic development during the first years of the existence of the U.S.S.R. has been described in detail in many books published in non-Russian languages. Here we shall only summarize the main landmarks of Soviet economic policy, and the most essential facts in its development; for unless

* Lenin, op. cit. vol. xiii, p. 209; vol. xiv, pt. ii, p. 164; vol. xv, p. 140.

† Lenin, op. cit. vol. xiv, pt. i, pp. 236, 250; vol. xv, pp. 41, 419, 516; vol. xvi, pp. 206, 448–9; vol. xvii, pp. 139, 355; vol. xviii, pp. 1, 129.

‡ Lenin, op. cit. vol. xiv, pp. 336–7; vol. xv, pp. 93, 150, 585; vol. xvi, pp. 71–2.

the main events which took place in the economic development of the U.S.S.R. during the period 1917–21 are borne in mind, many events of subsequent periods will not be rightly understood.

1. INDUSTRY

The existing conditions which the Soviet Government inherited in industry may be summarized as follows. Russian industry was not organized in monopolistic cartels or trusts. Only *trade* syndicates existed; they were common in heavy industry and in some branches of light industry.* Consequently there was no apparatus of monopolistic organization which the Soviet Government could take over as a basis on which to build up a central (State) organization. A very considerable part of the capital of the heavy industry belonged to foreign interests (especially French, English and Belgian).† This complicated the problem of the nationalization of industry. Industrial production was, on the one hand, very concentrated in some branches of heavy industry in the Ukraine, and on the other hand, widely dispersed among very small enterprises, especially in the production of consumer goods.‡ This fact, while facilitating nationalization of production in some branches of heavy industry, very much complicated the process in the industries producing consumer goods.

During the war of 1914–17, moreover, industrial productive capacity was mobilized for the production of war materials. Consequently there developed a two-fold process: a rise in the output of the war industries and some branches of heavy industry, and a decline in the output of the industries producing consumer goods. After the February Revolution of 1917 a process of decline in industrial production occurred in all branches of industry.§ In some branches of industry, many owners of factories closed their works; widespread strikes occurred, and attempts were made to

* See Cypirovich, *Syndicates and Trusts in Russia*; Lyashchenko, *The History of the National Economy of the U.S.S.R.*

† 90% of the joint stock of mining industries, 42% in iron, steel and engineering industries, 50% in the chemical industry, 37% in lumber and timber industries, and 28% in textile industries belonged to foreign joint-stock capital. From the total foreign joint-stock capital 32·6% was French, 22·6% English, 14·3% Belgian and 19·7% German. Lyashchenko, op. cit. pp. 598–9. P. V. Ol, *Foreign Capital in the National Economy of Russia*, pp. 11–29.

‡ See Lyashchenko, op. cit. pp. 558–62.

§ See figures in *Collection of Statistical Figures of the U.S.S.R. 1918–23*, pp. 168–71. Milyutin, *The History of the Economic Development of the U.S.S.R.* pp. 40–6. Rozenfeld, *Industrial Policy of the U.S.S.R.* pp. 63–4.

establish, by means of committees of factory workers, the control of factories by the workers. The intervention of the workers' committees considerably intensified the process of deterioration in industrial production which grew worse in the atmosphere of political, economic and administrative instability which speedily developed during the period between the February and October Revolutions of 1917. On the eve of the October Revolution of 1917 the production of all branches of industry was hampered by difficulties in obtaining supplies of raw materials and fuel. In addition, it was limited by the weakening in labour discipline and a decline in productivity of labour, and from the appearance of inflationary tendencies which disorganized the internal market.*

During the first months of Soviet power unorganized processes played a much more important part in industrial policy and in the evolution of industrial production than did the regulating measures of the Government: the Soviet Government, in the first months of its power, had no definite and *concrete* policy with regard to the method by which industry was to be nationalized and its administration reorganized. There were conflicting tendencies. The Government's policy was definitely aimed at nationalizing big enterprises in key industries, especially in the highly concentrated heavy industries, as well as some of the large enterprises in the light industries. It was even hoped that it would be possible, by some financial settlement with the former owners of the enterprises (a certain limited ransom for nationalized enterprises†), to get support in the organization of production from the former owners and managing boards of these enterprises. But at the same time it was expected that, during the transition period, private enterprises would continue to work alongside the concerns which had been nationalized, but under the general regulating direction of the State and under the supervision of worker-control committees. Accordingly, as early as 8 November 1917,‡ it was decided to create a Supreme Council of the National Economy (S.E.C.), which institution would deal with the 'organization of the National Economy and State finance and prepare the general norms and

---

* According to Prokopovitch, as early as 1916–17 the total industrial production fell to 70 % of that of 1913. Prokopovitch, *War and the National Economy*, p. 173.

† By giving the former owner of a nationalized factory either State bonds covering part of the cost of the factory or a portion of the shares of the State trust which would be formed from nationalized factories. Rozenfeld, op. cit. p. 97.   ‡ Lenin, op. cit. vol. xxiii, p. 36.

plans for the regulation of the economic life of the country'. (The S.E.C. was actually created by a decree of 5 December 1917.) On 14 November 1917 a decree introducing workers' control was published: 'in the interest of the systematic regulation of the national economy, in all branches of industrial and trade enterprises, in banks, agriculture, transport and co-operative enterprises, etc., employing hired labour, the workers' control of the production, purchases, storage and finance of the enterprises must be introduced.'*

This decree was aimed at bringing large nationalized enterprises in key industries under the jurisdiction and direction of the S.E.C. and at organizing and legalizing the violent, unorganized process of intervention by workers' committees in the 'control' of the management of enterprises.

The real process of nationalization, however, did not take place in a systematic way, but took the shape of quite crude, unorganized 'requisition'. Only some of the biggest factories were nationalized by the decision of the Council of People's Commissars (Sovnarkom R.S.F.S.R.) and the S.E.C. The majority of factories were nationalized or requisitioned by regional or local organizations.

The diarchy of former administration and workers' control was very short-lived. The two proved to be two hostile forces. In some cases owners either closed down their business directly or the management refused to continue to work under the new conditions and abandoned the enterprises; in other cases the factory worker committees expelled owners from their factories and took the management into their own hands. Very often a factory worker committee would consider the requisitioned factory as the property of the workers employed in it and carry on the business of the factory from this point of view. These syndicalist tendencies shown in the requisitioning of enterprises were very widespread.† Together with the growing difficulties in the supply of raw materials and fuel, and in transport, and the disorganization of the internal market, credit system and currency (see below), they helped to bring about an increasingly anarchic situation in the industrial system.

---

* *Decrees of the October Revolution*, pt. 1, pp. 96, 224.

† From October 1917 to June 1918, of 521 'nationalized' big factories only seventy-two were nationalized by decision of the Sovnarkom S.S.S.R. and S.E.C. and the rest by local organizations. Milyutin, op. cit. pp. 112, 115–16. See also Rozenfeld, op. cit. pp. 91–2; *October Revolution and Dictatorship of the Proletariat*, pp. 103–4.

In order to eliminate these syndicalist tendencies in local organization and the anarchy which accompanied nationalization, and to meet the emergency created by the Treaty of Brest-Litovsk, by the beginning of civil war and the steady decline of industrial production, it was decided to carry out disciplined nationalization of all key industries and to centralize the administration of nationalized industries in the hands of the S.E.C.

At the First Congress of the National Economic Councils (which took place between 26 May and 4 June 1918) it was decided to nationalize all branches of key industries, starting with the iron and steel, chemical, oil and textile industries; and a 'Statute for the administration of nationalized enterprises' was approved. The result of the first decision of this Congress was the publication of a decree of 28 June 1918 for the general nationalization of industry. The result of the second decision was the accomplishment of the conversion, in practice, of the S.E.C. from a general economic council into a central State institution for the general administration of all nationalized industry.

This decree of nationalization aimed at transferring all large-scale industries from private ownership to State ownership; it was stressed that nationalization of individual enterprises could be carried out only by the decision of the Sovnarkom R.S.F.S.R. or the S.E.C., and that nationalized enterprises must be transferred to the appropriate departments of the S.E.C. The leading personalities of the S.E.C. realized that this hasty nationalization of industry would result, in many cases, not in an increase but in a decline of industrial production. It was considered, however, that under the existing conditions (such as the impossibility of obtaining the collaboration of the former owners, the syndicalist tendencies in local organizations, and the general emergency situation) there was no other way out.*

In reality it proved to be impossible to limit nationalization to large-scale industries. It was found that large-scale industries depended on small industries for some of their supplies. Moreover, the majority of the most essential consumer goods were produced in small industries. Finally, orders given by the central power were not strictly observed by local authorities. Consequently, by a decision of the S.E.C. of 29 December 1920, 'all enterprises which are still in private possession and employ more than five workers using any kind of mechanical power or more than ten workers without

* See Central Committee of the Communist Party, *For Five Years*. Trotsky, *New Economic Policy of Soviet Russia and Perspective of the World Revolution*.

mechanical power' were nationalized. By this decision even small enterprises were nationalized, and the process of nationalization, in this period, was completed.

We shall not describe here the organization of the administration of industry in this period, as we shall have to refer to this question many times during the analysis of later stages in the development of the Soviet system.* We can only state that, in this period, an attempt was made at an extreme centralization of the administration and management of all industries. All branches of industrial production were centrally administered by a special chief department of the S.E.C. ('Glavki' and 'Tsentra', i.e. Chief and Central administrations) in which were concentrated all powers concerning particular industries and by which these powers were distributed among subordinate enterprises. The attempt was made to organize in a centralized manner the supply to subordinate enterprises of all materials required for production, to 'plan' their productive activities and to distribute their output on the basis of State-organized barter. All 'plans' were compiled in natural units without any economic consideration of net cost, prices, or of gains or losses from the economic as opposed to the technical point of view. Knowledge, on the part of the central departments of the S.E.C., of the enterprises subordinate to them was very superficial and had only a formal character. Technical and economic records of enterprises were generally not available; many archives and accounting materials were lost, and administrative links between the central organs of the S.E.C. and local organizations were as yet only in an embryonic state. The S.E.C. were forced to administer together with the key industries thousands of small enterprises. No wonder that under such conditions the majority of enterprises, with the exception of war industries and some key enterprises among the heavy and light industries, lived quite an independent life,† using the available stocks contrary to directions given by the S.E.C., with the aim of extending their productive life as far as possible and often producing not what was asked for by the centre but what could best be bartered under local conditions.

* The English reader can get a general idea of organization from Maurice Dobb's book, *Russian Economic Development since the Revolution*, pp. 99–106. See also Rozenfeld, op. cit. pp. 113–34.

† According to the 1920 census 37,226 industrial enterprises were registered as State enterprises, but only 6,908 of them were in the register of the S.E.C., the rest 'escaped' administration by the S.E.C. See Kritsman, *The Heroic Period in the Great Russian Revolution*, p. 129.

It is incorrect to speak of this period as forming the beginning of the planning of industrial production. Organization of the administration of industry took forms influenced not by the consideration of economic expediency but by the necessity of meeting the emergency situation which had resulted from the whole course of events in this period in which the industrial policy of the Soviet Government was only one card in the whole big game.

As a result of all these processes in industry as well as of others in other branches of the national economy, output very rapidly declined in all branches of industry, as can be clearly seen from the indexes of output calculated by the State Planning Commission (Gosplan).

Table 1

Industries...	Large-scale	Small-scale	Total
1913	100·0	100·0	100·0
1916	116·1	88·2	109·4
1917	74·8	78·4	75·7
1918	33·8	73·5	43·4
1919	14·9	49·0	23·1
1920	12·8	44·1	20·4

The output of large-scale industries, the administration of which was extremely centralized, declined much more rapidly than did that of small industries. Particularly large declines occurred in the production of the following materials: iron ore (in 1920 only 1·6% of the 1913 output was produced); pig iron (1920, 2·4% of 1913); steel (1920, 4·0% of 1913); cotton manufactures (1920, 5% of 1913); sugar (1920, 5·8% of 1913). In 1912, production of prime necessity goods amounted, per head of population, to 18·2 gold roubles, in 1920 only to 2·4 gold roubles. In 1912 manufactured consumer goods sold to the population were valued at 2,099 million gold roubles, while the value of these sold in 1920 amounted only to 262 million gold roubles.*

Such a situation in industrial production demanded a search for new methods of organizing, administering and managing industry.

But before describing the changes which took place during the next period, we must describe the processes which had taken place in the other sectors of the national economy.

* *For Five Years*, op. cit. p. 240; Rozenfeld, op. cit. pp. 155, 165, 166; *Collection of Statistical Figures of the U.S.S.R.*, 1918–23, pp. 168, 169, 200, 201.

2. AGRICULTURE

Pre-revolutionary Russia was an agrarian country. The agrarian population constituted the predominant part of the total population, while agricultural production furnished the main part of the national income of the country. Russia's agrarian problem differed in many respects from the agrarian problems of western European industrial countries, and without knowledge of the main roots of the economic and sociological problems which the Soviet Government inherited, it is impossible rightly to understand the agrarian policy of the Soviet Government and the course of events among the rural population and in the agricultural production of the U.S.S.R. Of course we cannot give here even an adequate summary of the historical origins of the agrarian problem in Russia. For this many pages would be necessary. But we find it necessary to recall some of the essential features of the agrarian problem with which the Soviet Government had to deal, not only in the first months of its power, but during a very long period to come.

The abolition of serfdom in Russia had taken place in 1861, i.e. only 56 years before the Revolution of 1917. Among the peasants of 1917 there were persons whose childhood and youth were spent under conditions of serfdom. The majority of the active agricultural population were only the second generation after the abolition of serfdom. But even after the abolition of serfdom neither the social status nor the economic rights of the peasantry were equal to those of the urban population; nor were they similar to the social status and economic rights of the farmers in western European countries.

The abolition of serfdom was realized on the following conditions:

(a) After the reform the peasants received for *use*, but not as private property, only the land which they had already used before the reform; that is to say, the land on which they had worked approximately only half of their working time, being obliged to spend the other half working on the estate of the landowner. In actual fact, in regions with good land, they received even less than they had cultivated before the reform,* and only in regions with poor soil did they receive a little more.

Consequently, after the reform, the peasants were unable to employ their labour fully on the land they received, and they were forced to look for an additional income either by renting land from

* In 21 goubernii of fertile 'black earth' soil they received, in total, 26·2 % less land than they had cultivated before the reform. In some goubernii the losses amounted to 44 %. Lyashchenko, op. cit. pp. 319–21.

or labouring on the estates belonging to their former landlords, to the State, Crown appanage estates, and to the monasteries and convents.

(b) Land was given to the peasants not as private property but only for 'permanent use' on condition that compensation was paid for the land granted to them.* The compensation was calculated on the basis of higher prices than those actually ruling for land in the different regions in this period. Thus the peasants were, in actual fact, obliged not only to pay a ransom for the land received for use but also, indirectly, what was equivalent to a certain amount as 'ransom' for his working capacity.

The total amount of compensation had to be paid in instalments to the State for 49 years. But the responsibility for the payment of these instalments lay on the 'peasant community' (obshchina), and all members of the community were jointly responsible for the payment of the compensation. Accordingly, members of the community were not allowed to leave the community without paying their full contribution, and their rights to alienate the land allotted them for use were very limited. Consequently, the peasants were tied to their community and could leave it definitely only after receiving its permission.

All land belonged de jure to the 'community', and the latter had the right of periodical redistribution of the land among its members according to the number of members in the peasant households ('number of eaters'). The peasant households received the land in separate plots, usually in different places, for use until the new repartitioning period. This practice of periodical redistribution of the land belonging to the community according to the size of families very much hampered the possibility of intensifying agricultural production.

Moreover, the forms of jurisdiction regulating the civil rights of the peasants were different from those which concerned the urban population. The limitation of their civil rights, associated with their inferior social status, were not completely liquidated by the reform. They continued not to enjoy equal civil and property rights with the former landowners and the urban population. By the reform, the power of the landowners over the peasantry was only liquidated de jure; de facto the peasantry continued to feel this

* Up to 1881 the former landowners retained their right of asking a peasant to work on their land for a certain number of days instead of paying the instalment of the ransom. In 1881 this privilege was definitely abolished. See details about the conditions regarding the payment of ransom, Lyashchenko, op. cit. pp. 321–4.

power in their restricted civil rights and their economic conditions. As we have seen, the peasant was under the necessity of renting land from the former landowner* or labouring on his estate, since the land he received after the reform had previously been cultivated by him in only half of his working time, and he now had to look for a larger money income in order to pay his share of the compensation for the land he received. The obligatory yearly instalments of the compensation were very often actually higher than the total money income derived from the land received by the peasant.†

(c) The amount of land received and the conditions on which it was granted for use did not provide the peasantry with possibilities of intensifying agricultural production. Households with small families, which accordingly received only a small amount of land from the community, could not even afford to keep a horse or breed livestock,‡ nor rent agricultural machinery.

(d) Only by renting or buying land from the estates was the road to 'enrichment' opened for the more enterprising and economically stronger peasant households. The establishment in 1882 of a special Peasants' Bank which enabled village communities or groups of peasants to receive credit to buy land from big estates made it possible for economically stronger peasant families to acquire land as private property. Slowly there began to develop a process of differentiation in the villages between well-to-do peasants who cultivated, in addition to their allotments received for use from the community, land bought as private property from the estates or alienated from economically less successful and impoverished peasant holdings. This process of differentiation§ between peasant holdings was speeded up by the land reform of 9 November 1906, the so-called 'Stolypin reform'.

* The dimensions of the renting of land can be illustrated by the following figures: in 1886–90 only 40% of the big estates did not lease their land, 39% leased all their land, and 21% partly cultivated their land and partly leased it. For 1896–1900 the corresponding figures were: 29, 51 and 20%.

† Peasants' arrears in the payment of their ransom steadily grew from year to year. See figures, Lyashchenko, op. cit. p. 373.

‡ According to the census of horses, between 1888 and 1891, 27·3% of peasant households were without horses, in 1900–29·2%.

§ According to the land census of 1905 the community land was divided among peasants as follows:

Groups	Percentage of households	Percentage of land
From 1 to 4 desyatin*	15·8	3·6
From 4 to 8 desyatin	33·7	19·0
From 8 to 20 desyatin	40·0	41·8
Over 20 desyatin	10·5	35·6

* Desyatin—approximately 2·6 acres.

After the widespread peasant insurrection of 1902–5 which had shown the Russian Government and the landowners what deep, latent, elemental revolutionary forces were concealed in the Russian peasantry, it was decided to create facilities for the speedy development of groups of well-to-do peasants as a basis for the conservative political stability of the country and as a means for increasing the productivity of agriculture. It was decided to create conditions for the liquidation of the 'community' ownership of land and to facilitate the transfer to private ownership of 'community' land at the time in use by the peasants. In actual practice this reform enabled the economically stronger peasant households to secure more land from the 'community' for their private ownership than the poor peasant holdings were able to secure, and more than that which remained, on the average, for those members of the 'community' who continued to cultivate their land on the basis of 'communal property' and not on the basis of private ownership.*

After the Stolypin reform the process of differentiation between peasant holdings was speeded up,† as not only did the economically stronger peasant households leave the 'community' with their relatively larger plots of land but they also purchased, through the Peasants' Bank, considerable amounts of land from the estates of the big landowners, since, after the peasant insurrection of 1902–5, landowners in many regions were quite willing to sell their estates.‡

(e) As a result of all these processes which developed in the domain of agriculture during the fifty years before the Revolution of 1917, the Russian agrarian question presented a complicated knot of political, social and economic problems. Ownership of the land was divided between the estates of the landed gentry, lands of the State and Crown appanages, estates belonging to the convents and monasteries, estates belonging to industrial and mercantile capitalists, and small peasant farmers privately owning land— and all this private property was still scattered in the sea of

---

* See description of 1906 reform—Lyashchenko, op. cit. pp. 622–3; or, in English, L. E. Hubbard, *The Economics of Soviet Agriculture*, pp. 44–5; there are some errors in Hubbard's description, but nevertheless it can be used for the general purpose.

† From 1907 to 1915 over 2 million peasant holdings left the 'community' and received from the 'community' land, as their private property, over 13 million desyatin of land or over 16% of the total 'community' land of Russia.

‡ See figures illustrating the differentiations among peasants on p. 13.

'community' land used by the majority of the agricultural population.*

The majority of the agricultural population worked on plots of land which provided them only with a very low standard of living, and considerable numbers of them (the poor peasants) did not even receive a sufficient income from their lands to provide their families with bare necessities. The poor peasants were thus forced to work as labourers or seasonal workers on the large estates and on the farms of the well-to-do peasants or do any kind of work that was available. They tilled their land with horses and agricultural machinery hired from richer peasant holdings or even leased all or part of their land to the richer peasants. These poor peasants looked with envy and a sense of grievance at the estates in the neighbourhood of their own poor holdings. They lived with the idea that the day would come when the land of those estates would be repartitioned among themselves in the same way as they used to repartition their 'communal' land. Every political party, seeking the support of the peasantry, had to satisfy this eternal, elemental aspiration of the majority of the peasantry of pre-revolutionary Russia.

The social alienation of the mass of the peasantry from the estate owners took extreme forms. The peasantry viewed the landowners not only as owners of 'their' land but as former serf-owners, social oppressors, who used their economic power in a

* Lenin gives the following approximate figures for the division of land, in 1905, among different owners:

	No. of owners (in millions)	Million desyatin of land	Average per owner
Poorest peasantry	10·5	75·0	7·0
Middle peasantry	1·0	15·0	15·0
Rich peasantry and medium estates	1·5	70·0	46·7
Big landowner estates, appanage Crown land, industrial and mercantile capital	0·03	70·0	2,333·0
Not divided in groups	—	50·0	—
Total	13·03	280·0	21·4

and he stresses that 30,000 big landowners own 70 million desyatin of land, whereas 10½ million poor peasants own only 75 million desyatin of land. Although his groups are somewhat conditional, these figures show the conception Lenin had in mind as regards the division of land when he started the October Revolution of 1917.

humiliating way for the peasantry. The hostility of the majority of the peasantry towards the estate owners had not only an economic but also a very strong social character.

In this lay the political and social aspects of the pre-revolutionary Russian agrarian problem. The peasantry craved for the distribution among themselves of the land of the big estates and for the disappearance of the landowners from their social horizon. But the satisfaction of these aspirations of the peasantry could not decide the economic aspect of the Russian agrarian problem; on the contrary, the repartitioning of land in itself might further hamper the development and intensification of agricultural production.

A peasant farm* is not only a producer but also a consumer of agricultural products. Under Russian conditions peasant farms cultivating less than 6 to 12 desyatin of land (depending upon regions and number of family)† did not produce for the market but, on the contrary, purchased some agricultural products in order to satisfy the needs of their families. Their money income was derived not from their land but from work in domestic craft industries or other trades, or from earnings outside their households. These categories of peasant farms, including not only 'poor peasants' but in some regions also part of the 'middle peasants', had a negative balance in agricultural production and were interested not in high prices for the main agricultural products, but, on the contrary, in low prices.

These peasant farms, with their existing quantity of land and of labour and number of family, could not start on the way toward intensified cultivation without changing their structure. Their prevalence in some regions created agrarian over-population in pre-revolutionary Russia, when it was considered that over 20 million peasants would either have to migrate to less populated regions, especially Siberia,‡ or be absorbed in other economic activities of the country. Only the withdrawal of this surplus agricultural population could make possible the intensifying of

---

* We use the term 'peasant farm' instead of simply 'farm', because the economic aspect of the majority of Russian pre-revolution 'peasant farms' substantially differed from that of the farms in Great Britain or the U.S.A.

† See regional figures, Prokopovitch, *Peasant Economy*, p. 240.

‡ The peasantry in over-populated regions persistently yearned to migrate beyond the Urals, but up to the beginning of the twentieth century the Government did not favour migration, and even during the last 20 years before the revolutions, migration was not organized on a large scale but progressed very slowly.

agricultural production and increase the marketability of agricultural products.

Under the existing conditions marketable agricultural products were supplied mostly by the estates and by the larger peasant farms and, to a much smaller extent, by 'middle' peasant farms.* Distribution of the land of the estates could not enlarge† the quantity of land in the possession of 15 million peasant farms so substantially as to make them fit for intensified cultivation or permit a substantial increase in the marketability of agricultural products. On the contrary, distribution of the land of the estates among the peasantry, under the conditions then existing, would lead to an immediate decrease in the market supply of agricultural products until either the surplus rural population could be absorbed by other branches of economic activity and the average size of farms increased, or until small farms could be combined to form larger productive units which would be able to afford the use of machinery, fertilizers, etc., and eliminate the division of acreage into small strips of land. But both these methods depended upon the development of industry, involving an increase of the industrial and urban population by the absorption of the surplus rural population, not to mention the difficulties in changing the traditional manner of production and consumption and the peasantry's whole outlook on life.

Such were the main political, social and economic aspects of the agrarian problem which the Soviet Government inherited from its predecessors.

Apart from these deep problems, the decrease in agricultural production during the war period (1914–17) created acute dif-

* The following figures give an idea, though not an accurate one (owing to the conditional composition of peasant groups), of the role of different producers in the total agricultural production of pre-revolutionary Russia (1913):

	Gross production		Marketable grain		Percentage of marketable grain
	Million poods*	%	Million poods	%	
Landowners	600	12·0	281·6	21·6	47·0
'Kulaks'†	1,900	38·0	650·0	50·0	34·0
Middle and poor peasants	2,500	50·0	369·0	28·4	14·7
Total	5,000	100·0	1,300·6	100·0	26·0

* Pood = 16·38 kg.   † Well-to-do peasants.

† See figures about acquisitions of the peasantry after the liquidation of private ownership of land on page 22.

ficulties in the supply of agricultural products.* The purchase of grain at fixed prices was introduced as early as 1915, and in 1916 it was even decided to introduce compulsory levies of grain (*khleb-razverstka*), though this measure was not carried out. After the February Revolution of 1917 the Provisional Government decreed a State monopoly of the purchase of grain,† but did not actually apply this decree and instead tried, by doubling prices for grain, to induce the peasantry to supply it in the necessary quantity. It was stressed, however, that if supplies were not increased voluntarily the Government would be obliged to apply military force. Such was the tension with regard to the supply of grain a week before the October Revolution (according to a statement of 16 October 1917 by the Minister of Food of the Provisional Government‡).

The Provisional Government postponed the decision regarding the main agrarian problem—the abolition of large estates—until a constitutional Government had been established. A few preparatory measures began to be applied in the organization of rural committees which would deal with the transfer of land from the estates to the peasantry. Consequently the Soviet Government had not only to think of some solution of the principal agrarian problem, but also to find this solution in an atmosphere of growing crisis in the supply of food to the urban and industrial population.

In order to win the political support of the peasantry, the Bolshevik Party not only proclaimed as the aim of their policy 'peace and land for the peasant', but, on the second day of the October Revolution (26 October 1917),§ published a decree for the liquidation of landed estates.

This decree established that: (*a*) private ownership of land by estate owners is herewith abolished without payment of any kind of compensation; (*b*) all land belonging to estate owners, Crown appanage estates, convents and monasteries, etc., with all their livestock, machinery, buildings and productive equipment, must be

---

* Mobilization of labour, decrease in production and import of agricultural machinery and fertilizers, mobilization of horses for military needs, and the decline in the supply of consumer goods, resulted in a very considerable decline in the production and marketing of agricultural products; the total sown area was reduced by 10 million desyatin (1914, 88·6 million desyatin; 1916, 78 million desyatin), gross production of grain declined from 7 milliard poods in 1909–13 to 6·9 milliard poods in 1916 and 5·1 milliard poods in 1917. See details, Lyashchenko, op. cit. pp. 637–9; Prokopovitch, *War and National Economy*.

† Decree of 25 March 1917.   ‡ Lyashchenko, op. cit. p. 640.

§ According to the 'old style', or on 8 November according to the 'new style', which we shall from now on use in all our quotations.

transmitted to the provisional custody and administration (until a Constitutive Assembly had been elected) of regional rural committees or to the district Soviets of peasants' representatives; (c) all damage done to property confiscated from the estates would be considered as a severe crime and would be punished according to the law, as all confiscated property must, henceforth, be considered as belonging to the whole people; (d) land belonging as private property to peasant farmers must not be confiscated.*

Thus this decree aimed only at transferring the land and productive equipment of the estates temporarily to the rural committees and district Soviets until a legal and concrete form of disposing of confiscated land and equipment would be established; and only then was the actual distribution of confiscated land and estate property among the peasant communities and their members to be carried out.

In reality, of course, the process of 'liquidating' the estates took quite different forms. Regional rural committees and district Soviets existed only in some places, and even in those places the 'elemental forces' of the peasantry overpowered any organized form of restraint in the 'confiscation' of the property of landowner estates.

In this liquidation of estates the social grievances of the peasantry towards landowners very often played an even more important role than economic interest, as the peasants very often burned and demolished the buildings and equipment of neighbouring estates. In the majority of cases, instead of transmitting the property of liquidated estates to the custody of committees and Soviets or peasant communities mentioned above, there took place a crude seizure and 'distribution' of property by individual peasants from neighbouring villages.† During this spontaneous 'confiscation' of the property of estates a great deal of property was destroyed and livestock slaughtered.‡ The distribution of the land of estates also took the form of crude partitioning of land by neighbouring peasant communities among their own members without any organized redistribution of the land among all the peasants of the district.

* This decree was supplemented by special detailed instructions including the main principles on which 'land rights' must be based in the future; but as these instructions, in this period, remained only 'paper law', we omit their description here.

† Very often richer peasants gained more from this 'confiscation' of property because they had carts and horses at their disposal whereas the poor peasants had no transport facilities.

‡ See facts in B. Milyutin, *Agrarian Policy of the U.S.S.R.* pp. 84–6.

2

For political reasons and owing to the absence of an administrative apparatus subordinated to the Central Government, the Central Soviet Government was, in general, during the first months only a spectator of this primitive process of partitioning the land of the estates, its main preoccupation being, during this period, to procure food supplies for the urban and industrial population.

However, as early as 19 February 1918 the Soviet Government published the 'Statutory Law concerning Land'. By this law all land (including land belonging to individual peasants and peasant communities) was proclaimed to be nationalized, and plots of land were to be given for use to all Soviet citizens who were prepared to work on them, the size of plots depending upon the number of persons in the peasant households. In this law it was also stressed that during the partitioning of land the organization of Kolkhozy (collective farms)* should be encouraged; and in November 1918 the Sovnarkom R.S.F.S.R. allocated a special fund to finance the organization of Kolkhozy. A further decree of 14 February 1919 already considered individual farm agricultural production as a transitional form of production to last only until collective productive units should be established ('Kommuns', 'artels',† and co-operative societies for joint tillage of land). In this policy of collectivization not only economic but also political aims were being pursued; as Lenin stressed at the Eighth Congress of Soviets in December 1920, 'it must be remembered that the individual peasants are the stronghold of the capitalist roots in Russia'.‡ The Decree of 14 February 1919 also decided that large State farms and Kolkhozy must be created on the basis of the former intensively farmed estates and the nationalized State land; and the right to organize Kolkhozy by their own initiative was given to State institutions and industrial organizations in order to procure supplies for persons working in these institutions and organizations.

At the Eighth Congress of Soviets in December 1920, measures for the planned increase in the productivity of individual peasant farms were suggested for the first time: peasants were asked to fulfil

* The Russian name 'Kolkhoz' cannot be adequately translated into English. Literally translated it means collective economy (*kollektivnoie khozyaistvo*) of productive units of peasants which cannot be identified with the farms in Great Britain or U.S.A. We shall in future use the term 'Kolkhoz' and will explain the organization of different forms of 'Kolkhoz' later on.

† Artels are a special type of co-operative association; we shall explain this later.

‡ Lenin, op. cit. vol. XVII, pt. II, p. 428.

their obligations towards the State by tilling their land according
to the best example of economy offered by the 'middle and poor
peasants' in the district; to fulfil the requirements as regards the
structure and norms of sowing planned by the State bodies;
regional districts and local agricultural committees were organized
which had to supervise the carrying out of measures for the planned
increase of the productivity of peasant farms.

Such were the main principles guiding agricultural policy, as
they were expressed in decisions of the Soviet Government.

The other measures of the Soviet Government, affecting the development of agriculture during this period, were interconnected
with its policy of procurement and distribution of food.

(a) The crisis in procuring supplies of grain for the town and
industrial population, which had already developed before the
October Revolution, became rapidly much worse. The amount of
grain purveyed declined catastrophically from month to month,*
and in the summer of 1918 the supply of bread in Moscow,
Petrograd and many industrial and rural consuming districts was
so short that the population began to leave these places, and deaths
from hunger were frequent.†

The peasantry willingly divided the estates and their property,
but were quite unwilling, in view of the catastrophic fall in the
purchasing power of money, to supply grain to the State purveyance institutions at the low prices fixed by law. The old
machinery of distribution had ceased to exist and a new one was
only beginning to be organized, while transport difficulties grew
enormously. The result was that although there were sufficient
quantities of grain in the country as a whole, many large towns,
industrial and rural consuming districts had practically no
bread.‡

* In November 1917 purveyance of grain by State purveying institutions
amounted to 641 thousand tons, in December dropped to 136, in January 1918
to 46 thousand tons, and in June 1918 the Central purveying organizations
could only get 2 thousand tons of grain.

† See description given by Lenin of the food situation in this period.
Collected Works, vol. xv, pp. 289, 316; vol. xvi, p. 262; vol. xviii, pt. i, p. 176.

‡ Thousands of people went with bags full of all kinds of 'exchange goods'
(old clothes, boots, watches, linen, etc.) to villages tens and even hundreds of
kilometres away in order to bring back food for their families or for speculative
trade. These 'bag-men' (*meshochniki*) played a very considerable role in supplying the town population with provisions. According to figures given by
Lenin they procured even more supplies than the State purveying organizations. Lenin, op. cit. vol. xxiv, pp. 509, 510.

(*b*) The Soviet Government decided to overcome these difficulties by emergency measures whose form and character changed many times. Here we shall merely enumerate the most important.* On 13 May 1918 a decree declaring a State grain monopoly was issued: all grain, except the grain needed for the maintenance of the families of peasant households and for sowing reserves, was to be delivered at fixed prices to the State purchasing bodies; violation of this order was to be punished by imprisonment up to 10 years with confiscation of property and expulsion from the peasant communities. But in spite of the danger of such severe punishment peasants refused to deliver their grain and preferred to hide it.

A decree of 11 June 1918 introduced the organization of 'village committees' of poor peasants (Kombedy) who had to help the State organizations to requisition grain from well-to-do peasants (kulaks). As a reward for their support in the purveying of grain, these Kombedy were entitled to a share of the supplies procured and of the industrial goods distributed among the villagers.

By a decree of 6 August and supplementary instructions of 20 August 1918, 'detachments of armed industrial workers and poor peasants' which carried out 'purveyance' of grain in various districts, and which had before been organized spontaneously, were sanctioned and centrally organized. These 'detachments' were armed and sent to districts where there was believed to be a surplus of grain in order to procure this grain at fixed low prices or, in case of refusal, to confiscate it; a part of all the grain procured belonged to the 'detachments', part of it was left to the local Kombedy, and the rest had to be delivered to the State distributing institutions. (The 'detachments' were also supplied with industrial goods which they had to distribute among the peasants who assisted in collecting the grain.)

These armed 'purveyance detachments' comprised, in 1918–19, between 20,000 and 45,000 men. On 21 April 1920 the 'purveyance detachments' were abolished,† and their task was taken

* To persons desiring to examine more closely the processes which took place in the relations between the peasantry and the Soviet Government, we recommend the literature marked in our bibliography on pp. 485, 487.

† The 'Kombedy' were officially liquidated in November 1918, as they often did not limit their activities to the purveying of grain but confiscated also private property of well-to-do peasants and not infrequently of middle peasants too; and in some districts their activity even caused the peasantry to rebel. However, they continued to exist in some districts in 1919, but as private local organizations of the poorest peasants.

over by special military detachments of the 'Kommissariat for internal security and combat against counter-revolution and speculation'.*

All these measures of the Soviet Government were carried out in an atmosphere of 'class war' in the villages (under the political slogan: 'With the support of the poor peasants, in alliance with the middle peasants—fight against the "kulaks"!'), and in conditions of civil war which either actually broke out in the more important agricultural regions (in northern Caucasia, Ukraine, the Volga districts, and Siberia), or separated these regions for many months from the territories which were governed by the Soviet Central Government.

The main results of all the measures of the Soviet Government described above and of the intervention of the spontaneous forces of the peasant rising in the domain of agriculture were as follows:

(a) Private estates were liquidated, but their liquidation did not take the forms prescribed by the decrees of the Soviet Government —the primitive forces of the peasant rising proved more powerful than the regulating and administrative power of the Soviet Government. Distribution of the land of the estates was not carried out in an organized manner. Land was directly taken possession of by neighbouring peasant communities and divided among their members. Cases of participation in the distribution of the land of estates by peasants who lived in districts far away from the estates were very rare, and migrations of peasants from over-populated regions to regions richer in land did not take place at all. Consequently, peasants in different districts received very different shares in the partitioned land of estates, according to the size of estates and the number of peasants in particular districts.

In most districts, land which had been bought by well-to-do peasants as private property with the aid of the Peasants' Bank was also divided among the members of the neighbouring peasant communities. In some districts even the land of peasants who had left the peasant community after the Stolypin reform was taken back into the common pool of the community and redistributed among its members. However, with the exception of a few districts only, a simultaneous distribution of all the community land was not carried out. In the majority of districts only the 'new' land, consisting of that of the confiscated estates, the privately owned land of well-to-do peasants, and the land of peasants who

---

* *Stages in the Development of the Economic Policy of the U.S.S.R.* pp. 48–9, 52.

had left the community after the Stolypin reform, was redistributed. Consequently peasants found themselves using, side by side with their previous strips of community land, 'new' strips of land received from the partition of the estates. The amount of this additional 'new' land varied very much in different regions (from 8·5 to 50 %, with an average of approximately 31 %,* of the amount of land previously used by the peasantry in a particular region). On the whole, the land cultivated by the peasants increased per head only from one-tenth of a desyatin to one desyatin in different regions.†

(b) Only on the fractions of land expropriated from the landed estates were Sovkhozy (State farms) and Kolkhozy organized (in 1920 in R.S.F.S.R. there were altogether 5,923 Sovkhozy and 10,426 Kolkhozy), and they received about 6–7 % of the total land expropriated from landed estates.

The Sovkhozy mostly included converted estates, on which sugar, spirits and starch had been produced and other industries working up agricultural products carried on, and other estates with specialized agricultural production. The economy of the Sovkhozy suffered very much from the lack of experience on the part of the managing staffs (which consisted mostly of industrial workers and revolutionary 'intellectuals'), and from a tendency to make the satisfaction of the needs of consumers, workers and employees of the Sovkhozy the first object of production. Consequently productivity of the Sovkhozy and the marketability of their products were very low.

Most of the Kolkhozy were organized by industrial workers and artisans who left the towns and factories, by demobilized soldiers and the poorest peasants, on the basis of former estates or agricultural machinery belonging to these estates. Their aim was to produce food almost exclusively to satisfy the needs of their members, and they did not play any significant part in the supply of food to the State distributing institutions.

(c) Peasants who disposed of their marketable surplus of food were unwilling to deliver food to the State purchasing bodies as, under the existing conditions of a catastrophic decline in the purchasing capacity of money and the supply of industrial consumer goods, these deliveries were practically gratuitous. Food was procured by compulsory methods in an atmosphere of 'class strife'

* 'Ten years of Soviet power in figures (1917–27)', *J. Statistics*, N. I–III, p. 138.

† Collected volumes under general title, *Land*, vol. I, pp. 29–31.

with the kulaks, i.e. with the peasants who, together with the
owners of the estates in pre-revolutionary Russia, were the main
producers of marketable agricultural products.

By means of compulsory methods the amount of food distributed
increased and the acute difficulty in supplying the town and the
industrial population was partly overcome,* but the peasantry
from whom the food was taken replied to these measures by reducing the production of foodstuffs.

(d) As a result of the processes described above there took place
a great decline in the output of agriculture. The sown area, gross
yield of crops and the number of livestock declined.†

Table 2

	Sown area in million desyatin	Gross yield of crops in million poods	No. of horses in millions	No. of cattle in millions	No. of sheep and goats in millions
1909–13	83·1	3,850	—	—	—
1916	79·0	3,482	31·5	49·9	80·9
1917	79·4	3,350	—	—	—
1920	62·9	2,082	25·4	39·1	49·8
1921	58·3	1,689	23·3	36·8	48·4

Apart from this great reduction in agricultural production there
also occurred a reduction in the marketable surplus of agricultural
products—the number of well-to-do peasant farms with large disposable surpluses considerably decreased and at the same time the
number of consuming peasant farms increased. Apart from these
underlying economically regressive processes the consequences
of the methods of compulsory procurement of agricultural products created, in some rural districts,‡ a difficult situation as regards
food and the prospects for the future development of agricultural

* Purveyance of grain by the State purveying organizations amounted in
1916–17 to 508·1 million poods; in 1918–19, 107·9; in 1919–20, 212·4; in
1920–1, 367·0; *Collection of Statistical Figures of the U.S.S.R.* 1918–23, p. 424.

† These figures do not refer to all territories of the U.S.S.R. but only to
territory on which the Census of 1920 was carried out and the same territory
for other years. *Collection of Statistical Figures of the U.S.S.R.* 1918–23, pp. 123,
131, 137, 146.

‡ In some districts, suffering from periodical droughts, in which special
seeds had to be used and reserves of grain had to be kept as an insurance against
the occurrence of drought years, these reserves were confiscated by procurement
'detachments' as grain surplus to the current consuming needs of the peasantry
in these districts. See figures for the amounts of purveyed grain from the districts
which were affected by the famine of 1920–1, B. Milyutin, *Agrarian Policy of the
U.S.S.R.* p. 132.

production, and also resulted, in some districts, in the rebellion of the peasantry.

In 1920 these processes were further aggravated by a very considerable failure of crops which affected fifteen regions with a population of over 20 millions and resulted in the notorious famine in the Volga districts in 1920–1.

The situation in agriculture therefore called imperatively for a change in some of the principles and methods of carrying out the agrarian policy and distributing agricultural products.

3. INTERNAL AND EXTERNAL TRADE

As regards internal trade the policy of the Soviet Government was merely to start by introducing State *control* over the activities of private trade in the key branches of trade, without immediate nationalization.* Control by the workers, introduced by a decree of 14 November 1917, aimed at controlling not only the production but also the sale and purchase of goods and raw materials. Alongside the workers' control of trade, it was also intended to introduce a State monopoly of trade in the most important goods and products. But in actual fact, this policy of allowing the co-existence of private trade and the system of workers' control and State monopoly was not realized in trade any more than it was in industry:

(*a*) The central power was not always able to enforce on local authorities the practical interpretation of its policy. These local authorities very often imposed monetary levies on representatives of the trading class, with the threat of confiscating the goods in their shops if these levies were not paid. Persons who refused or were unable to pay the amount of the contribution were often detained as hostages until the contribution was paid by relatives or trade associations. Consequently, many businesses closed down, either owing to the lack of liquid capital or for personal reasons. Many shops were closed owing to shortage of the goods in which they traded. There were many cases of goods being confiscated by the local authorities because the owners of stores and shops were accused of hiding goods and holding them back for speculative purposes, and of obstructing the orders of the authorities. A rapid rise in prices, due to inflationary processes in State finance and to a decrease in the output of all kinds of goods, speeded up the destruction of the fabric of internal trade.

* Lenin, op. cit. vol. xx, pp. 87–90.

(*b*) A State monopoly of trade in particular goods was introduced without any systematic, previously conceived plan. It was introduced as soon as difficulties arose in the trade in particular goods;* State monopoly in the autumn of 1918 already embraced all the most important goods and products, and the basis for complete nationalization of trade was thus practically established.

(*c*) But in spite of these measures, in the first years of the existence of Soviet power the free market was not liquidated, and private trade legally existed in all goods and products which were not monopolized by the State. In this period, consumers' co-operatives even continued, *de facto*, to work under the direction of their pre-revolutionary central organizations. However, the field of action of private and co-operative trade became steadily more limited, and that of State monopolies, methods of barter and centralized distribution by the State was steadily extended.

A decree of 21 November 1918 instituted the nationalization of all trade. And so ended the period of the co-existence of private and State trading. The Food Commissariat (Narkomprod) was entrusted with the purchase of all articles of personal and household consumption.

The decree provided for the setting up of a network of State and co-operative stores and distribution centres with a view to the supply and distribution of all consumer goods. Wholesale stores and retail shops of co-operatives were to be left under the direction of co-operative organizations, but controlled by the Narkomprod. Industrial commodities destined for mass consumption were to be

---

* On 30 November 1917, a State monopoly was introduced for agricultural machinery and implements; on 16 December 1917, for all textiles; on 27 December 1917, food commissions of the Soviets were ordered to take over the whole matter of food supplies; on 15 January 1918, the gold trade was made a State monopoly; on 7 March 1918, a State monopoly was introduced for matches, candles, rice, coffee and pepper. On 13 May 1918, a decree was published concerning 'food dictatorship', one of its clauses (Clause 3) running as follows: 'All those who possess surpluses of grain and fail to bring them to the delivery points, as well as those who squander their grain resources in the production of home-distilled spirits, are to be proclaimed enemies of the people and handed over to revolutionary tribunals, and those found guilty to be sentenced to imprisonment for not less than ten years.' This decree gave emergency powers to the Food Commissariat with regard to compulsory deliveries of grain and other agricultural produce, empowering it to apply armed force. Further, on 11 October 1918, the Food Commissariat ordered the taking over of stocks of chocolate, cocoa and their substitutes. On 13 November 1918, the S.E.C. decreed that all leather and hides be placed at the disposal of the State. On 14 November 1918, the purchase and distribution of oil seeds were monopolized.

delivered by the respective departments of the S.E.C. to the purchasing organs of the Narkomprod. The latter had to carry out the distribution of all foodstuffs and general consumption goods thus delivered through the intermediary of the wholesale and retail distribution network of the State and co-operatives. Co-operatives were to serve not only their members but all the population in their districts.

By a decree of January 1919 all sales of grain were prohibited, and compulsory distribution of cereals and fodder was instituted. Soon afterwards the sale of industrial crops was also forbidden and their compulsory assessment from peasant households decreed. We have described above the organization of the purveyance of agricultural products. Here we would only like to stress that in spite of the fact that trade in foodstuffs was proclaimed illegal and although the authorities tried to stop the practices of the 'bagmen' (*meshochnikÿ*; see above, p. 19) by setting up special armed 'pickets' along all lines of communication, 'bagging' continued until the policy of 'War Communism' was abandoned, as the authorities were unable to provide the urban and industrial population with a sufficient quantity of foodstuffs. Throughout this period of nationalization of trade, this 'bagging' was the only form of 'commerce' alongside the direct barter in which the urban consumers and the peasants engaged at the local illicit markets.*

The supply of the population with the *available* necessaries of life was carried out on the basis of a ration-card system, involving class differentiation. At first there existed neither unified basic rations nor ration categories extending over the whole country. At the end of 1918 four ration categories were introduced (with very different supplies of food for the different categories †). Later on, the number of categories increased, and by 1920 there were thirty different categories of population as regards the supply of consumer goods. By decrees of 14 and 24 January 1920 the existing thirty categories were abolished and replaced by five. In 1920, 35 million people were supplied through the centralized State machinery. (The peasantry was not supplied with foodstuffs, except in some regions where the predominant crops were industrial raw materials.)

---

* In 1918 groups of workers and employees were temporarily permitted to send their representatives to the villages for the purchase of food for their needs; afterwards even this was prohibited, but from time to time certain groups of the population were permitted to transport up to 1½ poods of food for their own use.

† For example, the first category was supplied with 35 lb. of bread per month, the fourth category only with 12 lb.

As we have seen above, the production of industrial goods and of food decreased to such an extent that the quantities available for distribution were very limited, particularly as a considerable part of the available supplies was to be allocated to the Red Army engaged in civil war. Consequently, the civil population could not be regularly supplied with even the most limited quantities of manufactured goods. Some goods disappeared completely as far as the mass of the population was concerned.

It must also be remembered that, during this period, only about one-ninth of the present European territory of the U.S.S.R. was not directly affected by the civil war and not cut off by the front line from the territories governed by the Central Soviet Government.

The result of all this in internal trade during the period of 'War Communism' was as follows:

(a) Internal trade, in the strict sense of the word, simply did not exist in the U.S.S.R. An attempt was made to organize forcible deliveries of agricultural products, to centralize the distribution of industrial commodities of mass consumption in the hands of the State distributing organs, and to distribute all foodstuffs and industrial commodities on a ration system with a 'class' basis.

(b) The whole network of trade relations established in the pre-revolutionary period was destroyed (with the exception of a part of the co-operative system which survived).

(c) As far as capital employed in private trade was concerned, it was a period of confiscations, requisitions and suppression of trade. Private trading in goods or money by private capital practically ceased to exist.

(d) Money, prices and credit ceased to play their usual role in trade. The rouble lost its purchasing power so rapidly that the population ceased to calculate exchange value in money and tried to use different kinds of goods as exchange 'money' (see below, chapter on Public Finance and Money). At the end of 1920 and the beginning of 1921, payment for foodstuffs and necessaries supplied by ration was abolished, as was payment for the use of post and telegraph services, rationed supplies of fuel, lodgings, communal services, newspapers, medical supplies and some other goods and services.

(e) Such an organization of the internal market could exist only as an emergency measure, in order to ensure distribution of the very scarce supplies of necessaries, in conditions of civil war and during the early stages of the development of the new administrative apparatus of the State. But this system did not offer any new means of securing the economic recovery of the country which was so desperately needed. It was no more than a temporary solution and had inevitably to be replaced by a new organization of internal trade, and it is well known that N.E.P. (the New Economic Policy) was first applied in the organization of internal trade.*

The internal market, in this period, was nearly completely isolated from the foreign market:

(a) On 29 December 1917 the Soviet Government issued a decree establishing a system of licences for exports and imports. The trade organizations which had existed before the Revolution were permitted to carry on foreign trade, but only on the basis of licences issued by the Foreign Department of the Commissariat of Trade and Industry. Foreign trade without licence was to be treated as smuggling. This intermediate form of organization proved as unworkable when applied to foreign commerce as it did in internal trade. It existed for only four months before being replaced, under a decree of 22 April 1918, by a system of State monopoly of foreign trade. According to this decree all foreign trade was nationalized and was henceforth to be conducted only by the appropriate department of the 'Soviet for Foreign Trade'. The object in introducing the State monopoly of foreign commerce was, in the words of its creator (L. Krasin): 'The Red Army must defend our country against possible military attacks. The monopoly of foreign trade must repulse all economic and financial intervention from abroad.' †

(b) The monopoly of foreign trade enabled the Soviet Government to exert control over all export and import transactions. It could not, however, protect the U.S.S.R. from the indirect economic and financial intervention of foreign countries. The blockade of the U.S.S.R., which was introduced by the Entente after the conclusion of the Treaty of Brest-Litovsk, was only lifted on 16 January 1920. The financial blockade, which took the form both of a refusal by leading French, English, American, Scandinavian and Estonian banks to take part in any credit transactions involving the U.S.S.R. and of a refusal to accept payment, even in Russian gold money, continued up to the middle of 1921. This blockade, together with the lack of export goods at the disposal of

* For a detailed description of the measures for and processes in internal trade during this period see literature mentioned in the bibliography, p. 485.

† Krasin, *Problems of Foreign Trade.*

the Soviet Government, resulted in the almost complete cessation of economic intercourse between the U.S.S.R. and the rest of the world.

(c) The volume of exports declined heavily and imports were limited to emergency purchases to meet the needs of the army and relief supplies for the civilian population.

The course of foreign trade in this period is shown by the figures for exports and imports from 1913 to 1920 (in millions of roubles, 1913 value) given in Table 3.

Table 3

	Exports	Imports	Balance
1913	1,520·1	1,374·0	+146·1
1914	835·0	1,109·0	−274.0
1915	274·0	870·0	−596·0
1916	237·0	862·0	−625·0
1917	137·0	802·0	−665·0
1918	7·5	61·1	− 53·6
1919	0·1	3·0	− 2·9
1920	1·4	28·7	− 27·3

In this period, therefore, foreign trade underwent the same process of deterioration as had the other branches of economic activity.

4. PUBLIC FINANCE, CREDIT AND MONEY

Developments in the domain of finance during this period provide another striking instance of the way in which reality moulded itself in forms quite different from those which the leaders of the Soviet Government had in mind. Lenin, in full accordance with Marxist teaching, shared the view that one of the first measures of the Socialist Government must be the centralization in the hands of the State power of control over credit. He stressed that without the nationalization of the banks a regulation of economic life was impossible.* But nationalization of the banks was not meant as the confiscation of the assets of the banks, or as the confiscation of private property deposited at banks. It was intended simply as a means for establishing real control over the banks and their activities. By the nationalization of banks 'the State will be enabled first to *review* all the main money transfers, later to *control*

---

* Lenin, op. cit. vol. xxi, p. 164.

them and further to *regulate* economic life, and finally to receive millions and milliards for big State financial operations without having to pay "commission" to the capitalists for their services'.*

Lenin further stressed that 'the big banks represent the potential State apparatus which we need for putting Socialism into practice . . . we must utilize this excellent apparatus, and make it even more integrated and all-embracing. One State Bank with branches in every rural district, in every factory—that is already nine-tenths of the Socialist apparatus. A general State accounting, and a general measurement by the State of the output and distribution of goods—that, it can be said, is a skeleton of a socialistic society.' †

According to these premises in the economic programme of the Party it was intended that the banks should be nationalized and merged into one Central Bank, and that commercial secrecy should be abolished. But the liquidation of the banks which did, in fact, take place was not originally intended. The programme of the Party also proposed: (1) the discontinuation of further issue of currency in order to stabilize the price level; (2) the reorganization of taxation by introducing a system of progressive income and property tax and a high indirect tax on luxuries.‡

Even in April 1918 (after the actual measures of the Government and developments in finance had already sharply deviated from the assumptions of the Soviet Government) Lenin stressed the fact that the main attention was now to be paid to the organization of strict accounting and control, and to raising the productivity of labour: 'We must convert banks into a unified apparatus for accounting and regulating the socialistically organized economic life of the country.... We must not forget that all our radical reforms will be unsuccessful if we do not achieve success in our financial policy.'§

Such were the main aims of the Party as regards financial policy. The measures actually taken and the course of events were quite different. As we shall proceed to show, the Soviet Government inherited the following situation as regards public finance and the currency:

(a) During the war successive State Budgets had showed heavy deficits, which had been met partly by the issue of notes and partly by loans (Table 4). As early as 1915–16, the State Budget deficit

* Lenin, op. cit. vol. xxi, p. 166.
† Lenin, op. cit. vol. xxi, p. 260.
‡ *Finance and Credit of the U.S.S.R.* p. 63.
§ Lenin, op. cit. vol. xxiii, p. 18; vol. xxx, p. 379.

amounted to over 75 % of total expenditure, and by 1917 it had risen to 81·7 %.

Table 4. *State Budget (in millions of roubles)*

	Revenue	Expenditure	Deficit	Note issue
1914	2,961	4,859	1,898	1,283
1915	3,001	11,562	8,561	2,670
1916	4,345	18,101	13,756	3,480
1917	5,039	27,607	22,568	16,403

(b) After the February Revolution of 1917 the printing press began to work very intensively. On 1 March 1917 the amount of paper currency in circulation was 9,950 million roubles (as against 1,630 in July 1914). In October 1917 (on the eve of the October Revolution) it was already 18,917 million roubles. That is to say, during the eight months of the existence of the Provisional Government the note circulation almost doubled.

(c) Prices, which were trebled between 1913 and February 1917, rose during the following eight months to a level nearly eight times higher than that of 1913. The price index was as follows: 1·00 in 1913, 3·02 in February 1917, 7·55 on 1 October 1917, and 12·85 on 1 November 1917. Consequently the Soviet Government inherited an already high inflationary financial situation.

(d) The Soviet Government inherited a very large and scattered network of credit institutions. The chief place was occupied by the State Bank, by mortgage banks for long-term credit (twelve big banks and a few smaller ones), commercial joint-stock banks for short-term credit (forty-six banks with 822 branches and agencies, including thirty-three abroad), and over 1,000 mutual credit companies. This credit system, in many of its aspects, differed from those in the other great European States, but it is unnecessary to describe these differences here. We will only stress the fact that the State Bank, in some respects, fulfilled the functions of a Central Bank, directed the credit policy of the whole Russian banking system, and had great influence on it, but at the same time its operational basis was not private deposits but public deposits and gold reserves; two big mortgage banks (the Nobles' Land Bank and Peasants' Land Bank) were closely interconnected with real estate. Joint-stock banks were very largely dependent on foreign capital (in 1914 over 40 % of the joint-stock capital of eighteen big banks belonged to foreigners) and were closely associated with large-scale industry. Mutual credit companies worked with small industries and businesses. Consequently none of these banks, nor the whole network of banks, could be considered as the prototype of a Central Credit apparatus which could be used for 'general State accounting...as a skeleton of a socialistic society'. Considerable reorganization would be necessary before the credit system could be used in this way.

Therefore the nationalization of banks, in the very first transitional period, had political rather than economic aims. The example of the Paris Commune which did not 'expropriate the expropriators' served Lenin as a warning of the danger which might face the Revolution if the banks were left in the hands of the 'bourgeoisie'.*

In accordance with the above-mentioned political and economic aims the only object of the first measures of the Soviet Government with regard to the credit system was to establish real control over the banks:

(a) On the second day of its seizing power the Soviet Government posted a military guard at the offices of the State Bank, but when a few days later the Soviet Government ordered the manager of the bank to place 20 million roubles at the disposal of the Government the manager refused to obey this order, and when it was repeated he called a meeting of the staff of the bank at which it was decided to refuse the demand of the Soviet Government and to start a strike. The Soviet Government replied to this by occupying the offices of the bank by military force on 20 November 1917, appointing a commissar of the Government to take the place of the manager, and inviting employees willing to collaborate with the new management to continue their work. Commissars of the Soviet Government were also appointed heads of many branches of the State Bank. Thus, in order to break at once the opposition of the bank personnel hostile towards the new regime, the State Bank was de facto taken over under the management of commissars appointed by the Soviet Government.

However, it was still hoped that it would be possible to establish some collaboration with private bankers. Private banks were permitted to draw a certain fixed sum every week from their balances at the State Bank on condition that this sum would be used for financing industries, and that the State would have the right of exercising control over the credit transactions of private banks. This control aimed, first of all, at preventing private banks from using their resources for political purposes (against the regime and

* Lenin, op. cit. vol. XII, p. 163.

against the economic measures of the Soviet Government) and preventing possible concealment of capital or transfer of capital abroad.

(*b*) In the event, this attempt of the Soviet Government to collaborate with private banks proved to be very short-lived.

The decree of the Sovnarkom S.S.S.R. of 12 November 1917 stated: 'Private banks are closed. Employees and managers still come to the banks, but they do not open the doors of the banks to the public. Workers cannot be paid their salaries because the banks refuse to pay the cheques of factories'; and the decree ordered the immediate reopening of banks (on 13 November) and the carrying on of business as usual, stressing that 'If banks would not reopen and cheques were not paid, all managers and members of the managing boards would be arrested and Commissars would be appointed in all banks...to secure order military guards will be posted at all banks.'*

Commercial secrecy was abolished. Payments from current accounts were limited to a certain sum in order to prevent large-scale withdrawals of deposits, but this limitation affected only deposits which were made before 1 January 1918. All sums deposited after that date could be disposed of freely.

All these measures, however, proved unsuccessful, and Lenin, in his speech at a meeting of the All-Russian Central Executive Committee (V.Ts.I.K.), gave the following justification for the necessity of immediate nationalization of private banks:

In order to establish control over banks we invited bankers to collaborate. Together with them we worked out measures to which they agreed. They agreed to receive funds on condition of full control over their accounts by us. But among the employees of the banks there were some to whom the interests of the people were dear and they said to us: 'They (the bankers) are deceiving you, hurry to suppress their criminal activities, aimed at doing you harm....' We know that this is a complicated measure [the taking over of banks]. None of us, even those who are experienced in economics, will be able to carry it out. We shall employ experts, men who are experienced in such work, but only after we have the keys in our hands. After that we can even consult ex-millionaires...we wished to proceed on the path of agreement with the bankers, we provided them with loans for the financing of industries, but they started sabotage on an unprecedented scale, and experience has compelled us to adopt other measures.†

On the morning of 27 December all private banks in Petrograd were occupied by military detachments, and the evening of the

---

* *Finance and Credit of the U.S.S.R.* p. 67.
† Lenin, op. cit. vol. XXII, p. 143.

same day V.Ts.I.K. accepted the decree for 'nationalizing the banks'.

(c) By the decree of 27 December 1917, banking was declared to be a State monopoly, all private joint-stock banks and banking houses were merged in the State Bank,* to which were transferred their assets and liabilities as well as the temporary managements of private banks. It was stressed that the interest of the small depositor must be fully protected. On the same day the inspection of safes was decreed. Safes were to be opened by owners in the presence of inspectors, all money found was to be deposited on personal current accounts in the State Bank, and gold coin or bullion was to be confiscated. On 29 December 1917 payment of coupons and dividends was discontinued and the transfer of shares prohibited.

On 26 January 1918 were decreed confiscation of all joint-stock capital of private banks and its transfer to the State Bank, annulment of all bank shares and the payment of their dividends. Other credit institutions, however, continued to exist up to the end of 1918 and some even up to the middle of 1919,† as they were not considered to be politically dangerous and the Government had its hands full with the organization of the liquidation of big banks and could not spare the personnel even for formally taking over the numerous credit institutions. By the middle of 1919 the nationalization of all banking institutions was completed and all private banks were merged in the State Bank, renamed the People's Bank. The Credit Chancellery and the Department of State Treasury were also absorbed in the State Bank.

All private insurance companies were also first put under State control and were liquidated at the end of 1918; insurance was proclaimed a State monopoly.

In January 1918 all State loans and foreign loans were annulled except for bondholders who owned not more than 10,000 roubles in internal State loans (they received the right to exchange these State loans for a new State loan of the R.S.F.S.R., but in reality this loan was not issued, and they were only credited by corre-

* The Nobles' Land Bank and the Peasants' Land Bank were abolished as early as 8 December 1917 as a consequence of the nationalization of land.

† In November–December 1918 joint-stock land banks, mutual credit societies and city public banks were liquidated; municipal and regional credit societies were abolished only in May 1919. On 2 December 1918 the liquidation of foreign banks and the nationalization of the Central co-operative institution (Moscow People's Bank) were decreed—the latter being reorganized as the co-operative section of the State Bank.

sponding sums on their accounts), and in December 1919 all regional (*zemstva*) and municipal loans were also annulled.

(*d*) Thus the nationalization of all credit institutions by the State and the concentration of all credit transactions in the People's Bank were *formally* achieved. But this 'nationalization' took place together with the ever-growing process of development of a money-less* economy and swift inflation which undermined the very basis of credit transactions and gradually led to the actual fusion of the activities of the People's Bank with those of the Commissariat of Finance. This deprived the People's Bank of its credit functions and converted it into a kind of State Central Clearing Office.

By the decree of 19 January 1920 the People's Bank was liquidated and its assets and liabilities were transferred to the Central Budgeting and Accounting Department of the Commissariat of Finance, which had to carry out the few remaining credit transactions. 'The only institution which, at any rate in outward appearance, kept the form of a bank, was the so-called co-operative section of the People's Commissariat of Finance, formed out of the former Moscow Narodny Bank; but even this institution, which preserved some feeble connexion with the old credit system, was liquidated in the beginning of 1922.'†

In the domain of public finance and money the chief developments were as follows:

(*a*) In the first months of the existence of the Soviet Government an attempt was made to collect the previously existing taxes and levies, and even in 1918 work was carried out for the adaptation of the old taxation system to the new conditions. But as the 'nationalization' of all branches of economic activities as well as the depreciation of money proceeded very rapidly, this source of State revenue played a very insignificant role.

From the very beginning of the existence of the Soviet, State methods of laying the representatives of the 'bourgeoisie' under contribution were widely used by the central and local Soviets and, during the first period, this source provided considerable sums.

---

* The financing of all nationalized enterprises was carried out by non-repayable grants from the State Budget. All production of enterprises was handed over gratis to the appropriate Glavki and Tsentra (Central departments of the S.E.C.) and all settlements between Soviet enterprises and institutions were carried out without money transfer, by means of book entries. The decree of 15 June 1920 even prohibited money payments among Soviet enterprises and institutions. Owing to the continuous depreciation of money the population shunned money exchange more and more and resorted to barter.

† S. S. Katzenellenbaum, *Russian Currency and Banking*, p. 152.

Only in April 1918 did the Commissariat of Finance try to stop such levies on the initiative of the local Soviets, as this 'undermined the sources of local as well as of State revenue'.* Other sources of revenue from taxation were extraordinary taxes. By the decree of 30 October 1918 the 'extraordinary Revolution tax of 10 milliard roubles' was put into operation and was levied on the better-off sections of the urban and rural population. The decree of 31 October 1918 'concerning extraordinary revolution taxes, to be set up at once by local Soviets for the satisfaction of their needs', authorized local Soviets to introduce extraordinary taxes in order to cover their budget deficits. These extraordinary taxes served as very substantial sources of revenue for the local Soviets, but in the revenue of the State Budget they played a very insignificant role.†

The main source for covering the expenditure of the State was the issue of money, and as disintegration of the money economy proceeded very rapidly, the *raison d'être* of imposing money taxes also diminished. By the decree of 8 February 1921 the collection of money taxes was discontinued.

(*b*) Since the money revenue of the State Budget from taxation covered only a small fraction of State expenditure, the Soviet Government had recourse to the printing press, without any formal declaration as to the extent of the issuing rights; and by the decree of 15 May 1919 it was permitted to issue as much money as was actually required for the national economy‡ (see Table 5). The

Table 5

	Revenue milliard roubles	Expenditure milliard roubles	Deficit milliard roubles	Issue milliard roubles
1917	5·0	27·6	22·6	16·4
1918	15·6	46·7	31·1	33·5
1919	49·0	215·4	166·4	164·2
1920	159·6	1,215·2	1,055·6	943·6
1921	4,139·9	26,076·8	21,936·9	16,375·3

designs of notes were changed many times, and in spite of the fact that money was expressed in the same units as before, the population, for psychological reasons, attributed a different purchasing power to different designs, some being considered 'better money'

* *Finance and Credit of the U.S.S.R.* p. 75.

† Instead of 10 milliard roubles the above-mentioned 'extraordinary revolution tax' brought the State Budget, up to the middle of 1919, only 1·5 milliard roubles, and, owing to the rapid depreciation of money in the meantime, the real value of this sum declined very considerably.

‡ Katzenellenbaum, op. cit. p. 69.

than others. Gresham's law, in this curious way, was operating as between different issues of paper money. Apart from the money issued by the Central Government, money was also issued by different Governments which were at war with the Soviet Government and even by the local authorities of some regions.

(c) The rate of depreciation of the rouble outstripped the rate of issue; this was due to the rapid decrease in the quantity and turnover of marketable goods and products, to the rapid growth of a moneyless economy, and to such psychological factors as the reluctance of the population to accept constantly depreciating money as a measure of value and its preference for barter, especially on the part of the peasantry.

Consequently the real revenue of the State Budget from the issue of money constantly decreased. The real value of all the circulating media (calculated on the basis of the index numbers of commodity prices—1913 = 100) was:* 2,200·6 milliard roubles on 1 November 1917; 488·5 milliard roubles on 1 July 1918; and only 29·1 milliard roubles on 1 July 1921; and the real monthly revenue extracted by the Treasury from the note issues shrank from 163·1 milliard roubles in November–December 1917 to 5·6 milliard roubles in the first half of 1921—in the last months of this period the real value of issue hardly covered the expenses of printing and organizing the distribution of the notes.

Disintegration of the monetary system proceeded so rapidly that at the end of this period paper money nearly ceased to serve as a measure of value and as a unit of accounting. In some districts the population even used different commodities as a means of exchange.

The programme of the Russian Communist Party, adopted at the Eighth Party Congress in March 1918, visualized that though during the transition from Capitalism to Communism the abolition of money is impossible, the gradual extension of moneyless settlements among enterprises monopolized by the State will 'prepare the ground for the abolition of money'. 'Moneyless settlements' acquired very great dimensions during the last years of this period,† and there even arose a project to replace money by a

---

* Prof. L. N. Yurovsky, *Currency Problems and Policy of the Soviet Union*, pp. 27, 28.

† By the decree of 2 May 1918 Soviet undertakings and institutions were asked to deposit all their money in the People's Bank or in the State Treasury and make all payments by means of drafts and cheques; by the decree of 13 August 1918 all money transactions among Soviet enterprises were to be done by book entries. The decree of 6 January 1920 extended this practice to co-operative undertakings, etc. See details, Yurovsky, op. cit. pp. 32–3.

stable unit of account in the form of a Labour Unit, but this project was not carried out and had no practical consequences which would deserve description in a summary survey.*

(d) As revenue from taxes and from the issue of money furnished less and less resources for the State Budget, requisitioning, taxes in kind and goods and products received from the nationalized enterprises began to play a great role in the State Budget. Taxation in kind (*prodrazverstka*) and requisition of grain, cattle and other agricultural products, as well as goods received from nationalized enterprises, were the Soviet Government's main sources for the supply of rationed products and goods to the population. If we also remember that the supply of factories with raw materials was carried out free of charge, that payments of wages and salaries were to a great extent made in kind, that free trading in grain and other commodities was prohibited, that in 1920 rationed goods were distributed free of charge, and that no charge was made for some State and communal services and dwellings—it will be clear that the sphere of money circulation became very limited and money gradually ceased to serve not only as a measure of value and unit of account but also as a circulating medium and means of payment.

The Soviet Government tried to regulate prices,† and all 'purchases' by the State and distribution of goods, as far as they were carried out on a monetary basis, took place at fixed prices. But these prices lagged so far behind the actual prices of the illegal free markets that they served only as a purely conventional means for the calculation of the total amount of different kinds of transferred goods.

Thus, in the domain of credit, public finance and money the measures of the Soviet Government, in this period, mostly took the form of emergency measures, influenced by the general aims of nationalization of credit and the struggle with the 'better-off' class, by the opposition to these aims of former governing bodies and personnel of the credit system, and by the developments which took place in industrial and agricultural production and on the internal market. The inherited financial system was destroyed, but

---

* See description of these projects: Yurovsky, op. cit. p. 34; Arthur Z. Arnold, *Banks, Credit and Money in Soviet Russia*, pp. 106–10.

† In January 1918 a 'committee for price regulation' was created whose duties were the fixing of prices for commodities, the distribution of profit among trading enterprises, and the definition of the expenditure of the trade turn-over. This was the first attempt to regulate prices; it remained only an attempt without practical consequences.

the newly established system had only an emergency character and could not be used for the task of restoring the productivity of the national economy—for this purpose it would be necessary to build up quite a new system for which not even the main institutions of the financial system of this period and the form of their activities could be used as building material.

5. LABOUR

The same divergence between aspirations and the actual course of events was seen in the domain of labour in this period.

The intention was to organize the participation of the large mass of the workers in the control and management of the national economy, to put into practice the most progressive legislation and raise the productivity of labour on the basis of the conscious effort of the worker who 'from now on works for himself'. All labour legislation, during the first year of this period, was inspired by these aspirations.

By the decree of 27 November 1917 there was instituted control by elected representatives of the workers over the activities of all enterprises. In all enterprises councils of workers and employees were to be elected, whose duty it was to look after the supply of fuel and raw material, normal production and fulfilment of orders, to control the activities of the managing boards and, at the same time, to help them in the organization of production and distribution.

Lenin visualized workers' control as a training of the workers in the management of enterprises, as a 'step towards Socialism'.* It was also thought that Trade Unions, though not directly intervening in the management of enterprises, would help in the organization of production by selecting cadres of managers, strengthening labour discipline and supporting, from 'below', the fulfilment of the orders of the management.†

The most progressive labour laws were promulgated. The decree of 11 November 1917 instituted an eight-hour day and limitation of overtime, prohibiting night work for women and for juveniles up to the age of sixteen, and underground work for women and for juveniles under eighteen. On 14 November 1917 new principles were introduced in the workers' insurance scheme which were

* Lenin, op. cit. vol. XXII, p. 451.
† *Party Resolutions*, pt. I, pp. 346, 378.

intended to extend insurance to all workers and employees without exception, to cover by insurance all losses through incapacity for work and unemployment, to introduce the payment of full wages in case of disablement, to organize complete administration of all insurance organizations by the insured persons, and to charge all the expenses of insurance on the enterprises. Further decrees of 13 and 31 December 1917 extended the benefits of insurance assistance in case of unemployment, sickness, pregnancy; by a decree of 14 June the right to two weeks holidays after a year of work and up to one month for workers in unhealthy occupations was instituted. The decrees of 31 January and 2 June abolished private employment agencies, and instead instituted recruitment of labour through labour exchanges, organized by Trade Unions at the local Soviets. These decrees also laid down rules for the approval of collective contracts, rates of wages, and conditions of work.

However, all this legislation remained mere aspiration and did not materialize.

(a) Workers' control, where it was introduced, did not limit its functions to mere control; more often the workers' committees took the management of enterprises into their own hands, which, through lack of experience and appropriate staff, led to the disorganization of industrial management. The breakdown was the combined result of opposition and sabotage by former owners and administrative personnel, the 'revolutionary antagonism' of the workers towards the representatives of the 'old regime', and anarcho-syndicalist tendencies among the workers, who very often considered the enterprises in which they were working as from now on exclusively belonging to themselves and placed their group interests above those of society. The workers became masters of the situation, factories and enterprises were in their hands, but they regarded them, especially during the first period of the Revolution, without any connexion with the whole national economy. On the contrary, they had an idea of industry as of a sea from which limitless wealth could be pumped without harm to it, not distinguishing between existing stocks and current production of their own factory.* 'Railwaymen considered that the railways must belong to them as their property, and the workers in the factories had the same idea.... Central committees of railwaymen, water-transport workers and factory committees took over the administration of

* *Herald of Labour*, 1920, no. 3, p. 91.

their respective enterprises.'* 'We have introduced workers' control by law, but it (the idea) has hardly begun to penetrate to the life and even to the minds of the mass of the proletariat.'†

(*b*) Instead of a rise in the productivity of labour there began a process of rapid decline and deterioration in labour discipline. Delays and absenteeism in industry amounted in 1919 to 191 working days, i.e. 65 % of the total working days in a year, and the productivity of labour declined to about 28 % of the annual and 47 % of the hourly productivity of 1913.‡

This decline in the productivity of labour was due to the deterioration in labour discipline and in organization, in the supply of fuel, raw materials and tools, to the rapid decline in the standard of living of the workers, and to the absorption of the most intelligent and energetic workers into the newly created administrative apparatus of the country.

Owing to the hardships experienced by the urban population and the population of industrial districts with regard to food, fuel, transport facilities, etc., there took place a great exodus of workers from towns back to the villages. Russian industrial workers, even during the last decades before the Revolution, did not completely sever their ties with the villages. A large number of them represented only the first generation of 'immigrants' from the villages; only in some branches of industry did the majority of workers consist of 'hereditary industrial workers'. Consequently, when living conditions in the towns became harder, masses of workers returned to the villages, where they participated in the distribution of the land of landed estates, in the organization of Kolkhozy and Sovkhozy, in the organization of productive co-operatives, in the formation of 'workers' detachments' for the support of the purveyance of agricultural products, and in handicraft industry.

The town population, in 1920, was reduced by 33·4 % in comparison with 1917, and in Moscow and Petrograd it was reduced by 58·2 % (by 2,326,000). Part of the town population was absorbed by the army, but the main mass of them went back to the villages.§ Owing to this exodus of industrial workers to the villages

* Collected volume, *The October upheaval and dictatorship of the Proletariat*, pp. 103–4. † Lenin, op. cit. vol. XXII, p. 451.

‡ Rozenfeld, op. cit. p. 330. Detailed description of the labour conditions in this period is given in a work by Strumilin, *Wages and Productivity of Labour in Russian Industry in* 1913–22.

§ 29 % of the workers of the engineering industry and about 29–34 % from the textile industries left for the villages (Markus, *Labour in a Socialist Society*, pp. 104, 107).

and their absorption in the army and in administration, and owing to the considerable decline in the productivity of labour, there arose a curious situation. In spite of the rapid decline in industrial production there was a great shortage of labour; there were more offers than demands for jobs on the labour exchange.* There even arose the necessity of mobilizing some categories of workers and prohibiting them from changing their place of work and, with the development of civil war, of introducing industrial conscription.

(c) The labour code promulgated in December 1918 instituted obligatory work for all citizens between the ages of 16 and 50 with the freedom to choose their occupation but with an obligation to accept any work in case of unemployment; unemployed workers could be transferred to any place of work according to the demand for labour. The code also instituted an obligatory standard of productivity of labour for all workers and reward for work, not only in money but also in kind by the supply of necessities.

In December 1918 registration and mobilization of all technical personnel were introduced. In January 1919 specialists in agriculture, as well as railwaymen, workers in water transport, and employees of some central institutions, were declared mobilized. On 29 January 1920 a law introducing conscription for all labour was promulgated. Strict limitations were imposed on changes of occupation and place of work, and all persons trying to shirk work were to be considered as labour deserters liable to prosecution. Special labour armies were organized and directed by central governing bodies of Soviets of Labour Armies. In general, by the end of this period, labour was conscripted, militarized, and attached to the place of work; 'Labour, like industry, was nationalized.'†

Some of the leading members of the Soviet Government, especially Trotsky,‡ saw in these labour armies and the conscription of labour not a temporary expedient called for by the emergency of civil war and the deterioration of all the productive sources of the country, but a new, permanent form of organization of labour in a Socialist society. When the civil war and the war with Poland came to an end, some of the labour armies were demobilized, some restrictions on changes of place of work and occupation were lifted, and enrolment for work was re-established on the basis of labour

---

* See Markus, op. cit. p. 106.

† Rozenfeld, op. cit. p. 135; see also Markus, op. cit. p. 95; *Stages in the Economic Policy of the U.S.S.R.* pp. 270–1.

‡ Trotsky, *Collected Works*, vol. xv, p. 180.

contracts. But the militarization of labour as well as other restrictions on the freedom of labour were not completely abolished until the introduction of N.E.P.

(d) The programme of the Communist Party, accepted at the Eighth Congress of the Party in March 1919, referred to wages policy in the following pronouncement: 'While aspiring to equality of remuneration for all kinds of labour and to total communism, the Soviet Government cannot consider as its task the immediate realization of this equality at the present moment when only the first steps are being made towards the transition from Capitalism to Communism.'[*] In reality, however, equalization of reward for different kinds of work did take place during this period. Reward was, in actual fact, not related to qualifications, skill or kind of work performed by a worker in spite of the fact that there existed formal wage schedules. According to data given by Strumilin wages of workers of the 12th category amounted to 232 % of those of workers of the 1st category in 1917, in June 1917 it was only 119 %, and in the first part of 1921 only 102 %; in other words, they were then nearly equal.[†]

As the purchasing power of money declined very rapidly, money remuneration began to play a much less important part in the total 'wages' of workers than the supply of bare necessities in kind. As early as the end of 1917 the supply of rationed goods made up 6·2 % of total wages, in the second half of 1918 wages in money made up 72·1 % and wages in kind 27·9 %, and in the first quarter of 1921 wages in money amounted only to 6·3 %, whereas payment in kind provided 93·7 % of total wages.[‡] According to data given by Markus, in 1918 real monthly wages of industrial workers (including supply of rationed goods, communal services and other rewards in kind) already amounted to only 40·9 % of the wages of 1913.[§] During the later period deterioration in real wages continued. Very often workers had recourse to illegal production of all kinds of goods from raw materials belonging to the factories, during their normal working time, in order to sell these goods privately and thus increase their income.

Thus the wage policy of this period was influenced not by any fixed principles but by the emergency situation, by the necessity of distributing the scarce, available supplies of necessities among all

[*] *Party Resolutions*, pt. i, p. 300.
[†] Strumilin, op. cit. p. 35.
[‡] *Stages in the Economic Policy of the U.S.S.R.* p. 274.
[§] Markus, op. cit. p. 20.

workers engaged in production without regard to their different qualifications and skill. And, of course, all the aspirations expressed in the labour legislation of the first year of this period (restriction of overtime, holidays, insurance, etc.) remained for the time being only intentions, not real possibilities.

Nor did this period create any *new, practical* form of organization of labour which could be used during the coming period of restoration in the productivity of the national economy.* On the contrary, the forms of organization of labour processes during the last years of this period proved to be only emergency forms which had to be changed under normal conditions of economic development.

6. GENERAL PLANNING

The comparison that has been made between measures taken by the Soviet Government and the actual course of events makes it evident that during this period the conditions did not exist for the application of planning in economic development. All the efforts of the State institutions were concentrated on restoring some kind of system in the administration of nationalized industries, transport, credit, etc. Nevertheless, attempts to organize *institutions* for planning were made from the very beginning of the period, and as some of these institutions continued to exist and played a considerable role in the administration and planning of the national economy in the subsequent period, we must at least register them in our summary survey.

In the chapter on industry we have already mentioned the organization of a Supreme Economic Council in the very first months of the existence of the Soviet Government. The S.E.C. was intended 'to work out the general patterns and plans for regulating the economic life of the country', and so to serve as a central organ for regulating and planning the whole national economy. In reality, as we know, it became merely a central institution organizing the administration of nationalized industries, and its activities were concentrated on the management of separate key branches of industry. During this period not even a general plan was worked out by the S.E.C. for the whole of industry. The activities of the

---

* Embryos of socialist forms of labour, so-called 'subbotniki' (voluntary work by groups of workers on Saturdays in order to accomplish some urgent task), expressed the new approach of workers to labour, but did not provide any practical example of a new form of organization of labour.

S.E.C. in this period, in principle but not in scope, were similar to those of the People's Commissariats of Agriculture (Narkomzem), Food (Narkomprod) and Labour (Narkomtrud).

An attempt to co-ordinate the interdepartmental activities of different institutions dealing with production and distribution was made by organizing, at the beginning of 1918, a 'Commission for Utilization' (Komissiya Ispolzovaniya),* whose duty it was to draw up plans for the allocation of all available goods and factory output between supply of the population and army, export and reserve stocks. But under the then existing conditions the activities of the Commission were absorbed, not by the allocation of goods and output according to plans worked out beforehand, but by the distribution of available goods and output according to the most urgent needs of the moment. It is true that plans for the utilization of available supplies of particular goods were prepared; but the discrepancies between plans and achievements were so considerable† that it could not be called planned utilization.

At the Eighth Congress of the Party in March 1919 a fresh attempt to create an organ for the central co-ordination of the activities of economic Commissariats was made by instituting a Council of Labour and Defence (S.T.O.) which was to function as an economic commission attached to the Sovnarkom S.S.S.R. At the same time Regional Economic Councils (Ekoso) were instituted for the purpose of co-ordinating the activities of the regional branches of the different Commissariats. But these institutions, too, limited their activities to attempts at co-ordinating the administrative orders of different Commissariats and their local branches, and not even an attempt was made to plan the development of the country's economy as a whole. Such an attempt was made for the first time only in 1920 in the famous 'Goelro' plan (a State plan for the electrification of Russia).

In the instructions for the composition of this plan it was stressed that: 'Together with the current, urgent task of organizing transport, eliminating crises in the supply of fuel and food, and organizing disciplined labour armies, there arises for the first time the possibility for Soviet Russia to approach a planned economic construction, on the basis of a scientific preparation and putting into practice of a State plan for the whole national economy.'

This plan already embraced plans for the reconstruction of

* It was instituted by the decree of 21 November 1918, but began to work only at the beginning of 1919.
† See *Stages in the Economic Policy of the U.S.S.R.* p. 99.

industry, agriculture and transport, worked out jointly.* There
arose many controversies about this plan among members of the
Party, and the following quotation shows what deep differences in
opinion existed among the then most influential Party members on
some of the principal questions of economic policy. Stalin, in his
letter to Lenin, wrote concerning the Goelro plan:

Excellent book. Masterly draft of a really unified and truly states-
manlike economic *plan* without inverted commas. You remember last
year's 'plan', proposed by Trotsky, for the 'economic resurrection' of
Russia on the basis of application of the labour of the mass of unskilled
peasants and industrial workers to the fragments of pre-war industry.
How pitiable, how backward in comparison with the Goelro plan!
A medieval handicraft man, who considers himself an Ibsen hero
[Trotsky], who is called upon to 'save' Russia by an old saga....And
what is the earthly use of the tens of 'unified plans' which so often, to
our shame, appear in our press—the babble of preparatory schoolboys.
...And another one, Rykov [Rykov was Chairman of the Council of
People's Commissars during the whole period of N.E.P.] with his
philistine 'realism', who continues to criticise Goelro, being completely
sunk in routine....†

This quotation shows what a deep antagonism of opinions existed
already at this time between Stalin, Trotsky and Rykov, and
throws an early light on the struggle against the opposition within
the Party which emerged later.

But the Goelro plan, in this period, was only a plan; it began to
be introduced into practice only during the period of N.E.P., together with the activities of the State Planning Commission
(Gosplan) which was instituted on 22 February 1920 and also
developed its activities only during the subsequent period of restoration of the national economy. During this period there existed
neither an institution in which general plans of development
could be elaborated nor an apparatus for the execution of plans.
Of course, the various economic Commissariats and institutions
worked out their current plans of activity but, as one author
rightly stressed, 'the existence of a multitude of independent
economic plans in reality meant the absence of a unified plan for
the national economy, i.e. the absence of "planning"'.‡ Only
during the following period did Gosplan begin to function as a
central planning institution, and conditions were gradually created
for putting into practice the principle of planning.

* See details in *Plan of Electrification of R.S.F.S.R.*
† Lenin, *About Electrification*, p. 66.
‡ Kritsman, *The Heroic Period in the Russian Revolution*, p. 115.

CHAPTER III. MAIN RESULTS OF THIS PERIOD

The general results of this period can be formulated as follows:

(1) During this period the Soviet Government succeeded in gaining control of the 'commanding heights' of the national economy. Large-scale industries, transport, banks, foreign trade, the main branches of the distributive system, municipal services, and even large private houses were taken over by Central Government institutions or by their local branches or local Soviets. Private capital almost ceased to exist, means of production were nationalized, financial capital was partly confiscated, and the remainder lost its value owing to the depreciation in value of the currency.

(2) While the consequences of the over-centralization of industrial administration and distribution were mainly negative, some foundations were laid for a new national economic apparatus. Some State institutions had accumulated experience in administering the key branches of industry, transport and distribution, in mobilizing manpower and in departmental planning.

(3) But the measures taken and the institutions set up succeeded neither in creating the conditions needed for a rise in the productivity of the national economy nor even in stopping the decline in it; on the contrary, they undoubtedly contributed to the destruction of the productivity of industry and agriculture, the deterioration in the transport and distributive system, and to the reduction of the productivity of labour.

(4) The main material resources on which the country lived during this period were provided not by fresh production but by existing stocks of raw materials, unfinished and finished goods inherited from the pre-revolution period, by compulsory requisitioning of agricultural products and by confiscation from the 'bourgeoisie'.

(5) The decline in the productivity of industry and agriculture did not cease but, on the contrary, increased in the last year of this period, although the civil war had ended. Consequently the deprivations, hardships and discontent of the mass of the population grew.

(6) Hopes of a revolutionary change of the capitalist system in other countries in the near future vanished.*

* During the First Congress of the National Economic Councils, which took place from 26 May to 4 June 1918, Lenin stressed that: 'We do not close our eyes to the fact that we cannot achieve a socialist revolution in one country

(7) It was realized by hard experience that the economic system set up could not be used for the restoration of the national economy without some amendment.

At the Tenth Congress of the Communist Party (in March 1921), which took the first steps towards the introduction of the new economic policy, Lenin made the following statement:

We are living in such conditions of impoverishment and ruin, of overstrain and exhaustion of the principal productive forces of the peasants and the workers, that for a time everything must be subordinated to this fundamental consideration—at all costs to increase the quantity of goods.... On the economic front, in our attempt to pass over to Communism, we had suffered, by the spring of 1921, a more serious defeat than any previously inflicted on us by Kolchak, Denikin or Pilsudsky. Compulsory requisition in the villages and the direct Communist approach to the problems of reconstruction in towns—this was the policy which interfered with the growth of the productive capacity of the country and proved to be the main cause of a profound economic and political crisis which confronted us in the spring of 1921 [famine, peasant uprisings in a number of places and the Kronstadt insurrection]. The new economic policy means the substitution of a food tax for requisitioning, it means a transition to the restoration of capitalism in no small degree. In what degree we do not know.... The fundamental question, from the point of view of strategy, is, who will the sooner take advantage of this new situation? Who will win? The capitalist whom we are now letting in through the door or even through several doors which we ourselves ignore and which will open independently of us and against us? Or the proletarian sovereign power?*

In such an atmosphere and with such ideological implications N.E.P. was inaugurated.

---

alone, even if that country were less backward than Russia and even if we lived under easier conditions than those created by four years of hard, distressing war.... We are deeply convinced that in the near future historic events will bring the west-European proletariat to supreme power, and in this respect we shall not be alone on the world arena as we are now. Through this, the road to Socialism and its embodiment in life will be made easier.' Quoted by Milyutin, *History of the Economic Development of the U.S.S.R.* pp. 149–50.

* Lenin, *Collected Works*, vol. XVIII, pt. I, pp. 67, 343, 344.

SECTION II. *PERIOD OF RESTORATION AND PREPARATION FOR THE RECONSTRUCTION OF THE NATIONAL ECONOMY*

CHAPTER IV. THE GENERAL AIMS AND POLICY OF THIS PERIOD

There has been much controversy over the substance of N.E.P. and the economic system which was created during this period. Many authors saw in N.E.P. a proof of the failure of the attempt to introduce 'Socialism' in the U.S.S.R., a failure of 'Marxism', a surrender of 'Socialist principles' to capitalism, a definite retreat from Socialism to State capitalism. Others, on the contrary, saw in N.E.P. only a 'respite' before a new and decisive attempt to introduce 'pure Socialism', a temporary retreat from 'Marxist' principles to 'capitalist practice', a tactical regrouping of forces and methods in the struggle to build up a Socialist State. And such conflicting views were expressed not only by foreign authors; some of them were shared by the different 'opposition groups' among the members of the Communist Party and by Trade Union groups which attempted to oppose the general policy of the Party in this period. The roots of these controversies lay in the very substance of N.E.P., which represented a dual system in which elements of Socialism, represented by attempts to plan parts of the economy, were combined with institutions typical of competitive capitalism.

It is clear from the statement by Lenin, quoted above, concerning the introduction of N.E.P., that the three immediate aims pursued by N.E.P. were: (1) 'at all costs to increase the quantity of products'; (2) to remedy the political crisis, i.e. to appease the hostility towards the Central Government shown by the peasantry and by a considerable part of industrial workers as the economic difficulties increased, and to end the growing alienation between villages and towns; and (3) to keep all the economic 'commanding heights' in the hands of the State and to use them for directing the restoration of productivity in such a way as to secure the victory of 'the proletarian sovereign power' over the newly released forces of 'capitalism'. But N.E.P. was not introduced as a system of measures thought out beforehand and systematically interconnected, clearly foreseeing the future forms of the development of the new economic system. From the very beginning it was hoped that it would be possible to limit the scope of the free market to local transactions, it was assumed that the free purchase and sale of both agricultural products and manufactured goods would be purely local, and that it would be possible to organize barter between towns and villages on a national scale. However, a few months of experience forced the Soviet Government to admit that the attempt to restrict free trading to local markets and organize barter was a failure. 'It was a failure in the sense that it degenerated into trade....None of our expectations have been realized, as the private market proved stronger than we, and instead of barter we had just ordinary sale and purchase. Be so good as to adapt yourselves to it [Lenin was addressing members of the Communist Party], otherwise the floods of trade, of monetary circulation, will submerge you.'*

Lenin was clearly aware of the fact that in admitting free trade, the country was necessarily adopting some of the institutions of the capitalist system, but in his opinion the path of her development was to be peculiar:

> State capitalism, such as we have it here, is not discussed in any theory or any literature, for the simple reason that all the normal implications of this word are attached to bourgeois government in a capitalist society. With us...it is not the bourgeoisie but the proletariat which rules the State. State capitalism in our case means capitalism *which we shall know how to restrict* [my italics] and to which we shall be able to set limits....It is that capitalism which we must circumscribe. ...And it depends on us what this State capitalism will be like. We have enough political power, we have also sufficient economic resources at our disposal....All we want is skill and this we lack.†

Moreover, Lenin repeatedly warned the Party that only an agreement with the peasantry could save the Socialist Revolution in Russia until a revolution should take place in other countries; only 'smychka', i.e. a union between the industrial workers and the peasantry, between town and village, could safeguard the Socialist Revolution in a country like Russia where the peasantry constitute the majority of the population.

The peasantry in Russia represented not only the main economic productive force but, after the Revolution, also an enormous latent political force. This political force was imbued with the 'petit bourgeois' psychology shown by owners of small properties, the

---

* Lenin, op. cit. vol. XVIII, pt. I, pp. 67–8.
† Lenin, op. cit. vol. XVIII, pt. II, pp. 31–2.

economic and political conditions of whose life did not encourage a rapprochement between them and the 'industrial proletariat', but, on the contrary, disqualified them from participation in the 'dictatorship of the proletariat'. It would take many years to transform this 'petit bourgeois' psychology of the peasantry into a Socialist psychology; it could be achieved only by changing the material basis and the technique of agricultural production, by its mechanization and co-operation. Only by these means could the Russian peasantry be drawn closely into the process of the 'socialistic rebuilding' of Russia. But for this it was in turn necessary first of all to develop industrial production; Lenin repeatedly stressed that the development of large-scale industry was the necessary prerequisite of the introduction of Socialism in Russia, and he emphasized that direct transition to Socialism would be possible only in highly developed industrial countries where

flourishing large-scale industries can immediately supply the peasantry with a sufficient quantity of goods, more than they had before (i.e. before the Revolution), and so create the right interchange of supplies received from peasantry and industry respectively. Only then would the peasants be completely satisfied, only then would they recognize that the new order is better than capitalism. If this question were treated on a world-wide scale, the necessary conditions would be provided. There are countries with an advanced large-scale industrial system which could at once supply the hundreds of millions of backward peasants. This is indeed the *basis* which is under our consideration.... But if a flourishing large-scale industry able to satisfy the peasantry at once with a supply of industrial goods does not exist, there is no other way by which a union between workers and peasants could be created, except trade. In this lies the basis and substance of N.E.P.*

Thus trade was regarded, for the time being, as the principal means by which the economic development of the country could be pushed ahead, and Lenin gave the members of the Communist Party the famous slogan: 'Learn to trade!'

Through trade it was hoped to increase both the supply of agricultural products for the urban population and that of agricultural raw materials for industries producing consumer goods. This would increase the output of consumer goods and supply the prerequisite for the development of the trade apparatus of State industry. The restoration of trade, of normal intercourse between town and village, would create conditions for the further expansion of industrial and agricultural production which, in its turn, would create a basis for the transition to a sound State Budget and

* Lenin's report to the Ninth Congress of Soviets on 23 December 1921.

national currency. Finally, all this would make possible the accumulation of capital in the socialized sector of the national economy as well as the restoration and further development of heavy industry, the capital and productive capacity of which had suffered greater ravages than any other branch of the national economy during the civil war and the period of 'War Communism'.

Such were the general aims and general tasks of N.E.P. which were envisaged at the time of the transition from the period of 'War Communism' to the new period of the restoration of the national economy. But the ways and means in which these aims and tasks would be moulded into the definite form of a new economic system were not clear at the beginning of N.E.P.; methods of trial and error were accepted as the inevitable price of a compromise between State and private economy in a period of transition.

We shall begin our brief survey of the concrete forms in which N.E.P. was expressed and the Soviet economic system moulded during this period with a description of the development which took place in trade.

CHAPTER V. INTERNAL AND EXTERNAL TRADE

INTERNAL TRADE

The main controversial problems of trade on which centred all the measures of the Government and the opinions of all the different opposition groups inside the Party were problems of price regulation and the development of private trade.

During the first two years of N.E.P. the task of restoring trade was placed in the foreground and trade, on the whole, developed spontaneously, aided by the revival of agricultural and industrial production. The attempt to limit free sales to local markets having failed, the restrictions on free trade were gradually lifted and the usual trading relations as regards all products and goods were, in principle, restored not only among private persons, but also among State enterprises and between State enterprises and private persons.*

* At first the peasants, after having paid the tax in kind, were allowed to sell their products and the local industries to sell their goods; later on State enterprises were allowed to sell part of their production on the market (December 1920), and still later to dispose of all their production freely. Private persons were allowed to trade in all products and goods in retail as well as in wholesale trade.

From the very first years there developed an intensive private trade in both agricultural products and manufactured goods. Its capital was composed of private funds which had survived the requisitions and confiscations of the previous period and from rapid accumulation of capital during the initial period of N.E.P., the period of the so-called 'squandering' of their goods by the nationalized industrial undertakings which, in the first year of N.E.P., very often sold their goods and even equipment below cost price in order to obtain working capital. Such 'squandering' was especially marked during the selling crisis of the summer of 1922, which exhibited the paradox of 'glut' in industrial goods in spite of the fact that the production of these goods was only just beginning to revive.* This 'squandering' provided great opportunities for the accumulation of private capital, as State trade had not yet developed a commercial mechanism of its own nor had it any experience in trade. During the first years of N.E.P. State enterprises, in their trade operations, generally used the channels of private trades, or the services of the 'Nepmen' as private traders were called.

However, from the very beginning of N.E.P. the process of developing co-operative trade and setting up a network of State trade, although slow and unorganized, went parallel with the development of private trade.

(a) By the decree of 7 April 1921, co-operatives were recognized as independent trading organizations no longer subordinated to the Commissariat of Supply (Narkomprod), and received the right to buy and sell freely goods of all kinds. Although the principle of obligatory membership was preserved, the introduction of a membership fee was permitted, and by the decree of 1 September 1921 the existing financial relations between co-operatives and the

---

* This 'glut' in manufactured consumer goods was due to many causes and mostly had a temporary character in the first transitional year of N.E.P. The supply of agricultural products to the markets was very limited owing to the very poor harvest of 1921 and the reluctance of the peasantry to dispose of the products; even the obligatory tax in kind, the collection of which was belated and, carried out with great difficulty, did not come up to expectation. The industries, on the contrary, endeavoured to sell all their available marketable stocks and current production in order to increase their working capital. A trade apparatus for the sale of industrial goods was only just beginning to be built up in big towns. The transport, monetary and credit systems were as yet only in the beginning of recovery. The result of all this was that during this short period of 1922 prices of agricultural products were relatively much higher than those of industrial goods, exchange equivalents were unfavourable to industry and some branches of industry experienced a 'liquidation crisis' and, in some cases, were even forced to cut down production.

State Budget were severed and co-operatives became independent of the State apparatus. By the decree of 20 October 1921 all their former property and industrial enterprises with existing stocks of raw materials and goods, which had during the previous period been nationalized or municipalized, were returned to the co-operatives, and all property which was actually being used by the co-operatives was given to them as their own private property. But neither this returned property nor the membership fee and profits furnished, during this initial period, sufficient financial resources to supply the working capital necessary for a rapid increase in the trade turn-over of the co-operatives. Commercial and bank credit partly helped to relieve their financial deficiencies, but these resources, too, were very meagre during this period. Owing to financial difficulties and deficiencies in organization (such as cumbersome State apparatus, high overhead expenses, desire for high profit, lack of experience), co-operative trade, up to 1923, developed only very slowly.*

(b) The development of State trade assumes two forms: that of the so-called 'Torgi' and that of the syndicates. The Torgi were formed from the appropriate trade departments of the Regional Councils of National Economy (Gubsovnarkhozy). They served mainly as channels for trade in goods produced by the local industries, but partly also for trade in goods received for sale from nationalized large-scale industries. In 1922 syndicates began to be organized by industrial trusts, first as a means of co-ordinating and organizing the trading activities of the trusts so as to prevent competition among them, and later as a wholesale agency for State trusts. During 1922–3† syndicates were organized for trade in the most important goods of mass consumption, such as textiles, leather, metals, oil, salt, matches, etc. These syndicates mainly carried on wholesale distribution, using the channels of private, co-operative and 'Gostorgi' trade for retail trade. In general, during the period of N.E.P. (1921–3), goods very often passed through five to seven stages of the commercial apparatus before reaching the con-

---

* At the beginning of this period an attempt was made to create workers' co-operatives quite independent of the general co-operative organizations, and at the Party conference of August 1922 a special resolution was passed, condemning these syndicalist tendencies in the trade unions and prohibiting the separate formation of special workers' co-operatives.

† In Soviet statistics the so-called 'economic year' from October to October was used during this period and not the ordinary January–December year, i.e. 1922–3 means 1 October 1922 to 30 September 1923.

sumer.* Apart from the delay involved, this raised costs enormously and consequently also final prices, which were sometimes six times higher than the original factory prices.†

The working capital of State trading organizations was provided by State institutions and State industries which participated as shareholders in the appropriate trading organizations and transferred goods to the State trading organizations to serve as a basis for the formation of capital. In addition, State industries provided the State trading organizations with fairly considerable credit in goods. During the first years of N.E.P. the banks played a much less important part in supplementing the working capital of State trade than the two above-mentioned sources.

State trade, during this period, served mainly as a channel for wholesale trade in manufactured goods. Its role in retail trade was much less significant than that of private trade. In 1922–3 the latter accounted for 75·3 % of the total retail turn-over, whereas State trade and co-operative trade respectively accounted only for 14·4 and 10·3 %.‡ Private enterprises accounted for 95·2 % of the whole distributive system in 1922 and for 91·5 % in 1923.§

Such was the position of State, co-operative and private trade channels at the end of 1923 when the famous 'scissors' crisis, followed by the 'liquidation crisis', attained its climax and excited a sharp controversy in the Party as to the attitude to be adopted towards the relation between industrial and agricultural prices. On this the fate of 'smychka' depended—the political union between workers and peasantry—and therefore the trend of 'class' differentiation in the villages as well as that of private trade.

To the question of the 'scissors' more attention has been paid by writers on Soviet economy than to any other question in the history of that economy: here we shall only recall some of the most essential facts concerning it and the crisis‖ of 1923 which must be remembered in order to understand subsequent tendencies in internal trade.

* For example: factory—warehouse of syndicate—warehouse of the Central co-operative institution—warehouses of branches of the Central co-operative institution—warehouse of regional co-operative—warehouse of district co-operative—warehouse of local co-operative centre—co-operative.

† *Economy of Soviet Trade*, p. 328.

‡ Ibid. p. 83.

§ *Stages in the Economic Policy of the U.S.S.R.* p. 302.

‖ A very informative description and theoretical analysis of the 'scissors' crisis is given by Maurice Dobb in his study *Russian Economic Development since the Revolution*, pp. 221–89.

The phenomenon of the 'scissors' and the crisis was quite simple in itself, but its causes and consequences were very complicated. After the crisis of the middle of 1922, when agricultural and industrial prices met on approximately the pre-war (1913) ratio, two opposed tendencies began to develop: on the one hand a fall in the prices of agricultural products, and on the other a rise in the prices of manufactured goods. The discrepancy between the two price levels consequently went on increasing—the two blades of the 'scissors' opened more and more. The wholesale price index of the Central Statistical Office for 1 October 1923, when the scissors were open widest, was 888 for agricultural products and 2,757 for industrial goods compared with 1,000 in 1913. In reality, exchange equivalents were much more unfavourable to agricultural products, as can be seen from the wholesale price index mentioned above. The exchange equivalent of agricultural products for industrial goods depends not on the relations between wholesale prices but on the ratio of agricultural *wholesale* prices for the main products to the *retail* prices of manufactured goods, as the peasants meet on the market on these terms. The discrepancies between wholesale agricultural prices and retail industrial prices were much greater than those represented by the above wholesale price indexes, since the retail prices of industrial goods were much higher than the wholesale prices, especially in private trade.

The 'scissors' were the main cause of the 'selling crisis' of 1923. The peasantry were again made to feel that they did not get a fair return for their products, and they refrained from purchasing industrial goods on such unfavourable terms of exchange. The demand of the Russian peasantry for industrial goods was very elastic, as they could have recourse to handicraft production of certain necessities such as linen, woollen textiles, home-made leather boots, or bast-shoes instead of leather boots, home-made soap, candles, and utensils made of wood and glazed clay, and their willingness to exchange their surplus of agricultural products for industrial goods consequently depended very largely on the price of the manufactured article in comparison with the income they obtained by selling agricultural products. However, upon the willingness of the peasantry to exchange their products for goods manufactured in towns depended not only the food supplies of the urban and industrial population and of those rural districts which were agriculturally not self-sufficient (the so-called 'agricultural consumption areas') as well as that of the districts which cultivated predominantly industrial crops (in particular cotton and flax), but also the supply of raw materials for industry, and in this way the whole development of industrial production.

The high industrial prices and their constant rise were the result of many causes. Because industry was only beginning to increase its output and was using only part of the productive capacity of each plant, overhead expenses were higher than before the war, when plants were more fully employed. Production was still very poorly organized and the administrative apparatus was cumbersome and expensive, a fact which also contributed to the increase of overhead expenses. Trusts were eager to enlarge their working capital and recoup themselves for the losses they had suffered during the period of 'squandering', and they endeavoured to achieve this by raising their rate of profit. Their monopoly position in the market resulting from the elimination of foreign competition (the State monopoly of foreign trade was preserved during N.E.P.) and the syndication of their wholesale trade enabled them to keep prices at a high level. Credit facilities provided by State credit institutions enabled trusts to accumulate stocks of goods and keep them from sale until the most favourable time for selling them, that is, when the peasants sold their harvest. The channels of trade were devious and expensive, and the rate of profit in retail trade was relatively high, especially in private trade, so that retail prices were very high in comparison with wholesale prices.

The downward trend of agricultural prices, too, was due to many factors. The revival of agricultural production proceeded more rapidly than that of industry, since a smaller proportion of the basic capital of agriculture had been destroyed. Such destruction had taken the form of an abnormal rate of slaughtering livestock during the civil war, especially in the Ukraine and in regions affected by famine, compulsory requisitioning of 'surplus' grain for the supply of the army and the towns, destruction of part of the agricultural machinery of the large estates, and failure to maintain a normal rate of replacement and repair of agricultural machinery and inventory. Moreover, the general principles on which agriculture was carried on remained unchanged by the nationalization of land, the organization of production being unaffected in principle. The agricultural tax in kind provided the greater part of the food supplies of the urban and industrial population, and consequently the Government prices for this part of the supplies served to prevent possible increases in the prices on such marketable products as still remained at the disposal of the peasantry. Peasants sold their products individually, while the purchase of the main agricultural products was already at this time highly concentrated by the introduction of State and co-operative distributive institutions. Export of agricultural products developed very slowly and consequently the internal market for the main agricultural products was more quickly saturated than was expected in view of existing marketable surpluses; the peasants continued to use the depreciating currency ('sovznak'), whereas industries and State institutions used a double currency, one stable and the other depreciating ('chervonets' and 'sovznak'). Agricultural circulating capital and stocks of durable manufactured consumer goods were in urgent need of replenishment owing to their great scarcity during the preceding years, and consequently peasants badly needed 'cash' which they endeavoured to spend immediately on manufactured goods. Besides, the peasantry had less opportunity of buying scarce manufactured goods than had the urban and industrial population, as the trade network was more quickly restored in towns than in villages, and the State and co-operative distributors in big towns and industrial centres were privileged as regards the supply of manufactured consumer goods. In addition, the urban and industrial population consumed a greater share of the smaller output of manufactured goods than in pre-revolutionary days.

Thus the 'scissors', from the economic point of view, hampered the further development of agricultural and industrial production and, from the political point of view, threatened 'smychka'. The 'scissors' had to be closed; but the problem was how to close them. A rise in the prices of agricultural products, the industrial situation being what it was, would result either in a lowering of the real wages of workers and Government employees or in a rise of the net cost of manufactured goods owing to the necessary corresponding increase in nominal wages and increased cost of agricultural raw materials. It would also slow down the accumulation of capital for the badly needed reconstruction of industry. A rise in the prices of agricultural products would also worsen the prospect of exporting these products, and, as they constituted the main export, this would reduce the possibility of importing urgently needed machinery. Besides, a rise in agricultural prices involved a political problem: the kulaks, being the principal owners of marketable products, would gain from the higher prices, and this would strengthen their economic position at the expense of the poor peasants, who purchased part of their food, and of the peasants of regions with a predominant cultivation of industrial crops.

On the other hand, a reduction of industrial prices would hamper the accumulation of capital in industry and consequently retard industrial reconstruction.

The question of the position and fate of private trade further complicated these problems of price regulation. Private capital, at this time, played a decisive role in retail trade; consequently whatever the decision reached with regard to price policy, it would have to be carried out largely through the channels of private trade. A reduction of industrial wholesale prices without any guarantee that a corresponding reduction would take place in retail prices would, in view of the existing scarcity of industrial goods, lead to an increased profitability of private trade and thus strengthen its position, which would be contrary to the general policy of the Government. To replace the private retail trade network by a network of State and co-operative trade was at this time impossible, owing to the insufficient amount of capital at the disposal of the Government which could be invested in State trade. Lack of experience, inefficiency and high overhead expenses of State and co-operative trade combined to make such a replacement impossible.

All the controversies and struggles among the different opposition groups in the Party, already mildly expressed at this period and growing in bitterness later, when new aspects of problems essentially the same revived the dissension, centred on the problems of the relation of industry and agriculture, the ways and means of accumulating capital for industrial reconstruction, the fate of the kulaks and of private capital, and the possibility of building up industry and establishing 'Socialism' in the U.S.S.R. without help from abroad and in the absence of a social revolution in other countries. We cannot, however, give here even a summary description of these controversies and of the views of different opposition groups in the Party, as this would lead us away from our main aim, which is to study the actual development of the Soviet system.*

At the sessions of the Thirteenth Party Conference and Thirteenth Party Congresses in 1924 it was stressed: (1) that the development of private trade must be checked by strengthening the position of co-operative and State trade; (2) the 'scissors' must be closed by reducing industrial prices, by closing the abnormal gap between wholesale and retail prices, by stricter regulation of prices and by raising the State purveyance prices for agricultural products;

* Good informative material concerning opposition groups in the period of N.E.P. can be found in Maurice Dobb's book, *Russian Economic Development since the Revolution*, pp. 254-9, 298, 317-22, 334, 336.

·(3) the existing elements of a general planning of trade must be strengthened by the conclusion of a general contract between industrial syndicates and co-operatives, by further centralization of the distribution of agricultural products in the hands of co-operative and State institutions, and by the gradual expulsion of private traders from trade in agricultural products and later from trade in scarce manufactured goods.*

The Peoples' Commissariat of Internal Trade (Narkomtorg), which in April 1924 replaced the Internal Trade Committee,† was entrusted with the task of 'mastering the market on behalf of State and co-operative trade at the expense of private, and especially private wholesale trade capital, and of exercising an effective control over the activity of private capital'; it was also entrusted with the task of 'regulating all trade and taking a leading part in determining the trade policy of all the enterprises in which State funds were invested'.‡

Let us now see how these tasks were fulfilled and what results were achieved.

(a) It was decided that co-operative and not State trade must become the main channel of retail trade because co-operatives were regarded not only as a more convenient form of trade during this period but also as providing a good schooling and means for developing a collective organization of the peasantry, first through consumers' and afterwards through producers' co-operatives. By a series of decrees, including those of 30 December 1923 and 20 April and 20 October 1924, the principle of voluntary membership and payment to the members of dividends on their purchases was re-established; co-operatives were given facilities for obtaining credit and received privileges in the payment of taxes and facilities for obtaining supplies of the most saleable manufactured goods. They gradually became the main channel for retail trade in manufactured goods and for the distribution of certain agricultural products.

(b) The purveyance of grain, meat and industrial crops was also gradually concentrated in the hands of special State and co-operative organizations. The number of these was reduced by

---

* *Party Resolutions*, vol. I, pp. 661–2. *Instructions of the Communist Party concerning Economic Questions*, pp. 172–4.

† The Internal Trade Committee was organized in 1922 and was entrusted merely with the task of unifying all legislation bearing on inland trade and studying the latter's development under new conditions.

‡ *Instructions of the Communist Party concerning Economic Questions*, p. 156.

fusions, and by 1926–7 the distribution of grain was centralized in the hands of nine main State and co-operative organizations (such as the Khleboprodukt, Tsentrosoyuz, Gostorg of the R.S.F.S.R., Gostorg of the U.S.S.R.) which gradually came to control the bulk of the purchases of agricultural produce. Between 76 and 78% of all marketable supplies of grain were purchased by these organizations.* Their purchasing plans were elaborated on the basis of statistical data from preceding years and the prospects of the coming harvest. The State financial institutions provided them with credits, and their purchases were facilitated by the despatch of larger supplies of manufactured goods to the rural districts during the purveyance period; in order to eliminate competition between different supply organizations the special regions were allocated to them.

The trade-regulating bodies gradually endeavoured in addition to extend their control over the remaining sales of grain not covered by planned purchases, the so-called 'Vneplanovyy Oborot' (non-planned turn-over).† This was done (1) by forbidding organizations and private persons not primarily concerned with trade in grain to trade in grain, and by compelling all persons and organizations trading in grain to register with the appropriate bodies of the Commissariat of Internal Trade; (2) by restricting the transport of grain by 'non-planned organizations' and private persons (forbidding them to transport grain from certain regions, establishing priority for grain purveyance by central organizations and different rates for the different traders in grain); (3) by restricting and even refusing credit to 'non-planned' organizations and to private traders; (4) by giving the central organizations priority in milling and restricting milling by private traders; (5) by demanding compulsory registration at corn exchanges of all contracts made by 'non-planned' traders, those who ignored the official price policy being 'invalid'; (6) by restricting and subsequently suppressing grain purchases by private traders in certain areas.‡

---

* *Inland Trade of the U.S.S.R. during Ten Years*, p. 178.

† Trade turn-over was divided into two parts, one part of it being 'planned turn-over', i.e. purchases and sales made by the State and co-operative organizations according to a preliminary plan, and the other being 'non-planned turn-over', i.e. sales and purchases not covered by the plan.

‡ Those who wish to study in detail the conditions in which private capital had to work in the U.S.S.R. during the period of N.E.P. will find a wealth of material in the following works: *Private Capital in the National Economy of the U.S.S.R.*, edited by A. M. Ginsburg, and *Private Trading Capital in the National Economy of the U.S.S.R.*, by M. M. Zhirmunsky.

All these measures were intended not only to make possible the extension of the planned purchases by the State and central co-operative organizations over the bulk of marketable grain but also to prevent the 'non-planned' trader from hampering the realization of the official price policy.

The desired concentration of the purchases of industrial crops in the hands of the central State and co-operative organizations was achieved in the same way and even more successfully.

From 1923–4 onwards measures were taken to restrict the number of organizations trading in industrial crops and other agricultural raw materials and to restrict them to trade in one kind of crops only. In 1926, by the decision of a special committee of the Commissariat for Soviet Labour and Defence which had been created for the purpose of rationalizing trade in agricultural raw materials, it was decreed that in future only two centralized organizations, one State the other co-operative, would be allowed to trade in specified agricultural raw materials (for example, flax 'L'nogostorg' and 'L'nocentr'; sugar beet 'Sahkorotrest' and 'Sel'skosoyuz'), and only in certain districts which would be allocated to them. Gradually these central purchasing organizations, by concluding contracts with the peasants covering all their future harvests, succeeded in controlling nearly all the marketable industrial crops and other agricultural raw materials. In 1927–8 planned purchases embraced 100 % of the total marketable cotton, 100 % of sugar beet, 98 % of flax, 98 % of tobacco, 80 % of hides, 92 % of furs, 70 % of wool.*

The regulation of prices for industrial crops and other agricultural raw materials demanded even more serious consideration than the regulation of prices of grain. In the U.S.S.R., as is well known, some regions either specialize in the cultivation of a certain kind of industrial crop, while in others the production of industrial crops is combined with that of grain. High prices for agricultural raw materials would, *ceteris paribus*, raise the cost of the corresponding manufactured goods with all the consequences that this would entail. Low prices, on the other hand, might ultimately result in the reduced cultivation of the crops concerned or in the substitution of one kind of crop by another. Violation of the normal relations between prices of foodstuffs and those of industrial crops might lead to an enlargement of the sowing area of grain at the expense of these crops. Great differences between the prices of cotton, wool, hides, etc., and those of the consumer goods pro-

* *Inland Trade of the U.S.S.R. during Ten Years*, p. 178.

duced from them, or insufficient supplies of those consumer goods
to the respective regions might result in a return to handicraft
production and so reduce supplies for industry.

At first, in order to regulate most effectively the purchase prices
for industrial crops, a system of two kinds of 'limit prices' was
used: 'maximum limit prices' above which the State and co-
operative purchasing organizations were not allowed to buy, and
'minimum limit prices' less than which could not be offered to the
producer of industrial crops. This system was applied to different
regions and different kinds of crops. Later on, a so-called 'convention price system' was introduced. On the basis of instructions
given by Narkomtorg, State and co-operative organizations were
to conclude conventions with the producers of particular industrial
crops regarding the conditions of delivery of their harvest (terms,
quality, price, fine for a breach of the agreement, granting of credit
to the producer). Narkomtorg fixed the basic prices, but provision
could be made in the conventions for the actual price to be 5–10%
above or below the basic price.

In order to facilitate the purveyance of foodstuffs and agricultural raw materials 'planned transfer of scarce industrial
goods' to the rural districts was introduced from the end of 1924.
The first plan for the transfer of manufactured goods, elaborated
for the autumn agricultural products buying campaign in 1924,
covered only three main agricultural regions, the Ukraine, the
North Caucasus and the Volga regions, and provided only for such
goods as textiles, metal utensils, leather goods, sugar and agricultural machinery. Later on, this planned transfer of manufactured
goods during buying campaigns was extended to other regions and
more goods were included; during the second half of 1925, plans
for the conveyance of the main industrial goods were already
worked out for all the regions of the U.S.S.R. These plans were
composed of two parts: 80–85 % of the total industrial goods intended for transfer to all the regions were allocated for immediate
distribution among the regions and 15–20 % were kept in reserve
as a planned supply at the disposal of Narkomtorg for later conveyance to different regions in order to make good any errors
which might have been made in the planned conveyance of the
main part. In this planned distribution of goods, special consideration was given to regions specializing in the cultivation of
industrial crops. More textiles and vegetable oils were allocated
for the flax-growing districts, more woollen goods to sheep-breeding
regions, and more textiles, bread, and vegetable oils, to cotton-

producing districts. At first, all the trade channels were used for trade in goods to be conveyed to the rural districts, but later on preference was given to the co-operative network.

By these methods of purveyance of the main agricultural produce through the centralized channels of State and co-operative organizations, the Soviet Government succeeded in acquiring the bulk of grain and agricultural raw materials according to fixed prices. Altogether, in 1926, co-operative trade accounted for 49·1 % of the total, State trade for 27·7 %, and private trade for 23·2 % of the total trade turn-over of agricultural products.

But the mastering of the purchase of the bulk of agricultural produce by centralized State and co-operative organizations at fixed prices alone was not enough to achieve complete control over the prices of agricultural produce on the local markets. Private turn-over, however small it might be, reflected free movements in the price of agricultural produce, and the existence of these 'private' prices, as we shall see below, played a very significant role when, in 1927–8, the central purveying institutions met with reluctance on the part of the peasantry to sell their produce at the fixed prices offered by these organizations.

The following were the outstanding developments in the trade in manufactured goods. After the crisis of 1923, syndicates gradually covered to an ever-increasing extent the wholesale marketing of the output of State industry. By 1926, 100 % of the wholesale trade of the oil and salt industries was carried out by syndicates, while 94·5 % of that of the textile industry, 93·1 % of that of the match industry and 87·5 % of that of the leather industry was syndicated. The trade turn-over of syndicates steadily rose,* and by general agreements among industrial syndicates and State co-operative trade agencies, the sale of all the main industrial goods as well as the supply of industrial crops to industry was gradually covered by them. The trade turn-over of Torgi through which the produce of local industries continued to be sold was also raised, though not as substantially as was the turn-over of the syndicates.† Private trade in manufactured commodities was reduced to an even greater degree than was private trade in agricultural pro-

---

* The trade turn-over of fourteen main syndicates in 1922 amounted to 444·2 million roubles, in 1923 to 790·1 million roubles, in 1924 to 1,565·5 million roubles, in 1925 to 2,621·6 million roubles, and in 1926 to 3,579·7 million roubles. *Economy of Soviet Trade*, p. 81.

† The trade turn-over of Torgi in 1923 amounted to 470 million roubles, in 1924 to 833 million roubles, in 1925 to 1,272 million roubles, and in 1926 to 1,336 million roubles.

duce; in 1926, 57·4 % of the total turn-over of manufactured goods was accounted for by co-operative trade, 32·5 % by State trade and only 10·1 % by private trade.

The general results as regards the total turn-over of retail trade in all goods and their distribution through the different trade channels are illustrated by the figures in Table 6.

Table 6. *Total retail trade turn-over (in million roubles)**

	State	Co-operative	Private	Total
1922–3	512·0	368·0	2,680·0	3,560·0
1927–8	2,408·8	9,341·2	3,406·6	15,156·6

The total retail turn-over increased nearly five times during this period, while private trade in 1927–8 was only 27·1 % higher than in 1922–3, and its part in the turn-over was reduced from 75·2% in 1922–3 to 22·4 % in 1927–8.

With regard to the number of trading establishments, the following changes took place. In 1923 their total number was 504,661, of which 461,100 or 91·4 % were private, while in 1927 there were 643,223 establishments, of which 500,275 or 77·8 % were private.† It is enough to compare the changes in the volume of trade with these figures of the number of trading establishments to realize that by 1927 not only did the part played by private trade sharply decrease in comparison with the first years of N.E.P., but private trade assumed the character of very small trade, mostly hawking and peddling. Thus the task of eliminating private trade as soon as co-operative and State trade could replace it was, in general, accomplished.

The task of assuring purveyance of the bulk of agricultural produce at the prices fixed by the Government was also in general achieved up to 1927.

The reduction of industrial prices proved to be a much more difficult task. Narkomvnutorg endeavoured, through the syndicates, to regulate the prices of manufactured goods by fixing prices of certain goods directly and by prescribing the rate of profit and the maximum permitted addition to the wholesale price by retail trading organizations. None of these methods was very successful, owing not only to technical difficulties but also to the fact that from the middle of 1925 onwards the demand for manufactured goods of mass consumption exceeded the supply, the so-called

* G. Neuman, *Inland Trade of the U.S.S.R.* p. 122.
† *Inland Trade of the U.S.S.R. during Ten Years*, p. 261.

'goods famine' began (we shall explain later why) and prices consequently tended to rise.* The Soviet Government tried to stop this by exercising pressure on industry for the reduction of wholesale prices and by stricter regulation of retail prices. The Council of Labour and Defence ordered that by 1 August 1926 retail prices for the main industrial goods must be reduced by 10 % as against prices existing in May 1926. This, however, was not achieved. On the contrary, prices continued to rise. In 1927 Narkomtorg together with S.E.C. started a campaign for the revision of wholesale prices of the main manufactured goods, and of the permitted rates of addition to wholesale trade prices by retail traders. This campaign for the reduction of prices spread from the central State institutions to the local Soviets (Ispolkomy), where special Committees were organized to support the campaign in the field of retail trade.

How great was the importance attached to the necessity of reducing industrial prices can be seen from the following resolution of the Plenum Communist Party, passed on 12 February 1927:

In the price problem are interwoven all the main economic, and consequently also political, problems of the Soviet State. The questions of establishing the right relations between the peasantry and the working class, of securing a common development of agriculture and industry, of the distribution of the national income and, closely connected with it, the question of the industrialization of the U.S.S.R. and the economic and political strengthening of the working class, as well as real wages, the consolidation of our currency, the strengthening of the position of the Socialist elements and the further limitation of the private-capitalist elements in our economy—all these questions rest on the problem of price.... The decisions of the Party and the State concerning the industrialization of our country, the development of agricultural production and the transition of its development in a Socialist direction—all these rest, at present, on the problem of reducing industrial prices.... The causes of the insufficient reduction of retail prices by co-operative and State trade are as follows. The rise in the purchasing capacity of the rural and urban population, which was not satisfied by the existing supplies of industrial goods, created a goods famine. On the other hand, the lack of sufficient capital in co-operative and State trading establishments intensified the latters' aspirations towards excessive accumulation of capital, not through rationalization of trading methods allowing a reduction of overhead expenses, but through high profit margins, and by making the most of their monopoly position under conditions of goods famine..... The maintenance of prices at a high level in the absence of competition, which is the main stimulus for

* The retail price index for industrial goods in October 1925 was 239 (1913—100), in January 1926 it was 248, and in May 1926 it was 271.

the improvement and development of a capitalist economy, and under conditions of a monopoly of production and trade protected by the monopoly of foreign trade, carries with it the danger of a bureaucratization of our productive and trading organizations and a relaxation of our efforts towards a steady improvement of production and trade....*

This quotation clearly shows how much importance the Soviet Government attached to the problem of reducing industrial prices. Many expedients were employed in order to enforce this policy on the trading organizations, such as the reduction of credit facilities, the reduction of goods supplies, and even the stopping of the supply of certain goods to trading organizations violating the official price policy, the obligatory display of official prices and disciplinary and penal responsibility of the managers and employees of shops not keeping to the official prices.†

All these efforts brought about some reduction of industrial prices, and the gap in the 'scissors' between industrial and agricultural prices was somewhat reduced (the general retail index for 1 January 1927 was 221 for manufactured goods and 188 for agricultural produce as against 100 in 1913); yet, in 1927, the relation of industrial and agricultural prices continued to be greatly to the disadvantage of the latter, as can be clearly seen from the figures given in Table 7. The table shows the goods which could be bought for the delivery price of 1 cwt. of rye paid to the peasantry by the State and co-operative trading organizations.‡ It will be seen

Table 7

	Cotton print m.	Sugar kg.	Salt kg.	Tobacco kg.	Kerosine kg.	Nails kg.
In 1913	23·72	14·60	165·8	6·52	41·53	24·36
In 1927:						
At co-operative prices	12·99	7·65	135·5	3·72	44·25	16·90
At private trade prices	10·91	7·45	86·5	3·52	38·75	13·77

that in 1927 the exchange value of rye in relation to cotton print diminished by almost half compared with pre-war times

* *Party Resolutions*, pt. ii, pp. 159, 160, 161.
† See details in *Bulletins of Financial and Economic Legislation*, 1927, nos. 3, 8, 13, 15, 23, 33.
‡ We take the exchange values and not the price indices of industrial and agricultural goods, for they reflect more accurately the relation of agricultural and industrial prices for the main classes of goods consumed by the agricultural population. *Inland Trade of the U.S.S.R. during Ten Years*, p. 82.

(54·8 % of the 1913 figures). For sugar the relation was also nearly halved (52·4 %). The exchange equivalents of delivery prices of industrial crops and essential industrial commodities were somewhat higher than those for grain (75–86% of the 1913 figures); but here, too, the position of agriculture was much worse than before the war. Thus it proved impossible to close the price 'scissors', and the latter continued to be unfavourable to agriculture.

These adverse agricultural prices in combination with structural changes which had taken place in agriculture (see below, pp. 134–6) were one of the main causes of the slow progress of agricultural production and the decrease of its marketability in the last years of N.E.P. In the chapters on industry, agriculture and labour below we dwell on the processes which took place in other branches of the national economy during the last years of N.E.P. and which must be borne in mind in order to understand fully the changes on the home market during that period. Here, however, we need only mention some of these processes in the national economy which found their reflexion on the home market on the eve of the introduction of the rationing system.

In industry, on the whole, the pre-war output from the point of view of quantity had by 1927–8 been restored, but this was the case mainly with regard to heavy industry, and the quality of production did not improve. In many a case this latter deteriorated as a result of deficient equipment service, wasteful use of raw material, excessive fuel and auxiliary materials expenditure, and the productivity of labour lagging behind the increase in wages. The increase in the number of workers and employees engaged in industry and the increase in wage bills were more rapid than the increase in the output of manufactured articles of general consumption and agricultural products. At the same time the Government endeavoured every year to increase its exports. Given a free play in the formation of prices on the home market, these circumstances would have naturally led to an increase in the prices of agricultural products and essential industrial commodities. But, as we have seen above, the Government adhered to its policy of not allowing an increase in prices, and by State and co-operative trade succeeded in controlling the expansion of the bulk of the country's trading operations. This control, however, given the policy of a rigid regulation of prices, instead of mitigating the contradictions between the growth of demand and that of supply, tended on the contrary to make them more acute. By fixing the prices of essential manufactured commodities below the level which would normally have resulted from the existing demand for them, a shortage of these goods was created and a discrepancy arose between their prices in private trade, which reflected the free market, and in State and co-operative shops, which carried out the instructions of the Government. On the other hand, the stabilization of delivery prices for agricultural produce, given a growing demand for it, also led to a severance between the delivery and the market prices and made the upper strata of peasants reluctant to deliver their grain and industrial crops to State and co-operative purchasing organizations at prices below the market level.

All this led, in the autumn of 1927 and spring of 1928, to the State purchasing organizations having to face the reluctance of the upper groups of the peasantry to effect deliveries imposed on them by the plan, at fixed prices. *The difficulties thus encountered in respect of grain deliveries had to be overcome, not by methods of economic regulation of trade, but by means of administrative emergency measures,* i.e. by compulsory confiscation of grain from well-to-do peasant households. Clause 107 of the Penal Code was applied, whereby those guilty of 'malicious increase of prices of goods by buying them up, hiding or withholding them from the market' were liable to 'imprisonment up to 12 months with or without the confiscation of all, or part, of their property', and in case of collusion between traders, to imprisonment up to three years with the confiscation of all property.* On the strength of this clause peasants who refused to deliver their grain at fixed prices in quantities laid down by the planning organs had not only all their grain, but also their whole property confiscated. As a result of these emergency measures grain deliveries were duly carried out but, by way of reply, the production of grain decreased (see pp. 325–6).

At the same time (1928) preparations began in industry for carrying out the Five Year Plan (F.Y.P.) for industrializing the U.S.S.R. The numbers of workers, the numbers of urban population, the financing of industrial construction were all on the increase, the result being an increase in the demand for agricultural produce, the output of which had decreased. This should have inevitably led to a sharp increase in the prices of agricultural goods, which, under the existing conditions, would have meant a holdup in the process of industrial reconstruction. The Government decided to combat the rise of agricultural prices by introducing the ration-card system for the sale of agricultural products to the

* *Collection of Codes of the R.S.F.S.R.* 4th ed. Moscow, 1928, pp. 681–2.

population. As early as 1928, ration cards for bread were introduced in a number of provincial towns, and from the beginning of 1929 in Leningrad and Moscow as well. The system was then extended to the whole of the Soviet Union. But the introduction of the ration-card system for bread, given the continued existence of the private market, however restricted, led to a still sharper cleavage between the delivery prices and the market prices. For instance, in the Ukraine in March 1928, the relation of the market price of rye to the delivery price was 126·3 %; in March 1929 it rose to 369·2 %; for wheat it was 117·3 and 429·3 % respectively. The average market price of flour in European Russia in April 1929 was 324·4 % of the price in April 1928.*

Given this enormous difference between market and delivery prices, the free market, no matter how small its dimensions, was bound to come into sharp conflict with the ration-card system introduced by the Government. The position as regards industrial commodities also grew more tense. Soviet papers of that period were filled with reports such as the following: 'Butter and sugar absent from the market, there is a crisis as far as timber is concerned, the position as regards manufactured goods is still worse, there are enormous queues...the demand being huge, no more than 20–30% can be covered by the supply...the same applies to leather goods and footwear...there is no roof iron....On the textile market a great tension prevails, the demand for all textiles, both in towns and in villages, remains unsatisfied....The villagers go to the towns for goods, stand in queues....Peasants produce receipts acknowledging deliveries of grain ranging from 50 to 500 poods, they would each of them buy 100–200 roubles' worth of industrial commodities, but all they are given is 20 roubles' worth', and so on.†

The market being in such a state, the Government could not confine itself to regulating the consumption of bread, but had to take the path of extending the number of regulated products and articles of general consumption and proceed with the final liquidation of private trade and private commercial intercourse. From 1929 N.E.P. was abolished in the field of home trade, and for it was substituted a totally new system of organized trade.

* *Ekonomicheskaya Zhizn*, 26 April and 1 May 1929. *Torgovo-Promyshlennaya Gazeta*, 6 April 1929.
† *Ekonomicheskaya Zhizn*, 14 November 1928.

EXTERNAL TRADE

When N.E.P. was introduced the principle of a State monopoly of *foreign trade* was retained in spite of the opposition of certain influential members of the Communist Party. Lenin advanced the following arguments in favour of retaining the monopoly: 'No tariff policy can be really effective in an era of Imperialism, an era of enormous discrimination between poor countries and very rich countries. In such circumstances any rich industrial country can completely defeat tariff protection. To do so it need only introduce an export bounty on the goods exported to Russia on which we levy a duty. Any industrial country has more than enough money to finance such a bounty, and consequently any industrial country can, with absolute certainty, defeat our home industries.'* Krasin, who was the actual organizer of the foreign trade monopoly and the first Soviet Ambassador to Great Britain, stressed that: 'Soviet monopoly of foreign trade is simply the application of the general Soviet principle of planned State regulation to the sphere of the foreign trade relations of the Soviet Union. Thus there is the closest mutual connexion between the foreign trade monopoly and the planned economy of the Soviet State. Without a foreign trade monopoly, the Soviet State could not carry out the State planning scheme.'

The following advantages can be gained from a State monopoly of foreign trade:

(*a*) It affords complete protection against the competition of other countries and against the interference of World Market prices with Internal Market prices. Such protection could not be achieved by mere import duties. To render the protection of import duties effective, it would have been necessary to make the duties almost prohibitive. But very high duties on imports would create great difficulties for exports because the other country on its part will introduce high import duties. A State monopoly of foreign trade makes it possible to conclude agreements with a so-called 'most-favoured nation' clause to make reciprocal concessions in tariffs, because imports could be controlled by internal licences and quotas irrespective of the height of import duties. As a means of protection such duties could have only a secondary importance. They might be used as an additional barrier, applied only in those cases where the specifications attached to import licences were made in general terms, as well as in the case of parcels sent by post and goods carried by travellers.

---

* Lenin, op. cit. vol. XXVII, pp. 380–1.

Of much greater importance would be import duties which could be used as a means of bargaining when concluding economic agreements with other countries. Soviet economists stressed that 'if we had no tariffs it would be very difficult for us to obtain any concessions from importing countries'.*

(b) A State monopoly of foreign trade makes it possible to regulate imports strictly according to the plan without any formal change in commercial agreements and without any changes in the tariff rates. Import licences are issued by the People's Commissariat of Foreign Trade or its subordinate bodies, according to a general import plan. And, as a matter of fact, import into the Soviet Union, during the later period, was carried out strictly according to plan. In the first period the need for importing certain foodstuffs and other consumer goods made it necessary to concentrate on the import of these items, but later on the import programme was carried out with the aim of supplying capital goods required for the development of industry, transport, and agriculture. The importation of goods for consumption was reduced to a minimum.

(c) Export, too, could be carried out more strictly according to plan. The State monopoly of foreign trade permitted the Government to determine the general structure of exports and to mobilize more fully the exportable resources of the country, since it was possible to consider export and import as united operations. Under the system of *free foreign trade* imports and exports usually appear as two separate operations. Importers and exporters work at their own risk, and profits or losses on imports are not compensated by the losses or profits on exports and vice versa. Export is carried out, generally, only with a view to obtaining individual profit and only when the home market cannot offer as profitable conditions for the disposal of the entire quantity of goods as can the foreign market. Only in the case of dumping is export carried out with temporary losses, but even there the ultimate aim is profit.

A system of State monopoly of foreign trade could treat the question of foreign trade profits in a different way. Both export and import would be viewed not as two commercially separate operations but as two aspects of one operation. The organizations dealing with export and import would be State organizations. Their capital would be part of the State finance, and the losses of one organization could be covered by the profits of the other. The Soviet trading organizations, like any other exporters, were of course anxious to obtain the highest prices for their goods and to buy imported goods

* Kaufman, *The Organization and Regulation of the Foreign Trade of the U.S.S.R.*

at the lowest possible prices; but when the level of world prices declined during a crisis the Soviet Union's only concern would be that the prices of articles which she imports should decline more rapidly than the prices of her exports. The result would be that for the same quantity of goods exported the Soviet Union would receive a greater quantity of imports.

(*d*) A State monopoly of foreign trade rendered it possible to regulate foreign trade not only according to economic aims but also according to political and social ones. The political aims, based on considerations of the desirability or otherwise of developing economic and political relations with a particular country, could be pursued by a corresponding transfer of import purchases from one country to another without formal changes in existing trade agreements with the country concerned.

(*e*) A State monopoly of foreign trade eliminated the necessity for the internal currency to be linked to the foreign currency. As all foreign trading was done by State organizations a special currency could be used for the accounting of foreign trade operations. This special currency could also be used for conversion into the currency of other countries, for the use of travellers and for remittances between private individuals in their transactions from abroad. And in actual fact, after the Soviet rouble had ceased to appear on the Foreign Exchange markets, the Soviet Government used a special rouble for the calculation of foreign trade and for the purpose of converting foreign currency in private foreign transactions (for travellers and for money orders from abroad) which served only as an accounting unit for all transactions in foreign currency (see pp. 102–3).

All these advantages of a State monopoly of foreign trade were reasons why the Soviet Government never deviated from this principle. The forms of regulating and executing foreign trade were often changed, but the principle of State monopoly of foreign trade was never infringed.

When the economic and financial blockade of the U.S.S.R. was lifted and the formal obstructions in the way of the development of foreign trade removed by the conclusion of the first temporary trade agreements with Great Britain in March 1921 and later on with other countries, foreign trade began to operate through two channels, through the central co-operative organizations (Tsentrosoyuz, Sel'skosoyuz, L'nocentr, etc.), and through mixed joint-stock companies of Soviet and foreign capital. These took the form of concessions for foreign trade under the control of the People's

Commissariat of Foreign Trade. Two kinds of companies were created—one for trade in special goods only, such as 'Rusholandoles' and 'Rusangloles' in the timber trade, and one for trade with a particular country, such as 'Rusavstorg', 'Rusgertorg', 'Sovpoltorg', i.e. for trade with Austria, Germany, Poland. The object of creating these mixed companies was to attract foreign capital and to use the experience of foreign companies as a school for the Soviet trading organizations. However, the companies did not attract a large amount of foreign capital and did not play a significant role in the international trade of the U.S.S.R.*

Thus, from the very beginning of N.E.P. and during the whole of its period, foreign trade was almost exclusively carried on by Soviet co-operatives and State trading organizations, under the general control of the People's Commissariat of Foreign Trade and its subordinate institutions. In the first years of N.E.P., however, strict co-ordination of the foreign trade activities of the various co-operative and State organizations was not always achieved, and they very often competed among themselves on the internal market in an endeavour to get the maximum possible quantity of goods for export. Sometimes the interests of export collided with those of the internal market. Stricter co-ordination of the trading activities of the different organizations began only after the fusion, in November 1925, of the People's Commissariat of Foreign Trade with the People's Commissariat of Internal Trade into one People's Commissariat of Trade, or Narkomtorg as it was called, and the creation of special joint-stock export and import organizations and syndicates.

These export and import organizations were henceforth closely interconnected with the economic institutions producing for or trading on the internal market in the corresponding export goods, or in need of import goods. They carried out their trade activities abroad exclusively through the corresponding departments of the trade delegations of the U.S.S.R. (Torgpredstvo) in the various countries.

The general aim of the foreign trade of the U.S.S.R. was not to export and import in order to obtain profit from these operations but to assist, through foreign trade, the development of the national economy. The need for importing certain foodstuffs and consumer

* In 1922–3 their turn-over in the total foreign trade turn-over of the U.S.S.R. amounted only to 3·8%, in 1923–4 to 3·6%, in 1924–5 to 2·7%, and in 1925–6 to 3%, but during the first years the role of these companies as regards certain highly profitable export goods was very significant. See details, Butovskiy, *Foreign Concessions in the U.S.S.R.* pp. 53–79.

goods, during the first years of N.E.P., was very great, as well as the need for importing capital goods for the restoration of industry and transport. This latter need did not diminish but, on the contrary, grew with the increasing industrial development of the national economy. The duty of exports was to provide, in the given period, as much foreign currency as possible to pay for the necessary imports even if this meant that exports were unprofitable and interfered with supplies for the internal market.* But the need to import was greater than the resources available for export and the yearly trade balance (see Table 8) was more often negative than positive. Since the Soviet Union did not have any substantial invisible exports during this period, but, on the contrary, paid considerable sums for foreign transport† and credit operations, the negative trade balance had to be paid in gold.

Table 8

	Export mill. roubles	Import mill. roubles	Balance
1913	1,520·1	1,374·0	+ 146·1
1920	1·4	28·7	− 27·3
1921	20·2	208·3	− 188·1
1922	81·6	269·8	− 188·2
1923–4	373·2	233·5	+ 139·7
1924–5	558·6	723·5	− 164·9
1925–6	676·6	756·3	− 79·7
1926–7	780·2	713·6	+ 66·6
1927–8	777·8	945·5	− 167·7
1928–9	877·6	836·3	+ 41·3
1929–30	1,002·3	1,068·6	− 66·3

* In the summer of 1925 it was stated in many cases that export was not only unprofitable but even impossible owing to the high prices prevailing on the internal market: 'Sometimes the domestic markets for timber, butter, eggs and grain are more active than those abroad' (M. Frumkin, *National Economy and Foreign Trade of the U.S.S.R.*); 'The export of most of our goods produces not only little profit, but at times involves us in loss' (*The Foreign Trade of the U.S.S.R. during Ten Years*, p. 206); 'Had the position [of the balance of payments] been more favourable, a number of articles which had to be sent abroad would not have been exported. For this reason the relative proportion of the unprofitable exports had increased and the exportation of a number of industrial and agricultural articles affected the interests of the home market, as these articles had to be exported although the home demand for such goods as butter, flax, cotton, textiles, cement and sawn timber remained unsatisfied' (*Statistical Survey*, no. 3, 1929, p. 75); 'Very frequently goods have been exported which would be very useful on the home market, but this has been done because we are in need of foreign raw materials and industrial equipment' (*Izvestia*, 21 August 1930).

† Kaufman estimated that the U.S.S.R. paid yearly about 50–60 million gold roubles for the services of foreign transport (*The Organization and Regulation of Russia's Foreign Trade*, p. 86).

The impossibility of paying for the required imports out of the proceeds of the export trade was due to the impossibility of raising sufficiently the volume of exports of agricultural products, especially foodstuffs (Table 9).

Table 9

	Foodstuffs	Raw materials and semi-manufactured goods	Animals	Manufactured goods
Exports (in million roubles)				
1913	878·5	522·3	34·3	84·9
1920	0·3	1·1	0·0	0·0
1921	1·5	18·1	0·0	0·6
1922	4·5	74·0	0·1	3·1
1923	125·2	79·0	0·0	1·6
1924–5	174·0	365·4	2·4	16·9
1925–6	289·4	354·1	2·9	30·3
1926–7	367·6	370·7	3·2	38·7
1927–8	234·7	455·2	3·2	84·8
1928–9	215·7	559·3	3·3	99·3
1929–30	274·3	625·4	1·0	101·6
Imports (in million roubles)				
1913	237·9	668·0	17·6	450·5
1920	1·1	4·4	0·0	23·0
1921	33·8	19·4	0·0	155·1
1922	93·3	39·9	0·0	136·6
1923	10·5	74·2	0·0	59·4
1924–5	203·5	347·2	5·1	167·6
1925–6	65·7	405·3	8·7	276·7
1926–7	58·4	425·3	8·6	221·3
1927–8	108·2	507·9	10·4	318·9
1928–9	72·1	455·9	11·0	297·3
1929–30	92·9	412·6	13·8	549·4

Before the Revolution agricultural exports paid not only the whole cost of annual imports of manufactured goods and such foodstuffs as were not produced or only insufficiently produced in Russia, but also partly covered the cost of imported raw materials and semi-manufactured goods. Only in 1926–7 did Soviet exports of agricultural products amount to more than one-third of those of 1913. This was the reason for the prevalence of a negative trade balance in the foreign trade of the U.S.S.R. during the period from 1920 to 1930.*

In spite of the fact that the Soviet State monopoly of foreign

* See more detailed study of the development of foreign trade during the period of 1913–30 in my study *The Foreign Trade of the U.S.S.R.*, published as Memorandum No. 2 of the Birmingham Bureau of Research on Russian Economic Conditions, Birmingham University.

trade made it possible to restrict imports in order to achieve a positive trade balance, the need to import, especially equipment and raw materials for industry, was considered so urgent that imports were maintained even in the face of the impossibility of paying for them by exports. It was not the fault of the planning of foreign trade or the functioning of the trade monopoly that the Russian foreign trade developed slowly and did not reach the pre-revolutionary level even at the end of the restoration period and was mostly carried on with a negative trade balance. The reason lay rather in the slow development of agricultural production and its marketability. On the contrary, owing to the monopoly of foreign trade more goods were mobilized for export than would have been possible under different conditions. Some goods were even exported at the expense of home consumption and without profit, indeed sometimes with loss, as they provided foreign currency for the payment of the required imports.

However, the centralization of the foreign trade in certain goods in the hands of huge State and co-operative monopoly organizations and the execution of small miscellaneous orders through the trading departments of 'Torgpredstvo' (trade delegations in particular countries) suffered from many defects, such as the cumbersomeness in the organization of the selling and buying of mass products, failure to time the utilization of a favourable market for particular goods, loss of time in executing orders for particular industrial equipment, and the overburdening of Torgpredstvo with small orders. These defects were tolerable while the national economy was being restored; but when the process of economic reconstruction began, coinciding with the beginning of the world economic crisis, the rationalization of the organization of the activities of the State monopoly of foreign trade by means of decentralization was considered urgent. This process began in 1930.

However, before describing this process and the events which took place subsequently in foreign trade, we shall give a general analysis of the development of the economic system and the national economy during the restoration period.

CHAPTER VI. PUBLIC FINANCE, CREDIT AND MONEY

The transition to N.E.P. started with the substitution of a food tax for the compulsory requisitioning of agricultural products,* i.e. in essence with a financial measure.

After the failure of the attempt to restrict trade in agricultural products to local markets and to organize barter between State enterprises, it was evident that fundamental changes in the organization of the finance and credit of the country were inevitable and the Ninth All Russian Congress of Soviets, which met in December 1921, by resolution stressed that in order to realize N.E.P. it would be necessary to adapt the financial policy to the new conditions and to effect a 'gradual transition to a stable monetary unit which is absolutely essential for trade turn-over...as well as for the realization of economic accounting among the State enterprises'.

The importance which was attached to the question of stabilizing the currency is clearly illustrated by the following statement of Lenin: 'What is truly important—is the stabilization of the rouble. We work at this question, to this task we ascribe a decisive significance. If we should succeed in stabilizing the rouble for a long period and afterwards for ever—that would mean that we had won.'†

But three years were to elapse before the Soviet Government introduced monetary reform and succeeded in stabilizing the currency. In order to do so it was necessary first of all to find ways and means for restoring a balanced State Budget, to create an appropriate credit apparatus and to accumulate sufficient resources.

In order to balance the State Budget it was necessary first of all to reduce expenditure, to relieve the State Budget of the need to subsidize State enterprises and local budgets, to build up a new fiscal apparatus and to create and multiply sources of revenue. Only in this way would it be possible to avoid the necessity of resorting again and again to the printing press in order to cover deficits in the budget. We shall enumerate only the most important

---

* The difference was that, before, the basic quantities of products to be left at the disposal of peasant households were fixed, and everything above these quantities had to be delivered to the State purveying bodies. The food tax meant that the amount to be delivered to the purveying bodies was fixed, any surplus being left at the free disposal of peasant households.

† Lenin, op. cit. vol. XXVII, p. 346.

measures and events in the field of State finance during the period before monetary reform was introduced in 1924.

(a) A series of measures aimed at reducing the expenditure of the State Budget. During 1921, payment for goods and services supplied by the State to enterprises and to private persons was re-instituted (decree of Sovnarkom S.S.S.R. of 5 August 1921). State-owned industrial enterprises were financially excluded from the State Budget and received the right to buy and sell on the market (decrees of the Soviet of People's Commissars of 4 and 27 October 1921). Many industrial enterprises whose costs of production were above the margin of profitability were temporarily closed. Some enterprises, especially small ones, were let to private entrepreneurs. It was stressed that the 'dependent psychology' shown by State enterprises would no more be tolerated, expenditure exceeding approved credit would be considered as illegal, and strict economy must be observed in spending State money (decrees of V.Ts.I.K. of 10 October 1921 and of Sovnarkom S.S.S.R. of 30 June and 12 August 1921). In order to cut down administrative expenditure a reduction of the network of administrative institutions and their staffs was undertaken. State control over the finance of State institutions and enterprises was strengthened by the fusion of the 'Workers' and Peasants' Inspection' (R.K.I.). This had been created by the decree of 7 February 1920 with the 'Central Control Commission' of the Party (Ts.K.K.). Its duty, in future, was not only to decide whether expenditure was justifiable but also to control its usefulness and expediency, and to stimulate economy in the expenditure of State enterprises. Later on, in addition to R.K.I. and Ts.K.K., a special body for control was created as the 'Financial controlling administration' of the People's Commissariat of Finance, and during 1921-2 all former employees of State financial institutions and insurance specialists were called upon to work in the newly constituted State financial apparatus.

A series of measures* aimed at separating local expenditure from the Central State Budget on the principle that local expenditure must be covered by local revenues. It was decreed that local revenues must cover expenditure on local Soviet administrative institutions, part of the expenditure on education, public health services, social security, transport and the cost of industrial and labour institutions of local significance.

* Decrees of the Council of People's Commissars of 22 August 1921 and 10 December 1921, Constitution of the U.S.S.R. of 1923, decisions of V.Ts.I.K. of 12 November 1923.

(b) The fiscal apparatus which had been completely destroyed during the previous period was gradually restored, and the sources of revenue of the State Budget began slowly to reappear. During this period taxation in kind co-existed with monetary taxation. By the decree of 21 March 1921 a tax in kind in grain was introduced and was supplemented during 1921 by one payable in potatoes, oil seeds, tobacco, and meat. Up to the end of 1921, therefore, there existed twelve taxes in kind paid in eighteen agricultural products. Apart from these there were other taxes in kind levied only on the agricultural population, such as land carriage tax (decree of Sovnarkom R.S.F.S.R. of 22 November 1922), and the peasant household tax (decree of V.Ts.I.K. of 25 May 1922). In 1922 all taxes in kind payable in agricultural products were unified in the 'consolidated tax in kind' (Edinyy Naturalnyy Nalog), which was calculated in poods of rye or wheat, but had to be paid in different products according to their equivalence to rye or wheat. In 1923 a further step was made in the unification of taxes paid by the peasantry by unifying all taxes payable in agricultural products, in money or in services in one 'consolidated agricultural tax' (Edinyy Selkhoz Nalog), which, however, continued to be calculated in poods of rye and wheat and was collected partly in kind and partly in money. The 'consolidated agricultural tax' became a purely monetary tax only in the beginning of 1924. It was considered impossible in a period when the restoration of marketing of agricultural products had scarcely begun, and money continued to depreciate, to pass on immediately to a monetary tax levied on the agricultural population.

But, parallel with taxation in kind imposed on the agricultural population, from the beginning of 1921 monetary taxation began to be restored. During 1921–2 excises on many 'packeted' goods such as wine, tobacco, matches, salt, sugar, and tea were introduced, together with a series of duties and levies. The first direct tax on the non-agricultural population was introduced in September 1921 (decree of 26 August 1921) as a trade or craft tax (Promyslovyy Nalog), levied at first only on private and co-operative trade and industrial enterprises. In 1922 this tax began to be levied on State enterprises as well. In 1922 an 'income-property tax' was introduced (Podokhodno-poimushchestvenyy Nalog); at first this also was levied only on private persons and private property, but it was extended to State enterprises in 1923. Besides these main taxes there existed many taxes for special purposes, such as the tax for the relief of hunger in 1921, the housing tax to finance house-building, and a special military tax for persons who were not called up for service in the army.

At the Eleventh Congress of the Party (which met from 27 March to 2 April 1922) it was emphasized that 'taxation policy must aim at regulating the process of accumulating resources by means of direct taxation of property and incomes. Taxation policy is the principal instrument of the revolutionary policy of the proletariat in a transitional epoch. But at the same time taxation policy must pursue a purely fiscal task—providing the greatest revenue from taxes'.

Thus from the very beginning of N.E.P. the dual task of taxation policy was stressed—redistribution of the national income, and the purely fiscal task—to provide the revenue of the State Budget. Taxation of all kinds in this period, however, was able to provide only a small part of the total revenue of the Budget—in 1922–3 taxes provided 30% (407 million roubles), and in 1923–4 about 40% (633 million roubles) of total revenue.

(c) Other main sources of revenue were non-tax revenues from State enterprises and State loans. Returns from State enterprises and properties during this period provided only a relatively small portion of the revenue, since State enterprises were only beginning to build up their economic activities on a sound financial basis. Gross non-tax revenues (during this period transport and communication services were included in the State Budget by their gross turn-over), however, nearly doubled between 1922–3 and 1923–4,* and this encouraged hopes for the future.

Owing to the conditions then existing of transition from a 'natural' to a monetary economy, from a depreciating to a stable currency, State loans were also of two kinds—loans in kind and loans in money expressed in units of the depreciating currency, but calculated on the 'gold basis'.

The first State loan was issued in May 1922 as a grain loan. It was issued for 10 million poods of grain. The bonds were sold for money, but were to be redeemed by the Treasury during the period from 1 November 1922 to 31 January 1923 by payment either in kind or in money at the option of the owners of bonds. Peasants were allowed to pay their taxes in kind with these bonds. The aim of this particular kind of State loan was manifold; to test the ground for the possibility of issuing further State loans, to stimulate

---

* In 1922–3 non-tax revenue amounted to 441 million roubles, in 1923–4 to 807 million roubles, of which revenue from transport was 364 and 630 million roubles for the respective years.

4

the extension of money economy among the peasantry since the latter were able to buy bonds for money but could pay their taxes in kind with bonds, and to create confidence in the currency as bonds were redeemable both in money and in kind at the option of the owner of bonds. Experience, however, showed that the peasantry used the bonds almost exclusively for paying their tax in kind (in this way 6·3 million poods of grain due in tax in kind were paid in bonds) or demanded repayment of redeemed bonds in grain (2 million poods of grain were paid by the State when bonds were paid off).* Only two more loans in kind were issued—a grain loan for 30 million poods and a sugar loan for 1 million poods of sugar issued on 15 November 1923—and the issuing of loans in kind was then discontinued.

The first monetary loan was issued in 1922 as a 6% loan of 100 million gold roubles for 10 years. Bonds were expressed in gold roubles, but were sold for paper roubles according to the gold rate of exchange. Subscription of this loan was not successful, and methods of compulsory subscription to it were applied among private entrepreneurs and partly also among State and co-operative enterprises.

All these sources of revenue were, however, inadequate to provide sufficient means for covering the expenditure of the State Budget. According to Yurovsky, at the beginning of 1922 only 2·7% of revenue was derived from taxes, as against 10·6% from State undertakings and properties, and 86·7% supplied by Treasury issues.† It proved impossible, during this period, to cover the deficit of the State Budget except by note issue, which continued to be one of the main sources of revenue until the very eve of the monetary reform of 1924. In this lay the main cause of the long postponement of the monetary reform.‡

Restoration of the credit system began with the establishment of the State Bank, the statutes of which were ratified on 12 October; it began business in November 1921. In a statement of V.Ts.I.K. it was explained that the purpose of establishing the State Bank of the R.S.F.S.R. was 'to assist the development of industry, agriculture and trade as well as to concentrate monetary transactions and

---

* *Finance and Credit of the U.S.S.R.* p. 100.

† Prof. L. N. Yurovsky, *Currency Problems and Policy of the Soviet Union*, p. 66.

‡ During the first quarter of 1922–3 the revenue from note issue covered 95·8% of the deficit of that quarter, in the last quarter it covered 54·2%; during October–December 1923 the revenue from note issue covered only 41% of the deficit of that quarter. Arnold, *Banks, Credit and Money in Soviet Russia*, p. 192.

apply other measures aimed at the establishment of a sound monetary circulation'.

The authorized capital of the Bank was supplied by a grant of 2,000,000,000,000 paper roubles from the Treasury which, at the time when it began operating, represented about 14–20 million roubles in gold.* Later on, further grants were made to the Bank from the Treasury in order partly to make good losses of authorized capital due to the continued rapid depreciation of currency. By a grant of 1 March 1922 the capital of the Bank was raised to 5,750,000,000,000 roubles and on 1 November 1922 to 130,750,000,000,000 roubles.

The Bank was allowed to grant short-term commercial credit and long-term investment credit against security to the State and co-operative enterprises as well as to agricultural producers and private enterprises in general. The Bank was permitted to carry out all the ordinary credit operations of banks. In the first year of its existence, however, it did not receive the right to issue notes. This was retained by the Treasury and only at the end of 1922 (by the decree of Sovnarkom S.S.S.R. of 11 October 1922) did the State Bank acquire the right of note issue. It was equipped with preferential rights in buying and selling gold and foreign exchange inside the country and in foreign transactions even after the abolition (in April 1922) of the system of compulsory surrender of gold and foreign currency exchange by individuals to the State. In February 1923 State and co-operative institutions were compelled to deposit in their current accounts at the State Bank any foreign currency in their possession. In this way, gold and foreign exchange were concentrated in the State Bank.

Great difficulties were experienced by the Bank during this period in safeguarding its capital under conditions of continued currency depreciation. Many 'insurance' devices were applied. Credit was calculated in 'gold' roubles and in commodities for the purchase of which credit was accorded, so that when credit was repayable it was paid according to the prices of the corresponding commodities at this time, and high depreciation interest was charged. But all these devices only mitigated losses in the capital of the Bank which resulted from conducting credit operations in an atmosphere of rapidly depreciating currency. Only at the end

* Different authors give different estimates for the gold value of the Treasury grant of 2 trillion roubles at the time when the Bank began operating. See Prof. S. S. Katzenellenbaum, *Russian Currency and Banking*, 1914–24, p. 156; *Finance and Credit of the U.S.S.R.* p. 106.

of 1923, when the new banknote 'chervonetz' substantially began to enter the note circulation, was the process of the depreciation of the capital of the State Bank brought to an end.

The State Bank was originally intended to be the only credit institution in the country. Accordingly, it was authorized to establish district offices, branches and agencies. On 1 October 1922 the State Bank had already 116 affiliates. It proved necessary, however, to permit the creation of other credit institutions in order to provide specialized credit services for different branches of economic activity catering for different clientèles and accumulating capital from different sources. In 1922 a number of such banks began to be created.

A general policy in this field was agreed upon at the above-mentioned Eleventh Congress of the Party, at which it was stressed that:

> The development of the trade turn-over of town and village...and, to an even greater degree, the development of trade turn-over on the foreign market cannot be speedy and successful but for the powerful assistance of credit, the regulation of which must be in the hands of the State. The creation of secondary credit institutions, controlled by the State Bank which would assist the concentration of free monetary resources for productive utilization, as well as the creation of a network of institutions for small credit operations (credit co-operatives) and local credit, must be undertaken within the limits set by the necessity of safeguarding the predominant role of the State Bank.

Thus the State Bank, after having ceased to be the sole credit institution, was intended to continue to exist as a central regulating and controlling bank for all the newly created credit institutions.

The first specialized credit institutions to be organized were the co-operative credit associations. By the decree of V.Ts.I.K. and Sovnarkom S.S.S.R. of 24 January 1922, all citizens of the Soviet Republics were allowed to organize credit associations and loan and savings associations. This decree emphasized the main task of the credit associations in rural districts, viz. the organization of mutual credit assistance to the poor and middle-class peasantry, to domestic industry and handicraftsmen, the mobilization of their monetary resources for the speedy development of agriculture and home industries and the relief of poor peasants and handicraftsmen from the necessity of having to resort to loans from rich peasants and private capital. Accordingly a very low membership minimum was fixed for these credit associations (fifty members) and their resources were to be derived from membership fees, from shares, loans and credit granted by the State institutions.

In order to support, direct and supervise these rural credit associations, the Soviet Government began, in accordance with the decree of 21 December 1922, to organize through the State Bank 'Agricultural credit societies' (Obshchestva selsko-khozyaistvennogo kredita) whose capital was to be derived from two types of shares—founders' shares, i.e. shares held by the founders of these 'Societies' (who were jointly the Commissariat of Finance and lately the State Bank, the People's Commissariat of Agriculture and the All-Russian Union of Agricultural Co-operation, lately the Consumers' Co-operative Bank) and shares held by the members and clientele of the rural credit associations and loan and savings associations. Thus there existed in these 'Agricultural credit societies' a combination of State and co-operative elements. The State, being the founder of these 'societies', provided part of their capital, regulated their activities and through them influenced the activities of rural credit 'associations'. Rural credit associations were built up on co-operative principles, and through their executive bodies were connected with the 'Agricultural credit societies'. At the beginning, however, both these kinds of rural credit institutions were financially very weak. Some of them were only credit institutions in name, since they were actually engaged more in trading than in credit operations. But as early as 1923, in order to co-ordinate and supervise the activities of local agricultural credit societies, republican agricultural banks began to be created in every Soviet Republic as joint-stock banks in which not less than 51% of the shares had to be held by State institutions. Finally, in February 1924, the Central Agricultural Bank of the U.S.S.R. was created, its authorized capital being provided by the State. The State Bank had to provide it with loans equalling the amount of its authorized capital. This bank was authorized to grant short- and long-term credit.

Thus, when monetary reform was introduced agricultural credit institutions consisted of a network of large numbers of small credit associations and loan and savings associations (purely co-operative credit institutions), and larger 'Agricultural credit societies' (mixed capital of State institutions and members of co-operatives). Above these were the republican agricultural banks (joint-stock capital with predominance of State capital) and, at the head of the entire agricultural credit system, the Central Agricultural Bank of the U.S.S.R.

A resolution of the Thirteenth Party Conference, which met on 16–18 January 1924, emphasized that 'the Soviet Government must help the peasantry also by increasing their working capital by (a) organizing cheap agricultural credit, (b) providing the peasantry with agricultural machinery and equipment on credit, (c) supporting agricultural co-operation, etc.' In all their measures regarding the peasantry the Soviet Government had to proceed from the necessity of giving help of every kind to the poorest and middle strata of the peasantry, and particularly to the Association for the Joint Cultivation of Land (Tovarishchestva dlia obshchestvennoi obrabotki zemli—T.O.Z.) in order to help them to free themselves from dependence on the kulaks.

This dual task which agricultural credit was called upon to perform—the support of the development of agricultural production, but with certain socio-political aims—influenced the whole credit policy of the agricultural credit institutions during this period.

In order to meet the credit needs of consumers' co-operatives in February 1922 (statutes approved on 16 February) the Consumers' Co-operative Bank (Bank Potrebitelskoy kooperatsii or, abbreviated, 'Pokobank') was founded. It was reorganized, in January 1923, as a general co-operative credit bank serving all types of co-operative under the name of All-Russian Co-operative Bank (Vserosiskiy Kooperativnyy Bank, or 'Vsekobank') and a similar bank for the Ukraine—All-Ukrainian Co-operative Bank (Vseukrainskiy Kooperativnyy Bank, or 'Ukrainbank')—was created. These co-operative banks, apart from the usual commercial banking business, were also engaged in long-term credit operations. During the early period of their existence these banks were hampered by the meagreness of their resources in spite of the fact that the State rendered them financial assistance. This, however, was not sufficient to meet the growing requirements for credit of the rapidly developing co-operative economy. At the same time, of course, until the general monetary reform had been accomplished co-operative banks suffered considerably from the currency depreciation.

The private sector, i.e. private enterprises of all kinds which had sprung up in the first year of N.E.P., at first resorted to the illegal money market and partly to the State credit institutions to meet their credit requirements. But from the middle of 1922 the Government permitted the organization of mutual credit societies (Obshchestva vzaimnogo kredita, or O.V.K.), whose numbers grew rapidly between the opening of the first in Petrograd in June 1922 and 1927. The organization of O.V.K.s was authorized by permits granted by the People's Commissariat of Finance, which latter had the right of approval of the Statutes, of fixing the amount of credit to be granted to members and of revising and compulsorily liquidating the O.V.K.s. The capital was provided by membership fees and they catered mostly for private wholesalers.

In order to meet the credit needs of individual branches of the national economy several specialized banks were organized in 1922: (1) The Commercial-Industrial Bank (Torgovo-Promyshlennyy Bank, or 'Prombank') which was organized on the initiative of State Trusts and syndicates as a joint-stock company which granted short-term credit as well as long-term industrial loans and loans for special purposes from special funds to State Industry and Transport. (2) The 'Elektrokredit' joint-stock bank for financing, originally, the electrification of agriculture. This bank was later reorganized as a bank for financing electrification in general, under the name of 'Elektrobank'. (3) The Russian Commercial Bank (Rossiiskiy Kommercheskiy Bank, or 'Roskombank'), the organization of which represented an attempt to attract foreign capital in collaboration with Soviet capital for extending foreign trade credit. It was organized by a Swedish company (Svenska Economie Aktiebolaget) and by the People's Commissariat of Foreign Trade. This bank, however, did not justify the hopes of attracting a large amount of foreign capital. Instead of concentrating on credit operations in connexion with foreign trade, it preferred to cater for internal trade and mostly for the private sector of it. Consequently, in April 1924, it was reorganized as Bank of Foreign Trade (Bank dlia Vneshney Torgovli, or 'Vneshtorgbank'). It was allowed to carry on all the usual commercial banking operations, but its activities were mostly concentrated on credit operations in connexion with foreign trade, and it catered almost exclusively for State and co-operative enterprises. (4) A number of municipal banks were organized from the beginning of 1923 as joint-stock banks with 'mixed' capital, i.e. they were organized by Regional Executive Committees (Gubispolkomy) which provided not less than 51% of the total capital stock, the other part of the capital being attracted from the private sector. These banks were organized with the aim of providing credit for municipal enterprises, to enable local populations to meet their needs for constructions of every kind and for local State, co-operative and private enterprises. The first of these banks to be organized was the Moscow City Bank (Moskovsky Gorodskoy Bank, or 'Mosgorbank'), which opened many branches. Municipal banks were gradually organized in nearly all regional centres. In the existing conditions of depreciating currency these banks were very reluctant to engage in long-term credit transactions, which was their primary task, and preferred commercial operations. In order to meet the urgent need for credit in co-operative housing construction and, later, to co-ordinate the activities of the municipal banks, the Central Bank for Municipal Economy and Housing (Tsentralnyy Bank Komunal-nogo Khozyaistva i Zhilishchnogo Stroitelstva, or 'Tsekombank') was created in January 1925, in the organization of which the People's Commissariats of Finance, Labour, Internal Affairs, the All-Union Soviet of Trade Unions, the main office of the State insurance of the U.S.S.R. and the Mosgorbank all took part. (5) In December 1922 the Government decided to establish Savings Banks, which began to open from the beginning of 1923, first in Moscow and Petrograd and afterwards gradually through-out the whole country. They were placed under the general ad-ministration of a special department of the Commissariat of Finance. Protection against losses in deposits owing to the de-preciation of money was obtained by accepting and paying back deposits in 'gold roubles', and people soon realized that it was a real advantage to deposit their spare money in Savings Banks and so to protect their savings from loss. Consequently, the number of branches and depositors and the total amount of deposits grew very rapidly. In March 1924, at the time of the Monetary Reform, over 2,500 Savings Banks were in existence with over 760,000 depositors and 18 million 'gold roubles' in deposits. Owing to this method of protecting the deposits of the large mass of the population from depreciation the Treasury suffered considerable losses. However, from the social and technical point of view, this loss was considered worth while. (6) A few special banks for credit operations in certain regions were also organized, such as the Far Eastern Joint-stock Bank, the North-Caucasian Bank, the Mid-Asiatic Bank, the South-Eastern Commercial Bank, and others.

Thus, during the first three years of N.E.P., a multifarious and widespread system of credit institutions developed, and at the end of 1923, i.e. on the eve of the Monetary Reform, there were over 150 main banks and credit societies with 750 branches and over 2,500 Savings Banks.

We have seen that the conditions in State finance at the begin-ning of N.E.P. did not permit stopping the use of the printing press as the main source for covering the deficit of the State Budget, and the note issue took on astronomical dimensions. During 1921 it rose from 1,168,597 million roubles to 9,845,195 million roubles.

In December 1922 there were already 1,479,219,306 million and in January 1923, 1,994,464,454 million roubles in circulation. Depreciation of the rouble followed this gigantic increase in the volume of money in circulation, but the rate of currency depreciation was somewhat slower in 1921–2 than that of the rise in the volume of money in circulation. The price index compiled by the Department for Labour Statistics in January 1921 was 16,800 (1913—1·0) in December 1921—138,000, in December 1922—16,440,000 and in January 1923—21,242,000.* This was due to the steady growth of trade turn-over and consequently to the increasing demand for money.

In order to relieve the population of the necessity of calculating in such astronomical figures the Government twice devalued the currency by ordering in November 1921 exchange of the 1922 rouble for all previous issues at the ratio of 10,000 roubles, and in October 1922 by making the rouble of the 1923 issue equal to 100 roubles of the 1922 issue or 1 million roubles of previous issues. These devaluations had only the technical effect of making accounting easier. They could not, of course, eliminate the depreciation of the currency and all its consequences.

Many devices were employed in order to find a stable measure of value under conditions of rapid currency depreciation—reckonings were made in the pre-war rouble, in the index rouble, in the pre-war gold rouble and in the commodity rouble—but they were all more or less defective substitutes for stable money. The need for a stable currency grew more and more urgent, especially if we remember all the problems of price regulation and relations between town and village, and between the socialized and private sectors which we described above.

The vast Budget deficit, however, could only be financed by increasing the note issue. It was therefore decided to continue to issue the depreciating currency—'sovznak'—and to introduce a stable currency with a limited sphere of circulation—the 'chervonetz'—alongside it.

By the decree of Sovnarkom S.S.S.R. of 11 October 1922 the State Bank was entrusted with the issue of the chervonetz—equal to ten of the pre-revolutionary gold roubles. Many precautions were taken to ensure the acceptance of this money as a stable currency. It was fully secured (25% of the issue was to be covered by gold and stable foreign currency; 75% by short-term bills, other short-term obligations, and by easily marketable goods). It was

* Arnold, *Banks, Credit and Money*, pp. 128–9.

not made legal tender but was accepted in payment made to or by the State in all cases where payments were to be effected in gold by law. The State Bank had the right to demand repayment in chervontzy of all credits granted in chervontzy, this measure guaranteeing the Bank the possibility of reverting to the issue of banknotes. The chervonetz was issued in very limited amounts and its issue was very carefully extended in accordance with the rate of development of the turn-over of the national economy and the possibility of note circulation. (On 1 January 1923, of the total volume of money in circulation, calculated in chervontzy, 97% consisted of sovznaks and only 3% of chervontzy, but on 1 October 1923 the sovznak accounted only for 25% of the total and the chervonetz already for 75%.)

It is not necessary to describe all the other technical measures which were taken in order to secure the stability of the chervonetz* and pave the way for monetary reform. It is sufficient to state that the steady penetration of the chervonetz in the circulation aided the rapid depreciation of the sovznak, and this process took on such catastrophical dimensions that, on the one hand, the revenue from the issue of the sovznak shrunk to negligible sums and so the profit of the Treasury from using the printing press in this way became negligible, and, on the other hand, the negative consequences of the continued existence of the rapidly depreciating currency parallel with the stable currency were aggravated by the development of industrial and agricultural production and the rise in the volume of credit transactions and trade. The need for immediate introduction of a single, stable currency was especially urgent when the 'scissors' crisis of 1923 threatened further economic development and involved certain major political questions. Consequently, in spite of the fact that the State Budget and foreign trade balance continued to be in deficit, it was decided to accomplish the process of transition to a stable currency by a definite monetary reform.

At the Thirteenth Party Conference in January 1924 (16–18 January), it was decided to undertake a monetary reform whose possibility of success was based on the anticipation that the following measures and processes took place in the development of the national economy; the abolition, in spring 1924, of all taxes in kind and their substitution by money payments, the stabilization of agricultural prices, and an improvement in the organization of

---

* The measures and processes which accompanied the introduction of the chervonetz are very ably and objectively described in Dr Arnold's study, *Banks, Money and Credit in Soviet Russia*, pp. 114–98.

trade in agricultural products which was to bring about a rise in the revenue from agriculture and a deeper penetration of agriculture by the money economy. The introduction of a stable currency was to bring about a decrease in the velocity of circulation, facilitating the regulation of prices and the improvement of the financial economy of enterprises, and it was thus hoped that the State Budget would be balanced and the printing press would definitely not be used for covering its deficits. The whole Party apparatus was mobilized in 1924 to support the successful conduct of the reform.*

The monetary reform was embodied in five main decrees. (1) The decree of 5 February 1924 ordered the issue of a new paper currency—State Treasury notes in the denomination of 1, 3 and 5 gold roubles which were accorded the right of legal tender. The amount of these in circulation was not to exceed 50% of the amount of chervontzy in circulation at the same date and had to be governed by the requirements of trade. The size of each new issue was to be under the control and decision of the Council of Labour and Defence. (2) The decree of 14 February 1924 ordered the cessation of the printing and issue of sovznaks, which were, however, left in circulation as before. (3) A separate decree of 7 March 1924 ordered redemption of the sovznak. The issue of the new paper currency, the cessation of the issue of the sovznak and its redemption were fixed at different dates for psychological and technical considerations, in order to persuade people that this was not only a new form of devaluation of the sovznak but really new money, and to find in the meantime a more adequate rate of redemption. The rate of redemption was fixed at 50,000 roubles of the sovznak of the 1923 pattern or 50,000,000 roubles of the sovznak of the pre-1921 pattern, and the redemption period was fixed at three months (April–June 1924). (4) The decree of 22 February 1924 ordered the minting and issue of silver and copper coins in the denomination of 10, 15 and 20 copecks and half-roubles in silver, and 1, 2, 3 and 5 copecks as copper coins. (5) From 1 July 1924 the emission of paper money to cover the deficits of the State Budget was ordered to cease.

These decrees, as we have seen, gave only the finishing touch to all the preparatory measures for the introduction of monetary

---

* In March 1924 the Central Executive Committee of the Party, in a directive letter to all Party organizations and in a statement 'concerning financial-economic measures in connexion with the conduct of monetary reform', gave detailed instructions as to what kind of support was needed for the successful conduct of the monetary reform.

reform, the accomplishment and successful prosecution of which was prepared by a series of measures not confined to the monetary sphere before and after the introduction of monetary reform.

After the accomplishment of the monetary reform a series of measures were introduced for placing the public finances on a sound basis and for increasing the revenue of the State. Here we shall only enumerate the most important of them.

As regards revenue: In 1924 the transition from taxation in kind to monetary taxation was completed. During 1924–7 the agricultural tax was gradually transformed into an income tax with progressive 'class' rates levied on the agricultural population. (In 1924–5 20% of peasant households, in 1925–6 25% and in 1927–8 35% did not have to pay the agricultural tax. At the same time the total amount of agricultural tax rose and consequently other groups, especially the richer ones such as the kulaks, were more heavily taxed.) The income-property tax was reformed in 1924 and 1926 as an income tax with highly progressive rates differing also according to the profession and social status of the taxpayer, being lower for workers, employees, co-operative home craftsmen and handicraftsmen, higher rates for non-co-operative individual home craftsmen and handicraftsmen and for some of the free professions, and much higher rates for persons with unearned incomes. From 1926 excess profit tax for private entrepreneurs was introduced. Excises were extended to larger groups of goods with higher rates for luxury and less essential goods and lower rates for the most essential goods. Many state loans were issued, for longer terms. During 1924–5 and 1926–9 five and fifteen loans were issued respectively. The average term of the 1922–5 loans was about three years, while in 1926–9 it was over eight years. Gradually a greater proportion of the profits of State enterprises was absorbed in the State Budget, and with the rise in the output and turn-over of State enterprises non-tax revenue steadily increased.

As regards expenditure: A series of enactments established a precise division of sources of revenue and direction of expenditure between the State Budget of the U.S.S.R., the State Budgets of Republics and the local budgets, with the aim of making each of them independently balanced budgets only formally united in one State Budget of the U.S.S.R.* It was decided to refrain from

---

* 'Statute of budgetary rights of the Union and Union's Republics' of 29 October 1924; 'Temporary Statute concerning local finance' of 29 October 1924; Decree of V.Ts.I.K. and Sovnarkom S.S.S.R. of 14 August 1925 concerning district (*raionnykh*) budgets; 'Statute concerning local finance' of 1926; 'Statute concerning budgetary rights of Union and Union's Republics' of 1927.

financing the development of the national economy from the State Budget on a large scale and to transfer the greater part of this task to the credit system. In actual fact, up to 1927, the role of the credit system in financing the national economy was greater than that of the State Budget. Control over expenditure was strengthened, and in 1926 the financial control department of the People's Commissariat of Finance S.S.S.R. was reorganized as State-finance Control (Gosfinkontrol), receiving the right and duty of inspecting the finance and underlying documents of enterprises, their cash and materials, not only retrospectively but also prospectively. Many campaigns were carried out for increased economy in the expenditure of State enterprises and institutions. In an enactment of V.Ts.I.K. and Sovnarkom S.S.S.R. of 11 June 1926 'concerning the regime of economy', a set of measures was introduced with the aim of achieving stricter economy in the expenditure of State enterprises and institutions. These included simplification and rationalization of the structure of institutions and enterprises, liquidation of certain institutions or their branches, reduction of staff, more effective use of resources and rationalization of the utilization of labour. In a resolution of the Fifteenth Party Conference (which met between 26 October and 3 November 1926) it was stressed that

the attention of the whole Party and of all Soviet institutions must be directed towards preventing any unnecessary or unproductive expenses. In accordance with the new economic task [the transition from restoration to reconstruction of the national economy] they must not confine themselves only to correcting minor defects in the administrative-economic apparatus, but must set themselves the task of revising the whole governing apparatus of national economy in order to improve it, and simplify and reduce expenses.... During the nine years which had expired since the October Revolution a very complicated organization of production, trade network, and credit institutions was created. Different links of this system often sprang up spontaneously. The scope of their activities was defined in quite a different economic situation. The lack of correspondence between the system of organization and the changed situation with its new tasks inevitably led to embezzlement of resources and the aggravation of bureaucracy.*

Thus, already in 1926, it was realized that a transition from restoration to reconstruction of the national economy would make necessary a revision 'of the whole governing apparatus of national economy set up during the period of N.E.P. and, as we shall see, as regards State finance, great changes in the methods of taxation and in the financing of development were introduced after 1930.

* *Party Resolutions*, pp. 126, 127.

The main features of the evolution of the State Budget of the U.S.S.R. during the period following the monetary reform up to 'the reform of Public Finance in 1930' are illustrated in Table 10.

In the years following the monetary reform revenue exceeded expenditure and there was consequently no need to use the printing press for covering budget deficits. Revenue from all sources grew steadily every year. Only the revenue from the agricultural tax varied, owing to special economic as well as political considerations peculiar to this tax. State loans were already a constant and quite important source of public revenue. Every year part of the savings of the population was used through the State Budget for financing the development of the national economy. In general, however, during this period the system of revenue of the State Budget did not differ in form from that of the pre-revolutionary Russian fiscal system (with some exceptions, such as the deduction from profits and the State loans policy), but, in principle, there was a great difference, since taxation policy was determined not only by fiscal considerations but by socio-political aims. This was illustrated by the differential rates of taxes for socialized and private sectors, favourable to the first and unfavourable to the latter, and for different groups of the agricultural and urban population.

As regards expenditure the principal difference between the pre-revolutionary Russian Budget and the budgets of other countries and that of the U.S.S.R. was that through the State Budget of the U.S.S.R. the national economy was constantly financed. Every year over 55% of the total expenditure of the State Budget was spent on financing the national economy. True, in this was included the gross expenditure on transport, which, along with the gross revenue, was excluded from the State Budget from 1932 onwards. If we exclude the working expenditure on transport, expenditure on the financing of the national economy amounted to about one fifth of the total during the period 1924–5 and 1926–7, and to over one-fourth in the following three years; it absorbed a still greater part of the State Budget after the financial reforms of 1930. As we have already mentioned, during the restoration period the national economy was financed to a greater extent through the credit system. Through the State Budget was redistributed a little over one-fourth of the national income, i.e. only about 5% more than in the pre-revolutionary State Budget (see Table 11).

However, in 1929–30, i.e. the year in which large-scale reconstruction work was carried out in different branches of the national

Table 10

	1924–5	1925–6	1926–7	1927–8	1928–9	1929–30
Expenditure in million roubles						
I. Financing of national economy of which:	1,629	2,245	3,067	3,796	4,784	7,681
(a) Industry	151	220	448	650	972	2,045
(b) Electrification	52	68	103	136	179	229
(c) Agriculture	171	210	204	279	548	1,099
(d) Transport and communications	1,074	1,567	2,045	2,335	2,669	3,421
(e) Food industry and trade	1	29	91	177	258	689
II. Social and cultural services	199	276	356	426	482	795
III. Administration and Defence	686	900	1,002	1,109	1,207	1,397
IV. State loans	66	118	101	300	317	406
V. Subventions to Allied Soviet Republics, local budgets and other financial institutions	325	441	615	669	1,299	1,744
VI. Other expenses	63	72	192	164	151	313
Total expenditure	2,969	4,051	5,335	6,465	8,241	12,335
Excess of receipts over expenditure	32·7	15·3	56·0	205·4	187·8	651·5
Revenue in million roubles*						
I. Revenue from taxation of which:	1,328	1,791	2,491	2,962	4,004	6,084
(a) Trade or craft tax	157	229	348	373	1,056	1,941
(b) Income tax	94	151	192	231	285	615
(c) Agricultural tax	326	252	358	354	449	406
(d) Excises	508	842	1,210	1,491	1,803	2,643
II. Non-tax revenue from which:	1,476	2,096	2,559	2,922	3,461	5,402
(a) Transport	992	1,427	1,712	1,948	2,336	3,100
(b) Communications	96	137	157	174	202	300
(c) Deduction from profit of State enterprises	123	172	308	382	418	1,004
(d) Revenue from State property	126	257	287	326	407	594
III. State loans	130	146	319	726	725	1,278
IV. Other revenues (including revenue carried over from previous years)	68	33	22	60	238	222
Total revenue	3,002	4,066	5,391	6,670	8,428	12,986

* *Socialist Construction of the U.S.S.R., Statistical Yearbook,* pp. 443–4.

Table 11

	National income (in million roubles)	Revenue of State Budget (in million roubles)
1913*	16,400	3,431
1925–6	21,230	4,066
1926–7	22,937	5,391
1927–8	25,342	6,670
1928–9	30,009	8,428
1929–30	33,963	12,986

* The figures for 1913 refer to the territory of the former Russian Empire.

economy, 38·2% of the national income passed through the State Budget and the State Budget later became the main instrument for redistributing the national income and for financing the development of the national economy.

We have seen above that on the eve of the monetary reform there already existed a multifarious and widespread system of credit institutions. The monetary reform provided a sound basis for further expansion of credit operations which joined and supported the general process of restoring the productive activity of the national economy. The number of credit institutions and their branches steadily grew up to 1927 as can be clearly seen from the figures given in Table 12. The total number of main credit institu-

Table 12

	Number of main credit institutions*		Number of branches*	
	1 October 1923	1 October 1926	1 October 1923	1 October 1926
State Bank	1	1	251	484
Prombank, Vneshtorgbank, Elektrobank	3	3	40	98
Co-operative banks	2	2	57	99
Agricultural credit system	26	72	75	214
Municipal credit system	13	50	39	222
Total	45	128	462	1,117
Municipal pawn shops	4	27	4	27
Mutual credit societies	54	283	54	283
Total	103	438	520	1,427
Comprising:				
All-Union Banks	4	7	319	647
Republican and regional banks	14	18	87	241
Local credit institutions	85	413	114	539

* *Finance and credit of the U.S.S.R.*, p. 126.

tions rose in three years more than four times and the number of their branches nearly three times. The State Bank, however, not only preserved but strengthened its role as the predominant credit institution and as a bank of banks. Table 13 shows the process of development of the main credit operations and the relative significance of the main banking institutions in the total credit operations during the period 1924–7.*

Table 13

	1924 Million roubles	1925 Million roubles	1926 Million roubles	1927 Million roubles
State Bank:				
Loans and discounts	599	1,425	1,902	2,174
Special loans	187	214	176	626
Deposits and current accounts	361	989	1,201	1,378
Banknote issue	522	757	857	1,027
Prombank:				
Capital	44	86	131	200
Loans and discounts	164	328	346	448
Deposits	104	224	180	147
Elektrobank:				
Capital	—	9	17	38
Loans and discounts	—	44	71	178
Deposits	—	15	16	13
Vsekobank:				
Capital	13	17	22	28
Loans and discounts	48	71	95	175
Deposits	24	52	56	72
Central Agricultural Bank:				
Capital	15	53	88	93
Loans and discounts	31	145	211	320
Deposits	—	11	6	10
Vneshtorgbank:				
Capital	18	30	39	43
Loans and discounts	38	90	96	107
Deposits	18	37	26	17
Mutual Credit Societies:				
Capital	3	8	16	14
Loans and discounts	9	31	52	31
Deposits	5	18	28	22

During the whole of this period the loans and discounts of the State Bank were more than double those of all other banks, and as early as 1924 deposits in the State Bank were more than twice

* This table is compiled from the rich statistical material collected by Dr Arnold in his study, *Banks, Credit and Money in Soviet Russia*, pp. 246, 294, 299, 304, 317 and 320.

and in 1927 more than four times larger than the total deposits in all other banking institutions.

The State Bank gradually became the main credit institution for providing short-term credit, especially when, after 1925–6, it became evident that deposits in the Prombank and the Vneshtorg-bank were beginning to fall and it was realized that this fall in deposits was not due to a change in the level of economic activity, but was due to the starting of a process of investment in the national economy. The State Bank, however, had special sources for short-term credit not available for other banks, that is, from the issue of banknotes and from Treasury deposits. From 1 October 1925 all funds of the Treasury offices (Prikhodnoraskhodnych kass) were transferred to the State Bank, and from September 1928 the State Bank undertook to collect the revenue and make payments on behalf of the State and local budgets.

Here it is necessary to stress that even at this period the activities of credit institutions in the U.S.S.R. not only developed in different surroundings, since their main clients were State enterprises and institutions, but that the main aims and principles of credit operations were different from those typical of the capitalist system.*

We quoted above a statement of V.Ts.I.K. and Eleventh Congress of the Party to the effect that the purpose of establishing the State Bank and other specialized banks was 'to *assist* the development of industry, agriculture and trade as well as to concentrate monetary transactions and conduct other measures aiming at the establishment of a sound monetary circulation...'—for the State Bank, and for specialized banks 'to *assist* the concentration of free monetary resources for productive utilization...within the limits of non-violation of the predominant role of the State Bank'. Thus to banks was allotted the role of ancillary economic institutions which were designed to *assist* the development of the national economy, but were denied the right of influencing it on their own account and using ordinary banking technique for this purpose. Accordingly, the aim of getting profit from credit operations and using it for investment activities was not to be pursued in banking transactions. Interest and discount rates were charged with the aim of covering operating costs, eventual losses and the building up of reserve capital, and were not influenced by the demand for

---

* We prefer the expression 'capitalist system' to 'competitive system' because nowadays in economically advanced countries purely competitive systems no longer exist, and, moreover, the meaning of the expression 'capitalist system' is so well known as to require no further definition or comment.

credit and the flow of deposits but were fixed arbitrarily in order to meet these technical aims. Soviet banks were restricted to the minimum functions of a banking system. They did not undertake any kind of investment (still less speculative) activities in stocks, bonds, sale of securities or commodities and the like. Long-term banks do not carry out mortgage operations. As price regulation and the regulation of foreign trade is carried out by direct methods used by the appropriate institutions for regulating internal and foreign trade, discount and exchange policy is not used for these purposes. Nor is it used for influencing price movements on the internal market or for controlling the flow of exports and imports. Discount rates as well as interest rates, as we have said, are fixed arbitrarily in order to meet costs, losses and accumulation of reserve capital. Generally speaking none of the so-called 'automatic devices' of credit techniques characteristic of the capitalist system is used by Soviet credit institutions—with certain exceptions as regards mutual credit societies. But the role of these societies in the total credit activities, as can be clearly seen from Table 13, was very insignificant, and from 1926 their activities began to shrink rapidly as a consequence of the exclusion of private enterprise from economic activities.

A certain amount of competition in attracting deposits did, of course, take place during this period among different banks, but it took quite different forms from those known in the competitive system. The special banks either made the condition that applicants for credit must also deposit their free money in the appropriate bank or endeavoured to secure orders from the appropriate Commissariat to the effect that enterprises or institutions subordinate to them must deposit their funds only with a certain bank. As it is not the aim of Soviet banks to get profit from their credit operations, this competition for deposits only expressed an endeavour to provide means for extending lending operations for their 'own' clients and reflected the cautious credit policy of the State Bank which was strict in using its right of banknote issue. Another essential characteristic of Soviet banks is that they serve as an instrument for carrying out not only economic but also socio-political directives of the Soviet Government. We have already mentioned, when describing the organization of agricultural credit, that credit was granted with the aim of supporting the poor and middle peasantry and collective farming and denying it to the well-to-do peasantry, i.e. granting credit to the economically weaker and not to the stronger in complete contrast to the ordinary credit practice in the capitalist system. Also if it is considered that from the point of view of general economic policy a certain enterprise should be supported by granting it credit, in spite of the fact that it cannot meet its credit obligations at maturity, it continues to be supplied with credit. Of course this is only done if this credit 'deficiency' is not due to inefficient or dishonest management, in which case the manager is removed. The enterprise is not denied credit if its output is considered necessary. The duty of Soviet banks is also, from one point of view, to help their clients to plan their financial operations and, from the other, to control the expenditure of loans granted. 'Automatic devices' for regulating credit operations are replaced by credit planning.

An attempt at credit planning was made as early as 1922. When the process of restoring the country's productive activities began, the demand for credit exceeded the supply, and it was necessary to allocate the scarce resources to satisfying the most urgent needs. Accordingly, crude general plans of redistribution of the available funds were worked out. After the monetary reform was accomplished, the State Bank began to compile detailed quarterly plans of basic assets and liabilities for the main office and less detailed ones (total balances) for its branches. In January 1924 a 'Committee of Banks' was organized at the State Bank, the members of which were composed of the chairman and the representatives of the Boards of the State Bank and other banks, representatives of the Commissariat of Finance, the S.E.C., the Commissariats of Internal and Foreign Trade and Gosplan. This Committee of Banks was entrusted with the task of co-ordinating the activities of all the main banks, drawing up general credit plans for all the main credit institutions and preparing proposals for the general credit policy for consideration and approval by the Commissariat of Finance of the U.S.S.R. All the main banks had to draw up quarterly, and later monthly, credit plans and present them to the Committee of Banks which, after co-ordinating them, had to send them to Gosplan and afterwards to the S.T.O. for final approval. The actual technique of credit planning was, of course, built up only gradually and not smoothly, encountering some opposition from leading special banks which endeavoured to preserve more independence in shaping their credit activities.

In the middle of 1927 a decisive step was made towards strict co-ordination of the credit activities of the different credit institutions. An enactment of V.Ts.I.K. and Sovnarkom S.S.S.R. of 15 June 1927, entitled 'Principles of construction of the credit system', decreed that (a) the State Bank was to be empowered to direct the credit activities of all credit institutions, giving it the right to have representatives in the councils and auditing committees of all credit institutions in which State capital predominated as well as supervising the activities of other credit institutions. The free reserves of the banks were to be deposited with the State Bank and so were the funds of the State Budget, savings banks, and State and social insurance; (b) a delimitation of clientele was fixed between the State Bank and specialized banks; every client concern was to use short-term credit as a rule and deposit its free funds in one bank only, in accordance with the character of its economic activity; (c) the bulk of short-term credit operations was to be concentrated in the State Bank and that of long-term credit operations in specialized banks which could grant short-term credit only to such clientele as was not allotted to the State Bank; (d) it was decided to strengthen the co-ordinating activities of the Committee of Banks which was from now on to be attached to the Commissariat of Finance of the U.S.S.R. After these decisions by the Government, the State Bank gradually acquired the real leadership of the credit system of the U.S.S.R. as the main institution for short-term credit and the main institution directing the general credit activities of the other banks.

With the growing expansion of reconstructive work and the building of new productive capacity a process of concentrating all short-term credit operations in the State Bank and long-term credit operations in the specialized banks steadily developed. In 1928 Prombank and Elektrobank were fused in one for long-term credit for industry and electrification. All the short-term credit operations of these two banks were transferred to the State Bank, and the fused bank was to carry out exclusively long-term credit operations.

In 1928 all branches of the Vneshtorgbank inside the U.S.S.R. were also wound up and their activities transferred to the State Bank. The general board of the Vneshtorgbank was to work in close collaboration with the foreign department of the State Bank. During 1928 and 1929, however, the short-term credit operations of co-operative, agricultural and communal banks gradually diminished and were transferred to the State Bank, the activity of these banks being more and more confined to the granting of long-term credit.

This process was quite a natural one if we remember that from as early as 1925–6, when the process of restoring the former productive capacity of industry in general was accomplished and a process of new investment in industry and other branches of the national economy began, deposits in specialized banks began to fall while the demand for credit quite naturally began to rise very rapidly. Under these conditions the State Bank, enjoying the right of note issue and holding the deposits of the Treasury and administrative institutions, was the main source of credit for the other banks, and in order to achieve a more planned distribution of available short-term credit funds it was thought that it would be better for the State Bank to concentrate short-term credit activities in its hands directly, instead of granting such credit indirectly through the channels of other banks.

Owing to this concentration of short-term and long-term credit operations in the State Bank and specialized banks respectively and the delimitation of clientele between different banks, credit planning became more and more effective and more closely related to actual credit resources and their distribution by different channels to clients.

Elements disturbing credit plans were the existence of commercial credit and the extensive use of the bill of exchange among State enterprises. However, after 1928, direct clearing settlements between enterprises began to increase, especially between syndicates and between syndicates and transport undertakings. As an experiment the State Bank introduced direct crediting of particular enterprises without discounting their bills of exchange.

All these processes of concentrating short-term credit in the State Bank and long-term credit in specialized banks, the growth of direct clearing settlements, the delimitation of clientele between different banks and the strengthening of credit planning paved the way for the credit reform of 1930–1, when the State Bank became the sole credit institution for short-term credit, commercial credit was abolished and the activities of long-term credit institutions were reorganized in order to meet the needs of large-scale financing of national economic reconstruction. We shall describe these processes later on.

As we have seen, the monetary reform was carried out on principles familiar in the reorganization of currency in other countries. After it was accomplished an attempt was made to introduce the chervonetz on the foreign market. This attempt met with only partial success. In 1924 the chervonetz was quoted on the exchanges of Riga, Tallinn and Harbin. To these were added (in 1925) exchanges in Rome, Istanbul, Kaunas, Teheran and Meshed, but the exchanges of London, New York and Paris continued to refrain from quoting the chervonetz. However, as early as 1926 the Soviet Government decided to divorce the chervonetz from the international exchange market. After March 1926 the sale of gold and foreign currency to private persons was discontinued and Soviet currency ceased to be redeemed in gold. In July 1926 the export of chervontzy, Treasury notes and coins was forbidden and, finally, in March 1928 their import was prohibited. After these measures the chervonetz became a purely internal currency, the exchange rate of which is fixed by a quotations commission at the State Bank according to the parity to the American dollar (1·943 roubles per dollar), and to other currencies depending on their terms of dollar exchange (9·458 roubles to the pound, 7·616 roubles to the 100 francs, 46·294 roubles to the RM., etc.).

Many explanations were given by Soviet and foreign authors of the reasons why the Soviet Government had introduced these measures for the insulation of Soviet currency from the foreign market. All available material leads us to the conclusion that the following main circumstances accounted for these measures. The memory of the catastrophic decline in the purchasing power of money in the previous period was still fresh in the minds of the people, and consequently there was a tendency, especially among Nepmen, to hoard gold and foreign exchanges as 'securities' (the well-to-do peasantry began to hoard silver coins in great quantities, particularly when in 1926 symptoms of a 'goods famine' became evident). Owing to the great shortage of consumer goods and the limited quantity of them being imported and differences in prices abroad and in the U.S.S.R., smuggling took on quite considerable dimensions. These contraband imports were paid for not so much in gold and foreign exchange smuggled from the U.S.S.R. as in chervontzy which were sold on the black market in neighbouring states at considerably below the official rates. Foreign concessionaries began to practise the buying of chervontzy on the black exchange markets abroad and using them for paying the wages of their workers. The Soviet foreign trade balance in 1924–5 to 1925–6 was highly adverse, and it was evident that for years to come the need to import machinery, raw materials, etc., for the restoration and reconstruction of industry, transport and other branches of the economy would increase, whereas the possibility of expanding export would be limited. Consequently it was necessary to build up reserves of gold and foreign exchange as a manœuvring fund to pay for imports in case of an adverse balance. The monopoly of foreign trade permitted the regulation of imports and exports by direct methods, and consequently it was not necessary to resort to the regulation of foreign trade through the usual exchange devices to protect the foreign exchange value of Soviet currency, especially as the leading foreign exchanges still refused to quote the chervonetz.

Under such circumstances it was thought more prudent and expedient for safeguarding reserves of gold and foreign valuta from uncontrolled leakage abroad to prohibit the export and import of Soviet currency, to put an end to the sale of foreign currency and gold to private persons, and to fix the ratio of exchange for foreign currency inside the U.S.S.R. As Soviet currency became a purely internal currency, the fixing of the rate of exchange served only for the purpose of accounting for foreign trade and all transactions connected with foreign trade and exchanging foreign currency in the case of foreign travellers and money orders from and to other countries.

The issue of currency was during this period kept as low as possible, guided, on the one hand, by a desire to preserve a stable currency and, on the other, by a desire not to permit monetary considerations to determine the possible rate of expansion of the productive activity of the country.

Table 14 illustrates the increase in the amount of money in circulation. The total amount of money in circulation grew yearly very considerably. The newly issued currency, however, was not

Table 14

	Banknotes in circulation mill. roubles	Treasury notes mill. roubles	Coins mill. roubles	Total mill. roubles	Index of the Bureau of Labour Statistics (1913—1·000)
1 Jan. 1924	—	—	—	321·9	1·823
1 Jan. 1925	410·8	229·2	74·9	714·9	1·976
1 Jan. 1926	726·6	387·7	149·6	1,263·9	2·106
1 Jan. 1927	796·7	397·6	160·0	1,354·3	2·067
1 Jan. 1928	1,002·9	479·8	185·1	1,667·8	2·052
1 Jan. 1929	1,090·7	730·4	206·8	2,027·9	2·168
1 Jan. 1930	1,501·0	1,028·2	243·8	2,773·0	2·206

used for balancing the State Budget, which from 1924–25 always showed a surplus, but only for credit expansion and mainly for crediting works first of economic restoration and afterwards of reconstruction.

The index of the Bureau of Labour Statistics (which we consider the most adequate index for judging price fluctuation in the

U.S.S.R. during this period) shows the rises in prices during 1924–6, thus indicating that there was in this period an over-issue of money as compared with the growth of output of consumer goods and services. Price regulation during this period, as we have seen above, was not sufficiently tightened up and consequently changes in prices apparently reflected the real changes in the purchasing power of money. In 1927 price regulation became more strict and steadily covered more and more items, especially after the introduction of rationing in 1929, and consequently changes in the price index did not adequately reflect the situation on the internal market. When prices are regulated, a rise in money circulation without an adequate rise in the production of consumer goods leads either to a goods famine or makes it necessary to introduce rationing. A rise in prices can be caused not only by over-issue of money but by the issue of money in accordance with the productive requirements of the country and the expansion of production and trade turn-over if the increased note issue is used to finance capital goods production and enlarge services without a corresponding enlargement of the production of consumer goods. As a matter of fact, this is what took place in the U.S.S.R., as we shall see from the description of measures and development in industrial and agricultural production and in labour during this period.

CHAPTER VII. INDUSTRY

In the instructions of Sovnarkom S.S.S.R. of 9 August 1921* on the introduction of N.E.P., stress was laid on the fact that the Soviet State was forced directly to administer an enormous number of different enterprises for the supply of which the available stocks of raw materials and other products were not sufficient. Consequently the State was quite unable to utilize rationally and economically even the existing stocks and productive capacity. In order to prevent a further decline in the national economy it was considered necessary to reorganize industry on the following principles: (a) The State, as represented by the S.E.C. and its local branches, was to concentrate under its direct administration only certain branches of industrial production, a certain amount of large-scale enterprises whose output was important for the State as a whole, as well as enterprises supplementary to and supplying

---

* *Collection of Government Decrees*, 1921, § 403.

these most important branches of industrial production. (*b*) All these enterprises were to be managed on the principle of rational economic budgeting. (*c*) Production in these enterprises could continue or commence only with the permission of the S.E.C. and only when their necessary supply of raw materials, technical equipment and working capital was assured. (*d*) Enterprises which were not included in the above were to be let to co-operative and other societies and to private persons. The Soviet institutions were to support this policy of letting enterprises in which the State institutions could not, at the time, organize production rationally, and especially the letting of small enterprises. (*e*) Enterprises which would be neither let nor taken over for administration by State organs were to be closed. The workers and employees of these enterprises were to be allocated to working enterprises, employed at State public works or registered as unemployed with the payment of unemployment allowances. (*f*) All enterprises which should have been nationalized according to the decree of 29 November 1920 but which in actual fact were not, were to be considered as not nationalized and their ownership restored to the former owners. The same applied to enterprises with less than twenty workers.* The Regional Economic Councils were to consider all applications for the restoration of small industrial enterprises to their former owners. (*g*) Large enterprises, technically well equipped and organized and suitably situated geographically, were to be organized in industrial combines, but the organization of such industrial combines was permitted only for State-owned and State-administered enterprises and not for private ones.

After these principles of N.E.P. for industry had been laid down, the following developments took place in the organization of industrial production during this period: (1) Large and important industrial enterprises remained in the ownership of the State. (2) Production in some of them was temporarily stopped and they were kept in a state of 'preservation' to enable a future renewal of their production. Most of the small enterprises were either leased to co-operatives and private entrepreneurs or denationalized and returned to their former owners. (3) Some of the existing enterprises were leased to foreign entrepreneurs and concessions were granted for certain new productions. (4) Some enterprises were organized as mixed societies with State and private capital. The result was as follows:†

* Decree of 10 December 1921.
† N. Vorobiev, *Town Industry of the U.S.S.R. according to Census*, 1923.

Of the 165,781 enterprises accounted for by census, 147,471 or 88·5 % were in the hands of private persons, 13,697 or 8·5 % were State enterprises and 4,613 or 3·1 % co-operative enterprises. The private enterprises were very small. While they accounted for 88·5 % of the total number of enterprises, they employed only 12·4 % of the total number of workers employed in industry at that time, whereas State-owned industries, accounting for only 8·5 % of the total number of enterprises, employed 84·1 % of all employed workers. The State enterprises employed an average of 155 workers, co-operative and private enterprises fifteen and two respectively.

Thus, owing to the process of denationalization and the leasing of small enterprises to private entrepreneurs the State freed itself of the necessity of administering small enterprises hastily 'nationalized' in the preceding period, but at the same time preserved for itself the administration of the main branches of industrial production concentrated in large enterprises. The 'commanding heights' of industrial production remained in the hands of the State, while private initiative was permitted to fill the whole sphere of industrial production not covered by State industry or to compete with the latter in similar productions, but on the basis of small-scale productive possibilities.

In the preceding period of 'War Communism', as we have shown, the management of State industry was confused by inept regulative interference with enterprises by the central bodies regulating industrial production. N.E.P., with its return to market conditions, asked for a fundamental reorganization of the relations between enterprises and regulating bodies. The former required more independence in organizing their production, but at the same time it was considered necessary for the S.E.C. to remain as a central body regulating the whole trend of the country's industrial development. The principle adopted was that the relations between the S.E.C. and the enterprises should be a combination of decentralization of administration and centralization of the general direction of industrial production. The search for a practical form of combination of these two principles influenced many changes which took place in the administration and management of industry during this and the following periods and, as we shall see later on, this reorganization of the relations of the central institutions regulating industrial production and the industrial enterprises themselves was not completed on the eve of the present war.

In the period under review the following main changes bearing on this question took place.

In the first years of N.E.P. centrifugal tendencies prevailed among State enterprises, as a reaction from the extreme administrative centralization of the period of 'War Communism'.

In accordance with the above instructions, State enterprises could be organized in industrial combines. These industrial combines were the prototype of the future trusts. Confronted by market conditions, enterprises endeavoured to free themselves of the 'tutelage' of the S.E.C. and its local branches, of having to deliver their products to the appropriate department of the S.E.C. and of receiving supplies from the latter. They preferred, after receiving financial means from the State central institutions, to dispose of their products and procure their supplies on the free market. This tendency was partly met by a series of decrees* which extended the independence of enterprises. Up to April 1923, however, when a decree defining the status of trusts was finally published, enterprises affirmed their economic independence more *de facto* than *de jure*. It is necessary to stress the point that Soviet economic law at this period, when speaking of industrial enterprise (Predpriyatie) meant the combination of industrial establishments (Zavedenie) or Soviet trusts, because only these trusts had the legal position of a juridical person, while individual factories were considered only as parts of trusts and were not granted the rights of independent juridical persons.

By organizing these combines or trusts it was intended to create from dispersed factories such combines as could concentrate production in similar or supplementary branches of industry more economically. Accordingly, three types of combines of industrial enterprises began to be organized: (a) combines of *similar* enterprises situated in the *same territory*, with the aim of concentrating production in the largest and best equipped enterprises; (b) combines of enterprises *not similar* but situated in the *same territory*, in order to facilitate the supply of raw materials, fuel, etc., to the united enterprises, especially in such developed regions as the Donbas, Urals, Central Moscow region and Briansk region; (c) combines of enterprises whose output had a special significance for the development of the national economy, such as oil and coal.

* Decree of 16 August 1921, extending the rights of enterprises as regards disposal of their financial and material resources; decrees of 4 and 27 October 1921, permitting to enterprises freer disposal of their products, etc. See details, Rozenfeld, op. cit. pp. 241–5.

In reality, however, trusts which sprang up during the first period of N.E.P. (the first of them were organized as early as June 1921) did not always adhere to these aims. Side by side with the large-scale trusts there sprang up a large number of rather small 'trusts' which included five or six 'factories', each employing only 10–20 workers. Thus these 'trusts' were industrial combines in the sense intended in name only; there existed trusts which were smaller than a small factory. There were many reasons for this. Reaction from the supercentralism of the period of 'War Communism' and consequent fear of concentration and the resistance of regional authorities which did not want unification into large trusts of enterprises considered advantageous from the regional point of view of these; instead of one big trust several small ones were organized. Inexperience in work under the new conditions of free markets, when it seemed easier to organize production and marketing in small enterprises, imperfect realization by the new administration (having behind it only experience of non-market methods of organizing production during 'War Communism') of the economic advantages of concentration of production were other factors.

In the resolution of the Twelfth Congress of the Party (17–25 April 1923) the developments which had taken place in industry from the beginning of N.E.P. were summed up as follows:

The transition from 'War Communism' to N.E.P. was accomplished to a considerable degree by methods of 'War Communism'. The grouping of enterprises, their division into trusts, the distribution of enterprises among trusts, and the granting of credit to them were to a considerable degree of a bureaucratic character. From the point of view of economic planning our trusts are as yet only rough drafts. Complaints from enterprises of the deficiency of working capital prove that the State placed under its administration more enterprises than was feasible in the existing economic condition of the country. This resulted in instability of enterprises, interruption of production and low utilization of productive capacity, which in their turn led to an extreme rise in the cost of production and shrinkage of the market with all the corresponding consequences.

The way out lies in the efficient concentration of production in the best equipped and geographically most suitably situated enterprises.*

A Central Committee for revising existing trusts was created. According to its decision some enterprises were temporarily closed, the smaller trusts liquidated, some being fused with others and

* Quoted by Rozenfeld, op. cit. p. 224. See, for more detailed description of the organization of industry during this period, pp. 213–25.

some, on the contrary, being split up into smaller trusts. This process of concentrating production rationally in combines of enterprises in the form of trusts continued throughout the whole period of N.E.P.

We say in the *form* of trusts because Soviet trusts can be compared with trusts in other countries only in form but not in essence.

According to a decree of 10 April 1923 (the first decree defining the legal status of trusts, which was amended only in 1927): 'By State trusts are meant *State industrial* [my italics] enterprises to whom the State has accorded independence in the carrying out of their operations in accordance with the statutes approved for each of them, acting on the principle of *commercial* calculation with the aim of *deriving profit*.' Thus only *State industrial* enterprises could be organized into trusts. It was their duty to endeavour to derive profit, but this profit had to be transferred to the Treasury except for a deduction of not less than 20 % to provide reserve capital, a contribution to the fund for improving the welfare of the workers of enterprises and a deduction for bonuses for managing personnel and for the workers and employees. The scale of these deductions from profit was fixed yearly by the S.E.C.

The Soviet trusts do not own the capital which 'belongs' to them. They can be liquidated, fused, and part of their capital can be transferred to other enterprises by decision of superior State institutions. Thus a Soviet trust is only a *form* for the administration of industrial enterprises by the State, but at the same time the State may or *may not* bear the eventual losses of trusts. A trust of its own decision may dispose only of its working capital. Only from the latter can creditors be compensated, while fixed* capital can be disposed of only with the permission of superior State institutions.

These different rights of trusts as regards the disposal of fixed and working capital were very important during this period when State and private enterprises coexisted. In the initial period of N.E.P., State enterprises, in the endeavour to increase their working capital, in case of losses or in order to meet credit obligations, very often drew on their fixed capital (especially during the liquidation crisis of 1922–3 when large-scale 'squandering' of equipment by the

---

* By fixed capital the Soviet law means all such inventory which cannot be destroyed by one act of production, by working capital all that which is used only once during a productive process. Consequently, for example, tools belong to fixed and raw material to working capital.

State enterprises took place) and part of it thus passed into private hands, and uncontrolled transfers of fixed capital from one State enterprise to another occurred.

Disposal of fixed capital depended on the decision of the Council of Labour and Defence (or S.T.O.). The S.T.O. possessed the following main rights with regard to trusts: (a) it approved the statutes of trusts and determined their fixed capital; (b) it could liquidate trusts; and (c) it approved the production plans of different branches of industry. The S.E.C., on the other hand, had the right: (a) to appoint and dismiss the board of directors of trusts and inspection committees; and (b) to carry out general supervision of the work of the trusts without, however, intervening in the actual administrative work of the trust. This supervision was to be carried out by the Inspection Committee which served as the 'eye' of the S.E.C. in the trusts.

The Soviet trusts of this period were thus only a form of concentration of the *productive* activities of State industry. The concentration of the *trade* activities of State industry was achieved by the organization of syndicates. The majority of syndicates were organized during the second half of 1922 by the initiative of the trusts in order to prevent competition among them on the then very limited market not only for their own goods but also on the market for supplies of raw materials for production.

Many of these syndicates 'inherited' stocks and capital from the former chief administrations of the S.E.C. of the period of 'War Communism', now abolished. This capital enabled the syndicates to obtain financial power over the trusts which, at this initial period, as we have seen, suffered from a lack of working capital. The majority of the syndicates were voluntary organizations founded by trusts, but some syndicates were compulsorily set up by the S.E.C., as, for instance, the oil, coal and salt syndicates. Two types of syndicates were organized: convention and trade syndicates. Convention syndicates regulated the allocation of regions for the sale of goods or purchase of raw materials, prices, the general conditions of the trading activities of united trusts, and their plans of production, while trade syndicates carried out the actual wholesale trade (inland and foreign) on behalf of the trusts. Already in 1923–4 half the total number of trusts were united in syndicates, and as regards the number of employed workers over 80 % of State industrial production was syndicated. The syndicates gradually concentrated the trading activities of State industry, the productive activities of which were concentrated by trusts. The statutes of the trade syndicates, their governing board and their liquidation had to be approved by S.T.O. and those of the conventions by the S.E.C.

According to a decree of 12 November 1923 the S.E.C. were empowered to carry out a general regulation of the productive and trade activities of State industry, supervise the activities of co-operative and private industries, administer according to their statutes those State enterprises which were recognized as being of importance for the State, examine the question of the organization of new forms of production and the introduction of rationalization in production, prepare industrial legislation and instructions regulating the activities of State, co-operative and private industry, and consider the question of the financing and crediting of industry.* To perform these tasks the following departments were organized in the S.E.C.: (a) 'Chief economic administration' (Glavnoe ekonomicheskoe upravlenie or G.E.U.), the main task of which was to prepare industrial legislation, consider questions of general industrial policy, prepare general production plans and supervise the general activities of syndicates; (b) 'Central administration of State industry' (Tsentralnoe upravlenie gosudarstvennoi promyshlennosti or Ts.U.G.P.), which had to make the decisions regarding the fixed capital of State industry, appoint the governing personnel of State industrial enterprises, and supervise the activities of trusts. In the Ts.U.G.P. 'directorates' were organized for the main branches of industrial production.

All State industrial enterprises, according to the importance of their production, their size and geographical situation, were divided into four main groups: All-Union industry which was under the regulation of the S.E.C. of the U.S.S.R.; Republican industry under the regulation of the S.E.C. of Union Republics; regional industry subordinated either to the Regional Economic Councils in larger regions or to so-called industrial bureaux in smaller regions; and local industry subordinated to local economic councils. It was thought that by this concentration of the function of planning in the G.E.U. and the administration of State industry in Ts.U.G.P., and by delegation of the regulating rights of the S.E.C. as regards industry of republican, regional and local significance to the corresponding decentralized economic councils, there would be achieved a healthy combination of decentralization of administration and centralization of planned regulation of industrial production.

Three years (1923–6) of experience, however, showed that the

* See details, *Collected Laws*, 1923, § 336.

distribution of the functions of administration, planning and regulating among Ts.U.G.P. and G.E.U. hampered the task for which it was intended, that of strengthening planned regulation of the development of industrial production. Planned regulation extended its scope only to industry of nation-wide significance, while republican and especially regional and local industry escaped planned control of its development. In 1926 a reorganization of the general administration of State industry was undertaken. Ts.U.G.P. and its directorates for different branches of industry were abolished and were replaced by chief administrations and committees for different branches of industry whose task it was to plan and regulate the whole production of a particular branch of industry. As regards All-Union industry, together with the planning and regulating function the chief administrations also strengthened their influence over the actual management of this particular branch of industry. Through the corresponding department of the S.E.C. of Republics the chief administrations strengthened also their influence over the development of republican, regional and local industries, those gradually covering by planned regulation of production all enterprises of the corresponding branch of industrial production. In order to co-ordinate the work of separate chief administrations and committees an Economic Planning Administration (Planovo-ekonomicheskoe Upravlenie or P.E.U.) was organized in the S.E.C. which replaced the former G.E.U. Its task, apart from the task of the former G.E.U., was to unify the work of chief administrations, prepare yearly plans of production and industrial capital construction as well as 'perspective' plans, for longer periods and more rigid administration of the activities of syndicates.*

In accordance with these decisions to strengthen the role of the S.E.C. in the planned regulation of industrial production, a decree was published in July 1927 considerably changing the basic law of 1923 concerning the statutes of trusts. In the statutes of 1923 it was stressed that trusts must 'act on the principle of commercial calculation with the aim of *deriving profit*', whereas the new statutes of 1927 stated that 'trusts are administered by the State institution defined in the statutes and act on the basis of commercial principles *in accordance with planned tasks* which have been approved by the said State institution'.† This State institution (the corresponding chief

---

* See detailed description of this reform in Sakharov and others in *Outline of Organization of Heavy Industry of the U.S.S.R.*

† See details, *Collected Laws*, 1927, § 392.

administration of the S.E.C.) had the right to fix the prices for the output of trusts, to order trusts to deliver goods to State organizations even at prices below the market price, and to regulate their productive plans. By these changes in the organization of the S.E.C. and in the statutes of trusts the planning and regulating intervention of S.E.C. in the activities of trusts was strengthened. Gradually also the activities of syndicates fell more and more under the control of the S.E.C. and they became in practice more departmental sections of the S.E.C. than independent associations of trusts. Trusts shifted their activities more and more from the financial and commercial side of the organization of industrial production to the organization of the technical side of it.

At the outset of the N.E.P. period, as has been generally indicated above, the trust alone enjoyed the rights of a legal personality. Factories, works, mines, etc., generally designated as 'establishments', were regarded merely as organs of the trust, and the commercial and financial transactions of an enterprise were left entirely in the hands of the trust. The trust was the link between production and the market. Many trust managers treated the establishments as passive units incapable of independent initiative; on the other hand, many large enterprises strove in every way to prevent the trust from interfering with their business activities, and even to break away from the trust. From 1924, when the 'Statute concerning the management of an enterprise forming part of a trust' came into force, the powers of these enterprises and establishments were gradually defined and expanded. Though the financial returns of all enterprises forming a trust were still merged into one, every establishment began to keep its own books and to make independent estimates of its production costs. By contract, the managing director of the establishment was responsible to the trust, but, within the limits of competence defined by the trust, he retained *de jure* powers to organize the production processes at the works under his control. Assignments in the form of definite orders (stipulating quantity, quality, date of delivery, prices, etc.) were given to the establishment and the establishment delivered the manufactured articles at cost price to the trust. It lay with the trust to ensure the supply of raw materials, fuel, products, and material and financial means requisite for the organization of production. The director had not the right to refuse orders placed by the trust even if they entailed loss; he could only lodge a complaint with the Praesidium of the S.E.C., but had no right to stop the execution of the trust's orders. All commercial transactions, such as placing and accepting orders, drawing up contracts for supplies and deliveries and disposing of the goods, were carried out by the trust. However, a director could be granted the right to dispose of a part of the output of his establishment and, to a certain extent, to place and accept orders, and to conduct various other commercial transactions.

In the early days of N.E.P., it was thought necessary to restrict the rights of the establishments in this way because the planning and regulating organizations would otherwise have found it impossible to deal with thousands of individual enterprises. However, as experience in industrial management deepened, the tendency to increase the powers of particular establishments—in so far as productive and economic activities were concerned—became more marked.

In line with the altered trust status, new 'Model regulations concerning an enterprise forming part of a trust' were published in 1927; the first paragraph reads as follows:

Factories, works, mines, exploitations and similar industrial enterprises, forming part of a trust, are administered by the management of the trust as one enterprise. The director manages the actual industrial enterprise; he is appointed and dismissed by the administration of the trust, and acts upon the principle of personal management in virtue of special regulations established by the trust....The director controls all the operations of the enterprise...he is responsible under the *criminal, civil and disciplinary laws* [italicized by author] for the upkeep of the property entrusted to him, and for running the business, particularly for observance of planned and economic discipline and the expenditure of credits strictly as appropriated.*

This decree stresses the unity of control vested in the director for the management of the enterprise; however, in the then prevailing circumstances the principle of personal management could hardly be put into practice, and this formulation rather reflects the desire to introduce the principle into industrial management than corresponds with actual conditions. *De facto*, during that period, the director was largely dependent on the works' trade union organ, the 'Zavkom' (the factory trade union committee) and on the Party cell, the organ of the Communist Party at the enterprise. Representatives of these organizations considered it their duty to supervise the director's activities, and usually interfered with his decisions. Many directors, anxious to ensure against failures in production or when attempting risky business operations, sought

* *Bull. Financ. and Econ. Leg.* no. 42, 1927.

for the sanction of the factory committee and Party cell to back their decisions. In fact an enterprise was not managed by the director acting on his sole responsibility, but by the so-called 'triangle': the director representing the management, the factory committee representing the works' trade union and the Communist cell, the 'eye' of the Party.

In February 1928 the S.E.C. issued the 'Fundamental regulations regarding the rights and duties of the administrative, technical and maintenance staffs of industrial enterprises' aimed at eliminating this divided authority in business management and at ensuring 'maximum freedom for the director as an executive, in accordance with the principles of "Khozraschet" (business accountancy).*...Henceforth, the director of a factory or works becomes the sole manager of the enterprise. Henceforth, he selects his own managerial staff...the trust has not the right to interfere in the internal affairs of the enterprise over the director's head but manages the factory or works exclusively through its director'. The same principle of personal management was to be the basis of the relationship between technical and maintenance staff within the enterprise; 'any administrative or technical worker can, according to an established procedure, lodge a complaint against the actions of his immediate chief.' The regulations defined in detail the rights, competence and duties of the director of the works, those of his deputies in charge of the technical side or of labour, those of the head of the production plan department, those of the chief engineer, the senior accountant, and the foreman of a workshop.†

However, the circumstances prevailing at this time did not favour the introduction of personal management. Factory committees and Party cells did not wish to surrender their positions and continued to view with suspicion the director's authority and the activities of the administrative and technical staffs; suspicions became particularly acute after the trial of the members of the 'Shakhty Counter-revolutionary Plot' in March 1928 (see p. 151). Factory committees and Party cells saw in pre-revolution specialists potential criminals plotting against the Soviet Government's policy

---

* There is no adequate English equivalent of the Soviet expression 'Khozraschet'. The notion implies that cost accounting is applied to definite quantitative and qualitative tasks prescribed by the plan as well as to financial results. We will retain the Russian word rather than adopt some misleading translation such as 'business accountancy'.

† *Torgovo-promyshlennaya Gazeta*, 2 February 1928.

and the working class. In these psychological conditions, it was difficult to expect that the administrative and technical staff would actually take advantage of their formal managerial rights, and Soviet industrial legislation had repeatedly to revert to the problem of establishing real personal management in industry.

An analysis of at least the fundamental facts and processes in the development of industrial production is necessary to understand the driving forces behind those organizational changes which took place in the structure of the Soviet system of national economy during its complicated evolution, and which were determined either by new requirements of economic policy or by new conditions in the actual development of the national economy.

When Lenin proclaimed the introduction of N.E.P. he emphasized that: 'Large-scale industry, its success and development are the fundamental and primary prerequisities for the building of Communism...it is the support of the *social* force which is establishing the industrial proletariat's communistic revolution. Therefore the fundamental task of economic policy directed to developing productive forces, is to strengthen large-scale industry.' 'Heavy industry needs State subsidies. If we do not find them, we are doomed as a civilized State, let alone as a socialistic State.'* Lenin's standpoint became the mainspring of the Soviet Government's policy not only in the period of recovery, but even more so in the reconstruction period of Soviet national economy.

The sorry plight to which industrial production was reduced at the end of the period of 'War Communism' has been shown above. Nationalized industry entered N.E.P. with its basic capital worn out and in need of large expenditure for repairs, and with a minimum of liquid resources mainly in the form of stocks of raw materials and of goods in production. The inherited working capital was reduced out of all proportion as compared with the inherited fixed capital, and this circumstance proved a determining factor in the development of industry in the first years of N.E.P. Being anxious to increase their working capital, the State enterprises threw on the market all they could sell even below reproduction costs to the detriment of the exhausted basic capital. Herein lay the real reason for that 'razbazarivanie', that squandering of industrial production which we mentioned in connexion with home-market conditions.

The shortage of working capital led to a reduced utilization of

* Lenin, op. cit. vol. xxvii, p. 348.

the fixed capital and this again to increased production costs. The cumulative effect of lack of experience among the new administrative staffs at the works, of shortage of skilled labour, due to circumstances prevailing in the period of 'War Communism', of low labour productivity and of high overhead charges resulted in the high cost prices of manufactured goods. The limited purchasing power of the population in the early days of the N.E.P. period, coupled with the tendency of State enterprises to flood the market with all that could be sold, brought about increasing competition; the necessity to eliminate competition was the real reason of that accelerated syndicalization of State industries which has been described above. By monopolizing the sale of manufactured goods, the syndicates enabled industry to maintain prices for manufactured articles at a high level. Another contributory factor was that agricultural production was recovering quicker than industrial production; already in 1923–4 the gross agricultural production reached 75 % of its 1913 level, whereas that of industry was only one-third of its figure for the same year. From 1924 the sale of manufactured goods underwent a change contrary to what had taken place earlier in the N.E.P. period; there was no longer any difficulty in disposing of manufactured goods, but on the contrary a dearth of commodities, particularly of most mass consumption goods, a rise in prices, and a deterioration in the exchange values of agricultural produce as compared with manufactured goods.

The requirements of an unsaturated market made it possible to keep prices at a high level without undue anxiety about reducing the cost of production. In spite of such a favourable conjuncture prevailing on the market since 1924–5, many enterprises continued to work at a great loss, as is shown in Table 15.

Table 15

	1923–4 mill. roubles	1924–5 mill. roubles	1925–6 mill. roubles	1926–7 mill. roubles
Profits of State industries	175	400	594	619
Losses of State industries	70	36	58	80
Of which iron and steel industries:				
Profits	21	51	48	54
Losses	29	19	25	32

Profits were derived chiefly from industries manufacturing articles of general consumption, whilst losses were mainly sustained by branches manufacturing means of production and in particular by heavy industry.* The redistribution of profits among enterprises working at a profit and those working at a loss, coupled with the financing of a considerable part of their capital expenditure from State funds, contributed to strengthen the centralizing tendencies in the organization of industrial administration and, in particular, the role of syndicates which tended more and more to become in fact departments of the S.E.C.; the same tendencies also served to strengthen the general planning and regulating role of the S.E.C. in the manner already described.

From 1924–5 onward the expenditure of State funds on financing industry exceeded the revenue derived by the budget from industry as is illustrated in Table 16.

Table 16

	1924–5 mill. roubles	1925–6 mill. roubles	1926–7 mill. roubles
Financing of industry and electrification:			
From the State Budget	181	266	610
From the 'Restoration of National Economy Loan'	—	148	37
From local budgets	2	9	28
From funds of the Communal Bank	9	37	50
Total	192	460	725
Revenue from industry:			
Income tax	36	61	63
Receipts from profits:			
State Budget	75	108	206
Local budgets	16	33	50
Subscriptions to the Recovery Loan	27	30	60
Other payments to the State Budget and State Bank	16.	24	37
Total	172	256	416
Balance: net contribution of State to industry	20	204	309

Already in the last years of N.E.P., the renovation and expansion of industry's basic capital was proceeding to a considerable degree at the expense of funds from the State Budget, and the amount of these subsidies grew yearly both absolutely and in comparison with the revenue derived from industry by the State and

* The Fourteenth Party Conference, held on 27–29 April 1925, in a special resolution 'On metal industries' demanded that 'the deficit of a number of trusts be liquidated and that this aim be made an urgent task not only for all organs of the Supreme Economic Council but also for Party and trade-union organs'. *The C.P. in Resolutions...*, p. 24.

local budgets. In connexion with the expression 'renewal and expansion' of basic capital, it should be explained that up to 1925 no increase but a reduction of the basic productive funds of industry was taking place,* and only from 1926 did the process of expansion begin in big industry. Up to 1925–6 capital expenditure was practically all absorbed by capital repairs. However, from 1925–6 substantial sums began to be allocated for expansion and re-equipment of basic capital, and for new construction, as is shown by the figures in Table 17 which relate to allocation of capital investments in the last three years of the N.E.P. period.†

Table 17

	1925–6		1926–7	
	Mill. roubles	%	Mill. roubles	%
Capital repairs	157·1	19·3	141·9	13·3
Expansion and re-equipment	446·9	55·2	598·9	56·1
New construction	100·3	12·3	219·2	20·5
Housing	106·7	13·2	107·8	10·1
Total	810·0	100	1,067·8	100
	1927–8		For all three years	
	Mill. roubles	%	Mill. roubles	%
Capital repairs	120·4	9·7	419·3	13·5
Expansion and re-equipment	690·5	55·7	1,736·3	55·6
New construction	325·9	26·3	645·4	20·7
Housing	103·4	8·3	318·0	10·2
Total	1,240·2	100	3,119·0	100

The figures show that during the last three years of N.E.P. the expenditure on capital repairs decreased absolutely and relatively, whereas expenditure on expansion and re-equipment and, in particular, on new building increased both absolutely and relatively. By 1926–7 the process of restoring inherited productive capacity and utilizing existing equipment was completed, and 1927–8 marks the first year of considerable industrial construction and of expanding productive capacity.

* The productive funds of big industry were estimated: in 1920 at 8,090 million roubles at prices of 1926–7, in 1921 at 7,930 million roubles, in 1922 at 7,935 million roubles, 1923 at 7,969 million roubles, in 1924 at 8,016 million roubles, and in 1925 at 8,105 million roubles. *Socialist Construction of the U.S.S.R.* 1936, p. 3.
† *Summary Production-Financial Plan for Industry for* 1927–8, Moscow, 1928.

Grants from the State Budget, bank credits to industry, the elimination of foreign competition by means of the monopoly of foreign trade, high prices for manufactured goods, restrictive measures against private enterprise in the field of industrial production—all were contributory factors enabling State industry to recover from the ruin of its capital and of production itself during the years of 'War Communism'.

In 1926–7 big industry had on the whole regained its 1913 prewar level (see Table 18). As can be inferred from these figures, the recovery of industrial production was progressing at high speed

Table 18

(In million roubles, in 1926–7 prices)			
	1913	1921	1922	1923
All large-scale industry Of which:	10,251	1,925	2,512	3,829
1. Production of means of production	4,290	814	1,090	1,785
2. Production of consumption goods	5,961	1,111	1,422	2,044
	1924	1925	1926	1927*
All large-scale industry Of which:	4,469	7,436	10,277	12,051
1. Production of means of production	1,959	3,121	4,304	5,372
2. Production of consumption goods	2,510	4,315	5,973	6,679

* There are discrepancies in the data afforded by various Soviet statistical sources for different years. We quote averages. For the purpose of describing the general trend of development of the industrial system and the development of industrial production these data may suffice. See *National Economy of the U.S.S.R. Statistical Handbook*, 1932, pp. 2–3; *Socialist Construction of the U.S.S.R. Statistical Yearbook*, 1934, p. 11.

and, by 1926–7, was on the whole up to the 1913 level. But if gross industrial production as a whole achieved recovery, the degree of recovery varied from one industry to another. Whilst coal-mining had reached 107 % of its 1913 production and oil industry 109 %, the production of iron ore was only 52 %, that of pig iron 70 %, and rolled iron 76 %, of the respective figures for 1913. The heavy metallurgy of the South, which had particularly suffered from the civil war, had not been able to recuperate its basic capital and productive powers by the end of the recovery period. These disparities in the recovery of various branches of production gave rise to a state of tension in industries that were lagging behind, and also hampered the development of the more successful. In the early years following the period of recovery, besides the general problem of expanding the productive possibilities of industry, another acute problem therefore was to call for considerable capital investment in the backward industries. And long before the first F.Y.P. for the reconstruction of the national economy had been drafted, partial 3- and 5-year plans for the reconstruction of heavy metallurgy were already under discussion.*

This recovery of the big industrial production up to the 1913 level was achieved by utilizing industry's inherited basic capital. But the population of the U.S.S.R. in 1926 numbered 147 millions as against 139 millions in 1913, on the same territory. Therefore the recovery of production to its pre-war level estimated in absolute figures meant its relative decrease per head of population. Moreover, small-scale industry and, in particular, home handicrafts which manufactured mainly articles of general consumption had not yet recovered to the same extent as big industry. This was due to the handicaps imposed on private industry and on craftsmen outside the co-operative associations—in particular to difficulties in purchasing raw materials which were bought up by the supply syndicates of big industry. The import of general consumption goods, compared with Russia's pre-revolution imports, were considerably reduced. As a result, the supply of manufactured general consumption goods on the market throughout the recovery period was below the level of pre-revolutionary Russia. At the same time the workers' and employees' wages fund grew faster than the production of goods (see p. 148), whilst in view of the special character of the development of the home market, as already explained, the urban and industrial population had better opportunities than the rural population for buying goods. Workers and employees got a relatively greater share of a smaller supply of articles of general consumption than had been the case in pre-revolutionary Russia. Therein lay the reason for that shortage of basic manufactured goods of general consumption which began to develop from 1924–5, and the reason why measures to bring down retail prices were doomed to failure. Moreover, the quality of production deteriorated, in the case of some articles greatly.† This deterioration in

* See the resolution of the Fourteenth Party Conference, 6 April 1925, in *The C.P. in Resolutions...*, p. 25.

† The Soviet press of the time is full of complaints about the poor quality of goods. We will cite here only a general appreciation given in a topical review of the development of industrial production. 'The quality of goods is going from bad to worse. The worst go to the remoter border provinces. That was so before the Revolution, too. But then the defective goods went through the special system of cheap rebate prices. Now the goods go at normal prices and that is the root of the evil. It has a great influence on rural districts where

quality was due to worn-out equipment, the poor quality of raw materials, mismanagement of production, declining skill among workers, and also undoubtedly to the subordinate position of the 'establishment', i.e. of individual factories and works in the general system of industrial administration, already referred to. This deterioration in quality and range of general consumption goods in the latter years of N.E.P. led to the paradox of 'over-supply' (*zatovarivanie*), that is, to the difficulty of disposing of some goods, amidst a general shortage of consumption goods. The Plenum of the Central Committee of the C.P. in February 1927, in a special resolution, stated that: '"over-supply" in the production of a number of branches of industry is due to the ill-assorted range and bad quality of the goods demanded by consumers' and 'noting the considerable deterioration in the quality of a number of manufactured goods in the past year (1926)', ordered 'that it should be considered a most important task of production in the current year (1927) not only to revert to the previous better quality of these goods but systematically to improve the quality of all industrial production, taking into account the growing fastidiousness of the consumer with regard to the quality of manufactured goods'.*

This problem of quality and the struggle against deterioration and for improvement of both quality and range of industrial production was, as will be shown below, on the agenda throughout the period of reconstruction of the U.S.S.R. national economy and up to the country's entry into the war in 1941.

The other shortcoming which persisted to the end of the process of recovery in industrial production was the high cost of production of manufactured articles: 'the average cost price of manufactured articles in 1926–7 as in the preceding years was double the pre-war average.'† Every year, starting with 1925–6 and the publication of the first 'Control figures of National Economy', industry was set the task of lowering the cost of production, but in 1925–6 instead of the 6 % decrease of production costs for industry as a whole demanded by the plan, there was an actual rise, averaging 2 %; and in 1926–7 instead of the required 5 % reduction, the actual decrease attained was only 1·8 %. The problem of reducing pro-

natural economy is reappearing. It leads to a decrease in the sales of flax, raw hides, furs, etc.' *Ekonomicheskaya Zhizn*, 13 and 29 May 1928; *Torgovo-promyshlennaya Gazeta*, 23 May 1928.

* *The C.P. in Resolutions...*, p. 163.

† *Bulletin of the Conjuncture Institute*, nos. 11–12, 1927, p. 69.

duction costs remained one of the most acute problems in the development of Soviet industry throughout the period just closed; every annual plan for the development of industrial production made provisions for reducing the cost of production, and yet no year saw it entirely fulfilled.

The reasons for such an unsatisfactory state of affairs with regard to the cost of production of manufactured goods during the period of recovery were largely the same as the reasons for the deterioration in quality. An unsaturated market and the virtual monopoly of State industry ensured the sale of goods at high prices and weakened any stimulus aimed at reducing production costs.

We noted in reviewing the evolution of industrial administration that even at the outset of the N.E.P. period private undertakings were restricted to small enterprises; *pari passu* with the growing output of State industry their part in the total industrial production systematically declined (see Table 19).*

Table 19. *Percentages of gross industrial production*

	State industry		
	1925–6	1926–7	1927–8
All industry	71·9	73·9	76·1
(a) Large-scale	89·6	91·3	90·9
(b) Small-scale	1·7	2·0	2·2
	Co-operative industry		
	1925–6	1926–7	1927–8
All industry	8·2	8·9	11·2
(a) Large-scale	6·4	6·5	7·4
(b) Small-scale	15·4	19·0	30·2
	Private industry		
	1925–6	1926–7	1927–8
All industry	19·9	7·2	12·7
(a) Large-scale	4·0	2·2	1·7
(b) Small-scale	82·9	79·0	67·6

It was only in the case of small undertakings that private industry retained its predominating position up to the very end of the recovery period. This fact must be borne in mind to understand the shortage of certain articles of general consumption which be-

* *Control Figures of the National Economy of the U.S.S.R. for* 1928–9, pp. 7,424–5.

came acute, as will be later shown in the years of the reconstruction period when the production of private industry fell sharply and in the case of certain articles almost ceased altogether, whilst the expansion of neither State nor co-operative industry could yet make up for its disappearance.

Both the character of private industry and its results in this period were logical consequences of the conditions in which private undertaking was allowed to work and of disadvantages which increased progressively with the recovery of the country's productive possibilities. From the outset of the N.E.P. period the fundamental policy adopted towards private industry was that it could be tolerated only in so far as the Soviet Government did not consider its existence a menace to the development of the State-managed big and medium-sized industries. As a consequence, private industrial enterprises exceeding a certain size could be organized only either as concessionary enterprises sanctioned by the Chief Concession Committee or else by way of renting State enterprises. Apart from the fact that no large private capital existed within the U.S.S.R. at the moment when N.E.P. was introduced, private enterprise naturally drifted more or less exclusively towards small industrial production. Yet restrictive measures designed for the 'economic regulation' of private enterprise increased with time. These restrictive measures were financial (heavier taxation of private than of State or co-operative enterprises and restrictions on credit), or affecting the supply of raw materials, or the use of transport facilities by rail and waterways, or directly prohibitive measures directed against building new enterprises manufacturing certain articles, etc.* These restrictive measures against private enterprise developed side by side with success in the recovery of the country's productive forces.

The attempt to enrol foreign capital in the concessionary undertakings of the U.S.S.R. proved even less successful. There were quite a number of concession-seekers. Between 1922 and 1927, 2,211 offers for concessions were received by the U.S.S.R. (705 in manufacturing industry and 208 in mining). The majority of offers came from Germany (782), Great Britain (223), U.S.A. (205) and France (174). Yet only 163 concession agreements were concluded

---

* More detailed information about conditions and results of the work of private capital in the N.E.P. period will be found in the numerous publications cited and analysed in my article 'Private commercial and industrial capital in the U.S.S.R.', published in no. 65, 1929, *Bull. Econ. Study of Prof. S. N. Prokopovich.*

(36 in manufacturing and 26 in mining industry). 'Nearly 50 % of the offers for concessions were declined because they affected objects which, for one reason or another, we did not wish to concede; 35 % were declined because those seeking for concessions did not dispose of sufficient capital. Lastly, 15 % of the proposals were refused because the conditions offered by those seeking to secure the concessions were unacceptable.'* By the end of 1927, out of the 163 concessions sanctioned, only 92 were still valid; of which 23 were not really concessions but rather agreements for providing technical help—patents, blue-prints, technical calculations—afforded to Soviet enterprises by foreign firms. There remained in 1927 in manufacturing industry only 23 real concessions in which only foreign capital was invested and 17 in mining.

Though some concessions occupied an important place in their special branch of production (Lena Goldfields in the gold or the Harriman concession in the manganese industry), their share in the general gross output of U.S.S.R. big industry was quite insignificant—in 1925-6 the output of concessionary industry was only 0·4 % of the total gross output of big industry, and in 1926-7 it was still less.† Generally speaking, the expectation that large foreign capital could be enlisted for investment in the development of industrial production did not materialize, and, toward the end of the recovery period, it became obvious that any further expansion of productive possibilities must be based exclusively on domestic capital accumulation. It may be remarked, incidentally, that towards the close of 1928 (on 15 September), on the eve of the inauguration of the first F.Y.P., a regulation of the Sovnarkom S.S.S.R. 'On the stimulation of the concession policy' was published; this contained the information that 'the Sovnarkom S.S.S.R. has approved a reference list of concessions which can be granted to foreign capital. Moreover, the Chief Concessions Department is authorized to enter into negotiations about other matters if the proposed concession is of interest to the State.' Apparently this was the last attempt of the so-called Right Wing of the Party to attract foreign capital for large-scale investment in

---

* V. Butovsky, *Foreign Concessions in the Economy of the U.S.S.R.*, Moscow, 1928, p. 32.

† My article 'The new regulations about concessions and the concession policy of the U.S.S.R.', published in no. 62, 1928, *Bull. Econ. Study of Prof. S. N. Procopovich*, gives a summary and an analysis of the principal material published on questions of the U.S.S.R. concessions policy during the years of N.E.P.

industry, and so to diminish the strain of domestic accumulation in the forthcoming years covered by the F.Y.P.*

Thus, in 1927, when the process of fully utilizing the inherited productive possibilities of large-scale industry was on the whole completed, the question of finding the further *means* to develop industrial production *within the country* became acute. The development of industrial production at any cost was, as we know, a fundamental tenet of the Party, because according to the Party's ideology the development of industry was an essential prerequisite to the 'building of Socialism in one country'. It should be remembered that in the last years of the recovery period an acute ideological and Party organization struggle was going on around the question as to how the 'industrialization of the country' could be brought about. As early as April 1925 (at the Fourteenth Party Conference), Stalin put forward the slogan of the possibility of 'building an entirely Socialist society in our country, with the moral approbation and the support of the proletarians of other countries, but without a preliminary victory of the proletarian revolution in other countries', in contrast to Trotsky's slogan of 'permanent revolution'; in December 1925 (at the Fourteenth Party Congress) the famous 'general line' of the Party was adopted; it demanded the maximum development of industry, 'the transformation of our country from an agrarian into an industrial one, capable by its own means of producing the necessary equipment'. In November 1926 (at the Fifteenth Party Conference) it was again emphasized that 'all the efforts of the Party and the Soviet State must be first and foremost directed to ensure such an expansion of basic capital as could bring about the progressive reconstruction of the country's whole economy on a higher technical basis.... One of the distinctive features and, at the same time, one of the main difficulties of the first stage of industrialization is that expenditure for capital construction will demand a considerable effort from the country's economy, whilst the results of new construction, that is, the output of the new factories and works, better in quality and cheaper in price, will reach the market only after a considerable lapse of time

* The directives of the Party for drafting the F.Y.P. were issued in December 1927, at the Fifteenth Party Congress; in 1928, Rykov, leader of the Party's Right Wing, which opposed accelerated industrialization and collectivization of agriculture, continued as chairman of the Sovnarkom S.S.S.R., but by November 1929, Rykov, Tomsky and Bukharin, principal leaders of the Right Opposition, recanted their errors in a letter to the Central Committee of the C.P., and on 20 December 1930, Rykov was removed from his post of chairman of the Sovnarkom S.S.S.R. and of the Labour Defence Council.

often amounting to several years.... The tempo of expansion of the basic capital will depend on: (*a*) the value of the accumulations of socialized industry; (*b*) the utilization through the State Budget of revenue from other branches of the country's economy; (*c*) the utilization of the population's savings through attracting them into co-operation, savings-banks, State loans, the credit system, etc.'*

To these general ideas determining the country's industrialization was added in 1927 the possibility of war in the near future.† In October 1927, the joint Plenum of the Central Committee and the Central Control Commission of the C.P. approved the 'Instructions for the drafting of a five-year plan for the national economy'. Paragraph 3 stressed that: 'Taking into account the possibility of an armed attack by capitalist states on the first proletarian state in history, it is necessary in drafting the five-year plan to devote the maximum attention to the speedy development of those branches of the national economy in general and industry in particular, which are most important for ensuring the country's defences and economic stability in war-time.'‡

Such was the background of the first F.Y.P. for the reconstruction of the economy of the U.S.S.R. It has seemed advisable to give this brief historical survey in order to show that the F.Y.P. was neither the product of the 'planning' institutions, nor that it was only 'confirmed' in May 1929, for ideologically and partly technically§ it had been maturing long before the process of recovery of the U.S.S.R. economy had been completed. The planning institutions did not work out the F.Y.P. on their intitative, the reverse happened: the task of hastily drafting it was thrust upon them. Nor could they follow a method of extrapolation, i.e. prolonging into the future the trends of earlier developments; their task demanded at once creative vision and the resolute will to achieve, i.e. they had to prepare a plan of what 'may and must be brought about by the utmost endeavours of the economic col-

---

* *The C.P. in Resolutions...*, p. 125.

† 'In breaking off relations with the U.S.S.R., the Conservative Government of Great Britain is pursuing the aim not only of weakening the economic power of the Soviet Union, but preparing the way for a possible direct attack on the U.S.S.R. Therefore a most important political task is...to carry out in the shortest time possible the necessary measures to prepare the country for the eventuality of the imperialistic states starting an economic blockade or an armed attack on the U.S.S.R.' Op. cit. p. 179.

‡ Op. cit. p. 197.

§ See S. Strumlin, 'First attempts at planning', *Planned Economy*, no. 12, 1930.

lectivity....'. 'It is the duty of the U.S.S.R. Gosplan and of the whole system of planning organs to translate general politico-economic standpoints and instructions issued by the Party into the language of concrete economic and technico-economic estimates, and to transform them into a plan of economic construction covering the forthcoming five years....It is a plan for the *radical* reconstruction of the productive foundations of our country.... Our country makes the unprecedented experiment of tremendous capital construction carried out at the expense of current consumption, at the price of a harsh regime of economy and by sacrificing the satisfaction of to-day's needs in the name of great historical aims.'*

CHAPTER VIII. AGRICULTURE

The description of the events and developments in agriculture in the years 1917–22 shows that of the complex political, social and economic problems involved in the agrarian question as inherited by the Soviet Government, only one—the liquidation of large landowners and the nationalization of the land—had been, in fact, solved before the introduction of N.E.P. The nationalization of the land had been carried out impulsively by the simple seizure of land, cattle, agricultural machinery and chattels by local peasant masses. No orderly redistribution of land between rural communities of different districts had been attempted and, therefore, the motley of peasant holdings, varying in size from district to district, was, on the whole, retained; especially as only a small percentage of the land belonging to rich peasants had been divided up by the poorer ones. Moreover, at the time, very few of the large estates were turned into State and collective farms, precursors of the future forms of large-scale land tenure. As a result of the manner in which land nationalization had been carried out, and although peasants had received additional land from the subdivision of large estates, in the country as a whole, holdings decreased in size. Consequently the economic aspect of the agrarian problem was not improved but further complicated. As before, peasant farming was on too small a scale to allow for the necessary intensification of agricultural production. Except for the upper

* *The Five-Year Plan of the U.S.S.R.'s Economic Construction*, vol. 1, pp. 9, 71, 74.

stratum of well-to-do farmers, individual peasants had not enough land for profitably using complicated agricultural machinery or for adopting intensive livestock breeding. Solely by uniting in some form of *producers'* co-operative associations could the peasant small-holders enter on the path of intensified and profitable production for the market. Amalgamation was the only course, for it was im-possible to increase the size of individual holdings both for economic and political reasons. Economically, it would have been necessary —under the existing conditions of land cultivation—to reduce the agricultural population by many millions, and to create conditions favouring the accumulation of production capital among the rich peasantry. This would only have been possible had an intensive development of industrial production, together with a growth of the urban population, been promoted by the influx of foreign capital investments. However, the recovery of the ruined in-dustrial production, and, in particular, new capital construction in heavy industry financed by the country's home accumulated capital, was possible only if a protective price policy for industrial goods was adopted, i.e. by the maintenance of relatively low prices for agricultural produce. In its turn, such a policy could but slow down the accumulation of agricultural capital. Moreover, ac-cumulation in individual peasant households, even when prices tend to favour agriculture, is a very lengthy process and cannot serve as a basis for a speedy solution of the problems of agrarian over-population and for the intensification of agricultural produc-tion. This is especially true when peasant holdings are subdivided to the extent they were in the U.S.S.R., and when the interests of peasant groups differ and even conflict according to the size of their plots and their resources. In the U.S.S.R., only the upper stratum of the wealthy peasantry had adequate resources to intensify pro-duction and increase marketable surplus. The prevailing mass of peasant households had neither enough land, nor cattle, nor other means of production to modernize their agricultural methods (see Table 20, p. 135). Moreover, the majority of poor peasants did not sell any basic agricultural produce (grain and livestock), but, on the contrary, had to buy them to meet their needs, and were therefore interested in keeping prices low. The 'middle' peasant—and he formed the foundation of the U.S.S.R.'s peasant population—could market only a very small surplus of his produce, and the possibility of his increasing production on his own account was therefore limited. Only by attaining the level of the upper group could he enter on the path of expansion and intensification of production. The policy of fostering the growth of the group of wealthy individual peasant households would have meant, under the existing circumstances, proletarianizing the poorer groups of peasants and weakening the importance of the middle peasantry. Such a policy was politically impossible; it was absolutely unacceptable to the Soviet Government. The Party's attitude to the rural population was founded on Lenin's view that the wealthy peasantry is the 'stronghold of capitalist roots'.

The policy of contributing to the growth of wealthy peasant households was not only politically unacceptable; it might also endanger economically the socialized sector of the national economy. Rich peasants, as producers of marketable agricultural surpluses, stood for high prices for agricultural produce; but, as has been explained, the recovery of industrial production called for a policy of relatively low prices for agricultural produce. Naturally, therefore, the interests of State industry and those of the rich peasantry ran the risk of clashing and, in fact, a conflict did arise when the restoration of industry's productive capital was completed and new construction in heavy industry began to be carried out on a large scale. It was impossible to exercise *direct* control over production carried out by millions of individual peasant households, and the indirect levers controlling agricultural production (prices, the system of purchasing agricultural stocks, the credit and taxation systems, etc.) were apt to prove inadequate for stimulating peasant producers to expand production so as to keep pace with the development of industrial production and the growth of the urban population. The rich peasantry, controlling a large proportion of the agricultural produce, might have used its economic power to obstruct the Soviet Government's policy of industrialization and thus transform its economic power into political power. Therefore, and apart from social and political principles, purely practical considerations of economic policy prevented the Soviet Government from favouring the development of the upper stratum of individual wealthy peasant households. But the policy of hindering the growth of the wealthy peasantry and affording full support to the development of the middle and lower groups of peasants, meant, under existing conditions of land tenure, choosing a very slow path for the development of agricultural production and particularly of marketable surplus.

Such was the tangle of economic and political problems in the field of agriculture which N.E.P. was called upon to solve. Moreover, in the field of agriculture the productive possibilities remained in the hands of millions of individual peasants, in contrast to other branches of the national economy where, in spite of the transition to N.E.P., the 'commanding heights' remained in the hands of the State economic machinery, e.g. in nationalized transport, industry, banking, foreign trade and other branches of the national economy where private enterprise was being readmitted but either within very strict limits or under the direct control of State institutions. The economic policy in regard to agriculture could be carried out only through indirect measures and not by regulating production directly as was the case in the socialized branches of the national economy. Therefore, in agriculture, the preparatory path leading to the necessary prerequisites for planning production proved much longer than in other branches of the national economy.

In this general survey, it is not possible to describe all the complex developments and governmental measures in the field of agriculture under N.E.P., but it seems necessary to point out at least the more important events, because without some knowledge of them it is difficult to understand and appreciate the planned measures and the evolution of agriculture in the ensuing periods of the Soviet system of national economy.

The general goal of N.E.P. was to achieve the recovery of production in all the branches of national economy which had been ruined in the course of the previous period, and to pave the way for a further socialization of the country's national economy. In agriculture the recovery of production could, however, at the time be achieved only through the personal initiative of individual peasant households. It was therefore imperative to free their personal initiative from restrictions. In consideration of this, N.E.P. while upholding the nationalization of the land—which continued to be regarded as State property, though in fact at the disposal of the peasantry—and while retaining the prohibition to sell land, recognized nevertheless the rights of the actual occupier to his investments in the land; moreover, it became permissible to lease land and to hire machinery, cattle and agricultural implements, and even labour within certain limits, whilst peasants were given full freedom to organize production and sell the produce of their holdings.

Naturally the right to rent land and to hire labour and agricultural machinery, whilst contributing to the recovery of production contributed at the same time further to split the peasantry into groups differing in wealth. Hence arose a complex ideological struggle within the Party and between various Party groups regarding the permissible limits to be set on renting and hiring, and also around the policy of taxation as applicable to different peasant groups. For instance, the extension of the right to lease land, to hire labour and means of production and certain rebates in the agricultural tax, approved by the Fourteenth Party Conference in 1925,* were regarded by the Left Wing (Trotsky's group) as a concession to the kulak, by the Right Wing (Bukharin, Rykov, and others) as insufficiently bold measures for raising agricultural production,† while the Centre (Stalin and others) considered that these measures were unavoidable concessions to the 'middle' peasant whose support the Party should enlist in the field of agriculture.

The fundamental Party standpoint was that among the rural social groups, the 'poor' are the *supporters* of the working class and of the Soviet government, the 'middle' peasant is economically an *ally*, and the kulak or well-to-do peasant is a *class enemy*. During the N.E.P. period this standpoint resulted in a whole system of governmental economic measures aimed at giving full support to the poor peasant, at supporting and collaborating with the middle peasant and restricting the growth of kulak farming. However, tactics varied according to vicissitudes in the recovery of national economy as a whole and of agriculture in particular, and also according to the course of the economic socialization of the country; and the measures adopted allowed for more or less liberty or restrictions on the rise of the socially and economically higher peasant groups. Thus, up to 1925–6, whilst the production of grain was recovering slowly, the agricultural tax was not assessed like the income tax and was not progressive. However, in 1925–6, after the greatest harvest of the N.E.P. period (see p. 325), the country's bread and fodder balance improved substantially, whilst the growing influence of the wealthy peasantry became apparent; so it was decided to increase the restrictive measures on the rich peasant households. In 1926–7 the agricultural tax became progressive for

* In particular, in 1925, a regulation was adopted allowing the leasing of land by a working household in all cases excepting that of the family giving up individual farming and losing its status of working household. Cf. *Bull. Financ. and Econ. Leg.* no. 9, 1925.

† 'Grow rich', was Bukharin's, the Right Wing ideologist's, slogan for the peasantry; his contention was that a wealthy peasantry was no political menace and would 'grow into socialism'. For further details on the internal Party struggle regarding the policy adopted at the time in rural districts, see *The C.P. in Resolution...*, pp. 50–2.

richer peasants. In the later years increasingly heavy taxes were imposed on them.* On the other hand, poor peasant households benefited not only from tax rebates, but received help in the case of crop failure, and were entitled to credit facilities and participation in the management of co-operative associations, etc.†

At the same time measures were taken (with the help of State subsidies) to develop agricultural co-operation and to attract to it the great masses of poor and middle peasants, whilst the admission of kulaks was strictly limited.‡ Whereas in the early years of N.E.P. agricultural co-operation developed mainly in the field of sale of agricultural produce and the supply of manufactured goods to rural districts, and in that of credit co-operation, i.e., in general, in trade turn-over designed to oust private enterprise acting as middle man in the exchange of urban and rural products, later on productive agricultural co-operation gained in importance, in particular co-operation for the joint cultivation of land without the socialization of means of production.§

In carrying out these measures the Soviet Government strove to differentiate the various social and economic groups in accordance with their general policy towards the peasantry. Economically, however, this policy led to a parcelling of peasant holdings and slowed down the pace of recovery of agricultural production,

---

* In 1926–7, 11·3 % of the peasantry (rural proletariat) paid no agricultural tax; 22·1 % (poor peasants) paid 1·3 % of the total sum brought in by the tax; 62·7 % (middle peasants) paid 72·9 % and 3·9 % (kulaks) paid 25·9 % of the total sum brought in by the tax. In 1928–9, 35 % of the homesteads paid no tax; 60·8 % paid 63·9 %, and 4·2 % paid 36·1 % of a much larger sum brought in by this tax. For details see *Statistical Survey*, no. 4, 1927; *Control Figures for 1928–9*; *Ekonomicheskaya Zhizn*, 24 April 1929; *Financial Journal*, no. 2, 1929.

† In 1925–6 the Government allocated 373 million roubles in aid to poor peasants suffering from the crop failure of 1924, and in 1926–7, 427 million roubles. Tax rebates to poor peasants amounted to 44 million roubles in 1925–6 and to 52 million roubles in 1926–7. For details see *The Development of Soviet Economy*, p. 295.

‡ In 1925, when the conditions of leasing land and hiring labour were facilitated in order to favour the middle peasant households, measures were also taken to strengthen the activities of the 'groups of rural paupers' and to prevent kulaks from participating in the management of rural co-operatives.

§ By 1925 the entire network of agricultural co-operation consisted of 54,813 co-operatives of various types, mainly sale-and-supply co-operatives, which comprised 6,589,000 peasant households, i.e. approximately 38 % of the total. By 1927 32 % and in 1928–9 45 % of all peasant households were members of co-operatives. In 1925 there were 3,124 associations for the joint cultivation of land, in 1927 4,627 and in July 1928 12,071. *The Development of Soviet Economy...*, pp. 215, 297, 314.

especially of its marketable surplus. Table 20 convincingly illustrates this.*

Table 20. *Total numbers of farms (in thousands)*

According to the 1916 census in the European part of the U.S.S.R.:

Peasant farms	15,535
Large farms	110
Total	15,645

In the U.S.S.R.	1924	1925	1926	1927	1928
Peasant farms	23,051	23,977	24,597	25,037	25,586
Collective farms	5·1	4·4	3·3	3·5	1·9
State farms	—	10·7	—	11·3	21·6
Total	23,056	23,992	24,600	25,052	25,609

	Numbers of individual farms* (in thousands)			Numbers of persons*		
	1924–5	1925–6	1926–7	1924–5	1925–6	1926–7
Proletariat	2,184	2,454	2,560	4,025	4,532	4,713
Farmers	20,209	19,955	20,213	107,919	106,558	108,010
Of which:						
Poor	5,803	5,317	5,037	25,245	22,664	21,106
Middle	13,678	13,822	14,280	77,870	78,539	81,045
Employers	728	816	896	4,804	5,355	5,859

* Employers comprised the following: (1) those who owned means of production valued at more than 1,600 roubles and either hired them out or employed hired labour for more than 50 working days per annum.; (2) owned means of production valued at 800 roubles and employed hired labour for more than 75 days per annum. The following groups came under the heading of poor peasants: (1) those without any draught animal and sowing an area of 4 desyatin and 50% of those with a sown area of 4–6 desyatin; (2) with one draught animal and a sown area of 1 desyatin. All others came under the heading of middle peasants. *Statistical Handbook*, 1928, pp. 42, 940.

Data for the R.S.F.S.R.

Farm sowing	% of farmers hiring draught animals			% of farmers hiring agricultural implements		
	1924	1925	1926	1924	1925	1926
Up to 2 desyatin	64·3	64·5	70·1	66·0	65·7	70·7
2–4 desyatin	34·4	34·4	37·0	36·3	36·7	38·8
4–6 desyatin	20·1	19·7	19·3	22·3	21·6	22·4
6–9 desyatin	12·0	12·0	11·1	14·5	14·8	15·6
9–15 desyatin	5·4	5·7	5·3	7·7	8·0	9·5
15 and over	1·5	2·0	2·9	2·7	3·0	3·4
Average total	38·0	38·2	36·6	40·0	39·7	38·8

* *Ten Years of Soviet Power, in Figures*, 1917–27, p. 168; *Statistical Handbook of the U.S.S.R.*, 1928, p. 82.

Percentage distribution of agricultural implements in the R.S.F.S.R. in 1926

	No. of farms %	No. of ploughs %	No. of sowing machines %	No. of harvesters %
Groups of farms:				
Without any or with sown area of less than 4 desyatin	75·1	57·1	12·9	11·8
With 4–10 desyatin of sown area	20·9	31·4	41·2	42·0
With over 10 desyatin of sown area	4·0	11·5	45·9	46·2

By the end of the N.E.P. period the number of peasant farms had increased by ten millions or 65 % as compared with the pre-revolutionary period. At the same time the numbers of poor peasants were decreasing very slowly, whilst the numbers of proletarians were even on the increase during the period 1924–5 to 1926–7. Some of the poor peasants rose to the level of middle peasant, others became proletarians. In the R.S.F.S.R. in 1926, 75·1 % of peasant households sowed up to 4 desyatin only; i.e. were consumers, whilst merely 4 % sowed over 10 desyatin. Moreover, the smallholders inadequately equipped with animals and agricultural machinery usually resorted to hiring them from the richer peasants. In 1926, on the average, 36·6 % peasant households hired animals, and 38·8 % hired implements. During the N.E.P. period the holdings of the upper stratum of peasants tended to decrease. Naturally, grain production, which is particularly dependent on the size of fields, recovered very slowly, and by the end of the N.E.P. period had not yet reached its pre-revolutionary level, either absolutely, or still less relatively to the increased population. As regards marketable surplus, it had considerably declined.* This slow recovery of agricultural production and of marketable surplus affected the home market in the manner described in the chapter on Home Trade (pp. 68–9); moreover, it should be mentioned that the difficulties encountered in 1927–8 on the agricultural produce market raised acutely the question of the immediate policy to be adopted in regard to agriculture. It became apparent that a permanent solution, not palliatives, was

* The marketable surplus grain in 1913 was 20·3 % of the total harvest, in 1924–5 14·3 %, in 1925–6 13·2 %, in 1927–8 12·1 %, and in 1928–9 11·1 %. Data of the State Planning Commission. *Bull. of the Conjuncture Inst.* nos. 11–12, 1927, p. 52. *Control Figures of the National Economy of the U.S.S.R. for* 1928–9, p. 230. For figures regarding the production of grain, see pp. 68–9.

needed to meet the current difficulties in the procurement of grain stocks, and also for the development of agriculture in general. The crisis was overcome by emergency administrative measures. The grain of rich peasants who had refused to deliver it at fixed prices to the State supply organizations was confiscated. 25 % of the grain confiscated from the kulaks was advanced as a subsidy to the village Committees of Poor Peasants for their part in the discovery and confiscation of the hoarded grain. Peasants who had hoarded grain were sentenced to imprisonment. The application of such extraordinary measures fanned the antagonism between various social and economic groups of the countryside, and assumed an acute and extreme character;* another result was the reduction in the extent of grain growing by grain marketing farmers.† The rich peasants preferred to reduce their sown areas rather than deliver their surplus at fixed prices to the supply organizations, especially because of the increasing discrepancy between the fixed and market prices (see p. 137). They hoped by economic pressure to compel the Soviet Government to alter both their policy of prices for agricultural produce and their general policy towards the better-off farmers.

Towards the close of 1927, when the collection of agricultural stocks encountered the first critical difficulties, there was, at the Fifteenth Party Congress, a sharp clash of opinions. The so-called Right Wing of the Party proposed the following policy: (1) to allow free play to market prices, resulting in a rise in the price of grain, even though this entailed slowing down industrial construction; (2) to give up the extreme measures applied against the kulaks, and obtain stocks of agricultural produce by buying them on a free market; (3) should grain collections fail, to import from abroad the necessary grain, even at the cost of curtailing imports of industrial equipment; (4) to contribute in every way to the development of individual peasant farming without fear of in-

---

* Rich peasants resorted to various way of concealing grain, burying it in the ground, hiding it in straw stacks, etc. On the other hand, local authorities occasionally 'confiscated' not only marketable surpluses but all the grain discovered as well as other produce. In their turn kulaks went as far as murdering members of Committees of Poor Peasants and local correspondents of newspapers. *Pravda*, 1 February 1928; *Ekon. Zhizn*, 17 February 1928; *Izvestia*, 12 and 19 April 1928.

† For data regarding the areas sown by peasant households in the principal districts producing marketable surpluses in 1928 as compared with 1927, see *Planned Economy*, no. 7, 1928, p. 102. *Economic Review*, 1928, no. 11, p. 94 and no. 12, p. 104.

creasing the wealthy peasant farming, and to slow down the development of State and collective farms. The Left Wing proposed on the contrary to proceed with the immediate liquidation of kulak farming and to change over to full collectivization. The Central group, which represented the so-called *general line* of the Party for the country's industrialization, stood: (1) for accelerating as much as possible the association of poor peasant households into producers' co-operatives, and the gradual extension of collectivization to the mass of middle peasants; (2) for substantially increasing State farms; (3) for firmly regulating prices of agricultural produce, and, in the case of a repetition of the difficulties with grain collection, to resort once more to emergency measures against kulaks; (4) for maintaining without deviation the policy of industrialization and the corresponding policy in foreign trade; in particular importing, instead of agricultural produce in short supply, agricultural machinery, thus creating a mechanized base for the State and collective farms.*

The policy of this *general line* began to be put into effect by a series of measures. (1) The production of poor peasants was aided by more credits, and means of production were supplied on a larger scale to the collective farms which they formed.† (2) It was decided to carry out a widespread campaign in favour of 'the adoption by the masses of poor and middle peasants during the forthcoming years of simple agricultural measures accessible to smallholders for ensuring a considerable rise in yield within a short time, in order to raise crop yields during the next five years by at least 30–35%'.‡ (3) It was decided 'to organize in the course of the next 4–5 years in the R.S.F.S.R. and in the Ukraine, new large grain-producing State farms in districts where the new State farms would not encroach on the lands already cultivated by peasants, with the aim of obtaining from these State farms a yearly yield of 100 million poods of marketable grain'.§ (4) It was decided to intensify measures for the collectivization of peasant households. Henceforth, the decision of the majority of the full members of the village community to change over to the joint use

* For details regarding the struggle within the Party, see *The C.P. in Resolutions...*, pp. 247–62. J. Stalin, *Leninism*, 11th ed., pp. 184–243. *Stages in the Economic Policy of the U.S.S.R.* pp. 237–44.

† Cf. the regulation of the Sovnarkom S.S.S.R., 'Concerning measures of economic aid to poor peasants', *Bull. Financ. and Econ. Leg.* 1928, no. 37.

‡ Cf. the regulation of the Fourth Session of the U.S.S.R. Central Executive Committee of the Fourth Convocation. *Bull. Financ. and Econ. Leg.* 1928, no. 52.

§ *The C.P. in Resolutions...*, p. 281.

of means and implements of production, was sufficient, and binding on the minority.*

Somewhat later, at the conference of Marxist Students of Agrarian Problems, Stalin thus formulated the political and theoretical reasons for multiplying State and collective farms.

The Marxian theory of reproduction teaches that modern society cannot develop without accumulating from year to year.... Our large-scale, centralized, Socialist industry is developing according to the Marxian theory of expanded reproduction...but small peasant farming still predominates in our national economy. Can it be said that our small peasant farming is developing according to the principle of expanded reproduction?...Not only is there no annual expanded reproduction in our small peasant farming, taken in the mass, but, on the contrary, it is not always able to obtain even simple reproduction. Can we advance our socialized industry at an accelerated rate having to rely on such an agricultural base?...Can the Soviet Government and the work of socialist construction be, for any length of time, based on two *different* foundations—on the foundation of the most large-scale and concentrated socialist industry, and on the foundation of the most fragmentary and backward, small-commodity peasant farming? They cannot. Sooner or later the end must be a complete collapse of the whole national economy. What, then, is the solution? The solution lies in enlarging the agricultural units, in making agriculture capable of accumulation, of expanded reproduction, and in thus changing the agricultural base of our national economy. But how are the agricultural units to be enlarged? There are two ways of doing this. There is the *capitalist* way, which is to enlarge the agricultural units by introducing capitalism in agriculture—a way which leads to the impoverishment of the peasantry and to the development of capitalist enterprises in agriculture; we reject this way as incompatible with the Soviet economic system. There is a second way—the *Socialist* way, which is to set up collective and State farms, the way which leads to the amalgamation of the small peasant farms into large collective farms, technically and scientifically equipped, and to the squeezing out of the capitalist elements from agriculture. We are in favour of this second way.†

* Cf. the regulation of the U.S.S.R. Central Executive Committee, 'General principles of land organization and land tenure' and the regulation of the Sovnarkom S.S.S.R. 'Programme of State measures for agriculture for 1927–8', *Bull. Financ. and Econ. Leg.* 1928, no. 11. *Izvestia*, 16 December 1928.

† Stalin, *Leninism*, pp. 277–8.

CHAPTER IX. LABOUR

The transition to N.E.P. necessitated a fundamental revision of the principles on which labour relations had rested during the period of 'War Communism'. Compulsory labour service and equal pay in kind had to be abolished, while mutual relations between trade unions and managements had to be re-established on a new basis. As already shown, a most progressive labour code had been introduced during the first months of the Soviet regime; but under the conditions of 'War Communism' this legislation remained more or less an aspiration for the future, and could not be put into practice. With the change over to N.E.P., the principle underlying this labour legislation, formulated in the first months of the Soviet regime, were confirmed anew by the Labour Code of 1922.

This code established an 8-hour working day for adults, a 6-hour day for young people of 16–18 years and also for workers employed underground, or in heavy work, or on work detrimental to health; a fortnight's holiday for all those in paid employment; the prohibition of child labour. Compulsory labour service was retained only in cases of *force majeure* calamities or to meet urgent State needs. These new statutes were not mere wishful thinking; they were to be strictly carried out in practice and it was the trade unions' duty to supervise their exact application not merely in private but also in all State enterprises. The Code laid down also fundamental rules for engaging and dismissing workers: the administration could require a candidate sent by the Labour Exchange to pass a test and, in the case of inadequate qualifications for the work, could refuse employment. If, however, the refusal was made on legally insufficient grounds, proceedings could be taken against the administration. A worker could be dismissed on the ground of criminal activities connected with his work and constituting a breach of the criminal law, which would have to be established as such by the competent judicial authority; or in the case of unjustified absenteeism during either 3 consecutive days or during 6 days in the course of a month. Moreover, by a decision of the wage-arbitration commission a worker could be dismissed if he were proved to be incapable of carrying out the work entrusted to him; or if he systematically failed to carry out the duties specified in the contract, or broke the internal rules of the enterprise; or if he systematically and through his own fault failed to achieve the norm of labour productivity fixed for his work. These norms were established by the administration in agreement with the trade unions. The administration of the enterprise was to inform the trade union within three days of every new engagement or of any proposed dismissal. The duty of supervising the enforcement of the rules for the protection of labour and the safety of those employed in a works fell upon the Labour Inspection authorities; no enterprise had the right to start work without the Labour Inspector's authorization. Trade unions were to supervise the strict observance by managements of rules established by law for the protection of labour and for safety, for social insurance and the timely payment of wages.

With the introduction of N.E.P., the system of social insurance became a reality; it had been proclaimed during the first months of the Soviet regime. but began to operate only with N.E.P. According to the law of 15 September 1921, later included in the Labour Code of 1922, social insurance covers every worker in paid employment, without exception, and provides benefits for the insured and the members of his family in cases of loss of labour capacity (unemployment, disablement, bodily injury, old age, sickness, death of the family's principal bread-winner, and, in the case of women, during pregnancy and child nursing). The social insurance funds are composed exclusively of employers' contributions, no contribution being paid to the fund by workers and salaried employees. The insurance funds are expended on free medical treatment and cures in rest-homes, spas, sanatoria, etc., on institutions for children, and on various other social and cultural forms of benefit to the insured.

Relations between trade unions and business organizations had to be entirely readjusted. In the previous period, the functions of trade unions tended to be merged with those of State institutions for industrial administration. Now, with the reappearance of the private employer and with State enterprises changing over to commercial methods including a profit system, the trade unions' fundamental *raison d'être*, i.e. the protection of workers' interests, came again to the fore. In regard to private enterprise the position of the trade unions was clear, they were to perform the same functions as under the competitive system, i.e. to protect hired labour against exploitation on the part of the employers. In regard to State enterprises the position was far more complex. On the one hand, it was pointed out at the Eleventh Party Congress at which the main tenets of N.E.P. were adopted, that it was 'unavoidable that departmental interests and departmental zeal should give rise to a certain clash of interests between the working masses and the directors of enterprises over labour conditions. Therefore in socialized enterprises it is indisputably the trade unions' duty to protect the workers' interests and constantly to correct the mistakes and the excessive demands of business organs, in so far as they are due to a bureaucratic abuse of State machinery'. At the same time a struggle between the interests of labour and of management is deemed inadmissible in cases when such a struggle is directed against the interests of the State, and not against an abuse of State interests by the management of a given enterprise. 'In the case of friction and conflict between individual groups of the working class and individual institutions and organs of the Workers' State, the trade unions must aim at the most speedy and smooth settlement of the conflict, with the maximum advantages for the workers' groups, represented by the union—provided these advantages can be put into effect without prejudice to other groups and are not detrimental to the development of the Workers' State and its economy as a whole. The only proper, healthy and effective method of settling conflicts and friction between individual sections of the working class and the organs of the Workers' State is for the trade unions to mediate through their corresponding organs, either by entering into negotiations with the corresponding business organ involved, on the basis of demands and proposals exactly defined by both parties, or by appealing to higher State institutions.' Disputes could be brought before the arbitration court (at first only trade unions enjoyed this right, but in 1925 it was also extended to the business organs), before the wage-dispute commissions, before the conciliation boards of the P. Commissariat of Labour and before arbitration tribunals.

On the other hand, trade unions were to collaborate in 'drawing the working masses into participation in the control of industry', to propose candidates, and to take part in nominations to posts in business enterprises and to State institutions concerned with economic affairs, while business enterprises when making new appointments were to consider trade union recommendations. Trade unions were also to foster a new labour discipline among workers, to help raise labour productivity and to oppose bureaucratic abuses in the organization of labour and production; they were also to participate in all State planning institutions. Furthermore, it was considered that 'production conferences held in factories, works and other large enterprises and economic units are

the best means of drawing the great working masses into a share in building up the Soviet economy, of inculcating in them the idea of the close dependence of the workers' interests on the Socialist State's economic success, and of promoting and educating new cadres of managers and administrators from among the workers'.*
Moreover, in 1926, Stalin emphasized that 'the programmes of production conferences must be broadened and their content enriched. Production conferences must consider fundamental problems of industrial development [previously production conferences mainly discussed problems of rationalization and technical improvement in the work of a given enterprise]. Only in this manner will it be possible to raise the activity of millions of the working class masses and make them conscious participants in industrial development'.

As planning was increasingly enforced in regulating the development of industrial production, the part played in planning by the trade unions necessarily increased. In 1927,

in order to ensure the participation of the trade unions at all stages in dealing with fundamental problems of production, the following procedure is established for the participation of the All-Union Central Council of Trade Unions and the Unions' Central Committee in the work of the institutions of the Supreme Economic Council:

1. The All-Union Central Council of Trade Unions and the Unions' Central Committee take an active part in all the work of the Supreme Economic Council and primarily in the examination of the following fundamental problems: (a) control figures, (b) the productive-financial plan, (c) the auditing of general balance sheets, (d) quality of production, (e) production costs, (f) economies, (g) enquiries and control, (h) capital construction, (i) rationalization and standardization, (j) appointments to managements of the principal institutions and (k) organizational problems.... Representatives of the [trade] unions enjoy the rights of members of the Collegium or Praesidium with consultative voice. A representative of the All-Union Central Council of Trade Unions participates in all the sessions of the Praesidium of the U.S.S.R. Supreme Economic Council with the right to a consultative voice.†

This dualism in trade unions' duties, involving on the one hand the protection of the workers' interests and on the other participation in the organization of production and the obligation to support measures designed to raise labour productivity and to rationalize production, etc., resulted in practice in frequent conflicts of interest and much confusion of these rights and duties. It was also the

* *The C.P. in Resolutions...*, pp. 60–7.
† *Bull. Financ. and Econ. Leg.* no. 14, 1927.

cause of that internal strife (between representatives of various trends of thought) regarding the aims of trade unionism, which culminated in the removal of Tomsky from the post of chairman of the A.U.C.C.T.U. in 1929, and in a reorganization of trade union administration and aims.

At the outset of the N.E.P. period, the aims of protecting the interests of labour and of improving the workers' material and cultural position prevailed over all other activities of the unions. However, trade unions often showed a so-called 'business bias', i.e. they either intervened in the management and administration of the enterprise (see above, pp. 115–17, measures to enforce personal management), or they used their authority to disguise measures taken by the administration contrary to the workers' interests, a phenomenon known as 'breaking away from the masses', or they assimilated their work to that of the enterprises' administration, preventing any conflict between workers and administration, and ignoring proposals made at production conferences. As planning became more and more the rule in industrial production and the socialized sector of industrial production gradually ousted private enterprise, these tendencies, peculiar to Soviet trade unions, became more marked, while their task of protecting the workers' interests faded more and more into the background.

In 1927, as has already been mentioned, the clause demanding that trusts should yield profits was omitted from the new Trusts' Statutes and replaced by the demand that they should develop production 'in accordance with planned tasks'. Similarly, trade unions were more and more made to focus their activities on problems of raising and strengthening labour discipline, on increasing labour productivity and on tackling problems connected with the reduction of production costs, the improved quality of production, etc.* These functions began to loom very large with the introduction of the first F.Y.P.; trade unions were then called upon to mobilize the efforts of the working masses to carry out a tremendous construction and expansion of industrial production programme in conditions of rationed supplies, of huge demands for man-power and the impossibility, temporarily, of raising real wages or of improving housing conditions on the sites of new construction, etc. A further treatment of these problems is given later when we come to deal with labour during the F.Y.P.

The introduction of N.E.P. also necessitated a revision of

* Cf. the very interesting study by M. and P. Joffe, *Trade Unions and the Planning of Industry*, Moscow, 1929.

wage-fixing methods. During the period of 'War Communism', the trade unions exercised absolute rights in the matter of wage-fixing. With the introduction of N.E.P., their role became that of a contracting party both in regard to private and to socialized enterprises. The fixing of wages was replaced by a system of free collective bargaining. Wages in kind were gradually replaced by purely money wages, and equal pay for skilled and unskilled work by a system of differential wages. Already at the Eleventh Party Conference, which met in 1921, it was emphasized that 'the direct interest of the worker in production and in raising labour productivity must be made the basis of wages rate policy'. In 1921-2 a unified scale of wages was worked out and gradually introduced. It established seventeen grades, of which the seventeenth was eight times as high as the first. According to this scale, apprentices were graded in the first six grades, workers up to the ninth, clerks and accountants up to the thirteenth, and managerial and technical workers up to the seventeenth grade. A highly skilled worker was paid 3·5 times as much as an unskilled worker. In introducing N.E.P., Lenin stressed that an increase in labour productivity must be achieved, 'not directly through enthusiasm, but with the help of enthusiasm through personal interest and personal motives'.*

In the N.E.P. period social incentives to work did not play any notable role. Wages were the main incentive relied on to raise standards of skill and intensity of work. But already during the N.E.P. period such forms of social distinction and awards for labour were introduced as the title of 'Distinguished scientific, technical and arts worker', and the award of the order of the 'Red Labour Banner', which also carried material advantages such as pensions for the holder and members of his family and exemption from income-tax or tax rebates.† Collective incentives to work (of various kinds) made their appearance only with the introduction of the F.Y.P.

In the early days of N.E.P., workers could be engaged solely through the Labour Exchange, and for a long time subsequently the practice, current under 'War Communism', of sending workers and employees, not always exactly corresponding to requirements

---

* Lenin, op. cit. vol. XXVII, p. 153.

† Regulation of the U.S.S.R. Central Executive Committee and of the Sovnarkom S.S.S.R., 'On the heroes of Labour' and 'On the institution of the statutes of the Order of the U.S.S.R. Red Labour Banner', *Bull. Financ. and Econ. Leg.* 1927, no. 32, and 1928, no. 40.

but mainly on the strength of their registration card, still persisted. About the middle of 1924 the obligation of engaging labour solely through the Labour Exchange was abrogated and it became optional for employers to offer and for workers to seek employment through the Labour Exchange; similarly the engagement of a worker sent by the Labour Exchange became optional and, conversely, the worker was not bound to accept work found through the Labour Exchange. These measures were taken to facilitate the absorption of the very considerable numbers of unemployed which appeared with the introduction of N.E.P. and continued in existence to the end of that period. According to figures issued by the Labour Exchange, registered unemployed numbered 160,000 in 1922, 641,000 in 1923, 1,240,000 in 1924, 1,017,000 in 1925–6, 1,241,000 in 1926–7 and 1,289,000 in 1927–8. The causes of this unemployment were the direct outcome of the developments which took place during the recovery period and have been described elsewhere; in particular, the gradual pace of recovery in industrial production, the need to cut down the country's administrative machinery for reasons of economy, changes in the population's social structure which resulted in a shrinking market for some professions, and above all, the influx of people from agriculturally over-populated rural areas into towns in quest of work and the establishment of unemployment relief. This unemployment was of a persistent nature and could only be overcome by a substantial expansion of construction and industrial production. The attempt to combat unemployment by traditional 'public works' methods is of some interest, as illustrating the economic ideas of certain Soviet leaders during the N.E.P. period. In an injunction of the P. Commissar of Labour, dated 18 May 1925, it was explained that 'public works are those works alone which are carried out with the sole object of providing labour assistance to the unemployed and which are financed from funds allocated by State, and local or public organizations'.* Obviously, palliatives such as public works could not eliminate persistent unemployment. It was brought to an end first formally (by stopping dole payments), and then actually, only towards the close of the second year of the first F.Y.P. Up to 1927–8 the recovery in the numbers of workers employed in the national economy as a whole and in large-scale

---

* *Bull. Financ. and Econ. Leg.* no. 4, 1925; cf. also the injunction of the P. Commissar of Labour of the R.S.F.S.R. 2 March 1927, 'On the manner of organizing and carrying out public works'. *Bull. Financ. and Econ. Leg.* no. 15, 1927.

industry in particular was only gradual, if these numbers are compared with labour employed in 1913.*

The problem of raising labour productivity became acute with
the introduction of N.E.P. It has already been mentioned that in
1920, on the eve of the introduction of N.E.P., the gross output
of large-scale industry had fallen to 12·8% of its 1913 figure,
and yet the numbers of workers employed were about 50% of the
corresponding 1913 figure. In 1921 the output per worker employed in large-scale industry was therefore roughly 2½ times less
than in 1913. A rapid rise in industrial production commenced in
1921, but the amount of labour employed grew simultaneously, so
that on the whole only towards the close of the recovery period did
the productivity of labour in large-scale industry reach its pre-war
level (see Table 21). The obstacles hampering recovery in labour

Table 21

	1913	1921	1922	1923	1924
Gross output of census industry in million roubles, 1926–7*	10,251	1,924	2,512	3,829	4,469
Workers employed in census industry (thousands)*	2,900	1,185	1,096	1,352	1,553

	1925	1926	1927	1928	1929
Gross output of census industry in million roubles, 1926–7*	7,436	10,276	12,051	14,754	18,337
Workers employed in census industry (thousands)*	1,939	2,272	2,392	2,598	2,860

* *National Economy of the U.S.S.R.; Statistical Handbook,* 1932, pp. 3, 11; *Socialist Construction in the U.S.S.R.; Statistical Yearbook,* 1934, p. 3; *The Five-Year Plan of the Economic Construction of the U.S.S.R.,* vol. 1, p. 144. The figure for 1913 covers not only workers but also employees in the census industry, while figures for the following years refer to workers only. To make them comparable, the 1913 figure should be cut down by 450 or 500 thousand, allowing for employees.

productivity were: deteriorating and worn-out equipment, poorer
quality of raw materials, decreasing utilization of production
capacity, increasing numbers of unskilled workers and employees
used on accessory work, waste of working time, the enterprises'
shortage of working capital, which led to stoppages when supplies

* In 1913 there were 11,250,000 persons in paid employment, of whom there
were 2,900,000 in large-scale industry. During the recovery period the yearly
averages of workers and employees grew as follows: whole national economy—
1924–5, 8,532,000; 1925–6, 10,173,000; 1926–7, 10,944,000; 1927–8, 11,350,000.
The corresponding figures for large-scale industry were: 2,107,000, 2,678,000,
2,839,000 and 3,072,000.

failed and caused delays in the payment of workers' and employees' wages (a condition which at one time tended to become chronic in several branches of industry), a considerable unproductive expenditure and a declining level of skill among workers; this last was due to the most able and enterprising workers either having transferred themselves to managerial, trade union or Party posts, or having left the enterprises during the civil war, and to the exodus of workers from town to country caused by the food crisis and the sharp decline of industrial production during the period of 'War Communism'.* Both labour discipline and the organization of industrial production had been unsettled by 'War Communism' and began to recover only in the course of the N.E.P. period.

The average yearly wages of workers and employees grew steadily and rapidly throughout the N.E.P. period as is shown in Table 22.† The slow recovery of labour productivity coupled with

Table 22

	1913	1923–4	1924–5	1925–6	1926–7	1928	1929
Whole national economy	—	—	450	571	624	703	800
Large-scale industry	292*	456	566	701	778	870	957

* Only *workers* in large-scale industry. All in roubles.

the rise in wages was the main reason for the high cost of industrial goods, against which numerous measures had to be directed, as we have shown in our survey of industry and home trade during the N.E.P. period. At the same time, between 1924–5 and 1926–7, the average nominal increase in wages was higher than the average increase in industrial output, estimated in current prices. This was one of the causes of the scarcity of mass consumption goods which began in those years.

Real wages of industrial workers reached the pre-war level by 1926–7 and, in 1927–8, on the eve of the introduction of the F.Y.P., they represented 122·5 % of the real 1913 wages.‡ Moreover, if to real wages are added the so-called 'socialized wages', i.e. the average per capita expenditure for social insurance, the fund for improvement of workers' living conditions, expenditure

* For further details regarding wages and labour productivity during the N.E.P. period, see Rozenfeld, *The Industrial Policy of the U.S.S.R.*; A. Rashin, *Wages during the Period of Recovery of the U.S.S.R. National Economy.*

† *Socialist Construction in the U.S.S.R., Statistical Yearbook,* 1934, p. 316.

‡ There are discrepancies in the data afforded by various statistical sources. The figure cited here is that of the Gosplan in the *Five-Year Plan of the National Economic Construction in the U.S.S.R.* vol. I, p. 146.

on housing, on trade unions' cultural services, on scholarships for workers and their children, etc.,* there can be no doubt that by the end of the recovery period industrial workers were better off, both materially and socially, than before the Revolution; and they were so both absolutely and especially in comparison with other sections of the community.

The above figures of the growth of the workers' and employees' wages, both in the national economy as a whole and in large-scale industry in particular, show clearly how much faster wages of industrial workers were growing than those of people employed in other branches of the national economy, and especially of those employed in administrative and cultural institutions. The salaries of social and cultural workers lagged noticeably behind the general pace of wage recovery. Even in the draft 'Control figures of the national economy of the U.S.S.R.' for 1928-9, i.e. the first year of the F.Y.P., it was proposed that 'in 1928-9 wages of social and cultural workers would amount to only ¾ (74%) of industrial workers' wages'.†

From the point of view of pay, the position of engineers, technicians and qualified administrative personnel was more favourable; in particular, managerial personnel could, in addition to their basic salaries, receive supplementary cash bonuses from special funds fed by deductions from profits. These bonuses were allocated for: (a) lowering cost while improving or maintaining the quality of production; (b) raising the profitableness of the enterprise without raising the prices of goods and without lowering their quality; (c) improving labour conditions without raising production costs. Similarly, employees in State and co-operative trading enterprises could receive monetary rewards, usually percentage bonuses on the enterprises' turn-over.‡ Nevertheless, on the whole the pay of engineering, technical and administrative personnel recovered at a slower pace than was the case with industrial workers' wages.

---

* In 1927-8 these socialized wages were estimated at 32% of individual wages: *The National Economy of the U.S.S.R.; Statistical Handbook*, 1932, p. 418. It is difficult to assess the exactitude of these computations, but the fact remains beyond doubt that these additional benefits were on the whole quite substantial, particularly from the social point of view.

† *Control Figures*..., p. 151.

‡ Cf. Regulation of the U.S.S.R. Central Executive Committee and of the Sovnarkom S.S.S.R., 'On the order of payment of rewards to members of managerial personnel in State enterprises and in joint-stock companies with a predominating share of State-held capital', and additional legislation on the subject, *Bull. Financ. and Econ. Leg.* nos. 13, 15 and 25, 1927.

During the N.E.P. period, and particularly during its latter years, industrial workers got a larger share of material advantages from the recovery of the national economy than did any other section of the population. Moreover, from the social standpoint they were in a certain sense first-grade citizens, whilst engineers, technicians and managerial employees were in the same sense only second-grade citizens.

During that period, the most important consideration in admission to the Party or appointments to responsible posts was the candidates' social origin and labour standing; conditions were more favourable and possibilities greater for those who came from workers' or poor peasants' families than for descendants not only of the former upper or possessing classes but even of employees. Children of engineering, technical and managerial personnel were at a disadvantage compared with workers' children for receiving a higher education. They did not themselves enjoy equal rights with workers in such matters as living space, or accommodation in rest homes and sanatoria, or for drawing insurance benefit, etc.

Moreover, managerial personnel and the rank and file of engineers and technicians had to work under conditions economically and juridically widely differing from pre-revolution conditions. According to Soviet law and particularly to Soviet legal practice, a large number of acts connected with business activity constitute economic offences; e.g. mismanagement of the business, inactivity or failure to take appropriate measures, obstruction of the normal activities of State enterprises, conclusion of agreements or contracts entailing losses to the enterprise or to the State, all were deemed offences, if they resulted in a dislocation of the smooth running of the business, or caused material damage, or disorganized the work of the public productive, supply, distributive or transport apparatus.* Legal commentators, for instance, defined business mismanagement as 'the crime of obstructing the plan for the recovery of the business or hindering its development'; 'secret sabotage consists in creating conditions or a setting which impedes the normal activities of a Soviet enterprise without any manifest or visible obstruction on the part of the saboteur; e.g. the head of an enterprise who through an apathetic and deliberately careless attitude towards his work wilfully tends not to fulfil the production plan of the enterprise entrusted to him.'† Economic crimes were

---

* *Criminal Code*, §§ 58, 109, 111, 112, 128 and 193.
† S. Kanarsky, *The Criminal Code of Soviet Republics, Text and Systematic Commentary*.

punishable by imprisonment for terms varying from six months to three years, with solitary confinement, and with or without confiscation of property; particularly serious cases entailed capital punishment (shooting) and confiscation of property. These laws came to be frequently applied against managerial and technico-engineering personnel after the memorable Shakhty trial, in March 1928, at which the outstanding coal-mining specialists were charged with fomenting a 'counter-revolutionary plot' to commit acts designed to undermine the production of the Donetz basin coal pits.

The Soviet economic press of the time was full of news items of the following kind: 'The position of managerial workers is now very difficult. Every specialist is branded as a criminal, in advance.' 'Nowadays the engineer often has to "stand to attention" and keep quiet. In such cases responsibility is of course out of the question. The necessity of keeping quiet, the impossibility of speaking one's mind and defending one's opinion is one of the most aggravating conditions of the work of a specialist in a factory.... When it is deemed necessary to accuse or attack a specialist, more often than not the charge brought against him is that he persecutes Party men. And only those who are subjected to these accusations know how difficult it is under the circumstances to defend one's good name.' 'News is coming through from many factories and works that labour discipline is deteriorating. Cases of leaving work early, coming to work drunk, of failure to attain normal output and rudeness to the technical staff are increasingly frequent. *The administration is afraid to embitter its relations with the workers.*' 'Under the present conditions the director lives under constant suspicion and persecution. For instance, proceedings have been started 27 times in the course of a year [1928] against the director of the Shaitan works on various trifling charges. The director of the Bereznikov works in the course of 8 months has been called upon 28 times to defend himself.' 'According to official statistics at every one of the large pits (at Shakhty, Donbass) every technician is to stand for trial. The morale among technicians is very low. "If you do thus you'll be brought to trial, and if you do otherwise you'll get sentenced to compulsory labour"; and their constant worry is the means of defence. Absurd things happen. A new technician is appointed to the pit. Before he has had time to get to know the job, a mishap occurs; and he, though innocent, is prosecuted.' 'The higher technical personnel finds no support among the lower grades of technicians, because they are dejected and terrified by threats of retaliation. Things have reached such a pitch that foremen beg to be shifted to ordinary work. Lately, cases of direct retaliation and physical violence have become more frequent.'*

Many more similar statements and even statistical evidence† could be quoted to show that engineering and technical personnel had to work in this atmosphere not as a rare exception but in fact very frequently. And this was one of the causes why it was proving so difficult to improve industrial management and to raise the qualitative standards of production. The working masses were intensely suspicious of the representatives of the pre-revolution engineering, technical and managerial personnel, whilst in that class itself, for many reasons, there did not always exist an entirely loyal, on the contrary there was sometimes an unco-operative and hostile attitude towards governmental measures and the new labour conditions.

These difficulties in the position of engineering, technical and managerial staffs increased, particularly in the first years of the F.Y.P., when they were called upon to carry out very strenuous plans for expanding production and organizing entirely new kinds of industrial production under difficult conditions—the absorption of masses of unskilled labour, a huge labour turn-over, lack of labour discipline and a deteriorating material condition due to 'class' differentiation against them in matters of rationing. A change in the attitude towards engineering and technical personnel came about only in 1931, after Stalin's famous speech, when a series of labour reforms were inaugurated, which will be analysed elsewhere.

* *Torgovo-promyshlennaya Gazeta*, 8 May 1928; *Ekonomicheskaya Zhizn*, 27 May 1928; *Torg-prom. Gazeta*, 13 December 1928; *Ekon. Zhizn*, 30 November 1928; cf. also similar news items in *Ekon. Zhizn*, 27 May, 2, 19 and 25 December 1928.

† Cf. e.g. statistics of disciplinary measures and sentences of hard labour in *Statistical Survey*, no. 5, 1930.

SECTION III. *PERIOD OF EXTENSIVE INDUSTRIALIZATION, COLLECTIVIZATION OF AGRICULTURE AND RATIONING*

CHAPTER X. GENERAL AIMS OF THIS PERIOD

As we have seen, N.E.P. accomplished its task of restoring the productive capacity of the country's economy and securing the predominance of the socialized sector. But at the end of the period of N.E.P. a new task arose, the task of the general reconstruction of the whole national economy. This task was embodied in the first F.Y.P. of reconstruction of the national economy. The putting into effect of this F.Y.P. called for the revision as well as reconstruction of the whole economic system which had been built up during the N.E.P. period.

The approved draft of the F.Y.P. is a publication comprising 960 pages, whilst reviews, comments and criticisms devoted to it run into thousands; we will try to withstand the temptation to add a few more dozen pages to this already voluminous literature. What we shall attempt is to set forth concisely only those principles of the F.Y.P. which it is absolutely necessary to remember for the understanding of the fundamental developments that took place in the country's economy and in the economic system of the U.S.S.R.

It was the so-called 'optimal draft' of the F.Y.P. that was eventually adopted, and not the 'initial draft' put forward for approval by the Gosplan. The initial draft was more cautious and took into account: (*a*) the possibility of a partial crop failure in the course of the five years; (*b*) the low level of foreign trade and the small increases in long-term foreign credits; (*c*) the relatively slow achievement of high-quality standards in the fields of construction, and of industrial and in particular agricultural production; (*d*) the relatively heavier burden of the defence programme for the national economy, the final scope being identical in both drafts. The optimal draft adopted assumed, on the contrary: (*a*) the absence in the course of the five years of any considerable crop failure; (*b*) a substantial expansion of foreign trade by means of greatly increased exports, and a much quicker flow of foreign long-term credits starting with the first years of the plan; (*c*) a sharp improvement in the qualitative side of the country's production, in particular during the two first years of the plan (reduction of production costs and of prices for manufactured goods, a sharp increase in the productivity of labour and a noticeable increase in crop yields); (*d*) the expenditure for defence to represent a relatively smaller share of the total expenditure.

The more cautious initial draft, with a similar scope for the re-organization of the country's economy, estimated—contrary to the optimal draft—that six years would be required to achieve it. The apprehensions expressed in the initial draft proved well grounded and were confirmed by events.

The construction of many industrial enterprises, mines, power stations, etc., included in the F.Y.P., had already started before the Plan was formally adopted and therefore independently of its financial provisos; these developments had to be continued, in any case.

The financing of industry's capital equipment was mainly based on the private accumulations of industry itself out of profits and allocations to sinking funds. Out of the planned capital investments in large-scale industry, controlled by the S.E.C., which amounted to 16,140 million roubles, 12,100 million roubles were to be obtained from profits and 3,575 million roubles to be covered by allocations to the sinking funds; that is, over 90% of all expenditure for capital investment in industry was to come from those intra-industrial accumulations. Advances from foreign credits to industry were planned to amount to 700 million roubles.

The success of this plan for financing industrialization from industry's own accumulations was dependent on a strict adherence to a programme both for the huge increase of industrial output and a simultaneous substantial reduction in the costs of industrial production. The gross output of industry as a whole was to increase annually, by 15·6% in the first year, rising to 21·4% in the last; with regard to large-scale industry, controlled by the S.E.C., the annual increase was to be 21·4% in the first year, rising to 25·2% in the last. As a result of these yearly increments the gross output of all industry in 1932–3 was to be 235·9% of the output for 1927–8, whilst that of large-scale industry, controlled by the S.E.C., was to reach 279·2% of its figure for 1927–8. A greater increase in output was planned in the means of production and a lesser in consumer goods (reaching, in 1932–3, 304% and 203% of the figures of 1927–8 respectively).

Production costs of manufactured articles were to decrease in the course of the five years by 35 %, whilst wholesale prices were to be reduced by only 24 %. The Plan was based on this annual reduction of production costs and the increase in output being both carried out to a time schedule which made possible the planned intra-industrial accumulation; in this way it was planned to secure 90 % of the money needed to finance investments in industry. To achieve such a considerable reduction in production costs, the qualitative side of work had to improve sharply and *quickly*; in particular, it was expected that the improvement in labour productivity in the course of the five years would be 110%, the decrease in the consumption of fuel 30 %, that of the construction index 50 %, etc.

Investments in industry and electrification during the five years were to amount to nearly five times the pre-revolution value of the basic capital of Russia's industry; the latter was estimated in 1913 at some 3·5 milliard roubles, whilst the investments in industry and electrification were to aggregate during the five years 15·6 milliard roubles (reckoned at their 1913 value). Thus, capital construction in industry was planned on an enormous scale, and the projects for capital construction in some branches of industry were the most thoroughly elaborated part of the Plan. They were not mere statistical calculations of a proposed increase of industrial production, or of improvement in the quality of work, or of financial resources for the Plan, etc., but actual plans for building definite power stations, factories, works, pits, etc. Moreover, much of the new building was to take the shape of 'huge electro-chemico-metallurgical combinats', that is, of groups of interdependent enterprises. If one member of the combinat was being built, it was necessary to carry out the construction of the other links, otherwise there was nothing to be gained from building the individual enterprise. Here lay one of the dangers of the Plan's construction programme, the more so since the fundamental objects of capital construction were enterprises of heavy industry, the output of which would come into use only long after they had begun building. Out of the total sum of 13·5 milliard roubles to be invested in the basic funds of industry controlled by the S.E.C., 9·8 milliard roubles were allotted to the output of means of production and only 2·9 milliards to that of consumer goods. Of the total funds invested in industry, 31·8 % was to be invested in the basic fields of metallurgy and machine-building, 17·6% in fuel, 10·4% in chemical, and 7·1 % in the building materials industries. As the essential aim of the F.Y.P. was to build heavy industrial plants, it was quite natural to expect that, should there be delays or curtailment in the funds available for capital construction, it would be the plans for the capital construction of industries manufacturing consumption goods that would be cut down, and not the plans affecting the heavy industry.

The success of the Plan depended not only on an exact achievement of the material and financial programme, but also entailed the tremendous task of training qualified personnel. To give but one instance: it was necessary to train for industry alone in the course of the five years 25,200 engineers, as against the 20,200 at the disposal of industry in 1927–8. Moreover, 'It was necessary to expand the practice of calling in foreign experts for all large-scale construction and so to organize it that the experts' survey would be a school for the young cadres of constructors in our country.'

Lastly, it must be emphasized that though the plan for the development of industry was the principal part of the F.Y.P., it was nevertheless only a part of the general plan for the development of the country's economy. The total sum to be invested in the country's whole economy during the five years was 64·5 milliard roubles, out of which only 16·4 milliards were earmarked for large-scale industry, 23·3 were allocated to agriculture, 3·8 to electrification, 9·9 to transport, 2·2 to home trade, 2·0 to education, 2·2 to municipal services and 5·9 to housing in urban areas. Here again the danger lay in the fact that should industry fail to achieve the financial plans, its construction plans would be carried out at the expense of other branches of the country's economy; in particular, at the expense of allocations for the reconstruction of transport, municipal services and housing, because investments in these branches were to come more or less exclusively from the socialized sector of the national economy, i.e. from moneys going through the channels of the State Budget and the State credit system.

In order rightly to understand the essence of the F.Y.P. and to appreciate all that was involved in its execution, one more important fact should be noted. At the time, the majority of serious critics of the F.Y.P. drew attention to the difficulties enumerated above and the dangers lying in the path of its successful fulfilment as far as industry was concerned. Many of these critics, including the author of the present study, supposed that the planners and the Soviet Government who approved the Plan had overlooked these difficulties and dangers. However, examining the facts in their historical perspective, we are driven to the conclusion that these difficulties and dangers were on the whole fully understood and appreciated not only by the authors of the Plan,* but also by the leading members of the Soviet Government,† and that nevertheless they decided to carry out the Plan in defiance of both difficulties and dangers.

The task set to the planning institutions was merely: (a) to work out a plan for the reconstruction of the country's economy and in particular to create new branches of industrial production requisite for a highly developed heavy and defence industry in the shortest possible time, and to embody these tasks in concrete objects for new construction and for the reconstruction of existing enterprises; and

* The authors of the Plan frankly admitted: 'One cannot shut one's eyes to the fact that from the point of view of planning, research, choice of sites, and also of qualified and trustworthy construction cadres, the programme of electrification, particularly considering the shortness of time, is insufficiently assured....There is no need to stress the special difficulties in the construction and production programmes of the oil industry. It is sufficient to indicate that in the programme for oil production, 4·5 million tons are to come from yet unprospected areas....One cannot underestimate the tremendous difficulties of the construction programme of the coal industry. It is sufficient to indicate that this programme is far from being secured by trustworthy exploitative prospecting, that practically no projects are yet at hand for the proposed series of large new pits and that the available technical forces of the Donetz basin are inadequate to carry out this programme within the strict time limits on which depends the country's uninterrupted fuel supply. However, this programme is a minimum and is *absolutely essential* to ensure the country's industrial development which is the leading idea of both drafts of the F.Y.P.' 'The country's five-year economic plan has to be approved and examined under particularly unfavourable prospects. Influenced by these unfavourable prospects some are apt to doubt the expediency of approving the prospective plan at the present moment. Our adversaries raise a great outcry about the obvious contradictions between the scope of the F.Y.P.'s constructive and productive tasks and the nature of the difficulties of the present juncture.' *Five-Year Plan...*, vol. I, pp. 29, 32, 36 and 38. 'The financing of this plan is like putting a steel ring on consumption', *Planned Economy*, no. 3, 1929, p. 283.

† 'Our plans suffer from a too statistical and an economically too generalized approach and often lack a thoroughly thought out and up-to-date technical basis. Too many of our controversies centre on how much money should be given to this or that plan and neglect discussing the technical basis' (Rykov). 'Planning of new construction was in many cases not up to the mark, and the technical and economic foundations often suffered from being out of touch with reality. The cost of construction in many cases falls wide of the mark of estimated suppositions.' 'The country proved able to mobilize large sums for capital construction, but on checking up, it was found that we are incapable of building well.' 'The effects of new enterprises do not come up to our expectations' (Mikoyan), *Ekonomicheskaya Zhizn*, 24 and 29 February and 2 and 18 March 1928; *Torgovo-promyshlennaya Gazeta...*, 14 March 1928.

(b) to indicate the economic and financial ways by which these tasks could be carried out, provided certain *tremendous efforts* were made by the population. The Soviet Government acted on the assumption that without a speedy reconstruction of the country's economy it would be impossible to solve those ideological problems for the sake of which the Revolution had been made; therefore a maximum endeavour to carry out this strenuous plan demanding stupendous efforts both from the Government and the population *must* be made, even in the face of those difficulties and dangers which were inherent in the adopted plan, and though they foresaw the possible necessity of modifying and adapting the Plan itself as well as the modes of its realization. It was expected that by mobilizing 'the creative efforts of the great masses of the population' many difficulties could be overcome and the desired *fundamental* results would be achieved. This element of *utmost endeavour* in the first F.Y.P. must be borne in mind when analysing the events that followed in the development of the U.S.S.R. economy.

The approved Plan covered all the fields of national economy; yet only the main points were worked out concretely and in detail. Even the plan for the development of industry, which had been worked out in greater detail than any other part of the F.Y.P., did not embrace all industry, nor even all large-scale industry, but only such industry as was controlled by the S.E.C. Thus, the Plan comprised parts very unevenly prepared: the general Plan referred to all industry, a somewhat more thoroughly worked out plan covered large-scale or so-called 'census' industry, the output of which accounted for 76 % of all industrial production, and lastly a really detailed plan was available for the industry controlled by the S.E.C.; the output of the latter amounted to 75 % of that of the whole 'census' industry. In drafting the plan for the development of industry, the planning organs had not only to take into account general governmental instructions and those of the central economic organs, but were under pressure from local interests— 'the working plans of the preliminary and capital work were in fact the outcome of collecting the desiderata of "localities". In sorting out the applications of localities for inclusion, a large part was played by data regarding the preparedness for such or such construction and also by the degree of activity of local communities.'* In consequence many cases occurred where projects, the technical case for which was accepted at 'face value' by the central authority

---

* *Industry according to Materials of the Central Control Commission of the C.P. and P. Commissariat of the Workers' and Peasants' Inspection*, p. 39.

without sufficient examination, were included in the Plan with a resulting loss of balance in the local distribution of new enterprise. These circumstances must also be borne in mind in appreciating individual facts which were mentioned in the Soviet press as 'breaches in the execution of the Plan'.

CHAPTER XI. INDUSTRY

Let us now consider what was taking place in industry after the adoption of this strenuous Plan for the development of industrial production.

We have seen that already, during the last two years of the recovery period, considerable investments were made in large-scale industry at the expense of the State Budget and partly at the expense of the credit system's funds. Considerable imports of equipment and raw materials for industry had taken place, and the numbers of workers employed by large-scale industry had increased. In the first year of the F.Y.P. the financing of industry from the State Budget and through the channels of the credit system expanded sharply, and so did imports of industrial equipment and raw materials, whilst the amount of labour in industry and on construction work also substantially increased. Even before the F.Y.P. was approved, industry had been set the task of expanding industrial production by 19% (*Control Figures of the National Economy of the U.S.S.R. for* 1928–9).

As a result of these measures, industry succeeded not only in fulfilling its set task of expansion of output but even exceeded it. Instead of the 19% increase planned by the Control Figures for large-scale industry or the 21·4% increase demanded for the first year by the F.Y.P., the actual increase amounted to 23·7%. Industry succeeded also in bringing down production costs by 4·2% as against the Plan's target figure of 7%.* However, this expansion in production was accompanied by a considerable deterioration in quality. The official governmental report emphasized that 'with regard to quality a definitely unsatisfactory position was observed already during the last years, but in 1928–9 it deteriorated very noticeably. Numerous complaints from con-

---

* Cf. the very interesting analysis of the correlation between the reductions of production costs in various industries in 1928–9 and the degree of renovation of their basic production funds: *Planned Economy*, no. 1, 1931.

sumers, trade and co-operative organizations, departments and industrial enterprises testify to the sharp decline in the quality of manufactured goods.'* In the Soviet economic press the explanation given for such an unsatisfactory position with regard to the quality of manufactured goods was the following:

Defects in the organization of the manufacturing processes at factories and works, lax organization of both the factory's productive-technical control and control of design, bad arrangements in the reception and processing of semi-finished and finished articles, absence of personal and material responsibility in the first place of the factory management and then of every individual worker, low standards of laboratory and testing work, lack of care among managerial and technical staffs for the qualitative course of technological processes, careless preparation of raw and other materials for the production processes, misunderstood and misapplied rationalization measures leading to over-simplification and over-drastic curtailment of individual processing operations, and also the reduction of production costs by an unthinking reduction of expenses essential to the production of standard quality goods.†

Two very significant factors are omitted from this enumeration: (a) the strain of the production expansion programme which forced the managements of enterprises—because their work was judged by the degree to which this programme was fulfilled—to concentrate on quantity, even if quality was deliberately lowered (e.g. by manufacturing narrower fabrics of simplified design and colouring, extracting coal and iron ore with an excessive amount of stone, smelting steel of inferior quality); (b) the shortage of properly qualified and responsible managerial and technical workers, particularly in new enterprises (cf. above, measures taken

* A year of the Government's work: *The First Year of the Five-Year Plan*, 1928–9, p. 155. Let us quote a few more significant statements: 'The drive to fulfil the quantitative tasks without simultaneous efforts to improve qualitative indices has found its reflexion also in the system of the Supreme Economic Council. It is now years since questions of quality have been systematically kept off the agenda and are solved amateurishly and only occasionally' (*Torgovo-promyshlennaya Gazeta*, 24 September 1930). 'The fact that the quality of production has deteriorated is no longer disputed....Our expectations that the dearth of goods would subside in connexion with the large expansion of production during 1928–9 are also far from coming true, because in many branches of the light industry the decline in the quality of production has reached the point at which the usefulness to consumers of the growing bulk of production no longer increases but declines' (*Torgovo-promyshlennaya Gazeta*, 24 September 1930). Cf. the very interesting attempt at evaluating the qualitative deterioration of some consumer goods in quantitative indices, in *Economic Review*, October 1929.

† *Torgovo-promyshlennaya Gazeta*, 8 October and 1 November 1929.

to enforce personal management). In 1929 in industry 43·7 % of the posts requiring higher technical training were held by people without any special technical qualifications, the so-called 'practicals', i.e. persons doing practical work in the corresponding branch of production without having undergone any theoretical instruction in the subject, whilst 59·7 % of the posts requiring secondary technical training were similarly filled by such 'practicals'.

Nevertheless, as already stated, the plan for the quantitative expansion of production in the first year of the F.Y.P. was on the whole exceeded. This success prompted an increase in the gross output of 32·1 % in 1929–30 instead of the 21·5 % increase proposed by the approved draft of the F.Y.P. It was hoped to reach such a high target for the expansion of production not so much because of an increase in the productive possibilities of enterprises following the expansion of industry's basic capital during 1927–8 to 1928–9, as because of an intensified utilization of the enterprises' productive possibilities. The number of workers employed in industry and on construction work was considerably increased, a campaign was started to promote workers, including women, to responsible posts, the campaign for a 'Socialist competition' was inaugurated, in August 1929 it was decided to adopt the non-stop week in enterprises and institutions, and a number of other labour measures were introduced (see pp. 213–18).

Grants to finance the development of industrial construction and of production increased steeply. Through the State Budget, 2,045 million roubles were allocated to industry as against 972 million roubles in 1928–9 and 650 million roubles in 1927–8, mainly from the huge funds provided by State loans (see Table, p. 95). The financing of industry by banks also increased, in particular through an increased note circulation (see Table 14, p. 104). Imports of industrial equipment and raw materials rose substantially in spite, and perhaps because, of the world crisis which had set in. The latter created serious difficulties for Soviet exports, but facilitated the placing of Soviet import orders and of obtaining foreign, though mostly short-term, credits.

As a result, industrial production made another leap forward— the gross output of large-scale industry increased by 24·2 %, in 1929–30.* Actually the year's planned target for the expansion of production was far from reached, but nevertheless the increase was

* There are discrepancies in the data provided by various Soviet statistical sources with regard to the increase of gross production, but these discrepancies are slight (1–3 %) and can be overlooked in the present study.

considerably above the average annual level proposed by the
F.Y.P. (21·5%). Moreover, the output of oil and of several
branches of the machine-building industry exceeded the planned
targets. Least successful of all, and lagging far behind the planned
increases, was the development of light industry; in particular, the
manufacture of cotton textiles even declined as compared with
1928–9.

Industry as a whole succeeded in reducing production costs of
manufactured goods, though far less drastically than had been
planned, with the result that the financial plan, which was based on
the reduction of costs being carried out to a time schedule, was not
fulfilled. According to a statement by the chairman of the S.E.C.
(Ordzhonikidze): 'This year [1929–30] we did not fulfil the task
of reducing production costs. Money ran out and we had to
borrow more than a milliard roubles from the bank.'*

The quality of manufactured goods continued to deteriorate
during the second year of the F.Y.P., and this deterioration was
caused more and more by the strain due to demands for expanding
industrial production.† In October 1930, an All-Union 'Quality'
Conference was held in Moscow in connexion with an exhibition
of rejected articles and mass consumption goods of substandard
quality from practically every branch of production.

However, enthusiasm for quantitative achievements was prevalent in the early years of the Plan. Many targets for the expansion
of industrial production confirmed by the F.Y.P. were reconsidered in the light of the successes achieved during the first and
second years of the Plan, and were altered in the sense of further
increases. The slogan 'the F.Y.P. fulfilled in four years' was put
forward.‡ A special plan was approved, the so-called 'special
quarter of 1930', i.e. the last quarter of 1930 which was to bridge
over the transitional quarter from the 'economic year' hitherto in
operation (from October to October of the following year) to the
normal calendar year; and the increase in industrial production

---

* *Za Industrializatsiu*, 2 February 1930.

† '1929–30, compared with the first year of the Plan and with the preceding
year, shows a deterioration in the quality of production in the basic branches of
industry.... This deterioration, particularly in the leading and key branches of
industry (coal, metal, machine-building, textiles, etc.) leads, owing to their
internal links and interdependence, to deterioration and disorganization in the
work of other branches of industry.' *Planned Economy*, no. 9, 1930, pp. 85–6.

‡ In particular, instead of the planned target of 10 million tons of pig iron
by the end of the five-year period, it was decided to aim at 17 million tons.
Izvestia, 28 September 1930, 7 and 9 December 1930.

for this quarter was to amount to 38·5 % of the figure for the corresponding quarter of the previous year. The quarter was proclaimed a 'shock' quarter in the expansion of production. Actually it proved possible to increase gross industrial production by only 16·7 %. However, an extra increase in industrial production was planned for 1931—production was to rise by 42·1 % in the course of 1931, instead of the 23·8 % increase demanded by the F.Y.P. for the year 1931–2. This strenuous task set to industrial production was the practical expression of the slogan: the F.Y.P. fulfilled in four years.

At the All-Union Conference of Industrial Workers, which was held in February 1931, a resolution was passed demanding

that the task of reducing production costs be made the concern of individual workshops, groups and workers, and that definite tasks be set to every worker, based on an annual plan of concrete rationalization measures; the S.E.C. to take proceedings against managerial staffs who reduced cost price by a deterioration in the quality and range of goods.*

Moreover, as another contributory measure for reducing production costs, the S.E.C. was instructed 'to enforce, by 1 September 1931, the adoption of piece-rate work in not less than 75 % of production'.† In its plan for 1931, the S.E.C. emphasized that

the reduction of the cost of production is the main qualitative task of the plan. Hitherto the attention and energy of managerial personnel, shock-workers, engineers and technical workers was focused more or less exclusively on the quantitative execution of the production programme. Inadmissible cases have occurred time and again when the reduction in cost price was achieved by lowering the quality of production. This must definitely cease. It must be remembered that every unfulfilled 1 % of reduction in industrial production costs deprives the proletarian State of 160–180 million roubles of socialist accumulation.‡

However, as shown above, the conditions of industrial organization which prevailed during those years of the Plan, developments in the home market, the position with regard to skilled and unskilled labour, and, not least, the extremely strenuous tasks of expanding industrial production, were so many factors adversely affecting the execution of these categorical demands to reduce production costs. In 1931, it again proved possible to expand production, quantitatively, by 20·5 %. Actually, this

* *Za Industrializatsiu*, 20 February 1931.
† Ibid. 3 June 1931.
‡ Regulation of the Supreme Economic Council, 30 January 1931, *Bull. Financ. and Econ. Leg.* no. 6, 1931.

expansion represented only 48·7 % of the target set by the annual plan for expanding production, and for the first time since the introduction of the F.Y.P. it fell below the increase proposed by the F.Y.P. for 1931–2 (23·8 %). Nevertheless, an absolute and very substantial increase had again been achieved.

At the same time, instead of the planned 8 % reduction on production costs, industry's average production costs rose by 6 % during the year. It was under the stress of these production costs results that Stalin, in 1931, made his statement that 'managerial staffs have long ceased to reckon, to calculate and to draw up a genuine balance sheet of income and expenditure'; reforms followed in industrial administration, and measures were taken to prepare for the abolition of rationing, to alter the technique of industrial credits, to enforce labour discipline and to raise its productivity. None the less, the quality of manufactured goods continued to deteriorate.* In spite of this unsatisfactory position on the qualitative side an increase of 38·2 % in gross industrial production was planned for 1932 as against 25·2 % proposed by the F.Y.P. for 1932–3; the reduction in production costs was to reach 7 %.

Industrial results for 1932 were less satisfactory than those for the previous 3⅓ years covered by the Plan. The production of big industry increased, according to some sources by 8 % and to others by 11 %, whilst production costs rose instead of decreasing; apart from this statement, no figures of the actual rise were given. According to an official statistical summary of the Central Board of National Economic Accounting of the U.S.S.R., the industrial plan for the gross production of large-scale ('census') industry had been carried out as shown in Table 23.† When they appeared, these figures aroused a number of questions among many authors, including the author of the present work. In the first place, there was the question as to the method used in calculating gross production

---

* 'Information collected by "brigades" of the S.E.C. which inspected a number of enterprises in the coal, coke and metallurgical industries reveals that in regard to quality the position is not satisfactory in these industries....Data from the metallurgical industry shows a sharp deterioration in the quality of metallurgical production in 1931 in comparison with the special quarter and the previous years. The output of substandard metal which does not conform to the set analytic test increases from year to year and from month to month.' *Za Industrialisatsiu*, 2 December 1931.

† *Summary of the Fulfilment of the First Five-Year Plan for the development of the National Economy of the U.S.S.R.* Moscow, 1933, p. 254. Unless otherwise stated, figures referring to the planned and fulfilled tasks are taken from that source.

Table 23

	In milliard roubles in fixed prices of 1926–7			1932 as % of	
	1928	1932	Planned by the F.Y.P. for 1932–3	1928	1932–3
All industry	15·7	34·3	36·6	218·5	93·7
Group A (means of production)	7·0	18·0	17·4	257·1	103·4
Group B (consumer goods)	8·7	16·3	19·2	187·3	84·9

in the so-called fixed prices of 1926–7. Many lines of production, in particular in the machine-building industry (the output of which according to official data had risen from 1·822 milliard roubles in 1928—in 1926–7 prices—to 7·363 milliard roubles in 1932), were only first introduced in the U.S.S.R. after 1928. How had the figures for the production of industries, which were non-existent in 1926–7, been calculated in that year's prices? Unfortunately, no explanation on the subject ever appeared in the Soviet economic press. Another question was raised by the fact that the published data regarding the fulfilment of the F.Y.P. referred only to large-scale ('census') industry, whereas the original F.Y.P. provided also for the development of small-scale industry, and therefore it was intended to raise the *total* gross production from 18·3 milliard roubles, the figure for 1927–8, to 43·2 milliard roubles in 1932–3. Unfortunately, no statistical information regarding the fate of small-scale industry during the years covered by the first Plan were ever published. However, taking into consideration: (1) that small-scale industry was mainly in private hands at the time when the F.Y.P. was introduced; (2) that the purchase of stocks of raw materials was monopolized by State and co-operative supply organizations and that even large-scale industry often found difficulty in expanding production owing to shortage of raw materials, particularly of raw materials for the manufacture of mass consumption goods; (3) that rationing prevailed throughout the national economy as well as a highly centralized system for distributing all available raw and auxiliary materials—there are good reasons to suppose that the output of small-scale industry considerably decreased during the years covered by the first F.Y.P. Moreover, the production of small-scale industry consisted more or less entirely of mass-consumption goods. Another objection to these summary figures regarding the fulfilment of the F.Y.P. is that they confound figures showing the growing output of large-scale industry manufacturing consumer goods with a corresponding increase in the supply of these goods to the population. Actually, however, an expansion of production only meant that the given articles were manufactured on a growing scale at large factories instead of being, as formerly, made at small enterprises, by craftsmen or at home. The following instances afford a good illustration: whilst the output of the large-scale food industry rose from 1·544 milliard roubles in 1928 to 3·485 milliard roubles in 1932, it is a known fact that the production of basic agricultural produce (e.g. grain, vegetables, products from livestock and poultry) in 1932 was below the 1928 level; similarly, the output of footwear by large-scale industry grew from 29,588,000 pairs in 1928 to 84,749,000 pairs in 1932, yet the numbers of cattle and consequently the resources of raw hides in 1932 were far below those available in 1928; moreover, this kind of raw material was not imported but on the contrary exported because of the adverse trade balance and the need to import industrial equipment. Obviously, if in 1928 a greater total quantity of raw hides was worked by small enterprises and craftsmen and big factories together, whilst in 1932, out of a smaller total quantity of raw hides a greater proportion was processed at large factories, it does not follow that the supply of footwear to the population had consequently increased. Unfortunately, similar confusions have often been made both by Soviet and by foreign writers.

Whatever the explanation of the difficulties mentioned in the figures of the F.Y.P. in the field of industry, the fact remains beyond dispute that quantitatively, during the years covered by the F.Y.P., industrial production did increase and very substantially. The fulfilment of planned tasks had admittedly been very uneven. Whilst, for instance, the output of industries manufacturing machinery and electrical equipment totalled 157 % of the amount demanded by the F.Y.P. for 1932–3, the output of heavy metallurgy (pig iron, steel, rolled metal) was only 67·7 %, that of the coal industry 89·2 %, that of the chemical industry 73·6 % and the production of consumer goods only 73·5 % of the respective planned quantities.*

Such an uneven expansion of industrial production created not only delays in the development of the more progressive branches of production, but often led to the manufacture of incompletely finished articles, or to changes in standards, and made it impossible

* For more detailed data on the movement of industrial production see p. 307.

fully to utilize productive capacities. It should be remembered that many of the large new enterprises were complex industrial combinations. Consequently, the first F.Y.P. bequeathed to the next the problem of organizing a normal and smooth co-ordination of individual industries. Moreover, it bequeathed a good deal of incompleted capital construction, as is illustrated by the figures in Table 24.*

Table 24

	In million roubles of the corresponding years		
	Expenditure on capital investments	In production	Incompleted construction
All large-scale industry	24,789	15,728	9,061
Of which: Group A	21,292	13,214	8,078
Group B	3,497	2,514	983

According to the F.Y.P. it was intended to invest a total of 19·1 milliard roubles, 14·7 milliards of which were allocated to the production of means of production. Nominally, in the course of the $4\frac{1}{3}$ years, investments exceeded the initial figure in large-scale industry as a whole by nearly 30 %, and by as much as 45 % in heavy industry. It is, however, known that prices rose continuously throughout the five-year period, and no comparison of the planned figures and the figures of actual expenditure is valid without allowing for changes in the price index. Unfortunately, Soviet statistical sources, as already mentioned, stopped publishing price indices in 1931. Even allowing for the increase in prices, however, it is clear that huge investments were made, and that 86 % of all investments were directed to heavy industry, while investments in consumption goods' industries were even at their nominal value below the planned figures.

The financing of such considerable investments in industry was made possible by the organization of the home market and of State finance in the manner already described. Materially, capital construction could be carried out thanks to the steady growth of labour employed on construction work (the number of workers and employees employed on construction grew from 723,000 in 1928 to 3,126,000 in 1932), to huge imports and, in the later years of the F.Y.P., also to home-produced equipment for the heavy and building industries.

* *Draft of the Second Five-Year Plan for the Development of the National Economy of the U.S.S.R.* vol. I, p. 422.

Nevertheless, a considerable part of the construction programme remained unfinished when the F.Y.P. came to an end. The need to complete this programme and to eliminate the discrepancies which had arisen in industrial production were among the compelling reasons for drafting another plan for the next five years. To conclude this brief and summary review of the fundamental developments in industry in the years of the first F.Y.P., one more fact needs stressing. In order to complete the quantitative programme in industrial production and still more in construction, a much greater number of workers and employees had had to be recruited than stipulated for by the F.Y.P. The number of workers and employees on construction work was 66 %, and those engaged in large-scale industry 57·1 %, above the planned figures. The total wages bill of all workers and employees employed in the national economy in 1932 was 208·4 % of the figure planned for 1932–3 and 404·4 % of 1928. These figures of workers and salaried employees and wages throw an additional light on the developments on the home market in the field of finance previously described, especially when it is recalled that a considerable part of the planned capital construction still remained unfinished after the F.Y.P. had come to an end, that the planned provisions for gross industrial production had only been fulfilled to the extent of 93·7 % and those of consumer goods—even taking large-scale industry alone into account—of only 84·9 %, while agricultural production as a whole declined during those years.

Unquestionably, it proved possible during the years covered by the first Plan to achieve in the aggregate a great expansion of productive capacity and of production itself. But it was admitted in the official reports of the results of the F.Y.P.: 'In the period of the F.Y.P. we succeeded in organizing enthusiasm and fervour for new construction, and achieved decisive successes....But that is not enough. Now we must supplement this with enthusiasm and fervour for *mastering* the new factories and the new technique, for a substantial rise in the productivity of labour and for a substantial reduction of production costs. *This is the main point at present*' (underlined by Stalin).* 'In the course of the second F.Y.P. we must focus our main efforts not on the quantitative growth of production but on improving the quality of production and on the growth of labour productivity in industry.'†

* Stalin, *Leninism*, p. 378.

† Report by Molotov, chairman of the Sovnarkom S.S.S.R., *Izvestia*, 12 January 1933.

We have seen that in the years immediately preceding the F.Y.P. the organs charged with planning and regulating the national economy tended more and more to interfere in market relations; the number of measures increased dealing with price-fixing, stocks of raw materials, sales of manufactured goods and credit operations, and financing expansion in the national economy from State funds. The 'commercial accountancy' of trusts and syndicates tended more and more towards a 'khozraschet', i.e. the fulfilment of commitments to increase production, lower production costs, improve the quality of goods, decrease managerial charges and expenditure on raw and other materials, under a general plan. From 1927 to 1928 wholesale (transfer) prices diverged more and more from commercial prices which existed on the non-controlled part of the market, and at the same time (1928) the S.E.C. began to place orders with production trusts for definite quantities of goods at definite prices. Moreover, from 1928 onwards, in order to provide encouragement for the development of particularly favoured branches of heavy industry, a dual price system for manufactured goods came into use, i.e. (1) differential prices for settling accounts between syndicates and industry, based on planned production costs; (2) uniform commercial prices for transactions between syndicates and the retail distributing system (see below, pp. 292-3). From 1928 to 1929 onwards, the trade in agricultural produce and foodstuffs was also reorganized and rationed supply substituted for the free market; free trading in foodstuffs and in mass-consumption goods was in the process of liquidation, being replaced by controlled supplies at fixed prices (see p. 234). Industrial enterprises were again deprived of the controlling influence of market conditions and of the free play of supply and demand. And the Sixteenth Party Conference in May 1929, at which the introduction of the F.Y.P. for the reconstruction of national economy was discussed, resolved that:

the fulfilment of the tasks confronting the Soviet people in regard to accelerated industrialization...calls for a systematic overhaul of the whole government administrative machinery, so as to bring it into line with our national economic system and the needs of socialist construction...it is necessary to take steps to transform the S.E.C. from the organ of economic planning which it has hitherto mainly been, into an organ of actual technical administration of industry...at the same time it is necessary to strengthen economic initiative in factories, works and individual workshops while reinforcing the part played by the trust in regard to the technical reconstruction of enterprises.*

* *Instructions of the C.P. on Economic Questions*, pp. 524-5.

It was decided to reorganize the administration of industry on the following basis:*

I. *The enterprise* must be the basic unit in industrial administration. Therefore the provision of the technical requirements of the enterprise, its proper supply organization, the efficient organization of its work, effective control of production, the selection of managerial staff with proper qualifications, and adequate internal independence for the individual enterprises—are the prerequisites of further improvement in the management of socialist industry. While scrupulously observing the productive and financial duties and limits imposed upon it by the general plan, an enterprise must be independent. Its management has sole responsibility for executing the production plan. A definite sum of money, *the amount of which is to be fixed annually by the industrial and financial plan*, is placed at its disposal. The *contract* to which the enterprise works, based on the industrial-financial plan, establishes the *estimated production cost* for the year and the respective fines in case of infringement of the contract stipulations.

II. *The Combine.* The present system of Glavki no longer corresponds with the requirements of the reconstruction period, particularly in matters of technical management. On the other hand, syndicates have gradually taken control of the actual management of the branches of industry with which they are concerned, and the majority have to deal with questions of production programme, capital construction, planning supply, distribution, etc. Consequently the work of a number of syndicates duplicates that of Glavki. Therefore, it is necessary *to liquidate the Chief Administrations* and to form industrial managements corresponding with the syndicates and working on the principles of 'khozraschet'.

The function of these combines is

to plan production, to plan and direct capital construction, to manage the technical side of one branch or another as a whole, to organize sales and supplies, to control commercial and financial activities, labour, the training and placing of trained personnel, and the appointment and dismissal of the managerial staffs of enterprises. Three types of combines in different branches of industry are being formed: (*a*) Combines confined to enterprises and trusts of All-Union importance. Such combines manage all the activities of affiliated industrial units in accordance with their functions as set out above. (*b*) Combines comprising enterprises of All-Union and also enterprises of local importance. Where enterprises and trusts are of All-Union importance, combines are to have the same functions as class (*a*) combines; where enterprises are of importance solely to a particular republic, combines assume the functions of

---

* The quotation of long extracts from this resolution is justified here, because of the concise description it gives of the actual position and the difficulties which confronted industrial administration in the years preceding the reform and also because it explains the essentials of the reform better than a general statement.

syndicates, with the addition of the following: planning of production and capital construction, general technical direction of rationalization and reconstruction, and the supervision of the training of skilled personnel. (c) Combines formed by enterprises and trusts of solely republican and local importance. In this case, combines assume only syndical functions to which are added: general inter-republican planning of production and capital construction, and the supervision of rationalization and, in particular, of technical reconstruction.

The combines' main task is to direct the technical-productive work of their affiliated enterprises and trusts. The technical direction of a combine must be organized on *functional* lines [as will be shown below, the application of this functional principle to technical reconstruction led in fact to an excessive subdivision of the management of technical processes among small sections of the special departments of the combines].

III. *The Trusts.* Enterprises may join the combines, when established, either through the intermediary of the trust, or directly. The trust must concentrate on the *technical direction* of reconstruction and, generally speaking, will *be deprived of sale and supply functions*. The trust's technical management is to be primarily based on the functional principle.

IV. *The Supreme Economic Council* must mainly focus its attention on drafting production and financial plans for the development of industry and its technical reconstruction, on co-ordinating the work of various branches of industry, on formulating principles for the current planning and control of industry, on supervising the execution of plans, and on staffing and training organs of management and control. The S.E.C. appoints and dismisses the managing bodies of combines, audits their balance sheets and accounts, allocates profits and losses, authorizes the expenditure of special funds, confirms statutes and statutory capital, examines and investigates the activities of combines, and fixes sale prices.*

After this reorganization of industry in 1929, the hierarchy of industrial administration was as follows: Praesidium of the S.E.C.; planning and technical, and economic administrations; three types of combines; the trust; the enterprise.

At the close of 1929 a decree of the Central Committee of the Communist Party concerning 'measures to improve the administration of production and to establish unity of control' was addressed to 'all Party organizations and all Party members'; this decree pointed out that

in spite of great achievements in industry, we have not yet secured the necessary order in the administration of enterprises: there is no sufficiently clear-cut and definite separation of functions and duties of the various factory organizations—between director, factory committee and Party cell. Cases of Party and trade union intervention in decisions

* *Instructions of the C.P. on Economic Questions*, pp. 641–6.

taken by the management about the work of the factory still occur. This leads to spasmodic and often wrong decisions in business matters, to mistakes and failures in the direction and management of the enterprise which are hushed up by Party cells and factory committees, and to a general decrease of the director's responsibility. On the other hand, there have been cases of an intolerant attitude of factory managements to Party and trade union organizations, when decisions taken by Party cells and factory committees, though legitimate and in accord with Party instructions, have been bureaucratically ignored, while industrial initiatives of the working masses were similarly ignored...the Party has more than once passed resolutions aimed at enforcing personal management in enterprises...this must be closely associated with the further development of the creative initiative and greater activity of the working masses in organizing and managing production. Henceforth:

(1) In organizing managements, it must be borne in mind that the *administration (the director) is directly* responsible for the carrying out of the financial-production plan and for all matters of production. The administration (director) is in charge of the administrative machinery as well as of all technical processes of the enterprise. All his orders affecting the functioning of the works are unconditionally binding on his subordinate administrative staff and on all workers whatever their standing in Party, trade union or other organizations. The administration of the enterprise directly appoints all the managerial and technical personnel, and in the relationship between director and workshop administration it is necessary to aim at broadening the rights of and affording a wider scope for the workshop administration, allowing it the right to choose the workshop's administrative and technical staff (foreman, 'brigade', etc.). When appointing or dismissing a worker the administration must take into account the opinion of Party and trade union organizations; if the latter disapprove of an appointment or dismissal, they are entitled to appeal against it to the higher Party, trade union or economic organ; but in the meantime the administration's decision holds good. The administration of an enterprise or workshop, whilst taking all necessary measures to enforce production discipline at the works, must at the same time harmonize their methods of organization and administration with the necessity of developing the creative capacity of the working masses, and introducing them to a share in the management of industry; proposals by them must be taken into account and use must be made of any that have been accepted, while the workers' initiative and inventiveness in proposing improvements must be encouraged in every way, and a sympathetic attitude should be adopted to their needs and to their criticisms of faulty technique or management.

(2) *The trade union organization* inside enterprises, whilst standing up for and defending the daily cultural, living and economic claims of workers, must at the same time energetically foster their interest in production and their initiative. Factory committees must take an active part—in particular at their production conferences—in discussing and working out the details of the main problems of production, of industrial and financial plans and measures of reconstruction in the enterprise;

they should see that suitable proposals made by workers are put into effect, and should collaborate in the rationalization of production and in improving the organization of labour, etc. Whilst regularly hearing the management's reports, studying materials relative to production and making reports thereon, the trade union organizations must not, however, intervene directly in the management of the enterprise and certainly not substitute themselves for the administration; on the contrary, they should in every way contribute to enforcing unity of control.

(3) *Party cells*, which are the foundation of the Party, particularly in enterprises, must take the lead in the political and economic life of the factory in order to ensure that the trade union and economic organs carry out the Party's instructions, but nevertheless they should not interfere in the details of the trade union or director's work, and particularly in the management's decisions affecting the functioning of the undertaking. The Party cell must contribute actively towards enforcing the principle of individual responsibility throughout the whole system of industrial administration. In no case should Party cells take the place of the administration in appointing the subordinate administrative staff; it is even less admissible that they should interfere with the administration's decisions regarding the placing of workers in workshops. When the principal members of the managerial staff, subordinate to the director, are appointed or dismissed, Party cells and factory committees may discuss these appointments and dismissals, but if they disapprove of a candidature they cannot veto the administration's decision but should refer the point in dispute to higher Party, trade union or economic organs. Similarly, cells must not substitute themselves for the factory committee.

The fundamental separation between the functions of Party, trade union and administrative organs does not exclude but, on the contrary, presupposes close collaboration, mutual help and a really comradely atmosphere in the works, to the exclusion, however, of any possibility of getting together and covering up one another's failings. When the production-financial plan is being worked out it should be discussed at conferences, workshop meetings and general factory meetings; this will help to bring to light the possibilities of raising the production programme, improving the position of the workers, increasing productivity of labour, lowering production costs, improving the quality of production, etc., and at the same time will help to prevent the breaking of the enterprise's internal rules and violations of labour discipline.

The Central Committee of the Communist Party suggest that Party organizations, trade union organizations and economic organs put forward workers more decidedly and energetically for managing and executive posts, gradually promoting them from post to post.

The use of new and experimental methods of rationalizing production involves risks and demands a thorough study and a good knowledge of the processes of production. When mistakes and shortcomings come to light it is necessary to distinguish between genuine mistakes and wilful wrecking.*

* *The C.P. in Resolutions...*, p. 812.

However, many difficulties and obstacles stood in the way of the reform of industrial administration. It was difficult to expect the principle of personal management to be carried out in the conditions prevailing during the years covered by the first F.Y.P. The majority of managing directors were Party men possessing neither adequate theoretical qualifications in engineering and economics nor a sufficiently long practical experience. Engineers and technicians trained in pre-revolution times formed only one-third of the staffs, and precisely these highly skilled specialists were under suspicion of not being loyal to the Soviet Government nor sincere in their support of the new ways of managing industry. In the course of the first years of the F.Y.P. several groups of specialists from various industries were brought to trial on charges of sabotage. On 24 May 1929 the O.G.P.U. announced the death sentences on the well-known pre-revolution railway experts von Meck, Velichko and Palchinsky; on 22 September 1930 it was announced that 'a plot by a counter-revolutionary wreckers' organization supplying the population with essential foodstuffs', headed by Prof. Riazantzev, Karatygin and others, had been discovered; the trial of the 'Industrial Party' led by Prof. Ramzin took place from 25 November to 7 December; and many other individual specialists in various branches of industry and stations of life were sentenced; a fact which naturally increased the suspicion and distrust of the trade union and Party organizations in factories not only towards specialists of pre-revolution standing but towards specialists in general; a real wave of 'spetz-baiting' swept at the time throughout all the branches of national economy.

On the other hand, during the same period a fierce struggle was going on within the trade union and Party organizations, and their whole machinery was being reconstituted on new principles. On 18 January 1929 Trotzky was banished; on 2 June 1929 Tomsky and with him the secretariat of the Central Committee of the T.U.C. were made to resign; Bukharin and Rykov's Right Opposition were in open struggle against the general Party line policy of industrialization and of collectivization of agriculture; on 27 November 1929 Bukharin was expelled from the Polit Bureau, and Rykov, Tomsky and others were cautioned that 'in the event of the slightest attempt on their part to oppose the line and the decisions of the Central Committee of the C.P., the Party would immediately take appropriate measures with them'; on 20 December 1930 Rykov had to relinquish the chairmanship of the Sovnarkom

S.S.S.R. and that of the Labour and Defence Council; all these events could hardly contribute to the establishment of the separation of functions between administration, factory committee and Party cell. Difficulties of organization and outlook were not the only obstacles to the establishment of personal management and of the principles of 'khozraschet'; this was hampered also by the tension brought about by extensive construction, exaggerated demands for increased production and the plan's maximum targets for expanding industry, by the need for mastering industries hitherto non-existent in the U.S.S.R. and the introduction of new technological processes which involved risky experiments and entailed charges of wrecking in case of failure. Production was hindered by limited supplies and by excessive centralization of management in the hands of unwieldy combines; the process of specializing the direction of industries on functional lines resulted in the trusts being deprived of the control of selling, supplying, building and even assembling—all these activities being transferred to specialized organizations of the combines—whilst the trusts exercised their activity only upon strictly technical matters. On the other hand, combines comprising numerous enterprises—anything up to 200, often scattered over large territories—could not really manage enterprises and substituted real guidance by 'red tape' and the issuing of 'plan' instructions based on average and general statistical indices.

A year and a half after the reorganization of the administration described above, none other than Stalin himself made the following official statement:

Why haven't we got personal management? We haven't got it and we shall not have it until we master technique. Not until there are among us, Bolsheviks, enough people thoroughly familiar with technique, economics and finance, shall we have real unity of control...we must master technique, we must become ourselves masters of the trade. *In the period of reconstruction technique decides everything.**

This was the famous slogan which dominated all questions of current industrial policy up to 1935 when Stalin threw out another slogan—'Personnel decide everything' (see p. 335).

Five months after this statement, Stalin made another speech in which he expounded instructions for the revision of labour organization, relations with specialists of pre-revolution training,

---

* Stalin's speech at the First All-Union Conference of Industrial Specialists, 4 February 1931. *Leninism*, ed. 1941, pp. 327, 330.

and the organization of industrial administration. He pointed out that:

We do not need *just any* kind of managing or engineering staffs. We need *such* managing and engineering staffs as are capable of understanding the policy of our country's working class and are ready to put it conscientiously into effect. Our country has reached a phase of development when the *working class must create its own industrial and technical intelligentsia* capable of making a stand for its own interests, which are those of the ruling class.

Further, the attitude towards representatives of the pre-Revolution technical intelligentsia must be altered: 'the Soviet Government could up to now practise but one policy towards them—the policy of smashing the active wreckers, dividing the neutrals and winning over the loyal'. During the latter years the representatives of the old school of technicians have been made to see that it is idle to hope for any 'intervention', for a 'change of heart of the Soviet regime and its speedy downfall' and:

we note definite signs of a new orientation on a part of this intelligentsia towards the Soviet power.... Wreckers there have been and wreckers there will be so long as we have classes and so long as we are encircled by capitalists, but it would be silly and unwise to see an uncaught criminal in practically every specialist or engineer of the old school. 'Spetz-baiting' has always been and still remains a harmful and shameful phenomenon. Hence, the task is *to change our attitude towards the engineers and technicians of the old school, to show them greater attention and solicitude, to display more boldness in enlisting their co-operation.*

Further, Stalin said:

Because of the unbusiness-like conduct of affairs the principles of 'khozraschet' have been completely undermined in a number of our enterprises and economic organizations. It is a fact that a number of enterprises and economic organizations have long ceased to reckon, to calculate and to draw up a genuine balance sheet of income and expenditure. It is a fact that in a series of enterprises and economic organizations such notions as a 'regime of economy', 'curtailment of unproductive expenses', 'rationalization of production' have long since gone out of fashion. Evidently, they assume that the Gosbank 'will advance the money anyway'. It is a fact that of late in a number of enterprises production costs have been mounting. From this it follows that it is no longer possible to exist only on the revenue from light industry, only on budget reserves, only on profits from agriculture...it is necessary to make heavy industry, and first and foremost, machine-building also yield a surplus. This requires abolition of unbusiness-like methods, mobilization of internal industrial resources, the adoption and enforcement of the 'khozraschet' in all our enterprises, a systematic lowering of production costs and increase of internal accumulation in all branches of industry without exception. . . it is further necessary that our present cumbersome combines, which comprise sometimes 100–200 enterprises, should be reduced in size and broken up into several combines. . . . Combines must be brought nearer to factories. . . it is necessary that our combines should replace management by collegium with individual management. The position at the present is that in the collegium of a combine there are ten or fifteen men, all writing papers, all carrying on discussions. To continue to manage in this way, comrades, will not do.*

After the issue of these governmental directives by Stalin further reforms were made in both the central management of industry and in the management of enterprises. In the course of 1931 many combines were reduced to smaller proportions and further specialized. Combines lost their function of planning production for a whole branch of industry, and their technical direction now extended only over a small circle of subordinated enterprises. Many combines were at once reorganized into trusts (in June 1931 there were only thirteen trusts in heavy metallurgy, by October 1932 they already numbered 152, and gradually most combines were transformed into trusts). Trusts reappeared as organizations directing all the productive activities of industrial undertakings. However, to co-ordinate the work of individual industries Chief Branch Administrations† of the S.E.C., which had been abolished in 1929, came again into existence; but their functions were now limited, and centred mainly on planning and co-ordinating the work of individual industries and not on directing their actual work. For the specialized technical guidance of enterprises and even more so for problems connected with technical reconstruction, the Praesidium of the S.E.C. was endowed with 'functional sectors' which dealt with particular problems of enterprises.

In January 1932 the S.E.C. was itself reorganized into three industrial P. Commissariats: the All-Union Commissariat of Heavy Industry (Narkomtiazhprom), the People's Commissariat of Light Industry (Narkomlegprom) and the People's Commissariat of Timber and Woodworking Industry (Narkomles).

This splitting of the S.E.C. into specialized Commissariats was, as we will see later, only the first step in the process of specialization of Commissariats according to industries, a process which continued

---

* From Stalin's speech at the conference of managerial workers, 23 June 1931. *Leninism*, 11th ed., pp. 341, 343, 344, 345, 346, 348, 349.

† See the Regulations of the Sovnarkom S.S.S.R., 8 September 1932. *Collected Laws and Orders*, no. 79, 1932, § 484.

up to the events of 1941. The subdivision of combined Commissariats into more narrowly specialized Commissariats was designed to bring them closer to the lower production units and so to improve their technical and detailed direction of the work of individual undertakings.

In the course of 1931–2 a series of regulations was issued tending to ensure a greater margin of autonomy to individual enterprises and allowing them to determine the use of their working capital and a proportion of their profits, and generally confirming the independence of the factory administration in the execution of the production and financial plan.* None the less, even in 1933 it was many times stated that

because of lack of knowledge and desire to master technique, economics, and finance, there existed a tendency to pass on 'functions', even if they formed an essential part of the management of a given sector, to other people in order to shirk responsibility. This resulted in the functional principle taking the place of the territorial or the territorial-production principles; the management of a production sector became subdivided between the manager of the sector and a series of 'functionaries'. Thus, for instance, at some large pits there was a manager of mechanization, a manager of ventilation, a manager of security apparatus, etc.†

In the course of 1933 further measures were taken, aimed at strengthening unity of control and at making one man responsible for the whole work carried out by the sector of production entrusted to his management. Detailed regulations were drafted regarding rights and duties of a 'brigadier', a foreman, the chief of a workshop, and those of the managing director of an enterprise, and they were given far wider powers in the field of management allotted to them at the enterprise than ever before. The number of

---

* We have enumerated here only some of the more important regulations; we refer those wishing to acquaint themselves with the technique of organizing industrial management during that period to: 'Liquid resources of State Combines, Trusts and other Industrial Organizations', *Coll. Laws*, no. 46, 1931, § 316. 'Amounts and Sources of Replenishment of own Liquid Resources of State Combines, Trusts...,' *Coll. Laws*, no. 64, 1931, § 433. 'Profits of Enterprises, Members of a Combine or Trust', *Coll. Laws*, no. 70, 1931, § 461. 'Amounts and Sources of Replenishment of own Liquid Resources of Combines, Trusts...,' *Coll. Laws*, no. 71, 1931, § 479; no. 14, 1932, § 78. 'Results of Endowing State Econ. Organizations with own Liquid Resources', *Coll. Laws*, no. 73, 1932, § 447.

† *Planned Economy*, no. 3, 1934, p. 85. Regulations of the Sovnarkom S.S.S.R. and the Central Committee of the C.P. entitled 'Work in the Coal Industry', *Bull. Financ. and Industr. Leg.* no. 12, 1933.

independent departments and sections of management, and the
administrative machinery of enterprises were reduced (the number
of employees in heavy industry decreased by 120,000 from
December 1932 to December 1933), whilst a further specialization
and reduction in size and increase in numbers of the Chief Departments of the Commissariat of Heavy Industry and its trusts took
place.*

So matters stood with industrial management as the first F.Y.P.
drew to its close and the second F.Y.P. was inaugurated; the latter,
incidentally, being confirmed only early in 1934, a year after the
official date of inauguration. During the years covered by the
first F.Y.P. industry had made very considerable quantitative
progress, but from the point of view of quality the results still left
much to be desired. At the Seventeenth Party Congress, when
the results of the first F.Y.P. were reviewed and the second
F.Y.P. for the development of the U.S.S.R. economy was adopted,
Stalin again stated officially that: '*Bureaucratic routine methods* of
management in the economic Commissariats and their departments...are still far from eliminated', that it was necessary 'to
liquidate the functional structure of the soviet-economic machinery
and to reorganize it on the productive-territorial principle, from
the lower units up to the P. Commissariats'. It was proclaimed
that 'the drive for *new construction* must be supplemented in the
second F.Y.P. by the drive for *mastering* new industries and new
technique, and by greatly increased labour productivity and
lowering production costs'.†

These fundamental principles of the Seventeenth Party Congress
were embodied in the following instructions for the reform of
industrial management introduced in 1934, i.e. on the eve of the
abolition of rationing.

A regulation of the Central Committee and of the Sovnarkom
S.S.S.R. decreed:

1. To liquidate the functional structure of the administrative
machinery in all soviet and economic organs, and to reorganize it from
the lower units to the P. Commissariats inclusive, on a productive-
territorial basis by forming within the P. Commissariats production or
productive-territorial Administrations *responsible for all managerial affairs*
of subordinate organizations and institutions; and by curtailing the
rights of the remaining functional organs, forbidding them to interfere
in the work of the lower units over the head of the Chief Administrations.

* See the regulations of the Sovnarkom S.S.S.R., *Bull. Financ. and Industr.
Leg.*, nos. 12 and 30, 1933.
† *The C.P. in Resolutions...*, pp. 240, 569, 587.

2. To strengthen the rights and duties of *local* provincial and republican organs for the development of local industry; to concentrate
in the Chief Administrations of the P. Commissariats only the management of enterprises of All-Union importance and to *hand over to local
organs some of the enterprises* which had hitherto been subordinate to
U.S.S.R. or republican organs.

3. *To abolish combines*, to decrease the number of trusts and expand
the *direct* connexions between the central economic organs, beginning
with the P. Commissariats, and their larger subordinate enterprises.

4. To make it the duty of the heads of all soviet and economic organs
personally to supervise the daily fulfilment by subordinate organs of the
decisions and orders of higher organs, and to forbid them to delegate the
duty of supervising fulfilment to secondary organs; and to liquidate
throughout the whole soviet and economic machinery the special super-
visory sections for this purpose.

5. To make it the duty of the heads of all soviet and economic institutions *personally to choose and allocate* managerial, engineering and technical workers, and at the same time to transfer considerable numbers of the
engineering and technical staffs from the offices to production.

6. To make it compulsory for heads of economic organs and enterprises to master the technical basis of their business and, for that purpose, to work out a 'technical minimum' for every industry which *must
be mastered* within a definite minimum time-limit by all managerial
workers.

7. To liquidate management by *collegium* in all fields of soviet-
economic work.

8. To form *advisory councils to the P. Commissariats*, each council
numbering 40–70 members and holding meetings once every two
months; at least half the members to be representatives of local organizations and enterprises. Concurrently, local organs of the economic
commissariats are to be reorganized and the representatives of the P.
Commissariats in the provinces are to be replaced by provincial departments of heavy, light and other industries; to be responsible for the
direction of the entire corresponding local industry and for carrying out
the instructions of the corresponding Commissariats; to ensure a reduction of staff by at least 10–15 % in the course of 1934, as compared with
the respective numbers approved in 1933, and also drastically to cut
down all forms of accountancy and reports throughout the administration.*

For the execution of these general government regulations for
the reorganization of administrative methods, not only in industry
but throughout the economic and Soviet administration, concrete
measures of practical reform were worked out.

Combines and their functional sections were abolished and
Chief Administrations based on the productive-territorial principle

* *Bull. Financ. and Econ. Leg.* no. 9, 1934.

were organized in their stead. Such was, for instance, the Chief Administration of the Moscow and Leningrad Provincial cotton industry, and the Chief Administration of the Ivanovo Provincial cotton industry. Each administration included a 'khozraschet' office for technical supply and a 'khozraschet' office for disposal of the production. Henceforth, Chief Administrations were 'wholly to direct the work, technique and finance of their subordinate trusts, enterprises, raw material and supply organizations'. Moreover, every Commissariat had departments, sections and groups for the direction of certain general questions affecting all the industries of a given Commissariat; for instance, the planning and economics department, the trade department, the statistical estimates section, the export and import group, etc. However, these departments and sections in contrast with the former functional departments had not the right to issue direct instructions to Chief Administrations, trusts or enterprises; they could only submit their proposals for approval by the P. Commissar, and only with his sanction were the proposals forwarded to the Chief Production Administrations.* Large enterprises were directly subordinate to the Chief Production Administration, whilst trusts acted as intermediaries for the others, the arrangement depending on the degree of concentration and the nature of production. Small undertakings were handed over to the newly organized Commissariats of Local Industry in the Allied and Autonomous Republics.† Moreover, along with the All-Union Commissariats of Food, Light, and Timber Industries, similar republican Commissariats were formed and took over enterprises of republican importance.

Thanks to these measures the burden of directing small and medium size enterprises was taken off the All-Union Commissariats which could now focus their attention on planning and regulating the work of the largest enterprises. On the other hand, the creation of Commissariats of Local Industry stimulated the effort to utilize local resources of raw materials, fuel, etc., and to make use of them at small and medium enterprises.

Responsible workers in economic organizations were obliged to take up courses in special technical subjects, relating to their business and to pass prescribed examinations; failing which, after a

* See the regulations on the reorganization of the administration in the Commissariats of Light and Timber Industries and of their local organs, *Bull. Financ. and Econ. Leg.* nos. 21, 27, 28, 29 and 30, 1934.

† See 'The formation of People's Commissariats of Local Industry in Allied and Autonomous Republics', *Bull. Financ. and Econ. Leg.* nos. 2, 22, 1934.

definite lapse of time, they lost the right to keep their posts. Many thousand engineers and technicians were transferred from managerial offices straight to production work in the shops.*

All these measures considerably improved the technical direction of industrial development during the fulfilment of the second F.Y.P., and it can be said that towards the close of the rationing period the problems of a rational technical organization of industry were being solved on the whole satisfactorily.

Before proceeding to analyse the substance of the second F.Y.P.'s industrial tasks the following facts must be mentioned. The instructions to draft a second F.Y.P. for the development of the national economy of the U.S.S.R. in the period of 1933-7 were adopted at the Seventeenth Party Conference which was held from 30 January to 4 February 1932, a year before the end of the first Plan. These instructions were still permeated by that spirit of maximum hopes and strivings to expand industrial production which was so characteristic of the first F.Y.P. period. Consequently, these instructions for the drafting of a second Plan again demanded tremendous quantitative increases in industrial production: 'to increase the production of the engineering industry by the end of the five-year period at least by $3-3\frac{1}{2}$ times compared with that of 1932 . . . to achieve by 1937 an output of electrical energy of at least 100 milliard kWh. as against 17 milliard, an output of coal of at least 250 million tons as against 90 million in 1932, to increase the oil output by $2\frac{1}{2}-3$ times, . . . to smelt 22 million tons of pig iron in 1937.'†

This resolution was adopted after the hearing of reports by the chairman of the Sovnarkom S.S.S.R. (Molotov) and the chairman of the Gosplan (Kuibyshev). However, a year later, after reviewing the results of the first Plan, and on the strength of reports by Stalin, Molotov and Kuibyshev, another resolution was passed in which the demands for expanding production were radically reduced: 'the annual increase of industrial production in the second five-year period should average not a 21-22 % increase, as in the first five-year period, but somewhat less, or 13-14 %',‡ and emphasis was laid on Stalin's and Molotov's statements to the effect that the drive of the second F.Y.P. was not so much for quantitative expansion of production as for a qualitative improvement in output.

* Concerning the enforcement of a compulsory minimum technical standard of knowledge among administrative workers of the Chief Administrations and of enterprises, cf. *Bull. Financ. and Econ. Leg.* no. 15, 1934.

† *The C.P. in Resolutions . . .*, p. 513.

‡ Ibid. p. 513.

None the less, a planned increase of 16·5% on the 1932 figure was approved for 1933, the first year of the second Plan; group A accounted for 21·2 % of this rise, and group B for 10·5.*

In accordance with these instructions the Gosplan worked out a very detailed draft of a second F.Y.P.† and submitted it for approval to the Seventeenth Party Congress which met from 26 January to 10 February 1934. Eventually, in the resolution of the Congress on the second F.Y.P., the tasks set for expanding production differed considerably both from the previous Party directives and from the Gosplan's detailed draft, as is shown in Table 25.

Table 25

	1937		1937 as % of 1932	
	Draft*	Approved†	Draft	Approved
Gross production of all industry (in milliard roubles at 1926–7 prices) Of which:	102·7	92·7	237·2	214·1
Production of means of production, group A	48·4	45·5	209·4	197·2
Production of consumer goods, group B	54·3	47·2	268·8	233·6
Commissariat of Heavy Industry	35·7	33·5	250·1	234·6
Commissariat of Timber Industry	3·6	3·6	202·4	200·0
Commissariat of Light Industry	23·5	19·5	300·0	248·8
Commissariat of Supply	13·1	11·9	282·7	256·1
Engineering and metal-working industries	21·4	19·5	227·4	207·0
Coal (million tons)	152·5	152·5	237·1	237·1
Crude oil and gas (million tons)	47·5	46·8	213·3	210·0
Pig iron (million tons)	18·0	16·0	292·4	260·0
Steel (million tons)	19·0	17·0	322·7	289·0
Rolled metal (million tons)	14·0	13·0	326·6	303·0
Cotton textiles (million metres)	6,250·0	5,100·0	229·8	188·0
Leather footwear (million pairs)	205·0	180·0	250·3	220·0

* *Draft of the Second Five-Year Plan...*, vol. 1, pp. 413–14.
† *The C.P. in Resolutions...*, p. 570.

Accordingly, instead of the average annual increase of industrial production of 18·9 % proposed by the draft, the approved increase was 16·5 %. Nevertheless, the expenditure on capital investments in industry remained the same as that proposed by the draft, i.e. 69·5 milliard roubles as against 24·5 milliards spent in the course of the first F.Y.P. Finally, in 1931, it had been planned to mine 250 million tons of coal in 1937, to produce at least 100 milliard

* Op. cit. p. 514.
† *Draft of the Second Five-Year Plan...*, vol. 1, 552 pages; vol. 2, 570 pages. Appendix to vol. 1, *Fundamental Objects of Capital Construction under the Second Five-Year Plan*, Moscow, 1934, 180 pages.

kWh. of electrical energy, to smelt 22 million tons of pig iron, but in the course of 1932–3 these tasks were considerably diminished, and by January 1934, the targets for 1937 were: to mine 152·5 million tons of coal, to produce 38 milliard kWh. of electrical energy and to smelt 18 million tons of pig iron.

After reviewing the extent of fulfilment of the first F.Y.P. and the experiment of carrying out the plan for 1933—that is, the first year of the second Plan—the Soviet Government evidently came to the conclusion that it was necessary to lower the targets for the quantitative expansion of industry in the coming years of the second Plan. For capital construction, however, the approved plan fully endorsed the draft proposals. Apparently, either the decision somewhat to slow down the pace of increasing industrial production was taken in haste and there was no time to revise the Gosplan's detailed draft (far more detailed than that of the first Plan), or else it may have been decided to maintain capital investment at the level proposed by the draft, in spite of the curtailment of the production programme.

It must be stressed that there was an essential difference between the capital construction programmes of the first and the second F.Y.P.s. As will be remembered, considerable construction was left incompleted after the first planned period. According to the draft of the second F.Y.P., 64·7 milliard roubles were allocated to capital investment to be expended as follows: on new construction—38·1 milliards, i.e. 58·9 % of all expenditure but only 21 milliards of this sum were assigned for capital construction, begun under the second F.Y.P., whilst 17·1 milliards were earmarked for completing works already under construction; the remaining 41·1 % to be allocated to the reconstruction and capital repairs of the existing plants and to other work. It is important to note that many of the new enterprises begun under the first F.Y.P. and still under construction were to be completed only towards the middle or the end of the second F.Y.P. period and a few even in the course of a third five-year period;* the expenditure for their completion, together with the money already spent on them during the first five-year period, added up to sums far exceeding the intital estimates. Evidently, the plans for enterprises to be completed in the course of the second five-year period were either altered and the expense of their construction increased by comparison with the initial estimates of the first F.Y.P. or else the estimates for capital construc-

* For more detailed data concerning the dates on which the construction of individual new enterprises was to start and to be completed and on their prices see *Fundamental Objects of Capital Construction under the Second Five-Year Plan.*

tion of the second F.Y.P. were calculated in 1933 prices, and the higher figure reflects the rise in price of construction work which had taken place in the interval. Otherwise there seems no explanation of the fact that in the official report on the fulfilment of the first F.Y.P incompleted construction is estimated at 9 milliard roubles, whilst the draft of the second F.Y.P. allocates 17 milliard roubles to complete construction left unfinished by the first F.Y.P.* Moreover, as already mentioned, the first F.Y.P. proposed to spend 19·1 milliard roubles on capital industrial construction, whereas eventually 24·8 milliards were spent, though of this only 15·7 milliards actually went into production. Undoubtedly, the roubles in these quotations vary in value and cannot be compared without allowing for the rise in prices; but no price index is available, nor is it possible to work out any such index on the strength of data published by the Soviet press.

Two other features of the capital construction programme of the second F.Y.P. are worth noting: during the first two years, practically all the allocations for capital industrial work were to be spent on completing construction left over from the first Plan, on expanding and rebuilding existing plants and on capital repairs;† whilst the considerable new construction programme proposed by the second Plan was to begin only in the third year of the five-year period. Thus, to a significant extent, the capital construction planned for the first two years represented the completion of construction remaining unfinished from the first five-year period; in other words, the construction programme of the first F.Y.P. was continued into the second. In the second place the increase in capital expenditure for group B industries in the second F.Y.P. was to be relatively greater than the increase in capital expenditure on group A industries, i.e. the second Plan devoted more attention to the renovation, rebuilding and new construction of industrial enterprises manufacturing mass consumption goods than had been the case during the first F.Y.P.‡ Taken absolutely, the tasks planned

* *Summary of the Fulfilment of the First Five-Year Plan...*, pp. 42, 47.

† Out of the draft's total of 9,474 million roubles allocated to industry for capital construction in 1933, only 550 were earmarked for new construction to begin under the second F.Y.P.; in 1934 the corresponding ratio was 1,180 million roubles for new construction out of a total of 11,889 million roubles. For details, see *Fundamental Objects of Capital Construction...*, p. 6.

‡ It was proposed during the years covered by the second Plan to invest 53·4 milliard roubles in capital construction of group A industries as against 21·3 milliard roubles invested under the first Plan, i.e. an increase of 150·8 %; it was planned to spend on group B, 16·1 milliard roubles as against 3·5 milliard roubles, i.e. an increase of 259·6 %. See for details *Draft of the Second Five-Year Plan...*, vol. I, p. 412.

for the second five-year period in the field of capital construction were again colossal, but this time they had a foundation in the very considerable capital construction and expansion of industry's productive capacity which had taken place during the years of the first F.Y.P. Relatively, however, the quantitative targets were more moderate than those of the first Plan. With regard to the quantitative side of work, the tasks were also more moderate; the reduction of production costs for industry as a whole was to be 26 %, the increase in labour productivity 63 %, whereas the first F.Y.P. had demanded a 35 % reduction in production costs and a 110 % increase in labour productivity.

One more remark regarding the second F.Y.P. The draft second F.Y.P. was worked out in greater technical detail than the first; nevertheless, out of a total of 1,300 pages of text and tables, merely five incomplete pages of text and three pages of statistical tables were spared for the purely financial aspects of the Plan. Table 26 expresses the summary of the financial plan.*

This is very significant. The system which had been evolved during the years of the first Plan to organize the country's finances and to monopolize the channels distributing the population's purchasing power (cf. chapter on Trade and Finance), made it possible to assume that the financial aspect of the Plan would encounter no difficulties and that finances would be adjusted to the course of the material processes of the country's national economy. The fulfilment of the Plan being dependent (a) on the successful utilization of the existing productive potentialities, (b) on the materialization of new construction, (c) on the growth of labour employed in all branches of the country's economic and cultural activity and (d) on the general wages fund—finances were to be moulded to suit the evolution of these processes. The financial plans of individual branches of production were, however, worked out in greater detail, because, apart from their importance for the work of these branches, they were to serve as indices controlling the fulfilment by enterprises of their qualitative tasks—in the way of reduction of production costs, increase in labour productivity, etc.

The experience gained in executing the industrial production plan in 1933 was one of the factors which led to the decision somewhat to modify the programme of industrial expansion during the second F.Y.P.

According to the annual control figures for 1933 drawn up on

* *Draft of the Second Five-Year Plan...*, vol. I, pp. 540-1.

Table 26

I. *Financial resources* (*in milliard roubles*)

	During the first F.Y.P. period		During the second F.Y.P. period	
	Absolute	%	Absolute	%
Accumulation of socialized economy Of which:	73·6	61·3	332·2	79·3
Profits	19·1	15·9	79·7	19·0
Turn-over tax	42·3	35·2	218·5	52·2
Depreciation of fixed capital	6·3	5·2	20·0	5·7
Mobilized resources of the population (mainly through State loans)	21·5	17·9	46·1	13·2
Miscellaneous revenues	18·7	15·6	20·5	5·9
Total revenue	120·1	100·0	348·8	100·0

II. *Allocation of financial resources* (*in milliard roubles*)

	During the second F.Y.P. period	1937 as % of 1932
Financing of national economy Of which:	208·2	147·0
Capital investments	114·2	125·0
Increase in working capital	26·4	141·5
Financing of social and cultural measures	75·4	214·9
Appropriation for Administration and Defence	19·0	172·0
Appropriation for State Loan Service	10·0	280·0
Miscellaneous appropriations	21·2	353·8
Total appropriations	333·8	171·7
State reserve	15·0	—
Grand total	348·8	183·0

the instructions of the Plenum of the Central Committee and of the Central Control Commission of the Party (see above), the plan was to increase industrial production by 16·5%, of which group A accounted for 21·2% and group B for 10·5%. But in the course of 1933 it was only possible to expand industrial production by 8·9%, of which group A accounted for 11·6% and group B for 5·5%, i.e. by only half the planned figure for the expansion of industrial production. This increase was admittedly achieved concurrently with a reduction in the number of workers and employees in industry (6,481,000 in 1932 and 6,222,000 in 1933) and with a decrease in production costs of 1·5–2%. However, there were again indications in 1933 that the quality of work was far from satisfactory.* So, in December 1933, the Central Committee and the Sovnarkom S.S.S.R. passed a decree, 'On responsibility for the output of defective goods', as follows: '(1) To ensure that criminal proceedings, involving court sentences of at least five years imprisonment, be taken against managers of trusts, directors of enterprises and members of managerial and technical staffs, guilty of producing defective goods or incomplete articles. (2) To make the Procurator's Office of the U.S.S.R. responsible for the rigid execution of the present regulation.'† And, in fact, this decree began to be applied in the case of managerial staffs of enterprises whose quality of production constantly deteriorated.

In 1933 a series of measures was taken to enforce labour discipline, to scale wages, to transfer engineers and technical workers from the administrative and managerial offices to production, and to increase the authority of the managerial and technical personnel, together with other measures regarding labour (see pp. 229–33). On the home market, free trade in agricultural produce was authorized to some extent, the role of commercial trade was increased and the system of rationing supplies was altered (see pp. 239–41). A Party purge was effected and admission of new members was temporarily suspended. The direct and indirect aim of all these measures was to achieve a drastic change in the quality of work of all economic organizations. And, in fact, 1934 marks the beginning of a change for the better in the quality of the work of industrial enterprises. The annual plan for 1934 demanded a 19 % increase in all industrial production, the share of group A being 21·7 % and that of group B 15·8 %. Actually, the gross output rose by 14·9 %, group A accounting for 20·1 % and group B for 8·8 %. Things were also stirring 'in regard to an improvement both in range and quality of the output of the light and food industries. This, however, is still virgin soil' (Kuibyshev).‡

* This can be illustrated by a few extracts from the report of the Party's Central Control Commission and the Workers' and Peasants' Inspection to the Seventeenth Party Congress: 'The number of accidents is very high. In the Donbass-energo (power system) 1,935 accidents occurred during the nine months of 1933 and in the Moscow-energo 1,158....Spoiled goods form a very high percentage of the output of some factories; for instance, at the "Stankomet" works in Moscow spoiled goods from mouldings reaches 26·5 %, that from the output of prepared casts 38 % and that from casting lathes is over 50 %....The Rostov agricultural machinery works states that out of 10,884 chains "galla" for combines, received by the works, 2,780, i.e. 25 % proved worthless....What is the total amount of spoilage? It has never been estimated. But it must be a matter of many hundred million roubles.' *Pravda*, 4 February 1934.

† *Ekonomicheskaya Zhizn*, 9 December 1933.   ‡ *Izvestia*, 12 January 1935.

In November 1934 a Government decree inaugurated the gradual abolition of rationing. In May 1935 Stalin came forward with the famous slogan—'Cadres decide everything'. A series of reforms in agriculture favourable to its development followed. In August the Stakhanov movement made its first appearance and led to a revision of norms of work and of the whole wages system. The new Constitution was in the making. All this left its mark on the processes of industrial production during the latter years of the second F.Y.P.

CHAPTER XII. AGRICULTURE

The Gosplan draft of the first F.Y.P. embodied in a more detailed way the views of the Party's *general line* on matters of agriculture, which we described in our survey of the development of agriculture in the N.E.P. period. However, it also echoed some Right Wing opinions of the Party on the development of agriculture in the forthcoming five years. The F.Y.P. aimed at raising the production of State and collective farms and in particular their production of marketable grain. It was planned to finance the development of State and collective farms largely from the State and the local budgets; these farms, it was hoped, would by 1932–3 provide 39% of all the marketable grain, i.e. roughly 'the same percentage as is now [1927–8] provided by the 10% of the rich farmers'.* However, it was also planned to expand the production of individual peasant farming. This is clearly shown by the figures of the F.Y.P. given in Table 27.

The authors of the F.Y.P. emphasized that

in summing up the results of the Plan as a whole, we arrive at the conclusion that in the course of these 5 years, individual peasant farming will play the principal part in the production of agricultural commodities, and therefore it must be one of the Plan's tenets to stimulate the poor and middle peasants to expand and improve their farming. Actually, individual farms will differ greatly by the end of the five-year period from what they were at the beginning. They will have largely joined in the co-operative movement, they will have been reconstructed, but, nevertheless, they will be individual peasant farms. . . . We would be deceiving ourselves if we asserted that the socialized sector—at least within the limits it will have reached by the end of the five-year period— could enable us to disregard the production of those groups of middle

* *The Five-Year Plan...*, vol. II, pt. I, p. 283.

peasants who produce marketable surpluses.... We will prevent in every way the rich peasant from becoming an exploiting peasant. But we should be wronging ourselves if we identified the peasant who thrives not on exploitation, but because he has mastered the methods of agriculture and reconstruction which we plan and preach, with the peasant who grows rich through exploitation.... We cannot imagine the Five-Year Plan fulfilled otherwise than in accordance with the decree of the Central Executive Committee regarding the raising of crop yields.

(i.e. the above-quoted decree dated 15 December 1928 regarding the raising of yields by 35 %).

Table 27

	1927–8		1932–3	
	Million roubles	%	Million roubles	%
Gross agricultural production:				
1. State farms	170	1·2	690	3·2
2. Collective farms	88	0·6	2,480	11·5
Total 1 + 2	258	1·8	3,170	14·7
3. Individual peasant farming	13,722	98·2	18,459	85·3
Total 1 + 2 + 3	13,980	100·0	21,629	100·0
Marketable surplus:				
1. State farms	104	3·6	550	8·6
2. Collective farms	24	0·8	1,060	16·7
Total 1 + 2	128	4·4	1,610	25·3
3. Individual peasant farming	2,772	95·6	4,754	74·7
Total 1 + 2 + 3	2,900	100·0	6,364	100·0
Total sown area (million hectares)	115·6	100·0	141·3	100·0
Individual peasant farming	113·3	98·0	122·4	86·6
Collective farms	1·1	0·9	14·5	10·3
State farms	1·2	1·1	4·4	3·1
Gross yield of grain crops (million quintals)	731·2	100·0	1,058·8	100·0
Individual peasant farming	715·3	97·9	895·8	84·6
Collective farms	7·2	1·0	119·5	11·3
State farms	8·7	1·1	43·5	4·1

In connexion with the F.Y.P.'s proposals for the collectivization of peasant holdings, already in the course of the first year of the F.Y.P. the financial, material and technical help afforded to poor peasants to organize collective farms was extended; tractors and other modern agricultural machinery were imported on a considerable scale and the organization of machine hiring, and

Machine-Tractor Stations was expanded.* Measures were also taken to put into effect the decision to organize large State farms.

As a result of these measures, in the course of 1928–9, the numbers of collective farms, and of peasant households amalgamated into collective farms, increased rapidly.† It has been shown above how numerous were the peasant households which suffered from a complete lack or a shortage of means of production and who were compelled either to hire machinery from richer farmers, or lease their land, or become farm hands. The formation of collective farms, especially since they received financial, material and technical aid from the State, undoubtedly represented for these groups an improvement on their previous conditions. Thus, in the early days of mass collectivization, collective farms were mainly organized by peasants least endowed with the basic means of production, and they usually formed the simplest type of collective farms, i.e. associations for the joint cultivation of the land.‡

* 'In 1929, the collective farms received more than half their assets in the form of State credits, and more than half their jointly owned funds were also supplied by the State, but in the form of unredeemable loans. Up to 1929, the contribution of the rural population towards the collective farms' assets was utterly inadequate.' *The Socialist Reorganization of U.S.S.R. Agriculture in the interval between the Fifteenth and Sixteenth Party Congresses*, p. 136. This statistical handbook is full of very interesting facts about the formation of collective farms before 1930.

The number of tractors in agriculture as a whole rose from 25,729 in 1927 to 29,702 in 1928 and up to 42,132 in 1929. *The Socialist Reconstruction of Agriculture*, 1930, no. 7, pp. 86–7.

† On 1 November 1927 in the entire U.S.S.R., collective farms numbered 14,832 and comprised 195,000 peasant homesteads; by 1 June 1928 the corresponding figures were 33,258 and 417,000, and by 1 June 1929, 57,000 and 1,003,000 respectively. *The Socialist Reorganization of U.S.S.R. Agriculture...*, pp. 124, 125.

‡ A comparison of the total percentage of peasant households collectivized with the relative proportion of landless peasants collectivized, as well as data referring to the means of production of peasant households amalgamating into collective farms, show that in 1929 'the first to join the collective farms were the peasant households least endowed with means of production'. *Socialist Reorganization...*, pp. 130, 177. Of the total number of collective farms in the U.S.S.R. on 1 October 1929, 7% were 'communes' (see definition, p. 495), 32% were 'artels', and 62% were associations for the joint cultivation of the land. *Socialist Reorganization...*, p. 131. Whereas 'the middle peasants amalgamate into less complex collective unions, the poor peasants form the main bulk of complex collective farms (i.e. communes and artels). The communes contain 70·9% of landless peasants, 74·3% horseless peasants and 70·0% peasants having no cow, whilst the associations for the joint cultivation of the land contain 29·4% landless, 48·1% horseless and 35·4% peasants having no cow'. *The Collective Farms of the U.S.S.R.*, published by the All-Union Council of Collective Farms, edited by E. P. Terletsky, p. 43.

On the other hand, in regard to kulaks, and with the aim of breaking their opposition to the stock procurement policy of the State, measures were taken to increase taxation, to exact the immediate payment of the agricultural tax and the immediate repayment of any loans to credit institutions, and to levy individually on kulak households an additional agricultural tax, as well as a tax for rural, cultural and welfare needs. Yet the autumn sowing of 1928 and the spring sowing of 1929 showed that the rich peasants were persisting in their policy of cutting down production, and it was obvious that it would not be possible to obtain the required stocks of agricultural produce without again resorting to emergency measures. Meanwhile, by contrast, the production of heavy industry had in 1928–9 exceeded the expansion scheduled by the F.Y.P. for that year, and construction work was being carried out on a larger scale and with the employment of more workers than had been planned. Thus, in the summer of 1929, the dilemma became acute as to whether the country's industrialization was to be slowed down, or the resistance of the upper stratum of the peasantry was to be broken and their production replaced by the introduction of large-scale collective farming.

In the summer of 1929 it was decided to change over 'from the policy of restricting the exploiting proclivities of the kulaks, to the policy of *eliminating the kulaks as a class*'.* This was the beginning

---

* The essence of this drastic change of policy towards the kulaks was strikingly formulated by Stalin in the following words: '...the kulak class, as a class, cannot be squeezed out by taxation measures and all sorts of other restrictions while the means of production are *left* in the hands of that class and it enjoys the right of freely using the land, while the law which permits the hiring of labour in rural districts, the law which permits the renting of land and the ban on the expropriation of the kulaks remain in operation.... Under the policy of restricting the exploiting proclivities of the kulaks, which does not contradict, but on the contrary, presumes the *retention* of the kulaks as a class for the time being. For the purpose of squeezing out the kulaks as a class, the policy of restricting and squeezing out the individual sections of the kulaks is not enough. In order to squeeze out the kulaks as a class we must *break down* the resistance of this class in open battle and *deprive* it of the productive sources of its existence and development (the free use of land, means of production, the renting of land, the right to hire labour, etc.). This is the *turn* towards the policy of eliminating the kulaks as a class. Without this, serious collectivization, let alone solid collectivization of the rural district, is inconceivable.... This has, apparently, not yet been grasped by some of our comrades. Hence, the present policy of our Party in the rural districts is not a *continuation* of the old policy, but a *turn* from the old policy of *restricting* (and squeezing out) the capitalist elements in the rural districts to the new policy of *eliminating* the kulaks as a class' (Stalin's italics). J. Stalin, *Leninism*, pp. 290, 298.

of the *second agrarian revolution* in the field of agriculture. In 1917–18 the agrarian revolution had eliminated private ownership of land and farming by landowners, but agriculture had continued to be carried out on the principle of individual farming. It was now decided to eliminate the rich peasantry as the mainstay of individual peasant production, and to change over to collective forms of agricultural production, i.e. to extend the abolition of private property from the land to other means of production as well. It was expected that within the coming years collective and State farms would take the place of individual farms as the basic producers in agriculture.

Numerous authors have devoted hundreds of pages to the description of the course of wholesale collectivization in rural districts.* Only the most important facts, necessary for the understanding of the further developments in the agricultural system of the U.S.S.R., need be mentioned here.

Wholesale collectivization was determined on the one hand by Government measures and on the other by a tide of impulsive actions on the part of peasant masses and the local administrative machinery. In the summer of 1929 the Government embodied its policy of 'eliminating the kulaks as a class' in the following measures: (*a*) Party organizations were instructed to contribute 'in strengthening the participation, leadership, and influence of the urban proletarian elements and the rural proletarian and semi-proletarian strata in the Kolkhoz (collective farm) movement'. Particular importance was ascribed to the organization of poor peasants' and farm workers' groups into simple producers' co-operative associations and into primary forms of collective farms (associations for the joint cultivation of the land), and to the development of 'a decisive offensive against the kulaks, obstructing and preventing by any means all attempts on the kulaks' part to penetrate into the collective farms. The Party must, by tenacious and systematic work, weld into the collective farms a nucleus of poor peasants and farm hands.'† (*b*) Another directive was: 'apart from strengthening the Kolkhoz movement by leading Party forces, to send in the forthcoming months [decision of the Plenum of the Party Central Committee, dated 17 November 1929] for work in the collective farms, machine-tractor stations, etc., no less than 25,000 industrial workers with adequate organiza-

---

* Cf. e.g. the bibliography and extracts from relevant literature on the subject in Sidney and Beatrice Webb, *Soviet Communism...*, pp. 233–40, 561–71.

† *The C.P. in Resolutions...*, p. 375.

tional and political experience. Trade unions must actively participate in the selection of these workers, choosing the most advanced.'*
(c) The tractor and agricultural machinery building programme
was expanded, and it was decided to start on the immediate construction of 'two tractor works with a capacity of 50,000 tractors
(caterpillar) each, of two plants manufacturing combine-harvesting
machines, on the expansion of works producing complex agricultural machinery, and on the production of chemical fertilizers,
etc.' (d) An All-Union Centre of M.T.S. (Machine-Tractor
Stations) was created and M.T.S. were to become centres of wholesale collectivization in entire districts.† (e) The All-Union P.
Commissariat of Agriculture was founded 'to co-ordinate the
development of the large State farms, collective farms, and M.T.S.,
to organize the supply of machinery, to direct electrification, agricultural credits and the training of personnel, and also to intensify
the work of expanding the enterprises processing agricultural
produce'.‡ (f) The importance of village soviets—'the organs of
proletarian dictatorship'—in the rural districts was increased.
In connexion with mass collectivization, 'the main task of the
village council's work was actively to participate in the drafting of
the collective farms' production plans'. It was decided to elect new
village soviets where the old ones 'had proved themselves incapable
of directing the Kolkhoz movement'.§ (g) In districts of complete
collectivization the law permitting individual peasant households
to rent land and hire labour was suspended, and the regional and
provincial executive committees, as well as the governments of
autonomous republics, were granted the right to apply 'all requisite measures to fight the kulaks, including the total confiscation
of kulak property and their deportation beyond the boundaries of
individual districts and regions (provinces)'.‖ The confiscated
property of the kulaks was to be handed over to the jointly owned
funds of collective farms as a contribution from the poor
peasants and agricultural labourers joining the collective farm.¶
(h) It was decreed that the basic form of the collective farm was to
be the agricultural 'artel', in which the following items were
socialized: 'all draught animals, agricultural machinery, livestock

---

* *The C.P. in Resolutions...*, p. 378.
  † Ibid. p. 376.   ‡ Ibid. p. 383.
  § Regulation of the Central Executive Committee, dated 25 January 1930.
Izvestia, 26 January 1930.
  ‖ *Coll. Decrees and Orders of the U.S.S.R. for* 1930, no. 9, § 105.
  ¶ *The Development of the Soviet Economy...*, p. 335.

yielding marketable production, seed stocks, fodder to the amount required for the upkeep of the socialized livestock, all buildings necessary for carrying out collective farming and all enterprises processing agricultural produce'.* (i) It was decided to collectivize not 20 % of the sown area as proposed by the F.Y.P., but 'to solve the problem of collectivization by collectivizing the greatest majority of peasant holdings; moreover, in such important grain-growing districts as the Lower Volga, the Middle Volga, the Northern Caucasus, collectivization can be on the whole completed by the autumn of 1930 or in any case by the spring of 1931; whilst the collectivization of other grain-growing districts can be on the whole completed by the autumn of 1931 and in any case by the spring of 1932'. It was ordered therefore to 'wage a decisive struggle against any attempts to delay the collective movement on the grounds of a shortage of tractors and agricultural machinery. ...Yet, the Party Central Committee utters a serious warning against any "decreeing" of the Kolkhoz movement from above, as this might create the danger of substituting a kind of playing at collectivization for an actual socialist emulation in the organization of collective farms.'†

Such were the measures decreed by the central authorities; but collectivization was also accompanied by a fierce struggle within the peasant masses and by arbitrary acts of local administrative authorities. The masses of poor peasants and farm hands transformed the 'policy of eliminating the kulaks as a class' into an opportunity of taking the law into their own hands, seizing the kulaks' entire property, extending 'confiscation' from the means of production to the personal chattels of the rich farmers' households, 'routing the kulaks and carrying out wholesale collectivization'.‡ Cases of murder, arson and the destruction of real property, movables and cattle were frequently perpetrated by both kulaks and poor peasants' and agricultural labourers' groups who were avenging former economic exploitation or social grievances.

The following are the chief examples of arbitrary acts of the local administrative authorities: 'the application of compulsory measures and coercion of middle and poor peasants when forming collective farms; the socialization of the artel members' small livestock and cows having only a personal consumption value; the

* Cf. the first model statute of an agricultural artel, *Pravda*, 6 and 7 January 1930.
† Decision of the Party Central Committee, dated 5 January 1930. *Pravda*, 6 January 1930.   ‡ J. Stalin, *Leninism*, p. 298.

extension to other districts of the pace of collectivization which experience justified and which the Party Central Committee had set for the grain-producing district alone; the hasty creation of communes without adequate material and organizational preparation; and the creation of lifeless bureaucratic organizations under the label "giant" collective farms; delay in the advancing of credits allocated by the Government to collective farms while collective farmers were deprived of the facilities granted to them by the Government; high-handedness in the administration of collective farms and the substitution of appointed managements and orders from above for the elected management; slighting of the middle peasant and failure to use his farming experience; extension to the middle peasant of measures directed against the kulaks' (*raskulachivanie*, disfranchisement, etc.).*

As a result of these Government measures, of the spontaneous action of the peasant masses and the arbitrariness of the local administrative authorities, collectivization was carried out at a staggering pace, exceeding all planned estimates, as is illustrated by the figures given in Table 28.† These figures indicate not only

Table 28

	20 Jan. 1930	1 Feb. 1930	10 Feb. 1930	20 Feb. 1930	1 Mar. 1930
Collective farms organized (thousands)	59·4	87·5	103·7	108·8	110·2
Numbers of collectivized peasant homesteads included in them (thousands)	4,393·1	8,015·1	10,935·1	13,675·1	14,264·3
Collectivized peasant homesteads as a % of the total number of peasant households	21·6	32·5	42·4	52·7	55·0

the pace of collectivization, but also that it was bound to be accompanied by excesses, disregard for the principle that collectivization must be voluntary, and gross organizational mistakes. According to the resolution of the Sixteenth Party Congress, 'In a number of districts these mistakes gave rise to not merely anti-Kolkhoz demonstrations, but in some cases to anti-Soviet demonstrations.... If these mistakes had not been corrected in time by the Party Central Committee, there would have been a danger of the

* *The C.P. in Resolutions...*, p. 423. Cf. materials regarding concrete cases of administrative arbitrariness, *Pravda*, 12, 14, 15 and 17 March 1930 and *Izvestia*, 18 and 20 March 1930.

† Communiqué of the P. Commissariat of Agriculture, *Izvestia*, 9 March 1930.

whole fabric of agricultural collectivization collapsing, and the very *basis* of the Soviet State—the alliance of the working class with the peasantry—exploding.'*

To ease the tension in rural districts, urgent steps were taken to stop further indiscriminate collectivization, to dissolve the unworkable collective farms formed hastily and in violation of the principle of voluntary collectivization. On behalf of the Government, Stalin made his famous broadcast and published his articles 'Dizzy with success' and 'Reply to collective farm comrades', in which he condemned the violation of the principle that the formation of collective farms must be voluntary, and the indiscriminate collectivization which disregarded the diversity of conditions in the various districts of the U.S.S.R. and the extent to which they were prepared for collectivization; he equally condemned the 'feverish pursuit of inflated collectivization figures', the practice of organizing communes instead of agricultural artels, the bureaucratic 'decreeing' of the Kolkhoz movement by individual representatives of the Government in a fit of 'excessive self-esteem and conceit', the practice of socializing not only means of production but dwellings, dairy cattle and small stock, and poultry, and similar distortions tolerated by local authorities in the formation of collective farms. The new model statute of an agricultural artel was published to serve as a basis for the formation of future collective farms. The statute confirmed the principle that the formation of collective farms must be voluntary and that individual farmers must also join voluntarily. Collectivized peasants were permitted to retain their dwellings with an adjoining allotment (garden, orchard, etc.), small agricultural implements necessary for its cultivation, dairy cattle for personal use, small stock and poultry; an exception was made to the rule prohibiting the admission into collective farms of kulaks, members of their families and all disfranchised persons; according to the new statute collective farms could admit those kulaks and disfranchised families, one member of which was a Red partisan, a Red soldier or Red sailor whether commissioned or in the ranks, or a village teacher loyal to the work of the Soviet Government, on the condition that he vouched for the members of his family. Other points, added to the statute, defined more precisely questions relating to collective farms' assets, the remuneration of their members' work and the distribution among them of the collective farms' yields.†

* *The C.P. in Resolutions...*, pp. 423-4.
† For details see the Statute of an Agricultural Artel, *Pravda*, 2 March 1930.

Instructions were given: (a) to Party organizations to refrain from any 'slighting of individual farming which will continue to exist for a relatively long time in a number of districts in the country.'* (b) To organize in the collective farms a system of promotion to managerial posts of personnel drawn from among the collective farmers, and to establish on State farms, at schools for rural youth, at universities, at agricultural technicums and second-grade M.T.S. schools, mass short training courses for collective farmers, and also to carry out mass political and educational work on collective farms. (c) Strictly to respect on collective farms the principle of socializing means of production alone, and even in communes 'not to substitute for this any unnecessary and harmful petty socialization of the mode of life'.† (d) 'Drastically to revise the F.Y.P. for the development of agriculture, bearing in mind the collectivization tempos set by the decision of the Party Central Committee of 5 January 1930 [cf. above, § (i), p. 195] and fully justified by experience, in order to ensure on this basis, *pari passu* with an accelerated development of grain and technical crops, the expansion and intensified development of livestock breeding, primarily by organizing special livestock State farms on the same lines as the grain-growing State farms, by forming on a mass scale, in collective farms, livestock-breeding farms yielding large marketable surplus, and by rapidly increasing the fodder base'.‡ (e) 'To double the credits allocated to collective farms for the current year [1929–30], i.e. up to one milliard roubles.'§ Moreover, a series of advantages was granted to collective farms; for two years their socialized draught animals were exempt from tax and so were cows, pigs, poultry and sheep, whether jointly owned by the collective farms, or individually by their members. By contrast, individual farmers were taxed on the basis of their previous year's sown area, if, in the current year, they had reduced it. Collective farmers and their families had priority claims on supplies of manufactured goods, and, in districts growing technical crops, on grain supplies; certain privileges were granted to collective farms growing technical crops.‖

These measures resulted in a considerable number of hastily formed collective farms being dissolved, and several million peasant households withdrawing from them; nevertheless, the numbers

---

* *The C.P. in Resolutions...*, p. 426. † Ibid. p. 427.
‡ Ibid. p. 424. § Ibid. p. 425.
‖ For further details see *Pravda*, 3 April 1930; *Socialist Agronomy*, 24 and 27 April 1930; *Ekon. Zhizn*, 20 April 1930.

both of collective farms and of collectivized homesteads which
remained exceeded the F.Y.P. figures for the collectivization of
agriculture to be achieved by the end of the five years (see
Table 29).

Table 29

	Numbers of Kolkhoz and of peasant homesteads in them*	
	1 March 1930	1 May 1930
Number of Kolkhoz (thousands)	110·2	82·3
Number of peasant homesteads amalgamated in them (thousands)	14,264	5,778
Collectivized peasant homesteads, as % of total number of peasant homesteads	55·0	24·1

* *The Socialist Reorganization of Agriculture...*, p. 126.

As the table shows, withdrawals from collective farms were substantial, but nevertheless some 5 million peasant homesteads, i.e.
nearly one-quarter of the total peasantry, remained amalgamated.
These remaining collective farms received large funds from the
confiscated kulak property and from the State.* Peasant households joining collective farms received more means of production
than they had owned before. Thus a basis and a springboard for
further collectivization had been created. The good 1930 harvest
contributed in consolidating the new collective farms. The kulak
resistance had on the whole been broken and, in spite of the
temporary drift away from the hastily formed collective farms, the
peasant masses understood that the slowing down of the collectivization pace was only temporary, and that collectivization, and not
the development of individual farming, remained the goal. This
was especially true since, even at the most critical moment, when
the mistakes of the collectivization campaign were recognized, it
was nevertheless officially stated that the struggle against misapplied collectivization policy did not mean that the policy of a
speedy collectivization itself was being abandoned; henceforth 'the
Soviet Government would give the collective farms privileges and
preferences over individual farmers... in respect of land, the supply

---

* On the whole, in 1930 more than half of the jointly owned collective farm
assets came from outside—from the State and from confiscated kulak property.
Cf. figures in *The Socialist Reorganization...*, pp. 248, 286, 287; *Socialist Reconstruction of Agriculture*, nos. 4, 5 and 7; *Planned Economy*, 1930, no. 10.

of machines, tractors, seed grain, etc., in respect of tax alleviation and in respect of credits'.*

From the autumn of 1930, in connexion with the grain-procurement campaign and the further pressure brought to bear on the remnants of kulak and well-to-do households,† the collectivization movement began spreading again and continued steadily throughout the following years (see Table 51, p. 327).

The stormy course of collectivization, with its ebb and flow, with the excesses committed by peasant impulsiveness and by the local administration, the difficulty of quickly devising satisfactory organizational forms for carrying out large-scale agricultural production by a recently collectivized peasantry, the shortage of experienced cadres capable of directing Kolkhoz production and the difficulty of organizing labour and distributing profits were, naturally enough, all factors affecting detrimentally the development of agricultural production in the first stages of mass collectivization. The most important adverse results were the losses in livestock and the reduction in grain production which lasted until 1933 (see Table 48, p. 325).

The main causes for the reduction in livestock were:

(1) The mass slaughter of cattle, during the anti-kulak campaign, by the rich farmers who owned a large proportion of the

* Stalin's article 'Reply to collective farm comrades', *Pravda*, 3 April 1930. In this official statement Stalin also condemned the wavering peasants who left the collective farms. 'In leaving the collective farms they are acting contrary to their own interests, for only collective farms offer the peasants a way out of poverty and ignorance. By leaving the collective farms they place themselves in a worse position, for they deprive themselves of the privileges and benefits which the Soviet government offers the collective farms', and it was also stressed that 'the policy of eliminating the kulaks as a class must be pursued with all the persistence and consistency of which Bolsheviks are capable'.

† On 4 January 1931 the Central Executive Committee issued an order 'to ensure the execution of the Party directive regarding the collectivization in 1931 of 50% of the poor and middle peasant homesteads, further successes in wholesale collectivization and, on this basis, the elimination of the kulaks as a class'. It was, moreover, emphasized that 'even the best aktivists of the village often overlook the kulak, and fail to understand that with the high speculative prices for bread, meat and vegetables prevailing on the market, individual middle peasant homesteads quickly grow into rich, kulak homesteads'. The Plenum of the Party Central Committee for the Ukraine gave the following directive on 6 January 1930: 'to carry out a merciless offensive against the kulaks along the entire front; the elimination of the kulaks from the districts of total collectivization and their deportation from the village must be a component part of the struggle waged by collective farms and poor and middle peasants for the success of wholesale collectivization.' *Pravda*, 21 September 1930; *Socialist Agronomy*, 4 January 1931; *Izvestia*, 6 January 1931.

cattle. Moreover, much of the livestock was slaughtered by peasants liquidating their farming before joining the Kolkhoz.*

(2) The mortality among livestock transferred to collective farms because, at the outset of mass collectivization, there was a shortage of premises for housing collectivized stock, and because the animals, particularly the young, were badly looked after.

(3) The difficulty of keeping and rearing livestock when the level of grain production was as low as it was in 1931 and 1932.

(4) The defective organization of State procurements of agricultural products demanded from the Kolkhoz, and uncertainty about private ownership of animals by collective farmers. This subject will be dealt with in more detail below.

To combat these adverse facts, various measures were taken; the most important were:

(1) It was proposed to refuse admission to collective farms to peasants who liquidated their livestock before joining; those who had already done so were to pay to the jointly owned funds of the collective farm contributions to the value of the animals they had sold before joining the collective farm.

(2) Strict penalties were decreed against those responsible for the stock in the event of its death.†

(3) Provisionally, instead of expanding the breeding of collectivized livestock, it was decided to assist collective farmers to acquire personal livestock.‡

(4) Measures were taken to improve the care of animals in existing Kolkhoz livestock farms and gradually to expand Kolkhoz stock breeding.

(5) Changes were made in the State procurement methods (see below).

The main causes for the drop in grain production in 1931–2 were crop failure and a deterioration in cultivation. The latter was due to the following circumstances:

(1) In agricultural as in industrial production, the main effort of the F.Y.P. was directed towards quantitative expansion, whilst

---

* Cf. *Ekon. Zhizn*, 30 October 1929; *Izvestia*, 27 December 1929.

† The penalty for slaughtering a horse or allowing it to die through the owner's fault was a fine of up to ten times the horse's value or imprisonment for up to one year. *Socialist Agronomy*, 12 December 1931.

‡ Cf. the regulation of the Sovnarkom S.S.S.R. and the Party Central Committee 'On the aid to collective farmers having no cow for the acquisition of cows', dated 14 August 1933 (*Izvestia*, 15 August 1933), and the regulation of the U.S.S.R. P. Commissariat of Agriculture, dated 15 June 1933.

insufficient attention was being given to the quality of production. The sowing programme of the U.S.S.R. P. Commissariat of Agriculture demanded a considerable extension of the sown area, and indeed in 1930–2 the sown area was substantially increased. But this extension was accompanied by a deterioration in cultivation. The increase in the number of tractors could not make good the losses in draught animals (horses and oxen)—especially in view of the inexperience in their use; so that the amount of agricultural work per unit of traction power at the outset of the collectivization period was greater than it had been before collectivization.* The dates for the principal agricultural operations (sowing, harvesting, autumn ploughing, etc.) were abnormally lengthened† and, all things being equal, this entailed reduction in yields and losses in harvesting.

(2) Inefficiency in the organization of collective farm managements, and shortage of experienced cadres, resulted in the principal agricultural works being carried out as 'shock campaigns', involving the mobilization of people not directly employed in agriculture, and transference of agricultural machinery from one district to another.‡ These measures made possible the achievement of the quantitative tasks, but the quality of work deteriorated.

(3) Frequent changes in the Kolkhoz managements and the shortage of trained personnel capable of using and maintaining the novel and unfamiliar agricultural machines had also an adverse effect on the quality of work.

(4) Faulty organization of labour, of its remuneration and of the distribution of the net income of the collective farms also impeded improvement in the quality of work. During this period the principal field works were carried out mainly in common, without definite tasks being assigned to definite groups. The remuneration for work and the distribution of yields did not take adequately into account either qualifications or the intensity of the work performed. In many collective farms, yields were distributed on the 'eating' principle, i.e. agricultural produce was shared out to the

---

* The numbers of horses fell from 34·6 million in 1929 to 16·6 million in 1933. The numbers of tractors rose correspondingly from 66·3 to 210·9 thousand, and their horse-power from 926,000 to 3,209,000; meanwhile the sown area rose from 118·0 million hectares in 1929 to 136·3 million hectares in 1931. For details, see figures on pp. 325, 331.

† Cf. data regarding the course of spring and autumn agricultural work in my articles in the *Bull. Econ. Study of Prof. S. N. Prokopovich*, nos. 80 and 84, 1930 and nos. 89 and 91, 1931.

‡ Cf. e.g. data in *Socialist Agronomy*, 12 February 1931.

families of collective farmers according to the number of mouths to be fed, and not according to the work performed by the family.

(5) Collective farms had not yet become stable production units, and, in various districts, no fixed forms of land tenure by collective farms had yet been established. Local authorities tended to form giant Kolkhózy alongside midget ones.* Re-allocation of lands among collective farms was frequently making for uncertainty in land tenure.

(6) Plans for the State procurements of agricultural produce were not yet strictly determined nor fixed in advance; the amounts of compulsory deliveries to State procurement organs were often established not beforehand but only after the prospects of the harvest became known, and were subject to alteration by local authorities. This introduced an element of uncertainty into the estimates of the collective farms as to the share of the State deliveries and the share to be distributed to their members. Moreover, the bad harvests of 1931 and 1932, combined with the rising needs of the quickly growing urban and industrial population, made the burden of State deliveries a heavy one, and the share of the harvest left to the collective farms was insufficient to remunerate the farmers' labour so as to take into account the quality and the quantity of their work.† This, naturally, weakened the inducement to intensify and improve work among certain groups of collective farmers, particularly among the formerly better-off middle-peasant groups. There were signs of antagonism within the collective farms between the formerly poor and middle peasants, who, on joining, had contributed in various degrees to the assets of the collective farm and who now saw its net income being allocated not in proportion to their respective initial contributions, but on completely different grounds.

(7) Lastly the dual position of the peasant household, as a member of the collective farm and as a household of not only consumers but of private producers as well, was still rather confusing. Boundaries had not yet been set as to how far the collective farmer's private production was lawful and inviolate, nor to what

* Cf. data in *Socialist Reorganization of Agriculture...*, pp. 237–8.

† Cf. data in *Socialist Agronomy*, 18 July 1932. Collective farms delivered to the State the following percentages of their gross yields:

1930	1931	1932	1933	1934
27·5	36·8	27·5	21·6	19·5

In 1928–9 the marketable grain surplus was only 11·1%. Cf. *The Socialist Agriculture of the U.S.S.R.* p. 630.

an extent he had the right to dispose of the marketable surplus of his private production.

A whole system of measures was devised by the Government to overcome the shortcomings and difficulties with which the working of collective farms had met at the time.

(1) To counter the bad timing of agricultural work, the plans for sowing, harvesting, autumn ploughing, seed selecting, and the maintenance of tractors (repairs, supply of fuel, spare parts, etc.), as well as those for other large-scale agricultural works, fixed not only their extent, but enforced definite dates, based on the nature of the district and such seasonal conditions as early or late spring, dry or rainy summer, the depth of the snow cover, etc. The speed and quality of work during the principal agricultural cultivation periods were subjected to stricter supervision.*

(2) Complex agricultural machinery was concentrated at M.T.S. and not on collective farms; skilled agro-technical personnel was being hastily trained and requisite premises erected for the machines. This improved technique and intensified the utilization of agricultural machinery, since the machines were here handled by more skilled personnel than on the collective farms, and since the same machines could service several collective farms; it also permitted the organization of special repair squads and generally contributed to improving the quality of agricultural work. In concluding contracts with the M.T.S. for carrying out definite cultivation work, collective farms pledged themselves to achieve definite agro-minima.† Moreover, the M.T.S. in carrying out work for the collective farms were in a position indirectly to control the degree of fulfilment of the collective farm's quantitative and qualitative plans.

(3) Measures were introduced to give stability of land tenure and also to break up giant collective farms into smaller units.‡

* Data for the beginning and completing of field work were established according to meteorological conditions of the corresponding year, and so were minimum qualitative norms of work. Cf. data in my article on the course of spring cultivation in 1931, *Bull. Econ. Study of Prof. S. N. Prokopovich*, 1931, no. 89.

† For details see 'Model agreement of M.T.S. with collective farms', *Izvestia*, 6 February 1933.

‡ The inalienability of the collective farms' land 'within the present boundaries' was proclaimed and any further re-allocation of land among collective farms was prohibited. Disputes regarding land boundaries were to be settled by local land commissions, and other measures were taken designed to make land tenure by collective farms stable. For details, see the regulation of the U.S.S.R. Central Executive Committee on the creation of stable land tenure by collective farms, *Izvestia*, 4 September 1932.

(4) Certain groups of collective farmers were made responsible for carrying out definite tasks. On collective farms 'brigades' were organized, and they were entrusted with certain jobs, at first just for the season and later for a whole year. Some brigades were subdivided into smaller groups or 'links', the members of which were also responsible for definite tasks.*

Gradually, in the remuneration of the collective farmers' work, skill began to be taken into account and piece rates to be introduced. Gradually, too, norms of labour were devised conforming to definite quantitative and qualitative indices. The payment of labour, in kind and cash, began henceforth to be based on the number of labour days worked.† The payment in kind consisted of advances before the harvest, followed by the distribution of the actual harvest, or rather of the share earmarked for distribution to the collective farmers and calculated according to the total number of labour days worked by the entire community and by each member in particular. The cash payments were made from the share of the general money fund which was earmarked for distribution among collective farmers in proportion to the number of labour days they had put in. The distribution of the Kolkhozy net income, both in cash and kind, and appropriations for various purposes were to conform to a general model.‡

From 1933 the method of State procurements was altered. The old formula of a contract for the supply of grain was abolished and replaced by fixed norms of grain per hectare to be delivered to the State by collective farms and by individual peasant households. These deliveries were no longer based 'on variable plans, but on

* Cf. the regulation of the ¡U.S.S.R. Central Executive Committee on the formation of brigades on collective farms, on their norms of work and on the remuneration of their labour. *Socialist Agronomy*, 11 February 1932.

† The norms of labour for every particular work were so devised that they could be completed by an average worker in one labour day. Therefore by achieving more or less than one norm in a day, the collective farmer earned more or less than the average remuneration for one day.

‡ After completing the deliveries of produce demanded by the State procurement plan and after setting aside seed and fodder stocks, the collective farms' managements distributed the remaining food and fodder grain among collective farmers according to the number of labour days put in by each one. In distributing fodder, the heads of livestock owned by members were taken into account so that those members who received no fodder could get other agricultural produce instead. All the collective farms' money funds were to be distributed to their members after the following appropriations had been made: refund of cash advances, payment of agricultural tax and insurances, and the allocation to the jointly owned fund; the latter appropriation amounted to 10–15% of the total income of the collective farms. For details, see *Socialist Agronomy*, 18 July 1932.

fixed unalterable norms, established by law, in order to give stability to farming and enable collective farms and individual peasants to estimate their income reliably. In no circumstances can counter-plans for grain deliveries be henceforth accepted.'* For the individual peasant the per hectare norms of State grain deliveries were established 5–10 % above those of collective farms in the same district. Similarly, fixed norms were established for meat deliveries for the period from 1 October 1932 to 1 January 1934, and collective and individual farmers could fulfil their obligations by delivering the type of animal or fowl they chose, and they could associate into groups for jointly meeting the State demands.† Consequently, collective farms knew exactly what their State deliveries of agricultural produce would amount to and could also be certain that any rise in gross yields would mean an increase in the quantity of produce left at the disposal of the collective farmers.

From January 1933, trading by collective farms became lawful. As already stated in the chapter on Home Trade, collective and individual farmers were granted the right to sell at local markets or at the collective farms' shops any surplus produce left after they had met their obligations regarding the State deliveries of agricultural produce. Moreover, trading by collective farms, their members and individual peasants could be carried on 'at prices prevailing on the market'; 'the existing republican and local taxes and impositions' were waived and 'incomes derived by collective farms and their members from the sale of their agricultural produce are not subject to the agricultural tax'.‡ Considering the very material differences between the fixed prices paid for State deliveries and prices then prevailing on the market, the income from collective farm trading represented an important additional source

* For details see the regulation of the Sovnarkom S.S.S.R. and the Party Central Committee, dated 19 January 1933, 'On the compulsory deliveries of grain to the State by collective farms and individual peasant households', *Izvestia*, 20 January 1933.

† For details see the regulation of the Sovnarkom S.S.S.R. and the Party Central Committee, dated 23 October 1932, 'On meat deliveries', *Izvestia*, 24 October 1932.

‡ For details see the regulations of the Sovnarkom S.S.S.R. and the Party Central Committee, dated 8, 11 and 20 May 1932, 'Concerning the plan of State deliveries from the 1932 harvest and the development of the collective farm trading in grain'; 'On the plan for State deliveries of livestock and trading in meat by collective farms, their members and peasants working individually'; 'Concerning the trade of collective farms, their members and peasants working individually, and the reduction in the tax on trade in agricultural produce': *Pravda*, 8, 11 and 20 May 1932.

of revenue for farmers (cf. Table 38 regarding prices and the volume of the collective farm trading, pp. 241, 243, 244, 254). The legalization of collective farm trading was expected to stimulate the 'economic initiative of the Kolkhoz masses' and open up 'an additional source of supply of agricultural produce to the urban population'.*

At the first congress of collective farm exemplary workers held in February 1933, Stalin proclaimed the slogan—'Make all collective farmers prosperous', i.e. he proclaimed the policy of fostering accumulation not only by collective farms but by individual collective farmers.† In order to contribute to the prosperity of the collective farmers' personal households, the State came to the assistance of those who had no cow, helping them to acquire 'on easy terms one million heifers in the course of 1933'.‡ Even members of agricultural communes were granted the right 'to acquire for their personal household a cow, small stock and poultry'. Moreover, the 'managements of agricultural communes, village councils and district organizations were to help members of agricultural communes to acquire and keep livestock, and, in distributing agricultural produce according to labour days worked, ensure to every communard fodder for his personal livestock proportionately to the number of labour days worked'.§

These measures were another step towards drawing the line between the collective farm's economy and the collective farmers' domestic economies, between the 'public' and the 'private' in agricultural production.

* *Ekon. Zhizn*, 8 May 1932; *Pravda*, 8 May 1932.

† Stalin justified the new policy as follows: 'Before, in order to become prosperous, a peasant had to wrong his neighbours, to sell to them dear and to buy from them cheap; to hire labourers and to exploit them a good deal; to accumulate some capital and, having strengthened his position, to attain the status of a kulak.... Now the position is different.... Only one thing is now needed to become prosperous collective farmers; that is, to work on the collective farm conscientiously; to make efficient use of draught animals, to cultivate the land efficiently and to cherish collective farm property.... We have now all that is needed to achieve our aim. At present our machines and tractors are badly used. Our land is not cultivated as well as it might be...we need only to improve the cultivation of our land to increase the quantity of our produce two-fold, three-fold. And this will be quite sufficient to convert all our collective farmers into prosperous tillers of collective farm fields.' J. Stalin, *Leninism*, pp. 417, 418.

‡ The State allocated 35 million roubles to help peasants having no cow to buy a heifer; grants amounted to 50 % of the heifer's value and were repayable by instalments in the course of one year. Regulation of the Sovnarkom S.S.S.R. and the Party Central Committee, dated 14 August 1933.

§ Regulation of the U.S.S.R. P. Commissariat of Agriculture, 15 June 1933.

In agrarian countries, agricultural production presents a twofold aspect because of the very nature of production and because of the population's mode of life. On the one hand, it is mass production for a market and, on the other, it is production to ensure a family's food requirements and also small-scale production of various subsidiary items peculiar to every district. This dual aspect gave rise to the idea of concentrating mass production of basic agricultural commodities required for 'public' needs (supply of urban and industrial population, export, accumulation of food reserves, etc.) on collective farms, whilst allowing small-scale personal production to be carried out privately by collective farmers to meet the consumption and day-to-day family needs, and also to produce additional marketable goods. Collective farms disposing of large fields and of a production base enabling them to mechanize and intensify agriculture surrendered some of their gross yield at State fixed prices to meet the public needs in agricultural produce, and also accumulated capital for the expansion of agricultural mass production. The difference between the prices paid by the State to collective farms for their agricultural produce, and the prices at which the State then sold it to the urban and industrial population, went to the State Budget. However, from the State Budget the money flowed back into agriculture in the form of subsidies to M.T.S., and in the form of supplies of fertilizers, vehicles, agricultural machinery, selected seeds, etc., made available to agriculture at reduced prices, because their production was financed by the State; the State Budget also financed agronomic research institutes, schools of agriculture, agronomic instruction, land reclamation works, etc.

The right granted to every collective farmer and later to agricultural labourers on State farms (see below) of carrying on their own small producer-consumer farming solved the problem of satisfying the personal consumption and day-to-day needs of a peasant family, and expanded additional and varied production including craftsmen's home production. This permission was of particular importance in improving livestock breeding, which required more personal attention, at least until well-equipped and well-staffed large-scale Kolkhoz breeding farms came into being; the same could be said of market gardening, poultry farming, beekeeping and other subsidiary production.

However, this division of the collective farmer's labour between the Kolkhoz and his own domestic economy and the fact that he derived his income, in cash and kind, from these two sources led certain groups of collective farmers to see a contradiction between 'public' and 'private' interests. Some collective farms tended to reduce their State deliveries of agricultural produce at fixed price so as to increase the share of produce earmarked for distribution among their members or for sale on the collective farms' market at high retail prices. Many collective farmers also tried to cut down the time they worked on the collective farm, though attempting by every means to get as large a share of the Kolkhoz produce as possible, and to concentrate on the expansion of their individual farming. Pilfering from Kolkhoz harvest and theft of Kolkhoz property were frequent, and so was sabotage of Kolkhoz production. The permission to carry on collective farm trading evidently increased the farmer's interest in his private production at the expense of public needs.*

A number of measures were taken in the course of 1933–5 to combat these tendencies. The most important were:

(1) Special political sections (Politotdely) were formed at M.T.S. and on State farms and '15,000 best and most proven Bolsheviks' were sent there to strengthen leadership and control over collective farms and the manner in which they performed their large-scale agricultural work.† As most tractors and machinery were concentrated at M.T.S. and since collective farms had to make contracts with the M.T.S. for carrying out the principal agricultural operations, it was possible through the M.T.S. effectively to control the nature of the collective farms' production and to estimate harvest prospects. Moreover, agronomic work brought the political sections of M.T.S. and State farms in contact with

* Stalin thus formulated the new situation: 'The peasant calculated in the following way, "collective farm trading has been proclaimed; market prices have been legalized; in the market I can obtain more for a given quantity of grain than I can get for the same quantity if I deliver it to the State—hence if I am not a fool, I must hold on to my grain, deliver less to the State, leave more grain for collective farm trade, and in this way get more for the same quantity of grain sold."...The collective farm is a socialist *form* of economic organization...everything depends upon the *content* that is put into the form.... As long as the peasants were engaged in individual farming they were scattered and separated from each other, and therefore counter-revolutionary ventures of anti-Soviet elements among the peasantry could not be very effective. The situation is altogether different since the peasants have adopted collective farming. Therefore the penetration of anti-Soviet elements into the collective farms and their anti-Soviet activities may be much more effective...therefore *who* stands at the head of the collective farms and *who* leads them is of the greatest importance' (Stalin's italics). J. Stalin, *Leninism*, pp. 399, 404, 405, 406.

† *Izvestia*, 21 February 1933. For details see *The Stages of the Economic Policy of the U.S.S.R....*, pp. 253–4.

8

Kolkhoz managements and allowed them to influence appointments to responsible posts at collective farms.* Thanks to the political sections 'a numerous *aktiv* of non-Party collective farmers rallied around the Party in its struggle against hostile class elements and for the Bolshevik strengthening of collective farms, the defence of the public, Kolkhoz and State property and for giving priority to State obligations. Socialist emulation and exemplary workers' movements developed on a wide front'.† Towards the end of 1934, these special political sections having attained their 'shock objectives' were reorganized into ordinary Party organs and merged into the existing district Party Committees, whilst a post of deputy director in charge of political work was created at every M.T.S.

In March 1933 intra-district commissions were formed 'to determine prospects and probable gross yields of grain crops'. The commissions were also 'to combat irregularities in accounting and forestall inexact estimates of the sown areas and gross yields aimed at defrauding the State'.‡

(2) Very strict measures were taken for safeguarding Kolkhoz property. Kolkhoz property (unreaped crops, stocks in warehouses, livestock, seed reserves, etc.) was to rank equal with State property, and it was decreed 'to inflict as a measure of judicial repression for theft of Kolkhoz and co-operative property the highest measure of Socialist defence—shooting, with the confiscation of all property, and, in the case of mitigating circumstances, a minimum sentence of 10 years' imprisonment with the confiscation of all property. No amnesty to apply to criminals sentenced for theft of Kolkhoz and co-operative property.'§

(3) Very strict penalties were also decreed for sabotage of agricultural work, fraud and evasion connected with the State deliveries of agricultural produce, and for evading work on the collective farm, etc. The importance of the measures justifies the

---

* During 1933 and 1934, 3,368 political sections were formed at M.T.S. and 2,021 at State farms with 17,000 and 8,000 political workers, respectively. *The C.P. in Resolutions...*, p. 612.

† *The C.P. in Resolutions...*, p. 612.

‡ They were 'directly to check information about sown areas, prospects, gross yields' and so give information about the expected volume of State deliveries of agricultural produce. For details see the Sovnarkom S.S.S.R. regulation, 5 March 1933, 'Statutes of permanent State commissions....' *Izvestia*, 6 March 1933.

§ For details see the regulation of the U.S.S.R. Central Executive Committee and Sovnarkom S.S.S.R., 'On the defence of the property of State enterprises, collective farms and co-operatives, and for the safeguard of public property', *Pravda*, 8 August 1932.

following long extracts from the government regulation on the matter.

The regulation on the defence of public property of 7 August 1932 [quoted above] is to be extended to persons convicted of sabotaging agricultural work, stealing seed, maliciously reducing the norms of sowing, wrecking ploughing and sowing work, and so causing deterioration and lower yields of the land, deliberately damaging tractors and machinery, and destroying horses, all of these offences are to be punished as theft of Kolkhoz property.

Any fraudulent accounting of Kolkhoz production, labour and harvest must rank as aiding and abetting kulaks and anti-Soviet elements, and as an attempt at stealing Kolkhoz property and consequently comes under the law of 7 August 1932 on the defence of public property.

The observance of agronomic rules must cease being the private concern of individual collective farms. In every district, the District Executive Committee, on the advice of the provincial agronomic institutions, must establish agronomic rules, the observance of which is obligatory for collective farms, collective farmers and individual peasants; the infringement of these rules to be punishable by reprimands, fines in cash and kind, public blame and by more stern measures in the case of transgressors maliciously damaging State land.

Any member of a collective farm refusing on insufficient grounds to carry out work entrusted to him by the collective farm is to be fined the equivalent of five labour days by the management, and, in the case of repeated refusal, expelled from the collective farm.

Every individual peasant who has retained the use of State land must sow and deliver produce to the State according to the plan established for him by the local soviet; in regard to individual peasants indulging in speculation and persistently refusing to cultivate and sow the land they occupy—as was the case in some districts of the North Caucasus—local authorities must resort to strict measures, finally depriving them of the land, and, in individual cases, as an extreme measure deporting them beyond the boundaries of the district to less fertile regions.*

Severe and firm measures were also enforced to ensure timely sowing and harvesting of crops; for this purpose local authorities were granted the right even to mobilize the peasant population for compulsory labour service; and detailed rules were issued on the care of livestock and its use in field work.†

All these measures contributed towards bringing about a complete change in agricultural production and furthering its develop-

---

* For details see the regulation of the U.S.S.R. Central Executive Committee, dated 30 January 1933, *Izvestia*, 31 January 1933.

† Cf. the regulation of the Sovnarkom S.S.S.R. dated 23 January 1933, 'On measures regarding spring sowing in the Northern Caucasus' and 10 February 1933, 'On preparing livestock for spring sowing'.

ment; they contributed to make land tenure stable, mechanization of agriculture was generously financed, financial aid was afforded to collective farms and collective farmers for intensifying their production, the economic initiative of collective farmers was stimulated (by remunerating quality as well as quantity of work, by enabling them to improve their domestic economies, by sanctioning collective farm trading, etc.), in brief, conditions for the development of agricultural production on the basis of honest and conscientious work on the collective farm were created, whilst severe penalties were inflicted on those hindering this development. Combined with a growing experience in the organization of Kolkhoz production and the realization by the basic masses of peasants that only honest work can improve their personal well-being, these measures led to a complete change in the development of agricultural production and towards its steady growth since 1933. In its turn, this growth made it possible to abolish the rationing of agricultural products in 1935.

However, much remained to be done to solve problems of stable land tenure, of improved organization of State and collective farms, of a more complex development of Kolkhoz production, especially in raising of livestock, for defining the position of domestic economies and labour relations as between the collective farm and its members, and lastly for improving methods of planning agricultural production.

CHAPTER XIII. LABOUR

In the field of labour, the F.Y.P. assumed that there would only be a substantial increase in the man-power employed in the national economy during the first two years of the F.Y.P., with 'a gradual slowing down of the tempo in the following years', in such a manner that the annual increase would average 6 % over the five years. Actually, as already mentioned in the chapter on industry, the plan was signally 'over-fulfilled' in regard to labour. Being anxious to achieve the high targets set for industrial expansion, the managements of enterprises enrolled more and more labour.

During the first year of the F.Y.P., workers were enrolled from among unemployed belonging to trade groups and only to a minor extent from among people seeking employment for the first time.

In 1929 the Labour Exchanges still had on their registers 811,000 unemployed belonging to twenty-six trade groups, of which only 299,000 were unskilled workers.* In 1930, however, the intake of new workers was mainly made up of people seeking employment for the first time, unskilled labour from rural districts accounting for a large share. On 11 October 1930 the P. Commissar of Labour issued a statement to the effect that unemployment was liquidated and the payment of dole stopped. On the strength of this decree, those still unemployed were to be directed to any work regardless of their trade. 'No reasons to refuse the work offered are to be taken into consideration excepting ill-health, confirmed by a hospital certificate'.†

In the same month, in connexion with the acute shortage of skilled labour which was beginning to be felt, the Party Central Committee issued the following regulation: 'On measures to secure man-power for the national economy according to plan, and to fight labour turn-over.' This regulation ordered the S.E.C., the U.S.S.R. P. Commissariats of Transport and of Labour 'to guarantee the training and distribution of man-power in their subordinate branches according to plan, by appointing to enterprises people personally responsible for the training and distribution of workers'. The P. Commissariat of Labour was to 'register the following categories at Labour institutions, apart from categories of workers hitherto eligible for registration: (a) members of workers' and employees' families who are not members of trade unions and who are temporarily out of work, independently of the length of the unemployment period; (b) children of workers and employees even if without special training and if they have not yet been in paid employment; (c) wives and widows of workers and employees, non-members of trade unions and without any special training'. It was proposed to direct all these people to work, and refusal by a registered worker to accept a job entailed his removal from the labour organ's register without the right to enter employment for a definite period.

Moreover, the P. Commissariat of Labour had the right in agreement with trade unions and on the application of business institutions to remove and *transfer skilled labour and specialists from less important branches of the national economy to the more essential* [i.e. coal

---

* *Statistical Survey*, no. 6, 1930.

† In April 1929, 1,741,000 unemployed were registered with the Labour Exchanges, in April 1930, 1,081,000; in January 1931, 236,000 and by 1 August 1931, 18,000. *Stages of the U.S.S.R. Economic Policy*, p. 282.

mining, heavy metallurgy, transport and large-scale capital construc-
tion] *and from one district to another*....Managers of institutions and
enterprises who defer the transfer of workers and administrative and
technical personnel, or wrongly use within the enterprises workers
skilled in trades of which there is shortage, or decoy workers and
technical personnel from other enterprises, or transgress the norms of
wages or work established by the collective contract, or engage labour
in excess of planned requirements as well as technical personnel attempting to dodge transfer to other enterprises or to other districts—are
liable to prosecution...in order to maintain cadres of skilled workers on
production *it is forbidden* in the course of the forthcoming two years to
promote workers from the lathe to any administrative offices whatsoever, promotion from the lathe to higher production and skilled work only remaining unaffected....Deserters [i.e. those who dodged transfer to
some particular work] and 'flitters' [i.e. those who drifted from one
enterprise to another in search of more favourable labour conditions]
are deprived of the right to be sent to work at industrial enterprises
for 6 months.

At the same time people who had worked at the same enterprise
for a long time, exemplary workers, and members of Socialist competitions, were to receive preferential treatment in the allocation of
living space, for leaves, cures at sanatoria, and could be transferred
to a category of workers entitled to a better supply of rationed
goods.*

These measures had to be taken because the demand for skilled
labour and specialists exceeded supply, and also because enterprises competed with one another in trying to engage such cadres
as were available, whilst workers searching for better housing conditions, better wages and, in particular, for a transfer to a better
rationed category, often moved from enterprise to enterprise,
causing what was known as labour 'fluidity'. This shortage of
skilled workers was further increased by the introduction of the
7-hour working day and the continuous week; the former measure
had been adopted in April 1927, but began to be put into practice
only in the first year of the F.Y.P. period, necessitating the enrolment of additional labour. The latter was introduced in enterprises and institutions, with the same effect, towards the close of
1929. With the aim of intensifying the utilization of industrial
capacity, a decree of September 1929 imposed a 5-day working
week (4 days' work and 1 day's rest) on all enterprises excepting
building and enterprises engaged on seasonal work, whilst in institutions where a 6-hour working day had so far been the rule a

* *Ekon. Zhizn*, 22 October 1930.

7-hour working day was now introduced.* The adoption of the continuous week 'required the enrolment of new skilled workers. The labour market could not fully meet the demand. Semi-skilled and even unskilled workers are now given work requiring experience and training'.† The Soviet press of the day was full of news from 'factories, works, plants under construction to the effect that the labour turn-over is constantly increasing, that enterprises, especially building jobs, are like transit yards where hundreds of new workers are daily engaged and as many if not an even greater number leave. Hence, no managerial or trade union worker, and indeed no worker in the Soviet economy, fails to refer to the labour turn-over when he has to explain a break-through on one or another sector of the economic front'.‡ Actually, labour turn-over did involve an exceedingly high proportion of workers, as is graphically illustrated in Table 30, which gives the numbers of workers engaged and dismissed as a percentage of the total average employed.§

Table 30

	Engaged	Left		Engaged	Left
1928	100·8	92·4	1932	127·1	135·3
1929	122·4	115·2	1933	124·9	122·4
1930	176·4	152·4	1934	100·5	96·7
1931	151·2	136·8	1935	91·6	86·1

Millions of workers flowed through enterprises, and labour turn-over reached its high peak in 1930, during the second year of the F.Y.P.

This high labour turn-over affected not only workers, but also the engineering and technical personnel. In May 1930 a regulation of the U.S.S.R. Central Executive Committee prohibited payment of increased salaries to engineers and technicians whose salary was 250 roubles or more, if they moved to other enterprises without obtaining permission from the management of their former employment. However, this rule did not extend to persons who left managerial offices for production, or were transferred to new enterprises, or went to remote parts of the U.S.S.R. Moreover, the salaries of engineers and technicians working on production were to be higher than those paid to engineering and technical personnel employed in administration, and they were also placed on an equal footing with workmen in regard to supplies of con-

* For further details see the Sovnarkom S.S.S.R. regulation dated 24 November 1929, *Coll. Laws*, no. 63, 1929, § 586.

† *Za Industr.* 22 May 1930.　　　‡ *Za Industr.* 12 September 1930.

§ *Socialist Construction in the U.S.S.R.*, Yearbook 1935, p. 504; 1936, p. 531.

sumption goods and improvements in housing conditions, while certain facilities were also granted to their families.*

The high labour turn-over among engineering and technical personnel and their tendency to avoid work on production were not so much caused by the lure of higher salaries as by the desire to find safer work, unconnected with production risks and with possible prosecution for failure to fulfil production plans or for mishaps in production. The comprehensive character of the laws against economic crimes, or rather their interpretation by judiciary authorities, has been shown. In the tense atmosphere created by demands for the expansion of industrial production and by the sentences passed on groups of specialists for wrecking and counter-revolutionary activities (see p. 151), the connotation of economic crime was still further enlarged in 1930. The following offences were to be tried by criminal courts: excessive demands for man-power and engagement of workers above requirements as estab-lished in the productive-financial plan, failure to ensure a timely supply of man-power and to train skilled workers, infringements of wage standards established by collective contract or fixed by the State, failure to carry out decisions reached at production con-ferences, wrong utilization of raw or other materials, failure to uphold labour discipline through slackness, etc.† Such a wide interpretation of economic offences, combined with the distrust surrounding engineers and technicians with pre-revolution training and frequent cases of 'administrative zeal' displayed by local agents of the criminal magistrature and other representatives of the law, explain clearly enough why in those years engineering and technical personnel did their utmost to avoid the responsi-bility for 'personal management', which the institutions responsible for industrial administration were so tenaciously anxious to en-force. Equally clear is the reason underlying statements of this kind in the Soviet economic press:

in the Donbass production risks are not popular, they have become a rarity, many specialists avoid them carefully and cautiously. Even in those cases where a responsible specialist puts forward a valuable sug-gestion or measure, he waits for somebody else to carry it out. The only form of activity acceptable at the pit is acting 'on higher orders'. Any decision of Ugol [the S.E.C.'s Chief Administration of Coal Mining] is carried out without the slightest healthy criticism.‡

* Cf. the regulation of the U.S.S.R. Central Executive Committee, *Ekon. Zhizn*, 14 May 1930.

† For further details see *Collection of Principal Regulations concerning Labour*, 1931, pp. 56, 58, 61 and 62.   ‡ *Za Industr.* 27 June 1931.

Such an atmosphere surrounding the conditions of work of the technico-engineering personnel could not but adversely affect the quality of the enterprises' work.

Moreover, production was adversely affected by the intake of low skilled and hastily trained workers...the output per worker is decreasing, labour discipline declining, absenteeism growing and spoilage increasing. The worst feature is that adequate skilled labour cannot be secured for the new works going into production this year (1930) and next. In one way or another the numbers will reach the required figure but their standards of skill will not be equal to the actual needs of production. The standards of skill are also declining at old works already in production. Apart from natural loss, we are confronted by a decrease of skilled workers due to promotion and transfer to work in rural areas [in the first years of the F.Y.P., agriculture was collectivized and agricultural work was mechanized to a considerable extent, necessitating the transfer of many thousand workers to rural districts to carry out this mechanization].*

During the first years of the F.Y.P., the Soviet economic press was full of statements about the acute shortage of skilled labour and the difficulty of providing anything like the adequate number of experienced skilled workers for industrial and especially for the new enterprises.†

Truly heroic measures were taken to train both skilled workers and technico-engineering personnel. Numerous schools known as F.Z.U. (factory and works apprentices' schools) were opened at enterprises to train apprentices for skilled trades, as well as evening courses for adult workers to train them without taking them away from work. In the course of the first F.Y.P. period, the F.Z.U. schools trained 450,000 skilled workers, but the number of workers and apprentices employed in large-scale industry alone rose during those five years from 2,691,000 in 1928 to 5,153,000 in 1932; consequently the greater number of new workers consisted of unskilled workers without any industrial experience. According to the labour census of 1929, only half the workers employed in industry had had industrial experience prior to the Revolution, and according to the census of 1930 only 42%. In particular in the Donetz basin, by 1930 miners of pre-revolution standing formed only 19·6% of the workers employed. Moreover, among new

---

* *Za Industr.* 1 June 1930.

† 'Practically in every trade there is a shortage of skilled labour and this is the worst bottle-neck in our development' (*Za Industr.* 19 August 1930). 'Rolling stock works are clamouring about the shortage of skilled labour as well as of engineers and technicians' (*Ekon. Zhizn*, 11 September 1930).

workers engaged in 1929, 1930 and 1931, the majority were under 22 years of age and women accounted for a considerable share. The number of women employed in large-scale industry alone grew during the years of the first F.Y.P. from 769,000 to 2,207,000, and their relative share in the total amount of labour employed increased from 29 to 35 %. Naturally, this deterioration in the qualitative make-up of the working force was reflected in the decline of labour discipline, increasing voluntary absenteeism, decrease of the workers' hourly output, and in deterioration in the quality of goods.

A similar process—immense expansion at the expense of quality—was going on in regard to technico-engineering personnel. In pre-revolution Russia enterprises were less well staffed with engineers and technicians than in other countries. A conspicuous drop in the numbers of engineers and technicians occurred during the first years of the Revolution and of the recovery period. According to an enquiry of the S.E.C. in 1928, on the eve of the adoption of the F.Y.P., specialists (engineers, technicians and 'economists'*) in the entire industry of All-Union importance formed only 2·27 % of the number of workers. More precisely, engineers and technicians with higher education formed 0·61 %, engineers and technicians with secondary education 0·60 %, and so-called 'practicals' 0·71 %.†

The F.Y.P. made provisions for the training of huge numbers of new specialists and, indeed, from the point of view of numbers, very considerable results were achieved.

As early as 1928, the U.S.S.R. S.E.C. and the P. Commissariat of Transport took over some of the university science departments from the P. Commissariat of Education. This measure aimed at specializing technical education by bringing it more into line with production requirements. A general reorganization of existing universities and higher technical schools took place in 1930. The universities' science departments were taken over by the corresponding branches of economic combines of the corresponding P. Commissariats and only Teachers' Training Colleges and Arts' Faculties remained under the P. Commissariat of Education. University courses were reduced to three years (except in medical schools, where courses lasted four years), and the necessity of presenting a dissertation or thesis to qualify for a degree was abolished;

---

* A specialized term covering all members of the staff concerned with the economic, as opposed to technological, sides of production.

† For details see *Torg.-prom. Gazeta*, 22 July 1928.

in fact, the level of university education declined, though of course this was not the purpose of the reform. The number of universities and higher technical schools rose greatly, as is shown by the figures in Table 31.* It should be remembered that not only was both

Table 31

	1928–9	1929–30	1930–1	1932
Universities (number)	129	151	537	645
Students (thousands)	167	191	272	394
Technicums (number)	1,054	1,111	2,932	3,096
Students (thousands)	208	236	594	754

secondary and higher education free, but that students were even awarded maintenance grants for the entire duration of their studies. The choice of a profession was determined by personal preference for a special subject, or, in the case of a workers' candidate, by his being sent to a definite educational establishment by the promoting organization, and lastly by the number of available places in the corresponding schools. Material considerations, i.e. salaries attached to the various professions, played a very minor part in the allocation of students to schools. The choice of a profession was not governed by the regulating influence of supply and demand for highly qualified labour, but by planned measures designed to secure definite contingents of specialists for the national economy. Detailed data about the number of students at universities and technicums indicate that the largest number were studying at institutions administered by the S.E.C., next, in decreasing numbers, were those in the institutions of the P. Commissariat of Education, the P. Commissariat of Agriculture and the P. Commissariat of Transport, while considerably fewer were studying other special subjects.

Undoubtedly the pace at which schools were established and the influx of huge contingents of students had an adverse effect on the organization of teaching and the assimilation of instruction by students. Two years after the Higher Education reform, in 1932, it was officially stated that in carrying out the reform

abuses had appeared, mainly apparent in the one-sided attention directed to increasing the network of educational establishments and the number of students, whilst insufficient attention had been given to the quality of teaching; the subdivision of specialization had also been carried too far; as a result some universities gave degrees to specialists whose stan-

* *The U.S.S.R.'s National Economy, Statistical Handbook*, 1932, pp. 512–13; *Socialist Construction in the U.S.S.R., Statistical Yearbook*, 1934, p. 406.

dard is that of engineers but not of fully qualified engineers. Nor did technicums always prepare properly qualified technicians for the national economy and for social and cultural construction.*

This intake by productive industry of tremendous numbers of specialists, whose training was inadequate for the posts they held, was also an important contributory factor in the decline of the quality of the enterprises' work. Nevertheless, certain positive trends were developing in the field of labour during the first years of the F.Y.P. which must be pointed out here. Among the new skilled workers pouring into industry from the F.Z.U. schools and among the young technico-engineering personnel, there was much valuable human material, literally thousands, who only needed practical experience to provide really valuable skilled cadres. For the time being their very quantity was detrimental to quality, but for the future this very quantity promised to spell quality. Moreover, from among this young generation thousands were called upon to become the leaven and nucleus of new forms of collective endeavours organized by groups of workers for raising labour productivity and improving methods, which came to be known as 'socialist competition'.†

The majority of foreign writers who have described the development of the national economy of the U.S.S.R. have viewed all forms of socialist emulation with scepticism, and have mentioned them, either as one of the peculiarities of the Soviet system, or merely for the sake of comprehensiveness, though denying them any serious effect in the development of the U.S.S.R.'s industry. In our opinion this conception is erroneous. During the years of the first F.Y.P., masses of workers without any industrial traditions were poured into enterprises, the shortage of housing for new workers was very acute (in particular in new industrial districts), and the supply of foodstuffs and even more the supply of mass consumption goods was barely adequate, while production and construction plans were extremely strenuous; in these conditions especially the collective social stimuli to raise production and the enthusiasm for producing and building not for the sake of direct, personal, material advantages, but in the name of future productive possibilities, was often of a tremendous importance. Those very groups of workers who initiated and popularized various

---

* For details see the U.S.S.R.'s Central Executive Committee's regulation regarding educational establishments, *Bull. Commissariat of Education of the R.S.F.S.R.*, no. 54, 1932, p. 715.

† 'Socialist emulation' would perhaps be a better rendering of this term.

forms of socialist emulation were the stabilizing element in industry and, with the support of the factory administration and the trade unions, fought such undesirable manifestations in the field of labour as the decline of labour discipline and of labour productivity, and the deterioration of the quality of work. Some outline, however sketchy, of the essentials of this socialist emulation of the time is called for.

In November 1928, on the eve of the F.Y.P., the Plenum of the Party Central Committee called upon 'all Party members to concentrate their efforts on overcoming economic difficulties and mobilizing all the creative powers of the working class in order to maintain at any cost the pace set by us for industrialization and socialization, and to carry out the proposed economic plan'.* And, indeed, at the end of 1928 the first 'shock brigade' came into being at a Leningrad textile mill (Ravenstvo), on the initiative of forty-nine young Communist workers who undertook to fulfil the plan for the output of yarn, to set an example of labour discipline, not to miss any working day, fully to utilize their working time, and to prevent machines from standing idle. With the support of Party and trade union organizations their initiative spread to other brigades, and three months later 30 % of the mill's workers had become 'exemplary workers'.†

In January 1929 the paper *Komsomolskaya Pravda* suggested the idea of organizing an All-Union Socialist competition among enterprises. On 5 March of the same year workers of the Leningrad factory 'Krasny Vyborzhets' published an appeal calling on workers of the U.S.S.R. factories and works to join in a socialist emulation for the fulfilment of the economic programme of the F.Y.P., for raising labour productivity, improving labour discipline and lowering production costs. Hundreds of factories and works responded to the appeal and entered the competition. In May 1929 the Party Central Committee issued a decree on the organization of socialist emulation among factories and works, and on 6 August 1929, a Sunday, on the suggestion of the A.U.C.C.T.U., the first All-Union Industrialization Day was held; the idea of this Industrialization Day, i.e. of working on a rest day 'for the Soviet land', was proposed by a workman in a letter to the *Leningrad Pravda*. In December 1929 the first All-Union Congress of shock brigades was held with great splendour in Moscow, and

* *The C.P. in Resolutions...*, p. 297.
† The usual translation of the Russian expression is 'shock worker', but 'exemplary worker' is preferable.

by 1 January 1930 29% of all industrial workers were taking part in socialist emulation and exemplary workers' movements. Later, the participation of working masses in various forms of socialist emulation and exemplary workers' movements expanded, and Soviet statistical sources give the following figures for workers taking part in competitions as a percentage of the total number of workers employed in industry:*

1930	1931	1932	1933	1934	1935
29%	65%	68%	71%	73%	72%

These percentages, of course, include workers who joined in competitions only formally, the so-called 'pseudo-exemplary workers', and the figures also cover cases of 'sham adoption of the principles of socialist emulation and exemplary workers' movements'; nevertheless, these facts do confirm how powerful and tenacious was the drive for socialist emulation, if even the unwilling felt bound to join.

Admittedly, exemplary workers enjoyed some material advantages; they were registered in a better supplied ration category, received permits for manufactured goods in short supply, obtained places in rest homes, sanatoria, etc. However, considering the large participation of workers in socialist emulation these were obviously but slight advantages, and could not be a decisive incentive to compete.

The obligations which at the time exemplary workers took upon themselves varied greatly in individual factories and at different times, but the following will serve as an indication: to surpass standards of output, to prevent spoiling by the fault of the worker, to keep equipment from standing idle either through his own or the administration's fault, to maintain his tools and working place in perfect cleanliness, to arrive to work on time, to make full use of working time, to take an active part in production conferences and contribute suggestions towards rationalizing production and, above all, by methods of mutual aid and by handing on working experience, to help laggards and bring them up to the level of the foremost exemplary workers. The description of exemplary worker was reserved for those who, apart from taking part in socialist emulation and achieving better results than their mates, also passed on their experience to others and set them an example of better work.

* M. Eskin, *Fundamental Ways of Development of the Socialist Forms of Labour*, p. 43.

The forms of socialist emulation varied with the actual problems occurring in the course of industrial development, or with the difficulties arising from the execution of plans for expanding production, eliminating defects in the quality of work, etc. Here are some examples: When in 1929 a shortage of metal became apparent, a month's drive to combat losses was announced at the suggestion of the Leningrad works 'Elektrosila'. In May 1930 one of the successful pits came forward with the idea of 'a public pull', i.e. in order to help other less successful pits to raise their productivity, the best labour organization of the successful pit was to give practical demonstrations of their experience. The A.U.C.C.T.U., owing to the success of the 'public pull' experiment by one pit, appealed to workers 'to pool the experience of the "public pull" among all factories and works. Brigades, pits, works failing to achieve the plan, are to be taken in tow by the public pull.' In July 1930 a new form of socialist emulation known as the 'cross productive-financial plan' made its appearance, i.e. the enterprise drafted its own productive-financial plan, aiming at higher targets than the official plan with the object of increasing production and improving financial results. Individual factories competed against each other along these lines. In 1931 the 'model quality shock brigades' and the 'khozraschet brigades' set themselves the task of raising the quality of work. In 1932 the so-called 'technico-production-financial plan' (Techpromfinplan) came into being; its slogan was: 'Given the same material means, on the basis of greater economy, better utilization of possibilities, better mobilization of force and better practical leadership, to give the country more and better production.' Upon receiving a production task, shock brigades scrutinized it for possibilities of improving the technological process, of economizing materials and equipment, of raising norms of output, etc. 1933 saw the introduction of the 'social-technical examination', which aimed at organizing a check on young workers preparing to use technically complicated machine-tools and so to increase the zeal and sense of responsibility of those training for the technical minimum or attending courses for increasing their qualifications. This movement grew to considerable proportions, and, as a result, by 1 July 1935, 700,000 workers in heavy industry passed the State technical examination. In 1935 appeared the so-called 'Otlichnichestvo', i.e. a movement the aim of which was to produce goods of excellent quality only; at the end of the working day the worker delivered his production which was graded as 'excellent', 'good' or just 'satisfactory'. The main purpose of the competition was to raise the quality of production.* Eventually, 1935 saw the birth of the famous Stakhanov movement, which will be dealt with below.

The trade unions, together with the Party organizations, took a most active and even leading part in the organization of these various socialist competitions. As already stated, on the eve of the introduction of the F.Y.P., trade unions were contributing on an increasing scale to the organization of labour designed to raise production, lower production costs, carry out planned directives, etc. With the adoption of the F.Y.P., trade unions concentrated their activities more and more on helping to carry out planned industrial programmes. It is well known that this change of orientation from the trade unions' traditional object of protecting the workers' interests against the employer, to that of affording help to the factory administration, gave rise to an internal struggle between old trade union leaders and supporters of the new trends which ended in the reform of the trade union administration, and the passing of trade union leadership into the hands of representatives of the new movement.

The Sixteenth Party Congress, which met in the middle of 1930, passed a special resolution 'On trade union problems in the reconstruction period', setting the trade unions

the goal of mobilizing and organizing the working masses for the purpose of building a socialist society. Trade unions must be the closest and most permanent collaborators of the State, whose political and economic work is directed by the conscious vanguard of the working class—the Communist Party.... All this alters trade union aims, demands of them a more active and direct participation in economic construction and an increased interest in production.... While struggling against bureaucratic abuses in the State and economic machinery, and promoting and training new thousands and tens of thousands of progressive proletarians, trade unions must fully co-ordinate their work aimed at improving the workers' material position and that dealing with production problems.... Socialist emulation and its offspring, the exemplary workers' movement, are decisive and fundamental factors vitalizing and improving trade-union work, and bringing wide working masses to participate in industrial management.... That is why socialist emulation and shock brigades must become the corner-stone of trade-union production activities in enterprises and workshops. A radical change in the work of the production conferences is made necessary by the development of socialist emulation and of the exemplary workers' movement.

* For detailed data on various forms of Socialist emulation see M. Eskin, *The Fundamental Ways of Development of the Socialist Forms of Labour*, Moscow, 1935; B. Markus, *Labour in the Socialist Society*, Moscow, 1939.

The shock brigade must become a primary cell for drawing workers into industrial administration. Exemplary workers are called upon to become the backbone of production conferences. The increasing importance of planning in the national economy, which determines for lengthy periods relations between various elements of the national economy, construction tempo and the workers' material position, makes it imperative for trade unions actively to participate in the drafting of economic plans. Moreover, it is necessary once and for all to do away with a bureaucratically formal attitude towards trade union participation in the drafting of the economic plan, both on the part of trade unions themselves and of economic and State institutions. Without directly interfering with the administration's operational work, trade-union organs must nevertheless combat personal management of a faulty bureaucratic type, and any disregard, on the part of management, of the productive initiative and self-expression of the masses. A most important function of all trade union organizations is the promotion of workers and members of the technical personnel who have most distinguished themselves, and in particular of exemplary workers to posts of factory directors, workshop stewards and their deputies.*

It seemed appropriate to quote this long extract giving a vivid picture of the work which trade unions were expected to and did carry out rather than to give a formal list of functions which distinguish the Soviet trade unions from trade unions in other countries.

Gradually these trade union functions of organizing labour and preparing and carrying out measures designed to regulate labour relations in industry expanded to the extent of merging with many functions of the P. Commissariat of Labour; this identity of functions of the P. Commissariat of Labour and of the A.U.C.C.T.U. was formally effected in 1933 when the Commissariat was merged into the A.U.C.C.T.U. The latter took over the general direction in all matters of social insurance, including control and guidance of trade unions on questions of social insurance, and the drafting for approval by the Sovnarkom S.S.S.R. of the summary social insurance budget and social insurance contribution rates. By a special decision of the A.U.C.C.T.U., labour inspection was organized according to industries and attached to trade union central committees and their local organs; labour inspection authorities retained the right to impose fines for infringement of the labour code. Rules and measures regarding safety devices and industrial hygiene were henceforth to be agreed by the corresponding trade union's central committee with the relevant depart-

* For further details see *The C.P. in Resolutions...*, pp. 428–36.

ment. It also became a function of the A.U.C.C.T.U. and of local trade-union councils to register collective contracts and to invalidate contracts contrary to the law. The A.U.C.C.T.U. were to submit to the Sovnarkom S.S.S.R. their conclusions on plans regarding labour (numbers of workers, wages fund, labour productivity, etc.) drawn up by Gosplan for approval by the Sovnarkom S.S.S.R.; and they were also to draft and submit to the U.S.S.R. Government an estimate of administrative expenses for social insurance and labour protection services.*

In this manner the A.U.C.C.T.U. embraced the functions of the trade unions' central administration and of the P. Commissariat of Labour.

Parallel with these measures from 1931 onward reforms were carried out on wages and the extension of piece-work rates, and eliminating hastily adopted and ill-prepared methods of intensifying production (the continuous week, the depersonalized use of lathes, and the functional subdivision of one production process among a number of workers), and strengthening the administrative legal provision for enforcing labour discipline and improving the material and social position of the engineering and technical staffs and their legal authority over production.

In a statement already quoted at a conference of managerial workers on 23 June 1931, Stalin sharply criticized the wages system current in the first years of the F.Y.P. when many establishments fixed wages scales obliterating 'any difference between skilled and unskilled work, between heavy and light work'. It is very significant that Stalin should have thought it necessary, quoting Marx and Lenin, to point out why it was time to do away with 'wage equalization' and to change over to a scale of wages strongly differentiated according to the degree of skill. 'To train skilled workers, to attach workers to the enterprises and end labour turn-over, we must give the unskilled worker a stimulus and a prospect of advancement, of rising...and the more boldly we do this the better.' At that time, the conviction still prevailed among Party (Left Wing) members and within trade unions, that grading wages is contrary to socialist principles, that they should not be graded but equalized. These convictions found their embodiment in actual measures designed to equalize wages paid for labour requiring various degrees of skill and favouring less qualified or un-

* For further details see the Sovnarkom S.S.S.R. and A.U.C.C.T.U. regulation, dated 10 September 1933 in *Coll. Laws of the U.S.S.R.* no. 57, 1933, § 333.

skilled work. Stalin's order was 'to put an end to labour turn-over, to abolish equal pay, readjust the wages system and improve the workers' living conditions'.

It also became evident that the continuous week designed to intensify the utilization of productive possibilities resulted in a phenomenon called depersonalization ('Obeslichka'), i.e. 'the absence of individual responsibility for work performed, or for lathes and tools', because different groups of workers used the same lathes in turn. The consequences of depersonalization were particularly detrimental to transport, as railway engines passed from one brigade to another and then to a third, and none in particular was responsible for their upkeep. As a result large numbers of engines were quickly worn out and went out of use. Stalin stated that 'some of our comrades hurried too much in introducing the continuous week and in their haste distorted it into depersonalization'. So the new directive prescribed 'the liquidation of depersonalization, the improvement of labour organization and the correct distribution of man-power'.

It became evident, too, that a radical change of attitude towards the technical-industrial intelligentsia was imperative. Its members were to be cleared of the sweepingly indiscriminate suspicions that they were not loyally carrying out the Soviet Government's measures and in fact wished to obstruct them; their material, living and social conditions were to be improved. As already indicated in the survey of industrial administration, the new policy prescribed 'a change of attitude towards engineers and technicians of the old school, greater attention and solicitude for them and more boldness in enlisting their co-operation'; at the same time providing 'the U.S.S.R. working class with their own technical-industrial intelligentsia [i.e. specialists of working-class and peasant descent educated in Soviet schools]...capable of understanding the policy of our country's working class and ready to put it conscientiously into effect'.

Meanwhile it was becoming increasingly difficult to recruit man-power, not only skilled, but unskilled also; the influx of man-power from rural areas was declining since the large-scale collectivization of agriculture had been carried out in 1929–30, while the practice of dividing the collective farm's profits equally among all its members was then the rule. In this connexion 'the organized recruiting of man-power by concluding contracts with collective farms and by mechanizing labour' (i.e. by using machinery for the most laborious processes, particularly in the timber industry, building, coal-mining, and in transport for the loading and unloading of freights) was prescribed.

These general instructions were gradually embodied in concrete measures of which some of the more important follow.

At first, in 1931, wages were adjusted only in the coal industry, on the principle of widening the gap between the lower and the higher grades of skill; then the reform was extended to the metal-working industries and to transport, and finally to other branches of industrial production. In the coal industry eleven grades were established, and wages rose not only from grade to grade, but differences in wages increased progressively: e.g. the difference between the first grade's daily wage of 1·60 roubles and the second grade's 1·75 roubles was only 15 kopeks or 9%, whereas the difference between the 5·75 roubles wage of grade 10 and the 7 roubles wage of grade 11 was 1·25 roubles or 21%. Moreover, for fulfilling the monthly norm of output and completing the full number of working days, underground workers received a 10% bonus. In other industries and in transport the wages scale was fixed on similar lines, i.e. wages rose not only absolutely but also progressively with increased qualifications. However, at the time, foodstuffs and mass consumption goods were rationed and the purchasing power of the rouble varied according to the supply category of its owner, with the result that the regulating effect of wages was considerably undermined.

The next step was made when the Sovnarkom S.S.S.R. and the Party Central Committee issued the regulation 'on the extended rights of industrial managements in the matter of supplying workers and improving the ration card system'. This regulation was made to 'combat allocation of foodstuffs and manufactured goods to absentees and flitters who do not actually work at enterprises', and 'to strengthen the director's powers'. The task of supplying the enterprises' workers devolved directly on the industrial managements; the whole machinery of the Closed Workers' Co-operatives (see p. 238) was transferred to them on long-term credits, complete with shops, chattels, cash, stock-in-trade, canteens and subsidiary resources such as market gardens, pigsties, dairy and poultry farms, fisheries, etc. Enterprises were equipped with Sections of Workers' Supply, and special deputy directors of workers' supply were put in charge of them. Henceforth, factory managements issued ration cards to workers and their families. Upon dismissal the worker and his family lost the right to use the ration cards for food and manufactured goods issued by the management, as well as the right to lodge in houses belonging to the enterprise or institution. This regulation gave the director a very effective weapon against labour turn-over, absenteeism and generally speaking all sorts of breaches of labour discipline, and at the same time enabled him to regulate real wages by distributing different kinds of cards according to the category into which the worker was placed.

A very drastic step was taken towards the close of 1932 to check absenteeism. This was a regulation of the Party Central Committee and the Sovnarkom S.S.S.R. dated 15 November 1932 ordering that workers and employees guilty of one day's voluntary absence from work should be dismissed and deprived of the housing accommodation allocated to them in the enterprise's or institution's houses. No worker or employee could be taken on by the administration of an enterprise without a certificate from his previous place of employment stating the reason for his dismissal. Moreover, managerial staffs, guilty of disregarding the Government regulation on absenteeism, were liable to be prosecuted before administrative or judicial tribunals.* In April 1934 a further regulation was published to the effect that 'all economic and soviet organizations, as a personal responsibility of the head of the institution, are to record in the labour book of the persons thus penalized, the penalties inflicted by the Commission of Soviet Control'.†

From 1931 'comradely-production tribunals' were set up in factories, works and State social and business institutions, whose duty it was to wage a 'struggle for the enforcement of firm production discipline and for carrying out the enterprises' or institutions' productive-financial plan, and to use all manner of cautionary and disciplinary measures against persons breaking labour discipline and internal order rules, and also those carelessly handling the property of the enterprise or institution'. General meetings of workers and employees of the corresponding enterprise or institution, or factory conferences, elected exemplary workers in enterprises, and exemplary employees in institutions, to sit on these tribunals. For definite breaches of labour discipline these tribunals had the right to inflict fines, to bring the question of dismissal before the administration, and to propose to the corresponding trade-union organization the expulsion of the culprit from the union for a definite period of time.‡

---

* For details see *Coll. Laws*, 1932, no. 78, § 475. *Bull. Financ. and Econ. Leg.* 1933, no. 13.

† For details see *Bull. Financ. and Econ. Leg.* 1934, no. 13.

‡ For details see *Coll. Decrees*, 1931, no. 14, § 160.

From December 1931 enterprises and institutions began to change over from the 5-day continuous week to a 6-day week broken by precisely fixed rest days. A struggle against depersonalization was also undertaken.* These measures did bring about a decrease in the labour turn-over and also led to an increase in the days actually worked; they diminished absenteeism and, on the whole, improved labour discipline (see Table 32). The application

Table 32

	Days of actual work*	Absence on insufficient grounds (days)*
1929	294·2	4·09
1930	252·6	4·49
1931	253·2	5·96
1932	257·2	5·96
1933	265·8	0·93
1934	265·4	0·67
1935	266·2	0·76

* *Socialist Construction in the U.S.S.R., Statistical Yearbook*, 1934, 1935, 1936.

of the piece-work system of payment became more widespread. In 1928, 57·5 % of the sum total of working hours worked in large-scale industry were paid on a piece-work basis; by 1932 and 1935 the respective figures had grown to 63·7 and 70·7 %. Meanwhile contingents of skilled workers coming from the F.Z.U. schools were increasing, as were those of workers trained at evening courses for adults without leaving production. Moreover, it was decided that every pupil upon leaving the F.Z.U. schools had to work for at least three years in industry according to his trade, before being entitled to enter a technicum or a university.†

It was decreed that from January 1933,

* Cf. the Sovnarkom S.S.S.R. regulation (dated 21 November 1931), *Coll. Laws of the U.S.S.R.* 1931, no. 67, § 448. At the All-Union Congress of Trade Unions held in May 1932, a resolution was passed demanding that 'depersonalization be done away with, and that at every lathe, every unit and every working place there should be a worker regularly working there and responsible for its upkeep. The Congress calls upon all trade-union organizations to enforce the maximum application of the piece-work system of payment as combining the growth of wages for individual workers with increased labour productivity and reduction of production costs. The Congress draws the trade unions' attention to the need of actually enforcing labour discipline, personal management and khozraschet and of raising the authority of the foreman and the engineer in the workshop and the enterprise'. *Trud*, 8 May 1932.

† For further details see the Central Executive Committee and the Sovnarkom S.S.S.R. regulation, dated 15 September 1933, *Coll. Laws of the U.S.S.R.* 1933, no. 59, § 357.

workers in all branches of the national economy on the U.S.S.R.
P. Commissariat of Labour's lists, of trades based on minimum technical standards of attainment, as proposed by business institutions and
approved by the P. Commissariat of Labour, are to begin mastering the
compulsory technical minimum.... After the stated time limits fixed for
taking the training, only workers, whether newly engaged or already
working at the enterprise, who have passed the compulsory technical
minimum examination will be allowed to work on complex combinations, machine-tools and mechanisms for which the technical minimum
is required.... It will be the duty of enterprises, and the responsibility
of their heads to provide the workers with the means for successfully
carrying out the training for the technical minimum (accommodation,
group instructors, educational appliances, etc.). Training courses are
to be held outside working hours, and attendance is compulsory twice
a 6-day week. Absence from the course is to be considered as a breach
of internal rules and of labour discipline.*

In December 1934 it was decreed that State technical examinations were to be introduced in heavy industry for the main categories of workers. It will be shown later that measures for raising
the workers' skill were further expanded after the abolition of
rationing and with the focusing of effort on raising quality of work.

From 1931 measures began to be taken for the organized recruitment of labour in rural districts. Business institutions were to
conclude agreements with collective farm managements 'for their
active collaboration in recruiting man-power', and individual
agreements with the recruited peasants regarding the conditions
of work at the enterprises. Moreover, and in the coal industry in
particular, trade-union and Party workers were to conduct an
organized mass-political campaign among workers urging them to
enter into a freely undertaken obligation to work for 2–3 years at
a given pit, those who had so committed themselves to be guaranteed accommodation and help in setting up houses, allotments,
etc. In order to regulate the recruitment of man-power, special
commissions were created, whose duty it was to estimate the labour
resources of individual districts, to deal with applications for man-
power sent in by business institutions, and to draft operational
plans for transferring man-power from one district to another.†
This method of recruiting labour was somewhat altered in 1938,
as will be shown later.

* For further details see the regulation of the U.S.S.R. P. Commissariat of
Labour, dated 11 December 1932, *Trud*, 27 December 1932.
† For details see the *Journal of the U.S.S.R. P. Commissariat of Labour*, 1931,
no. 29. *Coll. Laws of the U.S.S.R.* 1933, no. 25, § 148. *Coll. Decrees*, 1933, no. 46,
§ 194.

Measures were also taken to improve the material and social position of the engineering and technical personnel. A regulation of the Party Central Committee and the Sovnarkom S.S.S.R., dated 1 August 1931, granted to engineering and technical workers equal rights with workmen for receiving consumption goods, insurance benefits, places in rest homes and sanatoria, and housing accommodation. Moreover, 'considering the need to ensure for specialists favourable conditions of work at home, especially for raising their qualifications, engineering and technical personnel are, like responsible workers, to be entitled to additional accommodation'. This right to be housed on an equal footing with industrial workers, and even somewhat better, was an important step towards improving the living conditions of engineering and technical staffs, because the acute shortage of housing, particularly in the rapidly growing new industrial districts, had necessitated a very strict rationing of housing space.

Moreover, the children of engineering and technical workers were granted the same rights as workmen's children to enter educational establishments. From 1936 all educational establishments were opened to the children of all citizens whatever their social extraction.* The salaries of engineering and technical personnel were somewhat increased, percentage bonuses awarded for those who worked for long periods at the same establishment, and certain income tax reliefs were also granted.† Actually, these measures for improving the position of engineering and technical workers met at first with much local opposition, particularly in remote districts, where local Party and trade-union workers thought it 'politically inadmissible' to put measures favouring specialists into effect. However, gradually they came to be applied, and the position of the engineering and technical personnel improved with time.

The procedure for indicting managerial staffs and specialists for economic crimes was altered. Proceedings could be taken only with the sanction of the regional or provincial prosecuting magistrate, and in republics not subdivided into provinces only by the prosecuting magistrate of the republic; the preliminary consent of the corresponding economic organizations was required, and the investigation was to be carried out entirely by the examining magistrates. The investigating organs could summon managerial, technical and engineering workers to give evidence only with the

---

* For details see *Coll. Laws of the U.S.S.R.* 1936, no. 1, § 2.
† For details see *Coll. Laws of the U.S.S.R.* 1931, no. 48, § 322.

authorization of the corresponding prosecuting magistrate. The latter was himself liable to prosecution for issuing unjustified summonses. Thus, specialists had a fair guarantee of not being prosecuted for minor offences or even gratuitously by over-zealous local administrative and judicial authorities.

Towards the end of 1932, reforms were also undertaken in the sphere of education. It was decreed that 'in further expanding the V.U.Z. [i.e. in opening new and enlarging existing universities], special attention is to be given to avoiding unnecessary duplication, and the creation of midget universities'. Only holders of appropriate university degrees were henceforth entitled to occupy university chairs and teaching posts. Prospective university students had to pass entrance examinations, attendance at lectures became compulsory, and the duration of university courses was lengthened to 4 and 5 years, and that of technicums to 3 and 4 years; it was forbidden to mobilize students, and particularly senior university members, for all sorts of political and economic campaigns or to award degrees for shortened courses. These measures contributed to raising the standards of attainment in universities and technicums, and the national economy benefited by better qualified specialists.

These measures and many concurrent ones brought about those changes for the better in the qualitative side of the work of industrial enterprises and other branches of the national economy which, as we have described above, began to be felt in 1933-4, and became particularly apparent from 1935, when rationing was abolished.

CHAPTER XIV. INTERNAL TRADE DURING THE RATIONING PERIOD

The Soviet system of rationing consumption by the population was built up on quite original principles and differed very substantially from the systems known in other countries. Although it was built up gradually, underwent many changes, was not always strictly applied, and was altered in the light of experience, the Soviet rationing system aimed at attaining the following four main objects:

(1) The planned distribution of most of the country's marketable production and the regulation of the consumption of the whole population.

(2) The limitation of civil consumption on a differential and not on an egalitarian basis, planned from the point of view of production and not from that of consumption. This was intended to produce a rationing system aimed at supporting development of industrial production.

(3) The regulation of price of all the main consumer goods and the regulation of the demands of the population with the aim of achieving the planned absorption of its purchasing power.

(4) The making possible of capital accumulation in the national economy, the maintenance of the planned rate of industrial construction and investment for strengthening the defence of the country.

The main measures which the Government took to achieve these aims were as follows:

(a) The Soviet Government in the first place introduced measures for the distribution of marketable agricultural products. State purchasing organizations were ordered to cover, by contract purchases, the whole volume of marketable agricultural products and to introduce the practice not only of seasonal contracts but of annual contracts extending over a period of years. The collectivization of peasant holdings which began on a large scale in the autumn of 1929 greatly facilitated this task. The centralized State purchasing organizations, which in 1928-9 accounted for approximately 72 % of all marketable agricultural products, at the end of the first F.Y.P. (i.e. 1932) already covered 95·4 % of all marketable supplies of grain; as regards the industrial crops, nearly the whole gross output was purchased by the State and the co-operative purchasing organizations.* These purchases by contract had only formally the character of an agreement between agricultural producers and the State purchasing organizations. In practice they were a special form of compulsory delivery of agricultural produce to the State at fixed prices. In 1933 the contract system was abolished even in form,† and replaced by fixed quotas of delivery of agricultural produce to the State. These deliveries had, and still have, the character of taxation in kind. In addition to these centralized deliveries the State and co-operative purchasing organizations were gradually extended over 'decentralized purchases' or non-compulsory purchases at somewhat higher prices than those which were paid to the producers for the centralized deliveries. By

* G. Ya. Neiman, *Internal Trade U.S.S.R.* pp. 72, 249.
† *Coll. Laws of the U.S.S.R.* 1933, no. 4, § 25.

means of these 'decentralized purchases', State and co-operative trade aimed at including that part of the disposable marketable production that remained in the hands of agricultural producers.

Legitimate private trade in agricultural products was completely abolished and the entire volume of private trade, which in 1929 had amounted to 13·5 % of the total retail trade, had declined by 1930 to 5·6 % thereof, and by 1931 had practically ceased to exist. It is true that private trade in agricultural products con-

Table 33. *Total retail turn-over (without 'communal' feeding and Kolkhoz trade) in million roubles at current prices*

	Total turn-over	State trade and co-operative trade		Private trade	
		Total	%	Total	%
1923–4	5,399	2,283	42·3	3,116	57·7
1924–5	7,773	4,473	57·5	3,300	42·5
1925–6	11,732	6,769	57·7	4,963	42·3
1926–7	13,718	8,654	63·1	5,064	36·9
1928	15,157	11,750	77·5	3,407	22·5
1929	16,867	14,594	86·5	2,273	13·5
1930	18,625	17,582	94·4	1,043	5·6
1931	24,725	24,725	100·0	—	—
1932	35,504	35,504	100·0	—	—
1933	43,403	43,403	100·0	—	—
1934	54,772	54,772	100·0	—	—
1935	73,723	73,723	100·0	—	—

tinued to exist on a small scale, but it took the form of casual sales of small quantities by peasants in local markets, of the resale by illicit tradesmen or of sales by private individuals of rationed products in the local markets or of exchange of rationed goods.

Not until 1933 was the free market legalized in what was known as the Kolkhoz trade (see p. 241). The Kolkhoz as a whole, the collective farmers (Kolkhozniki), and the remaining individual peasants were allowed, after they had fulfilled their obligations regarding deliveries of agricultural products to the State, to sell the remainder on the local markets direct to the consumer without the intervention of a middleman. But this Kolkhoz trade was very limited in extent and existed only in local markets. In general, owing to the system of centralized deliveries together with the 'decentralized purchases', the Soviet Government during this period disposed, on an average, of about 95 % of the total marketable produce of agriculture and was consequently in a position to regulate strictly the direction and quantity of agricultural produce consumed at home and to allocate part of it for export.

All goods were first of all divided into two main groups known as 'non-market supply' and 'market supply'. The 'non-market' supply consisted of goods destined to provide for industrial needs, for the requirements of the army, for export and for other State purposes. The 'market supply' was also divided into two main groups of goods—'planned' and 'regulated'. The distribution of all the most important goods was planned, and the distinction between 'planned' and 'regulated' goods consisted in the degree to which their distribution was planned *centrally*. The 'planned' group of goods comprised the more important consumption goods and the scarcer commodities, and in this group allocation was planned in detail from the centre not only for distribution to the republics and regions, but also to the local trading organizations. The 'regulated' group included goods which were less scarce or less important for the general mass of consumers, and the planned distribution of these goods was less strictly centralized. These goods were simply allocated to the republics and central trade organizations, while the regional trade organizations arranged the details of their distribution.

Goods from the 'planned' group were transferred to the 'regulated' group according to the situation with regard to their production and to fluctuations in demand. In addition to these, the 'market supply' was divided into the following 'supplies':

(1) A supply of rationed goods to meet the needs of the urban and industrial population.

(2) A supply of rationed goods for the needs of the agricultural population.

(3) A supply for 'commercial trade' (see pp. 238–9), for the sale of products and goods in the State trading organization at higher prices.

(4) A special supply to meet the needs of foreign specialists and groups, known as 'Insnab' (*Snabzhenie inostrantsev*—supply for foreigners) and for the conversion of foreign exchange into commodities by private individuals, known as 'Torgsin' (*Torgovlia s inostrantsami*—trade with foreigners).

The greater part of the agricultural population was practically excluded from the supply of rationed bread and other foodstuffs.

The agricultural population was supplied in an entirely different manner from the urban and industrial population, as is shown below.

The number of rationed necessities were progressively increased until April 1932 as far as foodstuffs were concerned, and until the middle of 1931 as regards industrial goods. After these dates a contrary process began of reducing the number of rationed necessities and extending the free sale of these foodstuffs through the special network of commercial trade organizations.

(b) From the beginning of the introduction of rationing it was stressed that it was based on the principle of differentiation and not on that of unification. Rationed goods were supplied in different quantities to different categories of the population. But from the outset the unified system of classifying the population according to different categories was not fully elaborated. (One set of categories was introduced in Moscow, another in Leningrad and others in the other towns.) However, in 1930 the Government had already begun to unify the rations allowed to the different categories of the population. In February 1930 all towns were divided into two (later into four) groups, and all the population in these towns was divided into different categories on the basis of 'class—production —distinction'. The highest amount of rations was given to the 'special' group,* then to the first group, then to the second group and so on.†

By these differentiations the Soviet Government aimed at supplying larger quantities of necessities to the workers in the most important industries, to those engaged in heavy work and unhealthy occupations, and also to a special category of employees in the administrative machinery of the country. In 1932, in order to link distribution more closely with production, responsibility for the distribution of ration cards was transferred to the governing bodies of the enterprises and institutions in which particular workers were employed,‡ and rationing was thus even more closely linked with the position of the rationed person in industrial production. The employees of enterprises or administrative institutions were divided by their governing bodies among categories according to the character of their work. They were consequently

---

* This group comprised workers and employees of Moscow, Leningrad, Baku, workers in the mines of Donbass, Karaganda, underground workers in the Kuznetz Basin, metallurgical workers in the Donbass, Dnepropetrovsk, Magnitorsk and Kuznetz workers in engineering industry, in armaments and chemical industry, etc.

† For example, in September 1930 in Leningrad the first group received monthly per person: flour (apart from bread) 1 kg., and the fourth category only 500 g.; sugar, for the first group 1½ kg. and for the fourth 1 kg.; groats, first group, 1·8 and 0·7 kg. and so on. *Krasnaya Gazeta*, 29 August 1930. *Planned Economy*, nos. 2–3, 1931, p. 87. See also L. E. Hubbard, *Soviet Trade and Distribution*, p. 35.

‡ See pp. 228–9.

able to obtain greater or lesser amounts of the main rationed goods at fixed prices.

For the most important factories and administrative institutions special shops called *closed distributors* were also organized (Z.R., i.e. Zakrytye Raspredeliteli). The right to get products and goods in these shops was limited to those persons who, on the decision of the governing body, were 'tied' to this distributor. These 'closed distributors' supplied products and goods not only in greater quantities but also of better quality. For the workers and employees it was more important in this period to be put on the list of a particular category or to be 'tied' to one of the better 'closed distributors' than to get a rise in nominal wages. From 1933, important industrial plants began to organize a 'department of supplies for workers' (O.R.S.Y., i.e. Otdely Rabochego Snabzhenia) which had the right to obtain products privately purchased from the peasants and to organize market gardens, farms and poultry farms, and to rear cattle, sheep, goats, rabbits, etc., for catering for the needs of the workers and employees of these enterprises.

(c) It is quite understandable that with such a differential rationing system, the consumption needs of some categories of population were very inadequately provided for by rationed supplies. Wages of workers in this period varied very substantially, and expenditure on the rationed products and goods absorbed very unequal parts of wages in the different categories. In order to make it possible for some categories of population to buy a greater quantity of necessities than that allowed to their category, and at the same time to absorb the available purchasing capacity of the population in the channels of State trade and thus eliminate the possibility of extension of illicit private trade, the Soviet Government, side by side with the rationed distribution of necessities, also organized 'commercial' trade in those necessities that were rationed. As early as July 1929, at the same time that rationing of sugar was introduced, a special 'supply' of sugar was allocated for free sale to the population but at the higher 'commercial' prices. In December 1929 'commercial' trade was introduced for textiles, ready-made clothes, knitted fabrics and so on. From the spring of 1933 onwards 'commercial' trade in bread and other agricultural products was also introduced. Unrationed supplies of the same goods were sold at much higher prices than those that were rationed. Thus workers were enabled according to their categories to obtain a fixed amount of rationed products and goods at low prices, and also to purchase unlimited quantities at much higher prices in the

State shops; or were able to buy the same products at still higher prices on the black market. 'Commercial' trade was also the source of supply for those categories of the population which did not receive rationed supplies, especially for the agricultural population.*

In organizing 'commercial' trade the Soviet Government aimed at: (i) a still more differentiated supply, according to the differences in wages; (ii) absorbing the purchasing power of the population by State trade and accumulating, by means of price-differentiation, 'profits' from trade which accrued to the State Budget; (iii) checking the development of illicit trade in necessities; (iv) preparing the way for abolishing the rationing system (we shall return to this later).

Besides the general network of 'commercial' trade there also existed (as we mentioned above) special shops for providing the foreign colony with goods—Insnab and Torgsin. In Insnab foreigners could obtain rationed goods, in Torgsin it was possible for foreigners as well as for Soviet citizens to buy both Soviet and imported goods without restriction, but only in exchange for foreign currencies or precious metals. The aim of this special trade was not only to make it easier to supply the needs of foreigners but also to absorb their foreign exchange as well as that of Soviet citizens receiving money from abroad and the precious metals which were at their disposal.

(d) As regards the agricultural population, trade was organized according to the following principles. The great bulk of marketable agricultural products was delivered by producers to the State at much lower prices than those which were charged in the State

---

* The turn-over of 'commercial' trade in the towns has developed as follows (in million roubles):

1931	1932	1933	1934
662·8	3,820	6,296·3	13,000

The percentage of commercial trade of the whole State trade in the towns, in the different years, changed as follows:

	1930	1931	1932	1933	1934
Foodstuffs	4·1	1·9	4·9	7·8	7·1
Twelve planned industrial goods	7·4	19·0	37·5	39·6	57·8
Cotton textiles	29·0	56·5	64·0	64·3	75·0
Wool textiles	13·8	30·5	46·2	61·7	61·0
Knitted fabrics	—	29·7	77·0	58·5	63·8
Ready-made wear	3·8	6·0	46·3	46·3	56·0

G. Ya. Neiman, *Soviet Trade*, p. 239. *Soviet Trade*, no. 1, 1935, p. 80.

trade for the rationed products.* Consequently these deliveries to the State at low prices were in effect not purchases by the State organization but taxation-in-kind of agriculture. By these methods of organization of deliveries of agricultural products to the State the Soviet Government succeeded in raising the quantity of grain distributed each year, in spite of the fact that gross production in this period did not rise but, in some years, even declined, as is shown by the figures in Table 48, p. 325.

The agricultural population was supplied with rationed industrial goods according to the principles of 'Otovarivaniya' (exchange of goods for goods). In January 1929 the Commissariat of Internal Trade of the U.S.S.R. published the following order: 'All scarce industrial goods which are allocated for supplying the needs of the agricultural population must be sent to the local distributing centres according to the current deliveries of agricultural products.' Out of these industrial goods special stocks, amounting to about 30–40 % of all goods received, had to be reserved to meet the needs of the poorest peasants who made deliveries to the State and co-operative purchasing organizations. The remaining manufactured goods were distributed among the peasants who delivered grain to the State and co-operative organizations, but direct barter was forbidden. Nor was it permitted to sell manufactured goods to the full value of the agricultural produce delivered. In the regions where mainly industrial crops were produced and in the forest regions, the agricultural population was also supplied with rationed agricultural products. In these regions the rationing system was also based on the differential principle, according to the different groups of producers of industrial crops, and also on the 'class' principle, and varied with the rate of delivery of industrial crops.

Consequently the peasantry in the regions in which foodstuffs were produced were to deliver the greater part of their marketable agricultural products to the State at low prices and were able to get in exchange only very limited supplies of industrial goods at the low prices fixed for rationed goods; they were only able to buy other goods at very high prices in 'commercial' trade.

* For example, in 1932 the State purchasing body for the delivered grain paid 6 roubles 33 kopeks for 100 kg. of rye, and charged for the same rye for making flour a wholesale price of 22 roubles 20 kopeks, and for wheat the corresponding price was 8 roubles 52 kopeks and 27 roubles 75 kopeks. See more detailed data: S. D. Voloshin and L. S. Yampolskii, *Purveyance Prices for Grain on the delivery campaign*, 1932–3; E. S. Nikolskii and S. A. Skitaltsev, *Selling Prices on Grain.*

Similarly, peasants in the main regions producing industrial crops had to deliver all their products at low prices, and in exchange they received rationed amounts of foodstuffs and were able to buy very limited quantities of manufactured goods at low prices; for supplementary supplies they had to resort to 'commercial' trade. In actual fact, owing to the scarcity of manufactured goods in this period, and to the inability to meet the demand for them in the towns and in the industrial regions,* they were supplied to the agricultural population in very limited quantities (see Table 34). The disadvantages for the peasantry of having to deliver agricultural products to the State on such conditions, apart from other undesirable features which accompanied the collectivization of agriculture (see pp. 195-7), were the main causes of the reduction in the production of grain in this period. This decrease in agricultural production compelled the Soviet Government to make concessions to the peasantry by legalizing 'Kolkhoz trade'. By a Government decree on 6 May 1932, Kolkhoz and Kolkhoz farmers (Kolkhozniki) received the right to sell the remaining products at free-market prices on the local markets, once they had fulfilled their obligation to the State concerning centralized deliveries according to the planned requirements.

By legalizing the Kolkhoz trade the possibility of formation of free prices was again restored to the local market. The differences between centralized delivery prices and the prices of the Kolkhoz trade were, at this time, very great.† Besides the legalization of Kolkhoz trade, State purchasing bodies began from 1932 onwards to increase the above-mentioned decentralized purchases of agricultural products at prices somewhat higher than those paid for centralized deliveries.

Consequently, after 'Kolkhoz trade' had been legalized agricultural producers delivered and continue to deliver, up to the present, the greater part of their marketable products at fixed low prices. After meeting this obligation to the State, they can dispose

* The scarcest industrial goods were not supplied regularly even to the most privileged categories of workers. According to individual merits, diligent workers received special certificates (orders) for the purchase of these scarce goods.

† For example, in 1932 the delivery price for rye was 6 roubles 33 kopeks for 100 kg., and on the Kolkhoz markets in the Moscow region 1 kg. of rye flour cost 3 roubles 20 kopeks; the delivery price for oats was 5 roubles 60 kopeks for 100 kg., while on the Kolkhoz market the price was 189 roubles 70 kopeks for 100 kg.; the delivery price for beef was 50 kopeks, while on the Kolkhoz market it was sold between 9 roubles 60 kopeks and 11 roubles 10 kopeks.

9

Table 34. *Distribution of retail turn-over among foodstuffs and industrial goods (including 'communal catering') in million roubles*

	1928	1932	1933	1934	1935
Total turn-over	12,100·0	40,356·6	49,789·2	61,814·7	80,643·6
Of which:					
I. Foodstuffs:	5,814·1	22,219·9	29,264·9	38,494·5	53,399·7
(a) Retail turn-over	5,464·1	17,367·6	22,878·2	31,451·8	46,478·8
(b) 'Communal' catering	350·0	4,852·3	6,386·6	7,042·7	6,920·9
II. Industrial goods	6,285·9	18,136·7	20,524·4	23,320·2	27,243·9
Urban trade	8,093·2	27,571·9	35,148·8	45,689·6	58,441·2
Of which:					
I. Foodstuffs:	3,980·9	15,921·8	22,082·2	30,158·0	40,625·5
(a) Retail turn-over	3,680·9	11,737·7	16,381·6	23,817·2	34,425·5
(b) 'Communal' catering	300·0	4,184·1	5,700·6	6,340·8	6,201·0
II. Industrial goods	4,112·3	11,650·1	13,066·6	15,531·6	17,814·7
Rural districts...	4,006·8	12,784·7	14,640·4	16,125·1	22,202·4
Of which:					
I. Foodstuffs:	1,833·2	6,298·1	7,182·6	8,336·5	12,773·2
(a) Retail turn-over	1,783·2	5,629·9	6,496·6	7,634·6	12,053·3
(b) 'Communal' catering	50·0	668·2	686·0	701·9	719·9
II. Industrial goods	2,173·6	6,486·6	7,457·8	7,788·6	9,429·2

Retail turn-over divided between urban and rural trade and between State and co-operative trade (without 'communal' catering) in million roubles

	1928	1932	1933	1934	1935
Total turn-over	11,750·0	35,504·3	43,402·6	54,772·0	73,722·7
Of which:					
State trade	2,408·8	12,995·4	17,317·9	23,754·3	31,856·7
O.R.S.Y.	—	—	4,845·0	8,557·1	13,565·1
Co-operative trade	9,341·2	22,508·9	21,239·7	22,460·6	28,300·9
Urban trade	7,793·2	23,387·8	29,448·2	39,348·8	52,240·2
Of which:					
State trade	2,020·7	8,913·0	12,593·1	19,019·5	26,993·1
O.R.S.Y.	—	—	3,824·7	7,074·4	11,183·6
Co-operative trade	5,772·5	14,474·8	13,030·4	13,254·9	14,063·5
Rural districts trade	3,956·8	12,116·5	13,954·4	15,423·2	21,482·5
Of which:					
State trade	388·1	4,082·4	4,724·8	4,734·8	4,863·6
O.R.S.Y.	—	—	1,020·3	1,482·7	2,381·5
Co-operative trade	3,568·1	8,034·1	8,209·3	9,205·7	14,237·4

of their remaining marketable products either by selling them to the State purchasing authorities at somewhat higher prices ('decentralized purchase' of State organization) or by selling them at free-market prices on the local markets.*

(e) A substantial addition to the rationed supply of foodstuffs for the town and industrial population was 'communal' or 'public' catering, which was of great significance in this period.† 'Communal' catering was also organized on the differential principle: 'closed restaurants' existed for the use of the workers and employees of particular enterprises or administrative institutions, with discrimination in the supply of meals to the different categories; there were also restaurants open to everybody, but in these the meals were supplied at commercial prices.

As we have seen above there were, in this period, very different prices for similar products and goods. Five main price levels ruled for each kind of foodstuff, increasing steadily according as it was disposed of through the centralized delivery of agricultural products, through decentralized purchase, distributed by ration, sold 'commercially', or finally on the black market or in the Kolkhoz trade, respectively. As regards industrial goods, the price of rationed supplies (divided into two groups of prices—one for the urban and the other for the agricultural population) was the lowest, while those

---

* The apportionment of the marketable supply of grain was as follows (in percentages of the total):

	1932	1933	1934
Centralized deliveries	95·4	88·6	81·1
Decentralized deliveries	1·2	1·6	13·6
Kolkhoz trade	3·4	9·8	5·3

G. Ya. Neiman, op. cit. p. 249.

The sale of products to the State decentralized purchasing bodies was sometimes preferable to the sale of products on the Kolkhoz market owing to the possibility of receiving for the products sold manufactured goods at low prices; it also saved transport expenses.

† The total turn-over of the 'communal' catering services in the towns rose in this period as follows (in million roubles):

1929	1930	1931	1932	1933	1934
471	1,140	2,340	4,172	5,688	5,900

The total number of 'communal' catering establishments rose from 6,026 in 1929 to 30,115 in 1933. In 1932 70% of workers of the main industrial branches received their big meals in 'communal' eating-houses and, in 1932, meals were supplied on an average to 14·8 million persons daily. Besides these, in 1932, 12,500 eating-houses served the agricultural workers and forestry workers, supplying 5,240,000 meals daily.

of the 'commercial' trade were much higher (there also existed temporary intermediate prices, 'Srednepovyshennye'—'average raised prices'). Still higher prices ruled for goods sold in the special 'commercial' stores—'Unevermag'—in which were sold goods of better quality and greater variety. In addition to these there also existed special prices for products and goods purchased with foreign currencies and precious metals—'Torgsin'.*

Why did such a complicated price system exist in this period, why were prices not unified, what kind of motives guided the Soviet Government in introducing such price differences?

(a) As we have already pointed out, the Soviet Economic Press laid stress, during the period of N.E.P., on the principle that prices and wages in the Soviet system are the principal means for redistributing national incomes among different categories of the population; i.e. the main means for dividing up the national income into the part destined for consumption and that destined for capitalization. The first F.Y.P. as well as the second aimed at large-scale investment in heavy industry, so as to increase its capacity and the output of the war industries. In both these plans the Government also aimed at raising the output of consumer goods, but in reality consumer goods were produced in this period, especially during the first F.Y.P., in quantities quite insufficient to meet the effective demand of the growing industrial and urban population. Owing to the scarcity of manufactured goods for consumption and to the policy of industrialization which was pursued, it was necessary first of all to allocate them to the population concerned with the prosecution of industrialization and to curtail purchasing by the agricultural population. This was achieved, as we have already pointed out, by organizing central deliveries of the great bulk of marketable products to the State at low prices,

---

* Above we quote only prices which concerned the population. There also existed 'accounting' prices which were used inside the socialized sector for accounting purposes between syndicates, trusts, and enterprises of the State industry. The discrepancy between different prices can be seen from these examples (prices of 1932 in kopeks per kg.):

	Delivery prices	Rationed prices		Commercial prices	Kolkhoz market prices
Wheat	7–8	Wheat flour	19	450	580–650
Rye	5·2–5·8	Rye flour	14	280	320–390
Sugar	—		95	250	—
Butter	—		466	1,600–1,800	3,480–4,820

S. M. Gorelik and A. I. Malkis, *Soviet Trade*.

prices much lower than those which would have existed had the free market not been abolished. But centralized deliveries could not cover the whole marketable production of the main agricultural products (even though that was intended by the planning authorities), and a small part of the marketable production remained in the hands of the agricultural producer. The output of agricultural goods during this period lagged very much behind the growth of the population, especially the rapid growth of the urban and industrial population. Consequently, in spite of all formal precautions, the marketable products which remained in the hands of the agricultural producer were sold on the local market at much higher prices than those paid by the State for the centralized deliveries. The State purchasing authorities, as we have seen above, attempted to absorb these remaining marketable supplies in the State trade by means of 'decentralized purchase', paying somewhat higher prices than those paid for centralized deliveries. But the peasantry preferred to put up with all the inconveniences of illicit trade, which existed on the local market in this period, for the sake of getting the higher prices. Even the Soviet administrative apparatus with all its severity was unable to liquidate this private marketing. Besides this, in spite of the formal success of collectivization, agricultural production in the period did not rise and even partly declined, especially that of grain and livestock breeding. In order to combat the development of illicit trade and to provide additional stimulus for development of agricultural production it was decided to legalize the free sale of agricultural products on the Kolkhoz market at marketing prices. But at the same time the Soviet Government began to increase the quantity of the products which were sold in 'commercial' trade at lower prices than those which existed on the Kolkhoz market (although these prices were much higher than those of rationed supplies). The introduction of 'commercial' trade was intended to influence the level of prices on the Kolkhoz market. With the beginning of the increase of agricultural production which started after 1933, the tension in the balance of production and consumption of agricultural products began to lessen, and consequently the intervention of 'commercial' trade in free trade with agricultural products was more effective in reducing the price level on the Kolkhoz market.

As regards the urban and industrial population the Soviet Government first of all aimed at procuring a fixed minimum of necessities for the more important classes of the population at fixed low prices, and by this means at avoiding the need for rapid rises in the total wages bill. But, of course, owing to the insufficient production of agricultural products and still more of industrial consumer goods, and owing to the growing differences in nominal wages and the steady rise of the total wage bill, it was impossible to provide sufficient goods at fixed prices to meet the demand and exhaust the purchasing capacity of the urban and industrial population. A considerable part of the total purchasing capacity of the population could not be absorbed by rationed supplies. Rationing at *fixed* prices intrinsically assumes that a certain amount of the purchasing capacity of the population will be left unsatisfied. This unsatisfied purchasing power may ultimately result in the purchase of unrationed goods at rising prices. Even if this purchasing power is withdrawn into the State Budget by taxation or saving (i.e. by compulsory or voluntary saving) and is afterwards spent on building up heavy industry or on producing war materials and not on developing the production of consumption goods, there results only a redistribution of the purchasing power of the different classes of the population; and if rationing at fixed prices does not cover all necessities, a rise in the prices of non-rationed products is inevitable. By introducing 'commercial' trade at higher prices, it was hoped to absorb this unsatisfied purchasing power of the population and divert part of it into the State Budget.

(*b*) When the Soviet authorities for regulating internal trade fixed the prices for all products and goods which passed through the channels of the State and co-operative trade, they simultaneously fixed the percentage in the reckoning of prices which automatically had to be transferred to the State Budget.

The Soviet wholesale price system was composed of the following elements:

(1) Cost price for industrial goods, or for agricultural products, delivery prices plus the expenses of the wholesale purchasing organization.

(2) Planned profit of enterprises.

(3) Turn-over tax.

Turn-over tax is included in the wholesale price, and must be automatically delivered to the State Budget by the *wholesale* organization when commodities are sold to the retail trade organization. *By means of the turn-over tax the proceeds of all the differences in prices which existed between different branches of trade were accumulated into the State Budget* (see below, pp. 369–71).

Retail price was and is composed of the following elements:

(1) Wholesale price.

(2) Deduction for the State Budget of a certain percentage of wholesale prices which was paid to the State Budget by the retail trade organization, similar to the turn-over tax paid by the wholesale trade organization. This differed from the turn-over tax only because it was paid by the retail trade organization, and it was applied not to all but only to some commodities as a corrective of the general turn-over tax. The latter was calculated on groups of commodities and not on individual commodities, whereas the 'deduction' was applied to individual commodities.

(3) Expenses of the retail trade, which comprised expenses plus planned profit of enterprises.

(4) Transport expenses (these were fixed by the regulating authorities for some commodities only).

When the Soviet authorities for regulating internal trade fixed prices for commodities, they simultaneously fixed all the above components of the prices.

All goods, for the purpose of fixing of prices, were divided into three main groups: the first comprised those which were most important from the point of view of the development of the national economy and from the point of view of the consumption budget of the population. Prices for these were regulated by a 'Committee for marketable supplies in the Soviet Labour and Defence of the U.S.S.R.' These goods accounted for 55–65 % of the total marketable products of the country.

The second group of commodities comprised products less scarce and less important from the point of view of the development of the national economy and from the point of view of satisfying the needs of the mass of consumers. Prices for these commodities were fixed by the republican and district authorities which regulated the internal trade. This group accounted for 10–12 % of the total marketable output of the country.

The third group comprised mostly products purchased by decentralized organizations and goods produced by local industry and handicraft industry. The prices of these groups of products were fixed by the trading organizations themselves and needed only to be confirmed by the district trade-regulating authority.

We shall not enter into a more detailed account of which goods and commodities were included in the different groups and which elements of the prices were planned by different trade-regulating authorities.* We need only state that the most centralized were planned prices and separate components of the prices of the products and goods of the first category. The prices and components of the second group were planned more on a decentralized basis.

This system of discriminating rationing of the consumption of the population by differential prices (accompanied by corresponding financial measures) enabled the Soviet Government, in this period of great scarcity of necessities, to achieve:

(a) Assured supplies of minimum of necessities at low prices to those categories of the population which were most important for realizing the policy of industrialization and strengthening of the defence of the country proposed by two F.Y.P.s.

(b) Control of the distribution of the great bulk of the marketable products of the country and redistribution of necessities among different groups of the population.

(c) Redistribution of the national income and the purchasing power of the population for the purpose of industrializing the country, as is clearly evident from the figures given in Table 35.

Table 35

	Total turn-over of retail trade (without 'communal catering' and Kolkhoz trade)	Turn-over tax	Net retail turn-over	Total of receipts of the State Budget	Expense of the State Budget	
					On financing of national economy	On Army and Navy
	I	II*	I – II			
1931	24,725	11,643	13,082	20,342	16,507	1,288
1932	35,504	19,514	15,990	30,574	24,782	1,296
1933	43,403	26,983	16,420	40,153	25,058	1,421
1934	54,772	37,615	17,157	50,760	32,257	5,000
1935	73,722	52,026	21,696	67,488	37,200	8,200

* Turn-over tax was introduced at the end of 1930 and consequently we give the figures of the turn-over tax only from 1931.

The turn-over tax provided the main part of the receipts of the State Budget and nearly covered (in the last three years even exceeded) all expenses of the State Budget for financing the development of the national economy as well as expenditure on the defence of the country.

* More detailed description can be found in the following Soviet publications: *Soviet Trade*, S. M. Gorelik and A. I. Malkis, pp. 153, 161; *Economy of Soviet Trade*, editors L. P. Cotovskii, G. Neiman and V. Nodel, op. cit. pp. 394, 403; *Planned Economy*, no. 5, 1939, pp. 22–6.

(*d*) Allocation for export of considerable quantities of agricultural products and industrial consumer goods *in order to enable the State to import raw materials and equipment which were needed for the realization of the policy of industrialization.*

But this system of organizing the internal market involved many disadvantages:

(*a*) Centralization of the distribution of so great a part of marketable products was often followed by very inadequate supplies to various regions and to various trading organizations in the same regions. Seasonal goods often did not arrive in time at their destination or were not sent to the proper place. This involved a 'freezing' of goods in one region while the same goods were very scarce in other regions. Very often there occurred an interruption in supplying even those goods which were not scarce owing to defects in the centralized distribution.

(*b*) The distribution of goods was often planned on the basis of the abstract 'average consumer'. This was a cause of the 'freezing' and scarcity in different regions. Frequently the individual consumer was forced to readjust his demand to that of the 'average' consumer and 'to take what was given to him'. This planning according to the 'average' consumer and to the average choice of goods was one of the causes of the deterioration in the quality of the consumer goods produced. Industry often deliberately worsened the quality and the choice of the goods because the wholesale trade organization accepted goods according to the main planned groups of goods which were destined for a 'depersonalized' average consumer, without individual specification of goods.

(*c*) Consumers received little consideration in their purchases in the State and co-operative trade. They were treated as depersonalized 'units' and were served scantily. The choice of goods was very limited, and they were frequently compelled to accept 'forced assortments', i.e. to buy with goods they needed those goods which the salesman wanted to get rid of. The network of trading organizations was much smaller than in the previous period. In 1927–8, before the liquidation of private trade, there existed 481,435 shops and stalls of all kinds, while in 1930 there were only 163,000 and in 1935, 295,300 shops and stalls of all kinds (see Table 36).

All these defects in serving consumers were also familiar features of the 'communal catering'.

(*d*) Owing to the great number of institutions which regulated

Table 36. *Retail turn-over network divided into State and co-operative trade (in 1000's)*

	1930	1932	1933	1934	1935
Stores, shops and stalls, total...	163·0	224·9	284·4	285·4	295·3
Of which:					
State trade	23·6	39·5	62·1	67·4	101·9
O.R.S.Y.	—	—	10·9	35·8	37·2
Co-operative trade	39·4	185·4	211·4	182·2	155·2
Stores and shops, total	133·8	166·4	208·5	222·7	220·4

prices and their components, prices often differed from the 'planned' prices and were varied for the same goods in the different stores of the State and co-operative trade.* Besides the planned differences in prices, there existed also in reality many more differences.

(e) Owing to the inequality of rationed supplies at low prices for the different categories of workers and employees, nominal wages were only partly interconnected with the real wages. The rouble had quite a different purchasing power in the hands of the different categories of the population. This fact very much complicated the regulation of nominal wages and of incentives to increase the productivity of labour. Differences of supply to the workers of different industrial enterprises were the main causes of great 'fluctuations' of labour (see pp. 214–5). Multiplicity of prices also very much complicated calculation of the cost of production and the interrelations between different enterprises. The rouble lost significance as a universal unit of value.

All these disadvantages in the organization of the internal market in this period were very widely discussed and criticized in the Soviet Economic and Daily Press, and from 1933 onwards preparations began to be made for liquidating the rationing system and for the transition to a new organization of the internal trade on a non-rationing basis, and with a more unified price system.

* The Soviet Government had issued a decree ordering all stores to provide consumers with a price list to enable them to check the charged prices and also ordered every shop to keep a 'complaints journal' in which consumers were able to write their complaints about the defects of the service. But these measures had very little practical effect.

SECTION IV. *PERIOD OF INTENSIVE ENDEAVOUR TO IMPROVE THE COUNTRY'S ECONOMY AND ECONOMIC SYSTEM*

CHAPTER XV. THE ABOLITION OF RATIONING AND RECONSTRUCTION OF INTERNAL AND EXTERNAL TRADE

The abolition of the rationing system was prepared by many events which took place during the previous period:

(1) During the past period, as we have seen, the State trading organizations succeeded in mastering the distribution of the main bulk of consumer goods on the internal market.

(2) In the last years of the rationing period there began a steady increase in the output of the most essential goods (see Tables 23, 44). The quantity of agricultural products purchased by the State increased yearly (see Table 50).

(3) The rise in the number of workers and employees employed in industry, transport, etc., and the increase in urban population began to slow down (see Table 54). The demands of the industrial and urban population consequently increased at a slower pace.

(4) The export of agricultural products could now be reduced owing to the possibility of reducing imports (see p. 275).

(5) The rise in the turn-over of 'commercial' trade and the gradual reduction of differences between the prices of rationed and 'commercial' trade paved the way for the introduction of a unified price system.

(6) The trade network steadily expanded during the last years of the rationing period (see Table 36).

(7) Prices on the Kolkhoz market fell, owing, on one side, to the rise in the production of agricultural products and, on the other, to the reduction of prices in 'commercial' trade.

All these changes prepared the way for the transition from rationed to unrationed trade without, at the same time, diminishing the regulating power of the State on the internal market and undermining its control over prices.

The actual transition was only accomplished gradually. The decree of the Sovnarkom S.S.S.R. of 7 December 1934 ordered the abolition from 1 January 1935 of 'the rationing of bread, groats and other cereal products, the repeal of all existing fixed prices for these products and the introduction of unified retail prices according to the eight territorial zones;...an increase of the wages of low-paid workers and employees, scholarships for students and pensions and the allocation for this purpose of 4 milliard 200 million roubles from the State Budget [and] the liquidation of "otovarivanye" for all agricultural deliveries....'

By this decree a unified price system was introduced for cereal products, the unified prices varying only according to different geographical areas. In fixing prices in different areas, transport expenses, the relation between prices for bread and those for other agricultural products in these regions, and the structure of the trade turn-over in different regions were taken into account. At first only 1 kg. of bread at a time was allowed per person, but afterwards this restriction was removed. Rationing of other products and goods was gradually liquidated in 1935, and the process of derationing came to a close in January 1936. Prices for bread and other products were fixed at an average somewhat lower than those existing in 'commercial' trade during the last months of the rationing system, but much higher than those which had existed in rationed trade. Owing to this readjustment in price, the revenue from the turn-over tax on trade in agricultural products rose from 4·6 milliard roubles in 1934 to 20·7 milliard roubles in 1935 (see Table 59). This enormous rise in the revenue of the State Budget enabled the Government to carry out price readjustments in industry as well. Net cost in industry rose, owing to the increased expenditure on agricultural raw materials and increases in the wages and salaries of some categories of workers and employees. But by reducing the rate of turn-over tax and amount of deduction from the profits of industrial enterprises, a rise in the wholesale price for industrial products was prevented. The enlargement of the working capital of productive and trading organizations which were needed by industry and trade under the new market conditions was supplied from the State Budget.

Here it is necessary to emphasize that the abolition of the rationing system meant only that the population could buy unrestricted quantities of products and had freedom of choice. The Government continued to regulate prices with the same aims as before and retained control over the flow of goods to the urban and rural population and kept in force measures for the planned absorption of the purchasing power of the population.

But this freedom of choice of the population in spending their money incomes forced the Soviet trading organizations to re-organize the trading network, the methods of trade, methods of planning trade turn-over and methods of regulating and controlling prices.

We have said that the liquidation of private trade resulted in a considerable shrinkage of the trade network. In the first years of the rationing period the State and co-operative trade network shrank too, and the trade network only began to extend after 1932. After the abolition of rationing it was once more necessary to extend it, in order to improve the service to the population.

The basic and working capital for the new trading enterprises, as well as the additions to the working capital in existing enterprises, were provided by the State Budget. The utilization of the profit from the trade enterprises was also determined by trade-regulating institutions.

In co-operative trade the basic and working capital are, in general, supplied by membership fees.* In 1935 the co-operative trade network of the towns was transferred to the State trading organizations, and from 1935 up to the present time the co-operatives have concentrated on trade with the rural population.† In 1939 approximately 85% of all the purchases of the rural population passed through the co-operative network. This concentration of rural trade in the hands of the co-operatives was aimed at a further specialization of the trade network, attracting membership fees and strengthening the control of the population over the working of the distributive system in the rural districts.

In the towns, too, further specialization and differentiation of trade were carried out. The distributive system expanded considerably, and it was more rationally organized territorially (see Table 37).

Since rationing was abolished the main trade channels in U.S.S.R. have been State trade, co-operative trade and Kolkhoz trade.

State trade is carried out by wholesale trade organizations. The retail network belongs to different branches of industry, and to different Commissariats, especially that of internal trade.

* Members of co-operatives pay an entrance fee of 3 roubles and a membership fee of 50 roubles. In 1938 the membership fees accounted for 44·7% of the total basic capital of the co-operatives in the rural districts.

† In 1939 the urban network of consumer co-operatives consisted only of 2,231 trading units, whereas the total consumer co-operative network consisted of 179·1 thousand units.

Table 37. *Turn-over network of State and co-operative trade*

	1 January 1934	1 October 1938	1938 as % of 1934
Wholesale stores of State industry	718	2,046	285·0
Retail network of State and co-operative trade in 1000's: shops	222·7	239·7	107·0
Stalls in 1000's	62·6	115·0	183·7
Total	285·3	354·7	124·3

Co-operative trade is represented by the consumer co-operatives and productive co-operatives (co-operatives of handicraft workers, of Kolkhozy (collective farms) and of Kolkhozniki (collective farmers)).

Kolkhoz trade is carried out on local markets only by Kolkhozy as well as by individual Kolkhozniki and the remaining non-collectivized peasants; only in Kolkhoz trade does there exist a real free market. It is the only market in U.S.S.R. on which there exist free prices not directly fixed by the Government. The most characteristic feature of Kolkhoz trade is, however, the absence of the middleman; here the producers sell their products directly to the consumer.

State trade makes up the greater part of the trade turn-over. A smaller share is taken by the co-operatives and a still smaller one by Kolkhoz trade (see Table 38).

Table 38. *Gross retail turn-over (milliard roubles)*

	1936	1937	1938	1939
State trade	79·8	92·8	99·9	114·2
Co-operative trade	26·9	33·1	40·1	49·2
Kolkhoz trade	15·6	17·7	24·4	30·0

We have seen that during the period of rationing the quality of consumer goods deteriorated considerably. Trade was carried out on the basis of the needs of the 'average consumer'. Customers received no consideration, were treated as 'depersonalized units', and were 'forced to take what was given to them'. After the rationing system was abolished, trade-regulating organizations introduced many devices to eliminate the dependent mentality which prevailed during the period of rationing. Campaigns for 'cultural trade' were carried out during the whole of the recent period.

Soviet economic journals and newspapers in 1939 and 1940 continued to publish a great deal of material on the persistent defects in the organization of trade. On 13 July 1940, in an order issued by the People's Commissariat of Internal Trade and in another order issued by the Presidium of the Central Co-operative Union of U.S.S.R. and R.S.F.S.R., it was stated that: 'trade organizations were still paying insufficient attention to the quality of goods, that they continued to accept from industry and co-operative handicraft organizations goods of bad quality and non-standard goods, and continued to sell foodstuffs made of bad raw material.' It was decreed that in the future all trading organizations must reject inferior goods offered by industries, 'must see to it that goods delivered correspond to the approved standard, must examine all their available stocks and either return non-standard goods to the industries or sell them to the population at a lower price than that officially fixed'. Many other devices were employed with the same object.

Many of these defects of trade were gradually smoothed out, but some of them still existed in 1940; they were partly due to difficulties still existing in planning trade and organizing control over the distributive system.

After the liquidation of the rationing system, the main elements in the planning of trade remained, in general, the same. The planning institutions continued to plan:

(1) The total trade turn-over of all the main products and goods (the amount of agricultural products purchased and their sale to the population, the amount of industrial goods which must be allocated for trade, the main structure of trade, and the distribution of trade according to regions).

(2) The material-technical basis of trade (capital construction and development of the trade network, and preparation of trade specialists and personnel).

(3) The finance of trade (the amount of working capital allotted to the trading organizations, distribution of profits, credits, and the administrative costs of trade).

(4) Prices for all the main goods and products.

As before, all goods were divided into the following main groups:

(1) Planned industrial consumer goods.
(2) Regulated industrial consumer goods.
(3) Planned and regulated products.
(4) All remaining products.

In the period of rationing, as we have described above, the retail turn-over was planned on the differential standards of supply for the different sections of the population. After the rationing system was liquidated, the possible exercise of free choice by the individual in spending his money very much complicated the task of planning the trade turn-over. The State Bank of the U.S.S.R. (whose cash receipts and disbursement plans depend upon 85% of the proceeds of trade) tried to calculate the balance of the money incomes and expenses of the population on a quarterly basis, but experience proved that these balances were of little use in actually controlling the trade turn-over. Up to 1940 Soviet economists complained that statistical accounts of trade were still insufficient for the purpose of practical detailed trade planning. During the last few years before the present war, however, the P. Commissariat of Trade succeeded in supplying goods efficiently in approved assortments to the trading network. The Commissariat of Trade received the right to order industries to produce goods in approved assortments according to the information received from the trade network. In 1938 it received the right to exercise control in industrial enterprises as regards their fulfilment of the plan of production of consumer goods and the quality of goods produced.

One of the means of controlling the efficiency of trading organizations is credit. Credit is supplied by the State Bank to the trading organizations according to their approved plan of trade turn-over and, up to 1936, this credit was based on the average period of turn-over of all goods taken together, without distinction between the different rates of turn-over of different goods. The result was that trading organizations preferred to concentrate on trade in those goods which were in great demand and neglected trade in goods with slow rates of turn-over. The former was more profitable for the trading enterprises as they received credit for it for the average turn-over period. In 1936 this credit system was altered, and afterwards credit was supplied to the trading organizations 'for different periods in accordance with the individual periods of turn-over of different goods in different regions'.* The Soviet Economic Press, however, stated that the new differentially planned period of turn-over very often did not coincide with the actual requirements of the trading organizations in different regions.

The Soviet Economic Press also stated in 1940 that 'many trade

---

* Decree of Sovnarkom S.S.S.R. of 4 April 1936.

organizations rely on centralized supplies and do not sufficiently utilize local resources for the purpose of improving the supply of necessities to the population'.* According to the data of the turn-over of the forty co-operative unions of republics, regions and districts, their *decentralized* supplies of goods sold during the first quarter of 1940 amounted only to 11 % of the total turn-over. Soviet economists complained that 'local trade organizations do not encourage local production and local utilization of available resources, but prefer to get all their goods and products from the trading centre'.†

In 1939 many branches of industry ceased of their own accord to produce some kinds of goods and concentrated on the production of others in spite of the fact that this was in contradiction to planned requirements. They found it more profitable for themselves to produce one kind of goods and not the other. This was due partly to defects in the planning and regulation of prices.

We have given above a general outline of the planning and regulating of prices during the rationing period. After the abolition of rationing, prices continued to be planned with the same aims as before—the preservation of great differences between the delivery price for agricultural products and their selling price, and between net cost and selling price for the majority of industrial consumer goods; the absorption of all these price differences into the State Budget by means of the turn-over tax and deduction from profits, and finally the achievement by this means of a redistribution of the purchasing power of the population (see chapter on the State Budget).

The abolition of rationing did not change the structural inter-connexion between prices for different goods which had developed during the past period. *The total net cost of all consumer goods continued to represent only a fraction of the total wage bill paid to the labour employed in all branches of the national economy.* The purchasing power of the urban and industrial population, consisting of wages and salaries, exceeded many times the *net* cost of industrial consumer goods, owing to the fact that only a small fraction of the total labour employed in the national economy and in the administrative apparatus of the country was employed in the production of consumer goods. The amount of labour employed in the production of these goods and the rise in the output of these goods constantly lagged behind the development of the means of production and the

* *Problems of Soviet Trade*, no. 8, 1940, p. 11.
† *Planned Economy*, no. 9, 1940, pp. 126–7.

increase in the amount of labour employed in the other branches of the national economy. Consequently, the discrepancy between the total net cost of consumer goods and the total wage bill grew during the whole period of 1928–36, which was one of extensive construction of new industries, reconstruction of transport, improvement of the country's defence, and greatly increased expenditure on cultural health, educational work, etc.

In fixing prices for individual groups of goods the Soviet trade-regulating organizations were guided by the following main considerations:

(1) By the cost prices of goods.

(2) By the volume of goods available, taking into account the balance of supply and demand for a particular group of goods.

(3) By the need to stimulate the production of particular goods and consequently to create (or reduce) facilities for making a profit by the production of these goods (this can be achieved, as we have shown in chapters on Industry and Budgets, either by changing the planned net cost or by altering the rate of turn-over tax).

(4) By the need for economizing in a particular kind of raw material or replacing one kind of raw material by another.

(5) By the need for economizing in transport expenses.

(6) By the need for stimulating consumption of one kind of goods and restricting consumption of another.

(7) By cultural and social considerations in the extension or curtailment of consumption of certain goods (for example, prices for books and stationery were kept even below net cost, as were those of household soap, whereas prices for toilet luxuries were kept at a very high level).

Decentralized prices for agricultural products are also fixed by the State trade-regulating institutions, in spite of the fact that they vary according to different regions and different districts in the same regions. In fixing decentralized prices the specific conditions of regions were taken into account.

As a considerable part of the production of the handicraft and co-operative industries is produced from raw materials supplied by the State trading organizations, prices for these goods are also regulated by the State trade-regulating institutions. It was even suggested in 1940 that prices for products sold by the Kolkhoz and by the individual Kolkhoz farmer should be fixed by Executives of the Kolkhoz and that products should be sold only at these prices on the local market. But this suggestion was not applied on a large scale, and prices on the Kolkhoz market remain the only free prices in the Soviet Union. The trade-regulating organizations regulate Kolkhoz trade only indirectly by selling the same products at lower prices in the State and co-operative network if it is found necessary to intervene in the price formation on the Kolkhoz market. From the above description of the complicated motives which guided the fixing of price on particular commodities, it may be anticipated that trade-regulating organizations encounter many difficulties in the practical application of these principles. Soviet economists still insist that the price system suffers from many fundamental defects.

In 1939 it was emphasized that there existed different prices for similar products, not only in different regions but in one and the same region. There was no apparent cause for this except the confusion which existed in the regulation of prices. Very often prices hampered rather than stimulated the production and improvement of range of goods. In March 1939, at the Eighteenth Party Congress, the P. Commissar for internal trade stated:

There has been some confusion with regard to the fixing of prices; it was due to the fact that the wholesale price was fixed by the Government, whereas the retail prices were fixed by the local trading departments and branches, and by the regions and co-operative organizations, by adding an additional charge to the fixed price in order to cover overhead transport expenses, etc. Very often there occurred abuses in this direction. The Government has now adjusted matters by introducing *fixed* retail prices for most commodities; the consumer can now check prices with the price list approved by the Economic Council; and nobody has a right to change this fixed price.

At the beginning of 1939 fixed retail prices were introduced for all the main manufactured goods of mass consumption as well as for the majority of food products.

But even after the reform of the price-fixing regulations in 1939 Soviet authors asserted that some aspects of it were still confusing. For example, opinions still differed as to whether unified prices for the whole of the Soviet Union were preferable to zonal prices for different zones and about the methods of calculating the relation between net cost, rate of turn-over tax, and the amount of overhead expenses allowed, as a means of increasing the profits of the production of one or the other kind of goods. But we cannot enter here into a detailed description of these controversies, as it would also be necessary to elucidate the technique of price fixing, which is beyond the scope of this essay. We only state that owing to the accumulated experience of price regulation, and owing to the fact that the internal market for goods and products of the first necessity was never near saturation, the Soviet planning and trade-regulating institutions succeeded, on the whole, during the past few years before the present war, in solving satisfactorily the problem of price regulation in order to be able to achieve by it the main aims which we have described above.

After the end of the rationing system the total volume of trade turn-over rose yearly, nominally from 80·7 milliard roubles in 1935 to 174·5 milliard roubles in 1940. The turn-over of the State trading network rose from 63·1 milliard roubles in 1935 to 114·2 milliard roubles in 1939; co-operative trade rose from 18·5 milliard roubles in 1935 to 49·2 milliard roubles in 1940, and Kolkhoz trade rose correspondingly from 14·5 to 30·0 milliard roubles. Soviet statistical sources did not publish any price indexes, and consequently we cannot calculate the rise in the real amount of the trade turn-over. But we can calculate it indirectly by subtracting from the total turn-over the sums of the turn-over tax. We can thus get an approximate idea of the change which occurred in the real turn-over. Excluding turn-over tax retail turn-over rose from 28·5 milliard roubles in 1935 to 71·1 milliard roubles in 1939. In 1940, apparently, there occurred a reduction in the real trade turn-over in comparison with that of 1939 (see Table 39).

Table 39. *Gross retail turn-over (milliard roubles)*

	1935	1936	1937	1938	1939	1940
Gross retail turn-over* (milliard roubles)	80·7	106·8	125·9	138·6	163·5	174·5
Turn-over tax	52·2	65·8	75·9	80·4	92·4	105·8
Net retail turn-over	28·5	41·0	50·0	58·2	71·1	68·7

* State and co-operative trade.

In general, the Soviet Government succeeded in firmly regulating prices for the main goods and products of mass consumption and in stabilizing them during the period 1936–9. In 1940, apparently, prices for some goods and products began to rise again, as can be seen from the data concerning prices collected by the United States Embassy in Moscow (see Table 40).

After rationing was abolished a great improvement was achieved in the qualitative side of the work of State and co-operative trade. In spite of the increased outlay on the improvement of the technique of trade, overhead expenses diminished in comparison with the rationing period (see Table 41).

Table 40. *Prices for kilogram, litre and unit in roubles and kopeks**

	1. vii. 1936	1. vii. 1938	1. i. 1939	1. vii. 1939	1. i. 1940	24. i. 1940	10. iv. 1940
Rye bread	0·85	0·85	0·85	0·85	0·85	0·85	0·85
White bread (wheat)	1·70	1·70	1·70	1·70	1·70	1·70	1·70
Wheat flour (72 % extraction)	2·90	2·90	2·90	2·90	—	—	—
Potatoes	0·30	0·40	0·50	0·60	0·50	0·80	1·20
Sugar (lump)	4·10	4·10	4·10	4·10	4·10	5·50	5·50
Sugar (granulated)	3·80	3·80	3·80	3·80	3·80	—	—
Beef (for soup)	8·00	7·60	8·00	8·00	9·00	12·00	16·00
Mutton	8·00	8·00	8·00	—	—	14·00	18·00
Butter (second quality)	16·00	17·50	17·50	17·50	17·50	—	—
Milk (a litre)	1·30	1·60	2·10	1·70	2·10	—	2·10
Eggs (each)	0·40	0·65	0 75	0·75	0·85	—	—
Ham (smoked)	18·00	18·00	18·00	18·00	—	24·00	27·00
Sausage (ordinary)	10·00	10·00	10·00	10·00	10·00	13·50	16·00
Butter (first quality)	19·50	20·00	20·00	21·00	—	—	28·00
Cheese (best quality)	22·0	24·80	24·80	24·80	24·80	24·80	—
Salt	0·05	0·05	0·05	0·05	0·05	—	—
Laundry soap	3·00	3·10	3·10	3·10	3·10	—	—
Kerosene (litre)	0·47	0·47	0·47	0·65	0·65	—	—

Table 41. *Expenses on turn-over†*

	In million roubles		As % of turn-over	
	1932	1937	1932	1937
Wholesale trade organizations of industrial Commissariat	425·2	1,980·4	1·25	1·81
Wholesale trade organizations of Commissariat of Internal Trade and co-operatives	633·9	1,049·9	1·87	0·96
All wholesale trade organizations	1,059·1	3,030·3	3·12	2·77
All retail trade organizations	3,190·1	9,270·0	9·41	8·49
All branches	4,249·2	12,300·3	12·53	11·26
Expenses:				
On transport	1,046·2	3,503·9	3·09	3·21
On wages and salaries	1,760·1	3,956·8	5·19	3·63
On building and inventory	430·8	1,508·9	1·28	1·38
On packing and deliveries, etc.	92·6	668·6	0·28	0·61
On losses in goods	136·1	965·8	0·40	0·89
Travelling expenses	250·4	411·4	0·73	0·37
Credit expenses	126·7	403·4	0·38	0·37
On training personnel	111·1	199·1	0·32	0·18
Other expenses	295·1	682·4	0·86	0·62
Total	4,249·1	12,300·3	12·53	11·26

* *Quarterly Bulletin of Soviet-Russian Economics*, edited by Professor S. N. Prokopovich, no. 8, 1941, p. 126.

† *Planned Economy*, no. 6, 1939, pp. 129, 131.

The technique of price regulation, however, still experienced many difficulties as regards stimulating the production of particular goods. Cases of 'freezing' of trade in some goods and great scarcity in others were still very frequent; this was due not to production factors but to defects in the fixing of prices and the regulating of trade. One main problem remains still unsatisfactorily solved—that is, the problem of combining centralized planning and regulation of trade with the encouragement of initiative and autonomous responsibility of individual trading enterprises. Many measures were directed to this object during the last few years, but their positive effect is still far from adequate.

All these difficulties and shortcomings still apparent in home trade are, on the one hand, the historical outcome of the conditions from which the new organizational forms of Soviet trade sprang forth; and on the other they are generally inherent in any planned organization of the national economy.

In a sense, the Soviet system of home trade had to be created from scratch, on new principles and by new managerial and technical workers. Industry, transport, agriculture and other spheres of national economy when nationalized inherited basic capital, production traditions, a considerable proportion of the higher technical personnel and trained man-power, whereas State trade had to create anew a network of shops, trading habits and practically an entirely new personnel of managerial and other workers. Soviet trade lacked an inherited commercial base; it was the outcome of the struggle against the vestiges of private trade during which the heritage of the past had been liquidated. It did not inherit even all the buildings of private trade; at all events, they could not all have been used under a planned system of home trade. It was unavoidable that planned home trade should carry through a process of liquidating some of the scattered retail trading, which had sprung up in the course of history, in order to substitute a more rationally located trade network. This course would be unavoidable in any country where the system of chain stores in wholesale-retail trade has not yet been developed; and this was the case in pre-revolution Russia, where not only in retail but to a large extent in the wholesale trade too, property was still owned by individuals and not joint-stock companies. Therefore 'the nationalization' of private trade meant in actual fact the liquidation of the entire machinery of private trade and the loss of its managerial personnel. In the fields of industry, credit, agriculture, the former owners and to a certain extent the managerial workers could not be utilized under the new conditions of work; this was even more true of private trade. It has been shown how State trade developed gradually, parallel to the disappearance of private trade.

Another factor hampering the rationalization of Soviet trade was that its foundations had been laid at a time when conditions were such as to necessitate the introduction of rationing, i.e. distribution and not trade. These conditions fostered among the new personnel not the commercial habit of serving a consumer who buys goods and products freely, but the habits and ways of distributing goods among depersonalized ration-card holders. Only after the abolition of rationing was the Soviet trade machinery forced to adjust its attitude to the consumer freely choosing from among the goods offered. Naturally it took a considerable time to re-educate the commercial personnel and to reconstruct their methods of work. However, these were temporary difficulties due to the transition from private to State trade.

Difficulties of a more general and permanent nature consisted in the need to create a new attitude towards commercial activities, to replace the former profit motive by new motives to serve the consumer, to devise new incentives for rationalizing trade work and interesting managerial personnel in it. However, these problems of new forms in the organization of labour and allied problems which are inherent in this and other fields of the national economy under a planned system will be dealt with in later chapters.

These developments in home trade and the country's economy in general must have affected the organizational forms and the character of Soviet foreign trade. To supplement what has already been said on foreign trade in the N.E.P. period, a concise description is needed of the organizational changes and trends in foreign trade which marked the later periods of development of the Soviet economic system.*

We have seen that with the introduction of the first F.Y.P., private trade came to an end, while State and co-operative trade became primarily the distribution of existing commodities in a way conducive to the country's industrialization. Home trade developed into a system of centralized allocation of goods and products. Changes in the organization of home trade greatly contributed to centralize the earmarking of export goods and products. On the other hand, the enforcement of the F.Y.P. coincided with

* Further information on the subject will be found in a special study on *Foreign Trade Relations of the U.S.S.R.*, by the same author, now in preparation.

the world economic crisis. The task set for foreign trade was to expand exports in order to pay for the imports necessary to promote the country's industrialization. Endeavours to expand Soviet exports encountered ever-growing difficulties on the world markets. Consequently, foreign trade organizations had to concentrate their efforts chiefly on the sale of goods abroad and not on their procurement at home. These considerations were at the root of the reform of the foreign trade machinery which was carried out in 1930–1.

Early in 1930 (6 February) the existing export and import joint-stock companies were reorganized into monopolistic corporations which became the organs of the P. Commissariat of Trade. Most of the work previously performed by the P. Commissariat of Trade and the Trade Delegations was handed over to the new corporations. The latter, whether exporting or importing corporations, concentrated on trading in definite kinds of goods. The monopolies granted to them made it possible to put an end to the former multiplicity of organizations dealing in identical goods, both as regards export and import. Transactions with foreign firms were concluded as before by Trade Delegations, but the latter handed over to corresponding corporations the settling of accounts with their Soviet clients. Similarly, the technical preparations for the sale of exported goods and the placing of orders abroad were entrusted to the new corporations. The P. Commissariat of Trade concentrated mainly on questions of planning, general direction and control over foreign trade operations. On 29 November 1930 the P. Commissariat of Trade was split once more into two commissariats: the P. Commissariat of Supply of the U.S.S.R., which was to cater for the needs of the home market, and the P. Commissariat of Foreign Trade of the U.S.S.R., whose object was to specialize exclusively in problems of foreign trade. Early in 1931* the P. Commissariat of Foreign Trade was granted the right to have its own commissioners not only in allied and autonomous republics, in regions and provinces, but also at various points of importance to foreign trade. Moreover, in September 1931,† export 'conferences' (boards) were attached to the Sovnarkoms and Economic Councils of republics, and also to the praesidiums of regional, provincial and district executive committees and town councils; these conferences were to assist the commissioners of the P. Commissariat of Foreign Trade and the monopolistic export and import corporations. Gradually, in the course

* Regulation of the Central Executive Committee and the Sovnarkom S.S.S.R. dated 13 February 1931.
† Regulation of the Sovnarkom S.S.S.R. of 12 September 1931.

of the F.Y.P., all the main export and import transactions came to be handled by these corporations; they also performed planning functions in connexion with the commodities in which they specialized. As a consequence of this foreign trade reorganization, the policy of exporting and selling, or of importing any class of goods, was carried out from one centre working under the general supervision and direction of the P. Commissariat of Foreign Trade. The export corporations were henceforth exempt from the care of providing export funds—which they received from corresponding supply and industrial organizations—and could concentrate on the function of exporting and selling abroad the goods in which they specialized. Such an organization of the foreign trade turn-over contributed to the mobilization of the country's exportable resources and their sale under the crisis conditions prevailing on the world market; at the same time it secured the imports needed to carry out the policy of industrialization.

Although the conditions created by the world crisis were unfavourable to Soviet exports, and although in the early years of the F.Y.P. there was a shortage on the home market of many goods and products exported, the Soviet foreign trade turn-over reached its peak in those most critical years for world trade (for figures, see Appendix II, p. 275). During the world trade crisis, world prices declined so sharply that the volume of the U.S.S.R. foreign trade turn-over expressed in current prices gives quite a misleading picture of its volume in physical units. By weighting price changes, Soviet statisticians have calculated the physical volume of exports and imports, and Table 42 shows the physical volume of the U.S.S.R. foreign trade in the years 1929–37.

Table 42.

	1929	1930	1931	1932	1933	1934	1935	1936	1937
Index of physical volume of exports	100·0	135·7	146·1	127·8	118·5	102·9	90·5	68·2	68·4
Index of physical volume of imports	100·0	141·3	161·5	115·8	62·5	47·1	51·9	60·0	53·2
Index of physical volume of world exports	100·0	93·0	85·0	74·5	75·5	78·5	81·8	85·9	97·6

These figures show that the fluctuations in Soviet foreign trade in the years of world crisis are quite at variance with those for world exports in general. The objective of the U.S.S.R. foreign

* *The Foreign Trade of the Soviet Union,* edited by D. D. Mishustin, pp. 91–2.

trade was to contribute to the general economic plan for the country's industrialization. The export corporations were therefore set the task of mobilizing for export the maximum quantities of goods possible under existing production capacity, and to sell them in spite of the adverse conditions prevailing on the world market so as to secure the planned volume of imports. In fact, in spite of the unfavourable conditions of sale (the famous campaign against 'Soviet dumping'* and 'forced labour', and the sharp decline in prices on the main items of Soviet export), the physical volume of the latter in 1930–4 was above the 1929 level. However, the need of imports was too great to be met by the mobilization of the country's exportable resources, and the Soviet Government had deliberately to resort to an increase in its foreign indebtedness in order to secure imports vital to the fulfilment of the F.Y.P. Only after the latter had been carried out, and a base for further industrialization had thus been created, was a reduction effected in the physical volume of imports and concurrently in that of exports. Moreover, in the course of the second F.Y.P. it proved possible to curtail imports more than exports thus achieving a favourable balance of trade. From 1935 onward a favourable balance of payments was also attained (for data regarding the balance of payments of the U.S.S.R., see Appendix II, p. 276). The vital necessity to expand exports, at times to the prejudice of home needs even for agricultural produce, was now overcome. Herein lay one of the factors which led to the decision that from henceforth foreign trade operations should be transacted within the U.S.S.R., a transfer effected by the 1935 reform in the organization of foreign trade; this reform went hand in hand with the abolition of rationing on the home market.

The main provisions of the reorganization in the methods of work of the export and import corporations carried out in the summer of 1935† were as follows:

* In particular, the forced disposal of some Soviet exports at very low prices, described at the time as 'Soviet dumping' by the press, was determined not only by the need of selling export goods in order to obtain the foreign currency required to repay urgent short-term credits granted by importing firms, but was also due to the way in which Soviet foreign trade was organized in those days. Goods were exported and stored in the warehouses of the corresponding Trade Delegations according to plans made in respect of every country; sale plans, however, had to be suddenly altered and adapted to the rapidly deteriorating conditions of sale created by the spreading world crisis. Consequently it became necessary to clear stocks accumulated in the Trade Delegation warehouses at most unprofitable prices, not with the purpose of 'dumping', but for exchange, organizational and technical reasons.

† Regulation of the Sovnarkom S.S.S.R. dated 27 June 1935, 'Regarding the transfer of foreign trade operations into the U.S.S.R.'

(1) All export and import monopolistic corporations and mixed export-import and transport corporations were granted the right to enter into trade agreements with foreign firms without obtaining in every case the preliminary sanction of the P. Commissariat of Foreign Trade; agreements could be concluded within the U.S.S.R. or abroad; moreover, corporations were entitled to issue bills of exchange and to accept those of foreign firms.

(2) The delivery of goods by foreign firms was to be effected within the U.S.S.R. by the firms themselves. No longer were most Soviet exports sold from warehouses abroad where the actual goods lay stored, but they were sold c.i.f. and f.o.b. on the showing of samples, descriptions of goods and Soviet standards.

(3) Payments were effected within the U.S.S.R. and, similarly, disputes arising from contracts with foreign firms were also settled there.

(4) Some smaller corporations were liquidated and their business transferred to others.

(5) The chartering of ships was on the whole also transferred within the U.S.S.R. and taken over by the All-Union transport-dispatch corporations, while transport organizations with offices abroad were liquidated.

(6) The machinery of the U.S.S.R. Trade Delegations abroad was cut down, and most joint-stock companies with offices abroad were liquidated.

The transfer of export-import and freight operations back to the U.S.S.R. materially reduced administrative expenses payable in foreign currency, while the actual work connected with foreign trade operations passed entirely from the P. Commissariat of Foreign Trade and the Trade Delegations to the export, import and transport corporations.

The following are the main functions of export corporations*:

(a) To elaborate prospective export plans for those goods in which they specialized and to work out the relevant annual control figures and operational plans, and to submit them for approval in the established order.

(b) To put into effect the approved export plans by carrying out export operations on the basis of their monopoly.

(c) To work out and carry into effect measures for fulfilling export plans, improving the quality of the goods exported and raising the profitableness of export by such methods as the

* For details see *The Foreign Trade of the Soviet Union*, edited by D. D. Mishustin, pp. 77–80.

standardization of export goods, reduction in trade and overhead charges, better utilization of foreign markets, etc.

(*d*) To study prospects on foreign markets and firms' contracts.

Functions similar to those listed are also carried out by the import corporations; in addition to elaborating and carrying into effect measures for ascertaining the possibility of replacing imported by home-produced goods, they study the achievements of foreign production and commercial techniques, and carry out measures designed to introduce in the U.S.S.R. methods which have proved successful abroad.

Import corporations act as brokers to the Soviet economic organizations. Foreign trade corporations have offices and representatives at ports and other points of importance to their work. These offices and representatives, together with the commissioners of the P. Commissariat of Foreign Trade in republics, regions, provinces and other points important to foreign trade, are the main local agencies of the latter.

The main tasks of the commissioners of the P. Commissariat of Foreign Trade are:*

(1) To study local exporting potentialities, particularly with new items of export in view.

(2) To carry out measures designed to secure the fulfilment by republics, regions or provinces of their respective plans for the delivery of export goods.

(3) To supervise the fulfilment of export plans by local industry and procurement organizations, and the timely dispatch of export funds from their places of origin.

(4) To supervise the quality of goods earmarked for export and the work of State institutions controlling quality.

Export 'conferences', which exist in all administrative centres where the P. Commissariat of Foreign Trade has its commissioners, assist them in their work. In fact, the commissioners direct all the foreign trade organizations in the republic, region or province to which they are appointed. Corporations give to their local organs operational orders and general directives regarding definite types of goods for the republic, region or province as a whole; but the actual allocation of plans between districts, and the measures ensuring their fulfilment, are carried out whether directly or in-

* For details regarding the commissioners of the P. Commissariat of Foreign Trade see M. M. Zhirmunrsky, *The Organization and Technique of Soviet Export*.

directly by the commissioners of the Commissariat. In this manner, the commissioners co-ordinate the activities of all export corporations in any one area.

The P. Commissariat of Foreign Trade does not carry out any actual operations, but regulates, controls and directs the country's entire export and import work. The following functions come within the scope of its competence:

(1) To examine and ratify plans of export and import, submitted by the appropriate corporations.

(2) To direct and control the sale policy of export and import corporations abroad, and also to direct work connected with trade agreements.

(3) To promote the study of new items of export, the rationalization of export and import measures, the increase of exportable resources and the substitution of imported by home-produced goods.

(4) To scrutinize the corporations' financial and foreign exchange plans, to ratify their estimates of administrative and maintenance expenses, to fix norms of overhead charges, and to draft plans consolidating these various financial items.

Abroad, the P. Commissariat of Foreign Trade carries out its functions of regulating and controlling the entire foreign trade activity of the U.S.S.R. through the agency of Trade Delegations accredited to the various countries. The duty of every Trade Delegation is to regulate the trade of the U.S.S.R. with the given country, and in particular, to regulate and control the commercial activities of export and import corporations carrying out their transactions with that particular country. In latter years Trade Delegations carried out very little actual commercial work.

The planning of the entire foreign trade turn-over comprises the planning of export and import, and of currency circulation.*

In drawing up *plans of export* the following items are taken into account: the country's exportable resources, the prospects of their sale abroad and the U.S.S.R.'s commercial and political attitude towards various countries and different types of commodities. The fundamental method used in planning export and import, like that used in general planning, starts with the drafting of material balances of given commodities (see chapter on General Planning,

---

* A detailed account of the planning of Soviet foreign trade will be found in *The Foreign Trade of the Soviet Union*, edited by D. D. Mishustin; M. M. Zhirmunsky, *The Organization and Technique of Soviet Export*; L. Frey, A. Smirnov, G. Lopatin, I. Zhelezniakov, *The Financing of Foreign Trade.*

p. 444).* Under the direction of the P. Commissariat of Foreign Trade, export corporations in collaboration with their suppliers, work out plans for the delivery of export goods included in their list, as well as plans for their sale abroad. The P. Commissariat of Foreign Trade co-ordinates the corporations' export plans with the production plans of the P. Commissariats responsible for any of the given commodities and consolidates the drafts into a general plan of export and sale which it then submits to the Government for approval. The approved plans are transmitted to the export corporations for execution by their branches and local offices and the commissioners of the P. Commissariat of Foreign Trade in the corresponding republic, region, etc. The plan of exports consists of a long-range, an annual and quarterly plans; moreover, it includes, apart from the general plan covering all exported commodities, separate plans of exports to various countries which take into consideration the prospects of selling this or that commodity in the individual countries. In addition to the quantities to be exported and sold, profitableness, overhead charges, and the quality and standards of goods are also subject to planning.

The *planning of imports* is closely tied up with the long-range and annual national economic plans. On the basis of applications from various branches of the national economy for this or that raw material or finished article, and after taking into account the country's internal resources (stocks and production plans), the U.S.S.R. Gosplan draws up a general plan for the import of the goods required. The P. Commissariat of Foreign Trade co-ordinates the Gosplan's programme of imports with obligations arising from trade agreements with various states and also with the planned value of foreign currency receipts projected in the export plan; the resulting draft constitutes the general plan of imports.

---

* Example of material balances—flax.
A. Resources.

(1) Area under crop	Thousand hectares
(2) Yield per hectare	Quintals
(3) Harvest, gross	Thousand tons
(4) Retained for agricultural purposes	Thousand tons
(5) Marketable amount	Thousand tons
(6) Balance at the beginning of the year	Thousand tons
Resources, total	Thousand tons

B. Allocation of resources.

(1) To industry	Thousand tons
(2) For export	Thousand tons
(3) Reserves	Thousand tons

The Foreign Trade of the U.S.S.R...., p. 115.

Finally, annual import plans drawn up by the Gosplan and the P. Commissariat of Foreign Trade are examined, co-ordinated and ratified by the Government. Up to 1937, simultaneously with the import plan, the Government approved annual import quotas for various types of goods and for individual departments and organizations, and also the permissible dates of payment for the prospective purchases of foreign commodities, so as to bring them into line with the plan of foreign exchange receipts brought in by the sale of the goods exported. Since 1937 the apportionment of import quotas a year in advance has been maintained only for those goods which are distributed in the U.S.S.R. through the central agencies. Departments and institutions requiring other imported goods apply in every particular case for the Government's leave to import the requisite commodity or article, and upon their application being granted, receive the quota applied for. This change in the allocation of quotas was introduced because the improved balance of payments of the U.S.S.R., and an improved technique in the handling of import operations made for greater flexibility of the general import plan and allowed for adjustments in the course of its fulfilment. For some goods, mainly equipment, import quotas fix the value only, i.e. limits are fixed only to the value of the goods without any reference to their actual quantities; for other goods (raw materials and semi-finished articles) both value and quantity are specified. At the present time annual import plans are drawn up by the Department of Imports of the P. Commissariat of Foreign Trade in collaboration with the import corporations, whereas quarterly plans—which are operational plans—are drawn up by the import corporations on the basis of definite orders for imports sent in by organizations and institutions.

The planning of imports, like that of exports, takes into account the quantity of goods and their value, the countries from which the goods will be imported and the dates when payments fall due; moreover, the operational plan also includes a goods and firms plan stating with which firms orders will be placed. The purpose of this clause is to prevent the same foreign firms from receiving unco-ordinated orders from individual corporations or for individual goods. After the plan of imports has been approved, import corporations are issued with permits for foreign currency to the amount of their import quotas, indicating dates of payment and countries where purchases are being made or orders placed. No import corporation has the right to start carrying out its plan before receiving its permit for foreign currency. Import corporations carry out their clients' orders on a commission basis according to their contracts. The commission rates are fixed yearly by the P. Commissariat of Foreign Trade.

The *foreign currency plan* is based on an estimate of the balance of payments of the U.S.S.R. over a definite period, and consists of two parts: the commercial and the non-commercial foreign currency plans.

The commercial foreign currency plan includes plans of receipts from and payment for all export-import operations, freight expenses paid in foreign currencies, expenses for technical assistance also payable in foreign currencies and other expenses connected with foreign trade operations. The export plan fixes prices and values f.o.b. and carriage paid to the frontier of the U.S.S.R. The P. Commissariat of Foreign Trade scrutinizes the foreign currency plans of all corporations trading abroad and incorporates them into the commercial foreign currency plan.

The non-commercial part of the foreign currency plan is drawn up by the U.S.S.R. P. Commissariat of Finance on the basis of the foreign currency plans sent in by various departments. It comprises: receipts and expenses in foreign currency included in the State Budget, receipts and expenses arising from State loans subscribed to abroad, settlements with foreign concession holders, money orders not arising from commerce, revenue from and expenditure on the tourist trade, receipts from passengers using Soviet means of communication and other minor non-commercial items.

The commercial foreign currency plan of the P. Commissariat of Foreign Trade and the non-commercial foreign currency plan of the P. Commissariat of Finance are submitted together to the Government and, after ratification, become binding for the appropriate corporations and institutions. The foreign currency plan is drafted in roubles, but receipts and payments are made exclusively in foreign currencies at the rates of exchange fixed by the Department of Foreign Transactions of the U.S.S.R. State Bank.

All transfers of foreign currency and payments abroad are carried out by the State Bank within the limits set out in the foreign currency plan. This foreign currency plan must by no means be confused with the general financial plan of the foreign trade organizations. The latter is in every way similar to the financial plans of any industrial, commercial or other economic organization in the U.S.S.R., and the corporations' financial relations with the State Bank conform to the pattern common to all the other organizations working within the U.S.S.R. (see chapter on Finance, pp. 412–13).

This has been in broad outline the evolution of the organizational forms of Soviet foreign trade. This organization has enabled it, particularly in later years, to cope on the whole successfully with the tasks set by the economic plans, whilst achieving better results in import than in export trade. Although subject to the influence of conditions prevailing on the world market, the P. Commissariat of Foreign Trade has usually succeeded in carrying out the aims of the Soviet Government both as regards the volume of the foreign trade operations and also as regards the main commercial and political directives concerning various countries.

It is no exaggeration to say that the planning of the foreign trade proved to be more successful and technically more adequate than the planning of the home-trade turn-over. Whatever the chances of reorganization in other spheres of the Soviet system of national economy, it can be surmised that the principles elaborated in the field of Soviet trade with foreign countries are unlikely to be subjected to drastic changes in the future.

APPENDIX I

	Export (in million roubles)		Import (in million roubles)	
	I	II	I	II
1909–13	1,501·4	6,513·9	1,140·2	4,994·1
1913	1,520·1	6,596·4	1,374·0	6,022·5
1929	923·7	4,045·8	880·6	3,857·0
1930	1,036·4	4,539·3	1,058·8	4,637·5
1931	811·2	3,553·1	1,105·0	4,839·9
1932	574·9	2,518·2	704·0	3,083·5
1933	494·9	2,167·5	348·2	1,525·1
1934	418·3	1,832·4	232·4	1,018·0
1935	367·4	1,609·3	241·4	1,057·2
1936	310·3	1,359·1	308·8	1,352·5
1937	394·6	1,728·6	306·2	1,341·3
1938	304·1	1,331·9	320·5	1,422·9

	Total turn-over (in million roubles)		Balance (in million roubles)	
	I	II	I	II
1909–13	2,641·6	11,508·0	+361·2	+1,519·8
1913	2,895·1	12,618·9	+146·1	+573·9
1929	1,804·3	7,902·8	+43·1	+188·8
1930	2,095·2	9,176·8	−22·4	−98·2
1931	1,916·2	8,393·0	−293·8	−1,286·8
1932	1,278·9	5,601·7	−129·1	−565·3
1933	843·1	3,692·6	+146·7	+642·4
1934	650·7	2,850·4	+185·9	+814·4
1935	608·9	2,666·5	+126·0	+552·1
1936	619·1	2,711·6	+1·5	+6·6
1937	700·8	3,069·9	+88·4	+387·3
1938	624·6	2,754·8	−16·4	−91·0

The figures in column I are quoted as given in Soviet statistics before the devaluation of the rouble in 1935; figures for 1909–13 are gold roubles of 1913, and the territory that of pre-revolution Russia; figures for 1924–5 to 1935 are in 'chervonetz' roubles in force during that period; on the average the value of the rouble was 51·46 American cents; in later years, 1936–8, the value of the chervonetz rouble was fixed at 23·83 kopeks of the former chervonetz rouble; for comparison with data published prior to 1936, the coefficient 4·38 has been used. In column II the figures cited are those calculated by the Scientific Research Institute of the Monopoly of Foreign Trade, the exchange rate of the chervonetz rouble being 1 rouble = 4 frs. 25 cts., and later 1 American dollar = 5 roubles 30 kopeks.

APPENDIX II

	Export (thousand tons)	Import (thousand tons)	Total turn-over (thousand tons)
1909–13	24,590·8	11,240·7	35,831·5
1913	24,112·8	15,342·8	39,455·6
1924–5	6,169·0	1,863·7	8,032·7
1925–6	7,855·8	1,547·3	9,403·1
1926–7	9,573·0	1,846·5	11,419·5
1927–8	8,873·7	2,014·3	10,888·0
1929	14,145·0	1,936·7	16,081·7
1930	21,486·4	2,855·9	24,342·3
1931	21,778·9	3,564·4	25,343·3
1932	17,967·9	2,322·1	20,290·0
1933	17,916·3	1,236·1	19,152·4
1934	17,340·2	1,025·2	18,365·4
1935	17,190·4	1,259·1	18,449·5
1936	14,204·0	1,155·3	15,359·3
1937	12,969·4	1,285·8	14,255·2
1938	9,682·3	1,127·2	10,809·5

APPENDIX III

(Figures in millions of roubles, 1936 value, and % of total)

	Total Exports	Foodstuffs	%	Raw materials and semi-manufactured goods	%	Animals	%	Manufactured goods	%
Export									
1929	4,045·8	857·7	21·2	2,536·7	62·7	12·1	0·3	639·3	15·8
1930	4,539·3	1,434·4	31·6	2,414·9	53·2	0·1	0·0	690·0	15·2
1931	3,553·1	1,250·7	35·2	1,694·8	47·7	0·0	0·0	607·6	17·1
1932	2,518·2	566·6	22·5	1,347·2	53·5	0·0	0·04	604·4	24·0
1933	2,167·5	411·8	19·0	1,260·2	58·1	0·1	0·0	495·4	22·9
1934	1,832·4	295·8	16·1	1,104·4	60·3	0·2	0·0	432·0	23·6
1935	1,609·3	305·2	19·0	997·1	62·0	0·2	0·0	306·8	19·0
1936	1,359·1	182·0	13·4	907·7	66·8	0·1	0·0	269·3	19·8
1937	1,728·6	396·6	22·9	1,012·1	58·6	0·1	0·0	319·8	18·5
Import									
1929	3,857·0	322·4	8·4	1,681·9	43·6	55·4	1·4	1,797·3	46·6
1930	4,637·5	414·3	8·9	1,171·7	25·3	99·1	2·1	2,952·4	63·7
1931	4,839·9	204·8	4·2	930·3	19·2	114·9	2·4	3,589·9	74·2
1932	3,083·5	232·2	7·5	507·3	16·5	81·2	2·6	2,262·8	73·4
1933	1,525·1	69·4	4·6	388·6	25·5	59·5	3·9	1,007·6	66·0
1934	1,018·0	95·3	9·4	396·2	38·9	47·6	4·7	478·9	47·0
1935	1,057·2	92·3	8·7	464·1	43·9	41·1	3·9	459·7	43·5
1936	1,352·5	88·2	6·5	472·6	34·9	54·9	4·1	736·8	54·5
1937	1,341·3	85·9	6·4	669·0	49·9	46·1	3·4	540·3	40·3

APPENDIX IV

Balance of payments of the U.S.S.R. for 1935 and 1936.
In million roubles

Current items*

Receipts	1935	1936	Expenses	1935	1936
1. Receipts from sale of export goods (f.o.b. prices)	1,800	1,497	1. Cash payments for imports including overhead charges (c.i.f. prices) ...	860	1,328
2. Income from marine freightage (balance) ...	48	72	2. Expenses on technical servicing and assembly	23	23
3. Receipts from harbour dues and for the servicing of ships (balance) ...	11	2	3. Excess of State expenditure over State receipts abroad	57	55
4. Other receipts from transport (balance) ...	12	16	4. Interest on loans and credits (balance) ...	89	44
5. Receipts from insurance operations (balance) ...	6	2	5. Other expenses ...	—	62
6. Receipts from non-commercial transfers (balance)	62	7			
7. Receipts from the tourist trade and money spent by foreigners (balance)	29	35			
8. Other receipts	165	32			
9. Sale of gold	52	—			
Current items, total ...	2,185	1,663	Current items, total ...	1,029	1,512
			Excess of receipts over expenses on current items	1,156	151

Movement of credits and property held abroad*

Receipts	1935	1936	Expenses	1935	1936
1. Repatriation of property held abroad (balance) ...	—	71	1. Repayment of State and concessionary loans ...	—	46
2. Receipts from State loans sold abroad ...	8	—	2. Repayment of credits granted by foreign importing firms	694	354
3. Receipts from financial credits	—	242	3. Reduction of indebtedness made up of short-term export and bank credits	319	32
Movement of credits and property abroad, total...	8	313	Movement of credits and property abroad, total...	1,013	432
Excess of expenses over receipts in the movement of credits and property abroad	1,005	119	Increased balances of the Soviet banks' foreign currency accounts held abroad	151	32

* For details regarding the balance of payments of the U.S.S.R. see *The Financing of Foreign Trade*, by L. Frey, A. Smirnov, G. Lopatin and I. Zhelezniakov, pp. 236–43.

CHAPTER XVI. INDUSTRY

The abolition of rationing brought to the fore more acutely than ever the problem of improving the quality of work of industrial enterprises. From 1935 the drive was directed not so much towards expanding industrial production at any cost as towards improving the quality of its work. The increase in industrial production planned for 1935 was relatively less strenuous than any of the previous years of either the first or the second F.Y.P. It was limited for industry as a whole to 16% as against the 19% in 1934; for group A the increase was to be 19·4%, which was even below the actual increase achieved by heavy industry in 1934. The plan for lowering production costs was also moderate—a 3·7% reduction for industry as a whole in the course of the year. Altogether the plan for 1935 was more moderate, its whole character was less strained than those of previous years, and there was not such a drive to 'storm' industry.

In fact, the plan for 1935 was carried out more evenly, both in the sense of monthly achievements and in the sense that there were less discrepancies in the execution of the plan by individual branches of industrial production. As a result, for the first time since the introduction of the first and second F.Y.P.s, the tasks for the quantitative growth of industry were fulfilled by every All-Union Commissariat, aggregating a gross increase of output in All-Union industry of 23·6%; and in all industry, i.e. Union, republican, local and co-operative, the year's increase was 20% instead of the planned 16%. It also proved possible to achieve an improvement in the quality of goods. Nevertheless, in industrial reviews, attention continued to be drawn to the fact that 'losses from spoilt material are still very great....'. 'Elegance in design, colourfulness of fabrics, new fashions in shoes and knitwear, new varieties of crockery—are all introduced insufficiently by light industry and still do not satisfy the consumer....' 'The results of the past year show that light industry has not yet learnt to change its methods of work, and that the position is worst in regard to the fulfilment of the qualitative indices.'*

Encouraging results were obtained in regard to labour productivity and the reduction of production costs. For the first time,

* *Planned Economy*, no. 10, 1935, p. 55. *Lyogkaya Promyshlenost*, 28 December 1935.

labour productivity in the industries subordinate to the P. Commissariat of Heavy Industry exceeded the planned target, as did also the reduction of production costs.*

As a consequence of these successes the termination of State subsidies to heavy industry was raised for the first time, and the revision of industrial prices, already described, was started. In August, the Stakhanov movement was launched, on which great hopes were staked for raising the productivity of labour and the quality of industrial production (see p. 336). In December 1935 the Plenum of the Central Committee of the Party set heavy industry the task:

of developing an all-in Stakhanov movement, *starting in all the extracting industries* and primarily in the *coal-* and *ore-*mining industries, the oil industry, heavy and non-ferrous metallurgy, in construction, in production of building materials and in chemical industries not dependent on limited resources of raw materials. The principal aim in organizing the Stakhanov movement is to achieve a maximum increase of production and a reduction of production costs, assuming that the production programme is a compulsory minimum target. In machine-building the Stakhanov movement must be directed towards achieving a better use of metal, improving the utilization of machine-time and raising the quality of production. The P. Commissariat of Heavy Industry is invited to complete by 1936 the revision of technical standards of equipment and productive capacity, in order to increase these standards, and in revising new planned capacities to adopt these higher technical standards, as a rule. These technical standards determining the capacity of individual machine aggregates are to be established in accordance with the experience of the best Stakhanov workers...to proceed early in 1936 to the revision of standards of output ensuring a certain measure of increase, and as a preliminary, to convene according to the calendar plan approved by the P. Commissariat of Heavy Industry, branch conferences composed of factory and works directors, heads of workshops, engineers, foremen and Stakhanov workers; at these conferences the problem of revising the technical standards of equipment and capacities of enterprises as well as standards of output are to be worked out carefully, concretely and in detail.†

A number of measures were also drawn up to raise the standards of technical skill among workers and to revise wages (see p. 230–1).

In connexion with the great hopes staked on the Stakhanov movement and also on the organizational measures then carried

---

* The Plan demanded a 14·3 % increase in labour productivity; actually the increase attained 16·3 %. For further details on the work of heavy industry in 1935, see Plan no. 1, 1936.

† *The C.P. in Resolutions...*, pp. 630–1.

out in industry (see p. 338), the tasks planned for 1936 were again very high, both for the expansion of production and for the increase in labour productivity. The increase in gross output was planned as high as 23 %; it is characteristic that for the first time a faster tempo of increase was planned in light industry than in heavy industry, and the financing of light industry's capital investments was double the figure for 1935. It was decided to concentrate much more effort on speeding up production of mass-consumption goods, which was lagging so far behind the production of means of production and was so far from satisfying the growing needs of the population.

The results of 1936 proved even more satisfactory than those of 1935. According to official data, the gross output of industries subordinate to All-Union Commissariats increased by 30·3 % during the year, the gross output of medium and small-scale industry subordinate to P. Commissariats of allied republics also increased by 30 %, whilst the output of manufactured goods by small handicraft associations (co-operative) even increased by 41·8 %. It was stressed in publications reviewing industrial results that this considerable increase in industrial production was on the whole achieved not through an increase in the number of workers, but thanks to an increase in the productivity of labour and improved utilization of equipment and raw materials. However, it was at the same time emphasized that

things were less satisfactory in regard to mastering the economics and finance of enterprises, and in regard to business management standards. In this field, the results of 1936 cannot be considered as satisfactory. Industry had not fulfilled the plan for the reduction of production costs (though there had been a certain reduction in comparison with 1935). The share of substandard production (spoilt material, second and third grades, etc.) was in excess of the so-called norms and practically on a level with the last quarter of 1935. The plan for the accumulation of profits was on the whole not fulfilled. The inspection of books carried out in a number of enterprises and economic institutions during the second half of 1936 revealed the unsatisfactory state of affairs in accountancy, serious breaches of financial discipline and downright embezzlement of State funds.*

According to a statement by the P. Commissar of Light Industry:

Our quantitative achievements are lowered by a number of defaults in regard to qualitative indices, the productivity of equipment and the reduction of production costs, etc. The wages fund in light industry has

* *Ekon. Zhizn*, 6 February 1937.

been overspent to the huge amount of 170 million roubles. This extra expenditure, together with inadequate economy and poor utilization of raw materials, a high degree of spoilt material and lengthy stoppages have prevented light industry from fulfilling its task for the reduction of production costs.*

The results of extensively expanding industrial production in the conditions prevailing during the rationing period, of subsidizing industry from State funds and of artificially fixing transfer prices independently of cost prices, were still to be felt in 1936 and hampered a steady and substantial improvement in the quality of industry's work.

It will be remembered that in January 1937 the 'wreckers'' trials took place at which exhaustive evidence was given of 'wrecking' in industry; wrecking in carrying out the construction of industrial enterprises, in the co-ordination of this construction work and in the organization of production. Among the wreckers were the long-standing deputy P. Commissar of Heavy Industry, Piatakov, the deputy P. Commissar of Timber Industry, Sokolnikov, the manager of the Industrial Bank, Tumanov, and many other responsible workers from industry and the State Planning Commission. It is worth recalling this trial because the facts made public during the hearing as evidence of the wrecking activities of individual representatives of the 'Anti-Soviet Trotskyist Centre' vividly illustrate the defects under which industrial construction and production had often operated and the fact that at the time these defects were either overlooked or viewed as an inevitable if unfortunate result of the peculiar circumstances in which industry had to develop, and were not then considered to be wilful wrecking. In 1937 a purge of the Party and of the country's whole administrative machinery was carried out. A wave of prosecutions swept the country, prosecutions directed against individuals and groups of individuals accused of wrecking when drawing up plans for the reconstruction of factories, or in creating discrepancies between various kinds of production, and of other wrecking activities connected with the organization of production proper or of the financing of production, etc. According to a statement by Molotov:

Already [i.e. in March 1937, when the statement was made] hundreds of business managers in possession of Party membership cards have been unmasked, as well as 'non-Party' engineers and technicians, who held responsible posts in the institutions of the P. Commissariat of Heavy Industry and who for years indulged in criminal wrecking

* *Lyogkaya Promyshlenost,* 9 January 1937.

activities. May it be hoped that we shall succeed in quickly eradicating from industry all the ramifications of this criminal gang.*

The wreckers' trials of 1937 differed from the earlier 'Shakhty' and 'Industrial Party' trials by reason of the fact that in the latter the defendants in the dock were highly qualified engineers, non-Party members, whereas in the wreckers' trials the accused were more or less exclusively Party members, from among the 'administrators':

The Shakhty men had the advantage of technical knowledge over the Party men, but the present-day wreckers have no technical superiority over our men. On the contrary, our men are better trained technically than the present-day Trotskyist wreckers. Wherein then lies the strength of contemporary wreckers? Their strength is in their Party card, in their possession of a Party card. Their strength lies in the fact that a Party card wins political confidence and opens the doors of our institutions and organizations to them. The mistake of some of our Party comrades is that they have not understood this difference between old and new wreckers, between the 'Shakhty' men and Trotskyists.†

And from 1937 a general purge of the whole administrative and economic apparatus of the country set in and with it the removal from business posts not only of Trotskyists but of many other Party members, who held their positions in the economic system on the strength of former Party 'services' and not because they knew their job.

Incidentally, and as already observed here, the fact that the new Constitution of the U.S.S.R. was actually approved towards the end of 1936 suggests its close inner connexion with those widespread changes in managerial staffs, as well as with the developments in the field of labour in the period following the adoption of the Constitution.

At all events, the subsequent developments in industry show that the campaign against wrecking and the Party purge of 1937, with the numerous changes in the personnel of industry's managerial and production-administrative machinery which they entailed and the promotion to administrative posts of new cadres trained in special schools and grown to manhood during the first and second five-year periods, exercised not an adverse, but a beneficial influence on the development of industry.

The regulation of the Central Committee and the Sovnarkom S.S.S.R. concerning the 1937 plan of national economy stated that up to date, 'among serious defects are bad discipline in State insti-

* *Bolshevik*, no. 8, 1937, p. 137.   † Ibid., no. 7, 1937, p. 8.

tutions and a casual and careless attitude of economic organizations, particularly in fulfilling contract obligations, which result in impairing the plans for the supply of equipment, cause delays in construction schedules and swell production costs.... The Central Committee and the Sovnarkom S.S.S.R. draw attention to these defects and demand that managerial personnel wage a decisive struggle for their speedy elimination'. This criticism of the work of business organizations made by the U.S.S.R. Government on the eve of the last year of the second F.Y.P., stating the serious shortcomings still persistent in the work of industry, is quite sharply worded. Nevertheless, confidence that, in spite of these faults, industry would again be capable of achieving a very considerable expansion of production must evidently have been strong, for the tasks set to industry for expanding production in 1937 were again very great. A 20% increase in gross production was planned for industry as a whole, of which group A accounted for 19·5% and group B for 20·8%; for the first time it was stressed that 'the *fulfilment of the plan* (underlined in the original) by an enterprise must be judged not by the gross output, but by the output of finished and perfect production, the quality and range of which are fixed by the P. Commissariat. The Soviet of P. Commissars of the U.S.S.R. is authorized to issue instructions to the P. Commissariats of the U.S.S.R. and the Soviets of P. Commissars of [Union] republics regarding the means of assessing the fulfilment of the plan as established by the present decision'.* In the concluding lines of the plan it was stated that the fulfilment of the 1937 plan for national economy would not only mean the fulfilment but the over-fulfilment of the second F.Y.P. by industry as a whole and in regard to other fundamental tasks of the second F.Y.P.

This annual plan was approved on 29 March 1937, and on 29 April a statement was published by the Sovnarkom S.S.S.R. to the effect that 'the second F.Y.P. in regard to the most important branches of the national economy has been fulfilled ahead of schedule, and in U.S.S.R. industry as a whole was completed by 1 April 1937'.†

At the time, this statement raised many suspicions and doubts which were voiced in the specialist foreign press, among others by the author of the present study.‡ However, information published since makes it possible to establish more precisely the meaning and

---

* *The Plan for the National Economy of the U.S.S.R. in* 1937, Moscow, 1937, pp. 11, 13, 15.
† *Za Industr.* 29 April 1937.
‡ *Bull. Econ. Study of Prof. Prokopovich*, no. 135, 1937.

significance of the claim to premature fulfilment of the Plan; for greater clarity the figures already cited on p. 183 must be recalled (see Table 43).

Table 43*

	1937 according to the 2nd 5-year Plan	Annual plan for 1937	Actual fulfilment in 1937
Gross output of all industry in milliard roubles (in fixed prices of 1926–7)	92·7	103·0	95·5
Of which:			
Production of means of production (group A)	45·5	60·0	55·2
Production of consumer goods (group B)	47·2	43·0	40·3
Including:			
Production of electrical energy at district power stations (million kWh.)	24·5	28·0	25·4
Coal (million tons)	152·5	150·1	128·0
Crude oil and gas (million tons)	46·8	32·2	30·5
Pig iron (million tons)	16·0	16·0	14·5
Steel (million tons)	17·0	20·1	17·7
Rolled metal (million tons)	13·0	15·6	13·0
Chemical industry (milliard roubles in fixed prices 1926–7)	5·5	5·9	5·9
Metal-working industries (milliard roubles in fixed prices 1926–7)	19·5	30·0	27·5
Cotton textiles (million m.)	5,100·0	4,084·1	3,447·7
Linen textiles (million sq.m.)	600·0	310·0	285·2
Footwear (million pairs)	180·0	190·0	205·9

These figures show that the targets of the annual plan for 1937 for the gross output of industry as a whole were above those approved for the year by the second F.Y.P., but for individual branches of industry they were in some cases above and in others below. On the whole the fulfilment of the second F.Y.P. in 1937 exceeded the targets set by the F.Y.P. The over-fulfilment was particularly marked in the metal-working industry, which included the armament industry, while the output of light industry, particularly of textiles, fell short of the mark by a wide margin. In an official governmental report on the results of the second F.Y.P. by Molotov, it was stated:

We must declare that in the second five-year period the growth of heavy industry also outstripped that of industries manufacturing consumer goods. The main reason for this is that in the course of the second F.Y.P. we had to introduce important changes into the plan for

* *Second Five-Year Plan, approved by the Seventeenth Party Congress; The Plan for the National Economy of the U.S.S.R. in 1937; Results of the Fulfilment of the Second Five-Year Plan for the Development of the National Economy of the U.S.S.R.*

the development of industry; just as during the first F.Y.P. we were compelled by the international position to hasten the planned pace of the armament industry. This required a considerable intensification in the growth of heavy industry at the expense of light industry. But it must be admitted that now [i.e. in the third five-year period] *pari passu* with the desire still further to develop heavy industry, we must also speed up the whole industrial front manufacturing consumer goods.*

To appreciate the data on the fulfilment of the annual plans and the dynamics of the development of industrial production in the course of both five-year periods, the following important points must be underlined. Gross output as a whole was calculated at 1926–7 prices. Attention has already been drawn to the lack of information as to how such calculations were made in the case of industries which only went into production after 1926–7, i.e. the greater part of the metal-working industries. However, putting aside this methodological question, it must be emphasized that during the years covered by the two F.Y.P.s, and in particular during the years of the second, branches of large-scale industries, hitherto non-existent, came into being, and that the output of these branches accounts for an important share in the sum total of gross production of industry as a whole; e.g. according to the 1937 plan, the gross output of all heavy industry (at 1926–7 prices) was to be 52·4 milliard roubles, of which machine-building accounted for 30 milliards, whilst the share of the coal industry was only 1·4 milliards and that of non-ferrous metallurgy 1·6 milliards. The gross production of the whole timber industry was estimated at 6·8 milliard roubles; that of light industry at 21·8 milliards, and that of the food industry, including that of the Commissariat of Agricultural Supply, at 16·5 milliard roubles. At the same time, the gross production of such new branches of large-scale industry, as, on the whole, were the knitwear, garment and footwear industries, was to be 5·2 milliard roubles, whilst the output of the cotton industry, one of the oldest branches of Russian light industry, was some 5 milliards, and it was planned to manufacture 4,084 million metres of cotton textiles as against 2,227 million metres in 1913 and 2,742 million metres in 1928. Another and more striking example was that the gross production of bread by large-scale bakeries in 1937 was estimated at 2·3 milliard roubles, that of the confectionery industry at 1·4 milliards, butter at only 0·4 milliard and meat at 1·9 milliard roubles. All these—as large-scale industries—are new branches of industry created more or less entirely in the course of

* Molotov's report on the third F.Y.P. of the development of the national economy of the U.S.S.R. *Problems of Economics*, no. 3, 1939, p. 40.

the two five-year periods, and in particular in the latter years of the second Plan. Moreover, the value of the production of bread or of confectionery, expressed in roubles, is higher than that of the entire coal industry. Therefore, it may be argued that if the confectionery industry over-fulfilled its plan by some 10 %, this would cover a 10–12 % deficit in the coal industry, and in the final reckoning the plan would appear to have been fulfilled by 100 %. In the years of the two F.Y.P.s, the output of the metal-working, large-scale food, clothing and footwear industries grew annually; all these manufacture 'expensive' goods, and therefore the increase of gross production expressed in money leads to higher figures than the increase expressed in general physical volumes. Consequently, to form a more exact picture of the dynamics of industrial production in the course of the two five-year periods it is desirable to juxtapose the figures of gross production, estimated in 1926–7 roubles, with such data as are available for the output of individual branches of industry measured in physical units (see Appendix I, p. 307).

Industrial production in all branches of heavy industry clearly increased at a rapid pace, and this is particularly true of the metal-working industries. Much less successful was the development of the production of basic mass-consumption goods. In the official report on the fulfilment of the second F.Y.P. it was stated that an improvement of the qualitative indices in the work of industry as a whole had also taken place,

a lowering of the norms of consumption of raw and other materials and of fuel; a reduction of losses in production and an improvement in the indices of utilization of equipment as well as a reduction of overhead charges.... Independently of changes in the prices of raw and other materials and of fuel, certain branches of heavy industry have reduced the cost of production by 37 %, including the machine-building industries which have done so by 45 %, thus over-fulfilling the second F.Y.P.'s target.[*]

The capital construction programme was also carried out more successfully than during the first F.Y.P., when expenditure on capital construction had far exceeded the plan's provisions but only 60 % of completed construction had gone into production; during the second five-year period expenditure kept slightly below the plan and 87 % of the outlay went into production. As already mentioned, the capital construction programme of the second F.Y.P. had been more thoroughly worked out than that of the first

[*] *Results of the Fulfilment of the Second Five-Year Plan for the Development of the National Economy of the U.S.S.R.* p. 29.

Plan, and construction was carried out more evenly and with better co-ordination than had been the case during the first five-year period. The experience of the haphazard capital construction of the first Plan had not altogether been wasted.

As a result of this colossal capital construction carried out under the two F.Y.P.s, 80 % of the entire industrial output in 1937 was produced by newly built or completely reconstructed plants. This circumstance also contributed considerably to increase the productivity of industrial labour. Instead of a 63 % increase in the productivity of labour to be achieved in the course of the second five-year period, the actual increase amounted to 82 %; and this increase in the productivity of labour became the main source of increase in industrial production. Thus, in spite of all the difficulties and faults in the development of industry we have mentioned, it proved possible during the second five-year period not only to achieve an even greater increase in industrial production than had been achieved under the first Plan, but also substantially to improve the quality of planning both in capital construction and in industrial development, and at the same time to raise the quality of industrial work. Considerable success was also achieved in securing a more rational location of industries.

The third F.Y.P. for the development of the national economy was in its essence a continuation and a further intensification of the plan to industrialize the country, inaugurated by the first F.Y.P. Again the focal point was the development of industry, and in the first place of the production of the means of production. Out of a total volume of capital work estimated at 192 milliard roubles for the entire national economy (in current estimated 1939 prices), 111·9 milliards were to be expended on capital work in industry as against 58·6 milliards expended under the second F.Y.P.; of this 93·9 milliards were allocated to the production of the means of production, as against the 49·3 milliards expended in the course of the second five-year period, and 18 milliards on the production of consumption goods as against 8·8 milliards allotted to the same item under the previous Plan.* Thus, more than half of all invest-

* The figures quoted here and further on are those of the approved F.Y.P., and not those of the draft, worked out in detail by the U.S.S.R. Gosplan and submitted for approval, but which was somewhat altered in the process of confirmation. For a comparison of the draft figures and those cited here see *The Third Five-Year Plan for the Development of the National Economy of the U.S.S.R.* (1937–42). Draft. Gosplan-publishers, p. 238. The approved figures for capital construction in industry and transport, as well as for some branches of industry, surpass the corresponding targets of the draft.

ments were allocated by the third F.Y.P. to capital work in industry, and if the 37·3 milliards allocated to capital construction in transport be added—transport also represented further industrialization of the country—industry and transport accounted for two-thirds of all the country's expenditure on capital work. At the same time more attention was to be devoted than hitherto to the rational location of new capital construction:

under the third F.Y.P. in the location of new capital construction throughout the regions of the U.S.S.R. it is necessary to aim at bringing industry nearer to its sources of raw materials and to the districts consuming industrial production so as to eliminate unnecessary haulage over long distances, and also in order further to raise the formerly backward districts of the U.S.S.R.; and in consequence, to ensure in the basic economic districts of the Union a complex development of economy and to organize the mining of fuel and the production of such commodities as concrete, alabaster, fertilizers, glass, and mass-consumption goods of the light and food industries in quantities sufficient to meet the requirements of these districts. It is of particular importance to secure the supply of local fuel and of certain bulky products to those districts largely industrial whose dependence on great quantities of goods brought from afar has increased with their industrial growth and the rapid increase in their urban population.... To ensure due supervision in order that the decision of the Central Committee of the Party and the Sovnarkom S.S.S.R., prohibiting the construction of new enterprises in Moscow and Leningrad, be complied with, and to extend this regulation to Kiev, Kharkov, Rostov-on-Don, Gorki and Sverdlovsk, where the building of new enterprises is henceforth forbidden. To create during the third five-year period, in such *economically focal points* of the country as the Eastern regions, the Urals, and the Povolzhie [Volga districts], enterprises duplicating the work of enterprises hitherto unique in certain branches of machine-building and oil refining, and in the chemical industry, in order to meet any emergency in the supply of certain industrial products. To make provision for a more rapid growth in the volume of capital work and in the construction of new enterprises in the *Eastern and Far-eastern* regions of the U.S.S.R. To continue developing the metallurgical base of these regions, and consequently to erect three-quarters of all blast furnaces to be built under the third F.Y.P. in the Eastern districts. To create in the east of the U.S.S.R. a new important base of the textile industry to work up Central Asian cotton. To make provisions for a rapid development of coal-mining in the Far East and for the production of concrete in quantities sufficient to meet the regional needs.

In order to speed up construction and the going into production of productive capacities, and also to disperse new enterprises throughout the basic economic regions of the U.S.S.R., it is necessary to start a *campaign against gigantomania* in construction and to change over to the building of medium and small enterprises in all branches of the national economy. Not to allow in industrial construction the building of too narrowly specialized enterprises and to organize co-operation of enterprises within the economic districts.*

This demand for a campaign against 'gigantomania' in the construction of new enterprises was a reaction against that excessive enthusiasm for building 'super-giants', so characteristic of the first F.Y.P. Experience had shown that excessive concentration does not always pay economically (supplies of raw material transported over long distances, excessive specialization of production, long-distance transport of finished articles for disposal, etc.), that the construction of giant plants means a great time lag between the moment when building is started and the moment when the finished articles begin rolling off the conveyor belt, and that investments remain unproductive for too long, particularly if the building of works servicing production or of the factories consuming the 'giant's' production are ill-synchronized. Moreover, it was realized that concentrating on the construction of huge enterprises led to neglecting the construction of small enterprises which would have started producing within a shorter time, and could be better adapted to utilize local raw materials and to meet local demands for articles of greater variety.

Alongside with this enormous plan for new capital construction and for increasing the productivity of labour, the third F.Y.P. also made provisions for a tremendous increase of industrial production (see Table 44).

This table shows that the increase in gross production planned for the third five-year period was tremendous though its rate was slower than that of the first and second Plans (the average annual increase of all industrial production was planned to be 12·4 %). Once again the increase in gross production of means of production was to be greater than the increase in the production of consumer goods; and it is significant that in the textile and woollen industries the planned targets for 1942 were below those set by the second F.Y.P. for 1937 and about equal to what the first F.Y.P. had aimed at for 1932. Though the market for textiles and woollen articles was far from being saturated and there was a possibility of considerably increasing the programme for the construction of mills, provided investments in other branches of industrial produc-

---

* Resolution of the Eighteenth Party Congress on V. Molotov's report on the third F.Y.P. for the development of the national economy of the U.S.S.R. (1937–42).

Table 44

	1937	1942	1942 as % of 1937
Gross production of all industry (in 1926–7 prices), milliard roubles	95·5	184·0	192
Production of means of production	55·2	114·5	207
Production of consumer goods	40·3	69·5	172
Machine-building and metal-working	27·5	63·0	229
Chemical industry	5·9	14·0	237
Production of electrical energy (milliard kWh.)	36·4	75·0	206
Coal (million tons)	127·3	243·0	190
Crude oil and gas (million tons)	30·5	54·0	177
Pig iron (million tons)	14·5	22·0	152
Steel (million tons)	17·7	28·0	158
Rolled metal (million tons)	12·9	21·0	162
Aluminium (thousand tons)	46·8	162·0	346
Cement (million tons)	5·4	11·0	202
Cotton fabrics (million m.)	3,442·0	4,900·0	142
Woollen fabrics (million m.)	105·1	177·0	167
Leather footwear (million pairs)	164·2	258·0	143
Sugar, granulated (thousand tons)	2,421·0	3,500·0	144
Canned preserves (million tins conventional units)	863·0	1,800·0	206

tion were curtailed and the import of additional raw materials ensured, the Soviet Government nevertheless considered that, even in the course of the third F.Y.P., it was not possible to make such a change-over in capital construction or in the industrial production programme.

The need to expand the productive possibilities of heavy industry remained of major importance throughout the third five-year period, and continued to receive priority over the needs of expanding production of mass-consumption goods. Apparently, the international environment in which the third F.Y.P. was launched did not permit of a reversion even to the second F.Y.P.'s programme for expanding the production of mass-consumption goods.

Moreover, the third F.Y.P. demanded the creation of large State reserves.

The gigantic growth of industry and of the entire national economy in the course of the third F.Y.P. and the need to ensure its further un-interrupted development in connexion with the general State plan, particularly in view of the growing aggressive forces of Imperialism externally surrounding the U.S.S.R., demands the creation of *large State reserves*, primarily in the fuel, electrical energy and some of the defence industries, and also in the development of transport, correctly located in the corresponding regions of the country, so as to eliminate unproductive and distant cross-hauls, and to secure for the main economic centres of the country maximum supply from local resources.

The fulfilment of this condition necessarily led to a corresponding reduction of plans for expanding the production of consumer goods.

Lastly, as in the case of the two previous Plans, the third F.Y.P. demanded a considerable increase in labour productivity, actually a 65 % increase in the course of the third F.Y.P.. 'Out of a total increase in industrial production of 88·5 milliard roubles, 62 milliard roubles or 70 % of the increase will be obtained through the growth of labour productivity.' Very much more moderate was the demand for reducing production costs: in the course of the five years the reduction for industry as a whole was to reach 10 %.

During that part of the third five-year period which elapsed prior to the outbreak of hostilities with Germany, industrial output steadily continued to grow (see Table 45).

The rise in production in all branches of capital goods was very considerable. Much smaller was the rise in the production of consumer goods.* However, in the official reports it was stated that the annual plans were not completely fulfilled. In order to speed up production in all branches of industry which were particularly lagging behind planned requirements, a campaign for an 'All-Union Socialist competition' was inaugurated in July 1940 and continued up to the end of the year, in the coal, iron and steel, and oil industries and in non-ferrous metallurgy. A special monetary fund was allocated to reward the most successful of the competing enterprises, i.e. to reward the managerial and technical personnel and to distribute bonuses to workers and employees who had most distinguished themselves.

In the official report on the economic results of the year 1940, issued in February 1941 by the chairman of the Gosplan, it was however emphasized that: 'In spite of these increases in produc-

---

* In the three pre-war years (1938–40), the total output of the textile industry was: '10,870 million m. of cotton textiles, 335 million m. of woollen, 175 million m. of silken materials and 786 million m. of linen.' Thus, in these 3 years a total of 12,166 million m. of fabrics were produced. These figures indicate how low the per capita level of textile production still was. In the official 1940 report it was emphasized that all available quantities of flax, wool and silk cocoons were completely utilized, but the supply of these raw materials was below the productive capacity of the mills. Consequently, an expansion in the production of these kinds of textiles depended on an increased production of these textile raw materials.

Table 45

	1937	1938	1939	1940	1941 (Plan)
Gross output of industrial production in millard roubles in 1926–7 prices	95·5	106·8	123·9	137·5	162·0
Of which:					
Capital goods	55·2	62·6	73·7	83·9	103·6
Consumer goods	40·3	44·2	50·2	53·6	58·4
Production of coal (million tons)	127·9	132·9	145·9	164·6	191·0
,, oil (million tons)	30·5	32·2	*	34·2†	38·0
,, pig iron (million tons)	14·5	14·6	—	14·9†	18·0
,, steel (million tons)	17·7	18·0	—	18·4†	22·4
,, rolled metal (million tons)	13·0	13·3	—	13·4†	15·8
,, aluminium (thousand tons)	37·7	56·8	—	59·9†	99·4
,, copper (thousand tons)	99·8	103·2	—	164·7†	215·7†

* No figures for 1939 have been published.   † Estimated.

tion, the progress in the metallurgical and fuel industries cannot be regarded as adequate. The increase in the output of metals falls short of the provisions of the third F.Y.P. and is still not sufficient to meet the growing requirements of the national economy of the U.S.S.R.'* This quotation shows that in the course of the third F.Y.P. industry was urged as before to achieve great tasks in the expansion of production, and that the strain of quantitative expansion continued to hamper qualitative improvement in industrial production.

The quality of industrial production during the three years of the third F.Y.P. somewhat improved, though losses from over-consumption of raw materials, from wastage and spoiled goods, from failure to produce the planned selection of goods and to lower cost prices was still high,* and measures for reducing waste and for improving the quality and the choice of goods had constantly to be devised and introduced. On 13 July 1940 a new decree was published 'On the responsibility for the production of low quality or incomplete goods and for non-fulfilment of the official standards'. By this decree, directors of enterprises, engineers and inspectors of technical control became liable to prosecution and from 5 to 8 years' imprisonment, if guilty of producing bad-quality, incomplete or substandard goods; stronger measures were also introduced for technical control in the reception of goods and for the enforcement of fixed standards.

* N. Voznesensky, *Economic Results of the U.S.S.R. in* 1940 *and the Plan of National Economic Development for* 1941, Foreign Language Publishing House, Moscow, 1941, p. 11.

The abolition of the rationing system brought also to the fore-front questions such as price-fixing of manufactured articles, in-dustrial profit and returns, improvements in quality and range of goods; so that, generally speaking, problems of quality began to take precedence over those of technical reconstruction and of large-scale expansion of industry.

In his famous speech of 4 May 1935 Stalin pointed out that in order to create an industry

it had been necessary to make sacrifices...to economize on food, on schools, on manufacturing goods...to spend 3 milliard roubles in foreign currency, obtained as a result of a most rigorous economy, in-stead of using them to import raw materials and increasing the output of articles of general consumption...but now we have emerged from the period of famine in technique and we have entered a new period, a period of a famine in people, in skilled labour....Formerly we used to say: 'Technique decides everything', now this slogan must be replaced by a new slogan 'Cadres decide everything'.*

Incidentally, in our opinion this slogan, 'Cadres decide every-thing', was the driving force behind the new U.S.S.R. constitu-tion; it was stimulated by the desire to bring new people to par-ticipate in all the fields of the country's economic and cultural activities, new men who had grown to manhood among the wide masses of the population during the years of struggle for the technical reconstruction of national economy, 'non-party Bolshe-viks' capable of replacing the old cadres with a revolutionary past, who though 'heroes of the Civil War', had either become bureau-crats or proved themselves incapable of conducting current busi-ness in the new conditions of a qualitative reconstruction of the country's economic and administrative activities.

From 1936 the system of fixing prices was reorganized so as to do away with State subsidies and make industry self-supporting.

At the beginning of N.E.P., cost prices were based on pre-war calculations, a margin being allowed for changes in the ex-penditure on the main components. Subsequently, with the growing planning of transfer prices for industry, and the utilization of prices as a means to stimulate the production of certain types of goods, or to popularize substitutes and local raw materials and fuel on the one hand, and to regulate supply and demand on the other, a system of dual prices was introduced—planned prices for intra-industrial operations and market prices for transactions with the trade distributive network. From 1928 a dual price-list system

* Stalin, *Leninism*, ed. 11, pp. 488, 490.

was applied in many branches of industry—one list for transactions between syndicates and industrial concerns and another for those with the trade network. The price list intended for transactions with industries was based on a differential cost price which took into account the particular circumstances of production of this or that article in different enterprises and districts, while those quoted in the trade list for identical goods were the same for the entire district. After the 1930 fiscal and credit reforms (see chapter on Finance) and the 1929 industrial administration reform referred to above, the planning of cost and transfer prices was hardly related to the actual retail prices of manufactured goods. A price system isolated from the market began to function within industry. 'Notwithstanding considerable changes in retail prices during the period of rationing and the introduction of multiple differentiation in retail prices for identical goods, the level of industrial transfer prices (after deduction of the turn-over tax) scarcely altered during these years....By using taxation as a lever for retail price differentiation it became possible to leave unaffected the financial economy [i.e. the calculation of cost and transfer prices] of industry.'* It should be pointed out here that neither the enterprise's profits (both planned and actual) nor the turn-over tax is included in the factory's production costs. The sum total of factory cost price and commercial marketing expenses constitutes the 'commercial' or 'trust' cost price. The sum total of trust cost price and profit forms the so-called transfer price, less the turn-over tax. The transfer price plus the turn-over tax forms the wholesale price at which goods are delivered by the trust to wholesale trade. Profits and turn-over tax serve as levers for the redistribution of national income; they are fixed by the planning authorities and based on general considerations of a planned development of national economy (see, further, chapter on Finance). The rate of profit fixed bears no relation to the capital invested and depends on the needs for accumulation within a given enterprise for expanding its production. Generally speaking, the valuation of the existing productive capital is based not on the principle of what it has cost but what it will yield.

In the latter years appropriations to sinking funds were fixed at rather a high level in order to ensure better repairs and partly to accumulate capital within enterprises for further reconstructions. Thus, early in 1938, the following average industrial amortization

* Sh. Turetsky, 'Methods of Price Planning', *Planned Economy*, no. 3, 1936, pp. 133–4.

standards were fixed in the different commissariats (in percentages of the initial cost of working machinery, equipment, building and plant): P. Commissariat of Heavy Industry, 5·6%; P. Commissariat of Machine Building, 5·5%; P. Commissariat of Defence Industries, 5·5%; P. Commissariat of Timber Industry, 6%; P. Commissariat of Light Industry, 5·5%, P. Commissariat of Food Industry, 6%. These average standards are differentiated among the various industries and enterprises according to the types of their industrial equipment and plant, and the degree of intensity at which different industries are working and which determines the wear and tear of equipment and plant.*

During the period covered by the first F.Y.P. and in the first years of the second, the planned transfer prices in most branches of heavy industry were fixed below production cost, and the resulting losses incurred by enterprises were made good by State subsidies. This arrangement was prompted by the following considerations:

During the period covered by the first F.Y.P. it was necessary in the interest of industrialization to maintain low prices for the production of heavy industry. Low prices for metal and coal meant low prices for machines, thus creating an additional stimulus to the adoption of machinery in all branches of national economy. However, it was only possible to maintain low prices for heavy industrial production, in spite of high production costs, with the help of subsidies from the State Budget. During the first years of the second F.Y.P. it was necessary to maintain subsidies both because of these general considerations regarding industrialization, and also because it was impossible to bring the prices of heavy industrial production in line with production costs in the conditions prevailing in 1933 and 1934, when production costs in the extractive and other labour-absorbing branches of the heavy and timber industries were rising. To deprive heavy industry of subsidies, whilst the technique of production was still lagging behind and production costs high, would have led to a steep rise in prices for the products of heavy industry. Such a rise in prices would have dealt a blow to the entire price system of the country's economy. [Yet] the system of budget subsidies fostered, on the one hand, an irresponsible attitude among certain managers of economic organs, weakening the operation of 'khozraschet', and on the other hand gave a distorted picture of the actual economic state of an enterprise (the enterprises which worked best and carried out the plans for expanding output were just those that demanded the largest subsidies)....Budgetary subsidies encouraged

---

* Cf. the Regulation of the Sovnarkom S.S.S.R., dated 8 January 1938: 'On the utilization of sinking fund appropriations and the improving of repair work of industrial enterprises', *Bull. Financ. and Econ. Leg.* 1938, no. 2.

some managers to be irresponsible and negligent about finance: on the principle that 'anyway the budget will refund'. In this manner the enterprise's interest in the profitableness of its work was weakened.*

From April 1936, the coal-, peat- and iron-mining industries, heavy and non-ferrous metal industries, a number of chemical and certain machine-building industries, and the cement and timber industries were deprived of State subsidies; nevertheless, subsidies were temporarily maintained in several branches of heavy industry, because the discrepancy between their cost and transfer prices was so great that, had the subsidies been suddenly stopped, the prices of their goods would have soared out of proportion with that of other goods. Moreover,

in connexion with the application of the present measures, government enterprises consuming raw materials, fuel and equipment, the transfer prices of which have been increased, received supplementary working capital. To those branches of industry (light industry and other branches manufacturing mass consumption goods) for which the rise in the transfer prices of heavy industrial production has resulted in an increase of production costs, that could not be fully made good by higher efficiency, a rebate of the turn-over tax has been allowed, designed to keep retail prices unchanged and prevent them from rising.†

New transfer prices were fixed in accordance with the principle that a given *branch* should pay its way as a whole. The standard prices were based on the level of a particular industry's average enterprises, and a unified price list was issued for the whole of the U.S.S.R. However, at the time when subsidies were abolished and the price system altered, the cost price of similar goods manufactured at different enterprises often diverged considerably from the average;‡ therefore it was made the duty of Chief Branch Administrations

to regulate production costs and to redistribute accumulations properly among enterprises of the same branch of industry. *Pari passu* with profitableness in a given branch of industry as a whole, the role and importance of the more profitable enterprises are greatly intensified because their profits, resulting from a considerable difference between the transfer prices of an average enterprise and their own cost price, will

---

* *Planned Economy*, no. 5, 1936, pp. 76, 77; *Plan*, no. 9, 1936, p. 8.

† *Za Industr.* 11 April 1936.

‡ For instance, in 1935 the cost price of pig iron varied from 47 roubles 32 kopeks per ton at the Makeevka works to 75 roubles 37 kopeks at the Kerch works, and 94 roubles 04 kopeks at the Khabarovsk works of the Vostok-stal; the cost price of superphosphate varied from 42 roubles at the Chernorechensk works to 75 roubles at the Perm works of the Vostoko-khim (Eastern Chemicals).

be the only source for filling the gap between high production costs and the unified transfer prices at other unprofitable enterprises,

i.e. enterprises where production costs were above the average.

The Sales Branch organizations were made responsible

for ensuring not only that payments were made in good time to profitable enterprises for their output delivered at planned cost price, but that unprofitable enterprises should also be paid in good time the difference between production cost and transfer price for their production at a loss.... The redistribution of funds within an industry is not limited to covering the gap between production cost and transfer prices of the unprofitable enterprises at the expense of a greater profit from profitable industries. The timely redistribution of funds is of the greatest importance for investing profits in capital construction and replenishing the working capitals of enterprises to correspond with the growth of their production programme.*

In order rightly to appreciate the reason for such a system of price-fixing and for redistributing profits and losses within an industry, it should be remembered that the policy in regard to heavy industry was to obtain the maximum increase of output technically possible, even if production costs at some enterprises exceeded by far that of the averagely efficient enterprise.

After this reform in price-fixing for the output of heavy industry, Chief Branch Administrations were to redistribute profits within their branch of industry, in accordance with the planned targets, thus filling the role previously played by subsidies from the State Budget.

As a result of these new duties of the Chief Administrations, their competence in the matter of the sale of manufactured goods was extended.

Regulations issued by the Central Committee and the Sovnarkom S.S.S.R. on 15 June 1936 decreed:

To allocate to the Chief Administrations of the P. Commissariats of the heavy, light, food and timber industries, in addition to their productive functions, the functions of supply and sale as a consequence of the reorganization of the present 'khozraschet' offices for supply and sale into departments of the Chief Administrations. To grant the Chief Administrations of the P. Commissariats the rights: to enter into general and direct agreements for the sale and supply of products, to possess their own working capital, to dispose of bank credits for sale and supply operations, and to have accounts and current accounts at banks.

Hitherto, 'the Chief Administration was solely engaged in production, and the "khozraschet" offices for supply and sale were

* *Plan*, no. 9, 1936.

a kind of "autonomous province" in the management of branches of industry. The Chief Administration directed production for production's sake. This led to duality of control—on the one hand the Chief Administration, on the other the "khozraschet" sales offices'; but henceforth 'the Chief Administrations will be the operational headquarters of the production, financial, supply and sale activities of the industries they direct'.*

The Chief Branch Administrations were thus awarded exclusive and comprehensive rights to direct their branch of industry.

In order to stimulate the interest of managers in the profitableness of their enterprise's work and to help enforce personal management, an institution was created called the 'director's profits' fund'. This fund was fed by allocations amounting to 4 % from the net money profit of the enterprise earned according to plan, and 50 % of profits earned in excess of plan. The money of the director's fund is spent, with the sanction of the P. Commissar, or according to a prescribed procedure, and at the director's discretion on the following items in excess of planned expenditure: 50 % at least on housing for workers, engineers, technicians and employees of the enterprise; next, on improving their cultural and living conditions; on bonuses to managerial staffs and workers who have particularly distinguished themselves; on supplementary rationalization devices and on technical propaganda. The plan for the expenditure of the fund's money is established by the director in agreement with the works' trade union committee.†

With the increasing specialization of industrial production in the latter years of the second and the first years of the third F.Y.P., the need arose to specialize administration still further. It was no longer merely a question of directing a number of connected industries but a narrow circle of closely knit productive units; the need was also felt for bringing the specialized Chief Administration and even the P. Commissariat into closer contact with the actual management of the individual enterprises; and, indeed, in the course of 1937–40 some of the still unwieldy giant Chief Administrations were further reduced in size and several commissariats were split into a group of more specialized commissariats.

This reorganization was carried out by means of numerous measures, a description of which may be omitted here, for they did not alter fundamentally the principles underlying the organization of industrial management, but were only technical adjustments of

* *Za Industr.* 18 June 1936.
† Cf. Instruction in *Bull. Financ. and Econ. Leg.* no. 12, 1936.

the need to specialize industrial management within various industries. The P. Commissariat of Defence Industries was split off from the P. Commissariat of Heavy Industry, and, in 1938, was subdivided into four specialized commissariats; in its turn, the remaining Commissariat of Heavy Industry was split into six specialized commissariats, one of which, the Commissariat of Machine-Building, was subdivided again into three specialized commissariats. Similarly, other commissariats were split up; so that by 1940 the entire industry of the country was administered by the following Commissariats: Heavy Industry, Oil Industry, Coal Industry, Power Stations, Electrical Engineering, Shipbuilding, Heavy Metallurgy, Non-ferrous Metallurgy, Chemical Industry, Building Materials, Heavy Engineering, Medium Engineering, General Engineering, Defence Industry, Aviation, Armaments, Munitions, Food Industry, Meat and Dairy Industries, Fisheries, Light Industry, Textiles, Timber Industry, Cellulose and Paper Industries. The commissariats' Chief Branch Administrations were more systematically reorganized on a combined production and territorial basis; such were, for instance, the Chief Administration of the Donbass and Caucasian coal industry, the Chief Administration of the coal industry in the East, the Chief Administration of the coal industry of the Centre and the Urals.

This specialization of industrial administration in the hands of twenty-four Commissariats and scores of Chief Administrations brought to the fore the question of co-ordinating the work of these specialized commissariats, and led to a duplication in the Chief Administrations' work of technical servicing of enterprises, particularly in regard to sale and supply.

In 1940 Soviet economic publications were sharply criticizing the system of supplying industry with materials and machinery. It was emphasized that:

the evil of the present structure of supply organs is that alongside with the existing Chief Supply Administrations of the P. Commissariats with their network of offices, sections and warehouses, there is a similar network practically in every other Chief Administration. Prior to the reduction in size of the P. Commissariats, the parallel existence of a network of Commissariat supply sections together with a network of Chief Administrations' departments could be justified to a certain extent by the specific needs of individual branches of industry subordinate to the P. Commissariats; but now, since as a rule the P. Commissariats manage only one industry, there is no need for the parallel existence of these units. The number of supply organs of the Chief Supply Administrations and of other Chief Administrations of the All-Union Commissariats alone is roughly 5,000. They employ 126,000 persons whose salaries total 518 million roubles a year. The existence of such a large number of supply organizations employing a huge army of people is a consequence of the chaotic manner in which supply organizations were formed. Newly created Commissariats copied the structure of the supply organizations of those Commissariats from which they were created, though the amount of work at the new Commissariats was considerably less. It now happens that in many towns, where prior to the subdivision of the P. Commissariat of Machine-Building there was one department of the Chief Supply Administration with four specialized offices, that there are now, since the P. Commissariat was split up, three such departments and twelve specialized offices....Not having enough to do with the servicing of enterprises of their own Commissariat, the swollen supply organizations, seeking for income to cover the maintenance expenses of their network, have taken to purchasing materials not needed by their network and to reselling them elsewhere....Thus, many supply organizations have become 'commercial' enterprises and carry on trade instead of supplying their own enterprises with necessary material resources. Naturally, saddled with such an organization, the services of the supply organs cost the State dearly and add a heavy burden to industry's production costs.*

In 1940 the reorganization of the supply machinery was undertaken so as to eliminate duplication in the work of the supply organizations and to abolish those deemed superfluous;† but how far these measures proved a success it is difficult to say in the absence of any material published subsequently.

The problem of co-ordinating the activities of various Commissariats after their subdivision is analysed elsewhere.

CONCLUSION

The problem of improving the qualitative side both of capital construction and of production remained the main problem confronting Soviet industry.

The obstacles were twofold. Some were peculiar to those special circumstances which overshadowed the development of industrial construction and production in the U.S.S.R. during the period now elapsed; others are inherent in planned economy as such. In other words, some were problems of a local and temporary kind, whilst others were of a more general and permanent nature.

The policy of carrying out intensive and speedy capital construction and of demanding a tremendous expansion of industrial production created temporary obstacles both to an improvement in

* *Planned Economy*, no. 3, 1940, pp. 49, 51, 52, 55.
† Cf. *Coll. Decrees of the U.S.S.R. Government*, no. 10, 1940, § 255.

the quality of construction and to raising the quality of industrial work. The necessity of speedily carrying out enormous capital construction meant hasty planning, hastily prepared drafts and haste in the actual construction work. The obligation to fulfil strenuous plans for the expansion of industrial production resulted in a neglect of quality. A deterioration in quality was often even deliberately tolerated for the sake of fulfilling the quantitative plans; the standards of production including trimmings, colours, design were simplified, the choice of articles curtailed, thickness reduced, etc. Shortage of qualified managerial staffs, the low level of skill among workers, low-quality raw materials and an unsaturated market which absorbed the poorest goods were all factors which combined to affect the quality of production adversely.

These obstacles were, however, of a temporary nature and due to the policy of intensive and hasty industrialization. Other obstacles were of a more general and deep-rooted nature.

Under the competitive system of national economy, profits, prices and personal interest determine not only the direction and scale of capital construction and of production, but also exercise a controlling influence on the qualitative side of construction and production. In the U.S.S.R.—as might have been expected under a planned system of national economy—the selection of objectives for capital construction, their scale, and geographical location were not determined by profits, prices and personal interest, but by the basic aims underlying the development of the national economy, as adopted by the Government and embodied in a general capital construction and production plan. The explicit goal of industrializing the country determined not only the general direction of capital construction and production, but also concrete objectives within fixed time limits. The planning of quantitative tasks consisted in estimating existing material productive resources, in organizing the financing of capital works and the expansion of production, and in training and enrolling adequate specialist staffs and labour. Generally speaking, the planning of the quantitative side of production presents no difficulties—whatever the aims of the plan—provided the means of production are nationalized. There is no essential difference between planning the development of the production of means of production and planning the production of consumer goods, though some authors argue to the contrary on the basis that price-fixing for the means of production in a planned system of nationalized industry is wholly artificial, because the goods produced move within a closed circle of nationalized enterprises and do not come into direct contact with the market. If, however, the niceties of the argument about the influence of supply on demand and of demand on supply are waived, the only tenable proposition is that in the modern competitive system supply not only precedes demand but actually creates demand. Generally speaking, all production consists of the production of goods and commodities customary in a given country and the production of new goods and commodities. In regard to goods and products usually produced and consumed in a given country, the *status quo* inherited from the competitive system provides the basis for planning the quantity, quality and prices of production. In the U.S.S.R., as already shown, the *status quo* of 1913 and that of the end of the recovery period of national economy were the starting points for drafting the quantitative and qualitative plans in respect of identical kinds of production. In the case of new forms of production under present-day factory conditions, supply undoubtedly determines demand, and not vice versa. Apart from occasional individual orders to handicraft workers, the modern consumer does not give orders to the producer, the consumer merely approves—by buying—or rejects—by not buying—the choice of production offered by the producer, at the price demanded for the articles. Moreover, a change in price may transform a not wholly acceptable choice of the producer's, or a merely potential 'demand' for a given article, into an article acceptable to the consumer.

The consumer's behaviour does not alter, whether goods be offered to him by a private producer or by nationalized industry; it is indifferent to him whether he buys from a private shop or from a State trading institution. The consumer's controlling influence remains a *post factum* not an *ante factum* influence as much under a planned system of production as under the competitive system. The consumer of means of production, which move in the closed circle of nationalized industry under an appropriate system of industrial management, can exercise the same control over commodities and raw materials supplied to the enterprise as the consumer directly 'buying' those articles and raw materials under the competitive system.

Moreover, there is no fundamental difference in the estimates by a State or a private producer of the consumer's reactions to the goods supplied and to their prices. There are no reasonable grounds to suppose that unconnected and individual manufacturers can better estimate the consumers' needs for certain articles and commodities than would the management of rationally organized combines in the corresponding branches of industry. The question can only arise in regard to new articles and goods, and not in regard to customary lines of production and consumption. The contention that the producer's inventiveness creates new varieties of production and is the essential driving force in improving production is contradicted by the undeniable historical fact that inventor and manufacturer have hardly ever, if not indeed quite exceptionally, been one and the same person. Industrial inventions and improvements are, as a rule, made by technicians and specialists, and then utilized by manufacturers. Logically, there are no grounds to assume that creative initiative, provided its efforts are adequately stimulated, cannot be utilized as fruitfully for the benefit of industry under a planned system as under a competitive system. On the contrary, the abolition of proprietary rights over inventions and of secret patents and improvements in manufacturing processes, together with the mutual exchange of industrial information among enterprises, cannot but contribute to a fuller and more timely use of the creative initiative of those actually working for industrial progress, and remove anomalies in the utilization of industrial inventions which often occur under the competitive system (e.g. royalties limiting the wider application of an invention, the purchase of patents with the sole object of monopolizing rights, secrecy of invention hindering further improvements, etc.). The experience of the U.S.S.R. proves convincingly that methods for stimulating creative initiative can be devised under the planned system of industrial organization and that it does not 'dry up' as a result of the nationalization of the means of production.

It is equally difficult to agree with the view that private enterprise, activated by the profit motive and regulated by the price factor, is best suited to direct the country's capital investments and to distribute its productive resources so as to meet the population's needs. Apart from such phenomena as uncompleted factories, fully equipped plants standing idle or not working to full capacity, and cases of deliberate limitation of production or of the destruction of finished goods and commodities, owing to a miscalculation of the future market prospects, the very fact that many countries disposing of an abundance of raw materials and labour, and of possibilities for a more complex development of the national economy, do not make use of these possibilities, is adequate refutation of the contention that private enterprise is more efficient in distributing and using the productive resources of a country. The undisputably huge quantitative achievements of the U.S.S.R. in industry afford striking proof of the advantages of planned utilization of the country's existing material and labour resources and of planning its productive activities. Potentially, Russia possessed the same productive possibilities as the U.S.S.R.; the U.S.S.R., however, thanks to a planned utilization of existing potential productive resources in 12 years (1928–40), achieved results in the development of the national economy many times surpassing the results achieved by private enterprise in the course of the preceding 50 years (i.e. from the time of the abolition of serfdom and the elimination of formal obstacles to private enterprise to 1913).

The experience of the U.S.S.R. also shows that in spite of the plans not being always up to the mark or perfect in the elaboration of detail or in their estimate of the interdependence of individual branches of industry, or in the technical basis of constructional projects, and in spite also of planned tasks not always being fulfilled exactly, the growth of industrial production yearly achieved was nevertheless very substantial. Furthermore, the crisis of 'overproduction' was avoided at the very time when the national economies of the economically most advanced countries were suffering from a periodical crisis of production and sales.

The problem of improving the qualitative side of construction and production presented great difficulties to planned economy nevertheless; here the obstacles were due not only to temporary difficulties, but in view of the experience of the U.S.S.R. may be asserted to be of a more permanent and deeper order. The main difficulty lay in the problem of finding technical means of controlling the qualitative side of production to replace the role played in the competitive system by the producer's interest in improving quality, thus introducing new controls in line with the planned system of industrial development.

The private producer is *directly* interested that capital construction and production be carried out economically and, from the qualitative point of view, efficiently, for on this rests the success or failure of his enterprise and the scale of his profits. The director of a nationalized enterprise is not directly interested in achieving a maximum of economy and improvement in the qualitative side of his enterprise's work *unless the qualitative improvement programme is expressed in precise quantitative indices*, and his work is judged on the degree of their fulfilment. Accordingly, failure to fulfil the planned tasks will then involve penalties (e.g. dismissal, a drop in the salaries' scale, administrative censure, a sentence of imprisonment, etc.), whilst fulfilment and over-fulfilment will bring rewards (e.g. promotion, additional material remuneration, decorations, etc.).

The difficulty of measuring qualitative tasks in quantitative indices and of devising a system of control of the qualitative side of the enterprises' activities was the main cause for that unsatisfactory position with regard to the quality of production in the U.S.S.R., described above. The fixing of planned prices only partly solved the difficulty. Planned prices can be enforced simultaneously with a deterioration in the economy and technique of production. A different weighting in the expenditure on wages, raw materials, administrative expenses may eventually work out at the same planned price; e.g. an increase in administrative expenses and in expenditure on raw materials can be met by a saving on the workers' wages. While planned price may remain stable, the quality of the article may vary. Some of the facts already quoted from the history of the development of industrial production in the U.S.S.R. illustrate this difficulty of controlling quality solely by price. For instance, planned tasks for the output of certain textiles were fulfilled as regards metre output and planned prices, but the fabrics were thinner (owing to a saving on raw material), or of simplified patterns and colouring (saving on dyes and labour); or, crockery, glass and metal articles of general consumption were made heavy, clumsy, stereotyped, etc., because saving on labour offset losses on raw material, or because it was easier to manufacture such articles and so fulfil the planned quantitative tasks.

Realizing that prices did not adequately control quality, the Soviet planning institutions gradually evolved more detailed quantitative indices to reflect qualitative standards. Various production standards were established, the fulfilment of which was equivalent to raising the qualitative level; such were standards for the utilization of the equipment's capacity, standards for the consumption of fuel and raw materials (e.g. a norm of yarn per ton of raw material, of sugar per ton of sugar-beet, of alcohol per ton of starch, etc.), a norm of wages per article; and fixed standards for the quality of output were introduced. Consequently, the composite index represented by the cost price of the article could be attained only by fulfilling the fixed norms for every item in the productive process.

In the first F.Y.P. these quantitative equivalents of qualitative standards had scarcely been devised. In the second F.Y.P. considerable use was already made of them, in particular for some branches of heavy industry. In the draft third F.Y.P., indices of this type are worked out in detail for most important industries. The production plan of an enterprise aims at the expansion of production and the reduction of production costs by a definite amount; the fulfilment of these tasks, and in particular the reduction of production costs is, however, closely connected with the fulfilment of the corresponding technical requirements. The gap between the planned transfer price and the planned cost price reflects the planned profitableness or unprofitableness of the enterprise. The difference between the actual cost price and the transfer price reflects the level of efficiency of the management. The aim in instituting the director's fund has already been described; furthermore, other additional forms of award and incentive to the management for the successful work of their enterprises will be described in the chapter on labour. But it has also been shown that neither the application of technical indices to regulate the qualitative side of the enterprises' work, nor the establishment of additional rewards for improving quality was so far effective in stopping the output of substandard goods. Parallel with measures of control and encouragement, it became necessary to have recourse to administrative and judiciary penalties against the output of poor quality and substandard goods.

Apparently, the motive of personal interest in the economic activities of man remains fundamental, persisting even after the elimination of private ownership of the means of production and the adoption of a planned economy. The technical and economic indices of a synthetic and tangible character—price, norms, standards—may contribute something to the success of the work of managerial staffs, but prove inadequate to effect a permanent *improvement* in quality of work. For this end it is necessary to appeal to the personal interests of all who participate in the industrial processes—from director to workman—and to influence them personally either by incentives or penalties.

The fundamental difficulties of organization centred on the problem of balancing centralized planning and leadership in the development of industrial production against the necessity of decentralized management in the individual industrial enterprise. During the years of 'War Communism' an attempt was made to manage the entire activities of all enterprise from one centre. Experience proved that such a centralization of industrial administration was not practicable.

In the early years of the N.E.P. period, centrifugal forces

11

predominated in State industry and the part played by the S.E.C. hardly differed from that of industrial ministries in industrially developed countries. It became evident, however, that so long as trusts—even State trusts—were allowed a wide autonomy in the field of production it was difficult to carry out a co-ordinated and planned development of the country's industries taken as a whole. So, when the process of restoring inherited productive possibilities was practically achieved and new problems arose—building new industrial enterprises, mastering new industries, reconstructing existing plants—the necessity to plan and co-ordinate all these measures led to a marked curtailment of the individual enterprise's autonomy, particularly with regard to financial, supply and sale activities. An attempt was again made to centralize the management of these activities in the hands of the Commissariats' centralized industrial combines. The alternatives which then presented themselves were whether to concentrate the direction of the technical servicing and reconstruction of enterprises as well as the allocation of their profits and losses, of working capitals, of supplies and sales in the hands of the combines, or to divide up these activities among the Commissariats' specialized functional sections. How complicated was the evolution which led to a rational solution of this problem is shown by the changes described.

Another set of difficulties hinged on the vexed problems of enforcing personal management and delimiting the rights and duties of director, trade unions and Party control. Here the obstacles impeding a solution were not so much of a technical nature as social and political. The antagonism between representatives of the pre-revolution technical intelligentsia on the one hand, and workers' organizations and the working masses on the other, had to be overcome. We have seen above and shall see again, when dealing with the trials that took place in the field of labour, how the problem of industrial management met with great difficulties precisely on those grounds. Only when a new technical intelligentsia came into being and the principles on which the trade unions worked completely altered, did it become possible to overcome psychological obstacles and to enforce personal management in industry.

The adoption of 'khozraschet' and the improvement of the economic and financial element in production also met with great difficulties. The possibility of obtaining credits and subsidies weakened the necessity of achieving economies. The system of fixing prices and organizing the sale of manufactured goods did not provide any automatic control of the economic and financial activities of the enterprise. The latter had only an indirect incentive —execution of planned orders and the director's fund—to improve the economic and financial conduct of its work. It became necessary to devise a series of technical methods to control these activities of the enterprise, as is described in the chapters on Credit, Finance, Trade and General Planning of National Economy.

Yet, in spite of shortcomings and difficulties, a working system of industrial management, satisfactory on the whole, was created, and the current difficulties in the years immediately preceding the outbreak of war were not fundamental, but only such as could be solved by technical adjustments; they were mainly concerned with the organization of the technique of distribution of manufacture, and supply of enterprises. Moreover, it should be remembered that many of the defects in the work of the administrative system are the inevitable outcome of the continual change and reform called for by the recurrent need of adjustment to new problems and difficulties arising in the course of the development of industrial production and to new labour conditions, which we describe above and in the chapter on Labour.

APPENDIX I

Production of the most important branches of industry

	1913	1929	1933	1937	1938*
Engineering and metal industries (milliard roubles, 1926–7 value)	1,446	3,054	10,822	27,519	33,613
Engines	418	602	941	1,581	1,626
Goods trucks (thousands)	14·8	15·9	18·2	66·1	49·1
Motor cars (thousands)	—	1·4	49·7	200·0	211·4
Electric power (milliard kWh.)	1·9	6·2	16·4	36·4	39·6
Coal (million tons)	29·1	40·1	76·3	127·9	132·9
Oil (million tons)	9·2	13·8	22·5	30·5	32·2
Iron ore (million tons)	9·2	8·0	14·4	27·7	26·5
Manganese ore (thousand tons)	1,245	702	1,021	2,752	2,273
Pig iron (million tons)	4·2	4·0	7·1	14·5	14·6
Steel (million tons)	4·2	4·9	6·9	17·7	18·0
Rolled steel (million tons)	3·5	3·9	5·1	13·0	13·3
Copper (thousand tons)	—	35·5	44·5	99·8	103·2
Aluminium (thousand tons)	—	—	7·0	37·7	56·8
Cement (million tons)	1·5	2·2	2·7	5·5	5·7
Cotton textiles (million m.)	2,227	3,068	2,422	3,447	3,491
Woollen textiles (million m.)	95	100·6	86·1	108·3	114·0
Leather shoes (million pairs)	—	48·8	80·3	164·2	213·0
Raw sugar (thousand tons)	1,290	1,283	995	2,421	2,519

* Figures for 1938 are the last detailed data published in the Soviet Statistical Sources. Information concerning some branches of production only is available for 1939–40 and comparable tables with the preceding years (see p. 291) cannot be compiled.

Location of industrial production

Principal regions	1913	1929	1933	1938
	Coal production (million metric tons)			
Donetz basin	25·3	31·0	51·1	80·7
Kuznetsk basin	0·8	3·0	9·2	17·4
Urals	1·2	2·1	4·2	8·1
Moscow area	0·3	1·3	3·8	7·4
Eastern Siberia and Minusinsk basin	0·8	1·2	2·9	6·8
Far East	0·4	1·1	2·7	4·8
Kazakhstan	—	—	1·2	4·4
Total U.S.S.R., all regions	29·1	40·1	76·3	132·9
	Oil production (million metric tons)			
Baku	7·7	8·8	16·0	24·0
Grozny	1·2	4·6	5·0	2·8
Krasnodarskii region	0·09	0·2	0·8	2·3
Volga and Urals regions	—	—	0·04	1·3
Kazakhstan	0·1	0·3	0·2	0·6
Turkmenistan S.S.R.	0·1	—	0·2	0·4
Far East	—	0·02	0·2	0·4
Uzbek and Tadzhik S.S.R.	0·02	0·02	0·05	0·2
Total U.S.S.R., all regions	9·2	13·8	22·5	32·2
	Iron-ore production (million metric tons)			
Ukraine	6·4	5·6	9·0	16·1
Urals	1·8	1·8	4·2	7·7
Centre	0·6	0·5	0·7	1·4
Crimea	0·5	0·09	0·3	0·8
Siberia	—	—	0·2	0·5
Total U.S.S.R., all regions	9·2	8·0	14·4	26·5
	Pig-iron production (million metric tons)			
Ukraine	2·9	2·4	3·9	8·8
Urals	0·9	0·7	1·2	2·6
Siberia	—	—	0·3	1·5
Centre and Volga regions	0·2	0·2	0·4	1·2
North Caucasus and Crimea	0·2	0·03	0·4	0·4
Total U.S.S.R., all regions	4·2	3·3	6·2	14·5
	1913	1927–8	1932	1937
	Steel production (million metric tons)			
Ukraine	—	2·4	3·1	8·5
Urals	—	0·9	1·1	3·5
Centre	—	0·6	0·7	2·1
Volga regions	—	0·2	0·5	1·2
Siberia	—	—	0·05	1·6
North Caucasus and Crimea	—	0·09	0·4	0·8
Total U.S.S.R., all regions	4·2	4·2	5·9	17·7

CHAPTER XVII. AGRICULTURE

The abolition of rationing was not only an event of great economic significance, it was politically and psychologically the transition to a new era. It was the transition from a period of extensive reconstruction in all branches of the national economy, with its strenuous 'shock' solutions of urgent tasks, to a period of *consolidation* of the new system of relations and of a comprehensive effort to improve the quality of work throughout the national economy.

In agriculture this effort of consolidation found its symbolic expression in the new model statutes of the agricultural artel, adopted by the second All-Union Congress of collective farm exemplary workers, and later confirmed by the Government. The new statutes became the constitution of collective farms, regulating their internal organization and the right of collective farmers both as members of the collective farm and as proprietors of their domestic economies. These statutes regulated the life and work of the great masses of collective farmers throughout the next period, and an enumeration of their most important points is necessary.

(1) Kolkhoz land tenure was definitely settled. 'The land occupied by the artel is the property of the people and State; it is *conferred* on the artel for permanent use, i.e. *for ever*, and is neither to be sold nor bought, nor can it be leased by the artel.' Every Kolkhoz received a 'State certificate providing for the permanent usufruct of the land'. The act stated 'the precise boundaries of the land conferred on the artel; no reduction of these lands is permissible, though increases are allowed'.

(2) Limits were set to personal allotments. 'Homesteads at the disposal of the households of individual collective farmers (excluding the area under the actual dwelling) may vary from $\frac{1}{4}$ to $\frac{1}{2}$ ha., and in certain districts only may they amount to 1 ha., according to the conditions of the province and district as established by the Commissariats of Agriculture of allied republics on the instructions of the U.S.S.R. Commissariat of Agriculture.'

(3) The rights of collective farmers to own livestock for their personal use were extended and more precisely defined. The limits set were exactly specified and depended on the nature of the main agricultural production of the district. They varied from: 1 cow, 2 heads of young cattle, 2 sows with progeny, 10 sheep and goats,

unlimited amount of poultry and rabbits and 20 beehives in districts growing grain and technical crops, to 8–10 cows and their calves, 100–150 sheep or goats, 10 horses, 5–8 camels and unlimited poultry in districts of nomad stock breeding. Moreover, 'buildings necessary for housing livestock in the personal use of collective farmers, are not subject to socialization'. It was the artel's duty 'to expand the production of fodder, improve meadows and pastures and to come to the assistance of members of the artel who work conscientiously for the community, by ensuring, where possible, the use of communal pastures and, if possible, by distributing fodder for personal livestock in payment of labour days... to help those members who work conscientiously on production for the artel to acquire a cow and small stock and to serve with pedigree sires not only the Kolkhoz livestock but also livestock personally owned by members of the artel'.

(4) Contrary to the old statutes, it was now made possible to admit into collective farms 'the children of persons deprived of franchise who have been engaged for several years in public and useful work and have worked conscientiously, and also kulaks and members of their families who have been exiled for anti-Soviet and anti-Kolkhoz activities, and have given evidence of their reform in their new settlements by honest work and by conforming to the Soviet Government's regulations for a period of 3 years. Individual peasants who sold their horses less than two years before joining an artel and who have no seed, can be admitted to the artel provided they undertake to contribute from their income within the next 6 years the price of a horse and seeds in kind'.

(5) The new statutes also provided safeguards against arbitrary expulsion of members by collective farm managements. Henceforth, members could be expelled 'only upon a decision of the general meeting of the artel at which two-thirds of all the members are present', and the expelled member had the right of appeal against the decision of expulsion to the District Executive Committee.

(6) The new statutes laid down also, with more precision and in greater detail, the Kolkhoz management's rights and obligations, and increased its term of office from one to two years. The powers of the artel's general meeting to manage and control the community's life and work was strengthened, and so were its rights to protect individual members from arbitrary decisions on the part of the management.

(7) Lastly, the statutes emphasized that 'the artel undertakes

to carry out their collective farming according to a plan fully *conforming to the plans of agricultural production established by the organs of the Workers' and Peasants' Government* and to meet the artel's obligations to the State'.*

Throughout the following period these statutes of the agricultural artel remained no mere form, but were the actual system of rules governing the internal life and work of the collective farm and its relationship to government organs. It underwent no further change of principle, either legal or organizational, and thus definitely settled the relationship of collective farms with the State. But many problems of further development in agricultural production remained to be solved. We will enumerate here only the most important, together with the principal measures taken by the Soviet Government to overcome them during the last years of peaceful construction in the U.S.S.R.

Table 46 graphically illustrates the manner in which the gross production of collective farms was distributed.

Table 46. *Distribution of the gross yield of grain and leguminous plant crops in the collective farms of the U.S.S.R. as a whole for* 1938†

	In % of gross yield
Compulsory State deliveries at fixed price	15
State deliveries in payment for the M.T.S.'s work	16
Sales to State procurement organizations and co-operatives at decentralized prices and on Kolkhoz markets	5·1
Refund of State advances of seed	2
Allocations to the seed fund	18·6
Allocations to the fodder fund	13·6
Allocations to the fund for assisting invalids and children's nurseries	0·8
Distributed to collective farmers in payment of labour days	26·9
Miscellaneous allocations	2·0
	100·0

More than 90 % of the collective farms' marketable grain went to the State either in the form of compulsory deliveries or in payment of work done by the M.T.S., in both cases at fixed prices. This enabled the State to control the price of most grain. The same applied to an even greater extent to technical crops.‡ The live-

* For details see the *Model Statutes of an Agricultural Artel*, published in all the leading papers of the U.S.S.R. on 18 February 1935; English translation in the *Economics of Soviet Agriculture*, by Leonard E. Hubbard, 1939.

† The data refer to 220,385 collective farms investigated in 1938. Cf. *Socialist Agriculture*, 1939, no. 12, p. 63.

‡ In 1938 collective farms sold to the State either as compulsory deliveries or by contract 82% of their gross production of sugar beet and supplied another 17·8% of the crop as payment in kind for the M.T.S.'s work; 81% of

stock marketable production was somewhat less under State control. Precisely determined quantities of livestock produce (meat, wool and milk) were surrendered to the State at fixed prices by collective farms, their members and individual peasants, but the greater share of livestock was owned individually, and therefore a relatively greater share of livestock produce was sold not to the State at fixed prices, but either to State trading institutions or to co-operatives at decentralized prices or at the collective farms' markets.*

Table 47

	1933 in %	1937 in %	1938 in %
Taxes and dues (agricultural income tax, compulsory and voluntary insurance premium on Kolkhoz property, i.e. crops, livestock, buildings, etc.)	12·6	8·3	8·9
Allocations to the jointly owned funds (including repayment of long-term bank credits)	22·8	12·4	14·5
Production costs	27·9	25·7	19·2
Administrative and managerial expenses	3·4	1·8	1·5
Appropriations to the social fund	2·5	3·9	3·0
Distributed in payment for labour days	24·2	47·9	52·8
Miscellaneous expenditure	6·6	—	0·1
Total	100·0	100·0	100·0

Table 47 shows how the cash income of collective farms was distributed.† These figures show clearly the improvement in the

the cotton grown on irrigated lands and 90·1 % grown on non-irrigated land was sold to the State as compulsory deliveries, whilst 17·5 % of the irrigated and 0·5 % of non-irrigated went to M.T.S. as payment in kind. Similar data for other crops can be found in *Socialist Agriculture*, no. 12, 1939, p. 164.

* E.g. in 1938 the income from the sale of collective farm agricultural production (as a percentage of the total income from the given branch of production) was made up as follows:

	State deliveries, compulsory and contractual	Sales at decentralized prices	Sales on collective farms' markets
Produce from plant cultivation	62·9	15·9	21·2
Produce from livestock breeding	36·8	35·3	27·9
Produce from livestock slaughter	4·2	10·4	85·3

It must be borne in mind that the figures in the second and particularly in the third column refer to sales at higher prices than those in the first, and therefore this *cash* income should not be identified with the relative shares of the actual quantity of marketable produce. For details see *Socialist Agriculture*, 1939, no. 12, p. 64.

† *Planned Economy*, 1939, no. 8, p. 92. For details regarding the appropriations for various items on the average per Kolkhoz see *Socialist Agriculture*, no. 12, 1930, p. 66.

collective farms' financial position which was taking place in the pre-war years. The share of income spent on taxes and dues, on production and administration costs and on capital expenditure (allocations to the jointly owned fund) had considerably decreased in the period 1933–8, whereas the share of income distributed among collective farmers as labour-day dividends had more than doubled. The State set minimum and maximum limits to various appropriations; it fixed the relative shares to be allocated to administrative and managerial expenses and to the jointly owned fund, as well as the share of income to be divided among collective farmers.* These maximum and minimum limits set to the various appropriations from the collective farms' revenue were aimed at stimulating their financial self-discipline, at reducing their production costs, raising their profitableness, and at increasing the share of income distributed to members as labour-day dividends.

Since collective farmers were at the same time members of a producers' association and owners of personal producer-consumer undertakings, some of them were inclined to develop their own domestic undertakings beyond the limits set by the statutes of the agricultural artel. In some districts where labour-day dividends were not remunerative enough, either on account of infertile soil, or the one-sidedness of the Kolkhoz production, or slack cultivation,†

* E.g. in the Sovnarkom S.S.S.R. and Party Central Committee 1938 regulation, it was proposed to limit administrative and managerial costs to 2% of the total cash income of the collective farms; the appropriation to the jointly owned fund was estimated at 12–15% of all income (in grain-growing districts), and no less than 60–70% of all the income was to be distributed to collective farmers as labour-day dividends. The minimum limit set to appropriations to the jointly owned funds (12% in the grain-growing and 15% in the livestock-breeding districts and in districts producing technical crops) was designed to ensure a necessary annual increase of the Kolkhoz basic funds, whilst the maximum limit protected the Kolkhoz from too much enthusiasm for capital construction on the part of Kolkhoz managements. For details regarding the distribution of 'collective farms' income see the regulations of the Sovnarkom S.S.S.R. and the Party Central Committee in *Bull. Financ. and Econ. Leg.* nos. 11–12, 33–4, 1938; *Coll. Orders and Regulations of the U.S.S.R. Government*, 1938, no. 55, § 308.

† E.g. in 1938, 80·3% of all the collective farms distributed as payment in kind up to 3 kg. of grain and leguminous plants per labour day; 16·3% of them (38,981 Kolkhozy) distributed more than 3 kg., 1·6% (3,887 Kolkhozy) distributed from 7·1 to 10 kg. and 1·8% (4,365 Kolkhozy) distributed more than 10 kg. per labour day. *Socialist Agriculture*, 1939, no. 12, p. 67. On the average every collective farmer's family received as labour-day dividends:

	1932	1937	1938
Grain (poods; 1 pood = 36·11 lb.)	36·6	106·2	approx. 100
Money (roubles)	108·0	376·0	480

whilst work in the domestic economy—growing vegetables, raising poultry, home handicrafts—yielded better income, collective farmers evaded work on the collective farm.* In many collective farms this led to a shortage of labour and even delayed important seasonal field work; moreover, it hindered the intensification of Kolkhoz production and its development along more complex lines.

In 1939 decisive steps were taken to check such tendencies among collective farmers. A compulsory minimum number of labour days to be worked on the collective farm was introduced; it varied from 60 to 100 days a year. Failure to complete this minimum was considered as resigning from the Kolkhoz and entailed forfeiture of all the collective farmers' rights. Any encroachments on the collective farm's land in favour of its individual members and any increase of their personal allotments in excess of the limits set by the statutes of the agricultural artel were regarded as offences, and persons guilty of committing them were to be brought before criminal courts. Accomplices were also liable to prosecution. Collective farmers were liable to be expelled and deprived of their allotments for leasing them or allowing others to use them. The responsible administrative authorities were ordered to proceed at once with a survey of all allotments in the personal use of collective farmers and to return to the collective farms and to their general allotment funds any land held in excess of the established norms.

In districts where no land could be spared for collective farmers' allotments, as established by the statutes, migration to districts where land was more plentiful was suggested as a remedy.† Thus it

Socialist Agriculture, 1940, no. 4, p. 20. In 1938 only 16,235 Kolkhozy or 6·8% distributed meat and lard in payment for labour days. The majority of collective farms did not distribute meat and lard because their livestock breeding was yet inadequate. For details see Socialist Agriculture, 1939, no. 12, p. 68. For very informative material on the organization of labour and its remuneration see also Socialist Agriculture, 1940, no. 5.

* In 1938, 93·5% of the able-bodied collective farmers worked on collective farms; 22·6% of the farmers worked 50 labour days in the course of the year, 38·3% worked from 50 to 200, 18·1% worked from 200 to 300, 11·1% worked from 301 to 400 and 9·9% more than 400 labour days. For details see Socialist Agriculture, 1939, no. 12, p. 62.

† For details see the regulation of the Sovnarkom S.S.S.R. and the Party Central Committee 'On measures to safeguard the collective farms' communal lands from being squandered', 27 May 1939. Bull. Financ. and Econ. Leg. 1939, nos. 17–18. The survey of personal allotments carried out in 1939 revealed that the total land under personal allotments in excess of regulations amounted to 2·5 million ha. See The Development of National Economy, p. 526. Evidently the point of the above-mentioned decision to control the size of allotments was not so much the need to recuperate the 2·5 million ha. as the desire to emphasize

was once more made quite plain that the intensification of Kolkhoz production was the only path to the peasants' prosperity.

In the first years of collectivization, the main efforts of Kolkhoz production were directed towards increasing grain production. Measures to develop large-scale livestock breeding began to be taken only after 1934, when the first annual State plan for raising livestock was drafted. The reasons for leaving the development of livestock farming to the private initiative of peasant masses in the early stages of collectivization have already been referred to. From 1935, however, plans for the development of livestock breeding were issued along with plans for land cultivation, and measures were devised for stimulating the breeding of livestock by collective farms and for creating special livestock farms on every Kolkhoz. But in spite of considerable progress achieved in Kolkhoz livestock breeding the greater share of livestock, up to the very latest pre-war years, was still owned privately by the population (cf. p. 327). And yet the possibilities of developing mixed farming, of improving breeds and further substantially developing livestock breeding, were bound up with the growth of stock breeding on collective farms. Limits to the growth of stock breeding by individual peasants were set both formally (by the artel statutes) and practically (by the very size of their allotments).

On 8 July 1939 the Sovnarkom S.S.S.R. and the Party Central Committee issued a new regulation of great importance to stock breeding, entitled, 'On measures for developing communal live-stock breeding on collective farms'. The regulation decreed that three productive stock-breeding farms should be set up at every Kolkhoz, the compulsory minimum being two farms—one for cattle and the other for either sheep or pigs. At the same time the collective farms' compulsory State deliveries of meat, hides and wool were no longer to be assessed on the basis of their heads of stock, but on the basis of land owned by the collective farms. Under the old arrangement, the collective farms which owned more animals delivered more livestock produce, whereas under the new arrangement collective farms were obliged to supply fixed amounts of livestock produce according to the land they owned and independently of the size of their herds and flocks. It was henceforth to the collective farms' advantage to increase their numbers of stock so as to decrease the relative amount of compulsory de-

that collective farmers must consider Kolkhoz production as the *basic* production, and the cultivation of private allotments as a *subsidiary* economy solely designed to meet family food requirements.

liveries per head of stock owned. Collective farms were assessed on far easier terms than individual farmers.* Moreover, collective farms, upon completing their State deliveries, could supply to the State livestock produce due individually by their members, and so exempt the latter partially, or entirely, from State deliveries of livestock produce. Consequently it was to the collective farmers' advantage to improve the livestock position of the collective farm. Obviously such a system of State deliveries could be introduced only because most collective farms had already reached the position of being able to develop the raising of stock, and explains why this method was inaugurated only in 1939 (see Table 52).

In order to stimulate mixed farming in the Kolkhoz new methods of State procurement of other agricultural produce were also introduced in 1939. From 1940 the norms of compulsory deliveries of grain, potatoes, vegetables, oil-bearing seeds and grass seeds were no longer calculated on the basis of the area sown with these various crops but on the basis of all cultivated land belonging to the Kolkhoz. The area of cultivated land for assessment purposes included, apart from the actual fields, also vegetable gardens and new lands which, according to the State plan, were due to be ploughed up, as well as bogs due to be drained and shubberies to be cleared away; these lands were assessed the year after the reclamation work had been carried out.† Therefore, it was to the advantage of the collective farms to intensify their production and vary their crops, because they were to supply from every hectare of cultivated land certain requirements of produce to the State, and, by intensifying the utilization of the land, they relatively lightened the burden of their obligations. In this manner, changes in methods of State procurements were used as an additional lever to enforce planned measures designed by the Soviet Government for developing agricultural production.

In the first years of collectivization, State plans for agriculture controlled only the principal seasonal cultivation (spring and autumn sowing, harvesting, autumn ploughing, snow-drift prevention); later they tended to cover all the main agricultural production processes. For instance, the 'State plan for agricultural

---

* For collective farms, compulsory State deliveries were at the rate of $\frac{1}{2}$ to $4\frac{1}{2}$ kg. live weight per ha. of land, whilst domestic economies were assessed at 32–43 kg. per household, and individual peasants at 64–90 kg. per household. The exact amount, within these limits, depended on districts.

† For details see the above-cited regulation of the Sovnarkom S.S.S.R. and Party Central Committee, *Bull. Financ. and Econ. Leg.* 1940, nos. 7–8.

work for 1939', confirmed on 8 February 1939, laid down State tasks for spring and autumn sowing of all the principal crops (the plan laid down the total acreage and the dates according to republics and provinces, whilst local authorities fixed the dates and the amounts of every crop to be sown by every collective farm), dates for harvesting, for ploughing up fallow, deep harrowing, breaking up new land, sowing perennial fodder grasses, for the amounts of ensilage and hay to be stored, for the improvement of natural meadows and pastures, the use of fertilizers and manures, etc. Moreover, the 1939 agricultural plan for the first time set tasks for the principal vegetable crops (cabbage, cucumber, tomato, carrot, beetroot, onion and garlic). For the first time, too, a plan was issued for planting subtropical crops, fruit trees, soft fruit plantations, and vineyards. Concurrently with this plan for crop cultivation, a very detailed plan regarding stock breeding was to be enforced; it took into account every district, and made provisions for breeding both draught and productive animals during 1939; it contained separate plans for raising young animals by collective farms, for contracting and purchasing cattle from collective farmers to increase small Kolkhoz livestock farms and establish new ones; for breeding pedigree and for cross-breeding cattle at collective farms and by collective farmers, with similar plans for horses and sheep; and for developing a network of zootechnical and veterinary centres. The P. Commissariat of Finance was instructed to finance the necessary expenditure. 'The annual productive-financial plan of the M.T.S.', which was confirmed at the same time, set quantitative and qualitative tasks to M.T.S. for the tilling of Kolkhoz fields. According to this productive-financial plan, the M.T.S. were to conclude agreements with collective farms, to carry out during the year with their tractors and other agricultural machinery a definite amount of work, the precise qualitative indices of which were stated, as well as the dates for the completion of each type of work. Moreover, the M.T.S. undertook 'to give assistance to the Kolkhoz and strengthen its organization and economy by agronomic advice, by drafting its production plans and its estimates of profit and expenditure, by establishing a correct crop rotation, by helping the Kolkhoz to organize labour and to distribute its income, by training cadres and by establishing production accounting'. On their part the Kolkhozy undertook to provide field labour for permanent work on tractor-drawn ploughs, harrows and other 'coupled-up' machinery, to overhaul in good time Kolkhoz implements and to carry out certain agro-technical measures. As the plan for compulsory deliveries of basic agricultural produce was calculated on the basis of approved production plans,* it was in the interest of the Kolkhozy to carry out the planned tasks. Indeed, failure to fulfil the sowing programme did not exempt the Kolkhozy from their obligation to deliver the quota of produce, whereas if the plan was exceeded a greater share of produce was left at the Kolkhozy's disposal. Up to 1940 planned tasks set the Kolkhozy fixed not only the total crops to be sown, but specified their kind and respective amounts. In 1940, considering that the grain problem was on the whole solved and that collective farms had acquired sufficient experience, it was decided to abolish this procedure and not to issue the Kolkhozy with plans regarding 'the sowing of every crop separately and according to varieties', but to give them the right 'to carry out the distribution of crops according to their own judgement within the framework of their sowing programme'. This measure was aimed at stimulating the 'initiative of collective farmers to increase the yield of grain crops', allowing the Kolkhozy, in the framework of the grain-sowing pro-gramme, to vary their crops according to the soil, climate and economic conditions of the particular Kolkhoz, provided, however, that the compulsory state deliveries of the right kind of grain were unquestioningly fulfilled.†

This regulation was highly characteristic of the plans for the development of agriculture. The two aims of the plans were to ensure the production of certain amounts of basic agricultural pro-duce in the course of the season and the delivery of definite amounts at fixed prices to the State. In so far as these two aims could not be entirely left to the initiative of collective farms, the plans contained very definite and detailed instructions, but when the aims were being achieved, the peasants were given greater initiative for vary-ing production, distributing and utilizing the result of their labour.

Plans for agricultural production and plans for compulsory State deliveries of agricultural produce are closely linked. This is natural for a planned system of agricultural production. For on the fulfil-ment of the plan of agricultural deliveries depends not only the fulfilment of plans regarding other branches of the country's

---

* Cf. the corresponding Government regulation on the 1939 plan for agri-cultural works, *Bull. Financ. and Econ. Leg.* 1939, nos. 8–14. *Planned Economy*, 1939, no. 9, pp. 38–55.

† For details see the regulations 'Concerning the planning of sowing grain crops by collective farms' and 'Concerning the planning of kinds of grain crops by collective farms'. *Coll. Government Orders and Regulations*, 1940, nos. 1 and 3.

economy, but also the plan for financing any further development of agriculture itself. Expenditure on expanding agronomic education, agronomic research institutes, veterinary services in rural areas, expenditure on the construction of M.T.S., land reclamation, irrigation, raising pedigree livestock and assisting the agricultural population in case of crop failure and other natural calamities* is financed in the U.S.S.R. from the State Budget. The latter is to a great extent dependent on the fulfilment of the compulsory deliveries at fixed prices which enable it to finance measures for the development of agricultural production.

Thus planning in the field of agriculture comprises direct and indirect measures for achieving definite goals. The general plan lays down certain tasks, the fulfilment of which ensures the State's general aims for the development of the whole agricultural side of the national economy within a given period; but indirect pressures are also applied in order to contribute to the fulfilment of the general aims and to shape the character of the development of the country's agriculture; restrictions on the size of individual domestic undertakings, methods of procurement policy, limits set to the various items in the distribution of collective farms' income, the organization of agricultural exhibitions, etc., are all such indirect pressures. They supplement the planned measures by influencing the initiative of agricultural 'economic collectives', i.e. the collective farms. Unlike State industrial and agricultural enterprises (State farms), collective farms are independent associations of farming peasants. Therefore, in spite of the considerable influence exercised by administrative authorities over the choice of Kolkhoz managements, it would be difficult to achieve concrete production plans and the general agricultural objectives without the help of these indirect pressures on the collective farms.

Herein lies the main difference between the planning of agriculture and the planning of other branches of the national economy. Apparently, the co-existence of small subsidiary farming is indispensable alongside the large-scale producers' collectives (i.e. the State and collective farms). And it is worth noting that even members of agricultural communes, where the principle of col-

---

* Apart from voluntary insurance, the insurance of crops against possible destruction by natural calamities (hail, cloud-burst, storm, early frost, etc.) and fire, is obligatory in the U.S.S.R., and so is the insurance of livestock against epidemics and other abnormal causes of death, and that of buildings, produce and other agricultural property against damage due to definite causes. For insurance values and premiums in force in 1940, see *Collected Regulations, Decrees and Instructions on Financial and Economic Questions*, 1940, nos. 19–20.

lectivization is carried a step further than in the agricultural artel, and even labourers on State farms, have their own subsidiary farming.* Though fundamentally domestic undertakings exist to satisfy the food and day-to-day requirements of the peasant family, they also supplement the mass production. This is apparently peculiar to agricultural production where intensive utilization of soil and labour, at any rate for certain types of production, in small-scale farming (market gardening, rabbit breeding, bee-keeping, etc.) meets with as much success as in large-scale farming.

In certain respects, the planning of basic mass agricultural production—main crops and livestock—is fraught with fewer technical difficulties than the planning of industrial production, but in regard to secondary, subsidiary kinds of agricultural produce, planning has to fit in with the private initiative in production of the rural population. The experience of the U.S.S.R. definitely confirms this necessity.

It should be emphasized that, over and above the current planning of yearly tasks for the development of agricultural production, and apart from the long-term plans for the prospective development of agriculture, in the course of a lengthy period (the three F.Y.P.s), the planning of special tasks was being carried out in the U.S.S.R. on a large scale. The most outstanding examples of this planning of measures to achieve definite special aims were those inaugurated in 1940 for developing the production of Egyptian varieties of cotton in the Tadzhik S.S.R. and for greatly extending cotton growing in Uzbekistan, as well as measures to develop grain growing by State and collective farms in the east—the Altai and Krasnoyarsk regions and the provinces of Novosibirsk, Omsk, Cheliabinsk, etc.† These measures included huge irrigation works, the construction of new railways and the removal of existing railways to other localities, the migration of large numbers of the population, a very large housing programme, etc.

The description of other planned measures and the methods of long-term planning of prospective agricultural developments, especially under the third F.Y.P., falls outside the scope of this study, which is confined to a general survey of developments and an outline of planning of agricultural production in the U.S.S.R.

* For rules regulating the size of domestic economies of workers and employees on State farms see *Coll. regulations of the U.S.S.R. Government*, 1938, no. 45, § 268.

† For details about these measures see *Bull. Financ. and Econ. Leg.* 1940, nos. 1–2. *Problems of Economics*, 1940, nos. 5–6.

For the same reason no description of the organizational structure of the U.S.S.R. Agricultural Commissariats* is given here, though some summary statistical data regarding the development of agricultural production for the period elapsed are appended, as well as reference material on special points such as State farms, M.T.S., and a short note on the draft third F.Y.P.

CONCLUSION

The material analysed clearly shows how different *fundamentally* were the problems which had to be tackled in the transition to planned agricultural production from the problems of planning in the field of industry. This fundamental difference, particularly during the transition period, was not due to the inherent difference between agricultural and industrial production, but to other circumstances. In industry the transition from the competitive to the planned system of industrial production faced no *fundamental* difficulty in creating the *prerequisites* for concentrating and intensifying production, accumulating basic capital and increasing marketable production, whereas in agriculture these problems had to be solved *first* in order to create conditions permitting the planning of production.

The nationalization of large estates, normally accompanied by their subdivision,† solves only the social and political elements in the agrarian problem in countries where small peasant landownership is prevalent. In itself, it does nothing to prepare the ground for solving the economic problem, or to determine the way along which productive relations are to develop, nor does it create the conditions necessary for planning production.

The basic problems which had to be solved in the U.S.S.R., and which will have to be solved in every country of small freehold pro-

---

* For a description of the organizational structure of the agricultural commissariats, see no. 1, 1940 *Coll. Orders and Regulations of the Government*, 'On the structure of the U.S.S.R. P. Commissariat of Agriculture, the P. Commissariats of Agriculture of the R.S.F.S.R., the Ukrainian S.S.R. and the autonomous republics, and the regional, provincial and district agricultural sections'; also *Bull. Financ. and Econ. Leg.* 1938, no. 10, 'Statute of the P. Commissariat of grain growing and livestock breeding State farms of the U.S.S.R.'

† In a way this is the whole point of nationalizing the land of large landowners as opposed to the nationalization of factories and works. The breaking up of large estates and the distribution of these lands to land-hungry peasants is the very aim of democratic agrarian reforms. E.g. this was the essence of the agrarian reform in Czechoslovakia; and in many other countries where small peasant landownership is prevalent this demand for the division of large estates is one of the main points on the programme of peasant agrarian parties.

prietors, are the problems of production, which depend on capital accumulation, intensifying agriculture and increasing its marketable surplus. The limits to capital accumulation and to rational intensification of small peasant farming are set by the very nature of this farming. The size of holdings does not permit the profitable use of mechanized soil cultivation by personally owned agricultural machinery. Tractors, sheaf-binders, threshing machines, cultivators, seed selection apparatus, let alone combine-harvesting machines and other agricultural equipment improving the cultivation of soil, saving labour and preventing harvesting losses, are beyond the reach of the small farmer, because of the size of his holding and the income derived from it. Peasant households below certain limits, which may vary according to the country and the nature of basic production but are quite definite in each case, cannot afford to keep even a horse unless it is used for other purposes besides farming. A horse 'devours' a small peasant holding. The intensification of small peasant farming is possible solely through intensified physical exertion, and is limited to certain types of production, such as market gardening, poultry and rabbit breeding; it cannot be extended to the cultivation of basic agricultural crops and the breeding of livestock. Smallholders cannot take advantage of the mechanization of agricultural production even if they associate themselves in co-operatives, so long as they do not amalgamate their holdings into one block of land. This explains why *producers'* co-operation is so little developed even in countries where agricultural sales co-operation prospers.

Therefore any rational intensification of agricultural production —not through intensified physical exertion but through large-scale mechanization of production—requires the creation of sufficiently large individual farms or the amalgamation of peasant households into large producers' associations. This raises the further question of capital accumulation necessary for producers' associations. The accumulation of capital by smallholders is very limited and slow. This explains the well-known fact that the organization of co-operative agricultural machine societies was either subsidized from outside—by the State or by companies manufacturing agricultural machinery—or else they were organized not by small but by middle-sized or well-to-do farmers.

In the U.S.S.R., the creation of collective farms which merged the small plots into large land blocks met the fundamental need of increasing the scale of land tenure—the necessary *prerequisite* for the mechanization and the rational intensification of agriculture. The minimum appropriations from the gross income of collective farms to their jointly owned funds guaranteed a stable, gradual accumulation of production capital. The creation of the M.T.S. solved the problem of securing the advantages of complex agricultural machinery for mass cultivation work. Moreover, the size of land blocks held by collective farms and the size of the M.T.S. permitted not only the use of any type of agricultural machinery but also enabled the M.T.S. to be serviced by their own repair workshops and by skilled technical, administrative and agronomic personnel. The M.T.S. were made possible through the compulsory saving enforced by the policy of State procurements of basic agricultural produce at fixed prices. This system of compulsory saving was carried out through the channel of the State Budget, and it enabled the U.S.S.R., previously one of the most backward European countries agronomically, to accumulate in the space of a few years an enormous production capital—in agricultural machinery and buildings—and to mechanize the main branches of cultivation to a much greater extent than other countries had done in the course of a long period of history. Very considerable successes were also achieved in the improved servicing of agricultural production by qualified specialists and in improving the cultural and living conditions of the rural population (cf. Table 53).

After a period of unavoidable difficulties during the transition years when land relations were being completely recast (1929–32), substantial positive results were achieved in the planning of the development of agricultural production. The popular objection to planning in agriculture, i.e. that nature's intervention is likely to upset all plans, is too superficial to be taken seriously in scientific literature. It is precisely the planning of agricultural production that makes it possible to a considerable degree to nullify and offset the freaks of nature. The mechanization of large-scale agricultural operations, the shorter time needed for tilling and harvesting, the prevention of snowdrifts, irrigation works, the breeding of drought- and frost-resisting varieties of crops, correct crop rotation, the scientific utilization of manure and fertilizers, etc., all facilitate the struggle against the hazards of nature, and they can be better used under planned agricultural production than by the private efforts of individual farmers. The planning of agriculture presents also fewer difficulties than the planning of other branches of the national economy. The basic agricultural production consists of a small group of standard commodities. The fulfilment of quantitative and qualitative programmes can be controlled without difficulty because qualitative tasks are easily expressed in quantitative indices, e.g. definite standards of soil cultivation, of seed sown per unit of area, application of definite quantities of fertilizers, dates to be observed in carrying out mass field works, etc.* Actually, after the consolidation of Kolkhoz production had been achieved, plans for seasonal agricultural works were fulfilled in the U.S.S.R. in the latter years to the extent of 96–99 %. The planning of agriculture permitted the State and collective farms to achieve in a short time substantial and positive structural changes: the growing of wheat was expanded and in particular was extended to new districts, while the sowing of rye was curtailed; after a period of considerable expansion in the sowing of technical crops, the area under these crops was reduced with the object of obtaining higher yields from the sown areas; the acreage under perennial fodder grasses was increased to foster livestock breeding, etc. (cf. Table 49). Moreover, the 1939 plan for sowing proposed to reduce in some districts the areas sown to grain in order to increase those under feeding stuffs, and on the whole this was done. Thanks to the organization of State farms specializing in large-scale agricultural production it proved possible to bring under cultivation large areas of virgin soil in zones affected by droughts, in remote and sparsely populated districts, or to introduce varieties of production new to the district (see appendix on State farms), so that in 1939, State farms occupied an area of over 60 million ha. of which only 3 million ha. were 'old' State farm lands, i.e. lands which had formerly been large private estates on which the first State farms had been organized.

However, the experience of the U.S.S.R. also shows that in countries with a prevalently rural population it will be necessary in one way or another to decide the fate of private farming first, before proceeding to solve the problems of concentrating and intensifying agriculture, and creating the prerequisites for planning. Agricultural production differs from industrial production in that industrial workers produce as a rule articles 'for the market' and can only produce them in their factory, whilst in agriculture small personal farming can in theory yield the same produce as large-scale farming and, furthermore, commodities produced 'for the market' are at the same time commodities consumed by the household. The industrial worker can be absolutely indifferent to the

* The improved standards of cultivation allowed many collective farms to obtain higher yields per unit of sown area than were previously reaped off private estates in the same districts. E.g. in 1938 the grain harvest averaged 9·3 quintals per ha.; in 18,777 collective farms the yield was 10–12 quintals, in 9,883 it was 12·1–14 quintals, in 5,009 it was 14·1–16 quintals, in 3,010 it was 16·1–20 quintal and 1,227 collective farms harvested over 20 quintals per ha. For details, see *Socialist Agriculture*, 1939, no. 12.

Table 48

(mill. ha. / mill. quintals)	1913	1922	1923	1924	1925	1926	1927	1928	1929	1930
Sown area, total (mill. ha.)	105·0 (116·7)*	77·7	91·7	98·1	104·3	110·3	112·4	113·0	118·0	127·2
Grain crops	94·4 (102·7)*	66·2	78·6	82·9	87·3	93·7	94·7	92·2	96·0	101·8
Technical crops, total	4·6	4·0	—	5·8	7·2	6·8	7·2	8·6	8·8	10·5
Gross production (mill. quintals):										
Grain	801·0 (816)*	503·1	565·9	514·0	724·6	768·3	723·0	733·2	717·4	835·5
Flax-fibre	5·1	3·2	2·3	3·0	3·7	3·3	2·3	3·2	3·6	4·4
Cotton	6·8	—	—	—	—	—	—	8·2	8·6	11·1
Sugar beet	99·2	15·1	26·1	33·8	83·8	61·4	104·1	101·4	62·5	140·2
Horses (millions) [1916]	35·8	24·1	24·6	25·9	27·1	29·2	31·6	33·5	34·6	30·2
Cattle	60·6	45·8	52·9	59·0	62·1	65·5	68·0	70·5	67·1	52·5
Sheep and goats	121·2	—	—	—	115·8	123·1	139·7	146·7	147·0	108·8
Pigs	20·9	12·1	12·9	22·2	21·8	21·6	23·2	26·0	20·7	13·6

(mill. ha. / mill. quintals)	1931	1932	1933	1934	1935	1936	1937	1938	1939
Sown area, total (mill. ha.)	136·3	134·4	129·7	131·4	132·8	133·8	135·3	136·9	134·0
Grain crops	104·4	99·7	101·5	104·7	103·4	102·4	104·4	102·4	99·6
Technical crops, total	14·0	14·9	12·0†	10·7	10·6	10·8	11·2	11·0	11·1
Gross production (mill. quintals):									
Grain	694·8	698·7	898·0	894·0	901·0	827·3	1,202·9	949·9	1,054
Flax-fibre	5·5	5·0	5·5	5·3	5·5	5·8	5·7	5·5	6·4
Cotton	12·9	12·7	13·1	11·8	17·2	23·9	25·8	26·9	28·2
Sugar beet	120·5	65·6	89·9	113·6	162·1	168·3	218·6	166·8	210·2
Horses	26·2	19·6	16·6	15·7	15·9	16·6	16·7	17·5	18·3‡‡
Cattle	47·9	40·7	38·4	42·4	49·2	56·7	57·0	63·2	64·6‡‡
Sheep and goats	77·7	52·1	50·2	51·9	61·1	73·7	81·3	102·5	111·6‡‡‡
Pigs	14·4	11·6	12·1	17·4	22·5	30·5	22·8	30·6	32·5‡

	1928–32	1933–7	1938	1939
Average yields of grain crops (quintals per ha.)	7·5	9·1	9·3	9·3
Average harvests of grain crops (in mill. quintals)	735·9	944·7	949·9	1,054·4

* The figures in brackets were those given in Soviet statistical sources for the 1913 sown area and harvest up to 1930. In sources published after that date it was stated that detailed calculations showed the inexactness of these figures, and henceforth the officially accepted figures are those cited above without brackets.
† From 1933 the areas under technical crops were somewhat reduced in order to improve the quality of soil cultivation.   ‡ Estimates.

nature and volume of production and to the price of the article manufactured at his factory, but the peasant—in so far as he is not a hired labourer receiving merely a money wage—whether he works on his own farm or on a producers' collective farm is directly interested in the volume of his production, the manner in which the gross income is distributed and in the price of the commodity produced. Moreover, the peasant clings passionately to his farming because on the one hand, in theory at least, he can produce on his own plot the same commodities as yielded by large-scale farming, and on the other hand, under the capitalist system, if he gives up his farming for work in large-scale agricultural production he can expect only low wages and social degradation. Herein lies the sociological obstacle to the mechanization and intensification of agriculture. This circumstance, and not some peculiar feature of agricultural production, is at the root of the difficulty of changing over from petty peasant production to large-scale agricultural production.

In the field of industry, factory production has irrevocably displaced home handicrafts, but in the agriculture of agrarian countries craftsmen's production still bars the way to the adoption of mass mechanized production.

Table 49. *Structural changes in agriculture*

	1913 (thousand ha.)	1928 (thousand ha.)	1939 (thousand ha.)
Total sown area	104,998·6	112,992·4	133,987·3
Under grain crops	94,358·4	92,172·3	99,653·2
Of which: Wheat	31,654·3	27,730·2	40,925·8
Rye	25,813·3	24,646·8	17,833·8
Technical crops	4,550·5	8,615·4	11,073·9
Potatoes and vegetables	3,815·5	7,683·4	9,213·0
Fodder crops	2,050·0	3,871·5	13,952·0
Perennial grasses	Unknown	1,034·3	5,197·6

Table 50. *Marketable production (agricultural year)*
(million poods, 1 pood = 36·11 lb.)

	1926–7	1932–3	1937–8	1938–9
Grain	630·0	1,240·2	2,318·1	2,229·4
Cotton	32·6	73·4	157·1	164·0
Flax fibre	7·9	19·4	19·8	18·9
Sugar beet	373·7	373·4	1,309·5	998·0
Potatoes	182·8	352·1	713·2	492·3
Meat	75·6	42·9	89·4	125·4
Milk	264·0	274·6	489·3	500·0
Wool	0·2	2·5	4·9	5·4

Table 51. *The collective farms of the U.S.S.R.*

Year	No. of Kolkhozy in thousands	No. of homesteads in them millions	% of collectivized homesteads	Sown area of Kolkhozy million ha.	% of collectivized sown area	No. of Kolkhoz livestock farms thousands*	% of Kolkhoz sown area serviced by M.T.S.
1929	57·0	1·0	3·9	4·2	4·9	—	—
1930	85·9	6·0	23·6	38·1	33·6	—	27·4
1931	211·1	13·0	52·7	79·0	67·8	—	37·1
1932	211·1	14·9	61·5	91·5	77·7	63·7	49·3
1933	224·6	15·3	65·6	93·6	83·1	97·4	58·7
1934	233·3	15·7	71·4	98·6	87·4	136·1	63·9
1935	245·4	17·3	83·2	104·5	94·1	236·4	72·4
1936	244·2	18·4†	90·5	110·5	98·2	333·1	82·8
1937	243·7	18·5	93·0	116·0	99·1	370·5	91·2
1938	242·4	18·8	93·5	117·2	99·3	374·6	93·3
1939	241·1	19·3	—	114·9	—	406·5	94·0
1940	236·3†	19·2	—	117·6	—	605·5	94·5

* The fact that the number of Kolkhoz livestock farms is greater than the number of actual Kolkhozy is explained by the habit of counting the cattle, the sheep and the pig farms of one Kolkhoz as separate items.

† The decrease in the numbers of Kolkhozy which occurred from 1935, and the simultaneous rise in the numbers of collectivized homesteads, were due to the merging of small Kolkhozy, in a number of districts.

Table 52. *Relative shares of various categories of farms in the U.S.S.R. in 1938*

	Sown areas million ha.	%	Livestock ownership in %				Relative share of each in total agricultural gross production %
			Horses	Cattle	Sheep and goats	Pigs	
Collective farms	117·2	85·6	76·8	29·0	34·2	24·4	62·9
Collective farmers (personal homesteads)	5·3	3·9	4·7	49·3	46·2	49·8	21·5
All State and co-operative farming	12·4	9·1	12·5	7·3	10·5	11·0	9·3
Of which:							
State farms	—	—	4·0	5·1	8·6	7·1	—
Workers, employees and other groups of population	1·1	0·8	3·1	11·4	5·4	12·5	4·8
Individual peasants	0·9	0·6	2·9	3·0	3·7	2·3	1·5

Table 53. *Numbers of specialists in agriculture*

	1926	1938
Agronoms (thousands)	16·8	107·2
Surveyors, geodesists and topographers (thousands)	12·9	27·9
Veterinary surgeons	4·9	17·1
	1913	
Experimental agricultural research stations (units)	44	303
Scientific workers in agricultural institutes and at experimental stations	250	9,800
No. of experimental fields	78	507
No. of agrotechnical laboratories and seed control stations	18	2,720
No. of agricultural laboratories on collective farms	None	12,363

Public amenities and social service

	1914	1929	1939
Public libraries in rural districts	No data	20,894	61,636
Clubs in rural districts	88	29,984	95,274
Cinemas in rural districts	133	4,104	18,802
Agricultural newspapers	859	1,197	8,550
Circulation of agricultural newspapers (million copies)	2·7	9·4	37·5
No. of hospitals and maternity homes in rural districts	3,001	—	7,227
No. of hospital beds in rural districts (thousands)	49·0	—	178·9
No. of out-patient departments in rural districts	4,367	—	14,372
No. of doctors in rural districts	4,975	—	15,059
No. of cots in permanent nurseries in rural districts (thousands)	None	—	370·1
No. of cots in seasonal nurseries in rural districts (thousands)	None	—	3,490·9

	1914–15	1928–9	1938–9
Nos. of school children in rural districts (thousands)	6,117·2	8,667·3	22,087·8
Of which:			
In primary schools	6,065·0	7,679·8	9,144·5
In incomplete secondary schools	37·6	906·5	9,469·1
In secondary schools	14·6	81·0	3,474·2
Nos. of pupils in special agricultural schools (thousands)	18·6	—	803·1
Of which:			
At university agricultural schools	3·9	—	62·5
In secondary agricultural schools	3·5	—	136·9
Taking correspondence courses in agriculture	—	—	14·6
Taking mass training courses in agricultural subjects	11·2	—	589·1

From this point of view, the results of the U.S.S.R. experiment can have a high value for other agrarian countries. By combining collective farm production, which means large-scale methods of agricultural production, with the collective farmers' small personal subsidiary farming, an attempt has been made in the U.S.S.R. to solve the economic and the sociological aspects of the problem of agricultural production. In any country with a *predominantly agricultural population* the solution of the problem must begin with the creation of prerequisites to planning agricultural production and not with a discussion of the technique of this planning. This is why in this summary survey we have dwelt on the processes which re-moulded completely the agricultural system of the U.S.S.R. at much greater length than on the planning of agricultural production.

Economists and research workers should devote more attention than hitherto to the study of the sociological and economic structure of land relations and of agricultural production in different countries. Only a concrete knowledge of these problems, peculiar to each country, can give a basis for fruitful discussions on questions of planning in agricultural production. In the absence of such knowledge, 'theoretical generalizations' may suffer from sterile syllogisms based on abstract theories, so abundant in academic economic literature, which can at the best be regarded merely as useful mental gymnastics.

The statistical data of the general development of agriculture given in Tables 48–53, as well as the data of the M.T.S. and the State farms, are taken from the following sources:

Statistical Handbook, 1928.

The National Economy of the U.S.S.R. Statistical Yearbook, 1932.

Socialist Construction in the U.S.S.R. Statistical Handbooks for 1934, 1935, 1936, 1939.

Agriculture in the U.S.S.R. (statistical data), 1935.

Socialist Agriculture in the U.S.S.R. (statistical data), 1939.

The Sown Areas of the U.S.S.R. Statistical Handbook, 1939.

Results of the Fulfilment of the First Five-Year Plan for the Development of the National Economy of the U.S.S.R., 1933.

Results of the Fulfilment of the Second Five-Year Plan for the Development of the National Economy of the U.S.S.R., 1939.

Socialist Agriculture, no. 2, 1939, nos. 3 and 5, 1940.

Problems of Economics, no. 1, 1941.

Planned Economy, no. 11, 1939, nos. 4 and 7, 1940.

APPENDIX I

Machine-Tractor Stations and the Mechanization of Agriculture

The first M.T.S. came into existence in 1928 as co-operative tractor centres. In 1928–9 the 'Traktorotsentr', a joint-stock company with the participation of State and co-operative capital, was formed, some shares being acquired by collective farms. By 1930 'Traktorotsentr' owned 158 M.T.S. and 7,000 tractors. In 1932 'Traktorotsentr' was taken over by the State, and ever since M.T.S. have remained State property. The M.T.S. are entirely financed from the State Budget. The State Budget finances capital investments in the M.T.S. through the Agricultural Bank (Selkhozbank) and production, administrative and managerial expenditure through the State Bank (Gosbank). The money is either credited to the M.T.S. quarterly according to the degree to which they have fulfilled the State productive-financial plan, or else it is advanced for the forthcoming quarter.

Collective farms pay the M.T.S. for their work exactly fixed standard amounts in cash and kind stipulated in contracts drawn up according to a standard model. All such payments received by the M.T.S. from collective farms are credited to the State. By far the greater part of the complex agricultural machinery is concentrated at the M.T.S. As a rule one M.T.S. services several collective farms situated in the neighbourhood. In the first years of collectivization there were on the whole fewer M.T.S. to a greater number of collective farms than has been the case since. In later years many large unwieldy M.T.S. were reduced in size. In 1938, on the average, one M.T.S. serviced thirty-two collective farms aggregating together 17,200 ha., but in some cases one M.T.S. serviced less than ten and in other cases up to sixty collective farms. In the later years, the Soviet economic press was full of lively discussions about the standard optimum sizes of M.T.S. according to the prevailing crops and the various districts.*

* Cf. the very interesting material on the size of M.T.S. in *Problems of Economics*, 1940, nos. 5–6.

The following figures give some idea of the tremendous growth of mechanization in agricultural production in the U.S.S.R. in the course of one decade.

	1930	1931.	1932	1933	1934	1935
No. of M.T.S.	158	1,228	2,446	2,916	3,533	4,375
No. of tractors (total, thousands)	72·1	125·3	148·5	210·9	276·4	360·3
Of which:						
At M.T.S.	31·2	63·3	74·8	123·2	177·3	254·7
At State farms	27·7	51·5	64·0	83·2	95·5	102·1
No. of Harvester combines (total, thousands)	1·7	6·4	14·5	25·4	32·3	50·3
Average size of M.T.S. estimated according to:						
(a) Collective farms serviced	73	42	29	32	31	28
(b) Sown area worked (thousand ha.)	65·8	23·9	18·4	20·4	19·7	16·7

	1936	1937	1938	1939	1940	
No. of M.T.S.	5,000	5,818	6,358	6,501	6,980	
No. of tractors (total, thousands)	422·7	454·5	483·5	495·8	523·0	
Of which:						
At M.T.S.	328·5	365·8	394·0	—	—	
At State farms	88·5	84·5	85·0	—	—	
No. of Harvester combines (total, thousands)	87·8	128·8	153·5	—	182·0	
Average size of M.T.S. estimated according to:						
(a) Collective farms serviced	32	33	32	—	—	
(b) Sown area worked (thousand ha.)	18·3	18.5	17·2	—	—	

Mechanization of agricultural work in 1938

Ploughing by tractor-drawn ploughs	71·5% of total
Sowing by tractor-drawn seeders	56·7%
Sowing by horse-drawn seeders	30·5%
Harvesting by combines	48·4%
Harvesting by horse-drawn machines	43·1%
Threshing by mechanical threshers	95·0%

Electrification of agriculture

	1928	1932	1937	1938
Capacity of rural electrical power stations (thousand kW.)	29·0	53·0	145·5	162·5
Output of electrical energy (mill. kWh.)	34·8	74·4	184·2	237·0
Consumption by agriculture of electrical energy, derived from rural and other power stations (mill. kWh.)	35	86	330	382

Fertilizers supplied to agriculture

	1913	1928	1932	1938
Total (thousand tons)	188·0	234·1	922·8	3,216·3

APPENDIX II

State farms

Soviet State agricultural enterprises, known as Sovkhozy or State farms, were organized from 1918–19 and up to 1927 more or less exclusively on large estates which had belonged in pre-revolution days to private landowners, the Church and the State. Most of them were formed in the period between 1918–19 and 1921–2. During the N.E.P. period many State farms working either at a loss or with a very narrow margin of profit were liquidated; actually the total area under State farms which in 1921–2 had been 3,385,000 ha. had, by 1926, been reduced to 2,316,000 ha. However, in 1925, the Government decided to give the necessary financial and economic support to the existing State farms and to foster the creation of new ones; as a result the area under State farms rose to 3 million ha. by 1928. In 1928 the Government adopted the resolution already quoted to form new large State farms in districts where the land had not yet entirely been brought under cultivation by the peasants. The organization of State farms was financed from the State Budget and in the course of the two first F.Y.P.s the State invested some 15 milliard roubles in State farms. Construction of State farms during 1928–32 was carried out on an enormous scale, their numbers trebled and their sown area increased eightfold. However, in 1931 State inquiry commissions, upon investigation into the management of State farms, reported that many of them carried out their farming in 'an unbusiness-like fashion and displayed an inadmissible and criminal attitude towards State property'.* Gradually it became obvious that the causes for such an unsatisfactory state of affairs were not only the incapacity to organize farming on certain State farms, or the slackness and dishonesty of their managements, but also the cumbersome size and over-centralized administrations of large State farms. Numerous reforms, both of the central administration of State farms and of their methods of farming, were carried out from 1932 onwards. Broadly speaking the organizational problems were the same as those which had to be solved in the organization of industrial management which have been described above, only applied to agriculture. In the course of 1932–5 the size of many

---

* As formulated in the regulation of the Sovnarkom S.S.S.R. and the Party Central Committee, dated 27 November 1931. *Izvestia*, 28 November 1931.

State farms was reduced and between 1936 and 1937 a considerable number of the unprofitable ones were liquidated altogether, and their lands in many cases transferred to collective farms. The latter were moreover allowed to purchase on easy terms the livestock, buildings and other property of the abolished State farms.* On the whole, between 1934 and 1937 the area under State farms was reduced by nearly one-quarter (from 84·2 million ha. in 1934 to 60·3 million ha. in 1937). In this way the majority of the unprofitable State farms were either liquidated or reduced in size so as to place them in more favourable conditions for improving their farming.

The various phases in the development of State farms are illustrated by the following figures:

	1928	1932	1938
No. of State farms	1,400	4,337	3,992
Average no. of workers on them (thousands)	316·8	1,891	1,319·7
Basic capital (balance estimates) (mill. roubles)	451·5	4,030·6	7,716·1
Sown area (mill. ha.)	1·7	13·4	12·4
Tractors (thousands)	6·7	64·0	85·0
Their total h.p. (thousands h.p.)	77·6	1,043·0	1,751·8
Harvester combines (thousands)	—	12·3	26·0
Lorries (thousands)	0·7	8·2	30·6
Heads of livestock (mill. heads):			
Cattle	0·18	3·2	3·7
Pigs	0·06	1·8	2·8
Sheep and goats	0·75	5·7	7·0
Gross production:			
Grain (mill. quintals)	11·3	—	87·6
Cotton (mill. quintals)	0·1	—	1·4
Wool (thousand quintals)	21·0	—	186·0
Total gross production in fixed prices of 1926–7 (mill. roubles)	229·7	—	1,630·6
Marketable production supplied to the State:			
Grain (mill. quintals)	3·9	15·9	34·4
Cotton (thousand quintals)	130·0	406·0	1,381·7
Meat, live weight (thousand quintals)	—	1,536·0	3,549·0
Milk (mill. quintals)	1·2	6·9	16·2
Wool (thousand quintals)	20·0	125·0	201·0

In 1938 the average size of a grain-growing State farm was 23,400 ha., that of a dairy and meat-producing farm 28,600 ha., and that of a State farm raising sheep 108,500 ha.

* Cf. the Sovnarkom S.S.S.R. regulations regarding the liquidation of State farms or the transfer of some of their land to collective farms, in different districts; dated 10 February, 12 and 13 March, 14 and 20 July and 14 October 1936 and 27 and 28 February 1937 and published in the leading Soviet newspapers on the corresponding dates.

In 1938 State farms fell into the following categories, according to the nature of their farming:

	No.	% of total
State farms growing grain (including those growing seed)	471	11·7
State farms growing sugar beet	180	4·5
State farms growing special crops (tea, tobacco, rubber-bearing plants, etc.)	100	2·5
State farms growing potatoes, chicory and hops	77	1·9
State farms growing fibrous plants	63	1·6
State farms growing fruit and grapes	407	10·2
State farms breeding horses	119	3·0
State farms breeding cattle	755	18·9
State farms breeding pigs	650	16·3
State farms breeding sheep	200	5·0
State farms breeding reindeer and fur animals	39	1·0
State farms breeding poultry	95	2·4
Suburban and miscellaneous State farms	836	21·0
Total	3,992	100·0

An analysis of data regarding the expenditure, yields and production costs of State farms shows a marked improvement in their work in the later pre-war years.* Many achieved high profits and used model methods of farming. However, as late as 1939 some State farms still worked at a loss and their standards of farming were none too high. In 1940 the Government decision 'on measures for improving the work of State farms of the P. Commissariat of State Farms'† drafted a number of changes in the structure of the central administrative machinery of the P. Commissariats administering State farms, and covering the field of State farm expenditure, their deliveries of produce to the State and the system of paying managerial workers and specialists. Bonuses were awarded to managerial workers and specialists for fulfilling plans aimed at reducing cost price, and bonuses were introduced for workers who achieved the highest work indices. These current reorganizations, like the reorganization measures referred to in connexion with collective farms, were only current adjustments designed to improve the organization of State farm production and involved no change of principles. In the latter years, State farms like collective farms were established on a firm foundation and were gradually improving their standards of farming.

* Extensive and informative materials on State farms are to be found in *Planned Economy*, 1939, no. 11 and 1940, no. 12.

† Regulation of the Sovnarkom S.S.S.R. and the Party Central Committee, dated 17 March 1940.

CHAPTER XVIII. LABOUR

It has already been pointed out in surveying the development of industrial administration and production that the abolition of rationing compelled attention to the problems of improving the quality of industrial work, of giving up subsidies from the State Budget, and of revising the system of price fixing, etc. It became necessary also to achieve a drastic improvement in quality and organization in other branches of the national economy—in agriculture, transport, trade and in labour. Generally speaking, organization depends on the man, on his qualifications, and even more so on his psychology. The abolition of rationing was not only an economic, but also a social and psychological event of the greatest significance. For the mass of the people the abolition of rationing meant that the period of restrictions on the use of money was over, and there was a growing confidence in better supply, in improved cultural and living conditions, in the possibility, through personal efforts, not only of contributing to the growth of the country's productive capacity and prospects, but also in the direct and immediate possibility, through personal endeavour and by increased earnings, of improving one's own standard of living. These hopes were confirmed by the evidence of economic progress—the complete change in the development of agriculture since 1933, the expanding production and improved quality of mass-consumption goods, the very possibility of abolishing rationing, and the new wages policy. They were strengthened by the social and psychological results of the adoption of the collective farms' statutes of 1935 which placed land tenure on a stable basis, of the decision taken in February 1935 to draw up a new constitution for the U.S.S.R., of the Party's endeavours to train and promote new cadres, and of Stalin's slogan 'Cadres decide everything'; all these occurred before or in the months immediately following the abolition of rationing.

These economic, social and psychological factors lay at the root of the Stakhanov movement which made its appearance in 1935 and of the allied phenomena, such as the growth of labour productivity, further differentiation in the wages scales and improvement in the quality of work of industrial enterprises, transport, agriculture, and supply.

On 5 May 1935 Stalin had put forward the famous slogan: 'Cadres decide everything'. A few days later, on 15 May, at a conference of managerial workers and of the engineering and technical personnel of the U.S.S.R. P. Commissariat of Heavy Industry, the P. Commissar, Ordzhonikidze (a member of the Polit-Bureau and at the time one of the most influential members of the Party), demanded an improvement in the technical standards of output, an extension of the use of differential piece-rates, and also a revision of standards of utilization of enterprises' productive capacities. Stalin's statement, and these demands for a revision of standards and a new approach to the organization of productive processes, aiming at a greater increase in labour productivity, began to be widely discussed at production conferences and in the press. On 30 August, in the presence of the pit manager, of a representative of the Party and of the editor of the local paper, Stakhanov hewed out (in 6 hours) his record output of 102 tons of coal, thus earning 225 roubles for the shift, i.e. more than a coal-miner's average monthly wage. The essence of Stakhanov's achievement was a fresh analysis of the whole process of hewing coal, on the basis of which he introduced a new division of labour, separating principal from accessory operations. He also improved the use of the hewing hammer and adapted his methods to the peculiar nature of the coal seams. Stakhanov's results and the essence of his method received wide publicity in the press; they were discussed at production conferences, and aroused keen interest among Party and trade-union organizations, as well as among managements of enterprises and institutions. His experiment found numerous imitators not only in his own field, coal-mining, where his record was soon surpassed by other highly skilled and enterprising workers, but also in other branches of the national economy where his example awoke the creative initiative of many gifted and inventive workers. At the time, the press was full of news about the achievements of individual workers in various branches of industry, transport, agriculture, etc. The main contribution made by Stakhanov workers lay in the clearly per-ceived distinction between the basic process and the accessory and complementary operations; this allowed them to release the highly skilled worker from the necessity of performing functions which could be carried out by less skilled men. Moreover, the Stakhanov workers contrived to save time in the execution of definite produc-tion operations, either by changing the sequence of individual pro-duction processes, or by adapting the workers' motions to fit in more exactly with the movements of the machine, or by reducing the number of the worker's motions, or by more rationally arranging his working place, or his tools, auxiliary materials and finished articles, or by a change in the manner of supervising the work of individual lathes. To put it briefly, the records of Stakhanov workers were not due to any increased physical effort, but to a thorough understanding of a production process by experienced, highly skilled, imaginative and enterprising workers. It is characteristic of all Stakhanov achievements that they changed the old method of carrying out some definite production process, and, by a new approach to the division of labour and the utilization of working time, sharply raised the production results per unit of labour and time employed. Herein lies the essential difference between the Stakhanov movement and the older forms of socialist emulation, between a Stakhanov and a shock worker. The shock worker fulfilled and exceeded the old standard requirement, based on the old method of organizing the labour process, solely by bringing more zeal to the execution of his work and more personal effort. The course of the labour process and the relations between various stages of the production process remained, however, unaltered, whereas the Stakhanov worker revolutionized the old standards of output by rationalizing the production process. It can, indeed, be said that Stakhanov workers were pioneers and inventors in their own sphere. They could only arise from among those highly skilled workers who had been trained in special schools during the years of the first and second F.Y.P.s and had attained a high level of practical experience in their own trade.

The Stakhanov workers were initiating from below a revision of norms of output and of productive possibilities similar to that demanded from managerial and engineering and technical personnel by orders from above (cf. Ordzonikidze's demands above, p. 336). The managements of enterprises received instructions to encourage Stakhanovite experiments in every way,* to study results and to

---

* The following account graphically illustrates the manner in which managements staged some of the Stakhanov workers' records. At the conference of managerial workers of the P. Commissariat of Heavy Industry, the manager of one of the Coal Trusts made the following statement: 'When we organized shifts of Stakhanov workers—I am giving away the secret of success—members of the management, who were hurrying conveyor drivers, tram drivers and supervising the traffic, were stationed on the whole sector from the pillar to the working face.' The P. Commissar of Heavy Industry: 'Never mind. That can do no harm.' The Trust manager: 'Of course that can do no harm, and it does me no harm to be present at the larger pits at the time, and I have been to many pits, but it can hardly be expected that the pit manager should stand there throughout the shift.' The P. Commissar: 'So long as you have not trained the men, you'll have to stand. When they've been trained, they'll work on their own, but up to then you'll have to stand.' *Za Industr.* 16 January 1936.

introduce new standards of output based on these experiments; concurrently they were also to expand the use of differential piece-rates. Two months after the setting up of their first records, the Stakhanov workers held an All-Union conference; and, as early as December 1936, the Plenum of the Party Central Committee issued a regulation ordering the industrial commissariats and the P. Commissariat of Labour

to finish the revision of technical norms of equipment and of productive capacities in the course of 1936 in order to raise them.... The norms are to be established on the basis of the best Stakhanov workers' experience ...and discussed at branch conferences composed of the directors of works and enterprises, workshop stewards, engineers, foremen and Stakhanov workers.... In heavy industry the categories of workers required to take up the training for the compulsory technical minimum are to be extended with the aim of making, within the 3–4 coming years, the training compulsory for all workers in heavy industry* and the syllabus of the technical minimum is to be revised in the light of the new possibilities and problems of heavy industry...special courses of masters of socialist labour are to be organized for outstanding and Stakhanov workers without taking them away from production, and Stakhanov workers achieving a high labour productivity are to be admitted to these courses.

Similar demands to introduce compulsory training for all workers were made to the P. Commissariats of Light and Food Industries; moreover, in these industries training for the technical minimum was to be completed by all workers in the course of 1936 and 1937.†

These demands began to be met on a wide scale. The revision of standards of output in the sense of substantially increasing them was inaugurated in 1936, revision being based on rationalizations devised by individual gifted workers in the performance of their work. These increased standards were, of course, fixed much below the record norms achieved by individual Stakhanovite pioneers. Unfortunately, the Soviet economic press never published full statistical data of the scale of the increases, but judging from information available for individual industries, standards of output were raised by anything from 15 to 50 %. In the course of this revision, cases unavoidably occurred apparently where the introduction of new norms was formal and no corresponding and adequate adjustments in organization and technical conditions had

* Up to the time of the regulation the training for the technical minimum was compulsory only in the case of the 255 leading skilled trades in the heavy industry.

† For details see *The C.P. in Resolutions...*, pp. 627–35.

been made, with the result that workers found themselves incapable of fulfilling them and lost on their wages.* But on the whole, despite the difficulties of the transition period, the new standards began to be attained by the majority of skilled workers, and this led to the considerable expansion of industrial output and to the increase in labour productivity which marked 1936.

In connexion with the introduction of new standards, the method of paying labour according to a system of differential piece-rates became more widespread. By the end of the second F.Y.P. three-quarters of all industrial work was paid on a piece-work basis, and about one-third according to a progressive scale. Engineering and technical personnel, employees in trade, transport and other branches of the national economy were paid according to a progressive-premium system; that is, apart from their basic monthly salary they received bonuses in rising progression for exceeding planned tasks judged by both quantitative and qualitative indices. As for shop employees, they were entitled to bonuses for exceeding the plan for the sale of current consumer goods and for increasing the trading enterprise's monthly turn-over.†

Nevertheless, Soviet writers on labour questions point out that up to 1939 the fixing of wages continued to suffer from many defects. 'The fundamental evil in the system of pay in force during the two latter years of the second F.Y.P. was the superposition of an enormous number of various wage scales and rates resulting in confusion.' 'The crudest mistake in fixing wages lay in the multiplicity of bonus systems and in their arbitrariness.' 'The enforcement of equal pay for foremen, and engineering and technical workers occasionally resulted in some skilled workers earning more than engineers and foremen.' Abuses also arose from wrongly established relationships between time-work and piece-work; the wage of the time-worker was in fact often far below the basic rate

* 'The new norms have not been adequately propped up by the necessary organizational and technical measures. As, however, the norms had been revised, and labour productivity did not increase correspondingly, the result has been a reduction in wages. As a reaction there has been a drop in labour productivity and labour has been leaking away from the Donbass.' 'To-day the main difficulty is the failure to train collectives in Stakhanov methods of work. Hence, e.g. in the Donbass, high individual records and yet a low average standard of work in coal-mining as a whole....It is necessary, considering the new methods used by Stakhanov workers, to introduce changes into the technological processes and the organization of production, and also to train every worker in these new methods.' *Za Industr.* 30 June 1936. *Pravda*, 20 June 1936.

† For details see *Bull. Financ. and Econ. Leg.* 1936, nos. 12, 22–3, and 1939, nos. 19–20.

of the piece-worker, though the standard of skill required was similar; moreover, the piece-worker could increase his earnings, while the time-worker, because of the very nature of his work, had to be satisfied with the fixed wage established for the given type of work. As a result workers were loth to accept time-work, and sought transfer to work paid on a piece-work basis. In an attempt to retain man-power on works that could not be paid on a piece-work basis, managerial workers often resorted to all kinds of additional payments independent of the worker's results.

As a result of these shortcomings, managements often overspent the sums earmarked for wages by the plan, and

exceeded expenditure of State planned wages funds...but the wages funds in our country are a fundamental item in balancing State cash expenditure and the people's cash income; the circulation of the wages funds is a decisive fact determining the purchasing power of the urban and industrial population. In drafting the wages funds, the Soviet State takes into account the volume of the commodities' funds and the planned reduction in prices. In planning the cost of labour, the State takes into consideration the need to ensure a reduction of expenditure on wages per unit of articles manufactured. This must be achieved by the worker's output outstripping the planned rate of rise in wages, and therein lies the promise of any reduction in production costs.*

The planning of wages is one of the most important stages in the drafting of industry's financial and production plan. Annual plans for the development of industry always make provision for a rise in wages, labour productivity and in the general wages fund by specified percentages. Plans for savings banks, the total turn-over of home trade, revenue from the turn-over tax and from subscriptions to State loans and other financial-distributive plans for the national economy are made in connexion with the general wages fund.

The planning of wages and the degree of fulfilment of the plan are thus very important not only for achieving production tasks (for ensuring the flow of skilled labour into definite trades, for keeping an adequate balance between trades, raising labour productivity, etc.), but also for generally balancing production and consumption plans, within a definite time period, and from the point of view of both finance and distribution. In the years immediately preceding the war, problems of improving the system of wage fixing and of controlling the fulfilment of planned tasks for

* For further details regarding anomalies in the fixing of wages see B. L. Markus, *Labour in a Socialist Society*, Moscow, 1939, pp. 241–8; "Problems of Labour and Wages in the Engineering Industries", *Planned Economy*, 1939, no. 6.

the utilization of the wages fund, were a focal point in all discussions connected with labour. Between 1938 and 1940 wage scales were being revised with the purpose of giving first preference to wages in basic industries (coal, oil, heavy metallurgy), and of further differentiating pay for more and less skilled types of work. However, the revision aimed also at a greater uniformity of scales and the elimination of multiple and fractionary rates. In 1940 special 'wages commissions of the factory, works and local committees' were set up for the purpose of 'drawing the active membership of trade-union members to participate in solving problems of wages and of labour organization'. Commissions were formed of Stakhanov and exemplary workers, engineers, technicians and employees, numbering 3–21 members. Their duty was to organize socialist emulation and to discuss means of mastering production technique and of improving the quality of production; to organize schools for spreading Stakhanov methods; to study the application of the wage system in force at the enterprise or institution, and its influence on labour productivity; to consider the workers' and employees' representations regarding anomalies either in the amounts or irregularities in the payment of wages; to introduce proposals for adjusting wages, to be discussed at the factory or local committee; systematically to examine wages in various trades; to organize and carry out factory or workshop production meetings; to foster in every way the creative initiative of inventors and to organize, jointly with the administration, technical help for inventors and rationalizers.* 'In the case of the administration refusing to carry out in practice proposals made by the commission the case is to be transferred for discussion to the factory (or work-

---

* Up to 1938 the duty of supporting inventors fell upon the factory councils of inventors and the Inventors' Societies. In 1938 their functions were taken over by central, provincial, regional, factory and local trade-union committees.

In order to assist inventors (to finance experiments, help work out and test projects technically and economically, etc.) and to award prizes for inventions, special funds for the promotion of inventions and rationalizations were set aside by enterprises. Awards to inventors range from 100 to 100,000 roubles (according to a precisely established scale) and reach even 200,000 roubles in the case of inventions which render certain imports unnecessary or open up possibilities of exporting new kinds of production.

Plans for utilizing the more important inventions are worked out by the U.S.S.R. P. Commissariat, and the check up of all inventions is carried out by the corresponding P. Commissariats and the U.S.S.R. State Planning Commission. For details see governmental regulations regarding inventions, *Coll. Laws of the U.S.S.R.* 1931, no. 52, § 338; ibid. 1936, no. 39, § 334; *J. Inventions Committee*, 1931, no. 10, and *Bull. A.U.C.C.T.U.* 1938, no. 5.

shop) committee for appropriate measures to be taken.' Unfortunately, sufficient material regarding the way in which commissions carried out their wide range of functions has not been published in the Soviet economic press, so that no generalized opinion can be formed.

In the years preceding the war, salaries of engineering and technical workers were also revised and increased, and so were the salaries of employees. Moreover, in 1938, personal salaries were introduced 'for specialists and practical workers of particular value to a given institution, enterprise or organization, promoted to managerial work and having shown outstanding initiative and knowledge of the job.... Personal salaries can be fixed up to one and a half times the usual amount for the particular post, but must not exceed certain limits.'†

In 1938 these limits were fixed at 1,400–2,000 roubles per month, according to the various branches of economic activity. The average monthly earning of workers and employees in the national economy as a whole was at the time 288·6 roubles.

The statistics shown in Tables 54 and 55 give a general idea of the growth of labour employed and of wages. Unfortunately, no detailed information regarding the distribution of workers and employees, and the average wages in individual branches of the national economy since 1937, is available to us. These figures show

Table 54

Nos. of workers and employees in the national economy as a whole millions*		Average yearly wage of workers and employees in the national economy as a whole roubles*
1928	11·6	703
1929	12·2	800
1930	14·5	936
1931	19·4	1,127
1932	22·9	1,427
1933	22·3	1,566
1934	23·7	1,858
1935	24·8	2,269
1936	25·8	2,776
1937	27·0	3,038
1938	27·8	3,467
1940	30·4	—
1942 (plan)	32·0	4,100

* *Socialist Construction in the U.S.S.R., Statistical Yearbook for* 1934, 1935, 1936 and 1939. The Chairman of the State Planning Commission, Voznessevsky's report on the development of the national economy of the U.S.S.R. in 1940 and on the plan for 1941. *The Third Five-Year Plan for the Development of the National Economy of the U.S.S.R.*

† For further details see *Coll. Regulations of the U.S.S.R.* 1938, no. 39, § 229.

Table 55

	1932	1937	1937 as % of 1932	1942 plan	1942 as % of 1937
Numbers of workers and employees*					
All branches of the national economy	22,943	26,989	117·6	32,000	118·6
Of which:					
Industry	8,000	10,112	126·4	11,899	117·7
Construction	2,835	2,023	71·4	1,829	90·4
Railways	1,297	1,512	116·6	1,700	112·4
Waterways	146	180	123·4	230	128·1
Other transport	599	1,092	182·5	1,735	158·9
Communications (post, telegraph and telephone)	224	375	167·2	500	128·0
Trade	1,411	1,994	141·3	2,500	125·4
Communal feeding	515	396	76·8	560	139·1
Banking	128	193	150·2	230	119·3
Education	1,351	2,303	170·5	2,900	125·9
Arts	85	122	144·4	165	135·2
Health services	647	1,118	172·7	1,600	143·2
State and social institutions	1,833	1,743	95·1	2,000	114·7
Housing and municipal services	394	754	191·1	920	122·1
Other branches of the national economy, excluding agriculture	342	246	72·2	195	79·3
Agriculture†	2,858	2,483	86·9	2,650	106·7
Timber industry (Forestry)	196	248	126·4	325	131·1
Average wages of workers and employees per annum (roubles)*					
All branches of the national economy	1,427	3,047	213·5	4,100	136·0
Of which:					
Industry	1,434	3,005	209·5	4,166	138·7
Construction	1,507	3,087	204·8	4,285	138·8
Railways	1,463	3,271	223·6	4,187	128·0
Waterways	1,384	3,397	245·4	4,070	119·8
Other transport	1,539	3,218	209·1	4,119	128·0
Communications	1,333	2,356	176·7	3,440	146·0
Trade	1,351	2,528	187·1	3,109	123·0
Communal feeding	1,059	2,045	193·1	2,761	135·0
Banking	1,834	3,425	186·8	4,020	117·4
Education	1,633	3,442	210·8	5,034	146·3
Arts	1,989	3,757	188·9	5,072	135·0
Health services	1,248	2,455	196·7	3,435	139·9
State and social institutions	1,941	3,937	202·8	4,500	114·3
Housing and municipal services	1,409	2,306	163·7	3,113	135·0
Other branches of the national economy, excluding agriculture	828	1,241	148·7	1,416	114·1
Agriculture†	866	2,121	244·9	2,863	135·0
Timber industry (Forestry)	916	1,920	209·5	2,250	117·2

* *Results of the Fulfilment of the Second Five-Year Plan for the Development of the National Economy of the U.S.S.R.* pp. 104–6. *Socialist Construction of the U.S.S.R.* (1933–8), p. 138. *The Third Five-Year Plan*, pp. 199–200.

† Only workers and employees receiving wages are included in the figures for agriculture, i.e. only workers and employees hired by State and collective farms.

Table 55 *(cont.)*

	1932	1937	1937 as % of 1932	1942 plan	1942 as % of 1937
General workers' and employees' wages fund* (million roubles)					
All branches of the national economy	32,738	82,247	251·2	133,240	162·0
Of which:					
Industry	11,475	30,385	264·8	49,566	163·0
Construction	4,273	6,245	146·2	7,837	125·5
Railways	1,897	4,946	260·8	7,117	143·9
Waterways	201	610	302·7	936	153·4
Other transport	921	3,515	381·6	7,146	203·3
Communications	299	884	295·6	1,720	194·6
Trade	1,906	5,041	264·5	7,772	157·2
Communal feeding	546	809	148·2	1,519	187·8
Banking	240	660	275·1	925	140·2
Education	2,806	7,927	282·5	14,600	184·2
Arts	168	458	272·6	837	182·8
Health services	819	2,744	334·9	5,496	200·3
State and social institutions	3,560	6,864	192·8	9,200	134·0
Housing and municipal services	556	1,738	312·6	2,864	164·8
Other branches of the national economy, excluding agriculture	283	303	107·1	276	91·1
Agriculture†	2,474	5,267	212·9	7,587	144·0
Timber industry (Forestry)	180	476	264·8	731	153·6

See notes on previous page.

that throughout the years 1928–40, the amount of labour employed in the national economy increased annually. In particular, during the first F.Y.P. the intake of new workers was *huge*, and numbers practically doubled in the course of the five years. Under the second F.Y.P. the growth in labour employed proceeded at a more regular pace. Whereas during the first five-year period the increase in labour employed far exceeded the planned figures (the original F.Y.P. made provision for employing 15,764,000 workers and employees by 1932–3), during the second five-year period, on the contrary, the actual figures of workers and employees employed by 1937 fell short of the planned figure (according to the second F.Y.P., 29,641,000 workers and employees should have been employed in the national economy by 1937). Moreover, whereas during the first five-year period the rate of yearly increase of labour employed outstripped the rate of yearly increases in labour productivity, on the contrary, during the second five-year period labour productivity grew faster than the labour employed. For instance, in industry as a whole, the yearly increases in labour productivity were: in 1933 8·2 %, in 1934 13 %, in 1935 13 %, in 1936 21·4 % and in 1937 8·9 %. In 1937 the output per worker in heavy industry in roubles (at 1926–7 prices) was 209·3 % of what it was in 1932, instead of 162·7 % as foreseen by the second F.Y.P.; in construction the corresponding increase was 183·0 % as against the planned 175 %, in railway transport 147·9 % as against 143 %.*

The target of the third F.Y.P. for increasing labour productivity was below the actual increase achieved under the second F.Y.P., i.e. 65 % as against 82 % achieved during the latter period. In the years covered by the third F.Y.P. and up to the outbreak of war (1938–40), labour productivity continued to grow, and in large-scale industry was 38 % above its 1937 level.

The workers' and employees' average yearly wages were also rising from year to year. Discrepancies between the planned expenditure of both the first and the second Plans and the actual sums expended were very considerable. The average yearly wage in the national economy as a whole was to be 994 roubles by 1932–3, and the total wages fund 15,677 million roubles. Actually in 1932 the average wage was 1,427 roubles and the wages fund 32,738 million roubles. Similarly, under the second F.Y.P. the actual average wage in 1937 reached 3,047 roubles instead of the planned 1,755 roubles and the wages fund 82,247 as against the planned 51,808 million roubles. The processes already described on the home market had made it necessary drastically to alter the initial plans regarding wages.

The draft third F.Y.P. made provision for increases of labour employed in all branches of the national economy, excepting construction and some industries of secondary importance (cf. Table 55). Provision was also made for raising wages. The rises, however, expressed in absolute figures, were planned far below the actual rise in wages which had taken place during the second five-year period. However, if it is borne in mind that the rise in wages during the second F.Y.P. was to a large extent offset by the rising cost of living, whereas during the third five-year period it was planned to reduce prices for all basic foodstuffs and mass-consumption goods, it will appear that the proposed 36 % rise in the workers' and employees' wages between 1937 and 1942, for the national economy as a whole, represents in fact a much greater actual rise than appears from the nominal rise in the average wage.

* *The Development of the Soviet Economy*, edited by Prof. A. A. Aratiunian and B. L. Markus, Moscow, 1940, p. 484. *Results of the Fulfilment of the Second Five-Year Plan of the National Economy of the U.S.S.R.*, Moscow, 1939, p. 73. *Draft of the Second Five-Year Plan...*, vol. I, p. 418.

Space does not permit a discussion of the extent to which the wage-earners' actual standard of living altered in the course of the five-year periods, which would require a detailed analysis of the tremendous changes wrought in the general conditions—social and material—of the population's existence. The simple device of converting nominal—money—wages into real wages by means of a price index is out of the question, for no such price index is available. Moreover, even had such an index been available it would lead only to misleading results because of the enormous social and material changes which have marked the life of workers and employees in the course of the F.Y.P.s. Not only socialized expenditure on wage-earners (social insurance, expenditure on health services, education, housing, cultural and welfare improvements, etc.) would have to be taken into account as additions to wages, but notice would also have to be taken of such factors as the absence of unemployment, and the number of members in a family either in permanent employment or studying at the expense of the State, in institutions where education was free up to 1940 and students were in receipt of maintenance grants.

The very large number of women employed in all the branches of the national economy makes it obvious that the real standard of living of a worker's family in the U.S.S.R. depends on the earnings of several members of the family, and that, therefore, changes in the index of real wages cannot possibly be taken as a measure of the standards of living of a working family. Table 56 graphically illustrates the tremendous changes in the social and cultural life of workers and employees during the 10 years covered by the first and second F.Y.P.'s.

When radical changes alter the social and cultural conditions of life of great masses of the population, a simple index of real wages loses any significance as an objective measure of changes in the wage-earners' standard of living.

Table 56

*Numbers of pupils**

	1928–9	1932–3	1938–9
In elementary and secondary schools (thousands)	12,068	21,398	31,517
In universities and higher technical schools (thousands)	177	504	603

* See footnote on following page.

Table 56 (cont.)

Students in receipt of scholarships and maintenance grants, as a percentage of the total number of students*

	1933	1939
In universities and higher technical schools	50·3	90·6
In technical and other secondary schools for the training of cadres	59·8	85·8

Capital expenditure on municipal services in towns (in million roubles of the corresponding year)*

	Up to 1928	During the first F.Y.P.	During the second F.Y.P.
Total	620	1,961	6,488

Numbers of insured accommodated at the expense of the social insurance fund in sanatoria and rest homes*

	1928–9	1933	1937
In sanatoria (thousands)	80·7	176·2	495·8
In rest homes	466·8	973·9	1,750·3

Libraries, clubs, theatres, cinemas and health services*

	1929	1933	1939
Public libraries (thousands)	28·9	32·9	77·6
No. of books in public libraries (millions)	72·2	91·3	146·7
Clubs (thousands)	34·5	53·2	103·7
Theatres	153	551	787
Cinemas (thousands)	9·7	27·6	30·9
Hospital beds (thousands)	247	411	672
Doctors (thousands)	63·2	76·0	110·0
Beds in maternity homes and in maternity wards of hospitals (thousands)	26·9	42·7	131·1
Places in permanent nurseries (thousands)	62·0	600·9	748·2

Expenditure of State, collective farms, and public organizations, on social and cultural welfare per capita of population*

	1932	1937
Total expenditure (in roubles)	61·73	232·74

* *Socialist Construction in the U.S.S.R.* (1933–8), pp. 116, 124, 127, 128, 133, 135, 139 and 140. *Problems of Economics*, no. 3, 1939, p. 20.

Table 56 (cont.)

Number of women (workers and employees, in thousands)*

	1929	1932	1937	1937, % of women among workers of both sexes
In national economy as a whole	3,304	6,007	9,357	35·4
Of which:				
Large-scale industry	939	2,043	3,298	39·8
Construction	64	380	488	20·6
Transport	104	243	477	18·3
Trade ⎱	134	675	640	34·0
Communal feeding ⎰			236	62·2
Education ⎱	961	1,593	1,252	56·6
Health			725	72·4
State and public institutions ⎰			580	31·0
Agriculture	441	394	545	25·7

It is characteristic of the U.S.S.R. labour regime that, on the one hand, social incentives are fostered to encourage production and contributions to civilized life (e.g. socialist emulation, honours such as that of 'Hero of Socialist Toil' or 'Distinguished scientific, or arts worker', etc.), while, on the other hand, administrative and judicial measures are used to enforce labour discipline, regulate the distribution of labour, improve skill, etc. During the pre-war years many measures were taken in both directions. Here are some of the more important:

On 27 December 1938 new awards and decorations were introduced for those who particularly distinguished themselves in the field of labour. The title of 'Hero of Socialist Toil' became the highest reward, which, being 'the highest degree of distinction in the field of economic and cultural construction is awarded to persons who, by their outstanding pioneer activity in the field of industry, agriculture, transport, trade, scientific discoveries and technical inventions, have rendered particular services to the State, contributed to the rise of the national economy, culture, science and to the growth of the might and glory of the U.S.S.R.' The title carries with it the award of the Order of Lenin, the U.S.S.R.'s highest decoration, and entitles its holder to a number of material advantages and privileges. The medal 'For Prowess in Labour', like the title of 'Hero of Socialist Toil', is awarded for business and cultural achievements to workers, employees, engineering, technical and managerial workers who, because of 'their self-sacrificing labour·activity are the front-line fighters in socialist construction,

* *Problems of Economics*, no. 7, 1940, p. 112.

setting the example of a Stakhanov-like utilization of technique and achieving high standards of labour productivity, thus contributing to the advancement of science, technique and culture'. The medal carries with it also some minor material advantages. The medal 'For Distinguished Labour' is awarded to the same categories of workers in the same fields 'for outstanding exemplary work, high production standards and services rendered to the development of science, technique and culture'. This latter award also carries some small material advantages. In 1939–41 the Soviet press published the names of hundreds of workers in the national economy and in cultural walks of life to whom the title of 'Hero of Socialist Toil' had been awarded and the names of thousands of others who had received medals. In 1939 the so-called 'Stalin Prizes' to the value of 100,000, 50,000 and 20,000 roubles each were first awarded for outstanding material and cultural achievements.

It should be stressed here that all these rewards, both moral and material, were made for personal efforts and achievements, and did not depend on the type of work or its field of application; they were related to the *person*, not to the *nature of the job*. The underlying principle in remunerating labour was to differentiate between work varying in qualifications, responsibility, difficulty, effort, but not to differentiate it according to 'social' differences, such as the difference between physical and intellectual work, or work of a 'higher' or 'lower' category. It is significant that under the third F.Y.P., it was proposed to increase the average pay of workers more than that of engineers or technicians, and particularly more than that of employees. The discrepancies between the average pay of these categories were to be reduced (see Table 57).

Table 57. *Average wages in industry (in roubles)**

	1937	1942	1942 as % of 1937
Workers	2,820	4,050	144·0
Engineers and technicians	6,533	8,360	128·0
Employees	3,471	4,000	115·2

Whereas in 1937 the employees' average wages were 123% of the workers' wages, by 1942 the latter were to exceed the former, whilst the difference in pay between workers on the one hand and engineers and technicians on the other was to be reduced from 231% in 1937 to 206% in 1942. As a consequence, an average

* *The Third Five-Year Plan for the Development of the National Economy of the U.S.S.R.* (1938, 1942), p. 200.

employee, e.g. in a banking establishment, would earn in 1942 less than the average worker, and even an average employee in a State or public institution (the highest paid branches of clerical work) would earn in 1942 only 11 % more than an industrial worker.

Moreover, in the pre-war years, the Stakhanov movement was becoming a real mass movement, with the result that the difference in the earnings of a Stakhanov and an average worker doing the same kind of job was tending to decrease. Already by 1938 the proportion of Stakhanov workers in various branches of industry had grown to 41·4% of all industrial workers employed.* Evidently in this case the designation of Stakhanov workers is no longer applied to pioneers of new methods, but simply to workers achieving a high labour productivity and attaining the new high standards of output by using the principal innovations introduced into the corresponding production processes by Stakhanov pioneers.

In 1939 and 1940 a new trend in the Stakhanov movement made its appearance and became known as 'multi-lathes working' and 'plurality of trades'; this meant that one worker not only learned and was able to serve several lathes but knew also several trades; the aim of the movement was to increase labour productivity and enable one worker to change over from one kind of work to another.† Recurrent campaigns for socialist emulation were perseveringly carried out in those pre-war years with satisfactory results in expansion of production and improvement in quality.

Besides these social and psychological incentives, many other measures of administrative and judicial character were also adopted in the course of the latter years to enforce labour discipline and to regulate the distribution of labour. A regulation of the Sovnarkom S.S.S.R. dated 20 December 1938 decreed that henceforth workers and employees in all State and co-operative enterprises and institutions should be issued with Labour books, for recording the following items: 'Trade and information about work, transfer from one enterprise to another, reasons for the transfer, and also any praise or distinctions awarded.' Contraventions were not to be recorded in the Labour book. The purpose of this enactment was to exercise a stricter control over labour drifting from enterprise to enterprise. On 28 December 1938 the very important regulation of the Sovnarkom S.S.S.R. 'On measures to regulate labour discipline, improve the practice of State social insurance and to combat abuses in those matters' came into force. The regulation decreed that, 'a worker or employee who clocked in late

* *The Development of the Soviet Economy*, edited by Prof. A. A. Aratiunian, p. 496.
† For further details see *Problems of Economics*, nos. 2 and 7, 1940.

without sufficient reasons, or who left early for lunch, or returned late from lunch, or left the enterprise or institution early, or loafed in working time, was to be subjected to an administrative measure: censure or reprimand, or reprimand with caution of dismissal, or transfer to another less well paid work for a length of time up to 3 months or to a lower post...those guilty of three such infringements in the course of one month or of four in the course of two consecutive months to be dismissed for absenteeism'. Managers of enterprises and institutions were responsible to higher authorities for carrying out these measures and were liable to dismissal or trial for neglecting to carry them out. Workers and employees leaving of their own accord were to give a month's notice to the administration. In the case of a worker or employee dismissed on inadequate grounds, the pay for this involuntary absenteeism was to equal the average wage, but was payable for not more than 20 days; the management of the enterprise or institution, the factory committees and the wage-dispute commissions were to consider complaints of unjustified dismissal within 3 days, and judicial authorities within 5 days. The same regulation altered also the manner of granting disability allowances, leaves, accommodation in rest homes, pensions to old age and labour invalids, as well as maternity leaves to women, etc. Henceforth these benefits were made to depend on the length of employment at the enterprise or institution.* Workers and employees dismissed for absenteeism could not be re-engaged by the same enterprise or institution for the next 3 months. They could, however, immediately take up employment in any other enterprise or institution, but lost continuity of employment and were considered as entering employment for the first time, thus foregoing the rights and benefits acquired during previous employment.

On 27 June 1940 the Praesidium of the U.S.S.R. Supreme Soviet issued a decree 'On the change over to the 8-hour working day, the 7-day working week, and the prohibition to workers and employees of leaving enterprises and institutions without authorization'. The law introduced the 8-hour working day in enterprises previously working a 7-hour day and a 7-hour day in jobs where a 6-hour day had so far been the rule. All State, co-operative and public enterprises and institutions changed over from a 6-day week to a 7-day week, and Sunday became a common rest day. Workers and employees were forbidden to leave their enterprises and institutions and to transfer themselves elsewhere. Transfers could only be effected with the management's consent and were restricted to

* For further details see *Coll. Regulations of the U.S.S.R.*, 1939, no. 1, § 1.

certain cases specified by the law. To leave an enterprise un-
authorized was made an offence punishable, upon conviction by
a people's court, by 2–4 months' imprisonment; absenteeism was
punishable no longer by dismissal as laid down in the above-quoted
law of 1938, but by compulsory labour at the place of employment
for up to 6 months with a deduction of 25 % in wages.

However, this law, as well as other measures regarding the transfer of engineers, technicians, foremen, employees and skilled workers
from certain enterprises to others, and further restrictions on the
freedom of movements and penalties for breaches of labour discipline are already verging on war-time legislation and are not
the result of the normal evolution of the labour system. The
A.U.C.C.T.U. appeal commenting upon the introduction of this
labour law of 1940 stressed that its introduction was necessitated
because 'for our country there is a growing danger of war, the
international setting is pregnant with unpredictable events...to
strengthen further the defensive power of their country the working
class must face up to the necessary sacrifices'.

Other measures in the field of labour, carried out in the last
pre-war years, were designed to improve in practice the distribution of new cadres of specialists and the enrolment of unskilled
man-power, as well as to intensify the training of workers, particularly for industry and transport.

In 1938 the former practice of the universities of directing
students upon graduation to various jobs was abolished, and it was
established instead that the distribution of young graduates was to
be personally approved by the P. Commissar of the corresponding
branch of the national economy, who appointed each student to
definite work, at a definite place, stating the nature of the post and
the salary attached to it. Six months before students took their
Finals or presented their degree dissertations, the P. Commissariats were to interview them personally and to plan their
appointments. It also became the P. Commissariats' duty to 'keep
a personal register of all specialists with higher education and to
make arrangements enabling the P. Commissariat to follow any
transfers of these specialists to other work'.*

* The Party Central Committee's and the Sovnarkom S.S.S.R. regulation
(*Pravda*, 6 March 1938). Already since 1933 all students graduating from a
university or technicum had to work for 5 years at a definite point on production
fixed by the P. Commissariat to which the corresponding technicum or university was subordinate. To refuse accepting the appointment and making
personal arrangements for another job was regarded as an infringement of the
contract with the State and came within the jurisdiction of criminal courts.

This regulation reflects the fact that, in spite of the huge efforts made under the first and second F.Y.P.s to train specialists with higher and secondary education, the shortage in specialists continued to be acutely felt. Table 58 graphically illustrates the scale on which specialists had been trained under the first and second F.Y.P.s.

Table 58. *Specialists trained (thousands)**

	Universities	Technicums and special secondary schools for the training cadres
Total for 10 years (1928–37) Of which:	568·6	942·8
During the first five-year period (1928–32)	170·0	291·2
During the second five-year period (1933–7)	369·9	623·0

Numbers of young specialists having graduated from technicums and universities (in thousands)*

	1933	1934	1935	1936	1937	1938
Total excluding military specialists Of which:	34·6	49·2	83·7	97·6	104·8	106·7
Engineers, for industry and construction	6·1	14·0	29·6	29·6	27·6	25·2
Engineers, for transport and communications	1·8	4·0	7·6	6·6	7·1	6·1
Veterinary surgeons and zootechnicians	4·8	6·3	8·8	10·4	11·3	10·6
Economists and lawyers	2·5	2·5	5·0	6·4	5·0	5·7
Teachers for secondary and workers' faculties, technicums, and other workers in education and arts	10·5	7·9	12·5	21·6	31·7	35·7
Doctors; dispensing chemists and physical training specialists	4·6	2·5	7·5	9·2	12·3	13·6
Miscellaneous specialists	4·3	11·1	12·7	14·2	9·9	9·8

As stated already, the recruitment of unskilled labour, mainly from the rural population, was regulated since 1931 by agreements concluded between business organizations and collective farms. In 1938 it was stated that 'disorganization occurs in the recruitment of man-power. The estimates of recruitable labour from among collective farmers is badly organized in districts and provinces, as well as in republics, and as a consequence the enrolment is based on out-of-date information.... On the other hand, as a result of bad organization in the recruitment of workers on the part of the P. Commissariats, cases frequently occur when tens and even

* *The Social Construction in the U.S.S.R.* (1933–8). *Statistical Data*, p. 124. *Problems of Economics*, no. 3, 1939, p. 20.

hundreds of representatives of economic organizations are sent to the same province and to the same district to recruit workers. This leads to speculation in labour recruitment and gives rise to unhealthy competition between different organizations'. With the new regulation the control of labour recruitment was to be carried out by permanent commissions of the U.S.S.R. Economic Council and of republican Sovnarkoms in provinces, regions and districts.* From 1939 it became customary for every province to be attached to one P. Commissariat which, through a special recruiting official, had the right to enrol the man-power it required. Labour agreements were to specify the obligations undertaken by the economic organizations to help move the worker's family; and they were also to organize training courses to raise the skill of recruited workers. Throughout 1939–40 this problem of recruiting unskilled labour was much discussed in the Soviet economic press.†

The measures for training labour have already been described. During the years covered by the first and second F.Y.P.s the number of workers trained in all branches of the national economy was 5,952,000. Nevertheless, the shortage of skilled workers continued to be acutely felt, in particular in industry and transport, and as a consequence of this it was decided to create 'State Labour Reserves'. On 2 October 1940 a Government decree 'On State Labour Reserves' was published. This decree ordered that in special schools from 800,000 to 1,000,000 youths drawn from towns and collective farms should be yearly trained for skilled work in industry and transport. The P. Commissariat of the U.S.S.R. was authorized to conscript—should voluntary enlistment not meet requirements—all youths aged 14–15 years for training in the so-called 'Artisan and Transport Schools', and youths aged 16–17 for training in Industrial Schools. The training of the young people aged 14–15 was to last 2 years, and that of those aged 16–17 years for 6 months. During the training, all expenses, including maintenance, were paid by the Government. At the same time a Government decision introduced tuition fees in the upper forms of secondary schools and in the universities, where education had so far been free. From 1 September 1940 comparatively high fees (150–200 roubles per annum in secondary schools and 300–500

* For further details see *Coll. Regulations of the U.S.S.R.* 1938, no. 39, § 229.
† Cf. the very interesting articles on the sources of man-power supply in the U.S.S.R., the organization of its recruitment and a draft of the current man-power balance. *Problems of Economics*, no. 6, 1939. *Planned Economy*, nos. 9 and 11, 1939.

roubles in universities and higher technical schools) were introduced for tuition in the three senior forms of secondary schools, in
universities and higher technical schools. This measure was designed to make it somewhat more difficult to receive secondary and
higher education and to divert some of the school population towards Artisan, Transport and Industrial Schools. It was expected,
as a result of this measure, that even by 1941, 794,000 skilled
young workers would enter industry from these newly organized
schools.

In the years immediately preceding the war, the Soviet
Economic Press gave much prominence to discussions on defects
still persisting in the planning of wages and in methods of controlling the fulfilment of plans regarding wages. It was said that plans
regarding wages and the distribution of the wages fund continued
to be too general and not sufficiently detailed. The fund did not
fully cover the whole volume of wages paid out in all the branches
of the national economy. In drafting the distribution of the wages
fund sufficient details were not mapped out for every district, and
this made it difficult to plan home trade. The controls came into
action only when it became apparent that the wages fund was
being exceeded, and a stricter control of expenditure by banking
establishments was demanded.

However, all these measures to improve the planning of wages,
to organize more rationally the recruitment of unskilled labour, to
improve and expand the methods of training skilled workers, to
raise labour productivity, to distribute existing skilled workers and
specialists, etc., were only current technical adjustments to improve
the system in force, and did not involve any change in the principle
underlying the labour system which had been taking shape in those
pre-war years.

CONCLUSION

In summing up the results of the evolution in the field of labour
which has been going on in the U.S.S.R., it will be recognized that
some of the problems and difficulties were of a temporary kind and
due to the transition from the old system to the new, or to conditions peculiar to the development of the U.S.S.R. national
economy during the period now elapsed; whilst others were connected with fundamental difficulties in labour relations inherent in
a planned system of national economy.

One of the fundamental problems of the *transition* period was to
evolve a new relationship between the working masses and their

trade unions on the one hand, and the managerial and higher technical personnel on the other. Though these problems were more of a sociological than of an economic nature, they were problems, which, under one aspect or another, will have to be solved every time that the competitive system is being superseded by the system of planned economic organization of production and distribution. The problem of overcoming the psychological antagonism inherited from the competitive system, when the workers' interests, represented by their organizations, conflicted with those of the management and the higher technical personnel, loomed large among the difficulties confronting both the organization of the enterprise's management and the readjustment of labour relations. The masses took a long time to rid themselves of their psychological antagonism to representatives of the management and to authorities in general, and to overcome their resistance to administrative measures for raising labour productivity; conversely, many representatives of the former higher technical personnel found it very difficult to adapt themselves to the new ways of managing enterprises and to readjust their relations with trade unions and the working masses. This psychology of antagonism between workers' organizations and managements gradually died out, but only when a 'working class intelligentsia' drawn from among the working class itself and nurtured in the conditions of the Soviet system came into being, whilst, at the same time, various forms of social labour incentives were growing and expanding. Gradually, too, trade unions came to alter the aim of their activities and their ways of collaborating with managements of enterprises with the object of raising labour productivity, strengthening discipline and elaborating wage-fixing, etc. In this connexion, the evolution of the U.S.S.R. trade unionism is worthy of special study by any serious students of practical possibilities of transition from the competitive to the planned system of national economy.

The transition from the competitive to the planned system, in so far as it involves the nationalization of means of production, and completely alters former proprietary relations, unavoidably results in a change of occupation for many categories of workers (i.e. categories servicing and supplying the owner classes, manufacturing or trading in luxury articles, or occupied in the advertising, insurance, restaurant and tourist businesses, in jurisprudence, in some forms of banking, etc.); the transition also creates a special class of unemployed who have to learn new trades in order to be absorbed by other industries. Apart from the great upheaval wrought by the Revolution in its early years, by the civil war and the policy of

'War Communism', this was the main cause of the persistent unemployment which in the U.S.S.R. was overcome only by the
country's industrialization. The problem of unavoidable structural
changes in labour distribution which are bound to occur during
any transition from the competitive to the planned system of
national economy, involving the nationalization of means of production, calls for a serious study, because it turns on the distribution of labour between various occupations, a distribution peculiar
to every country. Unfortunately, so far, no detailed data on the
1939 census of the population have been published, and no general
analysis can be given of the structural changes in occupations. But
even scrappy and summary data show that in the period now
elapsed, very great changes have marked the population's occu-
pational make-up and have affected the sources of their means of
existence.*

Apart from these problems, due to the transition period and to
circumstances peculiar to the development of the U.S.S.R.
national economy during the period now elapsed (such as the hasty

* The following figures, though classified somewhat conventionally, are none
the less significant.

Class composition of the U.S.S.R.* (*in percentages*)

	1913	1928	1934	1937
Workers and employees	16·7	17·3	28·1	34·7
Collective farmers, craftsmen and artisans, members of co-operative associations	—	2·9	45·9	55·5
Individual peasants (excluding kulaks) and craftsmen and artisans non-members of co-operative associations	65·1	72·9	22·5	5·6
Bourgeois (landowners, wealthy and small urban bourgeoisie, shopkeepers and kulaks)	15·9	4·5	0·1	0·0
Others (students, pensioners, military, etc.)	2·3	2·4	3·4	4·2
Total	100·0	100·0	100·0	100·0

Numbers of people (*with families*) *according to the* 1939 *census**

	Millions	%
Workers in towns and rural areas	54·6	32·2
Employees in towns and rural areas	29·7	17·5
Collective farmers	75·6	44·6
Craftsmen, members of co-operative associations	3·9	2·3
Craftsmen, non-members of co-operative associations	1·4	0·8
Small holders	3·0	1·8
Non-labouring classes	0·06	0·04
Occupation, not stated	1·2	0·7
Total	169·5	100·0

* S. Sulkevich, *Territory and Population of the U.S.S.R.*, Moscow, 1940, pp. 14, 26.

intensive industrialization which necessitated the enrolment of un-skilled or poorly skilled labour, brought about an excessive labour turn-over, a temporary deterioration in labour discipline and labour productivity, and other temporary difficulties described by many foreign writers as unavoidable consequences of the Soviet system), the Soviet planning institutions had naturally to solve also problems of a more general character inherent in any planned system of national economy. The following were among the most important in the field of labour: problems of labour incentives, of labour discipline under conditions of full employment, of training skilled workers and specialists, and distributing them among indi-vidual branches of labour, and various problems connected with the technique of planning wages.

It has been shown how complicated was the solution of the problem of labour incentives. With the transition from 'War Communism' to N.E.P., compulsory labour service and equal pay in kind were on the whole replaced by the system of fixing wages inherited from pre-revolution times, though adapted to the changes which had altered the population's social composition. Pecuniary incentives and a differential system of wages were the fundamental regulators in distributing labour and rewarding effort. Social incentives to stimulate effort played but a minor part in the N.E.P. period. Measures designed to increase the im-portance of social incentives came really into their own only when planned economy began to be put into effect, that is with the introduction of the first F.Y.P. In spite of the existence of a dif-ferential system for supplying different categories of labour, the tendency for wage equalization persistently reappeared throughout the rationing period. An attempt was made to rely mainly on social incentives. However, experience showed that only excep-tionally can social incentives be effective *unless* they carry with them material advantages. Various kinds of *individual* endeavours stimu-lated by social motives—exemplary workers, 'Otlichniks', Sta-khanov workers—received not merely moral but also material rewards. The material reward gradually acquired more importance than when the first appeals to social motives had been made. If, for the average exemplary worker, the incentive to increase his endeavours during the enthusiastic drive for new construction was mainly an appeal to his public spirit—for the additional material rewards were too trifling to be the real driving motive—that can no longer be said of the average Stakhanov worker, for whom the expected material reward is a definite incentive. Similarly, whereas in the early days of social incentives, the achievements of outstanding specialists were rewarded by honours such as the title of 'Distinguished worker' in the corresponding field of work, or a decoration carrying with it very minor material advantages, in the latter pre-war years he could receive not only moral recognition but also a very considerable material award in the nature of a Stalin prize, or tax reliefs, pensions and other material advantages to which a decoration entitles its holder, to a far greater degree than before.

The importance of material advantages in addition to social incentives increased not only in the case of the individual, but also in the case of communal rewards, for outstanding achievements. If, previously, success in a socialist competition gained an enterprise mainly moral recognition, e.g. such as the 'model enterprise' challenge banner, in the later pre-war years the recognition was substantiated by considerable material advantages, e.g. money prizes from a special fund of competing enterprises to be expended on improving housing and welfare conditions, and also on paying out special cash prizes to some of the workers employed in the given enterprise.

It should nevertheless be emphasized that the material reward was *part* of and not a *substitute* for the social incentive. The Stakhanov worker received an additional award because he was a *Stakhanov worker*, i.e. an individual who has not only achieved definite material results in his work, but who also seeks to improve his work in order that others may profit by it, in order to stimulate others to work better and generally to raise labour productivity in a certain field. The recipient of the additional material reward must be either a pioneer or a member of a definite movement or of a group pursuing not personal aims but the public good. Purely selfish material motives were branded as grasping and self-seeking, and, if unmasked, closed any further possibilities of obtaining material advantages. A remarkable engineer, writer, artist, etc., can receive outstanding rewards if it is recognized by a competent jury that his work is useful to the community, but not because he is endowed with a certain acumen to utilize his abilities for personal material enrichment.

This fostering of social labour incentives and of social forms of group labour emulation is peculiar to labour relations in the U.S.S.R., and constitutes a new approach towards solving the problem of new labour incentives and stimuli to work. Experience has shown that under the planned system, when earthly goods are still scarce, it is as impossible to do away with material incentives as it is under the competitive system. It does not seem possible wholly to forego personal motives and material interests in order to raise labour productivity, to stimulate workers to improve their qualifications and in particular to interest managerial personnel in the qualitative side of their enterprise's work. It has been shown that differential piece rates came gradually to be widely applied, that special rewards were introduced for managerial workers (personal salaries, bonuses for achieving profits in excess of plan and for improving the quality of the enterprise's work), and that, generally speaking, wages became more and more dependent on the skill, intensity and responsibility of the work performed; yet, at the same time, great efforts were made to stimulate social labour motives and thus to counteract the use of material incentives, and to create a new psychological atmosphere in labour relations. Foreign students of the Soviet economic system, while emphasizing the use made in the U.S.S.R. of material incentives in the field of labour, have underrated the efforts to foster social labour incentives as well as their value and widespread application.

It is likely that under the planned system of national economy, as it develops and improves, and as the community's standard of living rises, the importance of social incentives will grow and replace purely material incentives. In so far as the planned system is bound up with the nationalization of means of production, with the ban on private undertakings using hired labour and the impossibility of any significant differentiation due to wealth among groups of population, work and particularly the work of managerial staffs will have to be stimulated by combining social with material incentives and not by relying exclusively on the latter. Though the U.S.S.R. experiment has so far been too short-lived to confirm beyond dispute that this is the way along which labour incentives are bound to develop under a planned system, it affords sufficient evidence for the need and possibility of using social labour incentives, and shows, moreover, that these are not limited to sporadic efforts of groups or to individual feats of a few 'saints', but are a persistent mass phenomenon. The history of labour relations and the development of the U.S.S.R. economy during the period now elapsed have given many mass examples of 'labour patriotism', and have shown that even in the economic sphere of human activity, motives other than material can be driving and creative forces, and that it is possible to mobilize social motives and the population's efforts and spirit of sacrifice for other aims than the destructive purpose of war.

The planned system, in so far as it presupposes full employment, cannot avoid a certain degree of compulsion and of administrative and material penalties to maintain labour discipline and combat irresponsibility and slackness among managerial staffs in the performance of their duty. In the absence of full employment, when an army of labour reserves is available, labour discipline is automatically enforced by the fear of losing one's job. Full employment may contribute in weakening labour discipline. The Soviet experience was that the abolition of unemployment led to a deterioration of labour discipline, such as excessive labour turn-over, rising absenteeism, late arrivals to work, idleness in working time, carelessly performed work, etc. To combat these consequences of full employment it proved necessary to resort to controlling the movement of labour by Labour books, the obligation to give a month's notice, etc., and to penalizing absenteeism, lateness and other infringements of labour discipline, by such measures as reprimands, transfer to less highly paid work, dismissal entailing the loss of benefits acquired during employment, etc.

Similarly, the planned system of national economy had to resort to administrative and judicial penalties in regard to managerial staffs when the harm done to the enterprise owing to their slackness and carelessness was not countered by their material responsibility.

Material and moral rewards can stimulate *creditable* labour endeavours, but to combat *undesirable* facts in the field of labour under conditions of full employment, material deterrents are not sufficient and they have to be supplemented by administrative and judicial penalties. In the case of wrongs to private property, modern society is not satisfied to demand restitution or amends for damage done (e.g. the return of a stolen article, or the defaulter's promise to honour his bill at a later date), but also inflicts penalties on the offenders. Similarly, a planned society will have to inflict penalties on transgressors of labour discipline and on managerial workers guilty of abuse or carelessness in the performance of their duties. Absenteeism, lateness at work, and the production of substandard goods, can be as harmful to the community as wrongs to private property under the competitive system. With full employment, economic pressure no longer contributes to uphold labour discipline, and has to be replaced by administrative and judicial penalties.

Doubtless, the special circumstances which marked the development of the U.S.S.R.'s national economy during the period elapsed gave rise to an acute and excessive use of penalties for enforcing labour discipline and the responsibility of managerial staffs, but to a certain extent the use of penalties is a logical outcome of full employment.

With the growing importance of social labour incentives and a better understanding by individuals of the interests of the community, the need for penalties against transgressors of labour discipline will decrease and so will their severity. However, as long as even in the most highly civilized countries the presence of a policeman in the street is the accepted guarantee against possible law-breaking, so long the need for repressive measures against transgressors of labour discipline may be regarded as equally unavoidable during the early stages of existence of the planned system of labour relations.

Under a planned system, labour incentives, both social and material, have to be used as motive powers; and similarly the enforcement of labour discipline requires a combination of reward and punishment.

The problem of training and distributing skilled personnel among different fields of labour was being solved in a twofold manner: by appealing to personal motives and by planned measures. The material remuneration for work took into account qualifications, endurance, shortage, responsibility, etc., of various types of labour, whilst additional advantages (pensions, length of paid leave, rest cures, maternity leave, etc.) were made to depend on the length of employment. Such a differentiation in payment for various types of labour had in the U.S.S.R., as under any competitive system, the function of stimulating the desire to raise skilled standards and of distributing labour among various fields.

However, the planned system presupposes definite aims in the development of the country's economy, whereas material labour incentives can be used only on a limited scale, and the automatic regulator, i.e. material advantages, may prove inadequate, in particular if a great structural change occurs in the country's economy; then material incentives have to be supplemented by planned measures for the training and distribution of labour. In the U.S.S.R. the training of skilled personnel and, to a great extent, their distribution among various fields of labour, and even between definite districts and enterprises, were to a considerable degree carried out in accordance with a planned programme. As stated already, the principal measures were: special schools for training young skilled workers, the training of workers in new trades without taking them away from production, State examinations for certain categories of workers to be taken within specified time-limits; moreover, technical schools were taken over by the administration of the corresponding economic commissariats, scholarships were allocated for definite professions, young graduates were directed to work at definite enterprises and to stay there for a compulsory minimum period, and various measures were introduced to transfer specialists from managerial offices to production, and even to assign definite categories of labour to definite districts and enterprises, whilst every encouragement was given to duplication of trades which permitted workers to move to different jobs.

Here again, the particular circumstances in which the national economy of the U.S.S.R. was developing gave rise to measures peculiar to those circumstances, whilst others will have to be taken under any planned system based on the principle that no great differences can be tolerated between the remuneration for physical or intellectual work, or vary in different spheres of human activity. Planning in this field of labour may present great difficulties in the transition period or when the country's economy is undergoing great structural changes, but when the planned system is once firmly established and the planned development of the country's economy is proceeding smoothly, this problem will offer fewer difficulties than the problems of labour incentives or of labour discipline under conditions of full employment.

Problems connected with other aspects of planning labour relations (i.e. planning the general wages fund and its distribution, planning the correlation of wages and labour productivity, setting up machinery to control the expenditure of the wages fund, etc.) are only adjustments of the planning technique and do not affect the principles governing labour relations under a planned system. The most complex problem in the technique of planning is, indisputably, the planning of the general wages fund and of its distribution, for it is linked up with the planning of prices and the production of consumption goods, i.e. with the general problems of planned production and distribution. As stated above, these problems of improving the technique of planning wages were the centre of attention for Soviet economists in the latter pre-war years. The analysis, however, of these purely technical questions of wage planning falls outside the framework of the present study.

It is, nevertheless, worth pointing out that problems of organizing the wages system and planning the general wages fund, as well as the technique of regulating prices and establishing a general balance of demand and supply, are fundamental problems which will have to be faced in any concrete attempt to plan the development of the national economy. It is therefore desirable that economists and research workers should devote more attention than hitherto to working out these problems in relation to the conditions prevailing in different countries.

CHAPTER XIX. PUBLIC FINANCE, CREDIT AND MONEY IN THE POST-N.E.P. PERIOD

The approved draft of the F.Y.P. made provision for the mobilization on a tremendous scale of the country's financial resources to finance the capital work and the cultural and welfare measures laid down in the Plan. Nevertheless, the financial programme 'relied on the levers of the financial system evolved in the course of the construction period now elapsed',* i.e. during the N.E.P. period. The pace set for the mobilization of resources was to be greatly speeded up, so that the planned works could be financed from the State Budget, the credit system, social insurance funds, and the redistribution of the accumulations of business organizations. Apart from the accelerated pace set for accumulation and for the unification of the 'hitherto notably disconnected elements of the financial system into a national unified financial plan', the F.Y.P. did not bring any important or fundamental innovations into the system as shaped by N.E.P. Even the traditional classification of taxes into direct and indirect was retained. The authors of the F.Y.P. did, however, make the following reservation: 'the particularly conventional financial estimates drawn up for the five-year period, and their dependency upon the other elements of the economic plan...make it necessary to place on the agenda— whilst the tasks of the F.Y.P. are still in the course of completion— the question of an all-round revision of our financial system so as to adapt it more perfectly to the conditions and needs of the construction programme inaugurated by socialist economics.'*

As already explained in the chapters on Industry, Labour and Agriculture, the financial plan was based: (*a*) on the growth of industrial and agricultural production being carried out to a time schedule, (*b*) on considerable improvements in the economic and

---

* *The Five-Year Plan...*, vol. i, p. 117. To save space the statistical estimates of the financial programme of the F.Y.P. are omitted here as having solely a historical significance.

financial work of enterprises (rising labour productivity and decreasing production costs), (c) on a difference of prices designed to intensify accumulation (the reduction of prices being made to lag behind the planned decrease in cost prices), (d) on the increasing importance of the socialized sector of the national economy, and (e) on an intensified mobilization of the population's resources through the channels of the credit system and the Budget. But the methods of mobilizing these resources were on the whole to be the same as in the latter years of N.E.P. Apparently, the authors of the F.Y.P. did not yet visualize exactly the path along which the reconstruction of the financial system of the U.S.S.R. was to be directed, since this system of financial relations was to concentrate anew by far the greater part of monetary turn-over within the socialized sector of the national economy. The first attempt at a new approach to the redistribution of financial resources within the socialized sector was made after the adoption of the F.Y.P., when, in connexion with the reorganization of industrial administration which began to be carried out in December 1929 (see pp. 170–1), the Party Central Committee suggested to the P. Commissariat of Finance and the U.S.S.R. Supreme Economic Council that the existing system for taxing State industries should be simplified and that a new system based on a single levy on the profits of enterprises should be elaborated. However, this proposal was never carried out.

The material analysed in the previous chapters shows that the actual developments which took place in the fields of industry, agriculture, labour and home trade during the first years of the F.Y.P. differed considerably from those envisaged in the Plan. The cost of capital construction far exceeded the planned estimates. The expansion of industrial production was achieved by employing considerably more labour than expected. Labour productivity and reduction in costs failed to keep in step with planned provisions. Accumulation within industry fell short of estimates. Consequently, in order to maintain the planned and actual rates of capital construction and expansion of industrial production, financing from the Budget and the credit system greatly exceeded the scheduled amounts; particularly since strained relations with Japan made it imperative to increase expenditure on the defence industries and on developing those heavy industries upon which armament factories are dependent. Furthermore, the onset of the world crisis, coinciding with the early years of the F.Y.P., adversely affected the U.S.S.R. foreign trade balance. More goods had to be exported for a lesser return, and this meant taking away more from the home market, and yet purchasing abroad less equipment and raw materials for industry and less goods than planned for the consumer, and being, nevertheless, faced with an adverse trade and payment balance (see pp. 274–5).

In agriculture, as we have seen, production fell instead of rising as planned. Rationing had to be reintroduced, and a system of price-fixing widely differing from that of the Plan had to be devised. All this was bound to affect finances, the more so since the socialization of the national economy was being carried out at a far greater speed than at first planned. Already in the early years of the F.Y.P. collectivization exceeded the targets set for the fifth year. On the home market the private sector was declining ahead of schedule, whilst centralization in industrial administration and in other branches of the socialized sector of the national economy was being considerably tightened up. The material side of the plan, i.e. capital construction and the expansion of industrial production, investments in State and collective farming, the training and enrolment of labour, etc., were being carried out—so finances had somehow to be adapted. During the first two years of the F.Y.P., this adaptation entailed the expansion of credit and currency, control over consumption and prices, and the mobilization of money through the State Budget by taxation, non-tax revenue and State loans (see pp. 95, 104).

The year 1930 saw two most important reforms—in January the credit reform and in September the fiscal reform. The credit reform gave the State Bank a virtual monopoly over the short-term financing of the socialized sector, put an end to commercial credits, and replaced them by a direct bank credit and a system of moneyless settlements for the bulk of payments effected within the socialized sector. This credit reform and the measures which followed in the field of credit will, however, be dealt with further on, after a description of the measures taken in the field of public finance.

In the introductory note attached to the fiscal reform bill, the following official explanation of its necessity is given.

With the growth and increasing strength of the socialized sector of the national economy and the sharp decline of the private sector, with the wider application of planning in national economics as a whole and in its individual enterprises, the present system of taxation no longer corresponds to the conditions and the organization of the national economy. The multiplicity of taxes and levies payable to the Budget, together with the considerable complexity of their assessment and collection, impede the regulation of production and exchange and, in particular, hamper price policy. The complex relations of the socialized sector of industry and trade with the Budget hinder the planning of individual branches and of the national economy as a whole. The need radically to alter the fiscal system has become more urgent in connexion with the reorganization of State industrial administration and the introduction of the credit reform.*

Thus, the reasons for the fiscal reform were not only of a technical, but of a deeper and more complex nature.

The fiscal reform divided the sources of all revenue into two channels: (*a*) revenue from the socialized sector of the national economy, and (*b*) mobilization of the population's resources.

Revenue from the socialized sector consisted of two main sources: (1) the turn-over tax, and (2) a deduction from profits of State enterprises and an income tax from co-operative enterprises. These two taxes replaced the former fifty-eight various kinds of payments made to the Budget by the State and co-operative enterprises.

The turn-over tax yields the largest item of revenue of the U.S.S.R. State Budget; moreover, it acts as a means for the redistribution of accumulations within the socialized sector of the national economy, and serves to regulate prices and exercise an indirect control over the finances of business organizations. Its manifold importance calls for a more detailed account of its nature.

The idea embodied in the turn-over tax is to collect in the State Budget *the difference between the cost of production of a commodity and the price it fetches as an item in the general expenditure on consumption of society.* Soviet economists have untiringly stressed that in the Soviet national economy prices are a planned category and are made to include both the costs of production and also planned accumulation earmarked for expanding production. The price of goods is not dictated directly by the production and accumulation needs of a given enterprise, but by general considerations aimed at balancing the supply of any given commodity with the effective demand for it (by effective demand is meant that the consumer both desires and is capable of purchasing the commodity at a given price). Generally speaking, under the competitive system too, price is, on last analysis, the fundamental agency in the redistribution of national income. This is even more so under a planned economy, when the volume of production is regulated, import and

---

* Regulation of the U.S.S.R. Central Executive Committee and the Sovnarkom S.S.S.R. dated 2 September 1930, on the fiscal reform.

export similarly planned, and consequently the amounts of goods reaching the market are fixed in advance. The actual cost price of these goods is equivalent to the wages paid out in the course of preparing and producing the goods. But their *social cost* is much greater than their immediate cost price, for it includes, apart from the expenditure on the labour employed in production, transport and the exchange of *goods*, also the expenditure incurred by society in remunerating labour not employed on material production, but in all those services without which any given production in modern society, or indeed the life of the individual as a member of society, would be impossible. The margin between the actual cost price of consumer goods and their social cost depends on the proportion of the population employed in the production of consumer goods, in the broadest sense of the word, on the proportion employed in the production of means of production and on that employed in various services. If the number of people employed in the production of means of production and in the various services grows faster than the numbers employed to produce consumer goods, then this margin between the immediate cost price of the goods and their social cost will increase, the social cost of goods being equivalent to the sum total of the expenditure of wage-earners in the period in question employed both in production and in the various services of society as a whole. When the national economy of the U.S.S.R. began to be industrialized, and cultural and welfare measures to be promoted, it was only natural to expect that this margin between social cost of consumer goods and their actual cost price, all other things being equal, would increase. Prices were so fixed as to take this margin into account and their various components being controlled by the plan, the margin was to accumulate in the State Budget, whence it was again directed into the national economy in order to meet the requirements set by the material and cultural development of the country.

It has been noted above that in fixing wholesale transfer prices for goods, Soviet regulating institutions take into account (1) the planned cost price, (2) the planned profit, and (3) the turn-over tax, the latter calculated as a fixed percentage of the wholesale-transfer price. The planned cost price and part of the profit retained by the enterprise (the other part is credited to the State Budget, cf. below) must ensure reproduction and accumulation within the enterprise. The turn-over tax is not directly nor immediately related to the results of the activity of a given enterprise, but represents the difference between the social cost of a given commodity expressed by the effective demand for it and the price components listed above.

All State and co-operative enterprises and collectivized economies selling *their own* production or the agricultural produce which they *themselves* procure are subject to the payment of the turn-over tax. As a rule, the rates of the turn-over tax are percentages of the wholesale-transfer price; in the case of most agricultural products, however, they are fixed monetary rates per quantity of the product sold (so many roubles or kopeks per quintal of grain sold).

The rates of turn-over tax are graded according to categories of goods and, in certain cases, according to the actual goods, and also according to the zone where the goods are marketed in the case of goods and products for which wholesale-transfer prices are zoned; they also depend on whether the goods are assigned for consumption by industry or by the general market. The principle of single imposition is strictly observed, i.e. a commodity, once taxed, moves then, tax free, from the producer to the consumer. In the case of individual goods manufactured from products taxed already, a second tax is, however, levied at a reduced rate, and in this case again the rates are scaled according to the class of consumers purchasing the goods (i.e. industry or the general market). In the case of foodstuffs and mass-consumption goods the tax is payable daily, for other commodities every 10 days, or on the actual turn-over for a fixed period. Such a procedure ensures a continuous flow of revenue to the Budget's account at the State Bank as the goods passing through the channels of the socialized sector are being sold.

Information regarding the gross and marketable production of industrial and agricultural goods, calculated at their wholesale-transfer prices, and information regarding the actual sale of these goods, together with the average rates of the turn-over tax are the data upon which the planned Budget receipts from the turn-over tax are based. Every P. Commissariat and State department bases their plan of receipts from the turn-over tax on this information. The All-Union Commissariats and departments then submit their plans to the U.S.S.R. P. Commissariat of Finance and the U.S.S.R. Gosplan, whilst in the allied republics, the republican P. Commissariats and departments submit theirs to the Gosplan and finance commissariats of their respective republics; similarly, provincial and regional organizations send in their plans to the corresponding local planning commissions and financial departments. On the basis of this information the P. Commissariats of Finance

13

and the provincial (regional) financial institutions draw up summary annual and quarterly plans for their territorial divisions. In the drafting of these plans the indices subjected to the most detailed scrutiny are the indices of sales of production, the production remaining unsold at the beginning and end of a planned period being taken into account, because any increase or decrease in unsold stock will influence the sum of realized goods and, *ipso facto*, the sum of receipts from the turn-over tax. Moreover, the average rates of the turn-over tax are reconsidered to make sure that they fit the planned range of production taxed according to different rates. Lastly, in drawing up quarterly plans, the seasonal factor in the sale of goods is taken into account, and also the manner and dates of payment of the turn-over tax. On the scale of the turn-over tax approved by the Government, the U.S.S.R. P. Commissariat of Finance bases the final plan of receipts from the turn-over tax for various territories of the U.S.S.R.

The amount of revenue from the turn-over tax depends on the *quantity* of goods sold by the socialized sector at the *planned wholesale-transfer price* and on the *rate* of the turn-over tax. The rate of the turn-over tax is therefore used as a means to adjust wholesale-transfer prices to the demand for and supply of a given commodity and to the cost of its production. If the quantity of the goods sold remains unaltered and the effective demand for them unchanged, whilst their cost price declines and, *ipso facto*, the margin between cost price and planned wholesale-transfer price increases, then the rate of the turn-over tax is raised; it is also raised if the cost price remains stationary, but the wholesale-transfer price is increased. Conversely, if the cost price rises, while the wholesale-transfer price is lowered, then the rate of turn-over tax is brought down. In this manner, the rate of the turn-over tax is used as an adjustment to alterations occurring or made in the basic components of price, i.e. cost price, planned profit and planned wholesale-transfer price, or in the sale of goods and products on the market. This role of the turn-over tax as a means for the adjustment of prices was widely practised in the period of rationed supply in home trade and in the transition period from rationed to unrationed trading. Having already touched upon the subject in the chapter on Home Trade, we shall give here only a few striking examples to illustrate this role of the turn-over tax in the adjustment of prices.

When bread was first rationed the difference between the procurement price of grain and the sale price fixed for bread sold to the population was slight (6·05 kopeks per kg. of wheat and 7·5 kopeks per kg. of white bread in 1931). Consequently, only an 8 % turn-over tax on the sale of bread was established.* Later, the prices of rationed bread were gradually raised (in 1932, 1 kg. of rye bread was sold at 12·5 kopeks, in 1934 at 50 kopeks), whilst the procurement prices were maintained practically unaltered. Therefore the margin between procurement and sale prices gradually increased, and this difference was allocated to the State Budget by means of a corresponding rise in the rate of the turn-over tax (in February 1933 the rate was raised to 30 % and in August to 76 %). A similar discrepancy between the 'commercial trade' and the procurement prices was credited to the State Budget by means of particularly high rates of turn-over tax. When in 1935 rationing was abolished, the price of bread and other products rose substantially. This in its turn made it necessary to revise the planned cost price of many commodities (because of increased expenditure on raw materials in industries processing agricultural produce and also because of increased wages paid to workers so as to make good the higher cost of living, etc.). All these price adjustments were made by altering the rates of the turn-over tax. Table 59† shows the planned and actual receipts of the Budget from the turn-over tax, in 1935 as compared with 1934, that is, during the transition from rationed to free trading, and gives an idea of this adjustment.

This table shows that the plans regarding turn-over and receipts from the tax were fulfilled in various degrees by different branches, but that on the whole, the actual revenue from the turn-over tax was 100·3 % of the planned estimate. This was achieved by adequate alterations in the rates of the turn-over tax as the course of sales of various categories of goods was being ascertained. Moreover, the transition from rationed to unrationed trade in agricultural products and rising prices, as well as the increased volume of their sales, increased the receipts from the turn-over tax from 4,574 million roubles in 1934 to 20,729 million in 1935. At the same time, though the actual turn-over of the light and timber industries increased, the receipt from the turn-over tax from these industries fell in 1935 as compared with 1934. The rising expendi-

* Figures are taken from the following sources which contain considerable material bearing on the question: *Procurement Prices and the Pricing of Grain and Sunflower-seed according to Quality for the* 1933-4 *Campaign*, Moscow, 1933; E. V. Nikolsky and C. A. Skitaltsov, *Sale Prices for Grain, Products derived from Grain and Oilseeds*; *Handbook of Retail Prices and Charges for the Moscow Province for* 1933, 1932 *and* 1933. *Bull. Financ. and Econ. Leg.* nos. 8, 10 and 31, 1933 and nos. 19 and 25, 1934.

† *Report on the Fulfilment of the State Budget for* 1935, Moscow, 1937.

Table 59

	Receipts from turn-over tax in 1934, million roubles	Taxed turn-over 1935, million roubles			Receipts from turn-over tax, 1935, million roubles		
		Planned	Actual	% of fulfilment	Planned	Actual	% of fulfilment
Heavy industry	4,081	17,874	19,755	110·5	4,695	5,272	112·2
Light industry	3,965	9,933	12,403	124·9	2,495	2,518	100·9
Timber industry	377	1,844	2,286	124·0	182	218	119·1
Food industry	6,685	15,589	19,548	125·4	7,709	9,734	126·3
Committee of procurement of agricultural products	4,574	28,332	25,030	88·3	24,000	20,729	86·4
Spirits	6,861	7,360	7,302	99·2	6,000	5,998	100·1
State trade	385	2,341	4,033	172·3	355	360	101·4
Co-operation:							
(a) Consumers	646	3,928	3,602	91·7	690	817	118·4
(b) Producers	780	5,300	4,676	88·2	506	487	96·3
(c) Other	123	1,080	517	47·9	125	59	47·4
Other branches (departmental industries, State farms, etc.)	797	4,685	4,088	87·3	817	666	81·5
Income from commercial trade	8,322	6,450	5,307	82·3	6,450	5,307	82·3
Reduction in the prices of some goods	—	-2,000	*	—	-2,000	*	—
Total	37,596	102,716	108,547	105·7	52,026	52,167	100·3

* The data regarding the fulfilled reduction in prices reflect the reduction of receipts from the corresponding branches.

ture on agricultural raw materials and on wages—particularly in the labour-absorbing timber industry—increased production costs and made it necessary to reduce the rates of the turn-over tax, since a corresponding increase in wholesale-transfer prices was deemed undesirable. The table also shows how widely different are the average rates of the turn-over tax for individual branches of the trade turn-over; in the institutions under the Committee of procurement of agricultural produce, the average rate was 82·8%, in heavy industry 26·6%, in light industry 20·3%, in co-operation 15·5%, and the average for the entire trade turn-over 48·0%.

The material reviewed in dealing with the development of industrial and agricultural production and with labour affords an adequate clue to the need for the existence of such differences between the actual cost prices and the wholesale-transfer prices of different categories of goods, and also shows why the rates of the turn-over tax are so high for some commodities and vary so widely from one category to another. In particular, the rates of the turn-over tax varied in 1940 from 0·5% (on some goods destined for industry) up to 84% (on vodka).*

Apart from its fiscal value and its role of price regulator, the turn-over tax also serves to control the activities of enterprises. The lower rates (0·5%) are indeed imposed mainly for the purpose of control. The correctness and completeness in the payment of tax is checked by auditing the monthly statements of the turn-over tax and the quarterly and yearly accounts submitted by enterprises and organizations. The items scrutinized are: the enterprise's total turn-over for the given period, the taxable turn-over, the correct application of various rates to different goods or categories of goods, the adequacy of the wholesale-transfer prices, and the financial position of the enterprise, in particular of its asset-and-liability indebtedness. Concurrently, the results of fulfilment of the productive plan and the punctual realization of product are checked too. Should any deviation from the plan come to light, it is the duty of the financial institutions to work out, *in consultation* with the economic institutions and the organization in authority, measures to remedy the deviation. The auditing of the turn-over tax accounts provides an opportunity of ascertaining whether the

* The rates of the turn-over tax are published regularly in the *Bull. Financ. and Econ. Leg.*, renamed in the middle of 1940 *Collected Regulations, Decrees and Instructions on Financial and Economic Questions*, and also in the *Collected Regulations and Decisions of the Government of the U.S.S.R.*

wholesale-transfer price adopted and the value of the tax rates are well chosen.*

Evidently the manifold functions of the turn-over tax met with many difficulties in practice, and up to the last pre-war years decisions were still being made about the degree to which the collection of the tax should be centralized (whether the tax be made payable by groups of enterprises or by enterprises individually) and the degree of detail in which rates should be graded (whether rates should apply to whole categories of goods or be worked out in detail for every one); similarly, the methods of assessment (whether on planned or actual turn-over) and methods of accounting (to apply to sums actually realized from the moment the goods were despatched or from the moment payment for them had been received) were still being settled.

During the rationing period and in the years immediately following, when prices were altered very materially (1935-7), the tendency was to scale minutely the rates of the turn-over tax, whereas in the latter years, on the contrary, a more unified scale of rates was coming into force, goods being grouped together and only exceptionally were specific rates established for individual goods; on the whole assessments were based on the principles which have been described above.

Another important source of the Budget's revenue from the socialized sector of the national economy are deductions from profits. All socialized enterprises have the right to retain part of their profits for the purpose of expanding production (capital, investments and increase of working capital) and for maintaining the director's fund. Deductions from profits are payable not on the planned but on the actual profits as established by the enterprise's accounts, but the rates of deductions are fixed in accordance with the enterprise's financial plan for the coming year. In this connexion, enterprises fall into three groups: (1) To the first group belong enterprises whose sources of income *equal* their requirements in liquid assets to carry out their approved productive-financial plan, and also enterprises whose needs in liquid assets

* Readers desirous of making a further study of this financial mainspring of the U.S.S.R. State Budget are referred to the following publications: The U.S.S.R. P. Commissariat of Finance's Instruction regarding the turn-over tax, *Bull. Financ. and Econ. Leg.* no. 12, 1939; K. Yanbukhtin, *Taxation in Conditions of Capitalism and in the Soviet Economy*, Moscow, 1934; I. M. Pushnov, *Methods of Financial Planning*, Moscow, 1937; *Finance and Credit in the U.S.S.R.*, edited by V. P. Diachenko, chap. x, 'The U.S.S.R. fiscal system', Moscow, 1938.

exceed their own sources for meeting their needs, their deficit being made good by grants from the State Budget. In this group by far the greatest portion of the profits is left at the disposal of the enterprises. The sole object of the minimum rate of deduction (10%) fixed for them is to check, in the process of levying this deduction, the fulfilment by the enterprise of its planned accumulation. (2) The second group consists of enterprises whose own sources of income exceed their needs to carry out their productive-financial plan, but whose plan at the same time prescribes expenditure on capital investment and an increase in their working capital. The rates of deductions from profits established for them vary from 10 to 81%. (3) The third group consists of enterprises whose own sources of income exceed their requirements in liquid assets, and whose plans make no provision for expenditure on capital investment or replenishment of working capital. The maximum rate of 81% on actual profits is levied in their case, because the remaining profits are allocated not to expansion of production but to the director's fund.

The amounts of deductions from profits payable to the Budget are settled quarterly, payments being made by monthly instalments. Financial institutions reach a closer approximation of the amounts due for every quarter in auditing the quarterly balance-sheets submitted. This auditing also affords an opportunity of checking the course of fulfilment of the enterprise's accumulation plan and its financial transactions. At the end of the business year, on the basis of the approved annual balance-sheet, final accounts regarding the deductions from profits are settled. When the balance-sheet is consolidated the sums of profits left to the enterprise for capital investment, for increasing its working capital and for allocations to its director's fund are finally fixed as well as the sums levied by the Budget.

Thus the deduction from profits takes away from the enterprise that part of its profits which exceeds its own needs for expanding productive capacity, and also serves to control the fulfilment by the enterprise of its accumulation plan and the proper use of its financial assets. This control supplements from another angle the control over the financial activities of the enterprise already exercised by the turn-over tax.

Many authors express their astonishment that these two basic sources of the Budget's revenue from the socialized sector are not merged into one, and some go so far as to see in this an anachronism surviving from the initial period of the reconstruction of the country's financial system. From the outline given it should, however, clearly appear that the two levies perform two completely different functions. The rates of the turn-over tax depend on the conditions of demand and supply of goods, and to a much lesser extent on the financial results of the enterprise's work. Should the enterprise fail to carry out its accumulation plan, this will affect only its financial resources (the amounts allocated to the expansion of production and to the director's fund, and also the amount of deductions from profits levied by the Budget); the revenue from the turn-over tax will not be affected. Any shortcomings on the financial side of the enterprise's work will affect the Budget's receipts only very slightly, since the bulk will be provided by the turn-over tax which is credited to the Budget as production is being realized at *wholesale-transfer prices*. Moreover, the discrepancy between the wholesale-transfer and the cost prices of many goods is so great that the abolition of the turn-over tax would result in large profits to enterprises and would weaken the inducement to observe any proper business accounting (khozraschet) and to run the enterprise economically. Furthermore, these profits would depend not on the enterprise's successful improvement of the financial side of its activity, but on general conditions of price fixing under planned economy which regulates production, prices and the utilization of the population's purchasing power, i.e. under special conditions of balancing effective demand for definite goods with their supply as determined by the development of the national economy of the U.S.S.R. during the whole preceding period. These reasons make it impossible to merge the turn-over tax with the deduction from profits. Their functions are complementary, both as regards accumulation in the State Budget of the income of the socialized sector of the national economy and as regards control of the financial side of the enterprises' work.

Apart from these two fundamental forms of receipts from the socialized sector, four other kinds of taxes are levied, but they are only modified forms of either the turn-over tax or the deduction from profits, made to apply to particular cases of turn-over or to co-operative and public organizations. They are: (1) A tax on the revenue payable by enterprises rendering paid services or manufacturing articles from their customers' materials. This tax is merely a modified turn-over tax. (2) A tax on cinema box-office receipts, which too is a form of the turn-over tax. (3) An income tax payable by co-operative and public organizations; it is a kind of modified deduction from the profits of co-operative enterprises which takes into account the fact that the co-operatives' and public enterprises' profits are not State property as is the case with State enterprises, but the property of those enterprises. Only a portion of these profits is appropriated to the State Budget. (4) A monetary income tax on collective farms, in force since 1936, which has superseded the former 'monetary agricultural tax on collective farms'. Its fiscal importance is secondary to its main purpose, which is to afford control over the financial activities of the collective farms. The tax is assessed on the collective farms' gross income (agricultural artels and communes paying 3%, and associations for the joint cultivation of the land paying 4% of their income). The assessment of the taxable income, the computation of the amounts due and the auditing of the annual reports of the collective farms, are carried out by tax inspectors who ascertain, in the process of auditing, whether the distribution of the collective farms' income conforms to the limits set by the Government to the various appropriations (see p. 313).

Apart from some minor additional dues, the entire contribution of the socialized sector to the Budget revenue, as far as taxes are concerned, is made up of these two basic and four supplementary taxes. Moreover, by subscribing to State loans, the socialized sector contributes towards the Budget a small part of its accumulation in the form of long-term credit. This latter form of redistribution of the socialized sector's accumulations through the Budget is identical with that which appears on the revenue side of the U.S.S.R. Budget under the heading of 'Enlistment of the resources of the population', and is effected by a subscription similar to State loans by the population.

The mobilization of the population's resources takes mainly the two following forms: (1) subscriptions to State loans and (2) an income tax, and a cultural and housing welfare tax, the latter assessed separately in the case of urban and rural populations. Several features in the organization of the population's contribution to the State Budget are so peculiar to the Soviet financial system that a brief account is called for.

As already stated in the outline of State finances during the N.E.P. period, State loans are not an emergency measure in the U.S.S.R.; they are not issued to cover a Budget deficit or to meet some other extraordinary expenditure, but are a permanent item on the revenue side of the State Budget. By means of State loans the liquid assets of the wide masses of the population are attracted into long-term credit, earmarked mainly for the country's industrialization.* In the absence of a market for capital, of shares of private concerns and private productive investments in the U.S.S.R., the mobilization of the population's resources for long-term credits is effected through organized subscription to State loans by the wide masses of the population. The State loans are actually subscribed by the masses. In the later pre-war years almost anyone with an individual income was a holder of State bonds—in 1937–8 over 50 million people owned State bonds. In connexion with this mass character of the U.S.S.R. State loans, the organization of their floating among the population is marked by peculiar features. Loans are raised either by collective subscription on a deferred payment basis or by sale of bonds for cash through savings banks. The deferment is usually fixed at ten months. Subscription is strictly voluntary, but of course social and psychological pressure is brought to bear (e.g. intensive savings campaigns in the press and propaganda at specially called meetings of workers and employees, the contagious example of Party members and of the most active groups of workers and employees, etc.). Participants in a collective subscription ask the accounting house of their enterprise or institution to deduct their share of payment from their wages. The bonds are handed over to subscribers when the last instalment has been paid off. Apart from these mass loans subscribed by the people, money is borrowed through loans subscribed by State enterprises and institutions with liquid assets set aside for special purposes (State insurance, savings banks, reserve capital of some enterprises and institutions). Gradually the importance of these loans subscribed by enterprises and institutions declined, because their excess liquid assets were to a large extent tapped by the redistribution of their profits through the State Budget and of their cash reserves through the credit system. Loans were issued either as interest-bearing bonds redeemable at par by drawings at definite intervals, or as both interest-bearing and lottery bonds which

* Practically all loans were issued under the slogan of the industrialization and defence of the country as their designations show: first industrialization loan of 1927 to the value of 200 million roubles; second industrialization loan 1928 for 499 million roubles; third industrialization loan 1929 for 829 million roubles; 'The F.Y.P. in 4 years' loan 1930 for 1,025 million roubles; 'The third decisive year of the F.Y.P.' loan 1931 for 1,935 million roubles; 'The fourth final year of the F.Y.P.' loan 1932 for 2,718 million roubles; the first issue of the second F.Y.P. loan 1933 for 3,076 million roubles; second issue of same 1934 for 3,402 million roubles; third issue 1935 for 3,965 million roubles; fourth issue of same 1936 for 4,832 million roubles; loan for 'Strengthening the defences of the U.S.S.R.' 1937 for 4,932 million roubles; 'Third F.Y.P.' loan 1938 for 5,928 and the same 1939 issue for 7,637 million roubles.

brought in income and were redeemable in both ways, or as separate interest-bearing and separate lottery issues, redeemable in the corresponding manner and yielding either interest or premiums. Up to 1936 a relatively high interest was paid on loans, and the average cost of credit to the State in interest or premiums on loans was about 10 %. In 1936, by means of the fourth issue of the second F.Y.P. loan, all previous mass loans were converted into 4 % interest-bearing bonds. Prior to 1936 loans were usually issued to mature after 10 years, since 1936 with a maturity of 20 years.

Table 60 gives an idea of the course, amount and structure of the U.S.S.R. public debt.* These figures show that the U.S.S.R. public debt has grown constantly from year to year; up to 1937 the debt both to the population and to the socialized sector was on the increase. However, after 1938–9 the debt to the socialized sector began to decrease. Though in absolute figures the U.S.S.R. public debt is considerable, relatively its burden decreases with the growth of the State Budget. Moreover, in the later years, the debt to the socialized sector consisted mainly of the debt to savings banks, which invest their stable annual balance of deposits in State bonds, and to the State insurance institutions, which similarly invest their reserve capital in State bonds.

Thus, by means of the State loans, almost the entire mass of the people's savings is redistributed by the State Budget. This is evident from a comparison of the figures below of the State indebtedness to the population with data regarding the movements of the population's deposits in savings banks, which are the principal custodians of the monetary savings of the U.S.S.R. population (see Table 61).†

The population's savings invested in State loans are several times as great as the sums deposited in the savings banks. Moreover, as the stable balance of savings banks is also invested in State bonds, it is no exaggeration to say that almost the entire stable savings of the U.S.S.R. population are in fact invested in State bonds.

If we now recall the figures regarding the U.S.S.R. annual general wages bill and compare them with the sum total of the population's visible savings (i.e. the State's debt to the population and the annual balance of the population's deposits in savings banks), it will appear quite obvious how ill-founded are the 'fears' of some authors and the 'hopes' of others that a class of 'rentiers'

---

* *Finance and Credit of the U.S.S.R.*, edited by Prof. V. P. Diachenko, pp. 264–5. For details regarding State loans and their role in the U.S.S.R., cf. ibid. pp. 258–67. *Planned Economy*, no. 7, 1940, pp. 11–24.

† *Finance and Credit of the U.S.S.R....*, p. 268.

Table 60

I. Debt to the population (in million roubles)

	Capital debt			Current debt	Total debt
	Total to all population	To workers and employees	To collective and individual farmers		
1 Oct. 1928	411·0	152·2	108·4	19·7	430·7
1 Jan. 1933	5,442·8	3,766·2	1,270·8	270·3	5,713·1
1 Jan. 1936	14,937·0	10,976·9	3,144·1	450·1	15,387·1
1 Jan. 1937	18,004·3	13,444·5	3,631·2	266·7	18,274·0
1 Jan. 1938	20,934·1	15,850·0	3,900·0	220·5	21,154·6

II. Debt to the socialized sector (in million roubles)

Total	To savings banks
833·4	290·3
4,328·6	1,286·9
7,182·8	2,557·2
8,287·8	3,556·7
7,610·9	4,652·9

III. Total debt (in million roubles)

Total	Capital debt
1,264·1	1,244·4
10,041·7	9,771·4
22,569·9	22,119·8
26,561·8	26,292·1
28,765·5	28,545·0

Table 61

	1933	1934	1935	1936	1937	1938
1. Balance of deposits on 1 Jan. of corresponding year (million roubles)	974·3	1,181·8	1,638·1	2,461·1	3,538·9	4,514·9
2. Increase in deposits in the course of the year (million roubles)	207·5	491·1	830·8	1,077·7	976·0	969·8
3. Average stable balance of deposits for the year (million roubles)	—	1,344·7	1,978·4	3,007·4	3,985·1	—

capable of living on the income from their monetary capital will gradually arise in the U.S.S.R. In 1937 (the last year for which the complete necessary data are at hand) the relevant figures were: the total wages bill, 82,247 million roubles; the population's savings invested in State bonds, 18,274 million roubles which, divided among 50 million bondholders, works out at an average of 365 roubles per bondholder; average stable balance of the population's deposits in savings banks, 3,985 million roubles, which, the depositors numbering 14 million, works out at 285 roubles per depositor; average interest on State bonds and on deposits in savings banks, 4%; and, lastly, average yearly wages of workers and employees, 3,038 roubles. These figures speak for themselves.

Up to 1936 restrictions existed on the disposal of bonds, and they could be mortgaged only with the preliminary approval of the corresponding committee for the sale of State bonds. Since 1936 this restriction has been abolished and the bondholder has the right to mortgage his bonds at a savings bank for 6 months and to obtain an advance of up to 30% of the value of the mortgaged securities. Bonds can also be bought and sold freely except in the case of speculatory purchase and resale; they can be donated and bequeathed, and income derived from them is not subject to tax.*

It proved possible in the course of the first F.Y.P. to mobilize by loans 9·5 milliard roubles for long-term credit, thus covering 18% of the capital construction outlay of the economy's socialized sector; in the course of the second F.Y.P. receipts from loans raised among the population ran to 19 milliard roubles, thus covering more than 14% of the capital investments made in the socialized sector during the second five-year period.

The U.S.S.R. system of taxing incomes possesses some characteristic features unknown to the taxation systems of other countries. There are two systems in force, one applied to the urban population and the population ranking as such, and the other to the rural

---

* The war loans issued since the outbreak of hostilities conform on the whole to the same principles as the previous loans, with some modifications, namely, the lottery issue is intended for the population, whilst the interest-bearing issue is intended for agricultural, craftsmen's and fishermen's associations and other co-operative producers' artels. All the income of the former issue is paid out in premiums and that of the latter in interest on coupons. It is very significant that the second State war loan issued on 5 June 1943 to the value of 12 milliard roubles was oversubscribed by 8,323 milliard in 7 days, the total sum subscribed reaching 20 milliard 323 million roubles; after such a success, subscription lists were closed. For details regarding the U.S.S.R. war loans, see *Collective Regulations and Orders of the Government of the U.S.S.R.* no. 3, 1942; *Izvestia*, 5 and 13 June 1943.

population. This differentiation is based on the fact that whereas the earnings of the urban population are in money, the rural population derives from its occupation an income the major part of which is in kind. Consequently the rural population pays its taxes partly in kind (cf. the compulsory deliveries of agricultural produce described above) and partly in cash. The income tax and a concomitant cultural and housing welfare contribution ('kult-zhil-sbor') are levied on the urban population according to a scale which varies with the sources of the taxpayers' income. The urban population liable to pay income tax and kult-zhil-sbor is sub-divided into the following groups: (1) Workers and employees and those ranking as such (co-operative craftsmen working either in co-operative enterprises or at home, but delivering production to their artel, scholarship holders, etc.); a high non-taxable personal allowance is granted to this category and low rates are fixed for both income tax and kult-zhil-sbor. In connexion with the con-siderable rise in wages which took place in the latter pre-war years the rates of taxes were revised* in conformity with the wage policy and the policy of stimulating the raising of qualifications and of labour productivity. (2) Professional men (writers, artists, doctors, etc.); the non-taxable personal allowance in this group is much lower, the tax rates higher and increasing in a steeper progression.† (3) Craftsmen and artisans, non-members of co-operative associa-tions and other persons deriving their income otherwise than from paid employment; the non-taxable personal allowances granted to this group are below those of group 2, whilst rates are higher and

* E.g. in 1934 the non-taxable personal allowance varied according to districts from 75 to 100 roubles of the monthly wage; in 1937 it was raised to 140–200 roubles and in 1940 brought down to 150 roubles. Rates altered similarly. In 1937 the rate of income tax was 2·38% and that of the kult-zhil-sbor 2·28% on an annual income of 5,000 roubles; the corresponding rates on an income of 20,000 roubles were 3·30 and 2·80% respectively; in 1940 the taxes paid on a monthly income of 150–200 roubles were 1 rouble 20 kopeks fixed rate and 3% of the sum in excess of 150 roubles; on a monthly income of 1,000 roubles and above, the fixed rate was 42 roubles and 7% off the income exceeding 1,000 roubles. Cf. details in *Bull. Financ. and Econ. Leg.* nos. 16–17, 1934; nos. 4–5, 1939; nos. 7–8, 1940; *Finance and Credit of the U.S.S.R....*, p. 246.

† E.g. in 1940 the non-taxable allowance was up to 1,000 roubles of the annual income. Incomes from 1,001 to 1,800 roubles paid 8%; incomes from 1,801 to 2,400 roubles paid 14 roubles 40 kopeks fixed rate and 3% of the in-come exceeding 1,800 roubles; incomes of 100,000 to 150,000 paid 11,364 roubles fixed and 25% of income exceeding 100,000; incomes of 300,001 and above paid 86,364 roubles fixed and 50% of the sums exceeding 300,000 roubles. The rates of the kult-zhil-sbor ranged from 3 to 3·25%.

their progressive increase steeper.* (4) Persons having an unearned income; no personal allowances are granted to them and
the rates of taxation are very high and increase in a particularly
steep progression.† Moreover, for the first category of taxpayers
taxes are levied separately according to each source of income,
whereas in the case of other categories, taxes are levied on the total
income whatever its sources. Heroes of the Soviet Union, Heroes of
Socialist Toil, and holders of U.S.S.R. awards are exempt, and the
pay of men in the forces is also tax free.

Thus the taxation system applied to the U.S.S.R. urban population is concerned not only with fiscal aims, nor is it based only on
the principle of progression, but it also pursues social and political
aims by taxing incomes not only according to their amount but
also according to their source. Incomes earned in State and co-
operative enterprises and institutions are taxed at privileged rates
and the taxation policy is linked to the wage policy; conversely,
incomes derived from private activities and especially unearned
incomes are taxed very heavily.

Similarly, the taxation system applied to the rural population
also pursues social and political as well as financial aims. The basic
monetary taxes paid by the rural population are the agricultural
tax and the rural kult-zhil-sbor. Taxpayers fall into three groups:
(1) collective farmers liable to tax on their domestic economies,
(2) individual working peasant households, and (3) households
having unearned incomes. The first group enjoy the lowest tax
rates, a more lenient assessment of the profits of their domestic
economies and exemption in special cases. Heavier taxes are levied
on the second and still more the third group. In particular, if
individual peasant households maliciously fail to fulfil their sowing
plans and compulsory State deliveries of agricultural products, they
forfeit any reliefs which would otherwise have been allowed (relief
in respect of Heroes of the Soviet Union, holders of awards, war
invalids or incapacitated menfolk, members of the household),

---

* In 1940 the non-taxable allowance varied from 500 to 800 roubles of yearly
income, according to districts; incomes of up to 1,200 roubles paid 4%; incomes
from 1,201 to 1,800 roubles paid 48 roubles fixed rate and 6% on the sum in
excess of 1,200; incomes of 24,001 roubles per annum and above paid 8,952
fixed rate and 60% on the income in excess of 24,000 roubles. The rate of the
kult-zhil-sbor ranged from 4.5 to 6%.

† Incomes of 5,000 roubles per annum paid 20.4% in income tax and 18%
in kult-zhil-sbor; incomes of over 20,000 roubles per annum paid 54.65%
income tax and 24% kult-zhil-sbor. Incomes exceeding 24,000 roubles per
annum paid 87% in tax.

whilst the tax recoverable is doubled. Households having un-earned incomes are taxed individually, i.e. not according to an average standard of profitableness, as other households, but on the actual income of the household as assessed by financial inspectors, while none of the reliefs usually granted to individual labouring peasant households are allowed.*

In addition to the cultural and housing welfare contribution, which is similar to that levied on the urban population, the rural population is liable to pay self-imposed contributions. The latter can, however, be imposed only by a decision passed at the general meeting of the village citizens. The general meeting at which the contribution is voted also discusses and fixes the necessary measures to levy the contribution and determines the rates for each category of taxpayers as well as the dates of payment in accordance with standards established by law.†

Moneys accruing from the social and cultural welfare contribution both from towns and rural areas are credited to the republican and local budgets and expended on welfare needs. Moneys received from self-imposed contributions remain at the disposal of the village soviet and must be expended on the purposes for which the contribution was voted. The village soviet must submit a report on the expenditure to the general meeting, and the correctness of the appropriations is checked by the rural auditing commission.

No account is given here of other minor taxes and local rates and contributions as they have no particular interest, and the revenue they provide for the State Budget is quite insignificant. They serve to meet small fiscal and technical needs. Incidentally, local rates and contributions, though part of the general Soviet taxation system, differ from State taxes in that they are differently imposed (by order of local authorities) and are entirely appropriated by local budgets.‡

As shown by the figures on p. 397, taxes and contributions paid by the population account for only a small part of the State revenue. Even the receipts from State loan subscriptions exceed the total revenue derived from taxes and contributions paid by the population. The fundamental source of revenue of the State Budget is the socialized sector of the national economy. The

---

* For details see *Finance and Credit of the U.S.S.R.* . . ., pp. 247–54; *Bull. Financ. and Econ. Leg.* nos. 25–6, 1939 and nos. 7–8, 1940.

† For details see *Finance and Credit of the U.S.S.R.* . . ., pp. 251–2.

‡ For a description of the small State and local taxes and impositions see *Finance and Credit of the U.S.S.R.* . . ., pp. 254–7.

revenue from this, and not the taxes paid by the population, provides the resources of the State Budget which are then redirected
to finance the development of the national economy and the social
and cultural welfare.

We have already touched upon the special role of the Soviet
State Budget in the financing of the development of the national
economy. Already during the N.E.P. period, particularly in its
closing years, many investments in the national economy were
effected through the State Budget. After the inauguration of the
reconstruction and new construction plans in various branches of
the national economy, the State Budget became the principal
source for the financing of these plans.

All industries, agriculture, forestry, transport, posts and telegraph, municipal services, housing, trade and other branches of
the national economy and cognate measures are financed from the
State Budget. The following are the main purposes of grant:
(1) capital expenditure, i.e. the construction of productive capacity;
(2) endowment of new enterprises with working capital and allocation of supplementary funds to enterprises already in production; (3) housing, cultural and social welfare measures, and
municipal services; (4) building, equipment, etc., of new schools;
(5) investments for the training of cadres and for the subsidizing
of science (scientific and research work, geological exploration and
prospecting, new inventions, dangerous experiments, etc.); (6)
capital expenditure on workers' supply institutions and the endowment and replenishment of these institutions with working capital;
(7) expenditure incurred in the early stages of enterprise and connected with the putting into production of new capital; (8) grants
to enterprises embarking on new production, to make good the discrepancies foreseen by the plan between planned cost and prices
established for these enterprises, i.e. planned losses (see pp. 292-4).*

Most important of these allocations for the financing of the
national economy from the State Budget are headings (1) and (2),
which account for the 90 % of all allocations; next come (7) and
(8), which were particularly important in the 1930-6 period, i.e.
at the time when new industries were going into production and a
very complex system of price relations was in force.

Money allocated by the State Budget for the financing of the
national economy is placed at the disposal of the enterprises

* For details see 'Classification for the fulfilment of receipts and expenses
of the State Budget of the U.S.S.R.', *Bull. Financ. and Econ. Leg.* no. 15, 1938;
Finance and Credit of the U.S.S.R. . . . , pp. 304–14.

through the agency of long-term credit banks as unrepayable grants. The financing of collective farms from the State Budget, which is effected through the Agricultural Bank, is, however, in the form of long-term repayable credits, the reason being that collective farms are not State, but co-operative enterprises.

The State Budget was the fundamental source of capital investment in the national economy, particularly during the period of intensive capital construction. In order of their decreasing importance, here is the list of the main sources from which capital investments into the national economy were financed: (1) Grants from the State and local budgets.* (2) Profits of enterprises earmarked for financing capital work. (3) Allocations to sinking funds from balances left after covering expenses on capital repairs. (4) Funds allocated by the Central Municipal Bank and local municipal banks, from resources transferred to them either by the Social Insurance or the Trade-Unions' Central Committee for financing housing, and from other special capitals of these banks. (5) Receipts from the sale of the property of enterprises and from the mobilization of their other internal resources for the purpose of capital investments.†

Figures quoted on p. 397 show what huge sums were expended yearly in financing the national economy and how great was the relative share of this expenditure in the total expenditure of the U.S.S.R. unified ('ediny') State Budget. The enormous grants

* The following figures (in million roubles) show the part of the State Budget in financing the country's economy:

	Total investments into industry, State trade and supply organizations	Of which from the unified State Budget	Share of the State Budget's allocation %
1931	7,466	5,897	79·0
1932	10,515	8,343	79·3
1933	9,774	8,145	83·3
1934	10,605	7,252	68·4
Total for 4 years	38,360	29,637	77·3

The Finances of the U.S.S.R. between the Sixth and Seventh Congresses of the Soviets (1931–4), Moscow, 1935, p. 23.

† E.g. the share of various sources in financing the industries of the U.S.S.R. P. Commissariat of Light Industry was as follows in 1938: total capital expenditure 850·1 million roubles, of which: grants from the State Budget, 477·6 million roubles; profits, 241·4 million roubles; sinking fund allocations, 81·7 million roubles; mobilization of internal resources for capital construction, 49·4 million roubles. *Finance and Credit of the U.S.S.R.…*, p. 308.

from the State Budget provided the money necessary for carrying out the plans for the country's industrialization. The State Budget played the part of the central agency where the wealth of the country accumulated and whence it was redirected to finance the planned tasks for the expansion of the country's productive capacity.

The part played by the budget system in financing social and cultural measures on a huge scale simultaneously with increasing the productivity of the country was also very great. It is preferable to speak here of the budget system rather than of the State Budget, because, though formally included in the State Budget, the expenditure on social and cultural measures is actually carried out mainly through local budgets (see below).

Like the national economy, social and cultural welfare measures are mainly financed by appropriations from the State Budget. Other sources are: (1) funds allocated for the purpose by the Social Insurance;* (2) additions to the wages bill to meet the expenses of training personnel; (3) allocations from profits of social and cultural organizations run on business principles (spas, press, dispensaries, etc.); (4) sums provided by trade-union and co-operative organizations for cultural and educational purposes, for organizing the leisure of trade-union members and the welfare of

---

* No account of the social insurance system (either the compulsory State or the voluntary insurance) has been given in the chapter on Labour or elsewhere, as this would involve us in many details outside the scope of this study. The following data from the social insurance general budget for 1938 will give some idea of how the funds are allocated:

	Million roubles
Total expenditure	5,900
Of which:	
Allowances and pensions	3,465·6
Children's welfare (allowances for nursing and care of infants, pioneers camps, etc.)	654·4
Rest homes, sanatoria and spas ⸱	1,034·2
Touring and mountaineering	50·0
Physical training	147·9
Nutrition allowances	99·6
Education (training of personnel and scientific institutes for the study of labour and social insurance)	84·1
Subsidies to mutual assistance societies	104·1
Medical inspection and labour inspection	98·0
Organizational and administrative expenses	80·0
Bonuses to insurance workers	5·0
Expenses of the Trade-Unions' Central Committee on allowances for temporary disablement	50·0

Finance and Credit of the U.S.S.R...., p. 318; details on the State and on voluntary insurance will be found in the same book, pp. 275–304.

their children; (5) sums appropriated from the directors' fund for cultural needs and improved living conditions of the enterprises' workers and employees; (6) sums provided by business institutions for scientific and research work, and for the training of personnel; (7) special funds from collective farms for cultural and welfare needs, and appropriations from self-imposed contributions set aside for this purpose. With the exception of appropriations from the budget and social insurance systems, all the above are expended as a rule in financing the cultural, educational and social needs of that community which provides the funds. All these sources financing social and cultural measures, however, are co-ordinated in a general financial plan for social and cultural measures, itself connected with the State economic plan for the same period. The plan of expenditure on social and cultural measures consists of two fundamental items, capital investment and operational expenditure; both fix in detail the standard rates of expenditure on every measure and on every operational expense so as to obtain similar qualitative standards in institutions of the same type. Special financial control inspectors supervise expenditure in the field of welfare.* Thanks to the tremendous subsidies lavished on both capital construction and operational expenditure by the budget system (see pp. 97, 392), it proved possible to put into effect the measures described in the chapter on Labour.

The other functions of the Soviet budget system, in particular the size and nature of appropriations for defence and administration, are omitted from this study, because, though differing in some respects from the function of budget systems of other countries, they do so rather in technique than in matters of principle.

There is, however, one feature of the Soviet budget system which cannot be entirely ignored, namely, the mutual relationships of the Union, the republican and the local budgets.

The budget system of the U.S.S.R. consists of: (1) the All-Union State Budget; (2) the State Budgets of allied and autonomous republics; (3) the local budgets, i.e. the budgets of provinces, regions, 'okrugs', districts, towns, villages and settlements. Up to 1938 the form commonly adopted in publishing summary budgetary data distinguished: (a) the unified ('ediny') State Budget, including the State Budget of the U.S.S.R. and the budgets of the allied and autonomous republics; (b) the combined ('svodny') budget, including local budgets in addition to the above; these local budgets

---

* For details regarding the content, drafting and methods of financing social and cultural measures see *Finance and Credit of the U.S.S.R.* . . . , pp. 314–22.

were included under one heading and were not subdivided according to republics; (c) the republic budgets, each of which was separately approved by the government of the corresponding republic after the unified budget had been passed. Usually, minor modifications were introduced in the course of their final approval by the republican governments so that the figures of republican budgets may vary slightly from those given in the unified State Budget of the U.S.S.R.,* such modifications allowing a closer adjustment of the provisional figures of the unified budget to the local needs of the corresponding republic. From 1939 the summary data published under the heading of 'The State Budget of the U.S.S.R.' include the budget of the U.S.S.R., the budgets of allied and autonomous republics, those of the local soviets and, moreover, the social insurance budget; so that according to the former terminology this is the combined budget with the social insurance budget included in it as well; the budgets of allied republics and of the autonomous republics and provinces which they incorporate, together with local budgets, were published as before. These changes were due to the possibility in the later years of planning local budgets with more precision and so including them more fully in the general budget system of the U.S.S.R. From 1939 the expression 'combined' budget disappears altogether from official publications and is superseded by that of State Budget of the U.S.S.R. The differences in terminology and in the form in which the U.S.S.R. State Budgets have been published must be borne in mind by students of the Soviet financial system in order to avoid the errors, commonly committed not only by foreign but even by Soviet writers, and due to a confusion of figures taken from U.S.S.R. budgets differently set out for different years. Table 62 gives a general notion of the correlation of separate items in the U.S.S.R. budget system.

As shown by the allied republics' formal budget estimates, republican revenues are considerably in excess of their expenditure, whilst local expenditure (including that of the A.S.S.R.) considerably exceeds local revenue. The discrepancies are made good by the transfer of funds from the republican to the A.S.S.R. and

---

* E.g. according to the bill passed by the Supreme Soviet of the U.S.S.R. on 29 May 1939, the R.S.F.S.R. budget of revenue and expenditure, as a part of the unified budget was fixed at 23·98 milliard roubles, but by the bill passed by the Supreme Soviet of the R.S.F.S.R. the final State Budget of revenue and expenditure of the R.S.F.S.R. was fixed at 24·60 milliard roubles. For details see *Bull. Financ. and Econ. Leg.* nos. 15–16 and 23–4, 1939.

Table 62

In milliard roubles according to estimates for corresponding year

	1939		1940		1941	
	Revenue	Expenditure	Revenue	Expenditure	Revenue	Expenditure
Combined budget	156·10	155·45	183·95	179·91	216·84	216·05
Union budget	117·37	116·72	141·09	137·05	170·48	169·69
Budgets of all allied republics	38·72	38·72	42·86	42·86	46·36	46·36
Of which:						
(a) Republican budgets	27·85	11·71	28·27	12·36	31·41	13·30
(b) Local budgets	10·87	27·01	14·59	30·50	14·95	33·06
(c) Grants from Union and republican budgets to A.S.S.R. and local budgets	16·13	—	15·90	—	18·11	—
R.S.F.S.R.	23·98	23·98	25·24	25·24	24·96*	24·96
(a) Republican budget	16·08	6·42	15·02	6·46	14·62*	5·48
(b) Local budgets	7·90	17·56	10·22	18·78	10·34	19·48
Ukrainian S.S.R.	6·54	6·54	8·10	8·10	8·29*	8·29
(a) Republican budget	4·68	1·93	5·38	2·26	5·57	2·16
(b) Local budgets	1·86	4·61	2·71	5·84	2·73	6·13
Bielorussian S.S.R.	1·30	1·30	2·14	2·14	2·13*	2·13
(a) Republican budget	1·13	0·48	1·67	0·72	1·74	0·70
(b) Local budgets	0·17	0·82	0·47	1·42	0·39	1·43
Azerbaidzhan S.S.R.	0·99	0·99	1·04	1·04	1·05	1·05
(a) Republican budget	0·81	0·39	0·84	0·39	0·83	0·40
(b) Local budgets	0·18	0·60	0·20	0·65	0·22	0·65
Georgian S.S.R.	1·15	1·15	1·22	1·22	1·23	1·23
(a) Republican budget	0·97	0·52	0·98	0·49	1·02	0·49
(b) Local budgets	0·18	0·63	0·24	0·73	0·21	0·74
Armenian S.S.R.	0·44	0·44	0·47	0·47	0·52	0·52
(a) Republican budget	0·39	0·21	0·40	0·21	0·46	0·23
(b) Local budgets	0·05	0·23	0·07	0·26	0·06	0·29
Turkmenian S.S.R.	0·50	0·50	0·53	0·53	0·53	0·53
(a) Republican budget	0·45	0·25	0·46	0·24	0·47	0·23
(b) Local budgets	0·05	0·25	0·07	0·29	0·06	0·30
Uzbek S.S.R.	1·44	1·44	1·49	1·49	1·61	1·61
(a) Republican budget	1·21	0·54	1·21	0·56	1·31	0·69
(b) Local budgets	0·23	0·90	0·28	0·93	0·30	0·92
Tadzhik S.S.R.	0·48	0·48	0·53	0·53	0·59	0·59
(a) Republican budget	0·43	0·21	0·47	0·23	0·54	0·26
(b) Local budgets	0·05	0·27	0·06	0·30	0·05	0·33
Kazakh S.S.R.	1·51	1·51	1·66	1·66	1·72	1·72
(a) Republican budget	1·35	0·59	1·44	0·63	1·51	0·66
(b) Local budgets	0·16	0·92	0·22	1·03	0·21	1·06

* The decrease in the budgets of the R.S.F.S.R. and of the Bielorussian S.S.R., and the small increase in that of the Ukrainian S.S.R. in 1941 as compared to 1940, is due to the formation of new republics (the Karelo-Finnish, the Moldavian, etc.) and to the transfer to their separate budgets of various items at the same time as territories previously included in the R.S.F.S.R., the Ukrainian and the Bielorussian S.S.R. were handed over to the new republics.

Table 62 (*cont.*)

	1939		1940		1941	
	Revenue	Expenditure	Revenue	Expenditure	Revenue	Expenditure
Kirghiz S.S.R.	0·39	0·39	0·43	0·43	0·48	0·48
(*a*) Republican budget	0·34	0·17	0·39	0·17	0·44	0·21
(*b*) Local budgets	0·05	0·22	0·04	0·26	0·04	0·27
Karelo-Finnish S.S.R.	—	—	—	—	0·49	0·49
(*a*) Republican budget	—	—	—	—	0·47	0·29
(*b*) Local budgets	—	—	—	—	0·02	0·20
Moldavian S.S.R.	—	—	—	—	0·46	0·46
(*a*) Republican budget	—	—	—	—	0·41	0·17
(*b*) Local budgets	—	—	—	—	0·05	0·29
Lithuanian S.S.R.	—	—	—	—	0·84	0·84
(*a*) Republican budget	—	—	—	—	0·75	0·45
(*b*) Local budgets	—	—	—	—	0·09	0·39
Latvian S.S.R.	—	—	—	—	0·90	0·90
(*a*) Republican budget	—	—	—	—	0·80	0·54
(*b*) Local budgets	—	—	—	—	0·10	0·36
Esthonian S.S.R.	—	—	—	—	0·53	0·53
(*a*) Republican budget	—	—	—	—	0·48	0·33
(*b*) Local budgets	—	—	—	—	0·05	0·20

local budgets. These transfers from the republican to the local budgets are necessitated by the special way in which monetary receipts and expenditure are apportioned between Union, republican and local budgets.

The following items of expenditure are met from the *Union Budget*: (*a*) the financing of enterprises and of economic measures of All-Union importance (i.e. industrial enterprises of this type, rail and water transport, communications, foreign trade, etc.); (*b*) the financing of social and cultural institutions and measures also of All-Union importance (i.e. the majority of establishments of higher education, scientific and research institutes, medical institutions); (*c*) defence, and the maintenance of the higher organs of the U.S.S.R. State Administration, the All-Union Courts of Justice and the central machinery of the Union and republican P. Commissariats; (*d*) the State loan service.

Republican budgets bear the costs arising from items similar to those of the Union Budget listed under (*a*), (*b*), and (*c*), with the exception of defence, but in regard to enterprises and institutions of republican importance only.

The following expenditure is met from *local* budgets: (*a*) the financing of local economy and economic measures of local importance (i.e. local industries, the construction of railway lines to satisfy local needs, municipal services, housing, etc.); (*b*) education (primary and secondary schools), health services (local medical institutions), pensions, physical training and other local social and cultural needs; (*c*) the maintenance of local government organs.

Most large industrial, transport and trading enterprises being of All-Union importance, the outstanding items of the Union budget are the financing of the national economy, whereas expenditure on social and cultural measures figures most prominently in local budgets.* In this way expenditure on items of All-Union importance is centralized, whilst other expenditure, chiefly concerned with social and cultural measures, is decentralized, with the aim of permitting a freer adaptation of expenditure to the particular needs of various districts, individual allied republics, autonomous republics and provinces, national 'okrugs' and districts inhabited by the different nationalities of the Soviet Union. The transfer of funds from the republican revenues to the A.S.S.R. and local budgets results in their being subsidized by the allied republics. The figures cited above show that in the national republics, the

* E.g. expenditure was apportioned as follows in 1935, the year for which we possess the most detailed data:

	Relative share of all expenditure of the combined budget %	Financing of national economy %	Social and cultural measures %	Administration %	Defence %
Union Budget	76·2	91·1	19·9	23·8	100·0
State Budgets of allied republics	5·2	2·6	18·3	6·0	—
Budgets of A.S.S.R. and local budgets	18·6	6·3	61·8	70·2	—
Total, combined budget	100·0	100·0	100·0	100·0	100·0

Finance and Credit of the U.S.S.R...., p. 340. For further details regarding the apportionment of expenses for various items and to various budgets see *Report on the Fulfilment of the State Budget of the U.S.S.R. for* 1935, Moscow, 1937. Incidentally, expenditure on social and cultural measures for 1939 and according to the 1940 provisional plan was apportioned as follows (in million roubles):

	1939	1940
Union Budget	6,892	8,120
Republican budgets	6,328	6,939
Local budgets	19,623	21,967
Social insurance budget	5,493	5,849
Total	38,336	42,875

local and not the republican budgets account for the greater part of the money expended, which means that funds are mainly spent on the social and cultural needs of these republics. But the funds for this expenditure are accumulated chiefly through the channel of the republican and not of the local budgets. This is due to the manner in which sources of revenue are apportioned between various budgets.

All budget receipts are either State or local receipts. The following are State taxes: the turn-over tax, the deductions from profits of enterprises and institutions of All-Union and republican importance—together with the subvarieties of the turn-over tax and of the deductions from profits described above—the revenue raised by State loans, the income tax and the kult-zhil-sbor paid by urban and rural populations, death duties and duties on donations, receipts from customs and from the mint, and other minor State receipts. The following make up the local revenue: deductions from profits of enterprises of local importance, rent collected from local trading and industrial enterprises and other small local rates and taxes. However, certain items of the State revenue, wholly or in part, are placed directly at the disposal of the allied republics and then transferred by them to local budgets. The rates of these allocations from the All-Union receipts to the republican and local budgets are fixed concurrently with the passing of the Union Budget.* The object of this procedure is: (a) to place the Union Budget in a position of authority over the main monetary sources of revenue; (b) to facilitate the regulation of the principal separate items of expenditure, thus co-ordinating expenditure with fulfilment of the budget revenue plans; and (c) to give local authorities an interest in the fulfilment of the budget receipt plans

---

* E.g. the great bulk of the general turn-over tax is appropriated to the Union Budget, whilst the whole of the receipts from the turn-over tax from collective farm trading and rural consumers' co-operation is allocated to the republican budgets and thence retransferred to the A.S.S.R. and local budgets. The deductions from profits paid by enterprises of All-Union importance are appropriated to the Union Budget and by those of republican importance to republican budgets, and by those of local importance to local budgets. In regard to State loans, 75% of the proceeds from bonds subscribed by workers and employees and 50% of those sold to collective and individual farmers are allocated to the Union Budget and the balances to republican budgets, which, in their turn, allocate 10 and 50% of each respectively to local budgets. The greater portion of the receipts from the kult-zhil-sbor and, in the Caucasian and Asiatic republics, the total receipts from this tax are allocated to republican budgets, and these funds also are forwarded to local budgets, etc. For details see *Finance and Credit of the U.S.S.R. . . .*, pp. 374–8, and also the annual decrees on budget estimates.

by making allocations transferred to them from the All-Union and republican budgets dependent on the degree of fulfilment of the plan.

Budgets are balanced by transferring expenses from one budgetary link to another in accordance with the course of realization of revenue plans. Such a method of balancing enabled the U.S.S.R. budget system, while carrying out the revenue plans, to register a surplus on the annual combined budget, and this despite the fact

Table 63. *Combined State Budget.* (*Union, republican and local budgets*)

	1938	1939	1940	1941
Revenue				
Estimated	132·6	156·1	183·9	216·8
Realized	127·4	155·9	178·1	—
Expenditure				
Estimated	131·1	155·4	179·9	216·1
Realized	124·0	153·1	173·3	—
Surplus				
Estimated	1·5	0·7	4·0	0·7
Realized	3·4	2·8	4·8	—
Turn-over tax				
Estimated	—	92·4	108·6	124·5
Realized	80·4	96·8	105·8	—
Deductions from profits				
Estimated	—	17·7	22·4	31·3
Realized	10·6	—	21·4	—
State loans				
Estimated	—	9·9	12·0	13·2
Realized	7·6	—	11·4	—
Taxes and impositions				
Estimated	—	6·4	9·7	12·4
Realized	5·0	—	9·4	—
State insurance				
Estimated	—	7·2	9·1	10·1
Realized	7·2	7·4	9·1	—
Financing of the national economy				
Estimated	—	59·3	57·1	72·9
Realized	51·7	59·1	57·1	—
Social and cultural welfare				
Estimated	—	38·6	42·9	47·8
Realized	35·3	38·3	41·7	—
Defence				
Estimated	—	40·9	57·1	70·9
Realized	23·1	—	56·1	—
Administration, Justice and the P. Commissariat of the Interior				
Estimated	—	11·6	14·2	—
Realized	9·6	—	—	—
Loan service				
Estimated	—	1·9	2·5	3·3
Realized	2·0	—	2·8	—

that practically every year the result of the revenue plans did not come up to expectation (Tables 63–65).

The U.S.S.R. budget system, both in regard to revenue and expenditure, is closely linked at every point with the economic plan, and the latter is usually approved together with the State Budget. The country's economic plan fixes the programme of capital work, the volume of production of various industries, the qualitative indices both for production and distribution (e.g. reduction of production costs, price movements, amount of accumulation in enterprises, etc.), the expenditure on social and cultural measures and on administration; the provisions of the economic plan determine also the expenditure on and the probable receipts from every branch (turn-over tax, deductions from profits and other principal taxes) and from the mobilization—by means of taxes and loans—of the resources of the people who derive their income from work in enterprises and institutions, the activity of which is fixed by the economic plan. The starting point for the planning of receipts of the U.S.S.R. budget system is naturally the data regarding the fulfilment of the State Budget and of the country's economic plan in the previous year, but this is only a starting point; the programme has to take account of the country's expanding economic and cultural activity in the ensuing year. The plan of material balances of the national economy (see below, p. 444) is the keystone on which rests the general financial plan and, in particular, the expenditure and revenue plan of the budget system. Budgetary estimates of expenditure take into account not only sources of budget income but also other sources of income for covering the expenses of the corresponding branches, such as internal accumulation, credits, assets redistributed between various units of the same industry, etc.*

* E.g. the 1940 capital investments plan apportioned expenditure as follows (in milliard roubles):

	Total	Of which	
		From State Budget	From the enterprises' own resources and other sources
All national economy	36·1	24·4	11·7
Of which:			
Industry	19·2	13·4	5·8
Agriculture (excluding investment by agricultural population)	1·2	0·9	0·3
Transport and communications	5·4	1·7	3·7
State trade and procurement	0·3	0·1	0·2
Municipal and cultural services	1·9	1·2	0·7

Table 64. *State Budget appropriations (according to items)*

	1935	1936	1937
A. Expenditure on financing the national economy:			
Industry: P. Commissariat of Heavy Industry	11,758	10,161	5,217
P. Commissariat of Defence Industries	—	—	2,329
P. Commissariat of Light Industry	1,173	910	1,604
P. Commissariat of Timber Industry	952	1,372	1,274
P. Commissariat of Food Industry	1,022	942	1,042
P. Commissariat of Local Industries	291	429	376
Cinema and photographic industries	128	262	163
Miscellaneous industrial construction	—	—	392
Industry, total	15,324	14,076	12,397
Agriculture: P. Commissariat of State Farms	2,235	1,825	2,064
P. Commissariat of Agriculture	4,887	5,875	6,995
Agriculture, total	7,122	7,700	9,059
Chief Administrator of Forestry and Afforestation of the Sovnarkom S.S.S.R.	—	—	390
P. Commissariat of Transport	3,598	4,212	4,699
P. Commissariat of Water Transport	1,024	1,434	1,133
Roads Administration of the P. Commissariat of the Interior	676	950	831
Chief Administration of the Arctic Sea Route	228	440	580
Chief Administration of Civil Aviation	228	289	301
P. Commissariat of Communications	271	360	546
Volgostroi	—	222	200
Moskanalstroi	—	—	243
Transport and Communications, total	6,025	7,907	8,923
State trade, supply and procurement organizations	4,893	4,443	3,036
P. Commissariat of Foreign Trade	90	52	20
Reserves Committee of the Council of Labour and Defence	700	1,592	1,688
Moscow underground railway	—	311	458
Chief Administrator of the hydro-meteorological services of the Sovnarkom S.S.S.R.	86	69	129
Miscellaneous expenditure on the national economy	914	1,431	3,876
National economy, total	35,154	37,583	39,586
B. Social and cultural welfare	18,700	21,291	26,605
(a) Financed directly by the State Budget	4,804	6,509	10,870
(b) Financed through local budgets	13,896	14,782	15,734
Of which:			
(1) Education (State Budget)	3,734	4,918	7,842
(2) Health (State Budget)	996	1,472	2,472
(3) Physical Training (State Budget)	20	29	44
(4) Pensions and Labour protection (State Budget)	54	90	511
C. P. Commissariat of Defence	6,500	14,815	20,102
D. P. Commissariat of the Interior	1,652	2,111	2,699
E. P. Commissariat of Justice and Procurature	886*	971*	149*
F. Administration			
G. State Loan Service	1,815	2,701	2,579
H. Grants to republican and local budgets	8,977	12,456	15,933
I. Bank settlements on account of long term investments	1,025	265	1,382
J. Reserve funds of the Sovnarkom S.S.S.R. and the Sovnarkoms of allied republics	1,962	857	1,855
K. Miscellaneous expenditure	226	444	345
Grand total	65,401†	78,715	97,119
Surplus	500	—	950

* For 1935 and 1936, expenditure on Administration, Justice and Procurature. For 1937 only on Justice and Procurature.

† Including 2300 milliard roubles representing the increased credit resources of the State Bank due to the revaluation of remaining seasonal raw materials and 95 milliards representing an advance to the Agricultural Bank for crediting collective farms' production.

Table 65

In milliard roubles

	1931	1932	1933	1934	1935	1936	1937	1938	1939	1940	1941 (Planned)
Combined State Budget	25·9	38·9	49·0	60·6	78·6	97·2	109·3	127·4	155·9	178·1	216·8
Total revenue*	23·4	34·6	44·3	55·1	71·7	88·8	104·3	127·4	155·9	178·1	216·8
Of which:											
I. Revenue from socialized economy:											
(a) Turn-over tax	11·6	19·5	27·0	37·6	52·0	65·8	75·9	80·4	96·8	105·8	124·8
(b) Deductions from profits	2·4	2·8	2·3	2·3	2·1	3·7	6·5	10·6	—	21·4	31·3
II. Enlistment of the population's resources:											
(a) State loans‡	3·3	3·9	4·4	4·3	4·8	4·9	6·0	7·6	9·9	11·4	13·2
(b) Taxes and impositions	1·0	1·6	2·8	—	—	—	—	5·0	—	9·4	12·4
Total expenditure†	23·4	34·4	39·8	52·4	68·1	86·4	100·7	124·0	153·1	173·3	216·1
Of which:											
I. Financing of the national economy	16·5	24·8	25·1	32·3	37·2	41·9	43·4	51·7	59·3	57·1	72·9
II. Social and cultural welfare§	3·4	4·6	5·8	6·2	8·8	—	—	35·3	38·3	41·7	47·8
(a) Education	2·7	3·7	4·9	5·0	8·2	13·9	16·3	18·8	20·6	22·7	26·6
III. Defence	1·3	1·3	1·4	5·0	8·2	14·9	17·5	23·1	40·9	56·1	70·8
IV. Administration and Justice‖	1·2	1·5	2·0	3·0	4·4	5·2	—	5·4	—	6·7	7·1

* Up to 1938 the income from and the expenditure on social insurance were not included in the State Budget. To give comparable figures for the entire period from 1931 to 1941, figures including social insurance are placed in the first column, and figures excluding social insurance in the second, and so up to 1937; figures for 1938 and the following years include social insurance. This arrangement has had to be adopted because budgets were published in this form in the Summary Data and the absence of other detailed information makes it impossible to extract the figures required. However, with the exception of the figures of the total revenue, the figures quoted in the principal subheadings are fully comparable in structure for the whole period 1931–41.

† Up to 1937 all revenue and expenditure and their subheadings are exclusive and from 1938 they are inclusive of social insurance.

‡ Including subscription by enterprises and institutions.

§ The data regarding expenditure on social and cultural welfare prior to 1938 are not comparable with those for 1938–41 because, up to 1937, the expenditure of local budgets on social and cultural welfare, a major item of these budgets, was not included in the State Budget, whereas it is so included since 1938. Data regarding education are comparable.

‖ Excluding expenditure on the P. Commissariat of the Interior; in view of the varying nomenclature of the items for different years, it has been impossible to extract comparable figures for over a number of years.

Concurrently with the complete programme of construction planned for every branch of the national economy, the Sovnarkom S.S.S.R. confirms the sums allocated for financing capital investments, which depend not only on the volume of the projected works, but on the planned targets for lowering construction costs, on changes in the material balances of materials and equipment, the position of the creditor-debitor indebtedness, etc.; the Sovnarkom also states the sources from which expenses are to be met. Therefore, the starting point of budget planning is a thorough analysis of data of the previous year's reports, and of the proposed material and financial plans for the coming year. The allocation of funds from the State Budget to the corresponding organizations is not effected automatically in accordance with the approved estimates, but in accordance with the actual course of fulfilment of their production plans by the organizations financed.

The need to modify and adjust the annual plan for the development of the national economy and social and cultural construction, gave rise to the practice of drawing up quarterly plans; similarly, the State Budget system has adopted the practice of quarterly plans. Quarterly budgets—cash receipt and expenditure plans—are approved for every quarter by the Sovnarkom S.S.S.R. in the case of the Union Budget, by the Sovnarkoms of the respective allied republics in the case of republican budgets, and by the corresponding soviets in the case of local budgets. On the basis of the approved quarterly cash plans, the U.S.S.R. P. Commissariat of Finance, the P. Commissariats of Finance of the allied republics and the local financial authorities establish monthly cash plans. The cash plan of the entire budget system, both as regards revenue and expenditure, passes through the channels of the State Bank.* A special institute of Financial and Budgetary Inspection has been established to enforce budgetary discipline. Its inspectors have the right to inquire into the reasons of an enterprise failing to fulfil its payments to the Budget, to investigate the enterprise's financial transactions and to report the facts coming to light to the organization to which the enterprise is subordinate. The P. Commissariat of Finance decides upon the forms to be used for bookkeeping reports and balance-sheets and issues instructions regarding their drafting; financial authorities have the right to participate in the examination of the bookkeeping reports and balance-sheets, to demand that enterprises and economic organs submit relevant material, to audit

* For details regarding the drafting, elaboration, approval and fulfilment of budgets see *Finance and Credit of the U.S.S.R....*, pp. 348–66.

on the spot book entries, reports and other necessary documentary evidence. Moreover the P. Commissariat of Finance has a section of Internal Control and a special Central Staff Commission, which supervises the compulsory registration of staffs in all institutions and economic organs and the correct expenditure of funds allocated by it for paying the staffs approved.* Thus financial control is not limited to the supervision of budgetary discipline, but carries out much wider functions.

The close connexion of the U.S.S.R. budget system with the country's economic plan and its social and cultural programme naturally result in the U.S.S.R. budget system playing a major part in the redistribution of the country's national income. Earlier, in the outline of the financial system under N.E.P., we noted that in the later years of the N.E.P. period, up to 40 % of the national income was redistributed through the State Budget. This role of the budget system has developed further since the application of the F.Y.P.s and the intensification of planning in all branches of the national economy, and in social and cultural activities (considered in their economic aspect). Unfortunately, figures for the U.S.S.R. national income are published only in the fixed prices of 1926–7, whilst budget data are published in current prices, and moreover, since 1931, no price indexes have been forthcoming from soviet sources. It is impossible therefore to estimate the share of the national income which passes through the channels of the budget system. However, the ever-increasing importance of the State Budget as redistributor of the national income can be surmised from a comparison of the figures in Table 64, which show the growth of the national income and that of the combined budget of the U.S.S.R.

In 1929–30 38·2 % of the national income (in identical prices) was redistributed through the State Budget; in the following years this percentage must necessarily have been greater, because the rate of increase of the combined budget was every year, and particularly in the 1930–6 period of intensive accumulation, considerably above the rate of increase of the national income.

The outstanding importance of the budget system as redistributor is a natural feature of any planned system where the means of production and the accumulation of productive capacities are nationalized, and where the character of the social and cultural

* To encourage the reduction of administrative and managerial expenses, 50 % of the sums economized are placed at the disposal of the heads of institutions to be distributed in bonuses to the employees of their institutions.

Table 66

	National income of the U.S.S.R. in fixed 1926-7 prices		Combined Budget in current prices	
	Milliard roubles	% of previous year	Milliard roubles	% of previous year
1931	40·9	—	25·9	—
1932	45·5	111·2	38·9	150·2
1933	48·5	106·6	49·0	125·9
1934	55·8	115·1	60·6	123·7
1935	66·5	119·2	78·6	129·8
1936	86·0*	131·2	97·2	123·6
1937	96·3	112·0	109·3	112·3
1938	105·0	109·0	127·4	116·6

* This tremendous growth of the national income in 1936 as compared with that of 1935 is to some extent a 'statistical' and not a real growth, since in 1936, in connexion with the abolition of rationing, the system of price fixing was altered and this apparently was reflected in the conversion of the national income into 1926-7 prices.

development of the country is determined by its economic plan and its social and cultural construction programme, and not by the private initiative of individuals, monopolistic economic interests and social and political groups. This question will be dealt with after an account of credit and money in the present-day Soviet financial system has been given.

The description given elsewhere (see pp. 96–102) of the evolution of the credit system in the closing years of the N.E.P. period shows that short-term credit came gradually to be vested in the State Bank, whilst the specialized banks' business became more and more the allocation of funds earmarked for capital construction. In fact, their long-term credit operations assumed the character of nonrepayable advances drawn from a redistribution of capital, accumulated in the socialized sector of the national economy, and from funds forthcoming from the State Budget.

The application of the F.Y.P. with its huge investment programme, the further centralization of industrial administration brought about by the reform of 5 December 1929, the hasty collectivization of agriculture which demanded large expenditure on the mechanization of agricultural production, were all factors necessitating centralization, specialization and planned distribution of credit resources. A series of measures had to be taken for the reorganization of credit, the first and foremost of which was the 1930 credit reform. This credit reform and the developments that ensued in the field of credit and money between 1930 and 1936 have been reviewed in several books in English,* and, unlike descriptions of other aspects of the Soviet economic system, these studies have been full and on the whole impartial; therefore, in this summary outline of the development of the Soviet economic system, only the most important events in the evolution of the credit and monetary systems need be stated, in order to help understand the general evolutionary trends of the whole economic system of the U.S.S.R.

The aims of the reform of 1930 were: (1) to concentrate all short-term credits in the State Bank and to grant credits to the enterprises and institutions of the socialized sector only in accordance with the plans approved for each of them. To achieve this, enterprises of the socialized sector were henceforth forbidden to issue commercial paper or grant credit, the State Bank being entrusted with all short-term credit transactions; (2) to concentrate in the State Bank all settlements by clearing between enterprises and institutions of the socialized sector.† At the time, in credit, as in other fields of the national economy, many among those at the helm of the economic apparatus cherished a firm belief in the 'plan', and in its virtue to function automatically as soon as established. Hence the credit reform too was imbued with the self-same faith in planned automatic regulation of credit relations. The credit needed by an enterprise or institution to carry out its productive-financial plan, i.e. the difference between its available working capital and the total amount of working capital necessary to put its plan into effect, was placed to its current account with the State Bank, and the State Bank then advanced to the given enterprise sums within the planned limits of its credit, and independently of how the enterprise or institution were fulfilling their planned production programme. Enterprises and institutions were naturally inclined to overstate their planned requirements in credit and so to secure for themselves a greater financial independence in the carrying out of planned production

* The fullest and best informed work is the already quoted book by Dr Arnold, *Banks, Credit and Money in Soviet Russia*; the factual material of the following two books is well worthy of attention, though the interpretation of the collected material is often far from impartial: W. B. Reddaway, *The Russian Financial System*, 1935 and L. E. Hubbard, *Soviet Money and Finance*, 1936.

† The fullest account of the 1930 credit reform is given in the compilation edited by A. A. Blum and B. M. Berlatsky, *The Credit Reform in Questions and Answers*, Moscow, 1930. The fullest account in English is to be found in Dr Arnold's work, pp. 345–63.

14

tasks. The transfer from the current account of one enterprise to that of another was effected automatically when the seller presented his invoice to the bank and without awaiting the buyer's acceptance. This obviously weakened the buyer's control over the quality of the goods delivered, since he could raise objections only post-factum—i.e. after his account had already been debited with the seller's invoice—as regards quality, assortment, date of delivery, packing, etc., not complying with the terms of his contract with the seller. Moreover, this automatic transfer from buyer's to seller's account resulted in some enterprises being unable to ascertain whether they had borrowed to the limit of their credit or not, for credits may have been exhausted before the goods had been delivered and acknowledged. Furthermore, the 1930 credit reform did not establish any demarcation line between the enterprise's or institution's own working capital account and the planned credit account; they were merged into one, and therefore transfers to the suppliers' account could be made not only from its credit resources but its own working capital as well. Consequently, an enterprise might find itself in the position of being unable to pay its current expenses such as wages or other current production needs. Sellers' invoices could also reach an enterprise after it had exhausted its credit and then it had to obtain supplementary credits from the Bank to meet the bills. This led to a general expansion of credit beyond the planned limits. Furthermore, no minimum limit was set to settlements effected through the State Bank; and a stream of petty accounts to be settled bètween enterprises and institutions of the socialized sector flooded the bank, causing considerable disorganization in bookkeeping, particularly in the first months following the reform. A number of Government measures taken in the course of 1931 helped to remedy many of the defects.

The first to be abolished was the automatic payment of sellers' invoices.* Henceforth the State Bank demanded either an *acceptance* by the buyer or an order ('*accreditive*') before paying—within the credit limits granted to the buyer—the seller's invoice, or else it made the payment from the buyer's *special account*. A minimum limit of 1000 roubles was set to moneyless settlements, and smaller bills had to be settled between enterprises in cash. Next, the State Bank ceased making advances 'on the basis of the plan', but made them dependent on the fulfilment by enterprises

---

* Sovnarkom S.S.S.R. regulation, dated 14 January 1931, *Coll. Laws*, 1931, decree no. 52.

and institutions of their financial plan.* The 'credit limit' of an enterprise or an institution was approved together with its financial plan, this credit limit being the sum of its bank credit which, however, could be used only upon the presentation of contracts concluded with other enterprises and institutions, and in so far as these were being carried out. In this way the granting of credits was limited not only by a definite ceiling (the 'limit') but made conditional on the fulfilment of contracts between enterprises. Enterprises were henceforth obliged to publish their balance-sheets and to submit them to the State Bank. The latter was given the right to apply sanctions against defaulting clients, namely, to stop their credits and to execute a forced sale of their securities.

The funds of enterprises and institutions held at the State Bank were henceforth subdivided into two independent accounts:† the working capital or so-called 'clearing' account, and the 'loan' account, which showed the enterprise's indebtedness to the State Bank. Every State enterprise was endowed with working capital sufficient to ensure its normal activities. If an enterprise had not at the time when this measure was introduced the requisite working capital, it was granted the necessary funds by a conversion of its indebtedness to the State Bank into working capital.‡ Any further replenishments of the enterprises' working capital were to be effected from their accumulations and, in the case of expanding activity prescribed by the plan, from subsidies granted by the State Budget. In estimating the working capital required by enterprises, so-called 'normatives' were fixed for each, i.e. the minimum stocks of raw and other materials necessary to carry on every enterprise's normal activity for a definite period of time; working capitals were such as to enable enterprises to maintain their 'normatives'. The enterprise alone was entitled to dispose of the money forming its 'clearing' account at the State Bank, and the latter had the right of debiting this account only in definite cases established by law.§

---

* Sovnarkom S.S.S.R. regulation, dated 20 March 1931, *Coll. Laws*, 1931, decree no. 166.

† Regulation of the Council of Labour and Defence (S.T.O.) dated 23 June 1931, 'Concerning the Working Capital of Combines, Trusts and other Economic Organizations', *Coll. Laws*, 1931, decree no. 316.

‡ The conversion involved a very considerable sum—6 milliard roubles. *The State Bank of the U.S.S.R. on the eve of the Seventh All-Union Congress of Soviets*, Moscow, 1935, p. 10.

§ Upon an order in court or an arbitration tribunal; on a decision of the financial authorities to recover tax arrears; in the case of outstanding bills and bank overdrafts.

Enterprises were expected to use their working capital only to meet expenditure on exactly specified normative stocks and on constant normal current expenses; supplementary expenditure was to be met by bank credits drawn from the 'loan' account. These short-term credits from the enterprise's 'loan' account at the State Bank could only be used for definite purposes, namely: (1) transit loans given against way-bills; (2) advances for seasonal production processes and expenses connected with the accumulation of seasonal stocks of raw materials, fuel, productive and auxiliary materials, or with temporary increased investments in uncompleted construction or with a seasonal accumulation of finished goods and production; (3) other temporary needs connected with production and the turn-over of goods. Thus every State Bank advance was made to meet expenditure for a specified purpose for a specified time, and it was guaranteed by goods and other material securities and the State Bank's right to debit the 'clearing' account of the enterprise or institution should the latter fail to repay the loan. Moreover, before granting the advance from the 'loan' account, the State Bank verified the position of the enterprise's 'clearing' account and only upon having satisfied itself that, within the normative limits, the enterprise's working capital was unable to meet the specified expenditure could it sanction the advance.* Consequently the bank checked the actual need for the advance and its correct appropriation for the purpose for which it had been granted. The division of the enterprise's assets into 'clearing' and 'loan' accounts achieved a technical differentiation and effected control of the general financial position of the enterprise seeking credit. By urging enterprises to make do with their own working capitals, the State Bank induced them to conform to the distribution of material stocks as established by planned normatives. In the later pre-war years (see below) it was proposed to reduce the enterprises' own working capitals and to increase their borrowings, so as to enable the State Bank to exercise greater control over all the financial transactions of enterprises.

Since in the course of 1931 these emendations of the 1930 credit reform were effected, no fundamental changes have been made in the organization of the State Bank's credit operations, the main effort being directed towards improving the technique of credit operations and towards strengthening the Bank's control over the financial transactions of the enterprises and institutions of the

* For details see *Finance and Credit of the U.S.S.R....*, pp. 160–2, 393–400; and Arnold, pp. 363–79.

socialized sector. Only a few of the more important changes in methods of crediting and in the organization of the State Bank's administration need be mentioned here. Up to 1933 trading organizations received credits on the same grounds as other business enterprises, i.e. advances were on the whole granted either to meet seasonal needs, or as transit loans against way-bills, or for other specific temporary needs. Towards 1933, when State trade was being reorganized prior to the abolition of rationing, it was decided to grant credits not for individual needs as hitherto, but for the general turn-over of the trading enterprise. Henceforth, the State Bank* was to credit—within planned credit limits—the whole turn-over of the enterprise in excess of the share which could be met from the enterprise's own working capital. Within the limits of the goods turn-over fixed for the enterprise and the time set to the 'normative average' turn-over of goods, the State Bank was to grant advances to pay for the goods bought by the enterprise, provided: (a) that each trading enterprise invested in the turn-over a specified sum from its own working capital; (b) that all the non-commercial activities of the enterprise were transferred to a separate balance-sheet so as to avoid the investment of working capital in these activities; (c) that there was no un-repaid indebtedness to the State Bank nor were bills pending for goods supplied. However, when rationing was abolished it became apparent that more elastic methods of crediting the goods turn-over and at the same time controlling individual commercial transactions of enterprises was needed, such a control being based not on 'average' turn-over times, but on a more individual approach to the enterprise's activities; hence a further adjustment was made in the practice of crediting the turn-over of trading enterprises. Credit 'limits' allowed to every commercial organization were abolished and the value of the credit was henceforth made to depend on the volume of the enterprise's turn-over. Instead of as formerly granting credits for an average turn-over time, credits were now allowed for time limits varying according to different categories of goods. This differentiated crediting of turn-over, based on different turn-over times for individual categories of goods, was designed to stimulate the speed of the goods turn-over, not only of the more saleable but of the entire range of goods; at the same time it provided the State Bank with an additional lever for controlling the fulfilment of tasks set by plan for the goods turn-over of the trading organizations.

* The Sovnarkom S.S.S.R. regulation of 16 August 1933.

The apparatus of the State Bank consists of a central administration or Main Office, with its Planning and Economic Departments, its Currency Department and its special Branch Departments situated in Moscow, and its numerous branches throughout the country. The developments which took place in the management of the State Bank, like those described in the organization of industrial administration, tended towards the creation at the Bank's Main Office of departments each specializing in crediting the operations of different branches of the national economy. In the course of the first F.Y.P. very large Branch Departments were formed, but later in 1932, and particularly since 1935, these Branch Credit Departments of the State Bank have been subdivided somewhat like the P. Commissariats and Chief Administrations which were split into smaller units as described in the chapter on Industry (see pp. 297–8), and with the same object of achieving a more specialized servicing of the corresponding branches of the national economy.* Apart from the central Branch Departments a whole network of provincial offices, branches, agencies and subagencies have come into existence throughout the country. The direction and management of these provincial branches is strictly centralized.†

A main branch is a local branch which performs the following functions: it grants credits to the business organizations operating in the territory served by the branch, settles their mutual accounts, participates in drawing up the State Bank's general credit plan,

* E.g. after the State Bank Credit Departments had been subdivided according to the Sovnarkom S.S.S.R. regulation of 15 June 1938, the former department for the crediting of the Heavy Industry was split into three departments for crediting the heavy, defence and machine-building industries respectively. Later, when a further subdivision of these P. Commissariats into more specialized commissariats was effected, the corresponding State Bank Credit Departments were similarly split up.

† The network of the State Bank's branches altered as follows:

	1 Jan. 1933	1 Jan. 1937	1 Jan. 1938
Main office	1	1	1
Allied republican offices	5	7	9
Suboffices in allied republics, excluding the R.S.F.S.R.	25	22	25
Provincial and regional offices in the R.S.F.S.R.	39	54	63
Urban offices	—	—	—
Local branches	2,129	2,699	2,926
Total	2,199	2,783	3,024
District agencies (not included above)	—	98	125

carries out operations concerned with the planning of money circulation and the issue and withdrawal of notes; transacts business on behalf of the specialized long-term credit banks; settles the cash accounts of budgetary institutions (i.e. institutions whose expenditure is paid from the State and local budgets); receives payments made to the budget and effects various re-allocations upon instructions from the financial authorities; and purchases gold and other precious metals and exchanges foreign for Soviet currency.* No further description of the structural interrelations of the various branch subsections will be given here, nor will any outline of their competence or their subordination to the central administration of the State Bank, because this pertains to the organizational technique of the U.S.S.R. credit system which we are unable to describe here. Nor can we deal with the organization of the system of the State Bank's clearing settlements; though in principle they differ from those accepted in other countries, in practice they use the same methods of banking technique.†

Apart from the credit and clearing operations described above, the State Bank carries out the following important functions: (a) note issue; (b) clearing operations with foreign countries, including the concentration in its hands of all foreign resources, the establishment of relations with correspondents abroad and the granting of credits to Soviet import and export organizations; (c) operations for the fulfilment of the State and local budgets' cash plans (collection of all tax and non-tax receipts, payments from budget funds within the limits of appropriations and estimates approved by budget institutions); (d) operations on behalf of specialized banks for financing and granting long-term credits for capital construction.

The topical subject of improving the work of the State Bank discussed in the Soviet press in the last pre-war years centred mainly on the problems of strengthening the Bank's control over the financial activities of enterprises and hence its control over the fulfilment of planned tasks. As stated above, when the accounts of the enterprises were split into the 'clearing' and the 'loan' accounts, enterprises were endowed with the minimum working capital

---

* For details see *Finance and Credit of the U.S.S.R.* . . . , pp. 411–12.

† Accounts are subdivided into two groups: intra-urban and local. The principal forms of intra-urban accounting is the acceptance, the 'accreditive' and the special account. Local transactions are settled by means of cheques, letters of credit, single or periodical mutual balance clearances and in some cases through the medium of special bureaux of mutual clearance. For details see *Finance and Credit of the U.S.S.R.* . . . , pp. 401–7.

requisite to meet their main necessary expenses, yet insufficient to cover all their needs in working capital, the supplementary funds being provided by short-term bank credits allowed for definite purposes and for exactly specified periods. In granting these credits the Bank was to analyse the enterprise's financial position and, in supervising the payments made from the credit, it could at the same time check the fulfilment of the financial-production plan. Consequently, the smaller the individual working capital of an enterprise, the greater its need in credits to carry on its business and *ipso facto* the greater the controlling role of the State Bank; eventually this control could be extended from occasional and single operations for which credits were granted to the entire financial activity of an enterprise. Proposals were persistently put forward for revising the existing 'normatives' and for increasing the amount of borrowed capital in the total working capital of the enterprise; from 1939 the State Bank began to make the size of bank credit dependent upon the satisfactory position of the enterprise's own working capital and of its correct utilization for planned tasks.* From 1939 also, the State Bank inaugurated the practice of advancing funds for the payment of wages only in so far as enterprises fulfilled their production plan; and in the case of budgetary enterprises (i.e. enterprises receiving funds from the State Budget) and similar organizations only if they actually em-

* For details see 'The struggle of the State Bank of the U.S.S.R. for business accounting [khoz-raschet] in the third five-year period', *Planned Economy*, no. 6, 1939; 'The State Bank in the struggle for economies in the national economy', *Planned Economy*, no. 3, 1940; 'The working capital of socialist industry', *Planned Economy*, no. 5, 1940.

The following figures graphically illustrate the correlation of own and borrowed working capital of enterprises on 1 July 1939, in %:

	Own working capital	Bank credit	Creditors
Total for All-Union industry	46·7	33·8	19·5
Of which:			
A. Production of means of production	55·6	24·8	19·6
(a) Coal industry	28·7	39·1	32·2
(b) Oil industry	47·8	25·1	27·1
(c) Heavy machine-building	78·4	11·8	9·8
(d) Timber industry	41·7	44·6	13·7
B. Production of consumer goods	36·6	47·1	16·3
(a) Textile industry	43·0	43·1	13·9
(b) Light industry	63·5	25·8	10·7
(c) Food industry	35·8	47·4	16·8

The production of consumer goods where seasonal expenditure is higher than in the production of means of production resorted more to credits.

ployed the numbers of workers fixed for them and paid at rates established by law.*

All these measures carried out or proposed on the eve of the war were designed not only further to increase the role of the State Bank as the central unique short-term credit establishment and as the clearing centre for settlements between enterprises of the socialized sector, but also to increase its control over the financial side of the activities of all enterprises and institutions.

The hasty mass collectivization made it imperative to reorganize agricultural credit, and this was carried out simultaneously with the general credit reform of 1930. The Central Agricultural Bank (see above, p. 85) was reorganized into the All-Union Agricultural Kolkhoz Co-operative Bank, and the former republican, provincial and regional agricultural banks became affiliated branches, whilst agricultural credit associations gave up their non-credit activities, such as the sale of agricultural products and the supply of industrial goods to the rural population, and were transformed into purely credit institutions for meeting the needs of local agricultural credit.

The huge capital investments in the national economy, carried out mainly as non-repayable subsidies from the State Budget, transformed the specialized banks into distributors of these funds, whilst their purely banking work came gradually to an end, particularly as the State Bank was monopolizing all short-term crediting. This process was precipitated in 1932 by the reorganization of the former specialized banks into 'special long-term investment banks'.† Four All-Union banking establishments, each specializing in one branch of the national economy, were formed: (1) the Industrial Bank or 'Prombank', whose duty it was to finance the construction of industrial State enterprises, transport and communication facilities, highways and also housing carried out by industrial P. Commissariats; (2) the Agricultural Bank (transformed from the Agricultural Kolkhoz Co-operative Bank) or 'Selkhozbank', whose duty it was to finance capital investments in State farms and M.T.S., and to grant long-term credits to collective farms; (3) the All-Union Co-operative Bank or 'Vsekobank', which, after the abolition of co-operative trading in towns (see p. 253), was reorganized into the Commercial Bank or

---

* Cf. the regulation of the Sovnarkom S.S.S.R., dated 5 August 1939.

† Regulation of the Central Executive Committee and the Sovnarkom S.S.S.R., dated 5 May 1932, 'Concerning the organization of special long-term investment banks'.

'Torgbank', for financing capital investment in State trading organizations and for granting long-term credits for capital construction of the consumers' and the craftsmen's and producers' co-operation; (4) the Central Municipal Bank or 'Tsekombank', with a network of local municipal banks, whose duty it was to finance and grant long-term credits for municipal, housing, and cultural welfare construction, such as schools, hospitals, clubs, etc., and, from 1938, also to finance industrial construction carried out by non-industrial commissariats, as, for instance, financing enterprises of the P. Commissariat of Health or of the Committee for Cinema Affairs.

The duties of these specialized banks included actual financing by means of non-repayable subsidies and long-term credits, funds being provided by the State Budget and by accumulations set aside for the purpose by enterprises (from profits, sinking funds, proceeds from the sale of basic means of production, etc.), which had to be deposited at specialized banks and could be used for capital construction only through the intermediary of the specialized banks; and clearing operations effected for their clients on the basis of approved plans, by allowing them credits and controlling the utilization for the right purpose of the funds advanced. The items thus controlled were: (a) the existence of a detailed technical project and estimate; (b) the prices paid for construction, cartage and assembly work, which were to conform to the estimates set out in the contracts; and (c) the expenditure on training personnel, on administrative costs, etc., which were also not to exceed the estimates. Banks were to cease financing construction work if expenditure on them exceeded the approved estimated cost or the quarterly grants allowed.

Payments were to be made according to the actual volume of work carried out and in conformity with the approved projects and estimates. Moreover, specialized banks, apart from the current control over the money advanced, were also to effect a *post-factum* control by auditing the construction accounts and inspecting the actual construction on the spot. If it is recalled how great the discrepancies were in industry between the outlay on capital construction and the capacities actually going into production during the first F.Y.P. (see p. 167), the urgent need for control by specialized banks over the expenditure of funds advanced for capital construction becomes obvious. The introduction of such a control brought about that complete change in the financial side of construction which was mentioned elsewhere (p. 285). Control over the expenditure of funds advanced for capital construction is indeed the main business of specialized banks.

In our opinion this particular activity of the specialized banks is not peculiar to Soviet banking but is inherent in capital construction under a planned system where means of production are nationalized. Under the capitalistic system the construction of an enterprise is usually undertaken by the physical or legal person who will, in the future, work the enterprise, and therefore the capital construction outlay is taken into account in the future cost of the enterprise's production. Prospective profits are actually gauged in relation to initial capital outlay. Under the Soviet system the two processes—the construction and the working of the enterprise—are both technically and financially unrelated. Construction is carried out by one set of organizations, and production by another. The latter is not the direct successor of the former, and the estimate of the enterprise's planned profits is not based on the capital expended on its construction. A special type of control over the financial side of construction in hand is therefore necessary, for funds sunk into it are not repayable, and the economical and purposeful utilization of outlay is controllable only during actual construction. This need for a specialized system of control over the expenditure of funds advanced for construction work is effected by specialized banks. The overwhelmingly greater portion of capital construction is carried out by setting *limits* to the funds allocated to any enterprise or business institution for any item of construction work; only in the case of minor objects of construction, and within very definite amounts, can the enterprise's director or the corresponding Chief Administration of a P. Commissariat have the work done on the so-called non-limit basis.

Apart from their principal work, to distribute non-returnable funds allocated for financing capital construction and granting long-term credits, and to supervise the utilization of the advances, specialized banks effect for their clients certain banking operations. They settle accounts with contracting building organizations, effect payments for building materials, equipment, cartage, etc., and perform other transactions connected with construction such as granting short-term credits to contracting building organizations to help them lay in stocks of materials required for construction work, to repair building machinery and vehicles, effect seasonal accumulation of materials and meet other definite temporary needs.

Specialized banks are institutions of All-Union importance and are therefore subordinate to the U.S.S.R. P. Commissariat of Finance. Their organizational structure differs in many ways from that of the State Bank. It is not possible here to enter into details, but it should be mentioned that all specialized banks except the Municipal Bank have branches and offices on the spot to carry out their banking operations and also representatives whose sole duty is to exercise control. The Municipal Bank has no branches, and local municipal banks act on its behalf. The largest branches are the provincial and regional offices whose main work consists of: collating material for annual and quarterly financial plans; drafting monthly operational plans; carrying out the actual financing on the basis of approved plans, projects and estimates; paying for the building work; granting short-term credits to contracting enterprises; acting as custodians of the savings of business organizations, and directing the work of the smaller branches, agencies, subagencies and inspectors groups.*

The cash plans drawn up by specialized banks are included in the State Bank's cash plan, thus linking these banks to the State Bank, which supervises their work in carrying out their cash plans.

As already stated, the credit operations of State and specialized banks are based on the credit plan.

The Credit Plan. The drafting of the credit plan begins with the study not of the credit institutions' credit plan, but of the credit and financial plans of enterprises and of economic organizations, their combines and institutions. They send in their applications for credit and cash determined by their approved productive-financial plan (Promfinplan) or their trading-financial plan (Torgfinplan) to the corresponding banking establishment, that is, the enterprises and economic organizations of local importance send their applications to the Bank's local branches, those of republican importance to the Bank's republican offices and those of All-Union importance to the Bank's Chief Administration. Every unit of the banking network has a planning section—at the bottom of the scale is the planning inspector or inspectors; higher up the ladder, in the larger offices, credit planning sections specializing in different branches of the national economy, and general planning sections; lastly, in the Bank's Main Office there are planning sections in every particular Branch Administration and coordinating groups of general planning, the whole system being headed by the Economic Planning Administration of the State Bank. On the basis of the credit plans sent in by business enter-

* For details see *Finance and Credit of the U.S.S.R....,* pp. 416–20.

prises and institutions and on the data regarding the financial resources available within the corresponding planning sections, the latter draw up provisional credit plans and transmit their consolidated plans for the district to the next higher unit of the credit system and thus, eventually, to the Bank's Economic Planning Administration. There the final draft is then co-ordinated with the general plan for the development of the national economy, with the State Budget and with the cash receipts and disbursement plans of the Bank, specialized and savings banks. After being approved by the Sovnarkom, this draft plan becomes operational, and copies of it are sent out for execution to the lower units of the credit system with explanatory instructions. Actually, it is the *quarterly* plans that are operational plans. The annual plan is drawn up as co-ordinating summary control figures connecting together the quarterly operational plans. Whilst the credit plan is being drafted and approved the transactions are carried out on the basis of the provisional plans.

The drafting of the State Bank's credit plan can be summarized as follows:*

Resources	*Appropriations*
1. Current accounts of State and local budgets.	1. For seasonal and temporary needs.
2. Current accounts of budgetary institutions.	2. Credits for goods turn-over.
	3. Transit loans.
3. State insurance funds.	4. Advances on 'accreditives' and special accounts.
4. Savings banks funds.	
5. Collective farms' current accounts.	5. The State Bank's reserves.
6. Current accounts of trade unions and public organizations.	6. Payments from the State Bank's profits.
7. Clearing accounts.	7. Withdrawal of notes from circulation.
8. Funds of specialized banks.	
9. Funds in clearing.	
10. Profits of the State Bank.	
11. Repayment of old debts.	
12. Increased currency circulation (note issue).	

The balance of the general credit plan is struck by an emissionary operation, i.e. by the issue or withdrawal of notes from circulation.

The Cash Plan. Through its balance, the credit plan is closely· linked to the State Bank's cash plan. The latter is like an appendix of the credit plan, and estimates the volume and sources of cash receipts flowing to the State Bank and their ensuing appropriation for the needs of the national economy. The procedure followed in drawing up the cash plan is very similar to that of the credit plan

---

* *Finance and Credit of the U.S.S.R. . . . ,* p. 409.

except for two major differences: (1) the cash plans of all enterprises, business organizations and institutions, whether of local, republican or All-Union importance, are submitted for discussions and approval to the State Bank's local branches, i.e. according to the location of these various establishments and not according to their importance; (2) though the cash plan is drawn up as a quarterly plan, it is the monthly plan which is an operational plan. Income and outgo of the cash plan are drawn up in connexion with the approved plans of work of the corresponding enterprises, economic organizations and institutions, and according to the latter's estimates.

The State Bank's cash plan can be summarized as follows:*

Receipts	*Expenses*
1. Proceeds of trade and public catering.	1. Planned wages.
2. Proceeds of rail and water transport.	2. Other forms of labour remuneration and scholarships.
3. Proceeds of the mobilization of the population's resources (according to data of financial authorities and State Insurance).	3. Disbursements for agricultural produce procurements.
4. Municipal receipts.	4. Payments from collective farms' accounts.
5. Increased balances of the collective farms' accounts.	5. Sickness benefits and other allowances paid out by Social Insurance and remunerations granted by State Insurance.
6. Post office receipts.	
7. Increased deposits in savings banks.	6. Subsidies to the post office.
8. Miscellaneous receipts.	7. Subsidies to savings banks.
9. Cash in hand at the beginning of the planned period.	8. Business transaction and other expenses.
10. Balance from reserve funds (note issue).	9. Cash in hand at the end of the planned period.
	10. Balance of refunds (withdrawal of notes).

Here again the balance is struck by issuing or withdrawing notes. The balances of the cash and credit plans coincide, because both are regulated by the emission order given by the State Bank's Emission Administration. The movement of funds listed under no. 10 in the above table of the cash plan can be effected only with the sanction of the Emission Administration.†

Currency Plan. On the basis of the approved economic plan, the Government forwards instructions to the State Bank every quarter regarding the issue of notes to meet circulation requirements in the forthcoming quarter. The planning of note issue under the Soviet

---

* *Finance and Credit of the U.S.S.R....*, p. 428.

† For details regarding the credit and cash plans see *Finance and Credit of the U.S.S.R....*, pp. 219–21, 408–11, 425–34; I. M. Nusinov, *Methods of Financial Planning*, maps out in greater detail both credit and cash plans; Arnold, pp. 386–403; L. E. Hubbard, *Soviet Money and Finance*, pp. 45–57.

system of planned economy presents far less technical difficulties than it would under the competitive system. The principal movements of commodities are predetermined by the economic plan. The plan also largely determines money disbursements. Moreover, by far the greater part of the turn-over of goods and the circulation of money, connected with payments to and receipts from the population, are made to pass through the channels of the socialized sector of the national economy. The main bulk of goods is handled by State trade and its close associate, co-operative trade. All prices, except those prevailing on the collective farms' markets, are planned prices. Price control is linked to the budget system through the turn-over tax. The greater part of the population's savings is also redistributed through the budget system by means of subscriptions to State loans and through the savings banks' stable balances which reach the budget through the State Bank. The mobile savings of the population, their 'till-money', is insignificant compared with the current cash resources associated with the total income of the population. Therefore money paid out to people employed in State enterprises and institutions in wages—which, too, are planned—and current income of other classes (collective farmers, artisans, professional men, etc.) are spent very shortly after it has been received. The population's 'deferred expenditure' is inconsiderable. The main currents of monetary ebb and flow pass through the channels of the State Bank along the following lines: The State Bank → payments to enterprises, business organizations and institutions → workers' and employees' wages → retail trade and payments for services made by the population to State, municipal and co-operative enterprises → payments of socialized sector and population to the State Budget → everything back to the State Bank (see above, the cash plan summary).

The economic plan determines the expansion of the production of means of production and of the general utility services; similarly, it determines the volume of consumer goods and personal services; the wages plan and adjustments in prices are made to fit the economic plan, and the currency plan—based on the Government's 'emission instruction'—is drafted to satisfy the requirements of the selfsame economic plan.

The currency plan is only an item of the cash plan which permits a balance to be struck; the cash plan is closely linked with the credit plan and the latter dependent on the general provisions of the economic plan and of the U.S.S.R. State Budget. The entire financial system of the U.S.S.R. is subservient to the economic plan, and only serves to connect and control the course of the economic plan; in no way does it, *itself*, influence economic processes.

It should be remembered that as early as the last years of the N.E.P. period, the rouble had become an entirely internal currency; its export from and its import into the U.S.S.R. were equally prohibited, and its exchange value for transactions in foreign currencies was fixed by the State Bank of the U.S.S.R. (see p. 103). The State Bank has a 'valuta' monopoly, that is, apart from the exclusive right of dealing throughout the territory of the U.S.S.R. in gold, silver, platinum and metals of the platinum group, whether in coin, ingots or raw, it also has the monopoly of all transactions in foreign currency, in all commercial paper denominated in foreign currency (bills of exchange, cheques, foreign money orders, etc.) and in foreign securities (shares, bonds, coupons, etc.).

All proceeds from exports and all 'valuta cheques' are directed to the State Bank. Similarly the State Bank settles all the U.S.S.R. foreign accounts, though some settlements, mainly with the Eastern countries, are effected through the Foreign Trade Bank, under the supervision of the State Bank. While settling accounts abroad on behalf of Soviet organizations and of the citizens of the U.S.S.R. in foreign currency, the State Bank settles its accounts with Soviet organizations at home or abroad and with all Soviet citizens in Soviet currency only. For all foreign exchange and gold received, the State Bank pays the Soviet organizations and citizens in Soviet currency. The rate of exchange of foreign currencies is fixed on the basis of the *planned* parity of the rouble and is published by the State Bank in a special exchange bulletin. This rate of exchange is entirely a *technical device* for computing foreign trade turn-over and settlements in foreign currencies. The rate was calculated through the gold parity of some foreign currency. Up to 1936 this was the dollar, 1·943 roubles to 1 dollar on the average. In 1936 and 1937 the French franc was used, but at 1 rouble to 3 gold francs; and after a further devaluation of the franc, at 4·25 francs. From July 1937, when the franc ceased to be a stable gold currency, the exchange rate of the rouble was again pegged to the dollar; and one dollar became equal to 5·30 roubles, while the exchange rate of the rouble with other currencies was adjusted accordingly.*

* The alteration in the exchange rate of the rouble effected in 1936 and the later adjustments were partly due to purely technical considerations of pegging

Owing to the monopoly of foreign trade, the foreign trade turn-over is regulated directly, i.e. by export and import plans, not by indirect methods, and, because the gold parity of the rouble has no direct bearing on its purchasing power at home, the fixing of the rouble exchange rate is a purely technical accounting device for calculating foreign trade operations and transactions denominated in foreign currency. In particular, gold is regarded in the U.S.S.R. as a kind of 'foreign exchange' transmutable into imported commodities. This view is clearly formulated in the following extract from the *Journal of the U.S.S.R. State Planning Commission:*

On the U.S.S.R. home market gold is not a commodity in itself and Soviet notes are not gold tokens. The main purpose of the Soviet gold reserve is to serve as an indispensable fund for settling accounts with foreign countries. In so far as the U.S.S.R. carries on trade with other countries and because gold in international trade is the world currency, the Soviet State must dispose of sufficient gold reserves to purchase and pay on the world market. At the same time the gold reserve has definite importance for ensuring the stability of Soviet currency because, potentially, it represents a certain mass of commodities which can be bought for gold on the world market.... Soviet money is directly bound up with commodities and only indirectly linked to gold, i.e. only in so far as gold is being used by the Soviet State for purchasing goods on the world market.*

In the socialized sector of the national economy of the U.S.S.R., money performs the function of a unit of account for recording cost of production and operating costs; and in this sector, money acts more as an instrument of planning production and costs than as a measure of value. Moreover, as already stated, in this sector clearing settlements are far more usual than cash payments.

In regard to the population, money in the U.S.S.R. carries out on the whole the same essential economic functions as it does under a competitive system, except that it cannot be converted by individuals into reproductive capital through the use of hired labour.

the rouble to the most stable foreign currency for convenience sake to calculate foreign trade turnover and payments made in foreign currencies, but partly it was due to the abolition of rationing and of the 'Torgsin'. The abolition of the 'Torgsin' (see p. 239) and the rise in prices on the home market following on the abolition of rationing would have placed foreign tourists in the U.S.S.R. at a disadvantage had the old rate of exchange been maintained. Therefore the same Government decree (14 November 1935) which abolished the 'Torgsin', instructed the State Bank to exchange foreign currency at the rate of 3 francs to the rouble and correspondingly to adjust the rates of other currencies. Only by a later decree (29 January 1936) was this new rate of exchange extended to all transactions in foreign money, and the gold reserve of the State Bank revalued.   * *Planned Economy,* no. 12, 1940, pp. 70–1.

While monetary circulation in the U.S.S.R. is regulated by the emission plan—which is closely linked to the State Budget, the State Bank's credit and cash plans—the purchasing power of money is dependent on the plan of economic and cultural development.

Foreign Exchange Plan.* Transactions with other countries are regulated by the foreign exchange or 'valuta' plan. The consolidated foreign exchange plan consists of two parts: the commercial and the non-commercial plans. The former is drafted by the P. Commissariat of Foreign Trade, and based on the plans of import, export and other organizations participating in the foreign trade turn-over; it includes also the State Bank's foreign exchange plan for operations abroad. The non-commercial part is drafted by the U.S.S.R. P. Commissariat of Finance and includes the expenses of maintaining diplomatic representation abroad, expenses and receipts from tourist traffic and other non-commercial operations involving foreign currency. The foreign exchange plan of the P. Commissariat of Foreign Trade together with that of the U.S.S.R. P. Commissariat of Finance form the consolidated foreign exchange plan which is submitted for approval to the Government and put into effect by the State Bank. The foreign exchange plan, which, at the same time, is the U.S.S.R.'s planned balance of payments, makes provision not only for the total volume of trade receipts and disbursements of foreign currencies, but details the balances of payments with different countries. The U.S.S.R. State Bank has a monopoly of all operations involving foreign exchange; therefore, on the basis of export and import plans and non-commercial plans either general or specific for each country, it can handle its funds of various currencies more successfully, and reduce to a minimum losses due to changed rates of exchange and to arbitrate operations more easily than individual banks in other countries. As a matter of technique, the foreign exchange plan, like the balance of payments, is calculated in roubles at the official rate of exchange.

CONCLUSION

Gradually, a real financial *system* was evolved in the U.S.S.R. and its branches; the financial-budgetary and credit systems were co-ordinated into a unified whole. The essential function of the financial budget system is the redistribution of the national income. The Soviet State Budget is *actively* linked, by its income and outlay

* For details regarding the foreign exchange plan and the technique of transactions in foreign currencies see *Finance and Credit of the U.S.S.R....*, pp. 438–48.

entries to the entire national economy. The savings of various branches of the national economy are accumulated through its agency (in the form of a portion of the goods' price, by means of the turn-over tax and by means of profits of State and co-operative enterprises) as well as the greater part of the productive accumulations of the population (by means of subscriptions to State loans, State insurance premiums, savings banks' deposits, etc.). It is also through the State Budget that the great mass of the population's money is directed not only to provide for administrative, defence, and social and cultural welfare expenditure, which are the principal items of budget expenditure in other countries, but also to finance the construction of new and the reconstruction of old enterprises in all the branches of the national economy and to replenish their working capital. Thus the objects of the entire population's collective 'saving' and 'investment' are achieved by means of the State Budget. From the point of view of productive investments this 'saving' and 'investment' is supplemented from the accumulations of the State enterprises, their sinking funds and part of their profits and from the collective farms' jointly owned funds. *Individuals* can accumulate only durable consumer goods, such as movable and real property, for their own personal use.

The role of the credit system is to redistribute temporarily liquid funds and control their expenditure according to planned appropriations, and, more generally, the economical management of affairs. It does not in *itself* influence the redistribution of the national income nor the 'saving' and 'investment' activities of the community. The liquid resources of the budget system deposited with the State Bank are one of the essential sources of short-term credit and permit expansion without resorting to the printing press. Budget funds provide the main source for financing works by means of non-repayable subsidies and long-term credits granted by specialized banks. Thus a close connexion is established between credit and budget systems.

The Soviet currency is not a managed but a *planned* currency. Whatever the reasons that may necessitate a change in the volume of note circulation, whether the plan of economic expansion or a failure in fulfilling its quantitative or qualitative tasks, these changes are bound to affect the State Bank's cash plan which covers the greater part of the country's currency circulation. The cash plan is linked with the State Bank's credit and emission plans, which, in their turn, are directly connected with the financial budget system of the U.S.S.R. The financial-budget system is the corner stone of the entire financial system, but nevertheless it only carries out the tasks set to it by the general plan for the country's economic and cultural development. Precisely because of this interconnexion of all branches of the U.S.S.R. financial system with the system's *direct* control over the financial processes of the country, the Soviet financial system succeeded in organizing the country's finances without introducing any disorganization or crisis in the development of the country's national economy. And this was achieved, though qualitative indices (reduction of cost in production and construction work, rise in labour productivity, level of savings within the country, etc.) often lagged behind quantitative indices, and the financial system had to make good breaches by currency and credit expansion, using the potentialities of the financial-budget system on a far greater scale than had first been planned (see pp. 154, 421). Because the cash plan is a monthly, and the credit and budget plans are quarterly operational plans, and moreover because they are interlinked and jointly adaptable, and because the Soviet financial system exercised a general control over transactions, the latter succeeded in making timely adjustments to the tasks set by the economic plan in the course of its fulfilment. The *raison d'être* of the Soviet financial system is to facilitate the fulfilment of the plan for the country's economic and cultural development, and the functioning of the system is entirely subservient to the development of economic processes and in no way determines their course.

Capital investments (without capital repairs) in milliards of roubles in prices of corresponding years*

	1st F.Y.P. Planned	1st F.Y.P. Actual for 4½ years	2nd F.Y.P. Planned	2nd F.Y.P. Actual	3rd F.Y.P. Planned
I. Industry	19·1	24·8	69·5	58·6	103·6
Of which:					
Group A	14·7	21·3	53·4	49·8	87·2
Group B	4·4	3·5	16·1	8·8	16·4
II. Agriculture	7·2	9·8	15·2	14·6	18·0
III. Transport	9·9	8·9	26·5	20·7	35·8
IV. Communications	0·3	0·56	1·68	1·16	1·75
V. Trade and distribution	—	0·94	1·68	2·06	2·56
VI. Social, cultural and administrative construction	—	5·6	18·8	20·8	26·6
Total socialized sector of national economy	46·9	50·5	133·4	114·7	188·2

APPENDIX II

Principal indices of the work of the State Bank of the U.S.S.R

	1934	1938
Single entry (gross) on all accounts included in the State Bank's balance sheet	2,838·3 mlrd. r.	8,300 mlrd. r.
Same, excluding transfers between branches	1,034 mlrd. r.	2,743 mlrd. r.
State Bank's clearing accounts balance	375 mlrd. r.	684 mlrd. r.
Average daily receipts on clearing accounts	1 mlrd. r.	2 mlrd. r.
State Bank's average daily cash receipts	163 mll. r.	360 mll. r.
Credit operations turn-over of the State Bank	140 mlrd. r.	475 mlrd. r.
Outstanding debt of the national economy to the State Bank (on 1 January)	14,222 mlrd. r.	44,953 mlrd. r.
Number of branches and offices of the State Bank	2,295	3,299

APPENDIX III

Currency circulation in millions of roubles

	Banknotes in circulation	Treasury notes and coins	Total
1930, 1 January	1,501·0	1,272·0	2,773·0
1931, 1 January	2,080·4	2,221·6	4,302·0
1932, 1 January	2,788·4	2,888·9	5,677·3
1933, July	3,356·2	3,468·8	6,825·0
1934, July	3,432·5	3,429·0	6,861.5
1935, July	3,838·3	3,895·4	7,733·7
1936, April	5,935·0	3,901·4	9,836·4
1937, January†	8,020·3	3,235·3	11,255·6

* Results of the Fulfilment of the First F.Y.P. p. 253. Draft of the Second F.Y.P., vol. I, p. 422. Results of the Fulfilment of the Second F.Y.P. p. 71. Third F.Y.P. of the Development of the National Economy of the U.S.S.R., 1939–42, p. 225.

† No figures available since 1937.

APPENDIX IV *Draft of a combined financial plan.* * Combined financial plan of the national economy for 19..

I. INCOME AND RECEIPTS

Entry 1	Accumulations			Mobilization of the population's resources	Other income	Total income of a combined financial plan	Grants and credits			Funds transferred from one financial plan to the next	Grand Total
	Profits	Turn-over Tax‡	Amortization				From State and local budgets	From long-term credit banks‡	From State Bank		
I. National economy											
(1) P. Commissariat of machine building											
(2) P. Commissariat of Timber Industry											
(3), (4), etc., similar items for other P. Commissariats and Departments											
National economy, Total											
II. Credit and financial institutions											
Of which:											
(1) State Bank											
(2) Long-term credit banks											
(3) Savings banks											
III. Insurance and public organizations											
Of which:											
(1) State insurance											
(2) Social insurance											
(3) Trade unions											
IV. Social and cultural institutions											
Of which:											
(1) Education											
(2) Health services											
(3) Social security and protection of labour											
V. Defence, administration, etc.											
(1) P. Commissariat of Defence											
(2) P. Commissariat of the Interior											
(3) Administration											
(4) Reserves and other funds											
(5) Loan service											
(6) Miscellaneous											
VI. Revenue of State and local budgets											
VII. Unappropriated reserves											
Receipts and income, Total (Balance)											

Comment on the Draft of a combined financial plan

The combined financial plan is not an operational but a co-ordinative plan. Its function is merely to co-ordinate individual financial plans which are the actual operational plans. The following are the principal individual financial plans which are included in the combined financial plan:

(a) The State Budget plan, the local budgets and the A.S.S.R. budgets plan;

(b) The financial plans of the industrial commissariats and the commissariats of agriculture, transport, trade, social welfare and culture and others, as well as those of co-operative and other departments;

(c) The State Bank's credit, cash and foreign exchange plans;

(d) The plans of the specialized banks which finance and grant credits for capital investments.

The combined financial plans of the commissariats and departments must clearly indicate their particular revenues and expenditure, receipts from the State Budget and other financial institutions and payments to the latter. They must include the plans of all the organizations belonging to the given commissariat or department. These combined financial plans are drawn up for each of their Chief Administrations and a combined plan for the whole commissariat, all of which are based on local data and instructions concerning the main items of the plan of national economy (such as the volume of production, cost price, capital construction, the going into production of new or reconstructed enterprises, etc.). The above plans are submitted for scrutiny to the planning and financial authorities of the U.S.S.R. (or of the appropriate republic in the case of republican commissariats). (2) After the annual and quarterly budgets have been ratified by the Council of P. Commissars of the U.S.S.R. (or of the appropriate republic), the P. Commissariats ratify the financial plans of their Chief Administrations, which in their turn confirm those of their subordinate trusts and enterprises. The latter must render account of the execution of these plans. Thus the combined financial plan of any P. Commissariat is closely interwoven with all the productive-financial plans of its enterprises; it co-ordinates the numerous financial plans of enterprises and trusts and through their intermediary is carried into effect.

For details see I. M. Nusinov, *Methods of Financial Planning*, pp. 54, 57. Cf. also the detailed Instruction of the Economic Council of the Sovnarkom S.S.S.R., 'Revenue and Expenditure Balances of the economic P. Commissariats and departments', *Bull. Financ. and Econ. Leg.* nos. 27–8, 1939.

* I. M. Nusinov, *Methods of Financial Planning*, pp. 64–7.

† P. Commissariats and Departments do not include in their income revenue brought in by the turn-over tax. The total amount of this revenue appears under heading VI, i.e. 'Revenue of State and local budgets'.

‡ Only those funds received from specialized banks and drawn from their special capital and similar funds are shown in this column. Funds received through the intermediary of specialized banks but actually provided by the Budget appear under the heading 'From State and local budgets'.

II. EXPENDITURE AND PAYMENTS

Entry 2	Financing investments	Increased working capital	Outlay on setting up new industries	Operational and other expenses	Total expenditure according to combined financial plan	Payment to financial system by:			Funds transferred from one financial plan to the next	Grand Total
						State and local budgets	Long-term credit banks	State Bank		
Headings I–VII as above for Entry 1										

CHAPTER XX. GENERAL PLANNING
THE PRE-REQUISITES OF PLANNING

In spite of the very difficult economic conditions which marked the introduction of N.E.P., some of the fundamental and, indeed, the most necessary prerequisites for the planned development of the national economy had been created. Different authors give different connotations to the word 'planning', and this leads not only to confusions in terminology but also affects the understanding of the very essence of the measures carried out in the field of Russian economy.* It seems, therefore, desirable to state at the outset what is meant by planning in the present study and what prerequisites are regarded as necessary to put such planning into effect.

Planning presupposes:

(1) The formulation of the aims pursued by the plan.

(2) The existence of planning machinery.

(3) The knowledge of what 'exists', that is, of the conditions prevailing at the start, of their elements and interdependence which will serve as a basis for the plan.

(4) The drafting of the plan, i.e. the embodiment of the general aims in concrete tasks, the fulfilment of which will result in the plan itself being fulfilled.

The existence of these four conditions allows the *drawing up* of a plan, but does not yet provide the requisites for *planning*, that is, of carrying out the plan.

The following conditions are necessary to make planning effective:

(1) The decision of the authority in power to carry out the proposed plan, i.e. the official approval of the plan and the issue of instructions and orders to put it into effect.

(2) The means of enforcing the execution of the plan, which must include the possibility of controlling the course of its fulfilment and of imposing penalties for failure to carry out orders issued by the planning authorities.

* In Dr Claude David Baldwin's *Economic Planning, its Aims and Implications*, the University of Illinois Press, Urbana, 1942, the reader will find an exhaustive summary of various opinions on questions connected with planning. A thorough analysis of the fundamental problems of planning in general will be found in *The Planning of Free Societies*, by Prof. Ferdinand Zweig, London, 1942, whilst *La planification soviétique*, by Dr Ch. Bettelheim, Paris, 1940, is perhaps the most detailed study of the principles of soviet planning to have been published outside the U.S.S.R.

Planning, in the full meaning of the word, is a reality when the execution of the plan is effected by means of direct orders and instructions. If, however, the planned aims are achieved by applying indirect measures, this cannot be regarded as planning, but should be termed control. For example, if the plan fixes the production of definite quantities of wheat, and orders and instructions are issued fixing definite figures for wheat production, this can be considered as *planning*; whereas the fixing of definite prices for wheat designed to stimulate or curtail the sowing of wheat and thus to achieve the desired wheat production can only be termed *wheat production control*.

Whatever the scope and importance of the measures taken (whether applied to single or to many enterprises, to branches of the national economy or even to the entire economy of a country), whatever the length of time for which these measures are taken (a number of years, a year or a fraction of it), whatever the forms and methods used in the drafting of the plans, no planning can, in our opinion, be effective unless the conditions listed above, and in particular the last, are satisfied. Only in so far as the enforcement of orders and instructions regarding planned tasks is being extended from a group of enterprises to a whole industry and then to the entire national economy, does partial planning become comprehensive, and finally complete economic planning comes to be achieved. Stalin has clearly stated that the obligation to carry out the plan is an essential feature of planning in the U.S.S.R. 'Admittedly they [i.e. under the capitalistic system] too have something akin to plans. But these plans are prognosis, guess-plans which bind nobody, and on the basis of which it is impossible to direct a country's economy. Things are different with us. Our plans are not prognosis, guess-plans, but *instructions* which are *compulsory* for all managements and which determine the future course of the economic development of our *entire* country. You see that this implies a difference of principle.'*

Partial, departmental planning became national economic planning in the U.S.S.R. when it became possible to draw up plans covering an ever-increasing number of branches of the national economy (their interdependence being taken into account), and, in particular, when it became possible to carry out these plans by means of orders and instructions.

A State Plan for the electrification of Russia (Goelro) was worked out as early as the period of 'War Communism'. It em-

* Stalin's speech at the Fifteenth Party Congress, Verbatim Report, p. 67.

braced a vast project for a general reconstruction of Russia's national economy. On 22 February 1921, on the eve of the introduction of N.E.P., the Government issued the following 'Statute for the setting up of a State Planning Commission':

(1) A General Planning Commission is being established in connexion with the Council of Labour and Defence (S.T.O.) for the purpose of working out a single, all-embracing State economic plan, on the basis of the electrification plan (Goelro) approved by the Eighth Congress of Soviets, and for general supervision of the execution of the aforesaid plan.

The economic problems first on the list, particularly those to be carried out at the earliest date, namely, in 1921, are to be elaborated in detail by the General Planning Commission or its sub-commission taking into consideration the existing economic conditions.

(2) The functions of the State General Planning Commission are as follows:

(a) To work out a general State Plan as well as the means and order for carrying it out;

(b) To examine and co-ordinate with the general State Plan all industrial programmes and planning suggestions of the various departments and regional economic organizations in all branches of national economy. To establish a rota for the execution of the same;

(c) To work out a series of general State measures for developing the knowledge and organizing the research necessary for putting the Plan of State Economy into effect, and for employing and training the necessary personnel;

(d) To work out measures for acquainting the general public with N.E.P., the means for its execution and the forms for the corresponding organization of labour.

(3) The State General Planning Commission, in carrying out its functions, is entitled to communicate direct with all higher State and central departments and institutions of the Republic.

(4) It is the duty of all the Commissariats and regional and local institutions to place at the disposal of the State General Planning Commission any information and material asked for, and to delegate responsible collaborators to provide the necessary explanations.

(5) All planning suggestions arising in commissariats and departments and connected with problems of national economy, and all production programmes are to be submitted to the State General Planning Commission for examination and co-ordination with the State General Plan.

(6) The Praesidium and members of the State General Planning Commission are appointed by the Council of Labour and Defence. The chairman of the State General Planning Commission is granted the right of personally reporting to the President of the Council of Labour and Defence.

(7) In carrying out its duties, the State General Planning Commission employs its own staff of collaborators. Moreover, the Commission is entitled to enlist the services of individual specialists both for permanent or temporary work in the Commission. It is likewise entitled to commission outside workers and remunerate them on a piece-work basis.

From the very outset, therefore, the Gosplan (State Planning Commission) was granted wide powers for working out the general State Plan for the reconstruction of the country's national economy. However, several years elapsed before the Gosplan drew up (towards the close of 1925) the first 'substitute' for an annual State economic plan in the form of 'Control Figures of National Economy for 1925–6', which, however, were not approved by the Government as a provisional plan for the development of the country's national economy. Only in later years were the Gosplan's 'Control Figures' gradually to become a genuine plan of national economy.

The first Plan of National Economy to be actually worked out by the U.S.S.R. Gosplan under the above title appeared only in 1931, and henceforth one was published every year. The cause for the prolonged delay which preceded the drafting of a first economic plan and the introduction of complete economic planning was the necessity of first creating the fundamental prerequisites for planning enumerated above.

Although after the transition to N.E.P. the 'commanding heights' in various branches of the national economy remained in the hands of the Government, nevertheless N.E.P. involved the co-existence of two distinct economic systems: the socialized and the private sectors. In the early years of N.E.P., the socialized sector occupied a dominating position in finance, large-scale industry, transport and foreign trade. In agriculture, petty industries and home trade, private enterprise played a leading part. It has been shown that, in regard to the socialized sector, the setting up of a system of departmental administration and the elaboration of departmental planning in the individual branches of the national economy proved to be a lengthy and complicated process. Even in industry, the sphere of national economy most dominated by the State, trusts and syndicates were obliged, up to 1927, in conformity with their statute, to achieve profits, as one of the main purposes of their production and trade activities. Only in the 'Model regulations concerning trusts' of 1927 was this particular point omitted and a clause substituted demanding that the activities of a trust be conducted 'in accordance with planned tasks, which have been approved by the appropriate State institution'. The process of controlling the development of industrial production exercised by the S.E.C. only gradually grew into planning; only gradually did *administration* by State departments (e.g. issue by the S.E.C. of orders to be put into effect by trusts and enterprises) and *control* (indirect measures designed to control production and disposal mainly through syndicates) develop into the *planning* of large-scale industrial production (e.g. drafting of provisional plans, issue of instructions and the introduction of measures designed to put these plans into effect). In the field of agriculture, throughout the N.E.P. period and until mass collectivization had been achieved, the grip of the State on the production and disposal of agricultural produce could be accomplished only by controls, i.e. by indirect measures. These measures, as already stated, consisted in various credit, taxation and social regulations, in the price policy, in methods of purchasing agricultural produce and other indirect ways, by means of which the Government intended to attain the desired modifications in the social structure of the peasantry and in the production and disposal of agricultural products. Gradually in home trade, and then only in so far as the growth of State trade and its associated co-operative trade reduced the importance of private trade, could control lead to a planning of the movement of goods and prices on the home market.

Generally speaking, during the first years of N.E.P., the commissariats concerned only gradually acquired the necessary experience of departmental planning within the various branches of the national economy. Similarly, during the early years of N.E.P., the U.S.S.R. Gosplan was mainly concerned with working out measures for planning and controlling certain 'crisis' sections of the national economy (such as the functioning of railways, corn prices, fuel supply, etc.).

The other fundamental prerequisite for nation-wide economic planning, i.e. the knowledge of what actually 'exists', together with the organized study of individual branches of the national economy and their interconnexion, was also satisfied gradually. Every act of planning, in so far as it is not mere fantastic castle-building, presupposes a preliminary investigation of existing conditions. Lofty aims are not sufficient for shaping the future. A thorough, not a 'general' knowledge of the initial situation, that starting point for the future, is imperative. This sounds a commonplace, but such a simple truth is frequently ignored by authors who write on planning or criticize the difficulties met with by planning in the U.S.S.R. During the N.E.P. period, so long as both the socialized and the private sectors co-existed, the possibilities for studying the developments which were taking place in the national economy remained unequal and dependent on the relative importance of this or that sector in a given branch of the national economy. The improving organization in the management of individual branches of the national economy enabled the Gosplan to obtain direct information from enterprises and institutions of the socialized sector. With regard to the private sector, however, it was necessary to rely merely on general indices and incomplete information. Therefore, even under the condition of properly equipped research staff and machinery, the degree of the Gosplan's knowledge of the actual position in any branch of the national economy depended on the relative importance of the two sectors mentioned above in any given sphere of the national economy.

Although the Gosplan, even in the early years of N.E.P., was able to obtain direct information of the progress of production and disposal in large-scale industry subordinated to the S.E.C., the same could not apply to small-scale industry, agriculture and private trade, information about which was not sufficiently precise. This naturally precluded the drawing up of an operational plan for any branch of the national economy taken as a whole.

Consequently only a system of planning was gradually evolved which made it possible to solve problems of planning and controlling individual branches of the national economy as a whole and eventually to tackle the drafting of a general plan covering the national economy of the whole country.

THE GROWTH OF THE PLANNING SYSTEM

During the N.E.P. period the planning system developed from two sets of organizations. On the one hand, special bodies were set up for general planning and, on the other, planning sections were being attached to the P. Commissariats and organizations governing the corresponding branches of the national economy. In describing the evolution of industrial administration and the processes which took place in the field of labour and home trade, an outline has been given of the development of departmental planning; an account only of the formation of the special machinery for general planning need be given here.

The shape of the future division of the country into economic regions were already apparent in the plan of the Goelro.* On

* According to this plan, the R.S.F.S.R. was to be divided into eight economic regions or districts: the Northern, the Central-Industrial, the Southern, the Volga, the Ural, the West-Siberian, the Caucasian and the Turkestan. *Electrification Plan for the R.S.F.S.R.*, Moscow, 1920.

4 November 1921, the Gosplan submitted to the Council of Labour and Defence a plan for the regional division of Russia on an economic basis, in which it was stated that:

Regional division must be founded on the economic principle. Every district thus created should represent an original and, wherever possible, an economically complete territory of the country, which—owing to a combination of natural characteristics, cultural values accumulated in the past, and with a population trained for production work—would constitute one of the links in the chain of the country's economy. Combining local resources with the capital values provided by modern technique and the General Economic Plan, the principle of economic completeness makes it possible to draft a programme for the economic development of the country based on the maximum utilization of every possibility with minimum outlay. At the same time, other important results are achieved: to a certain extent regions specialize in those industries for which they are best suited, and exchanges between regions are limited to strictly necessary and purposefully directed products of their respective production.*

It follows that from the outset, State Plan and planning system were so construed as to combine centralized management with decentralized planning executives. However, many years elapsed before these principles came to be translated into practice.

In the course of administrative reorganization and the division of the country into economic regions, planning institutions were set up in every republic and in every administrative and economic district; these planning institutions began working out yearly 'control figures and prospective plans for the economic development of their particular district'.† With the coming into existence of the State Planning Commission of the R.S.F.S.R. in February 1925, the setting up of republican State planning commissions, and provincial, regional and district commissions became strictly standardized. The pyramid of general planning commissions followed closely the administrative division of the U.S.S.R.; the U.S.S.R. Gosplan is the central State Planning Commission for the entire Soviet Union with gosplans in the allied republics and

* 'The Economic Regionalization of Russia.' *Report of the Gosplan to the All-Union Central Executive Committee*, 3rd session, Moscow, 1922, p. 55.

† For example, the Ural province was formed in 1923, and the same year on the basis of plans submitted by various industries, the first prospective plan for the Ural was attempted and an annual plan for 1925–6 actually drawn up. The Central Asiatic republics drew up their first economic plan in 1924. For further details see 'The Regional Section of the Economic Plan', *Planned Economy*, no. 3, 1936.

planning commissions in the A.S.S.R., provinces, regions, 'okrugs' and towns with a population of over 20,000. Each of these planning commissions is the central planning authority for its respective territory (republic, region, province, etc.), being at the same time subordinated to the planning commission of the larger territorial unit. Apart from these general planning commissions, departmental planning commissions are attached to the U.S.S.R. P. Commissariats, the P. Commissariats of allied republics and their subordinate sections, Chief Branch Administrations, trusts, enterprises and other administrative and economic units running the socialized sector of the national economy; the lower departmental planning commissions are subordinate to the higher ones on the same pattern as the general planning commissions. Here the principle of graduated subordination both in departmental and territorial-administrative (i.e. general) planning is brought into line with the principle of complex territorial planning, i.e. the plan drawn up by a general planning commission must include the plans of *all* the enterprises situated within the territory served by the given commission, irrespective of whether these enterprises are of All-Union, republican or local importance. From the point of view of administration, enterprises are subordinated to their superior managing bodies, but, parallel to this, their plans must also be submitted to the general planning commissions of the territorial subdivision in which they are situated; they thus form a component part of the general plan for the development of the national economy, which is drawn up by the corresponding territorial planning commission for all enterprises situated within its territory. Accordingly, the departmental plans of various branches of the national economy are co-ordinated with the general plans embracing the entire economy of a given territory, and, eventually, these plans are integrated into the general plan of the country's economy. Further details regarding the functions of the various units which form the planning system will be given below in the outline of the present-day work of the U.S.S.R. Gosplan and the territorial planning commissions.* This co-ordination in the work of the various planning units was evidently arrived at with the gradual expansion of planning work and the possibility of transforming controls into planning.

* Readers desirous to acquaint themselves in greater detail with the delimitation of functions of territorial planning commissions are referred to the regulation of the R.S.F.S.R. Sovnarkom, dated 16 June 1927: 'On the order for the co-ordination of planning work between the autonomous Republics and the central institutions of the R.S.F.S.R.' *Coll. Decrees*, 1927, no, 57, § 396.

THE VOLUME OF PLANNING

The scope of planning gradually expanded too with the growth of the planning machinery, its institutions and personnel, accumulating experience in the handling of economic processes and the increasing importance of the socialized sector. At first the Gosplan merely worked out measures to meet definite current problems and, therefore, corresponding sections such as the food, fuel, transport, metallurgy, agriculture, home trade, finance, conjuncture, etc. sections were set up.* The industry section of the Gosplan issued the 'Fundamental rules for drawing up the industrial plan' only in 1923, and actually drafted the first general industrial-financial plan for the entire large-scale industry subordinated to the S.E.C. of the U.S.S.R. as late as 1924, i.e. in the fourth year of its existence; prior to this only partial plans limited to certain industries had been drawn up. The first attempt to work out something resembling a general plan to cover the country's whole economy was made in 1925, when the 'Commission on Control Figures' of the U.S.S.R. Gosplan worked out the 'Control Figures for the national economy of the U.S.S.R. for 1925–6'. These control figures were an attempt to give a systematic survey of the preceding course of development of all the branches of the national economy, and, by taking into consideration the trends of development, to forecast their course during the following year; simultaneously a number of measures to solve the most urgent problems was put forward. However, these first 'Control figures', drawn up by the Gosplan for the U.S.S.R. as a whole, were not accepted by the Soviet Government as a suitable basis for planning the economic developments of the coming year; the 'Control figures for the national economy of the R.S.F.S.R. for 1926–7', drawn up by the Gosplan of the R.S.F.S.R., met with the same fate. The reason for this rejection was not due to any technical shortcomings of these control figures, but was dictated by deeper considerations and

---

* Lenin expressed in a rather picturesque way the need for the Gosplan, in the early years of N.E.P., to concentrate its main work on current problems: 'There is too much about electrification and too little about *current* economic plans.... When I was faced with the Communist "wise men" who babbled and wrote nonsense about the plan in general without having read the book *The Plan of the Electrification of Russia*, nor understood its meaning, I had to dig their noses into that book.... But in dealing with those who wrote it, I should have to drag them not towards but away from the book—to problems of current economic plans.... The present task of the State General Planning Commission is not to concentrate on that [i.e. the electrification plan] but to devote all its energy to working out current economic plans.' Letter to the Chairman of the Gosplan. Lenin, *Coll. Works*, vol. xxvi, p. 296.

matters of principle. In describing the processes which took place in the fields of finance, home trade, agriculture and to a lesser degree in that of industry, we indicated that, in the early years of N.E.P., the reconstruction of the system of economic relations was modelled on measures inherited from the pre-revolution system. The traditional and conservative mentality of economists and specialists in various fields of national economy is strikingly demonstrated by the nature of the 1924 monetary reform and in the State budgets drawn up in the N.E.P. period. The same conservative mentality, imbued with traditional methods of studying economics and economic theories inherited from the capitalistic system, is also noticeable in the way the first 'plans' for the development of the national economy were drawn up. In the last resort plans are man-made; as Lenin bluntly put it, that when seizing power 'we [Bolshevists] could foresee neither the form of the transformation, nor the pace of development of concrete socialists reforms. . nor is it possible by some *a priori* order to throw off or establish by a single stroke the forms of organization of the new society'.* What is true of forms is even more true of men who create the new forms and the new methods of reorganization of the economic system. In its methods of running the country's economy, N.E.P. was more or less a return to the old ways of the competitive system. Evidently circumstances were not the same in the socialized and in the private sector. Evidently also the aim was not only to rehabilitate the country's economy but also to adapt it to the new socialist order and to solve the problem of 'who'll get on top' by a victory of the socialist elements over the capitalist elements; nevertheless, these aims had to be attained in a setting of production and market relations which fundamentally differed little from a capitalist system. In the first years of N.E.P. irrational economic development overwhelmed any attempts at planning. As a result, the study of economic processes and the drafting of 'plans' for the development of the national economy followed the traditional path: study of conjunctures, application of extrapolation methods for establishing 'prognosis' of the future, stress laid on the static, not the dynamic equilibrium between individual branches of national economy, generally speaking the application of all the paraphernalia used by workers of conjuncture institutes for the study of the economic developments in capitalist countries. In this connexion it is significant that, apart from the Conjuncture Council of the U.S.S.R. Gosplan, there existed up to 1928 also a Conjuncture Institute

* Lenin, *Coll. Works*, vol. XXIII, p. 40.

attached to the P. Commissariat of Finance, and when it was closed down in 1928,* the Central Statistics Administration took it over 'to organize conjunctural statistical observations'; moreover, every administration in the U.S.S.R. was obliged 'to collect statistical conjunctural data in their respective fields of work after having settled with the Central Statistical Administration of the U.S.S.R., provisional plans and programmes for the manner of such collecting'.†

In their 'Control Figures for 1925–6' the U.S.S.R. Gosplan applied the methods of study of economic developments traditionally used in capitalist countries. One of the principal authors of these Control Figures, V. Groman, stressed that 'the methods and forms of changing society are dictated by the objective conditions of society and the objective trends of its development which are inherent in it. . . the achievement of pre-war relations, in which the conditions for economic equilibrium were expressed, provides to a great extent regulative norms, in the objective sense of the term, for the present economic process'.‡ Therefore the whole plan was thought of as 'an extrapolation of the events of the past projected into the future' and the proposed economic measures were to flow like a kind of tributary into the channels of this trend of development. For instance, the authors of the Control Figures drawn up by the R.S.F.S.R. Gosplan, noting the growth in the preceding year of the wealthier group of grain producing peasants, i.e. the economically and socially 'upper strata' of peasants, and stating that, 'the growth of the larger farming homesteads is based not only on the redistribution of means of production (exploitation),

* The work of the Conjuncture Institute differed little from that carried on in conjuncture institutes all over the world, and, from the point of view of methods, was strongly influenced by the Harvard School of Economic Barometers. Towards the fall of 1927, some members of the Institute openly criticized the Government's measures concerning industry and agriculture, accusing the policy of support afforded to industry as one leading to a crisis; the Institute's work was sharply censured by influential members of the Government and in 1928 the Institute stopped publishing its Bulletin; later, the leading members of the Institute were sentenced with a group of workers of the Gosplan and the Central Statistics Administration on charges of wrecking activities on the economic front. Cf. *The Bulletin of the Conjuncture Institute*, nos. 11 and 12, 1927; and *Problems of Conjuncture*, edited by N. D. Kondratiev.

† Regulation of the Sovnarkom S.S.S.R., dated 5 June 1928, *Bull. Financ. and Econ. Leg.* no. 31, 1928.

‡ *Planned Economy*, no. 1, 1925, pp. 88 and 98. Citation from *Social Economic Planning in the Union of Soviet Socialist Republics*, Report of Delegation from the U.S.S.R. to the World Social Economic Congress, Amsterdam, August 1931, pp. 62, 63.

15

but rather on the creation of such means of production by the households' own efforts', made provisions for a further increase of the upper peasant strata in the course of 1926–7. Such an interpretation of planning and such methods of drawing up plans obviously contradicted the principles of the Soviet Government whose aim it was to reform the national economy so as to increase the importance of the socialized sector and to introduce an entirely new set of economic relations. To base planning on the extrapolation of present trends, is indeed wholly to misunderstand the meaning of planning. For planning is essentially an act of the will, the choice of alternatives in the shaping of future developments. That which 'exists', i.e. the present state of the national economy, can only be a starting point but by no means the factor *determining* the future. For example, in the early years of N.E.P., private trade was developing quicker than State trade, the renting of land and the hiring of agricultural labourers were on the increase, in some districts the numbers of well-to-do peasants were rising, and the situation was more favourable to light than to heavy industry. However, it was the Government's avowed policy to intensify the development of State trade, to limit the rise of the well-to-do peasantry, to restore and further to develop the heavy industry, etc., i.e. to *overcome* the trends of development and not to foster their continuation. Consequently planned measures should have aimed at achieving these ends. But the Gosplan's first Control Figures were not inspired by any attempt at changing the system but were based on the extrapolation of tendencies apparent in the national economy and aimed at achieving an economic equilibrium modelled, on the whole, on pre-revolution and pre-war relations between industry and agriculture and resting on market relations. This approach in the drafting of the 'plan' and the measures of economic policy recommended therein, explain why the first Control Figures were unacceptable to the Soviet Government and were in consequence never ratified. Many economists and statisticians who held responsible posts in the Gosplan, the Central Statistics Administration and the Conjuncture Institute were made to resign, and the Party's control over these institutions was strengthened.* It should be emphasized that the U.S.S.R.

---

* In a publication of the Institute of Economics of the Communist Academy outlining the stages of economic planning, it is emphasized that, 'for many years a fierce struggle was waged within the planning institutions around the Control Figures—the wreckers and their opportunist supporters of both "left" and "right" orientation on the one side, and the small group of communists

Gosplan was at the time only an advisory body of the U.S.S.R. Council of Labour and Defence, and its task was merely to embody in concrete measures the instructions on economic policy issued by the Party and the Government.* The Supreme authority in matters of economic policy was the Council of Labour and Defence.

Economic Councils (Ekoso) attached to the U.S.S.R. P. Commissariats and to the Sovnarkoms of allied republics supervized the enforcement of the approved economic measures and co-ordinated the decisions taken by P. Commissariats and other economic

upholding the Party line in planning, on the other. At the same time, these years saw the elaboration of the planning technique and the often none too successful struggle for the liberation of this technique from the influence of wreckers'. *Stages of the Economic Policy of the U.S.S.R.*, op. cit. p. 121.

* The main points of economic policy were first considered by the Polit-Bureau and the Central Committee of the Party and were then submitted for approval by the Government. The following 'Plan of work of the Polit-Bureau, the Central Committee and the Plenum of the Central Committee of the Communist Party for 1926', gives an interesting picture of the problems discussed by the Party in those years. In 1926 the following were on the agenda: (1) The Control Figures for the national economy for 1926–7. Report of the Gosplan (Sept.). (2) Report of the Central Statistics Administration of the crop harvest in the current year (July). (3) The prospective five-year plan for the development of industry, according to industries and districts. Report of the U.S.S.R. S.E.C. and joint reports of the Central Control Commission and the Workers' and Peasants' Inspection (July). (4) The results of the application of the Trust Law from the point of view of its conformity with general economic policy. Report of the U.S.S.R. S.E.C. and joint reports of the Central Control Commission and the Workers' and Peasants' Inspection (May). (5) Report of the Chief Administration of the metal industry (structure and fulfilment of planned work) (May). (6) The position in the armament industry. Report of the Armament Industry Administration and the Revolutionary Military Soviet of the U.S.S.R., and joint reports of the Central Control Commission and the Workers' and Peasants' Inspection (July). (7) Report and accounts of the P. Commissariat of Finance for the first half of the year and joint reports of the Central Control Commission and the Workers' and Peasants' Inspection (May). (8) Course of fulfilment of the State Budget for 1925–6 and budget estimates for 1926–7. (9) Results of the work and development of the credit system of the U.S.S.R. (10) Report of the P. Commissariat of Trade (structure and work of agencies abroad, activities of export and import companies, etc.). Course of fulfilment of the export-import and of the foreign exchange plans for 1925–6 and plan for 1926–7. Practices and shortcomings of the trade network, etc. For details see *The C.P. in Resolutions...*, p. 103.

It is significant that appended to every report of any P. Commissariat is a joint report drawn up by the controlling Party (Central Control Commission) and Soviet (Workers' and Peasants' Inspection) authority whose duty it was to give critical appreciations on the reports submitted for discussion and approval by the economic institutions.

bodies.* May it be stressed once more that the planning authorities (the Gosplan, with its system of planning institutions and the departmental planning network) only worked out plans in conformity with Government directives; whereas the actual planning, i.e. the execution of planned tasks was the job of the corresponding P. Commissariats and other economic authorities. It seems necessary to insist on this distinction between the drafting of plans and actual planning, since so many authors when writing about 'planning' focus their attention on the elaboration of plans and omit to mention machinery, channels, and measures, which have to be devised and put into effect in order to make planning possible. In describing the developments which took place in the main branches of the national economy, an attempt has been made, in earlier chapters, to show how the prerequisites and conditions suitable for planning came to be evolved and planning made possible.

One of the most important technical prerequisites in the elaboration of plans is the organization of the necessary statistical observation over the processes taking place in the national economy. In the N.E.P. period such observations were to a considerable extent carried out according to the traditional pattern common to statistical institutes the world over. In the first years of N.E.P. a hierarchy of statistical bodies was established with the statistical sections of enterprises at the bottom of the ladder, the trusts', Chief Branch Administrations', P. Commissariats and territorial administrative centres' statistical sections higher up the scale, and, at the head of the system, the Central Statistics Administration of the allied republics and the Central Statistics Administration of the U.S.S.R.† This organization and programme of statistical observations were not closely linked to the problems of planning; only as late as 1931, when the U.S.S.R. Central Statistics Administration was reorganized into the Central Administration of Economic Accounting (Ts.U.N.Kh.U. S.S.S.R.) of the U.S.S.R. Gosplan, did the latter become entitled to 'work out and ratify the system of

---

* For details regarding the functions of the Economic Council of the Sovnarkom of the R.S.F.S.R., and illustrating the organization of similar economic councils in allied republics, see *Bull. Financ. and Econ. Leg.* no. 37, 1927.

† For details regarding the scope of the work done by the Central Statistics Administration of the U.S.S.R. and the Central Statistics Administrations of the allied republics, during the N.E.P. period, see the 'Statute of the Central Statistics Administration of the U.S.S.R.', in *Bull. Financ. and Econ. Leg.* no. 28, 1927; and the 'Statute of the Central Statistics Administration of the R.S.F.S.R.', *ibid.* no. 38, 1927.

indices of accounting for the entire national economy in conformity with the requirements of economic planning'.*

It was owing to all these circumstances that the Control Figures of the Gosplan became only gradually the actual basis of the annual operational plan and were gradually extended to include an ever increasing number of items of the national economy. The Control Figures of the national economy of the U.S.S.R. for 1926–7 already raised the fundamental questions: 'Which classes and groups in the Soviet Union are the bearers of its growing productive forces? In what directions is the economic power of the socialist and private sectors of the country's economy developing? What are the achievements of socialist construction and the dangers confronting them at the present stage of development of these productive forces?'† However, the central problem in these Control Figures was that of regulating market relations (cf. chapter on Home Trade). Many problems relating to the development of industry, agriculture, construction, labour, the State Budget and monetary circulation were dealt with from that particular angle. The authors of the Control Figures held the opinion that at the end of the recovery period, i.e. when production and correlation between various branches of the national economy would have reached the pre-war level, and the reconstruction period would begin, the rate of growth of the country's productive forces would slow down. The method of striking economic balances of certain commodities (such as the metal balance, the grain and fodder balance) was being applied already in the drawing up of these Control Figures. Its object was to eliminate the disproportions in the progress of these branches of the national economy as compared with that in others. Nevertheless, the Control Figures for 1926–7 as well as those for 1927–8 were approved only in part, but not as a single all-embracing plan of national economy. Parallel to the Control Figures, special plans were adopted for various industries, e.g. the 'Promfinplan' (productive-financial plan), drawn up by the U.S.S.R. S.E.C., the armament industries plan, the wages plan, the Budget and others. This was due not merely to the above defects in the composition of the first Control Figures,

---

* Regulation of the Sovnarkom S.S.S.R., dated 9 May 1931. Cf. also Regulation of the Central Executive Committee and the Sovnarkom S.S.S.R., dated 10 March 1932, 'Concerning the approval of the statute of the Central Administration of Economic Accounting of the Gosplan and also of Economic Accounting in the allied republics, provincial and district organs'.

† *The Control Figures of the National Economy of the U.S.S.R. for* 1926–7, p. 6.

but also to the fact that during the restoration period it only gradually became possible to extend planned action to whole industries and to change over from control to actual planning. Even as late as the end of the N.E.P. period, agricultural and small-scale industrial production as well as processes on the home market were only controlled and not planned. In 1928, in connexion with the difficulties in the supply of agricultural produce, it was officially stated by Stalin himself that, 'it would be a mistake to underrate the part and importance of planning. But it would be a still greater mistake to exaggerate the part actually played by the planning principle and to take it for granted that we have reached that stage of development when we are in a position to plan and regulate all and sundry. It should not be forgotten, that apart from elements susceptible to our planned action, there are those that resist; there exist, moreover, classes hostile to us, who cannot be overruled by the mere process of Gosplan planning'.*

One more feature in the scope and form of planning in the U.S.S.R. during the N.E.P. period must be mentioned here.

To critics who pointed out that it was utterly impracticable to plan the electrification of Russia at a time when the country's economy was on the verge of a catastrophe, Lenin replied: 'One cannot work without a plan covering a lengthy period and calculated to achieve important success'. A tremendous plan of work 'must be given at once, in a graphic, popular form, in order to captivate the masses by a clear and brilliant prospect (absolutely scientific in principle): To work! and in 10–20 years' time all Russia—industrial and agricultural—will be electrified!' But 'it is imperative specially to link up the scientific plan of electrification with the current practical plans and their actual fulfilment'.† 'The economic tasks first on the schedule, particularly those which are to be carried out in the nearest future, namely within the year 1921, should be worked out in detail by the General Planning Commission, the actual economic situation being fully taken into account.'‡ These quotations clearly formulate Lenin's differentiation between *prospective* and *current* plans. The prospective plan lays down the general lines of development for a prolonged period; the

---

* Stalin, *Leninism*. 'From a talk with the students of the Institute of Red Professorship, the Communist Academy and the Sverdlov University', 28 May 1928, p. 182.

† Quoted from excerpts published in *Planned Economy*, no. 3, 1936, pp. 11, 12.

‡ Lenin's Symposium xx, p. 23. Quoted from *Planned Economy*, no. 1, 1934, p. 12.

current plan transforms the general aims of the prospective plan into definite measures to be carried out at the present moment, and taking into account the existing economic conditions. The two forms of plans differ not only quantitatively (length of time) but qualitatively (in the degree in which the plan is immediately applicable in practice, detailed and adapted to prevailing circumstances). The Goelro was the first *prospective* plan for the reorganization of industry and agriculture in Russia on the basis of electrification. The approved draft of the first F.Y.P.* was the first *prospective* plan for the reorganization of the entire national economy and the social and cultural structure of the U.S.S.R. on the basis of a far-reaching plan of industrialization and collectivization of agriculture. It was a *prospective* plan, and as shown above its various parts had been elaborated in varying degrees of detail.† However, the prospective tasks of the F.Y.P. were set out most concretely not in a general economic plan, but again in the Control Figures of the national economy for 1928–9, i.e. for the first year of the five-year period, and later in the Control Figures for 1929–30. Only in 1931, i.e. the third year of the five-year period, did the Gosplan work out 'the National Economic Plan of the U.S.S.R. for 1931 (Control Figures)'; and henceforth, instead of the former Control Figures, an annual plan covering the entire national economy was drawn up every year. This change of title reflected the change in the volume of planning which had taken place since the introduction of the first F.Y.P.

In order to draw up the F.Y.P. for the country's economic and cultural development, the U.S.S.R. Gosplan and its network of republican and local planning institutions had to digest and co-ordinate the considerable experience gradually acquired in departmental planning; in particular, they profited by the S.E.C.'s experience in drafting plans for the development of industry.

---

* Several other prospective plans had been worked out before the approved draft of the F.Y.P. Cf. Deborin, Stagovich and Chernin, *Theory and Practice in the Planning of the National Economy in the U.S.S.R.* 1929. G. M. Krzhizhanovsky, *Problems of Planning*, vol. II, 1934. Strumlin, *Problems of Planning in the U.S.S.R.*

† In his political report of the Central Committee to the Sixteenth Party Congress, Stalin emphasized that, 'the F.Y.P. is for us merely a plan, adopted as a first approximation and one which need be altered, improved and rendered more precise on the basis of local experience of the working of the Plan. Only bureaucrats can think that the work of planning ends with the drawing up of a plan. The drawing up of a plan is merely the beginning of planning. Proper planned guidance is developed after the plan is drawn up, after it has been verified locally and rendered more precise in the process of fulfilment'. Quoted from *Planned Economy*, no. 1, 1934, p. 12.

Moreover, all planning sections of the commissariats of allied republics collaborated in drawing up the provisional F.Y.P. and so did scientific and research institutes and individual scientists, professors, engineers and specialists in the various fields of national economy.* Consequently both the materials and the methods of drawing up plans were checked by the general planning and departmental planning bodies; conversely, first-hand practical experience contributed to enrich the technique and the organization of drafting annual Control Figures.

In the course of elaboration of the provisional F.Y.P. the discrepancies in the development of individual branches of the national economy which has been widening in the N.E.P. period were startingly revealed. The planning authorities were, therefore, forced to turn their attention to co-ordinating the development of the various branches and to work out methods of balancing estimates. The discrepancies noticed in the degree of recovery of the manufacturing industries and the output of iron ore, pig iron and steel, and also coal, made it necessary to work out balances of raw materials, fuel, equipment and skilled labour. The 'scissors' between industrial and agricultural prices, between wholesale and retail, world and home market prices, demanded the elaboration of methods to co-ordinate and secure balance by the reduction of prices on manufactured articles and the rise in prices on agricultural products; they also called for measures designed to extend the State and co-operative trade network not only in regard to wholesale but also in regard to retail trade. Furthermore, the object of the first F.Y.P., being not only to promote the country's economic but also its cultural development, necessitated the setting up in 1928 of corresponding planning sections within the Gosplan to deal with measures for cultural development.

Thus, the Control Figures gradually grew from a *series* of figures and measures taken in separate industries into a *system* of figures knitting more closely together the planned measures to be taken in various branches of the national economy in the ensuing year.

* Cf. the regulation of the R.S.F.S.R. Economic Council, dated 11 August 1927, 'On the contribution of local organs and P. Commissariats of the R.S.F.S.R. to the drafting of the prospective F.Y.P. of national economy', *Bull. Financ. and Econ. Leg.* no. 37, 1927. Regulation of the Sovnarkom R.S.F.S.R., 'On the drafting of the prospective F.Y.P. for the development of the national economy and social and cultural construction in the R.S.F.S.R.', ibid. no. 32, 1928. Regulation of the Sovnarkom S.S.S.R., 'Fundamental statutes of the planning organs of the P. Commissariats of the U.S.S.R.', ibid. no. 31, 1928.

Only parts of the Control Figures for 1927–8 had been approved by the Government, together with special economic plans worked out by the corresponding commissariats. In 1928–9, however, the Government found it possible to discontinue the practice of examining and approving special plans for many individual branches of the national economy, in particular the passing of a separate production-financial plan for industry previously drawn up by the U.S.S.R. S.E.C.;* instead, the Government ratified the Control Figures for 1928–9 as a general draft plan for the national economy of the U.S.S.R. for that year. Even then the State Budget and some other special items (defence, wages plan), though closely linked with the Control Figures, were approved separately.

Nevertheless, in the introduction to the *Control Figures of the National Economy of the U.S.S.R. for* 1928–9, the chairman of the Gosplan found it necessary to stress the following facts:

We are building up a planned economy and we are still in the process of building it. It would, therefore, be as irrational to demand perfection from our calculations and the standard of our estimates as to expect the balanced proportions of any large architectural structure to be clearly discernable to all and sundry, while it is still surrounded by scaffolding. ...We are convinced that planned economy is one of the commanding heights—in fact, potentially the most important one—of our economy. We are introducing this system of planned economy, however, in one of the most backward countries technically, frequently in the painful conditions pertaining to the period of transition from private to socialized economy. There do not, nor can there exist any complete theories of such a construction. There are no precedents in history. Socialist construction, therefore, in its early stages cannot proceed otherwise than gropingly. And *wherever practice is in advance of theory, faultless creativeness is impossible.*†

The obstacles to the Control Figures becoming an all-embracing annual plan of national economy and cultural construction con-

---

* By its regulation of 16 August 1928, the Sovnarkom S.S.S.R. abrogated any further issue and approval by the Government of the State industry summary productive-financial plan. Instead, it was decreed that the 'planning of industry is carried out every year on the basis of Control Figures...the S.E.C. submits (*a*) provisional Control Figures for all State industry planned by it and (*b*) summarized information regarding all other industry. On the basis of the Control Figures of national economy approved by the Sovnarkom S.S.S.R., the S.E.C. establishes for the enterprises of All-Union importance directly subordinate to it and also for the S.E.C.s of allied republics annual production-financial tasks and annual plans of capital work. *Bull. Financ. and Econ. Leg.* no. 38, 1928.

† *Control Figures of the National Economy of the U.S.S.R. for* 1928–9, p. 2.

sisted not merely in the difficulties of *drawing up* the plan nor in the fact that planned measures were being carried out in one of the technically most backward countries. The difficulties were also due to the great discrepancies which existed within the various branches of the national economy in the possibilities of actually *carrying out* the plan. For instance, the planning of transfer prices in large-scale State industry had become possible after the consolidation of its administration in 1925, the planning of wholesale prices had likewise grown more comprehensive since 1925, when most of the wholesale trade turn-over had come under the control of the syndicates. On the other hand, the planning of retail prices for manufactured goods and particularly for agricultural produce was still only partial in 1928, and could be applied only within the insufficiently developed framework of State and co-operative retail trade. In the chapter on trade an account has been given of the emergency measures taken to achieve the planned reduction of prices on manufactured goods, and of the administrative—not economic—measures resorted to in 1927–8 to obtain agricultural products and to combat private trade which was jeopardizing the planned price policy. Prior to wholesale collectivization, agriculture could be influenced only through indirect measures, i.e. controls, not planning. Hence plans in the field of agriculture could be but tentative, not operational. Even in the field of industry and credit, the most socialized branches of the national economy, there were industries (medium and small plants not yet included in the S.E.C.'s plans and co-operative, private and craftsmen's production) and credit transactions (commercial credit granted by enterprises and institutions) still not subject to planning.

Only when private trading had been reduced to a minimum and the basic industrial and agricultural goods rationed, could a more comprehensive planning of the trade turn-over and of prices on the home market be introduced. The reorganization of industrial administration carried out in 1929 and the application of the 1930 credit and fiscal reforms created the prerequisites for a nation-wide planning of industry and credit. The collectivization of peasant holdings and the formation of a network of State farms extended planning into the sphere of agricultural production. Lastly, the reorganization of the trade unions and of the P. Commissariat of Labour, together with measures for training skilled cadres to put the F.Y.P. into effect, brought about the planning of labour.

The improvement in the drafting of plans due to a growing experience and a better co-ordination of departmental with general economic planning on the one hand and, on the other, the expansion of the socialized sector made it possible in 1930 to go over from the drafting of Control Figures to the elaboration of a national plan, covering the country's entire economy and cultural life, which henceforth was annually approved by the Government. Many governmental enactments of the Control Figures which had hitherto had only a regulating effect now became planned tasks compulsory for the corresponding branches of the national economy.

Nevertheless, as already stated, the draft F.Y.P. was markedly uneven in the elaboration of its programmes for various branches of the national economy, for it neither embraced all the enterprises of an industry nor were all its programmes worked out to the same degree of detail. Even the most thoroughly drafted part of the F.Y.P., i.e. the programme of industrial development, consisted of detailed plans of capital construction and production covering industries directed by the S.E.C., while plans for other big and medium industries were very general, and only tentative proposals were put forward as regards petty industries and handicrafts in spite of their importance as supplying consumer goods to the population. Also, in the first years following the adoption of the F.Y.P. it was not possible to carry out its various provisions to the same extent. Whereas the plan's quantitative targets were embodied in precise and controllable tasks and, on the whole, were faithfully fulfilled, its qualitative targets (such as the reduction of production costs, the raising of labour productivity, the improvement of standards and quality) were expressed only in general and summary terms; their degree of fulfilment was subject only to unsatisfactory methods of control and their actual fulfilment was equally unsatisfactory. In this connexion the planning institutions had to solve a most fundamental problem in the study of methods for drafting economic plans, namely the degree of detail to which a plan should be worked out. Should the national plan be just a general outline guiding the development of the various branches of the national economy and co-ordinating this development with a wide margin of initiative allowed within this framework to the economic organs responsible for carrying out the plan in practice? or alternatively, should the general plan be akin to a grand total of detailed specific tasks with the economic organs acting as mere subordinate executives? Experience alone could show the right course between too general a plan which would blur the concreteness of the tasks set and the too detailed plan which would cramp the creative initiative of economic workers and limit their chances of adapting the plan to the circumstances. The adopted course was to state the principal purposes of every annual plan and to set each branch of the national economy a few principal tasks, so that all efforts to fulfil the plan centred on these main objectives.

THE METHOD OF BALANCED ESTIMATES

With the wider use of the method of balanced estimates it became possible to achieve a co-ordinative planning of the development of related industries and to establish a closer connexion between measures taken in the different branches of the national economy. Just as for the normal working of any enterprise it is necessary to keep accounts and draw up a balance-sheet of material and monetary resources, i.e. to strike a balance reflecting the enterprise's work and the results achieved by the end of the year, similarly under the planned economy the resources of entire branches of the national economy, their interdependence and the call made upon them have to be balanced. As the drafting of balances expands from a group of related enterprises to the entire industry and thence to interbranch relations, later to be welded into a system of branch balances and eventually culminating in a general economic balance—so planning gradually develops from partial and loosely co-ordinated into all-embracing economic planning. This method of balanced estimates was widely applied in drafting the F.Y.P., but the balanced estimates themselves were far too general. When the F.Y.P. began to be carried out, its various provisions were fulfilled with varying degrees of success and the discrepancies in the development of individual industries became acutely apparent. Life itself brought the planning institutions to work out with more precision the balance-sheets of many branches of the national economy. As a result, the first annual plans devoted much attention to working out a number of material balances. By means of these material balances the kinds of products needed to fulfil the tasks set by the plan were determined, the respective shares to be provided by related industries were allotted, bottle-necks brought to light, plans of necessary capital work, of equipment and raw materials to be imported were established, and so were plans of corresponding exports. For instance, the fuel balance was arrived at by setting against the detailed estimates of production of the main kinds of fuel—coal, wood, oil, peat, gas and shale—the estimated consumption by transport, industry, the fuel industry itself, the population, etc.; moreover, the geographical location of fuel production and consumption was fully taken into account. Similarly, the balance of electrical power was struck by setting a detailed programme of power production against planned power consumption in industry, construction, transport, municipal services, rural areas, etc. General and partial balances of metals, equipment and building materials were drawn up on similar lines, and so were the balances of various kinds of manufactured goods (e.g. the balance of production and distribution of motor cars and the closely allied balance of rubber manufacture and import; the balance of tractor production and distribution in agriculture and the numbers to be imported to strike the balance, and so on). The grain* and textiles balances, and that of raw materials of animal origin were similarly worked out.

Nevertheless, under the first F.Y.P. these material balances applied only to the most important branches of the national economy, and were made use of to attain urgent 'shock' objectives planned; but by no means were they welded into a perfectly co-ordinated system of balance-sheets. As already shown, during those years planned measures sought to solve specific important current problems and, consequently, material balances were worked out for these 'priority links' of the general plan. Thus, the plan of intensive industrial construction made it urgent to work out balances of building materials and equipment, the latter entailing the elaboration of balances of metals; the plan to expand heavy industrial production necessitated the elaboration of fuel and power balances as well as balances of mining industries; the production plan of consumer goods called forth the elaboration of balances of agricultural raw materials, and so on. However, the Gosplan had not as yet set up sections of co-ordinative planning, i.e. sections co-ordinating separate material balances into a system

---

* The following items made up the grain balance:

A. *Resources*

1. Stocks in hand at the beginning of the year, of which:
   (a) In agriculture.
   (b) In industry.
   (c) In trade channels.
2. Harvest, gross (according to sectors).
3. Resources, total.

B. *Consumption*

1. Consumed by production:
   (a) Seed.
   (b) Livestock feed (urban and rural).
   (c) Industry.
2. Consumed by population and institutions:
   (a) Agricultural (according to groups).
   (b) Non-agricultural (according to groups).
   (c) Institutions.
3. Export-Import.
4. Stocks in hand by the end of the year, of which:
   (a) In agriculture.
   (b) In industry.
   (c) In trade channels.

of balances.* Incidentally, these sections of co-ordinative planning were formed only in 1935. In the drafting of the second F.Y.P. the method of balanced estimates was used both more widely, i.e. applied to a far greater number of branches of the national economy, and the balances themselves were worked out in greater detail and based on more precise data. Before drafting the second F.Y.P., and upon the instructions of the Sovnarkom S.S.S.R., the U.S.S.R. Gosplan circulated to the P. Commissariats of allied republics and to provinces questionnaires accompanied by explanatory notes concerning the principal indices required for drawing up the Plan. The information received from the provinces, together with the governmental instructions, enabled the U.S.S.R. Gosplan to work out summary control figures of the second F.Y.P. Then, on the basis of these control figures, the Gosplan sent more definite limits and directives to departments and districts for drawing up branch, republican, provincial and district five-year plans. Eventually these local plans were integrated by the Gosplan into the final draft of the second F.Y.P. for the development of the national economy.†

* After the re-organization of the U.S.S.R. Gosplan, effected in 1931, and prior to its second reorganization in 1935, planning was being carried out by the following sections constituting the Gosplan: the sections of power (fuel and electricity), industry, agriculture, transport and communications, consumption and distribution (i.e. organization of trading, and allocation of goods), labour (including the training of cadres, wages, + labour productivity), culture (including education, press, libraries, clubs, + broadcasting), science (the network of scientific institutions, the planning of scientific exploration and research), economics and statistics, and the organizational section whose duty it was to plan the work and the organization of the Gosplan itself.

† 'Aiming at a thoroughly scientific preparation and strictly scientific verification of the concrete problems and tasks of the F.Y.P., the Sovnarkom S.S.S.R. gave leave to the Gosplan to call 24 All-Union conferences and meetings. The P. Commissariats, the republics and provinces organized dozens of meetings and conferences to discuss their own problems and the industries subordinated to them. In this way, the problems of the second F.Y.P. came to be discussed by hundreds of scientific and research institutes, scientists specializing in the most varied subjects, by all the scientific élite of the country. Thus the second F.Y.P. compiled by the Gosplan was based not only on the information furnished by the planning system, but also on data worked out and thought out by thousands of institutions and organizations directly in touch with the corresponding branches of the national economy.' The regulation of the Sovnarkom S.S.S.R., dated 25 March 1932, and entitled 'Regarding the organization of the work of drafting the second F.Y.P.', proposed 'to secure for the work of drafting the F.Y.P. the co-operation of the widest strata of the working class'. The Central Committee of the Trade-Unions published (25 May 1932) a special appeal specifying exactly how and in what way workers, engineering and technical staffs and employees could take part in the elaboration of the F.Y.P. V. Halperin, 'From the experiment of drawing up the second F.Y.P.', *Planned Economy*, no. 3, 1936, pp. 72–3.

In the 'basic instructions for the drawing up of the second Five-Year Plan', published by the U.S.S.R. Gosplan, it was further emphasized that, 'in drafting branch and district plans it is necessary to apply the method of balances in order to check every variant of the proposed plans.... These balances must serve as a means of checking the correctness of the planned relations between individual industries within a given district and in regard to the national economy as a whole'.* In the provisional F.Y.P. this method of balanced estimates was in fact generally used to work out plans for all branches of national economy. Moreover, apart from the material balances of the separate branches, some composite balances were also worked out; such were the balances of man-power, of production and consumption, of the financial plan and of-production and distribution of the national income. Gradually branch balanced estimates began to serve as a basis for annual economic plans. They also served to control the course of fulfilment of quarterly plans for the development of individual branches of the national economy when in 1930 the U.S.S.R. Gosplan inaugurated the practice of such quarterly plans.

In striking balances the Gosplan not only co-ordinates separate production and consumption programmes into a balanced whole; it also checks whether applications made by departments, and projects submitted, agree with the general objectives of the plan for the development of the particular branches, and with tasks set for improving the work of the corresponding industries and the targets fixed for economizing in raw and other materials.†

The next step to improve the elaboration of material balances

---

* Basic instructions for the drawing up of the second F.Y.P. of the national economy of the U.S.S.R. (1933–7), Gosplan of the U.S.S.R., 1932, p. 7, quoted from *Planned Economy*, no. 3, 1936, p. 79.

† In drawing up the balance of electrical power, e.g. the Gosplan scrutinized the applications for power and the production plans of every branch of the national economy; moreover it compared the applications submitted with the quotas of electricity expended per unit of production at the foremost European and American enterprises. As a result the plan fixed new targets and norms for the enterprises.

Similarly, in drawing up the balance of equipment, the Gosplan not only co-ordinated the applications for equipment received from various P. Commissariats, economic organizations and social and cultural institutions; it also examined whether these applications corresponded to the approved projects and estimates, and the volume of capital work planned by any given commissariat or business organization, whether the achievements of modern technique were fully taken advantage of and no out-of-date type of equipment asked for, whether the planned utilization of the equipment demanded was correct and conformed to established technical norms, and how far the need for the amounts of every item of equipment was justified, etc.

was made in 1935 after the abolition of rationing. A regulation of the Central Executive Committee and the Sovnarkom S.S.S.R., 'On the reorganization of the State Planning Commission of the U.S.S.R.', issued on 15 April 1935, materially altered the structure of the Gosplan as it had so far existed. The Praesidium of the Gosplan was abolished and with it management by collegium. Instead, a chairman with far wider power, and a commission of seventy members were appointed. The latter were appointed by the Sovnarkom upon the recommendation of the chairman and were drawn from among leading members of the U.S.S.R. Gosplan and the local planning commissions and also from among scientists, technicians and cultural workers irrespective of their standing in individual departments and institutions. Two types of departments were set up within the U.S.S.R. Gosplan: (a) *departments of co-ordinative planning*, 'which elaborate the corresponding sections of the single national economic plan, supervise its fulfilment and solve problems of bringing into line the plans of various branches and districts, and work out the technique of planning'; and (b) *departments of planning of the various branches of the national economy*, which also supervise the course of fulfilment of the plan within these branches.

The enumeration of the principal departments which at the time constituted the U.S.S.R. Gosplan will give a clear picture of what problems came into its field of vision when drafting the annual plans; we therefore include here an outline of its structure.

A. *Departments of Co-ordinative Planning*

(1) Department of the co-ordination of production.
   (a) Section of production economics;
   (b) Section of production technique.
(2) Department of capital works.
   (a) Section of capital works co-ordination plan;
   (b) Section of the building industry and architecture;
   (c) Section of hydraulic engineering.
(3) Department of district planning.
   (a) Section of natural resources;
   (b) Section of the Central Industrial and Western districts;
   (c) Section of the Southern districts;
   (d) Section of the Volga districts;
   (e) Section of the Eastern districts;
   (f) Section of the East Siberian and Far-Eastern regions;
   (g) Section of the Transcaucasian, Uzbek, Turkmenian and Tadjik S.S.R.s and the Kirghiz and Kara-Kalpak A.S.S.R.;
   (h) Section of the Northern districts.

(4) Department of material balances.
    (a) Section of the co-ordination of material balances;
    (b) Section of the balances and plans for the allocation of metals and alloys;
    (c) Branch of timber balances and allocation plans for timber;
    (d) Branch of building materials balances and allocation plans.
(5) Department of financial plan.
    (a) Section of financial policy;
    (b) Section of Budget and credit;
    (c) Branch of national income.

B. *Departments of Branch Planning*

(1) Department of fuel and power.
    (a) Section of fuel balance and fuel supply planning;
    (b) Section of coal industry;
    (c) Section of oil industry;
    (d) Section of local fuel;
    (e) Section of electrification.
(2) Department of mines and metallurgy.
    (a) Section of heavy metallurgy;
    (b) Section of non-ferrous metals;
    (c) Section of rare metals;
    (d) Section of non-ore minerals.
(3) Department of engineering industry.
    (a) Section of rolling stock building;
    (b) Section of electrical engineering;
    (c) Section of general machine-building;
    (d) Section of heavy machine-building;
    (e) Section of agricultural machine-building;
    (f) Section of equipment balances and distribution.
(4) Department of chemical industry.
    (Three sections.)
(5) Department of timber industry.
    (Two sections.)
(6) Department of light industry.
    (Three sections.)
(7) Department of food industry.
    (Three sections.)
(8) Department of local industries and industrial co-operatives.
(9) Department of agriculture.
    (Six sections.)
(10) Department of railway transport.
    (Three sections.)
(11) Department of water transport.
    (Two sections.)
(12) Department of trade.
    (Two sections.)

(13) Department of foreign trade.
  (*a*) Section of import plan;
  (*b*) Section of export plan.
(14) Department of culture.
  (*a*) Section of education;
  (*b*) Branch of arts;
  (*c*) Branch of the press.
(15) Department of housing and municipal services.

C. *Independent sections*

Section of defence.
Section of labour and cadres.
Section of road and air transport.
Section of communication plans (post, telegraph, etc.).
Section of health services.
Section of training of planning personnel.*

Moreover, the following institutions are part of the Gosplan: (1) The Central Administration of Economic Accounting of the U.S.S.R. Gosplan; and (2) The Institute of Economic Research of the U.S.S.R. Gosplan and the All-Union Academy of Planning.

The changes in the structure of the Gosplan were chiefly designed clearly to distinguish between co-ordinative and branch planning sections. The former co-ordinated problems of interbranch and interdistrict planning, worked out methods of planning and drew up a unified economic plan. The latter elaborated the various component items of the Plan for the corresponding branch of the national economy. Branch planning departments and sections worked out the entire developments of their respective branches including capital construction, volume of production, technical and economic indices, numbers of workers to be employed, wages, labour productivity, production costs and the finances of their branch. Press comments devoted to this reorganization of the Gosplan laid stress on the duty of the sections planning the de-

* For details see *Bull. Financ. and Econ. Leg.* no. 11, 1935. In 1937 this structure of the U.S.S.R. Gosplan underwent certain modifications. The department of co-ordination of production was reorganized into the department of the combined plan with the following sections: general plan, labour, industrial production, cost price and plan fulfilment supervision. The section of labour and cadres was abolished. Instead, a branch for planned training of cadres was included in the department of culture. The Institute of Economic Research was also abolished and the Technico-Economic Bureau of the Chairman of the Gosplan was organized in its stead. The section of Defence was reorganized into the department of Defence with three sections: armament industries plan, mobilization preparedness of the national economy, and plan of the P. Commissariats of Defence and of the Interior. The organization of the department of fuel and power was likewise modified. For details see *Bull. Financ. and Econ. Leg.* no. 28, 1937.

velopment of individual industries to work out not only economic but also technical indices and indices reflecting the financial side of the enterprises' work.* It was suggested that apart from the economic and production plans, a unified technical plan of the development of the national economy was required. However, as shown later, the Gosplan elaborated its first technical plan only in 1941. The need to strengthen district planning, to make greater use of the experience and initiative of regional and provincial economic organizations and also of local economic possibilities was similarly emphasized. A reorganization of the republican gosplans and local planning commissions on the whole similar to that of the Gosplan was carried out as a result.† The Gosplan was also instructed to enforce a strict supervision of the Plan's fulfilment. Its former special section for the supervision of plan fulfilment was abolished and both co-ordinative and branch departments and their sections made responsible for checking the fulfilment of the Plan within their respective fields of planning.

THE SUPERVISION OF PLAN FULFILMENT

The possibility of supervising the fulfilment of the plan is, in our opinion, a fundamental prerequisite of planning. This supervision should pursue a twofold purpose: to control the fulfilment of planned tasks and to control the development of the national economy. The former entails the enforcement of government decisions, the detection of failures to fulfil the plan and the penalizing of such failure. The latter entails studying how the plan fits in with actual conditions and what causes the actual course of events to depart from the planned course; it also means devising suitable measures either to alter the plan (in the case of planning mistakes or the impossibility of carrying out the planned tasks under the given circumstances) or to take steps for achieving the planned tasks. However thorough the elaboration of the plan, it is always possible that its authors may have overlooked some circumstances, or the data and the notions which they had in mind did not exactly conform with the facts. The execution of the plan may meet with unforeseen or inadequately appreciated obstacles, or with human failings such as slackness, dishonesty or ill-will among those

* For details see V. Mezhlauk, 'Regarding the reorganization of the Gosplan of the U.S.S.R.', *Planned Economy*, no. 4, 1935.

† For details see *Coll. Decrees*, 1935, no. 19, § 183: 'On the reorganization of the State Planning Commission of the R.S.F.S.R. and of local planning commissions.'

responsible for putting the plan into effect. The supervision of plan fulfilment must call attention to the departures from the plan and suggest alterations to be made in the interdependent parts of the plan.

In so far as control ceases being sporadic and becomes systematic, and the shorter the time-lag between the departure from and the revision of the plan, the nearer planning moves from general guidance to operational planning. The elaboration of a plan, the issue of orders to put it into effect and control over its fulfilment are only different aspects of planning, and their combination is essential to operational planning. This may sound a commonplace. However, most authors writing about planning either completely overlook or devote but little attention to the need for devising some machinery for supervising plan fulfilment. Moreover, even in Soviet planning practice, this aspect of planning received much less attention than its other aspects. So much so that in a report on the third F.Y.P. for the development of the national economy of the U.S.S.R., the chairman of the Sovnarkom S.S.S.R., Molotov, found it necessary to stress that

planning cannot be considered good unless it takes into account the *course* of fulfilment of the plan. Unrealistic arm-chair planning is cheap enough. Planning is no mere piling up of tables and figures unrelated to the course of fulfilment of the plan. We need plans as a guiding line in our economic work. We need specific plans for branches and districts, covering years or shorter periods, adequately co-ordinating the various items of the plan and the time limits set to carry them out. According to *the results of the actual fulfilment of the plan*, it is necessary to introduce *emendations** in individual branches, districts and dates of fulfilment of the plan. We need plans to verify how our economic work is being carried out. If the plan is not bound up with plan fulfilment supervision, it becomes a mere scrap of paper. This applies to all our economic organizations and to our entire economic work. By seriously improving our plan fulfilment supervision we shall improve at the same time our economic work and the drawing up of our plans.

Hitherto we have not devoted due attention to plan fulfilment supervision. Time and again our enemies have taken advantage of this fact for their wrecking activities. We must put an end to this attitude and then our plans will play an even greater part in the country's economic life.†

The planning authorities met with more obstacles in devising effective means for checking up the fulfilment of the plan than in

---

* Author's italics.
† V. Molotov, *The Third Five-Year Plan for the Development of the National Economy of the U.S.S.R.*, Moscow, 1939, pp. 20–1.

the other aspects of planning. The network of planning authorities evolved only gradually, and the transition from partial planning to 'Control Figures' and thence to a nation-wide economic plan had been equally gradual. Yet, as soon as the socialized sector of the national economy came into existence, the need for some form of administrative control to ensure the execution of government decisions by economic organizations became apparent. So that the need for control preceded the setting up of the planning machinery and the introduction of planning. Throughout the N.E.P. the control over the activities of all commissariats and other economic organizations of the socialized sector was effected by the P. Commissariat of the Workers' and Peasants' Inspection of the U.S.S.R. and the republican P. Commissariats of the Workers' and Peasants' Inspection together with their local organs.*

At the same time, throughout the N.E.P. and up to 1932, the supervision of the course of development of the national economy was carried out by the conjuncture bureaux, which formed part of the U.S.S.R. Gosplan and of the gosplans of the allied republics. As their name suggests, they did not supervise the fulfilment of the plan, but studied conjunctures arising from the course of development of the national economy. Only in 1932 were these 'conjuncture bureaux' of the Gosplan reorganized into sections for checking the fulfilment of the economic plan; henceforth it became their duty to effect an untiring and constant control and 'to struggle' for the fulfilment of the plan.† At fixed intervals, in accordance with Government and Party instructions, all departments and organizations were to submit data showing the degree of fulfilment of the plan, and also practical proposals and projected steps called for by the degree of its fulfilment and any relevant information required by the planning commissions. Though the reorganization of the 'conjuncture bureaux' into sections for the checking of the fulfilment of the plan increased the Gosplan's hold over the course of its fulfilment, its supervision remained nevertheless somewhat academic and inadequately forceful in practice. In fact, the activities of economic institutions and enterprises continued to be subject to the permanent supervision of the

* Apart from the parallel to this central control with its local organs there existed the Party Central Control Commission whose duty was to supervise the enforcement of the Party line. However, the work of both the Party's and the Government's controlling organizations was closely interlocked.

† For details see the Sovnarkom's regulation, 'On the organization of the checking of the fulfilment of the national economic plan'. *Coll. Laws*, 1932, no. 52, § 233.

corresponding departmental hierarchy and occasional inspections held by the Workers and Peasants Inspection. Eventually departmental supervision gained in importance over the sporadic inspections held by the organs of the Workers and Peasants Inspection, particularly after a 'Fulfilment Commission' (Komissiya Ispolneniya), i.e. a central governmental commission whose duty it was to supervise the execution of all governmental decisions, was attached to the Sovnarkom S.S.S.R. Gradually all the control work previously effected by the Workers and Peasants Inspection passed to the Fulfilment Commission. Consequently in 1934 the P. Commissariat of the Workers and Peasants Inspection and its local organs were abolished as having achieved their purpose and their whole machinery was transferred to the Soviet Control Commission of the Sovnarkom S.S.S.R., which itself superseded the former Fulfilment Commission. The duties of the Soviet Control Commission comprised 'the systematic, concrete and operational supervision of the actual fulfilment of the most important Government decisions. . .the adoption of urgent measures for strengthening Soviet discipline and for correcting distortions coming to light'. Twenty subsections supervising the main branches of the national economy formed the central machinery of the Commission which also maintained permanent representatives in the allied and autonomous republics, regions and provinces. These representatives were to enlist the collaboration of local soviets, trade unions, engineering and technical sections, collective farms' aktivs, the press, and so on.*

The extensive functions of the Soviet Control Commission consisted, therefore, in the supervision of the fulfilment of the Government's decisions regarding national economy, and the Commission could inflict penalties for their infringement. The functions of the supervision organs of the P. Commissariats and their departments were similarly wide. At the same time, the U.S.S.R. Gosplan possessed neither the authority of the departments and the Soviet Control Commission nor the technical means of exercising supervision. Apparently herein lay the main cause for the Gosplan's inadequately organized supervision of plan fulfilment. However, with

---

* For details see the Statute of the Soviet Control Commission of the Sovnarkom S.S.S.R., *Bull. Financ. and Econ. Leg.* nos. 6, 7, 1934. At the same time the reformed Party Control Commission was 'to carry out its work in close collaboration with the Soviet Control Commission of the Sovnarkom S.S.S.R., co-ordinating the measures regarding joint decisions of the Party Central Committee and the Sovnarkom S.S.S.R.' Cf. *Bull. Financ. and Econ. Leg.* no. 7, 1934.

the growing authority of the U.S.S.R. Gosplan in the direction of the country's entire planning work and the creation of a competent machinery for carrying out supervision of plan fulfilment, this side of its work grew in importance. The splitting up of some of the P. Commissariats into smaller commissariats proved to be another contributory factor. The old commissariats governed vast branches of the national economy and were responsible for checking the fulfilment of the plan by their branches. The subdivision of the all-embracing old commissariats into more specialized ones reduced at the same time the scope both of their intersectional planning and of their plan fulfilment supervision. This placed before the Gosplan problems of coordinating the fragmentary planning of the separate branches; e.g. prior to its subdivision into a number of industrial commissariats, the S.E.C. was responsible for planning the entire large-scale industry; after its subdivision, the general planning of industry as a whole came to be replaced by a number of specialized sectional plans. The supervision of plan fulfilment was similarly split among specialized commissariats and consequently the Gosplan had to strengthen its co-ordinating supervision.

In 1938, when the results of the second F.Y.P. were being summarized and disproportions in the development of certain branches of the national economy became apparent, the U.S.S.R. Gosplan was again reorganized. The object of the reform was to strengthen the Gosplan's leadership and co-ordinative role in the planning work of P. Commissariats and departments and in the supervision of plan fulfilment. The new statutes emphasized that the U.S.S.R. Gosplan, apart from working out and submitting to the Sovnarkom S.S.S.R. national prospective, annual and quarterly economic plans, must also:

(1) Submit to the Sovnarkom S.S.S.R. its conclusions on the prospective, annual and quarterly plans drawn up by the P. Commissariats and other departments of the U.S.S.R. and the allied republics. Moreover, the economic plan of the U.S.S.R. Gosplan must first and foremost ensure a proper correlation in the development of the various branches of the national economy and elaborate measures to prevent disproportions in their development.

(2) In order to obviate possible breaches in the fulfilment of the economic plan, the Gosplan was to:

    (a) Verify the fulfilment of the State plan by the P. Commissariats, departments and enterprises;

    (b) Lay before the Sovnarkom S.S.S.R. problems and proposals arising from the verification of the fulfilment of the economic plan.

(3) To carry out the above tasks, apart from its central machinery, the Gosplan was to have its commissioners for supervising the fulfilment of the economic plans in republics, regions and provinces. The Gosplan's commissioners were appointed and recalled by the Sovnarkom S.S.S.R. on the recommendation of the Chairman of the Gosplan; they worked on the latter's instruction and were subordinated not to republican, regional and provincial planning commissions, but directly to the U.S.S.R. Gosplan.

The Gosplan had the right to demand from the P. Commissariats and other departments all necessary data and explanations necessary for the supervision of the fulfilment of the country's economic plan; similar rights were granted to Gosplan commissioners in republics, regions and provinces in regard to enterprises and economic institutions.

In this way Gosplan commissioners were responsible for plan fulfilment supervision and in a position to exercise it on the spot.

(4) The planning commissions attached to the Sovnarkoms of allied republics and to regional and provincial executive committees were to follow the instructions of the U.S.S.R. Gosplan in matters connected with both methods of planning and plan fulfilment supervision.*

The growing experience of the corresponding departments of the Gosplan in co-ordinative planning and in the methods of working out balances for individual branches of the national economy made it possible to draw up a far more comprehensive national plan and also to elaborate in far greater detail the material balances of the most important branches. As a result, also, the structure of the Gosplan was once more altered in 1938; the object of the reform was to give a wider scope to the department of the general plan of national economy and to share out more exactly the planning of various branches of the national economy. Apart from some minor alterations and additions introduced in 1939 and 1940, the 1938 structure of the Gosplan was very similar to that of 1940 quoted fully below (Appendix I).†

The reform of the Gosplans of allied republics and the planning commissions of regional and provincial executive committees was carried out on the same lines (cf. Appendix, Statutes of the

* For details see 'Statute of the State Planning Commission of the Sovnarkom S.S.S.R.', *Bull. Financ. and Econ. Leg.* nos. 3–4, 1938.

† Readers interested in the structural changes of the Gosplan effected in 1938, 1939 and 1940 can find the relevant decrees of the Sovnarkom S.S.S.R. in the *Coll. Regul. of the U.S.S.R.*, 1938, no. 7, § 41; *Bull. Financ. and Econ. Leg.* nos. 3–4, 1938; ibid. nos. 19–20, 1939; *Planned Economy*, no. 5, 1939, pp. 150–1; ibid. no. 5, 1940, pp. 124–5.

republican Gosplans and regional planning commissions on pp. 470–5).

In the later pre-war years, the planning authorities were focusing their attention on extending the scope and improving nationwide economic planning by extending the planning of balances, on bettering plan fulfilment supervision and district planning and on broadening the scope of planning so as to include not only economic but technical planning as well.

After the 1938–40 reforms of the Gosplan, the method of balanced estimates came to be used even more extensively than previously, while the actual procedure of drafting the plan was altered. Formerly, the elaboration of the plan began with production plans, and the method of balanced estimates was resorted to —somewhat *post factum*—in order to co-ordinate the planned production tasks. Now the elaboration of the plan commences with the appraisal of the main items of the branch and interbranch balance-sheets. The first step is to estimate the existing material, labour and financial resources. These estimates, termed preliminary balances, serve as a basis for shaping the general outline of the plan and correlating its various parts. They also serve to reveal bottle-necks existing in interbranch relations or within the branches themselves. Balanced estimates are brought into line with governmental directives and the requirements of those items of capital construction and production which are assigned priority; after which, preliminary balances are worked out in greater detail and become the basis of the production and distribution plans of the corresponding branches of the national economy. Next, agreement is reached with the corresponding P. Commissariats and economic organizations regarding the planned tasks, and the final draft of the corresponding balances is used for drawing up the capital construction, production and distribution plans approved by the Government. From the very structure of the U.S.S.R. Gosplan as it exists since 1940, it appears that the method of balances is a fundamental component part of planning in many fields of the national economy. Moreover, whereas previously only material balances were worked out and planned tasks determined only the general results of the economic activity of enterprises and organizations, since 1940 the balances of monetary receipts and expenditure of all economic organizations are included in the general plan, and the former tentative calculations of the population's monetary receipts and expenditure have come to be a regular balance-sheet of monetary receipts and expenditure.

Sample balance-sheets of the population's monetary receipts and expenditure will be found in Appendix IV, but an analysis of the methods of drawing them up falls outside the framework of this study.* Moreover, these balance-sheets were first included into the general economic plan only in the last pre-war year, and many problems regarding the methods of drawing them up were still in the process of elaboration. It was in 1940 also that the methods of drawing up a general balance of the national economy as a whole began to be discussed.†

In 1941 the Government instructed the U.S.S.R. Gosplan to work out a general plan for the economic development of the U.S.S.R. for the next fifteen years. This plan was to ascertain the internal economic resources and outline fundamental technical improvements which were to be based on the most modern technical achievements of leading Soviet and foreign enterprises in other technically advanced countries.

The U.S.S.R. Gosplan first elaborated a *technical* plan in 1940, i.e. a plan of the new technical improvements to be adopted in various branches of the national economy by 1941. Every P. Commissariat worked out definite programmes of the most valuable inventions and technical improvements already tried out which were to be mastered and applied. In drawing up this technical plan, the purpose of the Gosplan was to

take into consideration the latest achievements of world science and technique in order to introduce them into the leading branches of the national economy; to elucidate the latest inventions and technical improvements in use at home and abroad; to master certain most important inventions which have already undergone trials in our factories, but

* Readers interested in the methods of drafting the balance-sheets of economic organizations and in explanations of the technique of their elaboration are referred to G. Poliak, 'The balance-sheet of receipts and expenditure of economic organizations', *Planned Economy*, no. 7, 1940.

† One of the authors of the proposed draft of the general balance of the national economy thus formulated the purpose it would serve: '(a) fully to co-ordinate all branches of the national economy, saturating every pore of the plan with co-ordination; (b) to elucidate the general economic problems of a proper correlation in the development of the various branches, which can and must be solved by annual or prospective plans; (c) clearly to express in the indices and the general outline of the plan the principal planned balance connexions and its inner content and to formulate the country's economic balance as a whole; (d) to ensure conditions requisite for production throughout the national economy, and first and foremost in its priority items.' For details regarding draft balance-sheets of the entire national economy see V. Sobol, 'A blueprint of the national economic balance', *Planned Economy*, no. 6, 1940. M. Persitz, 'Plan and balance of national economy', *Planned Economy*, no. 9, 1940.

have hitherto been applied only on a limited scale. This is especially important in the case of substitutes and the economical use of materials in short supply, in particular modern machines manufactured in limited quantities. The 1941 Plan introduces only those most modern technical inventions and improvements which do not demand large capital outlay. The significance of the technical plan lies in the fact that the most important technical measures affecting various branches of industry and agriculture—such as the manufacture of machines according to the newest designs, the introduction of new technological processes, economies in fuel and materials of which there is scarcity, etc.—will be enforced as part of the obligatory State Plan. Considering that the 1941 technical plan is the first experiment in the drafting of a technical plan, it is made to include measures covering only some of the principal branches of the national economy, namely heavy and non-ferrous metallurgy, the engineering and fuel industries, the production of building materials, some branches of the light and food industries and the railway system.*

On the basis of this technical plan drawn up by the U.S.S.R. Gosplan and approved by the Government for 1941, every P. Commissariat was to work out detailed plans for introducing the most modern technique in the branches and enterprises subordinate to it. Thus, in the last pre-war year, the U.S.S.R. Gosplan extended its planning functions into the field of the technical development of the national economy.

* P. Kokurkin, P. Pashinin and J. Nikiforov, 'Problems of technique in the national economic plan', *Planned Economy*, no. 12, 1940, pp. 8–9.

Early in 1939 the previously independent Institute of Technical and Economic Information was transferred to the U.S.S.R. Gosplan; the Institute was called upon 'to extend technical and economic information in the following directions:

(a) P. Commissariat of Communications—latest achievements of world technique in the field of television, radio and cable communications.

(b) P. Commissariat of Timber Industry—mechanization of lumbering, problems of wood-chemistry, and paper and cellulose industry.

(c) P. Commissariat of Food Industry—introduction of automatic machinery.

(d) P. Commissariat of Light and Textile industries—artificial fibres, automatic machinery, maximum utilization of raw materials, in particular of short-fibred cottons, manufacture of substitutes, in particular of leather substitutes.

(e) Agriculture—new varieties of fertilizers, in particular concentrates, problems of mechanization and electrification.'

The Committee of Standards of the Sovnarkom S.S.S.R. enforces the introduction of standards in all the branches of national economy. 'The number of standards existing throughout the branches of the national economy, place the U.S.S.R. at the head of the world list. The total amount of standards is over 12,000.' V. Yemelianov, 'Problems of standardization in the U.S.S.R.', *Planned Economy*, no. 12, 1940, p. 14.

We have seen that in the later pre-war years much of the Gosplan's attention was devoted to plan-fulfilment supervision.* The problem was to organize *permanent supervision* over the progress of the plan and not only to sum up its results. In 1941 the Gosplan circulated forms of daily reports indicating the course of fulfilment of the plan for a number of manufactured goods, to be used throughout the first half of the year.† Articles devoted to the twentieth anniversary of the U.S.S.R. Gosplan emphasized Stalin's remarks that, 'only bureaucrats can think that planning work ends with the elaboration of the plan. The elaboration of the plan is only the beginning of planning. Real planning guidance develops after the plan has been drawn up, after it has been checked on the spot, in the course of its fulfilment, its improvement and adjustment'.‡ The main purpose of supervision was to *forestall* divergencies in the development of interdependent industries. Bearing this in mind the Gosplan, while supervising the progress of the plan, was to introduce necessary adjustments ('to correct mistakes occurring in the plan') and to submit to the Government measures for the prevention of possible disporportions.

In connexion with the growing importance of plan-fulfilment supervision, which, in the later pre-war years, was one of the principal routine occupations of the U.S.S.R. Gosplan, the U.S.S.R. Central Administration of Economic Accounting (Ts.U.N.Kh.U.)§ and its local organs were also reorganized.

---

* In September 1940 the Soviet Control Commission and Chief Military Control Commission were joined together and reorganized into the P. Commissariat of Soviet Control of the U.S.S.R. Apart from supervising the fulfilment of Government decrees, its functions included 'a daily, both preliminary and *post factum*, control of the accounts, custody and expenditure of State monetary funds and material values placed at the disposal of State, co-operative and other public organizations and enterprises...the carrying out of planned and sudden State inspections by order of the P. Commissar of State Control of the U.S.S.R. or the corresponding P. Commissars of State Control of the allied republics.'

For details see the enactment regarding the P. Commissariat of the State Control of the U.S.S.R. in *Coll. Regulations, Orders and Instructions on Problems of Finance and National Economy*, 1940, nos. 17–18.

† In particular such forms were issued to the P. Commissariat of Fuel and to various collieries, to show the output of coal and the progress of exploratory prospecting drilling; other forms showed the output of electrical power, pig-iron, steel and rolled metal, coke and the most important articles produced by the non-ferrous metallurgy, the engineering, chemical, building materials, timber, light and food industries and the volume of railway traffic.

‡ J. Stalin, *Leninism*, p. 413, quoted from A. Zelenovsky, 'Current tasks of the Gosplan', *Planned Economy*, no. 2, 1941, p. 20.

§ 'Accounting' is the nearest rendering of the Russian word 'uchet' which actually means statistical observations and not book-keeping.

Hitherto, the U.S.S.R. Central Administration of Economic Accounting, though attached to the U.S.S.R. Gosplan, was a more or less independent body; in February 1939 it was merged with the Gosplan and became one of its departments; the object of the reform was to subordinate economic accounting to the requirements of planning and plan-fulfilment supervision.* Forms of accounting and the collection of statistical data not necessary for the drafting of plans or their supervision were curtailed, while the work of the statistical sections of P. Commissariats and departments was made to fit in more closely with the statistical work of the Central Administration of Economic Accounting of the U.S.S.R. Gosplan, of the similar administrations of the republican Gosplans and local statistical organs.†

Early in 1940 the journal of the U.S.S.R. Gosplan still complained that

the gap existing between accounting and planning is being bridged over exceedingly slowly. As a result of this gap and the delays in sending in accounting data, the planning authorities cannot yet use the latter as a valuable instrument in plan-fulfilment supervision. Bureaucratic extravagances in accounting and records have not yet been done away with. Moreover, the Ts.U.N.Kh.U. has not yet produced a correct and full register of the most important indices showing the fulfilment of the economic plan. An urgent task is to bring the indices used by account-

* In this connexion it was proclaimed that, 'the Ts.U.N.Kh.U. must become actually not nominally a department of the U.S.S.R. Gosplan. Practical, daily, business contacts between accounting and planning workers must be established. Such living business contacts can alone prevent the bureaucratic gap between accounting and topical concrete problems of planning. It is necessary to free the Ts.U.N.Kh.U. of all work which the P. Commissariats and departments can carry out themselves under its methodological supervision. Lastly, one of the principal conditions for improving the organization of accounting is drastically to alter its methods of work and to ban the method of meaningless, summary average figures'. I. Pisarev, 'The work of the Ts.U.N.Kh.U. raised to the level of new tasks', *Planned Economy*, no. 1, 1940, p. 23.

† For details, cf. *Planned Economy*, no. 11, 1940, p. 126. Apart from its local statistical organs attached to the administrative hierarchy of the U.S.S.R. territorial subdivisions, the Ts.U.N.Kh.U. has special statistical agents in rural soviets and expert agricultural statistics commissions attached to district executive committees and also local inspectors of economic accounting. The inspectors 'check the accounting and statistical work and the correctness of the accounts and statistical data and information by auditing books and ledgers on the spot, i.e. in the rural soviet, on collective farms, on the sites of construction, at enterprises, etc., and also by inspecting individual homesteads and questioning citizens'. For details see 'Statute of statistical representatives attached to rural soviets and expert commissions on agricultural statistics attached to district executive committees', *Coll. Enactments*, 1930, no. 18, § 234; 'Statute of local inspectors of economic accounting', *Coll. Laws*, 1934, no. 42, § 331.

ing organs into conformity with those of the Plan, and to work out a minimum list of indices to be used in estimating the current progress of the Plan.*

It was natural that difficulties should have been encountered in the endeavour to improve the statistical work required for plan-fulfilment supervision, since Soviet economists and statisticians were pioneers in this sphere, as they had been in the elaboration of a methodology and technique of drawing up nation-wide economic plans. The existing world literature on statistics affords no theoretical, let alone practical solutions to many of the problems which life itself set to the Soviet statisticians; they themselves had to devise the necessary solutions, often by trial and error, and, consequently, mistakes and difficulties were not only likely, but unavoidably bound to occur.†

We have seen that, in the course of its development, the Soviet economic system gave birth to new institutions and an entirely new technique for directing economic processes and that the working ideas inspiring it differ essentially from those of the capitalist system of national economy. Economic textbooks, with their present-day theoretical knowledge intended for the study of the working ideas of an imaginary, no longer existing, purely competitive system of national economy,‡ are of little use nowadays for analysing the monopolistic economies prevalent in economically advanced countries; they are even less so to Soviet economists and statisticians for their practical work when drawing up economic plans or supervising their fulfilment. It is no exaggeration to say that the study of all the aspects of the planning technique elaborated in the U.S.S.R. during the last decade could provide extremely fruitful and instructive data for the revision of the many theoretical conceptions which still pervade academic economic and statistical literature.

CONCLUSION

We have already, in earlier chapters, drawn some conclusions about the planning of various branches of the national economy; only a few supplementary considerations need be added here.

* Editorial 'For a further improvement of planning work', *Planned Economy*, 1940, no. 3, p. 31. Also, I. Pisarev, 'The work of the Ts.U.N.Kh.U. raised to the level of new tasks', *Planned Economy*, 1940, no. 1.

† Interesting facts regarding the theoretical work of some Soviet statisticians is summarized in the article of F. Livshitz, 'Some results of a year's theoretical work by Moscow statisticians', *Problems of Economics*, nos. 11–12, 1940.

‡ We have in mind 'theories' on the free interplay of prices, supply and demand, the role of price in the maximum optimal utilization of resources, its role as regulator of labour relations, freedom of foreign markets, etc.

In general planning, as in the planning of separate branches of the national economy, some of the difficulties and problems which had to be overcome in the U.S.S.R. during the period now elapsed were temporary and transitional while others were of a more permanent nature. Partial planning in various branches of the national economy became possible more rapidly, while conditions permitting general economic planning were slower to materialize. The possibility of planning the development of the national economy during the N.E.P. period did not consist in the formal possibility of drawing up a plan, but in the fact that the State held, in the basic means of production, 'the commanding heights' of national economy. Centralized administration preceded even the introduction of partial planning in separate branches of the national economy. Even in the absence of any organized network of planning institutions or planning technique, the concentration of the basic productive resources of the country within the socialized sector made it possible to allocate these resources more or less according to a planned schedule and for the achievement of definite aims. The transition from partial to national planning became gradually possible with the growth of the socialized sector in importance at the expense of the private sector of the national economy. Planning developed not along one, but many lines. Planning and control were combined in varying proportions, according to the degree of development of the planning technique and, even more so, according to the changing economic circumstances which existed in the country's economy at different periods. Even in its latest stage of development the Soviet network of planning institutions can be termed pluralistic. For in spite of the strict hierarchy in which the structure is organized, both the general and the departmental planning networks (Union, republican, local, branch and departmental planning) are to a certain extent decentralized. The scope of planning expanded only gradually and even in the latter years alongside planning methods of direct and indirect control were still being applied (e.g. planned and controlled goods and prices, collective farm trading, individual allotments, local and craftsmen's industries, State, co-operative and personal property, organized and unorganized recruitment of manpower, and so on). The Plan itself is sufficiently flexible (prospective, annual, quarterly and in some cases monthly) to allow for revision and adjustment in the course of its fulfilment. All plans gave priority to 'leading links', other tasks and estimates being made to fit in with them. Experience showed that planning is not like some automatic clockwork which will carry on automatically once its relations and proportions have been established, but that it is more like a living creative organism in which the planning organs must be in constant touch with all the living tissues which constitute the organism of national economy. Plan-fulfilment supervision became a most important function of the planning authorities, and they had to devise practical solutions for an ever-increasing number of problems (e.g. the technical plan, the elaboration of qualitative indices for a quantitative control of plan fulfilment, the strengthening of planning co-ordination and parallel to this the need to increase decentralization in the management of individual branches of the national economy).

If attention is focused solely on the difficulties besetting the planning of national economy, the task may appear to be superhuman. However, the experience of the U.S.S.R. shows that by choosing certain 'leading links' at certain stages, by learning to control them and to plan the principal processes in the main branches of the national economy, it is possible to gain sufficient experience and devise an effective system for overcoming obstacles both apparent* (to the pure theoretician) and real which obstruct the path of economic planning. *Which* were the 'leading links' put forward and *how* the planning of the main branches was mastered in the various stages of development of the Soviet economic system—these are the questions to which the material reviewed in earlier chapters is directed. It is our hope that this material will enable the reader to draw his own conclusions and make his own generalizations.

One further point. To plan it was necessary to create the prerequisites which we enumerated at the beginning of this chapter, to mobilize the *will* of the nation for the desired aims and to find men capable of carrying them out. In the Government report on the third F.Y.P., some very interesting facts were given about the numbers of Soviet intelligentsia in 1937.

This expression, 'Soviet intelligentsia', has a profound significance. The figures below show not only the numbers of people employed in so-called intellectual work, but give an insight into

---

* Even a writer very critically disposed to the possibilities of economic planning is forced to admit, after an exhaustive account of all the theoretical objections against planning that, 'it is the writer's conclusion that economic theory as such offers no stumbling block to the attainment of a planned system, but that it is to the ethical and political implications that attention should be directed'. Claude Davis Baldwin, *Economic Planning, its Aims and Implications*, p. 172.

Table 67. *Composition of the Soviet intelligentsia in January* 1937

	Thousands
All responsible workers on the staff of institutions and enterprises	1,751
Of which:	
Heads of administrative institutions and institutions of the health and cultural services	450
Directors and managers of State industrial enterprises, workshops and departments, and their deputies	350
Chairmen of collective farms and their deputies, and managers of Kolkhoz marketing farms	582
Directors of M.T.S., State farms and managers of State livestock farms	19
Heads of producers' co-operative organizations	40
Directors and managers of shops	250
Directors and managers of canteens and other public catering establishments	60
Engineers and architects (excluding heads of enterprises and workshops)	250
Trained technical personnel	810
Agronomists	80
Other agronomic staffs (surveyors, agrotechnicians and zootechnicians)	96
Scientific workers (professors and other university staffs)	80
Teachers	969
Cultural and other educational workers (journalists, librarians, club leaders, etc.)	297
Arts workers	159
Doctors	132
Other medical personnel (assistants, midwives, etc.)	382
Economists and statisticians	822
Bookkeepers and accountants	1,617
Officers of Law (judges, public prosecutors, coroners, etc.)	46
University students	550
Other members of the intelligentsia (including the military)	1,550
Total	9,591

their qualitative standing. These hundreds of thousands of persons employed in various economic and cultural activities are, on the whole, people who have received their education and practical training in the years covered by the first two F.Y.P.s. The percentage of pre-revolution intellectuals among them is negligible from the point of view of both numbers and influence on the general course of events. The present-day intelligentsia is of Soviet formation and has grown up together with the Soviet system. As a result, its legal, social and material standing is quite different from what it was when the majority of white-collar workers were representative of the pre-revolution intelligentsia. The approach of the new Soviet intellectual to the current economic and social problems of the Soviet system is entirely different from that of persons born and bred under the capitalistic system of national economy and the social conditions of other countries. This sociological make-up of Soviet cadres must always be remembered by the foreign students when analysing the developments in the

Soviet economic system, both in its recent past and in the future. Many problems appear to the representatives of this new intelligentsia in a different light and they will tend to devise other solutions than would men who have grown up under different economic and social systems. The study of the developments taking place in the U.S.S.R. can, therefore, in our opinion, provide a wealth of instructive material to serious students of the economic and sociological problems of to-day.

APPENDIX I

Structure of the State Planning Commission (Gosplan) of the Sovnarkom S.S.S.R. (as approved by the Sovnarkom S.S.S.R. on 13 April 1940).

(1) The Chairman of the U.S.S.R. Gosplan, the deputy chairman of the U.S.S.R. Gosplan and the members of the U.S.S.R. Gosplan.
(2) Department of the General Plan of National Economy.
    Section of the General Production Plan.
    Section of the Balance of National Economy.
    Section of Production Costs.
    Section of Basic Funds and Capital Repairs.
    Section of the General Plan-Fulfilment Supervision.
(3) Department of Capital Construction.
    Branch of Building Industries.
    Section* of the General Capital Works Plan.
    Section of the Kuibyshev hydro-power Stations.
    Section of Water Power.
(4) Department of Finance.
    Section of Financial Plan.
    Section of Budget.
    Section of Credit.
    Section of Monetary Circulation.
(5) Department of Labour.
    Section of Labour and Wages.
    Section of Labour Balances.
    Section of Migration and Settlement.
(6) Department of Enterprise Location and District Planning.†

* A section is a smaller unit than a branch.
† This 'Department of Enterprise Location and District Planning' was subdivided at the end of 1940 into the following sections: Far-East and east Siberian districts, Ural and west Siberian districts, Central Asia and Kazakhstan districts, Transcaucasian districts, Southern districts, Central districts, South-Eastern districts, Northern and North-Western districts, Western districts (this section had subsections for Esthonia, Latvia and

Section of Inter-district Relations.
Section of Northern and Western Districts.
Section of Central Districts.
Section of Volga Districts.
Section of Urals and Western Siberia.
Section of Central Asia and Kazakhstan.
Section of Transcaucasia.
Section of Eastern and Far-Eastern Districts.
(7) Department of Fuel.
Branch of Fuel Balances.
Section of Coal and Shale.
Section of Oil and Gas (including artificial fuels).
Section of Peat.
(8) Department of the Balances of Materials.
Section of Balances of Iron and Steel.
Section of Balances of Non-ferrous Metals (including cables).
Section of Balances of Timber and Wood.
Section of Construction Supplies.
Section of High Grade Steels.
(9) Department of Balances of Equipment.
Section of Balances of Power Equipment.
Section of Balances of Lathes and Tools.
Section of Balances of Technological Equipment.
Section of Balances of Building Machinery.
Section of Balances of Vehicles.
(10) Department of Electrification.
Section of Balances and Distribution of Electric Power.
Section of Electric Power Production.
Section of Capital Works.
Section of Local Electrification.
(11) Department of Engineering.
Branch of Heavy Machine-building.
Branch of Middle Machine-building.

Lithuania), and a section of general district planning and location of enter-prises. These territorial departments were made responsible for:

(a) Drafting complex plans for the development of the national economy within their economic districts and checking up on the fulfilment of these plans;
(b) Working out measures for abolishing irrational and far distant haulage;
(c) Ensuring the rational location of enterprises within the economic districts;
(d) Working out plans for co-operation between enterprises situated in the same district.

In carrying out their work these departments of the U.S.S.R. Gosplan were to act in collaboration with the local Gosplan representatives and the planning commissions of the republics.

For details see *Planned Economy*, no. 11, 1940. Cf. also a highly interesting theoretical discussion on the principles on which the economic district is based in Prof. N. Kolosovsky's 'On the question of the economic district', *Problems of Economics*, no. 1, 1941.

Branch of General Machine-building.
Branch of Power Equipment.
Section of the Combined Plan.
Branch of Inter-departmental Co-operation.
(12) Department of Food Industries.
Branch of Fish Industries.
Branch of Food Industries.
Branch of Meat and Dairy.
(13) Department of Light Industry.
Branch of Textile Industry.
Branch of Light Industry.
Branch of Balances of Raw Materials and Unfinished Goods.
(14) Department of Agriculture.
Section of Plant Cultivation.
Section of Livestock Breeding.
Section of Technical Crops.
Section of Irrigation and Soil Amelioration.
Section of M.T.S.
Branch of State Farms.
(15) Department of Trade.
Branch of Goods Distribution.
Branch of Balance of Goods Funds.
Section of Trade Turn-over.
Section of Public Catering.
Section of Trade Network and Overhead Expenses.
Section of Mass-Consumption Goods.
(16) Department of Culture.
Branch of Education.
Branch of the Press.
Branch of Arts.
Branch of Higher Education and Scientific Institutions.
(17) Department of Natural Resources.
Section of Geodesy and Cartography.
Section of Geology.
(18) Department of Heavy Metallurgy.
Section of Pig-iron, Ore and Coke.
Section of Steel and Rolled Metal (including high grade and alloys).
Section of Capital Work and Equipment.
(19) Department of Non-ferrous Metallurgy.
Section of Mines.
Section of Non-ferrous Metals.
Section of Rare Metals.
(20) Department of Chemical Industry.
Section of Production and Balances of Basic Chemicals.
Section of Production and Balances of Organic Chemicals.
Section of Production and Balances of Rubber and Rubber Articles.
Section of Special Chemistry.

(21) Department of Air and Motor Transport.
   Section of Air Transport.
   Section of Motor Transport.
   Section of Roads.
(22) Department of Timber and Lumbering Industries.
   Section of Timber Stocks and Floatage.
   Section of Woodworking Industries.
   Section of Wood-chemical and Match Industries.
   Section of Cellulose and Paper.
   Section of Forestry.
(23) Department of Railway Transport.
   Branch of Goods Traffic and Exploitation.
   Section of Capital Works.
   Section of Industrial Transport.
(24) Department of Water Transport.
   Branch of River Transport.
   Branch of Sea Transport (including Arctic Route).
(25) Department of Agricultural Produce Procurements.
   Section of Agricultural Produce Procurements.
   Section of Flour and Groats.
   Section of Balances of Bread and Fodder.
(26) Bureau* of Prices.
   Section of Retail Prices.
   Section of Wholesale release Prices.
(27) Department of Local Industries and Producers' Co-operation.
   Section of Local and District Industries.
   Section of Producers' Co-operation.
   Section of Local Fuel.
(28) Department of Industrial Building Materials.
   Section of Building Materials.
   Section of Production and Balances of Sanitary and Technical
     Equipment.
   Branch of Building Parts and Assembly.
(29) Department of Housing and Municipal Services.
   Section of Municipal Services.
   Section of Housing.
   Section of Town Planning.
(30) Department of Foreign Trade.
   Branch of Exports.
   Branch of Imports.
(31) Department of Health Services.
   Section of Medical Institutions.
   Section of Nurseries and Maternity Homes.
   Section of Sanitation and Hygiene.
   Section of Medical Applicances.
   Section of Physical Training.

---

* A bureau is a smaller unit than a branch or a section.

(32) Department of Communications.
    Section of Communications (post, telephone, and telegraph).
    Section of Broadcasting and Television.
    Section of Hydro-meteorological Service.
(33) Section of Inventions (Patent Office).
(34) Bureau of Economies and Substitute Materials.
(35) Department of Cadres and Section of Planning Colleges.
(36) The Chairman of the Gosplan's Secretariat and the Control Section.
(37) The Institute of Technical and Economic Information.
(38) The Central Administration of Economic Accounting and its local organs (Central Statistical Institute Ts.U.N.Kh.U.).
(39) Local Representatives of the U.S.S.R. Gosplan.
(40) Council of Scientific and Technical Experts.
(41) The Council of the U.S.S.R. Gosplan.
(42) Administration and Staff Office.
(43) The periodical 'Planned Economy' (*Planovoe Khozyaistvo*).
(44) The State Planning Commission's Publishing House (Gosplanizdat).
(45) The Academy of Planning.
(46) The Moscow Institute of Planning.

APPENDIX II

Excerpts from the Statute of the *State Planning Commission attached to the Council of Peoples' Commissars of the R.S.F.S.R.*

1. The duties of the Gosplan of the R.S.F.S.R. Sovnarkom are:

(*a*) To work out and submit to the R.S.F.S.R. Sovnarkom prospective, annual and quarterly plans on national economy;

(*b*) To submit to the R.S.F.S.R. Sovnarkom their conclusions regarding the prospective, annual and quarterly plans drawn up by the P. Commissariats and departments of the R.S.F.S.R., the councils of peoples' commissars of the autonomous republics, the regional and provincial executive committees of the soviets (councils) of workers' delegates;

(*c*) To submit to the R.S.F.S.R. Sovnarkom their conclusions on the drafts of the most important enactments laid before the R.S.F.S.R. Sovnarkom by the P. Commissariats and departments of the R.S.F.S.R., the councils of peoples' commissars of the autonomous republics and the regional and provincial executive committees;

(*d*) To work out in detail individual problems of socialist construction in accordance with the instructions of the R.S.F.S.R. Sovnarkom, by request of the U.S.S.R. Gosplan or on its own initiative;

(*e*) To co-ordinate the prospective, annual or quarterly plans for the development of local economy with republican and All-Union economic plans;

(*f*) To appoint expert commissions for dealing with separate problems of the Republic's national economy;

(*g*) In accordance with the instructions of the U.S.S.R. Gosplan to work out and submit for its approval problems on the methods of planning the local and republican national economy.

2. The most important tasks of the Gosplan are as follows:

(*a*) To secure the maximum development of the national economy of the Republic, as well as its component regions, provinces and autonomous republics, based on the utilization of the local sources of raw materials and fuel;

(*b*) To ensure the proper location of enterprises with the view of avoiding long-distance and cross haulage and bringing production closer to its sources of raw materials and to the consumers of their goods;

(*c*) To guarantee in the plan of national economy of the R.S.F.S.R. a proper correlation in the development of the various branches of the national economy and the introduction of suitable measures to avoid disproportions within its framework.

3. The Gosplan is responsible for exercising constant control over the course of fulfilment of the plan of national economy and of the most important government regulations. For this purpose the Gosplan:

(*a*) Checks up the fulfilment of the plan of national economy by the P. Commissariats and departments of the R.S.F.S.R., the councils of peoples' commissars of the autonomous republics and the regional and provincial executive committees;

(*b*) Controls the execution of the most important government enactments concerning economic, social and cultural construction;

(*c*) Supervises the course of fulfilment of the plan by enterprises subordinated to All-Union authority;

(*d*) Submits to the R.S.F.S.R. Sovnarkom proposals arising from its control over the fulfilment of the plan of national economy and individual government regulations.

4. The Gosplan of the R.S.F.S.R. directs the activities of the planning commissions attached to the councils of the peoples' commissars of the autonomous republics, and the regional and provincial executive committees on all questions relating to the drafting of plans, verifies the nature and content of their work, issues instructions and assists them in matters of organization and methods of planning.

5. The Gosplan of the R.S.F.S.R. is entitled to demand from the peoples' commissariats and departments of the R.S.F.S.R. all data and explanations necessary for the drafting of economic plans and likewise for the purpose of verifying the execution of plans and Government regulations. It is likewise entitled to enter into direct communication with organizations and enterprises subordinated to All-Union authority, on questions concerning plans drafted by them, and data as to their execution.

6. The Gosplan possesses its own central machinery composed of the following departments and sections:

(1) Department of the general plan of national economy:
Section of labour planning and training of personnel;
Branch of production and balances;
Branch of raw materials and equipment utilization;
Branch of labour personnel planning;
Branch of cost price and prices;
Branch of the general plan.

(2) Department of the territorial plan:
Section of natural resources and inter-district relations;
Section of the organization of work and instruction of planning commissions;
Branch of the North-Western districts;
Branch of the Central districts;
Branch of the Volga districts;
Branch of the Ural-Siberian districts;
Branch of the East Siberian and Far-Northern districts;
Branch of All-Union economy;
Branch of the general territorial plan.

(3) Department of capital construction:
Section of building industry;
Branch of new construction and reconstruction;
Branch of capital repairs and extra-limit construction;
Branch of the general territorial plan.

(4) Department of material and technical supply:
Section of equipment;
Section of fuel allocation;
Branch of textile and leather goods;
Branch of metals and metal goods funds;
Branch of building materials funds;
Branch of the general territorial plan.

(5) Department of local industry:
Section of building materials;
Section of consumers' metal goods;
Branch of china, earthenware and glass industries;
Branch of the general territorial plan.

(6) Section of the fuel extracting industry.

(7) Section of timber:
Branch of woodworking and furniture manufacture;
Branch of lumbering.

(8) Section of light industry.

(9) Section of food industry.

(10) Section of producers' co-operation.

(11) Department of agriculture:
Section of State farms;
Section of vegetable, potato and fruit growing.
Section of soil amelioration;
Branch of the general territorial plan.

(12) Section of motor road and river transport.
(13) Department of municipal and housing economy.
   Section of housing and administration;
   Section of electrification;
   Branch of drainage and water supply;
   Branch of town planning;
   Branch of public baths and laundries;
   Branch of the general territorial plan.
(14) Section of trade:
   Branch of trade turn-over and stocks of agricultural products;
   Branch of the canteen, café and restaurant network.
(15) Department of culture:
   Section of education;
   Branch of press and printing;
   Branch of arts;
   Branch of political education and enlightenment institutions;
   Branch of the general territorial plan.
(16) Section of health services and social security.
(17) Section of finance.
(18) Section of mobilization.
(19) Section of planning cadres.
(20) Section of control and inspection.
(21) Governing Board of the educational institutions of the Gosplan attached to the R.S.F.S.R. Sovnarkom.
(22) Administrative office.
(23) Secretariat of the Gosplan Chairman.
(24) Secret branch.

Excerpts from the Statutes of the *Planning Commissions attached to the regional and provincial executive committees of the soviets* (councils) *of workers' delegates*.

1. The planning commissions attached to the regional and provincial executive committees of the soviets of workers' delegates are permanent commissions forming part of the regional and provincial executive committees, while at the same time part of the network of planning institutions directed by the R.S.F.S.R. Gosplan.

2. The commissions are responsible for:

(*a*) Working out the prospective, annual and quarterly plans for the economic and cultural development of regions and provinces, and submitting these for approval to the regional (provincial) executive committee and for examination to the Gosplan of the R.S.F.S.R. Sovnarkom and the Gosplan of the Sovnarkom S.S.S.R.;

(*b*) Laying before the regional (provincial) executive committee their conclusions on the prospective, annual and quarterly plans drawn up by the departments of the regional (provincial) executive committee;

(*c*) Working out, on the instruction of the Gosplan of the Sovnarkom S.S.S.R. and the Gosplan of the R.S.F.S.R. Sovnarkom, the regional and provincial executive committees and on their own initiative, problems of the development and rational utilization of the natural resources of the region or province, and likewise individual questions of economic and cultural construction;

(*d*) Checking up the fulfilment of their approved plans by organizations and enterprises situated within the territory of the region (province) and also the execution of individual government regulations regarding economic and cultural construction;

(*e*) Directing and assisting the work of the regional, municipal (town) and district planning commissions.

3. The commissions comprise the following sections:

Sections of the general plan; district plan; capital construction, and material and technical supply; power and fuel industry; district industry; timber (in regions and districts where forestry exists); agriculture; culture and health services; trade turn-over and stocks; housing and municipal services; roads and transport, and communications.

4. The commissions have the right to:

(*a*) Demand from the departments of the regional executive committee, and the institutions and enterprises under regional and district control, all data concerning their plans and the fulfilment of these; and also to communicate directly with organizations and enterprises of republican and All-Union importance within the territory of the region or province on questions relating to the drawing up or execution of plans;

(*b*) Demand from the regional (provincial) Administration of Economic Accounting statistical data and accounts requisite for the drafting of plans and the checking up of their fulfilment, within the framework of the existing accountancy system.

5. Each regional and provincial planning commission possesses an advisory council composed of members of the planning commission, workers co-opted from the planning sections of the regional and provincial executive committees, from the staffs of the provincial municipal and district planning commissions, and also scientists, specialists, workers and collective farmers, totalling in all 30–40 members.*

APPENDIX III

Statutes of the *District Planning Commissions*

(1) The district planning commissions enjoy equal status with the departments of the district executive committees. Their activities are subordinated to both the district executive committee and the planning commission of the corresponding A.S.S.R., region and province.

(2) The duties of the district planning commissions are as follows:

* For details see *Bull. Financ. and Econ. Leg.* nos. 10–11, 1939.

(*a*) To afford general methodological guidance to the departments of the district committees and to all enterprises and institutions of district importance in their work of drafting quarterly, annual and prospective plans;

(*b*) To work out a single (quarterly, annual and prospective) district plan of economic and cultural construction, covering industry, agriculture, producers' and consumers'' co-operatives and taking into account enterprises under provincial, regional, republican and All-Union authority;

(*c*) To control and supervise the course of fulfilment of the approved plans and to work out measures conducive to its success;

(*d*) To lay before the executive committee their conclusions concerning the draft district budget, and the report on its fulfilment as well as on the proposed measures put forward by district organizations;

(*e*) To study the existing and potential productive resources and reserves of the district with the object of their most fruitful exploitation.

3. The district planning commissions have the right to:

(*a*) Obtain from all departments of the district executive committee, rural councils and other district and rural institutions the drafts of plans and all data and information regarding their fulfilment;

(*b*) Obtain from all enterprises and institutions situated on the territory of the district and irrespective under whose authority, data and information necessary for drafting district plans; likewise information concerning the fulfilment of the aforesaid plans according to data submitted by these organizations to their senior authorities;

(*c*) Obtain from the district Economic Accountancy inspectors statistical data and accounts necessary for drafting the plan, within the scope of the existing rules on economic accounting and in conformity with the instructions of the regional, provincial and republican (A.S.S.R.) Administrations of Economic Accounting.

Balance-sheet of the monetary income and

	Total population		Workers		Peasants		Of... Collective farmers	
	(a)	(b)	(a)	(b)	(a)	(b)	(a)	(b)

I. MONETARY

A. Monetary receipts from State

	Total population (a)	(b)	Workers (a)	(b)	Peasants (a)	(b)	Collective farmers (a)	(b)
1. Wages	65,000	73,000	34,000	38,950	5,000	5,500	4,670	5,200
2. Collective farmers' monetary income derived from the collectivefarms	6,300	8,500	—	—	6,300	8,500	6,300	8,500
Of which:								
(a) Labour day dividends	6,000	8,100	—	—	6,000	8,100	6,000	8,100
(b) Other monetary income from the collective farms	300	400	—	—	300	400	300	400
3. Earnings of members of artels of the producers' co-operative associations	2,500	2,800	—	—	250	300	150	220
4. Receipts from the sale of products	4,500	5,000	—	—	4,400	4,900	4,050	4,670
Of which:								
(a) Agricultural products	4,000	4,400	—	—	4,000	4,400	3,700	4,210
(b) Non-agricultural products	500	600	—	—	400	500	350	460
5. Receipts for cartage	1,500	1,575	—	—	900	1,025	500	685
6. Pensions and allowances	4,200	4,800	1,600	1,875	650	720	620	700
7. Scholarships and maintenance grants	1,500	1,725	150	175	20	25	20	25
8. Monetary receipts from the financial system (interest and premium on loans and deposits, insurance benefits, credits, etc.)	1,600	2,000	560	690	550	710	535	700
9. Other monetary receipts	2,000	2,200	500	5,600	600	660	550	620
Total for schedule A	89,100	101,600	36,810	42,250	18,570	22,340	17,395	21,320

B. Monetary receipts from the sale of good

	Total population (a)	(b)	Workers (a)	(b)	Peasants (a)	(b)	Collective farmers (a)	(b)
1. Receipts from the sale of products on collective-farm markets	13,600	15,260	580	660	12,500	14,020	11,750	13,505
2. Income of craftsmen non-members of a co-operative association	450	360	—	—	—	—	—	—
3. Income from the sale of services	550	500	120	120	75	75	60	6
4. Receipts of monetary gifts	400	450	—	—	350	400	330	38
Total for schedule B	15,000	16,570	700	780	12,925	14,495	12,140	13,95
Total monetary income for schedules A and B	104,100	118,170	37,510	43,030	31,595	36,835	29,535	35,27

(a) Current year, anticipated fulfilment.   (b) Planned year.   All figures are convention

xpenditure of the population (in million roubles)

which:		Craftsmen		Employees, engineers, technicians and workers		Other groups		Total urban population		Total rural population	
Individual farmers											
(a)	(b)	(a)	(b)	(a)	(b)	(a)	(b)	(a)	(b)	(a)	(b)

INCOME

and co-operative enterprises

(a)	(b)	(a)	(b)	(a)	(b)	(a)	(b)	(a)	(b)	(a)	(b)
330	300	300	330	25,500	28,000	200	220	49,000	55,000	16,000	18,000
—	—	—	—	—	—	—	—	—	—	6,300	8,500
—	—	—	—	—	—	—	—	—	—	6,000	8,100
—	—	—-	—	—	—	—	—	—	—	300	400
100	80	2,500	2,500	—	—	—	—	1,750	1,920	750	880
350	230	100	100	—	—	—	—	—	—	4,500	5,000
300	190	—	—	—	—	—	—	—	—	4,000	4,400
50	40	100	100	—	—	—	—	—	—	500	600
400	340	600	550	—	—	—	—	600	550	900	1,025
30	20	100	110	700	800	1,150	1,295	3,000	3,465	1,200	1,335
—	—	5	5	75	85	1,250	1,435	1,500	1,725	—	—
15	10	50	60	410	500	30	40	1,200	1,470	400	530
50	40	100	110	650	710	150	160	1,500	1,650	500	550
1,275	1,020	3,505	3,765	27,335	30,095	2,780	3,150	58,550	65,780	30,550	35,820

and services to the population

(a)	(b)	(a)	(b)	(a)	(b)	(a)	(b)	(a)	(b)	(a)	(b)
750	515	210	235	265	295	45	50	550	630	13,050	14,630
—	—	450	360	—	—	—	—	320	240	130	120
15	10	200	150	—	—	—	—	380	350	170	150
20	15	—	—	—	—	50	50	50	50	350	400
785	540	860	745	350	380	165	170	1,300	1,270	13,700	15,300
2,060	1,560	4,365	4,510	27,685	30,475	2,945	3,320	59,850	67,050	44,250	51,120

N. S. Margolin, *Problems of the Population's Receipts and Expenditure Balance Sheet*, pp. 128–34

	Total population (a)	(b)	Workers (a)	(b)	Peasants (a)	(b)	Collective farmers (a)	(b)
								II. MONETAF
				A. Monetary expenditure in sta				
1. Taxes and other dues	3,350	4,250	850	1,020	1,920	1,950	1,670	1,76
2. Subscriptions to public organizations	825	940	410	470	60	75	57	7
3. Payments for services and orders placed	9,700	11,480	3,650	4,380	2,100	2,640	1,985	2,55
4. Purchase of goods and purchase of food from public catering	69,225	78,760	24,665	28,085	22,750	27,050	21,396	26,07
Of which:								
(a) In State and co-operative trading institutions	67,725	76,960	24,080	27,370	22,400	26,640	21,085	25,70
(b) From State and collective farms	1,500	1,800	525	715	350	410	311	37
Total for schedule A	83,700	95,430	29,575	33,955	26,830	31,715	25,108	30,45
				B. Monetary outlay in the purchase				
1. Purchase of goods on collective farm markets	13,600	15,260	5,360	6,090	3,100	3,410	2,760	3,10
Of which:								
(a) Agricultural products	13,000	14,600	5,100	5,800	3,000	3,300	2,670	3,00
(b) Non-agricultural products	600	660	260	290	100	110	90	10
2. Purchase of goods from craftsmen non-members of co-operative associations, and payments for orders placed	450	360	120	95	200	150	185	14
3. Payments for services	550	500	220	210	100	80	90	7
4. Payments of monetary gifts	400	450	250	280	—	—	—	—
Total for schedule B	15,000	16,570	5,950	6,675	3,400	3,640	3,035	3,31
Total expenditure, schedules A and B	98,700	112,000	35,525	40,630	30,230	35,355	28,143	33,76
								III. MONETAR
1. Membership fees of co-operative organizations	100	100	5	5	60	60	57	5
2. Subscription to State Loans	3,500	4,200	1,400	1,660	675	950	655	93
3. Increased deposits in savings banks	800	1,150	380	525	80	170	80	17
4. The population's increased cash in hand	1,000	720	200	210	550	300	600	35
Savings, total	5,400	6,170	1,985	2,400	1,365	1,480	1,392	1,50

(a) Current year, anticipated fulfilment.   (b) Planned year.   All figures are conventiona

which: Individual farmers		Craftsmen		Employees, engineers, technicians and workers		Other groups		Total urban population		Total rural population	
(a)	(b)	(a)	(b)	(a)	(b)	(a)	(b)	(a)	(b)	(a)	(b)
EXPENDITURE											
and co-operative organizations											
250	190	250	230	900	1,020	30	30	1,780	2,000	2,170	2,250
3	3	25	30	310	340	20	25	640	720	185	220
115	90	340	370	3,360	3,790	250	300	6,700	7,805	3,000	3,675
1,354	980	2,685	2,765	16,975	18,370	2,210	2,490	36,855	40,890	32,790	37,870
1,315	940	2,600	2,670	16,470	17,830	2,175	2,450	35,785	39,600	31,940	37,360
39	40	85	95	445	540	35	40	1,070	1,290	430	510
1,722	1,263	3,300	3,395	21,485	23,520	2,510	2,845	45,975	51,415	37,725	44,015
goods and services from the population											
340	310	760	800	4,065	4,615	375	346	9,585	10,770	4,015	4,690
330	300	730	770	3,870	4,400	300	330	9,200	10,350	3,800	4,250
10	10	30	30	195	215	15	15	385	120	215	240
15	10	15	15	105	90	10	10	170	130	280	230
10	5	30	25	190	175	10	10	350	320	200	120
—	—	—	—	—	—	—	—	—	—	—	—
365	325	835	875	4,420	5,015	335	365	10,505	11,670	4,495	4,900
2,087	1,588	4,135	4,270	25,965	28,535	2,845	3,210	54,680	63,085	42,220	48,915
SAVINGS											
3	2	25	25	10	10	—	—	10	10	90	90
20	20	135	145	1,220	1,365	70	80	2,400	2,800	200	350
—	—	40	50	285	385	15	20	600	800	200	350
50	50	30	20	205	180	15	10	360	355	640	365
27	28	230	240	1,720	1,940	100	110	3,370	3,965	2,030	2,205

N. S. Margolin, *Problems of the Population's Receipts and Expenditure Balance Sheet*, pp. 128–34.

BIBLIOGRAPHY

The economic literature published in the U.S.S.R. during the past 25 years comprises many thousands of volumes. Whoever wishes to compile a bibliography on special questions must consult *Knizhnaya letopis* in which all publications in the U.S.S.R. are enumerated. This Bibliography comprises only those sources which I consulted in the preparation of this study. These sources were selected from a more voluminous literature known to me because I thought that they were more suited to the aims pursued in the preparation of this study and because I hold that readers wishing to embark on a further study of questions described by me only in general terms, should consult this literature first of all.

This Bibliography gives only sources in the Russian language; the English titles are meant to serve for the orientation of readers as in my footnotes in the book I use the English and not the Russian titles. The titles of articles from journals, decrees, Government enactments, etc., given in English translations in the footnotes, are not included in the Bibliography, as it would make it too cumbersome. In the 'reference material' of my Bibliography I give only the titles of statistical sources, journals, etc., material from which was used in the book.

Sources in non-Russian languages are quoted in the footnotes directly and are not included, as well as titles of Soviet newspapers which are quoted in footnotes under their original Russian names, but in English transcription. The Bibliography is intended only for persons with a knowledge of Russian.

GENERAL SOURCES ON NATIONAL ECONOMY

BEILIN, A. E. Kadry spetsialistov S.S.S.R., ikh formirovanie i rost, pod red. I. A. Kravalya. 1935. *Specialist staffs in the U.S.S.R., their training and growth. Ed. by I. A. Kraval.*

Borba s poteryami v narodnom khozyaistve. Sbornik statey. 1930. *Struggle against waste in national economy. Coll. articles.*

CHERNOMORDIK, D. I. Ekonomicheskaya politika S.S.S.R. 1936. *The economic policy of the U.S.S.R.*

DEBORIN I CHERNIN. Teoria i praktika planirovania narodnogo khozyaistva S.S.S.R. 1929. *Theory and practice of economic planning in the U.S.S.R.*

DEN. Polozhenie Rossii v mirovom khozyaistve. Analiz russkogo eksporta do voiny. Statisticheskiy ocherk. 1922. *The position of Russia in world economy. Analysis of Russian pre-war exports. Statistical review.*

Dinamika tsen sovetskogo khozyaistva. Sbornik statey. 1930. *Dynamics of prices in Soviet economy. Coll. articles.*

Etapy ekonomicheskoy politiky S.S.S.R.; pod red. Veisberga, Kviringa, Saveleva. 1934. *Stages in the economic policy of the U.S.S.R. Ed. by Veisberg, Kviring, Savelev.*

GINZBURG, L. Upravlenie khozyaistvom v pervye gody proletarskoy diktatury. 1933. *Administration of national economy in the early years of proletarian dictatorship.*

God raboty pravitelstva. Materualy k otchetu za 1924–5, 1925–6, 1926–7, 1927–8, 1928–9. *One year of Government work. Data for the years 1924–5,* etc.

GRANOVSKY, E. L. Monopolistichesky kapitalizm v Rossii. 1929. *Monopolistic capitalism in Russia.*

KAKTYN, A. Novaya ekonomicheskaya politika i nozhnitsy. 1924. *The new economic policy and the 'scissors'.*

KAKTYN, A. O politike tsen. 1929. *On price policy.*

Khozyaistvennaya statistika S.S.S.R. Sbornik statey pod red. V. Den i B. Karpenko. 1930. *Economic statistics of the U.S.S.R. Coll. articles ed. by V. Den and B. Karpenko.*

Kontrolnye tsifry narodnogo khozyaistva na 1926–7 g., 1927–8 g., 1928–9 g., 1929–30 g., 1931 g. *Control figures of national economy for 1926–7,* etc.

KOVALEVSKIY, N. A. Razmeshchenie proizvoditelnykh sil na territoriy S.S.S.R. vo 2-oi piatiletke i genplane. Ch. 1-aya. 1932. *Location of productive forces within the territory of the U.S.S.R. under the Second Five-Year and the General Plans.*

KRITSMAN, L. Geroicheskiy period velikoy Russkoy revolutsii. *The heroic period in the great Russian revolution.*

KRZHIZHANOVSKIY, G. M. Problemy planirovania. Sochinenia T. II. 1934. *Problems of planning. Works.*

LARIN i KRITSMAN. Ocherk khozyaistvennoy zhizny i organizatsia narodnogo khozyaistva Rossii. 1920. *Survey of economic life and organization of national economy in Russia.*

LARIN, YU. Itogy, puti, vyvody novoy ekonomicheskoy politiky. 1923. *Results, ways and outcome of the new economic policy.*

LENIN, Sobranie sochineniy, III-e izdanie. *Collected works.*

LENIN i STALIN. Sbornik proizvedeniy k izucheniyu istorii V.K.P. (b). Vols. I, II, III. 1937. *Collection of works for study of history of C.P.*

LYASHCHENKO, P. Istoria narodnogo khozyaistva S.S.S.R. 1939. *The history of the national economy of the U.S.S.R.*

MARX, K. i ENGELS, F. Kommunisticheskiy Manifest, 5-oe izdanie, 1928. *Communist manifesto.*

Materialy po voprosu ob izbytochnom trude v selskom khozyaistve S.S.S.R. Trudy Gosudarstv. koloniz. Instituta, I, II, III. 1926. *Data on the question of surplus labour in the agriculture of the U.S.S.R. Transactions of the State colonization Institute.*

MILYUTIN, V. P. Istoria economicheskogo razvitia S.S.S.R. Izdanie vtoroie. 1929. *The history of the economic development of the U.S.S.R.*

Na perelome. Osnovnye voprosy khozyaistvennogo stroitelstva. Sbornik statey. 1927. *At the cross-roads. Fundamental problems of economic construction. Collected articles.*

Narodnoe khozyaistvo v 1920 g., 1922–3 g., 1923–4 g., 1924–5 g. *The national economy in 1920,* etc.

Narodno-khozyaistvenny plan na 1936g. 1936. *Plan of national economy for 1936.*

Narodnyi dokhod S.S.S.R. Pod red. Prof. D. I. Chernomordik. 1939. *The national income of the U.S.S.R. Ed. by Prof. D. I. Chernomordik.*

Nauchnye kadry i nauchno issledovatelskye uchrezhdenia S.S.S.R. Pod red. O. Yu. Shmidt i B. Ya. Smulevich. 1930. *Scientific workers and scientific research institutes of the U.S.S.R. Ed. by O. Yu. Shmidt and B. Ya. Smulevich.*

Novaya ekonomicheskaya politika i zadachy partiy. 1921. *The new economic policy and Party problems.*

O piatiletnem plane razvitia narodnogo khozyaistva S.S.S.R. Diskussia v Kom. Akademiy. 1928. *The Five-Year Plan of national economy and its development. Debate in the Communist Academy.*

Perspektivy razvertyvania narodnogo khozyaistva S.S.S.R. na 1926–7—1930–1. 1927. *Prospective developments of the national economy of the U.S.S.R. for 1926–7—1930–1.*

Pervaya Vsesoyuznaya konferentsia po planirovaniyu nauchno-issledovatelskoy raboty. 1931. *First All-Union conference for the planning of scientific and research work.*

PERVUSHIN, S. A. Dvizhenie volnykh tsen v gody revolyutsii (1917–21). 1921. *Movements of uncontrolled prices in the years of the revolution (1917–21).*

Plan elektrifikatsii R.S.F.S.R. 1920. *Plan of electrification of the R.S.F.S.R.*

Plan obespechenia narodnogo khozyaistva S.S.S.R. kadramy spetsialistov 1929–30—1932–3. 1930. *Plan for securing specialist staffs for the national economy of the U.S.S.R.*

PREOBRAZHENSKIY, E. Ekonomicheskye krizisy pri N.E.P-e. 1924. *Economic crises during the N.E.P.*

Problemy rekonstruktsii narodnogo khozyaistva S.S.S.R. na piatiletie (piatiletniy perspektivniy plan na V siezde Gosplanov). 1929. *Problems of reconstruction of the national economy of the U.S.S.R. for the five years (the prospective Five-Year Plan and the Fifth Congress of Gosplans).*

PROKOPOVITCH, S. N. Voina i narodnoie khozyaistvo. 1918. *War and the national economy.*

Promyshlennost i narodnoie khozyaistvo. 1927. *Industry and national economy.*

PUZISK. Kommunalnoe i zhilishchnoe khozyaistvo S.S.S.R. za 15 let. 1932. *Fifteen years of municipal services and housing in the U.S.S.R.*

Sbornik 'Oktiabrskiy perevorot i diktatura proletariata'. *October revolution and dictatorship of the Proletariat.*

STALIN. Voprosy Leninizma. Izdanie x, xi, 1939, 1941. *Leninism.*

STRUMILIN. Problemy planirovania v S.S.S.R. 1932. *Problems of planning in the U.S.S.R.*

SHTERN, A. B. Gosudarstvennoe finansirovanie promyshlennosty. 1924. *State financing of industry.*

Tekhnicheskaya rekonstruktsia narodnogo khozyaistva S.S.S.R. v pervoy piatiletke. Pod red. Granovskogo, Krzhizhanovskogo i dr. 1934. *The technical reconstruction of the national economy of the U.S.S.R. under the first Five-Year Plan. Ed. by Granovsky, Krzhizhanovsky and others.*

TROTSKY, L. Novaya economicheskaya politika Sovetskoy Rossii i perspektivy mirovoy revolutsii. 1923. *New economic policy of Soviet Russia and perspective of the world revolution.*

TROTSKY, L. Sochineniya. 1927. *Collected works.*

Tsentralnyy Komitet V.K.P. 'Za pyat let'. 1923. *Central Committee of the Communist Party 'For five years'.*

VEISBERG, R. E. Dengy i tseny. Podpolny rynok v period 'voennogo kommunizma'. 1925. *Money and prices. The black market in the period of war communism.*

VOLKOV, E. Z. Dinamika narodonaselenia S.S.S.R. za 80 let. 1930. *The U.S.S.R. population figures for the past 80 years.*

Voprosy sovetskogo stroitelstva; sbornik statey pod red. A. Alasheva i N. Chelyanov. 1934. *Problems of Soviet construction; coll. articles, ed. by A. Alashev and N. Chelyanov.*

REFERENCE MATERIAL
STATISTICAL SOURCES

XX let sovetskoy vlasti. Statisticheskiy sbornik. 1937. *20 years of Soviet power.*
Statisticheskiy ezhegodnik 1918–20. 1922. *Statistical Yearbook 1918–20. 1922.*
Statisticheskiy sbornik 1913–17. 1921. *Statistical Handbook 1913–17. 1921.*
Sbornik statisticheskykh svedeniy po Sojuzu S.S.R. 1918–23. 1924. *Collection of statistical figures of the U.S.S.R.*
Itogi desyatiletiya Sovetskoy vlasti v tsifrakh (1917–27). 1927. *Ten years of Soviet power in figures.*
Narodnoe khozyaistvo S.S.S.R. Statisticheskiy spravochnik 1932. *National economy of the U.S.S.R. Statistical Handbook 1932.*
Statisticheskiy spravochnik S.S.S.R. 1928. 1928. *Statistical Handbook of the U.S.S.R. 1928.*
Selskoe khozyaistvo S.S.S.R. (statisticheskiy sbornik). 1935. *Agriculture in the U.S.S.R. (statistical data).*
Sotsialisticheskoe selskoe khozyaistvo S.S.S.R. (statisticheskiy sbornik). 1939. *Socialist agriculture in the U.S.S.R. (statistical data).*
Posevnye ploshchadi S.S.S.R. Statisticheskiy spravochnik 1939. *The sown areas of the U.S.S.R. Statistical Handbook 1939.*
Sotsialisticheskoe stroitelstvo S.S.S.R. Statisticheskiy ezhegodnik 1934. *Socialist construction of the U.S.S.R. Statistical Yearbook. 1934.*
Sotsialisticheskoe stroitelstvo S.S.S.R. Statisticheskiy sbornik 1935. *Socialist construction of the U.S.S.R. Statistical Yearbook 1935.*
Sotsialisticheskoe stroitelstvo S.S.S.R. Statisticheskiy sbornik 1936. *Socialist construction of the U.S.S.R. Statistical Yearbook 1936.*
Sotsialisticheskoe stroitelstvo S.S.S.R. Statisticheskiy sbornik (1933–38). 1939. *Socialist construction of the U.S.S.R. Statistical Handbook (1933–38). 1939.*

FIVE-YEAR PLANS

Piatiletniy Plan narodnokhozyaistvennogo stroitelstva S.S.S.R. Vols. I, II, pts. I, II. *The Five-Year Plan of the economic construction of the U.S.S.R.*
Proekt vtorogo piatiletnego plana razvitiya narodnogo khozyaistva S.S.S.R. (1933–37). Vols. I, II. Plan razvitiya raionov. Prilozhenie k pervomu tomu. Osnovnye obiekty kapitalnogo stroitelstva vo vtorom pyatiletii. 1934. *Draft of the second Five-Year Plan for the development of the national economy of the U.S.S.R.*
Tretiy piatiletniy plan razvitiya narodnogo khozyaistva S.S.S.R. (1938–42). Proekt. 1939. *The third Five-Year Plan of the development of the national economy of the U.S.S.R. (1938–42).*
Itogi vypolneniya pervogo piatiletnego plana razvitiya narodnogo khozyaistva S.S.S.R. 1933. *Summary of the fulfilment of the first Five-Year Plan for the development of the national economy of the U.S.S.R.*
Itogi vypolneniya vtorogo piatiletnego plana narodnokhozyaistvennogo razvitiya S.S.S.R. 1939. *Results of the fulfilment of the second Five-Year Plan for the development of the national economy of the U.S.S.R.*

LEGISLATION

Bulletin finansovogo i khozyaistvennogo zakonodatestva za 1925–39. *Bulletin of financial and economic legislation.*
Dekrety Oktyabrskoy Revolyutsii. 1923. *Decrees of the October Revolution.*
Grazhdanskiy Kodeks. 1938. *Civil code.*

KANARSKY, S. Ugolovny kodeks sovetskykh respublik. Tekst i postateyny komentariy. 1924. *The Criminal Code of Soviet Republics, text and systematic commentary.*

SAVELIEV, M. i POSKREBYSHEV, A. Direktivy V.K.P. (b) po khozyaistvennym voprosam. 1931. *Instructions of the Communist Party concerning economic questions.*

Sbornik postanovleniy, prikazov i instruktsiy po finansovo-khozyaistvennym voprosam za 1940. *Coll. regulations, orders and instructions on problems of finance and national economy.*

Sobranie postanovleniy i rasporyazheniy pravitelstva S.S.S.R. za 1939–40. *Coll. orders and regulations of the U.S.S.R. Government.*

Sobranie postanovleniy pravitelstva S.S.S.R. za 1939–40. *Coll. decrees of the U.S.S.R. Government.*

Sobranie uzakoneniy i rasporyazheniy rabochego i krestyanskogo pravitelstva S.S.S.R. za 1921–38. *Collection of Government decrees.*

Sobranie zakonov i rasporyazheniy S.S.S.R. za 1921–38. *Collected laws and orders.*

Ugolovny Kodeks 1926. *Criminal Code 1926.*

V.K.P. (b) v resolutsyakh, resheniakh siezdov, konferensii i plenumov Ts.K. Chast I (1898–1924), 1932. Chast II (1925–39), 1941. *The Communist Party in resolutions and decisions of its congresses, conferences and plenums of the Central Committee.*

JOURNALS

Bolshevik. *Bolshevik.*
Bulleten ekonomicheskogo kabineta. Prof. S. N. Prokopovitcha. Prague. *Bulletin of the economic study by Prof. S. N. Prokopovich.*
Bulleten Komissariata po Prosveshcheniyu R.S.F.S.R. *Bulletin of the Commissariat of Education of the R.S.F.S.R.*
Bulleten Konjunkturnogo Instituta. *Bulletin of the Conjuncture Institute.*
Ekonomicheskoe obozrenie. *Economic Review.*
Izvestiya narkomtruda S.S.S.R. *Journal of the U.S.S.R. P. Commissariat of Labour.*
Planovoe khozyaistvo. *Planned Economy.*
Problemy ekonomiki. *Problems of Economics.*
Sotsialisticheskaya rekonstruktsiya selskogo khozyaistva. *Socialist reconstruction of agriculture.*
Sotsialisticheskoe selskoe khozyaistvo. *Socialist Agriculture.*
Sotsialisticheskoe zemledelie. *Socialist Agronomy (newspaper).*
Statisticheskoe obozrenie. *Statistical Survey.*
Vestnik finansov. *Financial Journal.*
Vestnik statistiky. *Journal of Statistics.*
Vestnik truda. *Herald of Labour.*
Vneshnyya torgovlya. *Foreign Trade.*
Voprosy sovetskoy torgovli. *Problems of Soviet Trade.*

INDUSTRY. HOME TRADE

ARONOVICH, M. Nepreryvnoe proizvodstvo. 1930. *Continuous production.*
BEREZOV, N. F. Razmeshchenie chernoy metallurgii. *Location of heavy metallurgy.*
BERNSHTEIN-KAGAN. Vvedenie v eckonomiyu promyshlennosti. 1926. *Introduction in the economics of industry.*
BOLOTIN, Z. Voprosy snabzhenia. 1934. *Problems of supply.*
BYALY, I. Problema vosproizvodstva v khozyaistve S.S.S.R. 1930. *The problem of reproduction in the economy of the U.S.S.R.*

Chastnaya torgovlya S.S.S.R. Sbornik. 1927. *The private trade of the U.S.S.R.*
Chastny kapital v narodnom khozyaistve S.S.S.R. Sbornik. 1927. *Private capital in the national economy of the U.S.S.R.*
Chetyre goda prodovolstvenoy politiki. 1922. *Four years of food supply policy.*
DEZEN. Bankovoe kreditovanie promyshlennosti. 1926. *Bank credits to industry.*
Dinamika rossiyskoy i sovetskoy promyshlennosti vsvyazi s razvitiem narodnogo khozyaistva za 40 let. (1887–1926). T. I, ch. I, 1929; T. I, ch. II, 1929; T. I, ch. III, 1930. *The dynamics of Russian and Soviet industry in connexion with the development of the national economy for 40 years (1887–1926).*
Ekonomika sovetskoy torgovli. Pod red. L. Gatovskogo, G. Neimana, V. Nedelya. *The economics of Soviet trade. Ed. by L. Gatovsky, G. Neiman, V. Nedelya.* 1934.
Fabrichno-zavod. promyshlennost S.S.S.R. Vyp. I, 1928; vyp. II, 1929; vyp. III, 1929; vyp. IV, 1929; vyp. V, 1929. *The U.S.S.R. industry, its factories and works. Vol. 1, 1928; vol. 2, 1929; vol. 3, 1929; vol. 4, 1929; vol. 5, 1929.*
GIRSH, YU. Ekonomika torgovli. 1927. *The economics of trade.*
GRINEVETSKIY. Poslevoennye perspektivy russkoy promyshlennosti. 1919. *Post-war prospects of Russian industry.*
GROMYKO i RYAUZOV. Sovetskaya torgovlya za 15 let. Statistiko-ekonom. sbornik. 1932. *Fifteen years of Soviet trade. Statistical and economic survey.*
ITIN, KULBERT, MOLOCHEK, YAKHNICH. Ekonomika i planirovanie sotsialisti-cheskoy promyshlennosti. 1934. *The economics and planning of socialist industry.*
Kapitalnoe stroitelstvo promyshlennosti (perechen vystroennykh novykh fabrik). 1928. *Industrial capital construction (list of newly built factories).*
Kolkhoznaya i individyalnaya krestyanskaya torgovlya. 1936. *Collective farm and private peasant trade.*
Kolkhoznaya torgovlya v 1932–4. 1935. *Collective farm trade in 1932–4.*
KONDRATIEV. Rynok i ego regulirovanie vo vremya voiny i revolyutsii. 1922. *The market and its control during the war and revolution.*
Kontrolnye tsifry piatiletnego plana promyshlennosti na 1928–9—1932–3. 1929. *Control figures of the industrial Five-Year Plan for 1928–9—1932–3.*
KRON. Chastnaya torgovlya v S.S.S.R. 1926. *Private trade in the U.S.S.R.*
KURSKIY. Razmeshchenie promyshlennosti v pervoy piatiletke. 1934. *Location of industry under the first Five-Year Plan.*
KVIRING. Ocherki razvitia promyshlennosti S.S.S.R. 1917–1927. 1929. *Essays on the industrial development of the U.S.S.R. 1917–27.*
LOKSHIN, A. Analiz kapitalnogo stroitelstva i finansov prompredpriyatia. 1936. *Analysis of capital construction and finances of industrial enterprises.*
LOKSHIN, A., Kratkiy ocherk razvitiya promyshlennosti S.S.S.R. 1933. *Short survey of the industrial development of the U.S.S.R.*
LOKSHIN, A. Organizatsia upravlenia promyshlennostyu S.S.S.R. *The organization of the U.S.S.R. industrial administration.*
Materialy rasshirennykh soveshchaniy prezidiyma V.S.N.Kh. S.S.S.R. s mestnymi organami. 1926. *Minutes of the augmented conferences of the Praesidium of the Supreme Economic Council of the U.S.S.R. with local organs.*
MOSHINSKIY, YU. I. Ekonomika i organisatsia obrashchenia sredstv proizvodstva v S.S.S.R. 1936. *The economics and organization of the circulation of means oj production in the U.S.S.R.*
Na novykh putyakh. Itogi N.E.P.-a 1921–2. Vyp. III. Promyshlennost. 1923. *The new course. Results of the N.E.P. 1921–2. Industry.*
Nauchno-tekhnicheskoe obsluzhivanie promyshlennosti. Sbornik. 1934. *Scientific and technical servicing of industry. A symposium.*

NEIMAN, G. YA., MAKAROV, M. Tekstilnaya promyshlennost S.S.S.R. 1927. *The textile industry of the U.S.S.R.*

NEIMAN, G. YA. Vnutrennyya torgovlya S.S.S.R. 1935. *The home trade of the U.S.S.R.*

NIKOLSKY, E. V. i SKITALTSEV, S. A. Prodazhnye tseny na zerno, produkty ego pererabotki i maslosemena. 1933. *Sale prices for grain, products derived from grain and oilseeds.*

ORDZHONIKIDZE. O zadachakh tyazheloy promyshlennosti i stakhanovskom dvizhenii. 1936. *The objects of heavy industry and the Stakhanov movement.*

ORLOV. Devyat mesyatsev prodovolstvennoy raboty sovetskoy vlasti. 1922. *Nine months of the food supply activities of the Soviet Government.*

Osnovnye momenty rekonstruktsii promyshlennosti S.S.S.R. 1930. *Principal phases in the industrial reconstruction of the U.S.S.R.*

Otpusknye i roznichnye tseny i torgovye nakidki na promtorvary. 1936. *Release and retail prices and commercial charges on manufactured goods.*

PERTSOVICH. Sovetskie tresty i sindikaty (organizatsia krupnoy promyshlennosti S.S.S.R.). 1925. *Soviet trusts and syndicates (the organization of the U.S.S.R. large-scale industry).*

PISAREV, RYAUZOV, TITELBAUM. Osnovy statistiki sovetskoy torgovli. 1936. *The bases of Soviet trade statistics.*

Potreblenie i spros v S.S.S.R. Sbornik. 1935. *Consumption and demand in the U.S.S.R. A symposium.*

Promyshlennosts po materialam Ts.K.K.V.K.P. (b) i N.K.R.K.I. Sbornik pod red. Rozengoltsa. 1930. *Industry according to data of the Central Control Committee of the Communist Party and the P. Commissariat of the Workers' and Peasants' Inspection. Ed. by Rozengolts.*

ROZENFELD. Promyshlennaya politika S.S.S.R. 1926. *The industrial policy of the U.S.S.R.*

Roznichnye i optovye organizatsii. Itogi godovoy perepisi 1935. 1936. *Retail and wholesale trade organizations.*

SAKHAROV, CHERNAY, KABAKOV. Ocherki organizatsii tyazheloy promyshlennosti S.S.S.R. 1934. *Outline of the organization of the heavy industry of the U.S.S.R.*

Sindikaty S.S.S.R. v tsifrakh i diogrammakh za 5 let, 1923–4—1927–8. 1928. *The U.S.S.R. syndicates in figures and diagrams for five years.*

Sotsialisticheskaya promyshlennost i khozyaistvennoe pravo. Sbornik. 1935. *Socialist industry and economic legislation. A symposium.*

Sotsialisticheskaya sorevnovanie v promyshlennosti S.S.S.R. 1930. *Socialist emulation in the industry of the U.S.S.R.*

Sovetskaya torgovlya. 1935. *Soviet trade.*

Sovetskaya torgovlya. Ekonomicheskie i organizatsionnye izmenenia za 1935–6. 1936. *Soviet trade. Economic and organizational changes in 1935–6.*

Sravnitelnye koeffitsienty kachestva produktsii. Sbornik. Stenograficheskiy otchet. 1926. *Comparative qualitative production coefficients. A symposium. Verbatim report.*

Svodny proizvostvenno-finansovy plan promyshlennosti na 1927–8. 1928. *Summary production-financial plan for industry for 1927–8.*

Teoruya i praktika vreditelstva v sovetskoy torgovle. 1932. *The theory and practice of wrecking in Soviet trade.*

TSYPIROVICH. Sindikaty i tresty v Rossii. Petersburg, 1918. *Syndicates and trusts in Russia.*

UVIRA, R. Uchet sotsialisticheskogo predpriyatia. 1937. *Accounting in a socialist enterprise.*

VASILEVSKIY, SHLIFSHTEIN. Ocherki kustarnoy promyshlennosti S.S.S.R. 1930. *Essays on U.S.S.R. handicrafts.*

Vnutrennyya torgovlya S.S.S.R. za X let. 1928. *Ten years of the U.S.S.R. home trade.*

ZHIRMUNSKIY. Chastny torgovy kapital v narodnom khozyaistve S.S.S.R. 1927. *Private commercial capital in the national economy of the U.S.S.R.*

AGRICULTURE

Agrarnaya politika v resheniakh siezdov i konferentsiy R.K.P. (b) s 1917 po 1925. 1926. *Agrarian policy according to decision of Party congresses and conferences, 1917–25.*

Agrarny vopros i sovremennoe krestyanskoe dvizhenie. Vypusk 1. Sbornik statey. 1935. *The agrarian problem and the contemporary peasant movement. Vol. 1. Coll. articles.*

ALMAYKIY, ARINA, BERESOVSKIY i drugie. Doxody, nakopleni i finansovoe khozyaistvo v kolkhozakh. 1937. *Revenue, accumulation and finance economy in Kolkhoz.*

AZIAN i VELIKEVICH. Arendnye otnoshenia v sovetskoy derevne. 1928. *Leasehold in the Soviet village.*

BITSENKO, A. A. K voprosam teorii i istorii kollektivizatsii selskogo khozyaistva S.S.S.R. 1929. *Contributions to the theory and history of the collectivization of agriculture in the U.S.S.R.*

BROYNOV. Klimaticheskie i selskokhozyaistvennye raiony Rossii. 1924. *Russia's climatic and agricultural zones.*

CHELINTSEV, MATYUKHIN, NIKITIN. Dinamika krestyanskogo khozyaistva. 1928. *The dynamics of peasant farming.*

ELIZAROV. Likvidatsia kulachestva kak klassa. 1930. *The liquidation of the kulaks as a class.*

Finansovo-khozyaistvenny spravochnik kolkhoza. 1936. *The collective farm's handbook on finance and economics.*

GAISTER, A. Dostizhenia i trudnosti kolkhoznogo stroitelstva. 1929. *Achievements and difficulties of Kolkhoz construction.*

GAISTER, A. Rassloenie sovetskoy derevni. 1928. *Class differentiation within the Soviet village.*

GEIFERT, V. Selskoe khozyaistvo S.S.S.R. (1917–25). 1926. *The agriculture of the U.S.S.R.*

Gosudarstvennaya kreditnaya pomoshch kolkhozam i kolkhoznikam za period ot 6 do 7 siezda sovetov S.S.S.R. 1935. *State credit assistance to collective farms and farmers within the period between the Sixth and Seventh Soviet Congresses of the U.S.S.R.*

Gruppovye itogi selsko-khozyaistvennoy perepisi 1920-go goda (po gubern. i raionam). 1926. *The 1920 agricultural census returns according to groups (provincial and district).*

Itogi razrabotki krestyanskikh byudzhetov v gruppirovkakh po doxodu. 1930. *Study of peasant budgets grouped according to revenue.*

K voprosu o sotsialisticheskom pereystroistve selsk. khozyaistva. Materialy N.K.R.K.I. S.S.S.R., pod red Yakovleva. 1928. *On the problem of the socialist reconstruction of agriculture. Materials of the U.S.S.R. P. Commissariat of Workers' and Peasants' Inspection.*

KAMENEV, L. Nalogovaya politika v derevne. 1923. *Fiscal policy in rural districts.*

KAVRAISKIY, V. i NUSINOV, I. Klassy i klassovye otnoshenia v sovremennoy sovetskoy derevne. S predisloviem Syrtsova. 1929. *Classes and class relationship in the present-day Soviet countryside. With foreword by Syrtsov.*

KHLEBNIKOV, V. N. Sdelshchina v kolkhoze. 1937. *Piece work on the collective farm.*

KHRYASHCHEV, A. I. Gruppy i klassy v krestyanstve. 1926. *Peasant groups and classes.*

KINDEEV, K. Kollektivnye khozyaistva. 1927. *Collective farms.*

KIRILLOV, I. A. Ocherki zemleustroistva za 3 goda revolyutsii (1917–20). 1922. *Essays on land and land tenure during three years of revolution* (1917–20).

KIY. Ot krestyanskoy obshchiny k sotsialisticheskoy kommune. 1918. *From the peasant 'mir' to the socialist commune.*

KNIPOVICH, B. N. Ocherk deyatelnosti narodnogo komissariata zemledeliya za tri goda (1917–20). 1920. *Report on the activities of the P. Commissariat of agriculture for three years* (1917–20).

Kolkhozy nakanune XVI-go siezda V.K.P. (b). 1930. *Collective farms on the eve of the Sixteenth Party Congress*

Kolkhozy v 1929. 1931. *Collective farms in 1929.*

Kolkhozy. Pervy vsesoyuzny siezd selskokhozyaistvenykh kollektivov. 1929. *First All-Union congress of agricultural collectives.*

Kolkhozy S.S.S.R. Pod red. E. P. Terletskogo. 1929. *The collective farms of the U.S.S.R. Edited by E. P. Terletsky.*

Kollektivizatsia sovetskoy derevni. Predvaritelnye itogi sploshnykh obsledovaniy kolkhozov v 1928 i 1929. 1930. *Collectivization in the Soviet village. Preliminary results of a comprehensive study of collective farms in 1928 and 1929.*

Komitety bednoty. Sbornik materialov, T. I. 1933. *Poor peasants' committees. Collected data. Vol. I.*

KONYUKOV, I. A. Kollektivnoe zemledelie. 1925. *Collective farming.*

KONYUKOV, I. A. Trudovye zemledelcheskie arteli i kommuny. 1923. *Labouring agricultural artels and communes.*

Krestyanskoe dvizhenie v 1917. 1927. *The peasant movement in 1917.*

KRITSMAN, L. Klassovoe rassloenie sovetskoy derevni. 1925. *Class differentiation in the Soviet countryside.*

KUBANIN, M. I. Klassovaya sushchnost droblenia krestyanskikh khozyaistv. 1929 *Class significance of parcellations of peasants' homesteads.*

KUBANIN, M. I. Proizvodstvennye tipy kolkhozov. 1936. *Types of productive collective farms.*

KUVSHINOV, I. S. Osnovnye voprosy organizatsii krupnykh sovetskikh khozyaistv. 1930. *Basic organizational problems of large-scale Soviet farming.*

LATSIS, A. Agrarnoe perenaselenie i perspektivy borby s nim. 1929. *Agrarian over-population and how to combat it.*

LATSIS, A. Sovetskie khozyaistva. 1924. *Soviet farming.*

LIBKIND, A. Agrarnoe perenaselenie i kollektivizatsia derevni. 1931. *Agrarian over-population and agricultural collectivization.*

LUGOVSKIY, K. G. Kolkhoznoe dvizhenie na perelome. 1929. *The collective farm movement at the cross-roads.*

LYASHCHENKO, P. I. Ocherki agrarnoy revolyutsii Rossii, T. I. 1923. *Essays on the agrarian revolution in Russia.*

MARKEVICH. Mezhselennye mashinno-traktornye stantsii. 1929. *Machine-tractor stations.*

MASLOV, P. Perenaselenie russkoy derevni. 1930. *Russian rural over-population.*

Materialy po istorii agrarnoy revolyutsii v Rossii. Pod red. Kritsmana. Vol. I, 1928; vol. II, 1929. *Materials for the history of the agrarian revolution in Russia. Ed. by Kritsman.*

MESHCHEREKOV, V. Natsionalizatsia i sotsializatsia zemli. 1918. *The nationalization and socialization of land.*

MESYATSEV. Zemelnaya i selskokhozyaistvennaya politika v Rossii. 1922. *Land and agricultural policy in Russia.*

MINTS. Agrarnoe perenaselenie i rynok truda v S.S.S.R. 1929. *Agrarian overpopulation and the labour market in the U.S.S.R.*

Na novykh putyakh. Itogi N.E.P-a (selskoe khozyaistvo). 1923. *New ways. The results of the N.E.P. (agriculture).*

NIFONTOV, V. P. Produkty zhivotnovodstva S.S.S.R. 1937. *Animal products of the U.S.S.R.*

NIFONTOV, V. P. Zhivotnovodstvo S.S.S.R. v tsifrakh. 1932. *U.S.S.R. livestock breeding in figures.*

NIKULIKHIN, YA. Sotsialisticheskaya rekonstruktsia selskogo khozyaistva v pervoy piatiletke. 1934. *Socialist reconstruction of agriculture under the first Five-Year Plan.*

OGANOVSKY, N. P. Ocherky po ekonomicheskoy geografii Rossii. 1922. *Essays on the economic geography of Russia*

O proizvoditelnosti truda v kolkhozakh. Narkomzem. 1935. *The productivity of labour on collective farms.*

OSINSKIY. Gosudarstvennoe regulirovanie krestyanskogo khozyaistva. 1920. *Peasant farming and State control.*

Otkhod krestyanskogo naselenia na zarabotki v S.S.S.R. 1926. *Peasant population drift to seasonal work in the U.S.S.R.*

PERSHIN. Uchastkovoe zemlepolzovanie v Rossii. 1920. *Strip land tenure in Russia.*

PESHKOV, P. Naemny trud v krestyanskom khozyaistve S.S.S.R. 1928. *Hired labour in U.S.S.R. peasant farming.*

PROKOPOVICH, S. N. Krestyanskoe khozyaistvo. Berlin, 1923. *Peasant economy.*

ROZENBLYUM, D. S. Zemelnoe pravo R.S.F.S.R. 1929. *R.S.F.S.R. land legislation.*

Sbornik 'O zemle'. 1921. *Collected volume, 'Land'.*

Sdvigi v selskom khozyaistve S.S.S.R. mezhdu xv i xvi part. siezdami. Statisticheskie svedenia po sel. khoz. za 1927–30. 1931. *Changes in U.S.S.R. agriculture between the Fifteenth and Sixteenth Party Congresses. Statistical data on agriculture for 1927–30.*

Selsko-khozyaistvennaya nauka v S.S.S.R. 1934. Sbornik statey. *The science of agriculture in the U.S.S.R.* 1934. *Collected articles.*

Selskoe khozyaistvo S.S.S.R. Ezhegodnik 1935. 1936. *The agriculture of the U.S.S.R. Yearbook for 1935.*

SHUVAEV, K. M. Staraya i novaya derevnya. 1937. *The old village and the new.*

Sotsialisticheskoe pereustroistvo selskogo khozyaistva S.S.S.R. mezhdu xv i xvi siezdami V.K.P. (b). 1930. *The socialist reorganization of U.S.S.R. agriculture between the Fifteenth and Sixteenth Party Congresses.*

Sovkhozy k 15-oy godovshchine oktyabrya. Sbornik. 1932. *The State farms on the eve of the fifteenth anniversary of the October Revolution.*

Spravochnik dlya politotdelov M.T.S. i sovkhozov. Agrotekhnika, mekhanizatsia zhivotnovodstva. 1935. *Handbook for political sections of M.T.S. and State farms. Agrotechnics. Mechanization of stock breeding.*

URALSKIY. Unichnozhenie protivopolozhnostey mezhdu gorodom i derevney. 1932. *The abolition of contradictions between town and countryside.*

VATULIN, B. Proizvodstvenno-finansovy plan sovkhoza. 1935. *The State farms' production-financial plan.*

Vazhneishie reshenia po selskomu khozyaistvu. Dlya politotdelov, M.T.S. i sovkhozov. 1933. *Principal decisions on agriculture. For use by political sections, M.T.S. and State farms.*

VERMENICHEV, I. Za sotsialisticheskoe pereystroistvo derevni. 1929. *For the socialist reconstruction of the countryside.*

Vliyanie neyrozhaev na narodnoe khozyaistvo Rossii. Ch. I, II. 1927. *Influence of crop failure on the national economy of Russia.*

Voina krestyan s pomeshchikami v 1917. 1917-y god v derevne. Vospominania krestyan. 1927. *The peasant war against landlords in 1917. The countryside in 1917. Peasant reminiscences.*

VOLF, M. M. Puti rekonstruktsii selskogo khozyaistva v piatiletie. 1929. *Ways and means of agricultural reconstruction within the five-year period.*

VOLKOV, E. Z. Agrarno-ekon. statistika Rossii. 1924. *Russia's agrarian and economic statistics.*

Vsesoyuznoe soveshchanie po edinomu selsko-khoz. nalogu pri Narkomfine S.S.S.R. 1–8 II, 1927. 1927. *The P. Commissariat of Finance's All-Union Conference on the single agricultural tax.*

YAKOVLEV, YA. Ob oshibkakh khlebo-furazhnogo balansa Ts.S.U. i ego istolkovateley. 1926. *The mistakes in the bread and fodder balance of the Central Statistical Administration and its commentators.*

YAKOVLEV, YA. Voprosy organizatsii sotsialisticheskogo selskogo khozyaistva. 1935. *Problems of the organization of socialist agriculture.*

Za krupnye kolkhozy. 1929. *The case for large collective farms.*

Zadachi i perspektivy kolkhoznogo stroitelstva. Proekt piatiletnego plana. 1929. *Objects and prospects of Kolkhoz construction. Provisional Five-Year Plan.*

Zhivotnovodstvo S.S.S.R. 1930. *Livestock breeding in the U.S.S.R.*

LABOUR

Arkhiv istorii truda v Rossii. 1921. *Archives of the history of labour in Russia.*

BAEVSKY. Fondy kollektivnogo potreblenia (ob urovne zhizni proletariata S.S.S.R.). 1932. *Funds of collective consumption (the U.S.S.R. proletariat's standard of life).*

Borba na dva fronta v oblasti ekonomiki truda. 1932. *A two-front struggle in the field of labour economics.*

Budzhety rabochikh i sluzhashchikh. Vyp. 1. Budzhet rabochey semi v 1922–7. 1929. *Workers' and employees' budgets. Vol. 1. The budget of a working-class family in 1922–7.*

Ekonomika truda. Ch. I, II. 1933. *Labour economics. Parts I, II.*

ESKIN, M. Osnovnye puti razvitia sotsialisticheskikh form truda. 1936. *Fundamental ways of development of the socialist forms of labour.*

GINDIN. Regulirovanie rynka truda i borba s bezrabotitsey. 1926. *The regulating of the labour market and the struggle against unemployment.*

GOLTSMAN i KAGAN. Starye i novye kadry proletariata S.S.S.R. 1934. *The old and new cadres of the U.S.S.R. proletariat.*

GRISHIN, Z. Sovetskoe trudovoe pravo. 1936. *Soviet labour legislation.*

GUKHMAN. Chislennost i zarabotnaya plata proletariata S.S.S.R. 1926. *The numbers of the U.S.S.R. proletariat and their wages.*

GUMILEVSKIY, P. Budzhet sluzhashchikh v 1922–6. 1928. *Employees' budgets in 1922–6.*

KABO. Pitanie russkogo rabochego do i posle voiny. 1926. *Pre- and post-war diet of the Russian worker.*

KAGANOVITCH L. O zadachakh profsoyuzov S.S.S.R. na dannom etape razvitia. 1932. *The objects of the U.S.S.R. trade unions at the present stage of development.*

KALISTRATOV, YU. Zarabotnaya plata v S.S.S.R. i v kapitalisticheskikh stranakh. 1931. *Wages in the U.S.S.R. and the capitalist countries.*

KISELEV, YA. i MALKIN, S. Sbornik vazhneishikh postanovleniy po trudu. 1938. *Collection of principal regulations concerning labour.*

LIVSHITS. Problema zarabotnoy platy v Sovetskoy Rossii. 1922. *The problem of wages in Soviet Russia.*

MARKUS, B., Trud v sotsialisticheskom obshchestve. 1939. *Labour in the socialist society.*

MORDUKHOVICH, Z. Na borbu s tekuchestyu rabochey sily. 1931. *Combat labour turn-over!*

Naemny trud v Rossii. 1927. *Hired labour in Russia.*

Oktyabrskaya revolyutsia i fabzavkomy. Ch. 1-aya, 1927; ch. 11-aya, 1927. *The October Revolution and the factory committees. Part I, 1927; part II, 1927.*

RASHIN, A. G. Zarabotnaya plata za vosstanovitelny period khozyaistva S.S.S.R. 1928. *Wages during the period of recovery of the U.S.S.R. national economy.* 1928.

RASHIN, A. G. Formirovanie promyshlennogo proletariata v Rossii. 1940. *Formation of industrial proletariat in Russia.*

Sbornik vazhneishikh postanovleniy po trudu. 1931. *Collection of principal regulations concerning labour.* 1931.

SEREBRENNIKOV, G. N. Zhenskiy trud v S.S.S.R. 1934. *Female labour in the U.S.S.R.*

SHVERNIK, N. Profsoyuzy S.S.S.R. nakanune vtoroy piatiletki. 1932. *The U.S.S.R. trade unions on the eve of the second Five-Year Plan.*

Sovetskoe trudovoe pravo na novom etape. Sbornik. 1931. *A new stage of Soviet labour legislation.*

SPERLINA, A. Proizvoditelnost truda v promyshlennosti v 1-oy i 2-oy piatiletke. 1934. *The productivity of labour in industry under the first and second Five-Year Plans.*

STRUMILIN, S. Zarabotnaya plata i proizvoditelnost truda v russkoy promyshlennosti v 1913–22. 1923. *Wages and productivity of labour in Russian industry, 1913–22.*

TSIBULSKIY, V. Politika zarabotnoy platy v S.S.S.R. za 15 let proletarskoy diktatury. 1932. *Wages policy in the U.S.S.R. for the 15 years of proletarian dictatorship.*

Trud v S.S.S.R., Statisticheskiy spravochnik. 1936. *Labour in the U.S.S.R., a statistical handbook.*

VAINSHTEIN, A. Zarabotnaya plata. 1937. *Wages.*

V.K.P. (b) o profsoyuzakh. Sbornik resheniy i postanovleniy siezdov, konferentsiy, plenumov Ts.K.V.K.P. (b). 1933. *The C.P. and trade unions. Collected decisions and resolutions of Party congresses, conferences and plenary sessions of the Central Committee of the C.P.*

Voprosy truda na novom etape. Sbornik. 1931. *A new stage in labour problems. Symposium.*

Vtoraya piatiletka i zadachi profsoyuzov. 1932. *The second Five-Year Plan and trade-union aims.*

VVEDENSKIY. Zhilishchnoe polozhenie fabrichno-zavodokogo proletariata S.S.S.R. 1932. *Housing position of the U.S.S.R. industrial proletariat.*

YOFFE. M. i P. Problema proizvoditelnosti truda. 1931. *The problem of labour productivity.*

YOFFE, M. i P. Profsoyuzy i planirovanie promyshlennosti. 1929. *Trade unions and the planning of industry.*

FINANCE

ATLAS, Z. V. Dengi i kredit (pri kapitalizme i v S.S.S.R.). 1930. *Money and credit (under capitalism and in the U.S.S.R.).*

BELKIN, G. A. Oblozhenie pribyli predpriatiy obobshchestvlennogo khozyaistva. 1934. *Taxation of profits of socialized economic enterprises.*

BLUM, A. A. i BERLATSKY. Kreditnaya reforma v voprosakh i otvetakh. 1930. *The credit reform in questions and answers.*

Budzhetnaya sistema i ediny finansovy plan S.S.S.R. Sistematicheskiy sbornik obshchesoyuznogo zakonodatelstva. 1933. *The budget system and the unified financial plan of the U.S.S.R. All-Union legislation, systematized handbook.*

Budzhetnaya sistema S.S.S.R. Sbornik zakonov i instruktsiy. Sostavil Glezin, pod red. Dyachenko. 1937. *The budget system of the U.S.S.R. Collected law and instructions. Compiled by Glezin.*

DANILOV, D. V. Mestnye nalogi i sbory. Pod red. Dolgova i Dunaevskogo. 1936. *Local taxes and levies. Ed. by Dolgov and Dunaevsky.*

Denezhnaya reforma, snizhenie tsen, zarabotnaya plata. Dekrety i postanovlenia. 1924. *The monetary reform, price reductions and wages. Decrees and regulations.*

Dengi i denezhnoe obrashchenie v osveshchenii marksizma. Sbornik. 1923. *Money and currency circulation from the Marxist point of view. A symposium.*

DMITRIEV-KRYMSKIY. Sovremennye banki i kredit v S.S.S.R. i zagranitsey. 1924. *Modern banks and credit in the U.S.S.R. and abroad.*

Finansy i kredit S.S.S.R. Pod red. Prof. V. P. Duachenko. 1938. *Finance and credit in the U.S.S.R. Ed. by Prof. V. P. Duachenko.*

Finansy S.S.S.R. mezhdu 6 i 7 siezdami partii (1931–4). 1935. *The finances of the U.S.S.R. between the Sixth and Seventh Congresses of the Soviets (1931–4).*

Gosudarstvenny Bank nakanune 7-ogo Vsesoyuznogo Siezda Sovietov. 1935. *The State Bank of the U.S.S.R. on the eve of the Seventh All-Union Congress of Soviets.*

KANTOROVICH. Izderzhki obrashchenia v S.S.S.R. 1933. *Overhead charges in the U.S.S.R.*

KARPENKO. Finansovaya statistika (statistika nalogov i byudzhetov) 1929. *Financial statistics (taxes and budgets)*

KATSELENBAUM. Denezhnoe obrashchenie Rossii, 1914–24. 1924. *Russia's currency circulation, 1914–24.*

KUZOVKOV. Finansovaya sistema v period pervonachalnogo sotsialisticheskogo nakoplenia. 1923. *The financial system in the early period of socialist accumulation.*

LEVIN, A. YA. Banki i vneshnyaya torgovlya. 1926. *Banks and foreign trade.*

LEVITSKIY. Valyutnaya politika S.S.S.R. 1926. *Foreign exchange policy of the U.S.S.R.*

MARGOLIN, N. S. Voprosy balansa denezhnykh dokhodov i raskhodov naselenia. 1939. *Problems of the population's receipts and expenditure balance sheet.*

Mestnye finansy S.S.S.R. Brigada pod rukovodstvom Prof. N. N. Rovinskogo. 1936. *Local finances of the U.S.S.R. Prof. N. N. Rovinsky et al.*

Nalogi. Sbornik dekretov, instruktsiy i tsirkulyarov za 1921–2. 1922. *Taxes. Collected decrees, instructions and circular for 1921–2.*

Nalogi s oborota. Izd. Narkomfina. 1936. *Turn-over taxes. Published by the P. Commissariat of Finance.*

NUSINOV, I. M. Metodika finansovogo planirovania. 1939. *Methods of financial planning.*

Obzor finansovogo zakonodatelstva 1917–21. 1921. *Survey of financial legislation for 1917–21.*

Ocherki po teorii deneg i kredita. Pod red. Trakhtenberga. Izd. Inst. krasnoy professury. 1930. *Essays on monetary and credit theories. Ed. by Trakhtenberg. Publication of the Institute of Red Professorship.*

Osnovy finansovoy sistemy S.S.S.R. Sbornik statey (M. I. Bogolepov, K. O. Shmelev, I. I. Reyngoldts i dr.). 1930. *The foundation of the U.S.S.R. financial system. Collected articles.*

Otchet ob ispolnenii gosudarstvennogo budzheta za 1935. 1937. *Report on the fulfilment of the State Budget for 1935.*

PERVUSHIN. Volnye tseny i pokupatelnaya sila russkogo rublya. 1922. *Uncontrolled prices and the purchasing value of the Russian ruble.*

PREOBRAZHENSKIY. Teoria padayushchey valyuty. 1930. *The theory of devaluating currency.*

Rekonstruktsia sistemy nalogovykh i nenalogovykh iziatiy. Sbornik. 1930. *The revision of the system of taxes and non-tax deductions. A symposium.* 1930.

RONIN, S. Inostranny kapital i russkie banki. 1926. *Foreign capital and Russian banks.*

SHENGER, YU. R. Razvitie i organisatsia kreditnoy sistemy S.S.S.R. 1934. *Development and organization of the U.S.S.R. credit system.*

SOBOLEV. Osnovnye voprosy reorganizatsii kreditnoy sistemy S.S.S.R. 1929. *The basic problems of the reorganization of the U.S.S.R. credit system.*

SOKOLNIKOV, G. YA. Finansovaya nauka. Vyp. I, II. 1930. *The science of finance.*

SOKOLNIKOV, G. YA. Finansovaya politika revolyutsii. T. I, 1925; T. II, 1926; T. III, 1928. *The financial policy of the revolution.*

Trudy Moskovskogo Finansovo-ekonomicheskogo instituta imeni tovarishcha Kaganovicha. Vyp. I, II. 1934. *Transactions of the Moscow Financial Economic Institute named after com. Kaganovich.*

YANBUKHTIN, K. Nalogi v usloviakh kapitalizma i v sovetskom khozyaistve. 1934. *Taxation in conditions of capitalism and in the Soviet economy.*

Zadachi i perspektivy goskredita S.S.S.R. 1927. *Problems and prospects of the State credit of the U.S.S.R.*

FOREIGN TRADE. FOREIGN CAPITAL

BAKULIN, S. N. i MISHUSTIN, D. D. Vnesniya torgovlia S.S.S.R. za 20 let. 1918–1937. Statisticheskiy spravochnik. 1939. *Foreign trade statistics of the U.S.S.R. for 20 years.*

BUTKOVSKIY, V. Inostrannye kontsessii v narodnom khozyaistve S.S.S.R. 1928. *Foreign concessions in the U.S.S.R.*

Eksport S.S.S.R. Spravochnik-putevoditel. Sostavlen Zhirmunskim. 1935. *Export of the U.S.S.R. Guide and reference book. Compiled by Zhirmunsky.*

Finansirovanie vneshney torgovli. (Frey, L., Smirnov, A. i dr.). 1938. *Financing of foreign trade. A symposium.*

FRUMKIN, M. Narodnoe khozyaistvo i vneshniya torgovlya S.S.S.R. 1927. *National economy and foreign trade of the U.S.S.R.*

KAUFMAN, M. YA. Organizatsia i regulirovanie vneshney torgovli Rossii. 1925. *The organization and regulation of the foreign trade of the U.S.S.R.*

KRASIN. Voprosy vneshney torgovli. 1928. *Problems of foreign trade.*

XV let borby za monopoliyu vneshney torgovli S.S.S.R. 1927. *Fifteen years of struggle for the monopoly of the U.S.S.R. foreign trade.*

MISHUSTIN. Vneshnyya torgovlya i industrializatsia S.S.S.R. 1938. *Foreign trade and the industrialization of the U.S.S.R.*

OL, P. V. Inostrannye kapitaly v narodnom khozyaistve Rossii. Leningrad, 1925. *Foreign capital in the national economy of Russia.*

PETRYAKOV. Vneshnyya torgovlya i narodnoe khozyaistvo S.S.S.R. 1927. *Foreign trade and the national economy of the U.S.S.R.*

ROZENGOLTS. Vneshnyya torgovlya S.S.S.R. v novykh usloviakh. 1936. *The foreign trade of the U.S.S.R. in novel conditions.*

Sbornik deistvuyushchikh dogovorov i inykh khozyaistvennykh soglasheniy S.S.S.R., zaklyuchennykh s inostrannymi gosudarstvami. 1935. *Collection of acting pacts and other economic agreements concluded between the U.S.S.R. and foreign states.*

Selsko-khozyaistvenny eksport S.S.S.R. 1930. *Agricultural exports of the U.S.S.R.*

SIGRIST. Vneshniya torgovaya politika S.S.S.R. v mezhdunarodnykh dogovorakh. 1927. *Foreign trade policy of the U.S.S.R. in international agreements.*

Sovetsko-amerikanskie otnoshenia, 1919–33. 1934. *Soviet-American relations, 1919–33.*

TANIN, M. 10 let vneshney politiki S.S.S.R., 1917–27. 1927. *Ten years of U.S.S.R. foreign policy, 1917–27.*

Torgovye otnoshenia S.S.S.R. s kapitalisticheskimi stranami. 1938. *Trade relations between the U.S.S.R. and capitalist countries.*

Torgovye otnoshenia S.S.S.R. so stranami Vostoka. 1938. *Trade relations between the U.S.S.R. and the East.*

Vneshnetorgovy transport; pod red. A. D. Keylina. 1938. *Foreign trade transport; ed by A. D. Keylin.*

Vneshnyaya torgovlya S.S.S.R. k XVII siezdu V.K.P. (b). 1934. *The foreign trade of the U.S.S.R. at the time of the Seventeenth Party Congress.*

Vneshnyaya torgovlya Sovetskogo Soyuza; pod red. D. D. Mishustina. 1938. *The foreign trade of the Soviet Union; ed by D. D. Mishustin.*

Vneshnyaya torgovlya S.S.S.R. za x let. 1928. *The foreign trade of the U.S.S.R. during ten years.*

ZHIRMUNSKIY. Organizatsia eksporta. 1938. *The organization of export.*

MOST FREQUENTLY QUOTED ABBREVIATIONS

A.U.C.C.T.U. = All-Union Central Council of Trade Unions.
Centry = Central Administrations of S.E.C.
C.P. = All-Union Communist Party.
F.Y.P. = Five-Year Plan.
Glavki = Chief Administrations of S.E.C.
Goelro = State Plan for Electrification of Russia.
Gosplan = State Planning Commission.
Gostorg = State trading organization.
Kolkhoz = Collective farm.
Kolkhozy = Collective farms.
M.T.S. = Machine Tractor Stations.
Narkom = People's Commissar.
N.E.P. = New Economic Policy.

P. Commissariats = People's Commissariats.
Polit-Bureau = Political Bureau of Central Committee of Communist Party.
S.E.C. = Supreme Economic Council.
Sovkhoz = State farm.
Sovkhozy = State farms.
Sovnarkom S.S.S.R. = Council of People's Commissars of the U.S.S.R.
S.T.O. = Council of Labour and Defence of the U.S.S.R.
T.O.Z. = Association for the Joint Cultivation of Land.
Ts.U.N.Kh.U. = U.S.S.R. Central Administration of Economic Accounting.
V.Ts.I.K. = All-Russian Central Executive Committee.

Toz. Association of peasant farms for the Joint Cultivation of Land, the purpose of which is to combine their labour, draught animals and agricultural machinery for the mass joint field work.

Artel. Much more close association of peasant farms in which all main productive resources (land, machinery, implements, productive buildings and so on) are commonly owned and labour united for all agricultural work. In individual ownership are left dwelling houses, small plots of land, minor implements, certain amount of cattle, poultry and so on for the private use of peasant farms.

Commune. Association of peasants with more complete common ownership of all means of production than in Artel, with the common share not only of the whole proceeds of the member's labour but also of dwelling-houses and all amenities belonging to the commune.

INDEX

17

17*

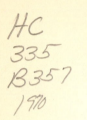